HELEN HUNT JACKSON

*The publisher gratefully acknowledges
the generous contribution to this book
provided by Barclay and Sharon Simpson
and by the General Endowment Fund of the University
of California Press Associates.*

Helen Hunt Jackson

A Literary Life

KATE PHILLIPS

University of California Press

BERKELEY   LOS ANGELES   LONDON

University of California Press
Berkeley and Los Angeles, California

University of California Press, Ltd.
London, England

Title page images: Helen Jackson (inset) and manuscript
of *Ramona.* Both courtesy Special Collections, Tutt
Library, Colorado College, Colorado Springs, Colorado.

Library of Congress Cataloging-in-Publication Data

Phillips, Kate
  Helen Hunt Jackson : a literary life / Kate Phillips.
     p. cm.
Includes bibliographical references and index.
  ISBN 0-520-21804-3 (cloth : alk. paper)
  1. Jackson, Helen Hunt, 1830–1885. 2. Women and literature—West
(U.S.)—History—19th century. 3. Authors, American—19th
century—Biography. 4. West (U.S.) in literature. 5. Indians in
literature. I. Title.

  PS2108 .P48 2003
  818' .409—dc21

                                                    2002013309

Manufactured in the United States of America

12 11 10 09 08 07 06 05 04 03
10 9 8 7 6 5 4 3 2 1

If it be true, as some poets think, that every spot on earth is full of poetry, then it is certainly also true that each place has its own distinctive measure; an indigenous metre, so to speak, in which, and in which only, its poetry will be truly set or sung.

Helen Hunt Jackson, "Chester Streets"

Contents

Illustrations

Prologue

A flock of sheep weave past scrub brush and cacti, trailing their shepherd down the sloping hillside, across the dirt-floored stage, and out of sight. Later, the hillside springs to life as more than a hundred Indians pop out from behind scattered rocks, men and boys bare-chested, their silhouettes bold against the blue April sky. Mexican dancers and musicians send up flashes of color and song. A posse of American cowboys makes a sudden appearance, whooping and hollering, horses kicking up thick swirls of brown dust. And there, at the center of this ersatz historical California, our heroine and hero struggle for their very survival.

This is the Ramona Pageant, an elaborate outdoor theatrical adaptation of Helen Jackson's 1884 novel, performed almost every year since 1923 in the chaparral country of Hemet, California, ninety miles east of Los Angeles. The pageant is the longest-running open-air play in the United States; more than two million people have seen it. While the show's enormous cast is always made up mostly of local volunteers, over the decades some rising stars have filled the paying title role: Raquel Welch was Ramona in 1959, Anne Archer a decade later.

I made my own first visit to the pageant on a spring weekend in 1990, when my parents and I took my grandmother to see the show. She was eighty-seven years old then, approaching the end of her life. She was small and frail. The afternoon was very hot, even by Hemet standards; the Ramona Bowl fried in the sun. My grandmother struggled to maintain her cool with giant therapeutic sunglasses, an old white tennis visor, and frequent trips to the shaded restroom area. She had read and reread Jackson's novel over the years, and had long dreamed of seeing it enacted at the pageant; she did not want the heat to ruin this special day. In the end, we managed to make it through most of the show—a testament to my grandmother's strong will, and to her love for the story of *Ramona*.

She adored everything about it. Set in the decades following the 1848 American takeover of California, *Ramona* depicts a time when early Californians—Indian, Spanish, and Mexican—struggled to maintain their hold on a pastoral land against the encroaching order of American industrialism. My grandmother admired the beautiful orphan Ramona, Jackson's half-Indian, half-Scottish heroine, who patiently endures an unhappy youth on the Southern California ranch of her austere Spanish guardian, Señora Moreno. She thrilled in Ramona's love affair with Alessandro, a dashing Luiseño Indian from Temecula, and pitied the young couple as they struggled to set up home in one Indian village after another, only to be driven away by greedy, unscrupulous white settlers. At the pageant, like other spectators, my grandmother jeered these settlers, never mind that many of us were their descendants. (Hoping to leave illness behind, to begin life anew, my great-grandparents first arrived in San Diego County from Massachusetts and Minnesota during a late-nineteenth-century land rush on the area. They seem to have been an ordinary, good-enough sort of people, but their new lives were made possible only by the earlier, brutal takeover that Jackson depicts in *Ramona*.) My grandmother identified not with the settlers but rather with Ramona and Alessandro—lonely people, like herself, who were losing their place in a rapidly changing world.

In a sense, the strength of my grandmother's enthusiasm for *Ramona* was a sign of her age. During the fifty years following the novel's appearance, people around the country felt a similar passion for the book, which had been a bestseller upon publication. My grandmother had an aunt back in St. Paul, Minnesota, who was named after Jackson's heroine, as were many other women well into the twentieth century. In Colorado, at the remote spot high on Cheyenne Mountain where Jackson was buried in 1885, countless pilgrims paid homage to the beloved author, piling up stones and branches on top of her grave until they eventually created such a clutter with their tributes and picnic debris that in 1891 Jackson's husband had her body removed to a private cemetery. Between 1910 and 1936, four major Hollywood films were made of *Ramona*—Mary Pickford, one of my grandmother's favorite actresses, was the first movie's silent star. The theme song "Ramona," written by Mabel Wayne and L. Wolfe Gilbert for a 1928 United Artists adaptation starring Dolores del Rio, became an international hit. In Southern California, Jackson's novel was transformed into local legend. Restaurants, streets, and whole towns were given Ramona's name, and a vast tourism industry developed around the fictional events in the book, generating tens of millions of dollars in revenue.

Today *Ramona* no longer attracts such fervent recognition. Yet it does maintain a significant cultural presence in Southern California. There is the ongoing Ramona Pageant, of course; and ever since the novel's first publication, local residents and historians have continued to tussle over which places and people Jackson knew in the area and used as inspiration for her story. Rancho Camulos in Ventura County, on which Jackson loosely based the Moreno estate, is even now being renovated as a museum. More broadly, throughout the region countless Spanish-style strip malls and real estate developments, with their stucco exteriors, arched porticos, and red-tiled roofs, recall turn-of-the-twentieth-century Spanish Colonial Revival and Mission Revival architectural movements, trends that were partly inspired by popular enthusiasm for scenes evoked in *Ramona*. The novel's literary presence can also still be felt. While *Ramona* is read in many places—it is currently available in English in paperback and audiocassette editions, as well as electronically on the Web, and it has been widely translated—it has always been of special interest to Southern Californians. During the decades of the novel's greatest popularity, the Los Angeles Public Library purchased more than 1,000 copies in an effort to meet the demand of local readers; many other Southern Californians bought the book themselves, ensuring it continuous sales. *Ramona* has also taken an important place in the literary history of Southern California. The first novel about the region ever published, it is the founding work in a powerful local dystopian tradition. With Ramona and Alessandro, who wander through Southern California as through a nightmare world, isolated, dispossessed of their rightful connection to the land, and longing to be consoled for the ruin of their dreams, Jackson created the first figures in the long line of disappointed, deracinated heroes who populate the later Southern California fiction of writers as diverse as Nathanael West, Evelyn Waugh, Thomas Pynchon, and Joan Didion.

Who was Helen Jackson, and how did she arrive at this seminal regional vision? For years now I have tried to find answers to these questions. Motivated initially by my grandmother's enthusiasm for Jackson and her work, I later formed a sustained interest of my own, discovering Jackson to be a complicated, witty, immensely resolute woman, and a writer of considerable power. While *Ramona* was perhaps her most significant literary achievement, she was prolific in several genres during the two decades of her career, 1865 through 1885, writing not only fiction but also poetry and creative nonfiction. Her work in each of these forms is worthy of substantive attention. I have therefore organized this book by both genre and chronology. After an overview of Jackson's life and work, I make an extended examination of her formative influences and then address each of her various types of writing roughly in the order in which she began to devote attention to them.

Jackson was not given to explicit theorizing of her own work. Even so, many disparate sources have provided me with evidence in my investigation of her intellectual life. Above all, her literary interests and beliefs can be discovered by examining her published writings, which she wished to speak for themselves, and also by judiciously considering the occasional comments on literary matters that punctuate her private correspondence. Locating and making use of these sources has involved a good deal of literary sleuthing. Much of Jackson's work was never collected but is available only in its original periodical form, and these pieces are sometimes hard to identify; she published not only under her most common literary signature, "H.H.," an acronym for "Helen Hunt," but also under a variety of pseudonyms and anonymously. (The name "Helen Hunt Jackson," now universally applied to Jackson, includes the surnames of both her first husband, Edward Hunt, and her second husband, William Jackson. She never used this combined name either in publishing her work or in referring to herself.) Jackson's private letters are scattered across the country in dozens of libraries; I have located fifty-five with Jackson holdings. Some letters that were available to previous commentators have been lost, including a number that were in existence at least as late as 1939, when Ruth Odell published the first and only creditable biography of Jackson, *Helen Hunt Jackson (H.H.)*. I know something about the contents of these missing letters through references to them in published works, but I cannot know how my analysis might have been altered had I been able to review them—nor, for that matter, how the probable future discovery of other, now unsuspected Jackson letters might bear on the portrait I draw here. There are no absolute truths in biography, only lesser and greater degrees of accuracy and understanding.

Still, I have examined most of the 314 letters on which Ruth Odell relied, and also a great many others, a large portion of which only recently became available. For a long time Jackson's survivors and descendants maintained strict control over access to the papers in their possession, but after the Jackson home in Colorado Springs was demolished in 1961, the family began a series of donations to the Tutt Library of Colorado College in Colorado Springs. As late as February 2001, Helen Jackson's great-grandnephew, William ("Bill") S. Jackson III, phoned me from Denver with news that he had just discovered a suitcase full of long-missing Jackson letters while cleaning an upstairs storeroom; after sharing them with me, he presented them to the Tutt Library, where they now take their place alongside another very recent donation from Bill's sister, Jean. In all, I have read, transcribed, and studied more than thirteen hundred letters written by Jackson to friends, family, and business associates. These letters have allowed me to correct a number of misperceptions about Jackson and to understand her life and career in new ways. My work has been facilitated by Jackson's careful dating of her correspondence, but slowed by her often difficult handwriting, which, as she herself realized, began to deteriorate when she was in her twenties from the small, tidy cursive of a contemplative youth to the larger, hurried scrawl of active adulthood.

Jackson left behind almost as few explicit comments about her emotional life as about literary matters. She did not keep diaries.[1] (She did make sporadic notes in pocket date books, but these notes were simply about her daily activities, not her inner life, and only eight of these date books remain in existence today.)[2] When she was young, she wrote lengthy letters about her feelings to her friends and her guardian Julius Palmer, sometimes recording her observations over a span of several days in what she called "journal letters"; but once she became a professional author, she began to save her daily observations for print and to guard her discussion of intimate matters in letters. In 1869 she insisted to her sister Ann: "You always have been & I suppose always will be, my dear sister, urging me to write what you call 'personal letters.' I *can't* do it.— & as for '*feelings*' that is still more out of the question."[3] She was more forthcoming in correspondence with her second husband, William Jackson, but even to him she wrote her more private passages on separate pages, instructing him to burn them after reading: "It is best to have no record anywhere of anything we don't wish to share with strangers after we are dead."[4] By the time of her second marriage, she was famous, and her knowledge that biographers and editors were always eager for access to authors' private letters and unfinished, unpublished manuscripts heightened her reluctance to have any such writings survive her. In 1883 she and John Greenleaf Whittier commiserated over lunch in Boston about the "new terrors added to death" since Nathaniel Hawthorne's son Julian had recently taken the "blasphemous liberty" of publishing his unfinished romance, *Dr. Grimshawe's Secret*.[5] When her own death approached, she instructed associates in San Francisco and New York to burn all of the letters and manuscripts she had stored in temporary desks in those cities, and she asked her husband to destroy immediately "every scrap of writing," including "old letters," "notebooks," "rough draughts," and "mss verses," that remained in her home in Colorado Springs.[6]

In fact, Jackson had always asked certain friends to destroy her letters or at least to ensure that they should never fall into unwanted hands. This is why so few of her letters to her beloved mentor Thomas Wentworth Higginson remain in existence and perhaps also why much of her early and late correspondence with her closest female friends is missing. According to Higginson, Jackson could be "a most hazardous correspondent" where her emotions were involved; he believed that for this reason she had personally destroyed many of her old letters before she married William Jackson in 1875.[7] These probably included not only letters from Higginson, but also those to and from her first husband. Jackson was aware that evidence of old intimacies might wound present loved ones, and she herself had little interest in reawakening buried emotions by the perusal of old correspondence. Once, when her sister Ann was sick and claimed to enjoy "reading over old letters as an assistance to convalescence," Jackson scoffed, "I can't imagine anything that would make me ill quicker."[8]

Not only was Jackson extremely circumspect about discussing her personal life in writing, but she also did everything in her power to prevent journalists and critics from discussing her, though she was eager to see them address her work. Following the Civil War, popular interest in the private lives of authors and other prominent figures grew steadily. Jackson detested this trend, and published two essays on the subject. In "Glass Houses," she criticized both readers and publishers for succumbing to "the silly and vulgar passion of people for knowing all about their neighbors' affairs." In "The Old-Clothes Monger in Journalism," she accused writers who hounded celebrities in print of "patch[ing] out their miserable, little, sham 'properties'" from "scraps from private letters, bits of conversation overheard[,] . . . impudent inferences and suppositions, and guesses about other people's affairs."[9]

Unable to "bear" having her personal life "discussed, or even *mentioned,*" Jackson never submitted without struggle to being "vivisected for the gratification of a vulgar curiosity."[10] She tried to convince editor friends at newspapers not to mention anything in their pages about her doings—"I hate newspaper paragraphs about my movements," she told Whitelaw Reid, managing editor of the *New York Tribune*[11]—and she avoided both reporters and biographers. Toward the end of her life, her pride in keeping herself out of all "biographical notices" and "bevies of 'Famous Women'"[12] was wounded when she mistakenly let down her guard and spoke with two women journalists. One of them, Helen Bartlett, published as interviews extracts from conversations that Jackson had considered entirely confidential. In an article for the *Journalist,* Bartlett not only described Jackson as "a woman of high-strung nerves, as both her manners and her conversation only too plainly indicate," but also focused her piece less on the author than on Jackson's negative opinions of other famous writers—egregious distortions of her actual comments, according to Jackson.[13] The other woman, Alice Wellington Rollins, wrote an article for the *Critic* that made what Jackson considered a "needless revelation to the world" of her habit of spending her Sundays in pleasure outings, rather than at church. "It is all my townspeople can do to keep from *stoning* me for my Sunday outings—How much more strangers," Jackson complained to Joseph Gilder, the editor of the *Critic.*[14] She was especially upset over Rollins's portrait since, at the urging of her more public husband, she had willingly met with Rollins in her own home. She bitterly regretted having spoken with Rollins and Helen Bartlett, and her hatred for newspaper profiles was sealed. "They are sickening; insuperable; one is ready to disappear from the face of the earth altogether, to escape them," she told the writer Charles Dudley Warner. "There is no punishment severe enough for those who write & journals that publish such things."[15]

Because Jackson eschewed biography, I have had recourse to only a very few portraits written by her contemporaries. Moreover, her hostility toward inquiry into her personal life has presented something of an ethical dilemma, for I have certainly relied on "inferences" and "scraps from private letters" in my analysis. I have found some justification for my transgression in the fact that Jackson herself was curious about the personal lives of other authors: the memorandum book she kept during an 1880 visit to Scotland is filled with notes on the private life of the poet Robert Burns, for instance, which she later worked into a published travel essay, "A Burns Pilgrimage."[16] Even more to the point, almost all of her travel essays feature biographical sketches of ordinary people she met on her journeys, and scarcely knew—her own published "guesses about other people's affairs."

PART ONE

An Introduction to Jackson's Life, Career, and Literary Reputation

Staying Power

Helen Maria Fiske, a girl destined to become one of America's most critically acclaimed and financially successful writers in the decades following the Civil War, was born on October 14, 1830, in Amherst, Massachusetts, a rural college town of some 2,500 inhabitants.[1] She learned repeatedly in her own early life the need for perseverance, a lesson that she would later elaborate as the central theme of her writing.

Her father, Nathan Welby Fiske, was an orthodox Calvinist minister who had become a professor of Latin and Greek at Amherst College, a conservative Calvinist stronghold, in 1824. Her mother, Deborah Vinal Fiske, was also an orthodox Calvinist. Both Nathan and Deborah Fiske were writers: Nathan wrote and edited several books, including a mammoth *Manual of Classical Literature* that he worked on for almost a decade during Helen's youth, and Deborah wrote a handful of children's stories in addition to charming letters.[2] Like all orthodox Calvinists, Mr. and Mrs. Fiske believed that human beings were naturally depraved as a result of Adam's original sin, and that God granted salvation from depravity only to a chosen few, whose fate, like that of all people, was thereby predestined, and who would become aware of their election by God through an irresistible conversion experience. In their writings, both were self-conscious dogmatists, for they considered it their duty to help lead readers to God by promoting Christian morality. When directing Helen's education, they worked toward the same goal. Above all, they emphasized the duty of contented submission to God's ordering of events on earth, which they expected their daughter to demonstrate by going about her daily business cheerfully and industriously, even under difficult circumstances.

In some respects, Helen's early home life was conducive to cheerfulness. Family relations seem to have been quite happy. There were frequent visits from young cousins, from Nathan's sister Maria, and from Deborah's father David Vinal, a practical-minded, gruff, but loving man. While Helen's parents experienced their share of marital tension, they were clearly devoted to each other. In his journals, Nathan Fiske calls his wife Deborah his "dear companion," and in letters to her he often comments on the pleasure he takes in her company: "To have a companion, an equal, whom you love & by whom you are loved, who is one with yourself in every dear interest for time & eternity," he tells her, is "blessedness." Deborah's letters to her husband also express loving fidelity. "As to prayer for you," she writes in one, "I shall as soon forget to pray for myself."[3] Helen was aware of the love between her parents, and long after her youth had passed, she wrote about it in one of her stories for children:

> My mamma came home one evening just at dark. I was lying on a sofa in a dark corner, where she could not see me, and papa was sitting by the fire. She went up to his chair and kissed him, and burst out into such a laugh, as she said, "Darling[.]" . . . It makes the tears come into my eyes even now, to remember how my papa and mamma used to love each other. Since I have grown up, and have seen what men and women really are, I know how wonderful it was.[4]

Helen's parents were as devoted to her and her sister Ann, often called "Annie," as they were to each other. Their attention to Helen and belief in her capabilities instilled in her a firm, enduring sense of self-confidence. And even though Helen was four years older than Ann, and left home to begin attending boarding schools when Ann was only eight, the two sisters enjoyed a warm relationship. They spent time together during school vacations; after both were grown and married, they visited each other and traded frequent letters on domestic matters. When Helen became a professional writer, the two sisters grew further apart in temperament and opinions, but their steady exchange of letters continued. Helen delighted in her role of aunt to Ann's six children—especially her namesake, a niece named Helen.

Although the atmosphere in the Fiske home was nurturing, Helen began when very young to experience a series of losses and sorrows that would eventually give her early life an aspect of unremitting misfortune. When she was three, her one-year-old brother Humphrey died. When she was four, her only living grandmother died. When she was eleven, she lost her best friend, Amherst faculty daughter Rebecca Snell. Throughout her childhood, her mother suffered terribly from tuberculosis (then called "consumption"), America's deadliest disease in the early nineteenth century. Any Amherst neighbor who met Deborah would have understood the ominous significance of what one called her constant "coughing and panting and sinking."[5] She had trouble eating and sometimes weighed as little as seventy-nine pounds. Her doctors prescribed conventional treatments, advising her to avoid bookish endeavors and to adopt a mild diet, take mild exercise, and seek mild climates whenever possible. When she was especially unwell, they ordered her to maintain "*perfect quietness* and *entire* rest from talking, walking, working and everything," including "family cares & toils."[6] At these times, Deborah would sometimes leave her family and go to Charlestown to stay with her paternal uncle Otis Vinal and his wife Martha, who had cared for her in her teens. On other occasions, she would send Helen and Ann away to the homes of relations or to boarding schools in various Massachusetts towns.

This habit of separation at times of illness was to have a profound emotional impact on Helen. When away from her family, she grappled with intense homesickness, at the same time feeling that she must subordinate her own needs to the common effort to preserve her mother's health. In 1841, when she had been sent to stay with family friends in nearby Hadley and her mother was off in Boston, she wrote plaintively to her father as Thanksgiving approached: "I thought we should be comfortably settled at home but instead of that we shall be scattered at the four ends of the earth."[7] For her mother, she made an effort to be braver. "I wish you would begin to think of coming home not that I am homesick. No I should be wicked and ungrateful if I were," she told her.

> But you know "there is no place like Home" and I begin to long to see you . . . now that the novelty of being "Miss Helen or Miss Fiske" as I am generally called has worn off. . . . I hear nothing but "How do you do Miss Fiske, When do you leave town Miss Fiske, I should be very happy to have you call on me Miss Fiske." I am utterly sick of it and you cannot think how I want some body that I can talk to as I do to you.[8]

Two years later, at boarding school in Pittsfield, Helen was again struggling to be mature for her mother. "I have been '*awful*' homesick since I've been here but I hope I've got over it now," she wrote. "If it is true as folks say 'you never are homesick again after you have been *really* so once' I am sure I never shall be again for I've been 'seasoned' this time for certain."[9]

Consumption and anxiety about consumption dominated Helen's childhood. Her mother's pain was ever-present, as was the possibility of separation from her, temporary or final. In addition, Helen's father had chronic bronchitis, and by the late 1830s, according to his journal, he showed signs of "incipient consumption."[10] On several occasions ill health forced him to take breaks from work. And as if concern for the lives of her parents were not already much to bear, Helen herself suffered frequent and severe sore throats. From age six to age eighteen, these sore throats were, she would later testify, "the haunting misery of my life."[11] During most of the nineteenth century, tuberculosis was thought to be a hereditary rather than a contagious disease, and the Fiskes worried that Helen had inherited her mother's illness: Deborah had suffered sore throats like Helen's as a child, before her disease advanced, and Deborah's mother had died of consumption when Deborah was only two. "When Helen is unwell it makes me so nervous," Deborah admitted to a cousin.[12] When apart from Helen, Deborah sent detailed advice in letters. "I have been thinking that you may possibly have a sore throat," she wrote in one,

> But if you do, you know that there is nothing which can be done for them, but to keep still and quiet, and be patient, and take small doses of salts occasionally and drink lemon water or cream of carbon water, and live very light, which you always choose to do rather than swallow where there is no space. You must be *very careful* about taking colds, for you know colds bring on the inflammation in your throat— never pull off any article because you are "so *hot,* you shall certainly *melt,*" wait till you have become cool by *keeping still.*[13]

Deborah died on February 19, 1844, when Helen was thirteen. Away from home at boarding school in Pittsfield, Helen slipped into a protracted period of depression. To make matters worse, her father's consumption began to advance, and in 1846 his doctors recommended an entire change of climate. He set off on a trip—to Palestine, a place he had long wished to visit, and where he hoped, as his wife used to hope, that new surroundings might revive him. Sadly, he died there, of dysentery, in May 1847. He was buried on Mt. Zion.[14] In boarding school as usual, this time at the Ipswich Female Seminary, Helen finally received the news of her father's death in July. She was devastated. As upon her mother's death, she had been given no chance to say goodbye or to offer comfort, a circumstance that would grieve her for years. Now, at age sixteen, she was an orphan. In losing her father, moreover, she lost the one person on whom she had come entirely to depend for intellectual companionship. She felt "a *separation,* a *want of congeniality,* an utter *impossibility* of sympathy" between herself and those around her, and often cried for feeling "all alone" in the world. She became, in her own estimation, "a sad, unamiable, half-misanthropic silent girl," her life a "confused medley of mistakes, wrong doing, wishes, aspirations, vanities, absurdities, miseries."[15]

Fortunately, a more peaceful and happier phase of life soon began. Helen's grandfather Vinal, a successful Boston contractor and lumber dealer, arranged for Julius A. Palmer, a Boston lawyer, to assume guardianship of his two granddaughters, while he himself supported them financially. Helen never spent an extended period of time with Julius Palmer's large family, but she became very close with one of Palmer's children, Lucy, and especially with Julius Palmer himself. For several years in early adulthood she wrote to him frequently and with unusual candor.[16] "Never in my life have I had a friend to whom I could speak so unreservedly," she told Palmer when she was nineteen.[17] When she was twenty-one, she described her feelings for him in a letter to an old friend of her mother's: "all the love which my heart held for father, mother, home—*all*, has centered on him."[18]

In the fall of 1851, Helen went to live for a year with the family of Julius Palmer's brother, the Reverend Ray Palmer, in Albany, New York. There she met Edward Hunt, a civil engineer and lieutenant in the Army Corps of Engineers, assigned to river and harbor duties. She was immediately impressed by his intellect and good looks, and soon afterward by his warm heart. After a six-month engagement, they were married, on October 28, 1852. Right away, Helen felt her "inner life" become more "calm," less racked by "storms."[19] Indeed, she was "almost *too* happy to trust the future."[20] After nearly two months of marriage, she told Lucy Palmer that she still felt the same "passionate delight—the almost wild bliss" that had thrilled her on first getting to know her husband.[21]

Very quickly, however, her old experience of sorrow and separation returned with a vengeance. Illness seemed to stalk the Hunt family much as it had the Fiskes. In 1853 Helen gave birth to a son, Murray, who died of a brain tumor before his first birthday. The year 1855 was marred by the deaths of both her mother's Aunt Vinal and one of her own closest friends, Henry Root. In December 1855 Helen had a second son, Warren Horsford, nicknamed "Rennie." She doted on him. Still, in the few letters that survive from this period of her life, no member of the Hunt family ever seems entirely healthy; Edward, in particular, is generally only "*pretty* well."[22] In 1857 Edward was ordered away from his usual postings along the Atlantic seaboard to Key West. He tried desperately to have his orders revoked, writing to a superior that he feared the climate in Florida not only would aggravate his own digestive disorders, which had for several years kept him "more or less miserable" and "only able to work by extreme effort," but would also be entirely out of the question for Helen:

> Mrs. Hunt is never well in warm weather & depends on the bracing effect of winter for renewing the wastes of summer. She is of delicate constitution, & could not rally her strength after being prostrated by a Southern climate. I should therefore not expect to take her to a Southern Station.
>   Thus an order to the South is to me a virtual decree of divorce, & a consignment of myself to the tortures of bilious dyspepsia & fever.[23]

Despite his pleas, Edward was sent to Key West. From 1857 through 1862 he lived there for the better part of each year, superintending the construction, and at the start of the Civil War the defense, of Fort Taylor. He also spent two months in Texas and California, planning the fortifications of Galveston Harbor and of Lime Point, San Francisco. Later, he was involved in the Union campaign in the Shenandoah Valley. During this period, the Hunt family was able to live together only in the summers, when Edward was stationed in various locations in the Northeast. While Helen had her good-natured son to keep her company, and delighted in teaching and playing with him, she found these separations from her husband difficult. She often urged him to "retire."[24] Finally, in 1863, Edward was recalled from Florida to work in a place more accessible to his family, New York City. But that autumn an accident occurred while he was experimenting in the Brooklyn Navy Yard with a weapon of his own design, the "Sea Miner," a device that involved a new way of firing torpedoes from a ship. According to Helen, "a valve which should have been *opened* was left *shut*—& the hold was consequently filled with the gas from the gun powder discharge."[25] Edward collapsed from asphyxiation, suffered a concussion, and died in the Brooklyn Naval Hospital on October 2, 1863, just three weeks shy of the Hunts' eleventh wedding anniversary.

Having spent her entire adolescence in full mourning dress, from the time of her mother's death until the spring of 1850—a period, as Helen calculated, of "*seven* years, with the exception of a short interval before my father's death"[26]—Helen put her dark mourning clothes back on. She also began writing her letters on black-bordered mourning stationery. In the years to come she would seldom speak of Edward's loss, preferring instead to bear her suffering in silence; but when she became a professional writer she would allude to it in poetry and in an early short story, "The Elder's Wife." There her heroine Draxy Miller is at first dazed, and later earnestly determined to carry on, after her husband's death in an accident. In the period immediately following Edward's death, Helen made efforts to have the government continue his work on the Sea Miner, arguing that not to do so would "be a cruel injustice, to his reputation, & a poor return for his devotion" to the Union cause;[27] and she dedicated herself wholeheartedly to Rennie. Within a mere eighteen months, however, Rennie contracted diphtheria while they were visiting Ann in West Roxbury, Massachusetts. After three days of acute illness he died, on April 13, 1865, at age nine.

Rennie's death was a devastating blow to Helen, a catastrophe greater even than the loss of her husband. She would never entirely recover. In 1882 she revealed the depth of her lasting sorrow in a letter to an acquaintance. After recounting the long, terrible night of Rennie's death, an ordeal during which Rennie was tender toward her and brave, she confided: "My boy would be a man now—twenty-seven years old. But every moment of that night is as vivid to me as if it were yesterday. I shall never be so old that I can think of it or of him without tears."[28]

While Helen would never cease to feel the pain of being childless, she emerged from her early years of loss and sorrow with highly effective methods for coping with trouble. She found strength in the practice of Christian submission, working to remain cheerful and industrious no matter what the circumstances; and she found escape from any lingering psychic turmoil through frequent travel and relocation. While these behaviors were initially acts of will, modeled after the teaching and example of her parents, in time they became habitual, instinctive responses. They also became essential both to her ability to write and to the content of her work.

Jackson was not naturally given to submission—quite the opposite. When she was a child, her parents considered her rebellious and moody, a "wild witch cat" in comparison with her placid sister Ann.[29] One family acquaintance, describing the Fiske girls, said that "Annie was a tender little girl but Helen was tough & hardy, & would wrestle or fight at almost any time or anybody."[30] In one of the few published writings in which the adult Jackson seems to have written fairly directly of her own early experiences, "The Naughtiest Day of My Life, and What Came of It," she describes for young readers a day on which she and a childhood friend, Rebecca Snell's sister Mary, skipped school and ran away for a frolic in the woods.[31] Helen, a little towheaded, green-eyed girl, who liked to climb fences and walk on walls, was thrilled by the illicit adventure, and cared little for the trouble she knew she must be causing at home; there, her parents and grandfather were in a desperate state of worry, and classes were canceled at Amherst College so that students and faculty could join in searching for the lost children. In adolescence, Helen was still earning a reputation as the "naughty sister."[32] When Julius Palmer became her guardian, she warned him of her temperament. "Annie will *never* be any trouble to any one, I *know,* and I will *try,*" she said, admitting that the effort would be difficult because she had an "inconsistent heart."[33]

As an adult, Jackson remained inconsistent, moody, and impulsive. She continued to experience occasional bouts of severe depression, such as those she had suffered on the death of each of her parents, and she had many more periods of protracted low spirits—times when she felt, as she once told her sister, a "*simple prostration,*" a "sense of weak good-for-nothingness."[34] More often, she was in noticeably high spirits. She was known for living intensely, moving and speaking quickly, and expressing unusually strong reactions to people she met, "sudden fancies" in which she placed lasting trust.[35] One of her closest friends, Sarah Woolsey, explained these fancies: "She loved, when she did love, with her whole heart, but she hated as thoroughly as she loved, and what she hated or doubted she resisted. Her will was like an iron rod; you could influence but never bend her." Like many who knew Jackson, Woolsey thought her friend's unpredictable vivacity made her a unique and charming companion. "She was daring, defiant, audaciously frank, and her keen sense of humor dealt unsparingly with constituted authorities," Woolsey said. "She was the most vital creature, without exception, that I ever knew." Other people were sometimes frustrated by Jackson's impetuousness. According to Woolsey, even Edward Hunt was occasionally "perplexed and distressed" by his wife's "snap judgements."[36]

Despite her notable inconsistencies, Jackson had by adulthood fashioned a single outward response to her own shifting moods and to the vicissitudes of life. Invariably, she worked to maintain an attitude of Christian submission. In her case, submission did not mean acknowledging herself helpless in the face of God's will and clinging anxiously to hope in his mercy, for she soon renounced Calvinism in favor of the more optimistic creeds of Unitarianism and Transcendentalism. Instead, she looked on submission as a more practical-minded, nonsectarian habit of accepting circumstances that she could not control and manifesting her acceptance through cheerfulness and earnest application to work.

Her response to Rennie's death illustrates her manner of dealing with adversity. After shutting herself up for a while at the home of friends, where she wrestled alone with her losses, she finally emerged in the world as outwardly cheerful as ever, determined to accept her misfortunes without rancor. In addition, she set herself industriously to work: her first publication, a poem titled "The Key of the Casket," appeared in the *New York Evening Post* on June 7, 1865, less than two months following Rennie's death. From this time forward, she devoted herself to forging a literary career, working with such extreme diligence and regularity that she would one day refer to herself as "a martinet of ardent system."[37] When she had firmly established herself as a writer, she told her sister: "there have been a great many things in this world I have not liked, but of which I have made the best." She assured friends who continued to express concern over her many early reverses that she remained "content, always, and sometimes glad."[38] And whenever she was confronted with new afflictions, she spoke of them with pointed resignation: "I should be a brute & deserve a worse thing to come on me, if I grumbled," she would say.[39]

Over time, Jackson's efforts to keep cheerful and productive in the face of difficulty became an integral part of her identity. She considered it a point of honor to triumph over circumstances by means of willpower. "I scorn to complain," she once explained to a friend, and she would always dislike people who acted "sulky."[40] The extent to which her outward cheer was merely the product of habit and determination, rather than a true reflection of her inner feelings, varied with her situation. In the years immediately following her loss of Edward and Rennie, she mostly used good humor as a conscious means of establishing control over her life, as a sort of second skin behind which she could hide her misery and pain. In 1870 she published an essay, "Friends of the Prisoners," in which she obliquely acknowledged her dual manner of living. Claiming that all people are prisoners of their own sorrows, she argues that the best way to alleviate "bitterness" is to deny it through a discipline of cheer: "We keep our fetters out of sight, we smile, we sing, we contrive to be glad of being alive[.] . . . How bravely and cheerily most eyes look up! This is one of the sweetest mercies of life, that 'the heart knoweth its own bitterness,' and, knowing it, can hide it."[41] Two years later, she explicitly admitted to a long-estranged friend, Mary Sprague, that her own cheer was little more than a mask. "I keep a brave face—partly from pride I am afraid—partly because of my temperament," she wrote. "But the heart of me is sorely tired out."[42]

Not long after making this confession, Jackson entered upon her years of greatest personal happiness, a time when her outward cheer more directly reflected inner peace and joy. In the mid-1870s, illness led her to move away from her native New England to Colorado Springs, Colorado Territory. There, she met William Sharpless Jackson, an executive with the Denver and Rio Grande Railroad and a rising banker. William patiently courted her, helping her to mend from her early sorrows and also from a later period of frustrated affections. Friendship grew into love, and they were married on October 22, 1875. Their early years together were joyous. And though they would later struggle with several personal sources of friction and be kept a good deal apart, they remained dedicated to each other. William's support for his wife's work eventually helped her achieve the greatest satisfactions of her career.

In the coming chapters, I discuss how Jackson's parents and a succession of later teachers first taught her to value submission as a virtue, and how, in turn, she came to endorse this virtue in her writings. She also internalized her parents' obsession with illness, including their anxiety about her own health and their manner of trying to cope with chronic sickness through relocation. Because she had been often separated from her parents at times of illness, and was subsequently separated permanently from them by death, she had by the age of twenty endured what she considered the lamentable experience of living in ten different residences. Moreover, she had come to associate relocation not only with poor health but also with loneliness and trying to feel better about loneliness. In the process she had laid the foundations of a complex psychological wanderlust: for the rest of her life both her physical and mental health would be dependent on changes in location.

In her extant correspondence, Jackson mentions her personal health troubles more often than any other topic. In letter after letter, she describes how she is shut up in various rooms, on various couches, for days or weeks; in letter after letter, she cancels or makes only tentative plans for seeing friends because she fears to venture out of doors. As a rule, Jackson never felt well for more than six months at a time. "I feel about my body as I do about a person who has repeatedly deceived me," she wrote to one of her doctors in 1873. "I have no faith in anything short of a long probation."[43]

Over the course of her life she endured a vast, baffling variety of ailments. In some of her letters it is difficult to discern exactly what is wrong with her, or even if she truly is ill; it might be closer to the truth to say that she thinks she is ill. At times, she seems to exaggerate her symptoms in an effort to avoid an onerous social obligation. During the summer of 1876, for instance, she told correspondents that she had so strained her eyes and neck in looking over the

Centennial Exhibitions in Philadelphia that she required two weeks to recover. Yet there is no doubt that she often suffered a great deal, and that she possessed a remarkable capacity for productivity in the midst of discomforts that could make it nearly impossible to lie down, eat, or even breathe. She had weak eyes, frequent headaches, a "bilious" condition, and teeth so bad that she eventually resorted to dentures. Three times, during two trips to Europe and again at the end of her life, she believed she had contracted malaria. To her sister, she once defined her "same old troubles" as "indigestion—constipation &c," caused by "having worn out my digestive apparatus, by *brain* excitements, & malarial poison combined."[44] Above all, she suffered from severe respiratory troubles. Though she did not state it in so many words, she seems to have lived in fear of dying from the same disease that had shattered the lives of her parents. For instance, because she had watched her mother waste away from tuberculosis, she always paid great attention to what she ate and wished to be "fleshy."[45] A modest five feet, three inches tall, she eventually came to weigh 170 pounds.

Jackson never did develop advanced symptoms of tuberculosis, but her worries over her "old lung trouble" were not unfounded.[46] She was almost certainly infected as a child, and throughout her life she continued to have severe sore throats. At different times, she attributed this "throat burning," or irritation of what she sometimes jokingly called her "(mu-cuss) membrane,"[47] to various maladies including catarrh, laryngitis, the common cold, influenza, diphtheria, and seasonal allergies, which Jackson knew as "rose cold" or "June cold." For the most part, however, she blamed chronic bronchitis, the illness that had plagued her father at the height of his battle with tuberculosis. When she was nineteen, Helen reported to Julius Palmer that she had been to see the same New York throat specialist who had examined her father shortly before his fateful trip to Palestine; this specialist had diagnosed her with chronic bronchitis "precisely similar to my *father's,* except that the disease had not extended so far." The doctor ordered the immediate removal of her tonsils, and told one of her teachers, who passed on the opinion to Helen, "that it was a wonder that with all the consumptive tendencies of our family, I had lived so long."[48]

By middle life, Jackson had come to think of "bronchitis" as her "old arch enemy."[49] This enemy assaulted her with such frequency and regularity that she was on intimate terms with its every maneuver. Her letters are filled with discussions of whether it is "past the time" when "the illness" should arrive, whether a particular "attack" is worse than another or perhaps more "comfortable and natural," and when she might expect "the merciful period which will bring suspension of the torture."[50] To combat her sore throats, Jackson took bed rest and consulted homeopathic doctors. A relatively popular form of alternative medicine in mid-nineteenth-century America, homeopathy involved taking minute doses of toxins (including, in Jackson's case, arsenic) in order to promote the body's natural tendencies in illness, rather than trying to counter those tendencies through the standard pills, tonics, blisterings, and bleedings.[51] More important, because doctors were increasingly recommending extended journeys to women with respiratory illnesses, as they had long recommended them to men, she arranged her entire life around frequent changes of climate in an effort to stave off the onset of sickness and the low spirits that often accompanied it.[52]

Since germs and contagion were not well understood in Jackson's time, she believed that bad climates and localized pockets of unhealthy "air"—in her living quarters, or in sudden atmospheric phenomena such as wind, dust, and electrical storms—were directly responsible for triggering her illnesses. She therefore moved with the seasons, at least twice a year, working to avoid both harsh winters and enervating summers. Constantly in motion, she made a succession of temporary homes for herself in various boardinghouses and hotels. In warm weather she frequented mountain resorts in rural New Hampshire and Massachusetts; at the start of her career she passed many winters at Hannah Dame's boardinghouse in Newport, Rhode Island; she so often occupied two quiet, comfortable rooms at the south side of Boston's Parker House, on School Street, that she considered the hotel "my own inn";[53] and she made innumerable stays in New York City at both the Brevoort and the Berkeley Hotels. Only when she married William Jackson in 1875 and settled in Colorado Springs did she have a permanent home, but even then she continued to travel for health to lodgings in the East and later in California.

Jackson often expressed sorrow that she was "a bit of drifting seaweed," a "world-wanderer," an "ancient pilgrim" who could not even "*imagine* how it would seem to live in *one* place."[54] After she finally did establish her home with her second husband, she was frustrated at having to keep up her seasonal travels. "Here am I," she lamented to one friend, "for thirty years driven like a leaf from pillar to post, by one destiny after another—And after, in my old age, I did get what looked like a permanent anchorage, a dear sweet home, climate must needs rear up & attack me & compel me forth again, every autumn!"[55] Her own disappointment led her to express special sympathy for wanderers and exiles in her published writings. "This is one of the saddest sights in the world," she wrote in one children's essay: "a man or a woman running from one climate to another climate, and from one doctor to another doctor, trying to cure or patch up a body that is out of order."[56]

Yet the truth is that Jackson felt saddest when she did not have the distraction of frequent movement. According to Sarah Woolsey, she once confided that the reason she had never established a home for herself before her second marriage was that she feared "loneliness would smite me every time I entered the door."[57] After she did have her permanent home in Colorado, she clearly continued to journey not only for health purposes, and to renew her literary contacts, but also to stave off feelings of loneliness and melancholy. She admitted to friends that she was never entirely happy in her home when her husband was away on business. And in 1879, when she was suffering from a bout of depression, she turned to travel, explaining to her husband, in a letter written from a train headed east, that she needed to be "on the move again" in order to "feel better."[58]

Travel did make Jackson feel better. She was curious about the world and took delight in visiting new places and meeting local people. Her precarious health never kept her, when well, from active adventuring. In years when the cross-country journey took at least a week, she spent long days and nights alone in trains, moving frequently between the East Coast, Colorado, and California. From the time of her first clandestine tramp through the woods outside Amherst, she was especially fond of rural exploration. "It seemed to me that I should like to go on walking from grove to grove and field to field as long as I lived," she later wrote of that formative experience. "I think a sort of insanity had taken possession of me, from my delight in the freedom and the out-door life. I love it well enough now to understand how I must have felt then."[59] She liked flowers and plants, and knew a good deal about them; she took regular nature walks in search of new botanic specimens, which she often carried home as decorations for her lodgings. According to Sarah Woolsey, who sometimes accompanied Jackson on hikes through New England woods, "At each discovery her bright face would wear a look like some happy wild thing's, a look with no yesterday in it and no regrets."[60] She particularly loved mountain scenery, and considered herself a "passionate mountaineer." She once told a friend, "I shall sit at the foot of mountains till I die. They are the only things I love, except now and then a man, or a woman."[61]

Like her practice of submission, Jackson's habit of travel and exploration gave shape to her career, becoming the tangible force behind her eventual development as a regionalist writer. And in turn, by association with the personal fulfillment she came to find in her literary career, travel became ever more important as a means of maintaining her psychic well-being.

Jackson first began to write in earnest early in 1866, when, after publishing a handful of poems based on her early losses and one essay—works that appeared mostly in the *New York Evening Post*—she took up residence for the winter in Newport, Rhode Island. She was familiar with the town, having lived there for a time during her marriage to Hunt, when she had enjoyed the "constant *tonic*" of the local climate,[62] reputed to be healthy for consumptives. More important, Newport was known as a literary center, and she had decided to act on a long-standing desire to become a writer. Perhaps intentionally, she moved into the same boardinghouse where Thomas Wentworth Higginson was living with his invalid wife, Mary Channing. A man known today mostly for his role as advisor to Emily Dickinson, Higginson had by 1866 begun to establish his reputation as a writer and important arbiter of literary taste. He quickly became Jackson's literary mentor.

Higginson was to have a profound influence on Jackson's literary career, second only to that of her parents. From the beginning, he urged her to perfect her prose and to practice writing in a wide variety of genres, including travel sketches, essays on domestic topics, literary reviews, and editorials. At the same time, though, because he believed that her true talent lay not in prose but in poetry, he encouraged her to direct her best energies as an artist to her poetry, to think of her prose as a secondary endeavor, a means of earning money. Under his sway, Jackson considered poetry her primary art form throughout the first decade of her career. Her assessment was solidly reinforced by the praise "H.H." quickly began to receive for her poems from readers of what became her primary literary outlet, the weekly *New York Independent,* and also from some of the most powerful American poets and critics of her time, including Ralph Waldo Emerson. Toward her prose writing, on the other hand, Jackson maintained until the mid-1870s an attitude that was more a journalist's than an artist's: she kept an eye out for useful material in her surroundings and everyday experiences, with the goal of working her observations into prose that she could sell to the periodical press.

Though for a long time Jackson placed top priority on poetry, it was actually in her prose that she gradually discovered her deepest literary concerns. As she moved about from place to place, taking close notice of whether local environments and inhabitants might promote her health and happiness, and whether she should perhaps set up one of her temporary homes, she naturally took a keen interest in regional identity and difference. This interest immediately made itself felt in travel essays, and later in fiction.

In the earliest years of her career, just following the Civil War, Jackson wrote many New England travel sketches for the *New York Evening Post* under the pseudonym "Rip Van Winkle." Styling herself after Washington Irving's famous fictional character, who sleeps through the Revolutionary War and then awakens to find himself in a new nation, Jackson adopts a narrative attitude in her early travel essays of bemused wonderment at the changes occurring in post–Civil War America. In particular, she expresses nostalgia for the fast-disappearing countryside of places like the Amherst of her youth, depicting these rural hamlets as profoundly threatened by industrialism, which was spreading rapidly through the United States at this time.

In November 1868, Jackson took a break from her New England wanderings and Newport winters and went off to spend more than a year in Europe. In the travel essays she wrote at this time under her now familiar signature "H.H."—some of which were published in newspapers while she was away and others, after her return, in the prestigious *Atlantic Monthly* and in a volume by

J. R. Osgood—she began devoting more attention to brief portraits of individual people. Her talent for character portrayal was significant and, along with her considerable descriptive powers, raised her nonfiction writing above the level of most other newspaper journalism. After she returned to the United States, her new enthusiasm for character portraiture combined with her burgeoning interest in America's newly industrializing rural corners. As they fused, she began to find a lasting focus for her prose: humble people, usually women, of various ethnic backgrounds, whose good cheer and diligence enable them to cope with change at home, at work, and in the broader world.

Taken as a whole, Jackson's travel essays offer a paradoxical critique of the industrialization of America. She intended them to constitute what she called, in a significant early title, "A Protest against the Spread of Civilization." In this context, she did not intend the word "civilization" to mean culture or comfort, which she always appreciated, but rather the negative side effects of rapid industrialization: the invasion of charming rural places by new railroads, businesses, and masses of people. Related to the problem of industrialization in her mind was what she considered the generally "out-of-breath," "utilitarian, money getting, money spending spirit of the age," when many people seemed inclined to ignore beauty and human compassion in their hunger for material possessions and practical advances—a "new kind of railroad tie, or mowing machine, a cheaper light, or a swifter wheel."[63] In her essays, Jackson attempted not so much to discourage American emigration to new areas as to encourage new emigrants to respect the rights and dignity of their predecessors. Yet despite her best intentions, her essays actually served to promote the very "spread of civilization" they protested. Jackson's own touristic presence helped transfigure the rural places in which she took up temporary residence, and the essays she wrote about those places encouraged readers to join her in visiting them.

The contradictory nature of Jackson's travel essays became especially apparent after she settled in Colorado Springs in the mid-1870s. The eastern half of Colorado, where Colorado Springs is located, had become part of the United States with the 1803 Louisiana Purchase and was relatively well-known to Americans. But the rest of the territory—that portion west of the Continental Divide along the Rocky Mountains and, according to the 1819 Spanish Treaty line, south of the Arkansas River—had been nominally controlled by Spain and then Mexico, and in many places held by the Utes, up until the 1848 Treaty of Guadalupe Hidalgo. This area had not been much visited by Americans before the territorial era began in 1861; along with the rest of Colorado, it did not become a formal part of the Union until the coming of statehood in 1876, three years into Jackson's residence. Everywhere Jackson journeyed in her new home, she encountered distinct evidence of the effects of American expansion. As she watched and reported, a local mining boom turned empty spaces into bustling industrial towns, and settlers from the United States usurped political and economic supremacy from longtime Indian and Hispanic residents.

Jackson criticized the escalating destruction of Colorado's natural environment and sympathized with the area's original inhabitants: from the time of her move, her writings begin to reflect an increased empathy for America's embattled ethnic minorities. Nonetheless, her main loyalties in her Colorado essays remain with those American settlers responsible for colonizing and developing the West. After all, her new hometown of Colorado Springs had been founded only as late as 1871, two years before she arrived, upon lands previously belonging to two Mexican estates; Jackson herself was one of the Anglo-American pioneers who transformed this once scarcely inhabited place into a town that by 1874 boasted 3,000 residents, enthusiastic developers who erected some 250 buildings every year. Jackson's new husband, moreover, was a leader in the railroad and banking enterprises that were spearheading change throughout the region. As usual, Jackson's travel writings offered what was in effect a tacit invitation to other Anglo-Americans to follow in her footsteps. They therefore served, like the work of other frontier writers, to solidify the American expansion they described.

After her move to Colorado and her remarriage, Jackson continued to write, prolifically, in all of the genres she had originally practiced. But she made one significant change: she dedicated herself increasingly to fiction, eventually coming to think of poetry as her "old trade," an activity she undertook as a "rest" from more difficult work.[64] She had first begun to publish short fiction in 1871, under the pseudonym "Saxe Holm," and she continued to publish Saxe Holm stories throughout her career, mostly in *Scribner's Monthly* magazine. The Saxe Holm stories were very popular, and speculation about their authorship added much to their visibility. Jackson thought of the stories as "light fiction,"[65] however, and turned them out almost formulaically: she quickly developed a standard heroine, a unidimensional being who changed little over the course of Jackson's career in the short story. Possessed of an artistic sensibility and an inspired connection with her natural environment, the Saxe Holm heroine is unerringly cheerful and industrious—a rather heavy-handed example of righteous living for her fellow characters, and for readers.[66]

In the second half of her career, Jackson was not satisfied to remain only within the boundaries of the Saxe Holm stories; she wished to try writing longer, more nuanced fiction. In February 1876, at the age of forty-five, she sat down to write her first novel. Published later that same year, *Mercy Philbrick's Choice* is the partly autobiographical tale of a young woman's decision to forgo the uncertain rewards of romantic love in order to pursue a career as a poet; as such, it is that relatively rare thing, a female artist's coming-of-age story, or *Künstlerroman*. It is also a New England regional novel, in which Jackson's long-standing interest in America's rural corners and the women who struggle to persevere in them makes itself felt as an essential element of her story. In 1877 Jackson published another New England novel, *Hetty's Strange History,* and in 1878 she published a Colorado novel for children, *Nelly's Silver Mine.* Roberts Brothers, a prominent Boston firm, published *Mercy* and *Hetty* anonymously and *Nelly* under the "H.H." signature; all these books received a good deal of critical and public attention.

Mercy and Hetty are more fully developed characters than the heroines of Jackson's short stories, and their relationships with their regional environments more conflicted. While they both exhibit the Saxe Holm heroine's exemplary cheerfulness and industry, their virtues of submission function not simply as tools of didacticism but also as foils for more complex textual and societal pressures. Their indomitable cheerfulness and industriousness are intended to make them admirable and immediately winning to readers, so that they will remain sympathetic whatever they might eventually do: from choosing a career over domesticity, like Mercy, to running away from a husband and taking up paid work under a false identity, like Hetty.

After publishing *Hetty's Strange History,* Jackson began intermittent work on another adult novel, in which she hoped to make good on the real gains she had made as a fiction writer. But she never completed "Elspeth Dynor," for in the autumn of 1879, a new interest began to absorb all her attention. She was visiting Boston, struggling through travel and activity to overcome low spirits, when she attended a lecture by Ponca Chief Standing Bear. Standing Bear spoke on the miseries his agricultural people had endured since the federal government had forcibly removed them from their ancestral homelands in Dakota Territory to Indian Territory, in what is today Oklahoma. He and his translator, the Omaha Indian Susette La Flesche, appealed powerfully to the deepest preoccupations of Jackson's imagination: each epitomized the dignified rural person struggling to carry on in the face of industrial expansion whom she had long been celebrating in her travel essays and fiction. Moreover, the Poncas' status as homeless wanderers recalled Jackson's own early experience as an orphan, when repeated misfortune had first taught her the meaning of perseverance.

Until learning of the plight of the Poncas, Jackson had never demonstrated much interest in reform movements, though she was always drawn to the company of social activists and had grown up in an environment supportive of moral evangelism and even, to some extent, Indian rights. She had been too busy with her career. What is more, she believed that women who wanted to improve society should dedicate their energies to improving their own homes. To that end, she wrote many domestic essays explaining her beliefs about child care and home management. (In these essays, somewhat paradoxically, she idealized home life and endorsed domesticity for women, despite the enjoyment she herself found in her career and independent travels.) Having learned of the plight of the Poncas, however, she set aside her usual writing projects to devote herself to helping them and other Indians. She could no longer believe, as she had in the past, that all reform efforts not directed toward the "field" of "home and private life" were merely "trivial, dilatory, ineffective."[67] Indeed, she became convinced that no good American should be able to "feel happy in his own home again so long as these helpless creatures remain in our borders without home, freedom, or the protection of the law."[68] For the next six years, until she died, she worked as what she called an "advocate of the Indians' rights."[69] She worked mostly alone, channeling her politics into written exposés, a muckraker before the word was coined. While earlier in her career she had written both out of love for art and for money, now she wrote with a distinct social purpose, discovering in this purpose new fonts of inspiration.

Jackson's efforts as a reformer can be divided into two phases. In the first, she labored feverishly on behalf of the Poncas, writing articles and engaging in an acrimonious epistolary debate with Secretary of the Interior Carl Schurz. She also researched and wrote *A Century of Dishonor* (1881), one of the first serious historical studies of federal Indian policy. In the second phase, she took special interest in the plight of Southern California's "Mission" Indians.[70] In 1881–82 and again in 1883, she traveled through Southern California, visiting almost twenty Indian villages and reservations: first on assignment to write articles about the area for *Century Magazine,* and then as a United States government agent, commissioned to write what would become her official *Report on the Condition and Needs of the Mission Indians of California* (1883). When her nonfiction writings failed to bring relief to Southern California's Indians, she tried to rouse general readers through a piece of reform fiction, making a return to novel writing with *Ramona* (1884).

What Jackson wanted Congress to grant American Indians was what many Indians wanted for themselves: an end to violent oppression and removals to Indian Territory; government adherence to existing treaty provisions; protection of ancestral lands and established reservations; and individual legal rights within the United States, including citizenship, the right to travel freely off reservations, and the right to testify in court.

In recent years, some scholars have argued that Jackson's writings actually served to undermine Indian culture, by helping to bring about a national atmosphere conducive to the Dawes General Allotment Act of 1887. This legislation, passed two years after her death, instituted individual ownership of Indian lands and ushered in a half century of destructive assimilationist government policy. Jackson's published and private writings certainly do not express any desire for such an outcome. Like most people of her time, she was fairly ethnocentric, but over the course of her life she became a champion of tolerance and grew to possess an unusual appreciation for racial, ethnic, and religious diversity. Unlike most of the hundreds of Anglo-Americans who worked to change federal Indian policy at the end of the nineteenth century, she was neither an evangelical Protestant nor an assimilationist.[71] Once, in suggesting to a fellow activist that she try to have a teacher sent to the Mission Indians, Jackson specifically warned: "But don't have it a *religious* teacher[.] . . . If any man is going in there to try to *convert* them to Protestantism, he would better stay away."[72] It is true that her research, her personal interviews with Indians, and above all her desire to counter grasping white industrialists and pioneers convinced her that some Indians would find individual rather than collective ownership the best means of legally securing their lands. In her opinion, many whites argued that Indians " '*will not* settle' on lands 'after the fashion of white people' " simply so that they could feel morally absolved in stealing Indian lands.[73] It is also true that she was on friendly terms with Massachusetts senator Henry Dawes, whom she considered "a good friend to Indians,"[74] and who later promoted the General Allotment Act. But it is highly unlikely that she would have supported the General Allotment Act's particular plan for bringing about individual ownership, which included selling off unallotted lands—and resulted, tragically, in a drastic reduction of Indian landholdings. During her lifetime, she opposed severalty bills framed by Senator Alvin Saunders and Schurz on the very grounds that they were intended not so much "for the purpose of benefiting the Indians," but instead for "opening millions of acres of land for white settlers."[75] She wished, perhaps above all else, to make Indians secure in possessing the broadest possible land base.

The efforts she made in this regard were remarkable for her time. In the two decades following the Civil War, the United States waged war against many Indian tribes, engaging in more than two hundred battles and extensive guerrilla warfare so that its citizens could spread out across the continent. Most Americans who lived in the West near Indian communities were not sympathetic to their plight, nor were many residents of Colorado and California sympathetic to Jackson's reform efforts. She encountered constant hostility. In Colorado, white hatred of Native Americans had reached a peak just before Jackson undertook her work, when, on September 29, 1879, a number of Utes murdered an Indian agent and kidnapped his wife and daughter. According to Carlyle Channing Davis, a Colorado journalist during Jackson's time there, Jackson "was quite without a genuine sympathizer with her work in the entire State of Colorado," where most white residents believed "the only good Indian was the dead Indian."[76] California had an even more dismal history of racism. Earlier, in the north, American settlers eager to get rich during the midcentury gold rush had perpetrated some of the most vicious atrocities against Native Americans ever seen; in 1851 genocide was an official government policy, with Governor Peter Burnett assuring the state legislature that "a war of extermination will continue to be waged between the races until the Indian race becomes extinct."[77] In 1883, when Jackson visited Southern California to report on the condition of Indians there and to determine which areas might be set aside as reservations, American settlers eager to exploit the area's agricultural and residential capacities were again in a frenzy of greed for Indian lands. Several local newspapers attacked Jackson. The *San Luis Rey Star,* for instance, called her a "busy body" and "a meddlesome feminine pet" of the new secretary of the interior, Henry Teller, and urged her replacement by a man more sympathetic to white land claims.[78] One woman who traveled through the area shortly after Jackson's visit noted that her concern for "the Indians and their wrongs" remained "a most unpopular one in this region," and that Jackson herself was remembered as "dictatorial, possessing none of the womanly attributes."[79]

Because she was already sensitized to American mistreatment of Indians when she first visited Southern California in the early 1880s—and because in her travels there she finally met and spoke with Indians in the sanctity of their own homes—Jackson was more outraged over the bitter realities that the American "spread of civilization" entailed for racial minorities in California than she had ever been in Colorado. The southernmost region of the state, once known as the "cow counties," had supported a pastoral economy under Spanish and Mexican rule; now American agriculture, industry, and urbanization were radically transforming the area. As Jackson visited long-established Indian villages, wealthy Hispanic, or *Californio,*[80] ranches, and new American towns, she met the sort of dignified, persevering people she always liked to write about; yet among the newly conquered population she also met many who were unable to persevere in their traditional ways despite their best efforts. Many Indians, in particular, were being run off their lands and brutally persecuted by white American settlers, who were backed up by the authority of American law.

In her California travel essays, Jackson's main sympathies are not with American settlers but with the area's earlier inhabitants. For the *Independent* and *Century Magazine,* she penned some of the first positive portraits of California's Indians to appear in the national press. And, fascinated by stories and written accounts of what life in California had been like in the years leading up to the advent of American "civilization," she formed a new commitment to historical research and narration, turning some of her travel essays into chronicles of the area's Spanish and Mexican periods.

In *Ramona,* the story of the tragically thwarted love between a half-Indian, half-Scottish orphan girl raised on a *Californio* ranch and a Luiseño Indian named Alessandro, Jackson continued to work with her usual methods of regional description and character portrayal; but now, for almost the first time, she made "a protest against the spread of civilization" the main theme of a piece of fiction. *Ramona* offers an almost unmitigated denunciation of U.S. imperialism in California, presenting the region in a dystopian light, as a paradise gone bad. Señora Moreno, Ramona's Spanish foster mother, has fond memories of her youth, when she married an important Mexican general and became proprietress of the vast Moreno estate; Alessandro, Ramona's Indian husband, remembers a happy childhood in the Indian village at Temecula. But since the arrival of the Americans, which takes place before the opening of *Ramona*, California has become a miserable place for Alessandro, Señora Moreno, and most other Indian and Hispanic characters in the book. In marked contrast to Jackson's earlier work, the protagonists of *Ramona* have been deprived of their rightful connection to the land; and though Ramona meets her difficulties with an attitude of Christian submission, her efforts to remain cheerful and industrious avail nothing.

Jackson based the sufferings of her Indian characters in *Ramona* on actual recent occurrences, for which she wanted readers to demand reparation. But at the same time she was well aware of the extent of American prejudices. She therefore attempted to create a heroine so sympathetic that white readers would set aside whatever racial antipathies they might feel and, in coming to care about this one individual, wish to help all Indians. She made her heroine Ramona even more entirely pure and virtuous than her usual Saxe Holm heroines, and she also gave Ramona some of the same poignant experiences that she herself had suffered in early life—her orphanhood and homelessness, her loss of husband and children, and her painful effort to persevere. In addition, she intentionally devoted much of the first half of the novel to picturesque descriptions of life on the Moreno estate and romanticized allusions to life in California under Spanish and Mexican rule. "In my Century of Dishonor I tried to attack people's consciences directly, and they would not listen," she explained to a friend after completing the novel. "Now I have sugared my pill, and it remains to be seen if it will go down."[81]

In fact, while *Ramona* found many readers upon publication, most cared more for the story's sugar coating—for charming Ramona, her romance, and Jackson's romanticized, in some respects erroneous version of Spanish and Mexican colonialism—than for the book's later depiction of the terrible subjugation of California's Indians under American rule. Readers and critics tended to view the novel as mere history or myth, not as a presentation of current outrages that still needed to be redressed. Like Jackson herself, many Americans felt a nostalgic longing for the sort of preindustrial, pastoral existence depicted on the Moreno ranch; but few could believe that any real Indians were as admirable as Jackson's heroine and hero. "I can recall no approach to [Alessandro] among the tribes I have known," noted Elizabeth Custer, the widow of General George Armstrong Custer and a writer on western life. "In Mexico last year I saw one who fits the character in appearance, but it hardly seemed to me that he had that lofty nature."[82]

Early in 1885, during another visit to California, Jackson told a correspondent that she was "positively sick" over the tendency of readers to view *Ramona* as a mere idealization.[83] In fact, she was sick not only in spirit. In a matter of months she would be gone, dying, as more than once during the course of her wandering life she had feared that she might, in the hired bed of a boardinghouse.

Like the grasp of the American nation, Jackson had moved during her lifetime westward across the land, ending her journey an entire continent away from her Massachusetts origins. In the course of her travels, she had won a prominent national reputation. During the weeks following her death, she was canonized from coast to coast. The *Nation,* bulwark of the eastern literary establishment, ran an article by Thomas Wentworth Higginson arguing that Jackson's prose demonstrated more "marked ability" than that of most American writers, and speculating that the news of her death might "carry a pang of regret into more American homes than similar intelligence in regard to any other woman."[84] California's premier journal, the *Overland Monthly,* proclaimed that Jackson's "reputation for literary excellence and finish" was "scarcely surpassed by a contemporary writer," and in particular praised her travel essays on California and Colorado as the first to treat America's new West in the manner of "worthy literature."[85]

For about fifty years, Jackson's fame endured. New editions of many of her works were published, as were calendars and books of Jackson quotations. Jackson's poetry was taught to children in school and frequently anthologized. Of all Jackson's writings, her novel *Ramona* retained the highest status. In 1893, it was one of only three contemporary novels held by more than 50 percent of American libraries.[86] In 1921 it received positive critical attention in both *The Cambridge History of American Literature* and Carl Van Doren's *American Novel.* In 1936 Herbert Jenkins, vice president of Little, Brown and Company (which had earlier absorbed Jackson's own publisher, Roberts Brothers), wrote to tell William Jackson that *Ramona*'s total sales to date were "approximately 437,800 copies," not counting sales from another publisher's "cheap edition" of 100,000 copies. "We have never had a novel which has had such a continuously large sale in regular and higher priced editions over a long period as 'Ramona,' " Jenkins claimed.[87]

Ramona has retained some popular following up to the present day. It has never been out of print. Starting in the 1930s, however, when critics and members of the newly institutionalized academic field of American literature began promoting strict realism in literature, most assessments of Jackson began to take on a patronizing tone and to dismiss her writing as "sentimental" or "melodramatic."[88] For example, in 1939, when Ruth Odell published her biography of Jackson, promotional materials for the book referred to Jackson as one of America's "best-known" writers.[89] But when the literary critic Howard Mumford Jones reviewed *Helen Hunt Jackson* for the *Boston Evening Transcript,* he demonstrated little real knowledge of Jackson and her work, or even of the biography he was evaluating. His essay is filled with errors, among them his claim that Jackson "wasted about twenty-five years writing sentimental poetry and even more sentimental prose" before she came to *Ramona*—which Jones describes, oddly, as "a better book than it has any business to be."[90]

Critics continued to dismiss Jackson on the grounds of "sentimentality" for several decades, never bothering to look very deeply into her career. In general, literary scholars mentioned her work, if at all, only in order to comment on its failings: the mediocrity of her popular poetry proved the contrasting greatness of her friend Emily Dickinson, for instance; her romanticized portrait of early California in *Ramona* proved the weakness of her vision as a social activist. But today it is possible to begin to evaluate Jackson's work more fairly. Over the past thirty years, a broader critical environment has emerged, as scholars have worked to recover the reputations of many forgotten women writers and to reinterpret the meanings of "sentimentalism" and "regionalism" in nineteenth-century literature.

Some aspects of Jackson's work can with justice be labeled "sentimental," embodying both the excessive emotionalism denoted by early critics' use of the word and what literary critics employing the word more recently have pointed to: a nineteenth-century American tradition of literature about domestic matters and private emotions, which reached its height of popularity in Harriet Beecher Stowe's *Uncle Tom's Cabin* (1852). In general, this tradition represented a belief that by promoting individual morality and harmonious homes, literature could help bring about a better society.

Current understandings of sentimentalism as a significant literary genre began to emerge in the 1970s.[91] In 1985 Jane Tompkins made a vital contribution to the developing body of theory when she argued, in *Sensational Designs: The Cultural Work of American Fiction, 1790–1860*, that women's sentimental fiction did not function simply as a compensatory pleasure, aimed to keep women contented within the domestic sphere, but was actually a type of political weapon: in appealing to women's emotions, sentimental fiction inspired them to take charge of their lives, even to demand widespread social change. Recent influential evaluations of sentimentalism have followed Tompkins's lead. Perhaps most significant, contributors to Shirley Samuels's volume, *The Culture of Sentiment: Race, Gender, and Sentimentality in Nineteenth-Century America* (1992), have demonstrated that literary sentimentality had important implications for America's identity as a multicultural nation: the genre made use of "discursive models of affect and identification" that "linked individual bodies to the national body," thereby serving to "effect connections across gender, race, and class boundaries."[92]

Jackson herself, like her early-twentieth-century critics, used the word "sentimental" in a negative sense, to refer to writing she considered melodramatic, inadequately crafted, and, in fiction, excessively dependent on piety and marriage for plot resolution. In an essay titled "Hysteria in Literature," she argued that no intelligent person should "tolerate" work that was "unreal, over-wrought, and melodramatic" in "atmosphere and execution"; she especially condemned what she called " 'field tactics' for souls," or narratives of the "ex-ceptionally pathetic and romantic careers of sweet and refined Magdalens."[93] She frequently expressed scorn for writers she thought of as sentimental, in-cluding the popular contemporary American fiction writers E. D. E. N. South-worth and Josiah Holland, and the British poet Felicia Hemans, a favorite from the previous generation.[94] She insisted in private letters that she was not a "sen-timentalist" and that she could "distinguish between melodrama and true art"; she was devastated when the *Nation* once defined her poetry as "sentimen-tal."[95] Conversely, she was delighted whenever her writing was praised as "masculine." Like reviewers who used this word as an adjective for literary praise, she admired a "manly method" of "quiet" and "repression," criticizing the work of most American women who published as too effusive.[96]

Jackson's writing in most genres is free of the "overwrought" emotion she disdained as "sentimental." Yet in some of her poetry and fiction, even as she celebrates emotional stoicism in the uncomplaining perseverance of her literary subjects, her effort to render these subjects exemplary can lead her to emotional operatics: her subjects possess inordinately intense feelings about nature, art, spirituality, and other people, and they inspire melodramatic expressions of rapture in those around them.

This accentuation of private emotion makes it possible to classify a portion of Jackson's work as belonging to the sentimental genre as it is defined today. Except in some of her domestic essays, Jackson did not promote domesticity in the narrowest sense, for women who work for pay are the favored subjects of her fiction and travel essays, and she invariably presents these women as digni-fied and praiseworthy. Furthermore, the homes she depicts in her writings are not the sort of conventional, pious, confining nuclear spaces described by Bar-bara Welter and other scholars of nineteenth-century America's separate woman's sphere; Jackson believed a home could be formed by a group of friends as well as by relations, by poor people as well as by the rich, in "any house, however small, in which love dwells," and she thought all members of a home deserved to achieve individual fulfillment.[97] Still, she always wrote of happy domestic life and motherhood as among the most desirable things in life, her sense of their importance heightened by the pain of her own early losses. Her exemplary female subjects invariably possess talent for creating pleasant homes, including special genius for home decoration. (Jackson's interest in in-terior design, like her interest in homes generally, was rooted in personal expe-rience: in her many years of passing through boardinghouses and hotels, she learned to carry along a select stock of vases, fans, pictures, and other decora-tive items, which, together with the leaves and plants she gathered on nature outings, helped make each of her temporary residences feel more like one permanent dwelling.) Like writers today defined as "sentimental," Jackson intended her literary portraits of domestic life to serve as a broader commentary on society. Within her writing as a whole, the ability of good people to succeed in creating nurturing homes serves as a trope for societal well-being—the human spirit triumphing despite the material pressures of industrialization—even as the inability to create homes, as in some of Jackson's western travel essays and especially *Ramona,* signifies a society gone wrong. *Ramona* is Jackson's most typically "sentimental" work, and she intended it as such: quite self-consciously, she constructed her story to engage the emotions of her readers in the hope that they would be galvanized to demand social reform. Together with Jackson's Saxe Holm stories, *Ramona* played a major role in the continued significance of Romantic idealism in American literature in the latter half of the nineteenth century.

While some elements of Jackson's work can clearly be labeled "sentimental" in the sense in which that term is used today, her central literary vision as expressed in her travel essays and fiction—where she both celebrates the persevering inhabitants of America's less industrially developed regions and explores differences among rural regions, including differences in dialect and ethnicity—is best labeled "regionalist." This term, like "sentimental," can be unjustly restrictive and even pejorative, because the work of the nineteenth-century women authors to whom these terms are usually applied is generally more complex than such labels would indicate, and also because these terms are most often used only for female writers, when they might just as well be applied to many male writers.[98] Nonetheless, it is both appropriate and useful to discuss Jackson's work within the context of regionalism: Jackson herself thought of her travel essays and fiction within a similar context, and current theories about regionalism can offer insight into the broader significance of her work.

A literary tradition that emphasizes the defining influence of place on human beings, regionalism in the nineteenth century featured description of local environments, usually rural backwaters where individuality could thrive away from the homogenizing influence of national industrialization, and also of local folkways; it included written imitation of local vernaculars. Regionalism first took firm hold in America in the 1860s New England fiction of Harriet Beecher Stowe and the California fiction of Bret Harte; in the following decades it became what Richard Brodhead has called the "dominant genre" and "principal place of literary access in America."[99] The genre was defined mostly by women writers who, like Jackson, envisioned their work in contrast to the previously dominant woman's tradition of sentimentalism.[100] Jackson was among the first American women writers to maintain a sustained focus on regionalism: she began to publish what may be defined as regionalist travel essays in 1865 and regionalist fic tion in the early 1870s, while the nineteenth-century regionalist writers who are best known today, Sarah Orne Jewett (1849–1909) and Mary Wilkins Freeman (1852–1930), did not publish their important works until after Jackson's death.

During Jackson's own era, writing with a regional focus was generally called "regional realism" or "local color," the latter term an allusion to paintings that depicted everyday, local scenes. Jackson never explicitly referred to herself as a local color writer. Like most regionalists, she did not theorize her own work; and because she wrote most of her fiction under pseudonyms and for a long time did not admit to many people that she was a fiction writer, she rarely discussed that portion of her regionalism in letters. (She had no qualms about calling herself an "artist," and along with her female regionalist peers constituted the first generation of American women writers to seek and be granted critical prestige as such.)[101] Still, she did make a number of indirect allusions to her regionalist sensibility in her private correspondence. In 1882 she told Thomas Bailey Aldrich, the editor of the *Atlantic Monthly,* that "there was nothing in the world" she "liked so much as to travel, and try to reproduce the pictures" she saw, and that she considered such work "as legitimate art, as to paint a landscape or a village interior." At the same time, she made an indirect comparison of her vision to that of Jean-Baptiste-Camille Corot, a recently deceased French painter known for his landscapes.[102] The following year, after a trip through "seven deserted mining towns" in Colorado, she told a friend, slyly, that "a novelist" could "pick up no end of local coloring in this land."[103] And the year after that, when writing *Ramona,* she explained to Thomas Wentworth Higginson that though she had for "three or four years longed to write a story that should 'tell' on the Indian question," she had been able to begin such a story only after extensive knowledge of Southern California had given her sufficient "local color for it."[104] Later, she was thrilled when Horace Scudder's review of *Ramona* for the *Atlantic Monthly* compared her work to that of the seventeenth-century Spanish painter Bartolomé Esteban Murillo, whose exquisite "coloring" and portraits of ordinary people she had long admired.[105]

In addition to alluding in her private correspondence to her own interest in "local color," Jackson singled out the works of other regionalist writers for praise in her letters, as I will discuss in chapter 7. She also made positive references to regionalism in some of the anonymous literary reviews that she published over the course of her career in the *Independent, Scribner's Monthly* and its successor *Century Magazine,* the *Atlantic Monthly,* and the *Denver Tribune.* For instance, in a *Scribner's* review of John De Forest's *Overland* (1871), she argues that regionalism is the natural mode for American novelists. While rightly criticizing De Forest's southwestern novel as sensationalized, she praises both it and his recent South Carolina novel *Kate Beaumont* (1872) for putting to rest an ongoing critical debate over whether there could ever be "a good novel which is truly American." To Jackson's mind, De Forest's novels prove that there could be, by the very fact of their adroit regional specificity:

> To be sure, each is strongly sectional, in geography of plot and in tone of coloring; but they are none the less genuinely American for all that. There are as yet many Americas. Probably there always will be; and it is the overrating of the bearing of this condition on the future American novel which has created the misgiving as to its probability. But it seems illogical. Nobody disputes that a faithful picture of Devonshire people has as good a right as one of Regent Street and London Terrace to be called a picture of English life. So with *Overland* and *Kate Beaumont*.[106]

Although Jackson argued in this review of De Forest that regionalism was inherent to American literature, and though she expressed her own regionalist sensibilities in her private correspondence and in her work, she has received little critical attention as a regionalist writer. Scholars of regionalism have concentrated mainly on writers who made one particular region their own, whereas Jackson wrote not only about her native New England but also about her adopted home of Colorado and about California—especially Southern California, where she lived and traveled for a total of only about one year. To classify Jackson as a regionalist, narrow frameworks must be widened to incorporate her focus on these three different regions, and also to take into account her travel writing, which was as much a part of her regionalist enterprise as was her fiction. Further, Jackson can be defined as a regionalist only if we accept that in her western work, she wrote not simply about older, marginalized communities but also about new, newly industrializing enclaves of miners and pioneers. And finally, we must allow for the fact that Jackson's prose, like that of many regionalists, is not entirely free from sentimentalism. Indeed, her "regionalist" focus on place is closely allied to her "sentimental" focus on home, and she never abandoned her penchant for idealized character portrayal even as she tried to render characters true to their specific regions.

Jackson formed her career in the midst of a broad, gradual movement in American literature away from Romanticism, with its focus on the picturesque and noble and its ethos of spiritual transcendence, toward realism. Like many writers of her time, she maintained a predilection for Romanticism, especially Hawthornesque and Emersonian idealisms, even as her central literary vision was realistic, or more particularly regionalist. Thus in a review of the works of William Morris Hunt, her favorite American painter, she argued that "all true and masterly characterization in any art" must manage to render "universal" human emotions, to offer "an interpretation of a great spiritual idea, a rendering of a type," and that talent for infusing character with ideal meaning was of a higher order than that for realistic portraiture.[107] Yet her main aim in her fiction and travel essays was to depict the everyday realities of ordinary people in various places. She strove to make her depictions regionally specific, as is testi-fied, for instance, in her efforts to mimic distinctive speech patterns. While these efforts often resulted in clunky sentences—in this respect, Jackson had a good deal of company among the regionalist writers of her day—she made them in the name of accuracy. Once, when a proofreader at the *Atlantic Monthly* sug-gested that she not use both "the" and "te" to represent the definite article when quoting the broken English of a travel essay subject, she demurred: "but that was exactly the way she talked: sometimes one, & sometimes the other.—If you think it is better to be false to fact, & true to probabilities, & make her consis-tent, they can all be altered to 'te's—but it would be like most of the consistency in this world a lie."[108]

Scholars tend to agree on the major historical forces that inspired post–Civil War writers like Jackson to document American regional variation. While liter-ary America was preoccupied throughout the nineteenth century with American national identity and with expressing what made that identity unique, in the 1860s, the Civil War, a catastrophe brought about by regional differences, in-creased general awareness of the diversity of American people and places, and made understanding this diversity seem crucial to societal well-being. Writers worked to create a forum for understanding. In this respect, it is telling that Jack-son's only stories that deal specifically with the Civil War, "Joe Hale's Red Stock-ings" and "A Four Leaved Clover,"[109] are about not battles but romantic unions between people of different ethnicities and regions, made possible by the upheaval of the war. With the beginning of the Second Industrial Revolution, general in-terest in understanding American diversity was heightened by the growth of cities, where formerly rural Americans and an increasing number of European immi-grants lived and worked in proximity. Interest in diversity was also stirred by the growth of transportation. Expanding railroad networks enabled increasing num-bers of people to visit unfamiliar regions, including the Far West, where Ameri-cans like Jackson struggled to make sense of their encounters with embattled In-dians and the subjugated people of America's other recent war, that with Mexico.

While scholars generally agree on the historical circumstances that encour-aged many late-nineteenth-century authors to write about American diversity, opinions are divided as to the ends served by the representations of diversity that they produced. Critics also see different meanings in the strong tendency of regionalists like Jackson to write about rural lifeways, and to depict rural Americans as quietly persevering in the face of an industrialism that is often evoked only vaguely, as unspoken context. Many students of regionalism, in-cluding Judith Fetterley, Marjorie Pryse, Josephine Donovan, and the contrib-utors to *Breaking Boundaries: New Perspectives on Women's Regional Writing* (1997), see regionalism as a subversive genre. In their view, regionalists offered a critique of patriarchal, white-supremacist industrial capitalism by their very depiction of places at the margins of the nation's centers of power, and of people marginalized by gender, ethnicity, and class, as self-sufficient and persevering; most regionalists did not specifically discuss industrialization because their aim was to celebrate ordinary people and the rhythms of life that endure regardless of societal change. Proponents of this view of regionalism argue that regionalist authors felt a sympathetic identification with the marginalized people they described.[110] According to Nancy Glazener in *Reading for Realism: The History of a U.S. Literary Institution, 1850–1910* (1997), their writings served the interests of these people.[111]

Other commentators on nineteenth-century regionalism have argued that the genre served the interests not of the people it depicted but of its readers: upper-class, urban members of the establishment who bought the high-culture journals that published regionalism. Recent scholars of this persuasion write in the wake of colonial studies, and also Benedict Anderson's influential argument, in *Imagined Communities: Reflections on the Origins and Spread of Nationalism* (1983), that literature functions to coalesce a people's sense of nationhood. They argue that regionalism offered elite readers strategies for coping with the rapid changes of the postbellum years. It not only enabled readers to look back with a satisfying sense of nostalgia on a more rural America, performing what Richard Brodhead has called a "cultural elegy" for the "supersession of local cultures by the new national culture modern transportation and marketing opened up," but it also gave them opportunities to rehearse their desires for class dominance: it enabled them to imagine "Americans different in habits, speech, and appearance from a norm this form help[ed] render normative," and to indulge their new "leisured outlook" in a form of "experiential imperialism," whereby they entered at will into the lives of people different from themselves.[112] Eric Sundquist has similarly likened the reading of regionalism to a form of "colonialism" in which participants in America's rising "spectator culture" proscriptively mapped "America's psychological space." Amy Kaplan has argued that by "consuming images of rural 'others,'" well-off urbanites found cathartic relief from the "more explosive social conflicts of class, race, and gender" that surrounded them.[113]

Jackson's regionalist writing seems to have reflected motivations and served purposes discussed by scholars on both sides of the debate over regionalism's function.[114] I have mentioned the ambiguous nature of the "protest against the spread of civilization" that she offered in her travel essays: the essays promoted interest in visiting the very places Jackson wished to protect.[115] In a similar way, her attempts to idealize the human subjects of her travel essays and fiction, even as she tried to render them regionally specific, reflected ambivalent purposes. By portraying them as demonstrating the same commitment to uncomplaining perseverance that she herself possessed, she could achieve a sense of reassurance about her own position in society: people different from herself, if they practiced Christian submission, would not harm her. In this regard, individual members of ethnic minority groups became what Jackson in one private letter referred to as just "so much 'material,' "[116] to be ranged beneath the sway of her writing.

Usually, though, she felt what in that same letter she called a "positive affection" for the people and characters she wrote about, and her habit of attributing her own values to them was an expression of personal identification. A sense of solidarity is evident throughout her regionalist writings. Unlike most of the authors with whom she might be compared, in her western travel essays she rarely exoticizes or sensationalizes the lifeways of the area's diverse inhabitants. In her novel *Ramona,* she expresses solidarity with oppressed groups by inverting the ordinary regionalist method of transcribing local vernaculars: only white American settlers speak in dialect in the novel, whereas the words of Indian, Mexican, and Spanish characters are set down in a heightened, formal English, a language intended to distinguish them as the societal "norm," the legitimate offspring of the land. Moreover, Jackson's work has always been read not only in the eastern United States, where it was published, but also, and often most enthusiastically, in the West. In his 1879 *Short Studies of American Authors,* Thomas Wentworth Higginson noted that her popular poems were "repeated and preserved in many a Western cabin, cheering and strengthening many a heart."[117] Jackson confirmed this statement in her 1882 date book, where she twice recorded meeting people in the remotest parts of rural Southern California who knew and cherished her work.[118]

Jackson was inclined to sympathize with the people she wrote about, rather than to stand apart from them, a condescending observer, because she always thought of herself as a rural person. As a young adult she prized the cultural offerings of Boston and New York, and later she conducted much of her professional life in these cities; but her only permanent homes were in small towns—Amherst, which she continued to visit occasionally even after her father's death, and Colorado Springs. As she aged she expressed increasing hatred for the industrial, unnatural aspect of cities. "If I were God, I would not let such a thing as a city exist on the face of my fair and beautiful world," she once told William Jackson.[119] It was in small-town Massachusetts, in the home of her parents and amid traditionally religious surroundings, that she first learned to feel this way, and to cultivate the values that would become central to her regionalist vision.

PART TWO

"Their teaching in the heart of their child"

Earliest Influences

2

Lessons from Father and Mother

My father had a great deal of ambition with regard to my education. I was his favorite child. He took the most unwearied pains in teaching me, and I now ascribe whatever mental culture I may have, to the *habits* which he formed in me, at a very early age. I did almost worship my father[.] . . . To win a word of praise, to see him smile as he often would when I had recited a lesson remarkably well, was my highest ambition, when a child. I can distinctly remember when I was not more than five years old, seeing him look *significantly* at mother, when I had made some rather old remark. I knew that he was proud of me, and the thought was ever before me. It was unfavorable in its influence, in some respects: it inclined me to vanity, and yet it was a most powerful incentive to exertion. And perhaps after all that could hardly be called unfavorable in its influence, which led a child to bend every energy of mind and soul to the gratification of a parent.

JACKSON TO JULIUS PALMER, March 8, 1850, HHJ2

I inherited nothing from either of my parents except my mother's gift of cheer.

JACKSON IN ADULT LIFE, exact date unknown, quoted in Sarah Woolsey, "H.H."

When Jackson was nineteen and twenty, and struggling to find her place in the world, she went through a phase of reassessing the effects of her upbringing. She was moved to examine her feelings by a new, close friendship with her guardian Julius Palmer. Her letters to Palmer from this period contain her only extended extant comments on her relationship with her father. In one of them, excerpted in an epigraph above, she emphasizes the huge intellectual influence he had on her in youth: he closely supervised her education, and she made it her "highest ambition" to please him with her attainments. In working to satisfy her father, she formed lasting "habits" of diligence in her studies, to which, as she entered adulthood, she ascribed all of the "mental culture" she had as yet obtained.

Years later, however, she told her friend Sarah Woolsey that she had "inherited" nothing from her parents, except her "mother's gift of cheer"—her ability to demonstrate cheerfulness in the face of adversity. It is true that Jackson's parents did not leave her a financial inheritance: following her father's death, she was supported by her maternal grandfather, David Vinal, who left her and her sister Ann his entire estate upon his own death in 1854; it provided Jackson with a comfortable income for life.[1] It is also true that Jackson's mother had a naturally ebullient temperament, which set a standard for Jackson. Yet Jackson's ability to persevere in the face of adversity actually represented an inheritance not only of her mother's "gift of cheer," important as that was, but also of her father's "habits" of diligence—a legacy that new intellectual influences had perhaps obscured by the time she spoke with Woolsey.

In fact, Jackson inherited a number of personal characteristics for which she never explicitly gave her parents credit, but which would prove fundamental to her writing career—from the set of attitudes about health that led her continually to travel to her literary inclination itself and a belief that writing should be spiritually uplifting. Indeed, no other person or writer would ever have such influence over Jackson's writing as her parents had. That they died long before her career began did not lessen but quite possibly increased their influence: unable to confront her parents directly, she was turned back on herself, to work out her inheritance in writing.

Jackson's father, Nathan Welby Fiske, was the son of a Weston, Massachusetts, farmer and veteran of the Revolutionary War, also named Nathan Fiske, who was neither learned nor very religious. But Nathan Welby's pious mother instructed her five children rigorously in the Westminster Catechism. Moreover, there had long been Calvinist ministers in the Fiske family—including yet another Nathan Fiske, of Brookfield, Massachusetts, who in the eighteenth century had been a prolific writer of moralistic newspaper essays.[2] Nathan Welby's own dedication to the Calvinist faith began in 1814, when, during his sophomore year at Dartmouth College, a student revival led him to conversion. After graduating from college, he paused for only a few years—one in which he served as principal of an academy in Maine, and two in which he worked as a tutor at his alma mater—before he entered the Andover Theological Seminary, a training ground for conservative Congregational ministers. He graduated three years later, Phi Beta Kappa, and was ordained as an evangelist on September 25, 1823, at the age of twenty-five.

The Reverend Elias Cornelius delivered the sermon that day in Salem's Tabernacle Church, on Exodus 14:15: "Speak to the children of Israel that they go forward." In the manner then customary, Cornelius cast America's Christians as the true children of Israel, permanently bound, as such, to "labour for the conversion of the world."[3] Jackson's father took his duties as an evangelist very seriously. After his ordination, he moved to Savannah, Georgia, to proselytize among seamen. But Fiske was by nature a scholarly, introverted man, and within less than a year he began considering various academic positions. In 1824 he accepted the offer of a professorship in Latin and Greek languages from fledgling Amherst College, a Congregational institution that, like most in western Massachusetts at the time, still adhered to the sort of orthodox Calvinism that Fiske had learned in seminary.

Fiske would stay on in Amherst for more than twenty years. In 1828 he married Deborah Waterman Vinal; within the next four years Helen and Ann were born, and the family moved into a permanent home on South Pleasant Street. During these years, before paved roads, sewers, or electricity, Amherst was a quiet, rural town, notable for its lack of growth and industrial development, and also for the unchanging Puritanical thinking of its small population.[4] Yet even in a town where strict Calvinism was the norm, and at a college founded to further that religion, Nathan Fiske stood out for the degree of diligence with which he carried out his professional duties, and for the fixity with which he proselytized submission to the Calvinist God from each of his positions as professor, minister, scholar, and father.

Among his colleagues at Amherst College, some dozen devout men, Nathan was known for being erudite, yet so narrowly focused on his duties that he gave little license to his imagination and occasionally lost sight of how his behavior affected other people. "For nothing, perhaps, was Professor Fiske more remarkable, than for his *industry and perseverance*," writes the Reverend Heman Humphrey, president of the college during most of Nathan's tenure there, in his 1850 *Memoir of Rev. Nathan W. Fiske.*[5] While Humphrey praises Nathan's diligence and the work that he accomplished by it, he portrays him as so "eminently systematic in the division and improvement of his time," so "eminently a man of order," that he came to view the world in a manner that was "rather microscopic than telescopic." Humphrey explains, "He never was entranced by mere moonshine in his life; but if his extraordinary cautiousness saved him from mistakes, I think it sometimes repressed invention, and circumscribed the range of his active and powerful mind."[6] According to the Reverend Professor Edward Hitchcock, who became college president after Humphrey retired in 1845, Nathan was "not well fitted to come in contact with men in the rough and tumble of life." Though he had a satirical sense of humor, for instance, he misjudged its effects, so that it often "wounded deeper than he intended." Hitchcock noted, "He seemed to want what scholars are so apt to want—a knowledge of common things, so that when they mix with men they do things, which though not wrong, are odd, and are laughed at. They shrink away from the world and live in a sort of seclusion."[7]

Like the faculty, students at the college respected Nathan's intellect and morality, but considered him rather narrow-minded. They ridiculed what they viewed as his obsession with Greek particles.[8] Many suffered under his method of pedagogy, which one defined as "rigid, beyond that of most men whom I have known."[9] In addition, though Amherst students were a pious lot—a large percentage of them went on after graduation to become Congregational ministers—they saw Nathan as unusually determined in his efforts to proselytize. "Professor Fiske loved the truth and was tenacious of it," explained one. "His countenance, gestures, and whole manner, bespoke his clinging to the truth."[10] The pedantic nature of Nathan's religious instruction, in particular his habit of asking rhetorical questions rather than directly stating his beliefs, led one student to exclaim: "I can never forget his sanctity, stolidity, repulsion inspiring as he asked me *not talked*—about sanctification regeneration &c!"[11]

Nathan was aware of his questionable reputation at Amherst College. Awkward and shy, he knew that he seemed a "mere student" in comparison with the other faculty, who were by contrast men of "easy and good manners."[12] In 1831, after delivering an ill-attended lecture, he felt that he had "utterly *failed,*" and lamented to his wife: "Mr. Abbott is exceedingly popular; Mr. Hitchcock is lauded to the skies . . . on poorer Mr. F. everybody turns an eye of a sort of *condescending* respectfulness."[13] A decade later, he was miserably humiliated when some students shaved his horse's tail as a prank. "I am as sick as you are of your connection with Amherst College," Deborah tried to console him, no doubt wounded herself, for over the years she had taken in several students as boarders. "You work very hard, and get *no thanks,* nothing but your daily bread and *insults.*"[14]

Nathan coped with his difficulties by means of a disciplined perseverance that he would seek to instill in his daughter as well. Possessed of a firm belief that "God knows what is best for individuals & for the world," he always submitted to God's will under even the most trying circumstances. Over the years, he viewed the constant illnesses that afflicted his family as God's "servants," sent to foster their spiritual improvement.[15] He expressed grateful resignation upon the deaths of two infant sons: David Vinal, who lived only a few weeks after his birth in 1829, and Humphrey Washburn, who was born in 1832 and lived less than a year. He turned his obituary sermon for his closest friend, the Reverend Royal Washburn, into a lesson on "cheerfulness" and "happy resignation" in the face of adversity.[16] He even thought of his wife's death as the "discipline of God."[17] By comparison, his ongoing troubles at Amherst were of little moment. He resigned himself to them completely, if anything becoming ever more single-minded in his dedication to his work and to evangelism.

Every day, he arose by five and went to bed at ten, the intermediate hours almost entirely filled with labor. He carried a heavy teaching load. During his first decade as a professor, he taught classics, including the Greek and Latin languages, and, for several years, Greek literature and belles lettres. During his second decade at Amherst he taught "moral philosophy," the other major humanistic study of his era, which encompassed not only topics classified today under the social sciences but also epistemology, aesthetics, and ethics. He also offered public lectures: in 1830–31, 1840, and again in 1842, he toured the Northeast, speaking on various subjects in American history and geography. Preparations for his many lectures absorbed so much of his time that by 1836, Deborah Fiske had come to think of the "huge pile of volumes" that he used for research as a "sister wife."[18] In addition to teaching, Nathan had many administrative duties at the college, including keeping the chapel records and soliciting funds to keep the school running. He was so zealously committed to the latter enterprise that in 1832, when travels to procure funding were keeping him away from home for months, he told Deborah that given the "imperious urgency of duty," he would have been willing to travel for years.[19]

Entwined with Nathan's collegiate duties were a number of ministerial duties: in addition to proselytizing continually to his students, he took his turn along with other ordained faculty in preaching to them in the college chapel, and he also often preached in town. According to Heman Humphrey, Nathan devoted an unusual amount of effort to his preaching: though he never intended to publish his sermons, and "although ninety-nine out of a hundred readers would have said that the first draft needed no revision," he left behind manuscripts that were "very much interlined" with corrections and emendations.[20] Some of Nathan's colleagues described his labored sermons as too abstruse, too strenuously "metaphysical and scholastic," for popular tastes.[21] But however obscure his particular topic might be, Nathan's main intention in his sermons was always to make his listeners understand the necessity of Christian submission, or what he calls in one sermon the "entire subjection of the soul" to God[22]—and this message was always perfectly clear. Indeed, Nathan was known for preaching with particular "power" during the four periods of religious revival that stirred Amherst College during his time there.[23]

As a child, Helen heard some of her father's pointed sermons. She seems to have admired their strengths, for in adult life she always expressed pleasure in meeting people who had read the sermons reprinted in Humphrey's *Memoir* of her father, and she once urged the ministry on a young friend by assuring him that the glory of speaking in a pulpit could make up for any "necessities and embarrassments" associated with clerical life.[24] In her youth, moreover, she was a daily witness to the diligence with which Fiske applied himself to his college duties, especially his writing. Over the course of his career, Nathan wrote a number of books and scholarly essays: like his sermons, they all, however varied in nature, were ultimately aimed at proselytizing his religion.[25] His single-minded industry served as a powerful example for Helen, later inclining her not only toward diligence and perfectionism in her own career but also toward a desire to make her writing uplifting.

Nathan's major literary undertaking was a textbook, an extensively anno-
tated and expanded translation of a *Manual of Classical Literature* by the German literary historian Johann Joachim Eschenburg.[26] He began work on the
Manual in the fall of 1834, and in the course of preparing four successive editions labored on it until the summer of 1843. Throughout Helen's childhood,
from the time she was four until she was almost thirteen, her father spent most
of his time absorbed in this project.

Nathan's *Manual* is a work of imposing erudition; it contains more than 650
dense pages of materials pertaining to Greek and Latin literature and art, of
which more than a quarter is Nathan's contribution to the original. The *Manual* attests to his knowledge of ancient and modern languages and to his respect
for classical literature, which he had been studying since college. Yet while
Nathan appreciated classical literature, and states at various times in his *Manual* that he hopes his book will promote "better understanding" of it, his ultimate hope is that knowledge of the ancient pagan beliefs recorded in classical
literature will inspire his readers toward a deeper Christianity: properly to understand the classics, as properly to understand anything in Nathan's view, is
to gain in "knowledge of God and of Jesus Christ, 'whom to know is *eternal
life.*' "[27] Throughout the *Manual,* he bends his subject matter toward lessons in
Christian morality. His discussion of the Greek New Testament, for instance,
includes a lengthy digression on the New Testament in general. His commentary on the meaning of its books typifies his didactic, and also his competent,
but somewhat cumbersome, literary style:

> There is irresistible evidence, that they are from the pens of men who wrote as they
> were moved by the Holy Ghost, and contain the infallible rules of faith and practice
> for us as the intelligent moral subjects of the Great Ruler of the universe. . . . It is
> only by giving earnest heed to these books, that we can cleanse our ways from sin,
> or obtain part in the life and immortality which they and they only have brought to
> light.[28]

Because Nathan saw his *Manual* not only as a textbook but also as an important piece of moral didacticism capable of transforming the souls of its readers, he devoted himself to it with fervor. "It would not be far from the truth to
say that he was always in his study when his health would allow," writes Heman Humphrey. "Call when you might, you would find him at his desk, with
pen in hand, or poring over his text book and classics."[29] Nathan's relentless
toil exhausted his energies and strained his relations with his family. In his journal, he records the severe toll taken on his health by his "diligent & labourious
application" to each edition of the *Manual:* in 1839, for instance, the "immense" task "of preparing the copy & examining the proof" for the third edition "proved too much," and "symptoms of an incipient consumption" forced
him to give up work of every kind for almost a year.[30] Immediately upon his re-

covery, plans were made for the stereotyped fourth edition. Nathan was tormented by fears that the publishers of this new edition would steal his profits from the book, and he was so overburdened with preparing new copy that he had little time left over for parenting. In 1842, when Helen went through a period of great loneliness, having been sent away to Charlestown to spend three months with the family of her mother's beloved Aunt Vinal in order to ease Deborah's burdens, Nathan's work on the *Manual* kept him from granting her repeated requests that he come to visit her. What she received, instead, were long letters from her mother, apprising her how "*very* busy" her father was, struggling to supply his publisher with as many as "sixty or seventy pages a week."[31] At long last, her father did come, but his visit was only an addendum to a business trip to Boston, where he needed to examine some recently published books.

Not only was Helen well aware of her father's dedication to his scholarly work, but she also knew of his determination to evangelize with his writings, for he wrote a number of didactic works for children. Helen kept a copy of one of them in her personal childhood library: *The Story of Aleck: or, Pitcairn's Island. Being a True Account of a Very Singular and Interesting Colony,* which Nathan published anonymously in 1829.[32] In this purportedly nonfiction work, Nathan recounts the history of Pitcairn's Island in the South Pacific, focusing on the awakening to God, under the guidance of Christian missionaries, of the "ignorant and wicked" natives and the evil pirate castaways who once lived there. While Nathan strives to keep the attention of young readers by portraying his hero Aleck as a real-life Robinson Crusoe, he never disguises his intention to present a moral lesson. He reminds his readers that God is always watching them, "just as he saw the pirates, who could not escape from the punishment of their sins, although they fled to a desert island." He concludes his book with a chapter of "Reflections Suggested by the Narrative," in which he advises: "take the Bible for your daily teacher, and friend. Read it carefully. See what it tells you to feel, and feel so. See what it tells you to do, and do so."[33]

It is likely that Helen learned what the Bible expected her to feel and do from another of Nathan's works for children, *The Bible Class Book,* a Sunday school pamphlet that he coauthored with his Amherst colleague and former theology school classmate, the Reverend Jacob Abbott. "There are many things which every person who lives ought to do, and many things which every person ought not to do," say Fiske and Abbott in this pamphlet. "The Bible points out these things, and thus teaches all our duties."[34] Among the many duties that Fiske and Abbott list and annotate, they emphasize the duty of "patient submission," to be demonstrated in the further obligations of steadfast cheerfulness and industry. Their discussion of the "duty of contentment and cheerfulness" is more lengthy than their discussion of any other. They also place special emphasis on the "duty of diligence in business," arguing that diligence is not only an earthly duty but also an eternal one: "the rest of heaven consists in exemption from fatigue and suffering, not from employment."[35]

In addition to witnessing her father's steadfast efforts to preach and to practice Christian submission, Helen received his direct instruction. From her earliest years, both of her parents were intimately involved in her general education: according to the adult testimony of her sister Ann, Helen was "a very uncommon child," intellectually precocious, and her parents "took the very greatest pains" in teaching her.[36] When Helen was a toddler, her parents went over daily readings in the Bible with her. From the time she began at age four to attend a succession of private day schools in Amherst, including Mary White's, Miss Baker's, and Miss Nelson's, they supplemented her education. Her mother supervised her progress in reading, spelling, composition, and domestic arts such as sewing, while her father instructed her in foreign languages, including, from the age of five, Hebrew and especially Latin. When Helen began in 1841 to attend schools outside of Amherst, they continued to direct her education through letters. While Helen's father and mother both emphasized the attainment of an attitude of Christian submission as the ultimate goal of all education, her father was more single-minded in urging its pursuit. He was also more determined to see Helen conduct her studies in a diligent and sober manner. In teaching her, he employed the same strict pedagogy and narrow focus on Christian duty for which he was known at Amherst College. Because he had ultimate authority over Helen's education—sole authority, following Deborah's death in February 1844—his efforts were enormously influential.

Helen was a smart and studious girl who liked to please her parents. She found studying with them "delightful,"[37] and also made good progress at school. In 1841, when she was staying with family friends in Hadley, the Dickinsons, she wrote to her mother about her studies at the local school: "I am very much interested in all of them and am trying to see how far I can proceed."[38] The following year, when she had been sent to stay with the Vinal family in Charlestown, where she attended Miss Austin's school, the Vinals reported in a letter to Helen's mother that Helen was "quite ambitious about her studies," even "disposed to study evenings although there is no need of it, and we do not like to have her."[39] Helen sent her mother a listing of her six-day class schedule and reported with pride that Miss Austin had told Aunt Vinal that "I was a very good girl and she was very much *interested* in me."[40]

Though Helen needed no encouragement to be diligent, in her father's opinion she needed help learning to channel and sustain her efforts. "Be more patient in learning one thing first, & then something else," he told her. "Your constant danger is that you will run from one thing to another & lose the power of self control & perseverance."[41] Even when Helen was away from home he closely monitored her Latin studies, examining her translations through the mail and suggesting various additional exercises. He was so exacting in his scrutiny and demands for thorough and methodical study that Helen only truly began to enjoy Latin when she was away in Hadley, studying under a Latin teacher who was "not half as strict as pa."[42] Back at home in 1842, probably before her trip to Charlestown, she wrote her father a poem, begging him for a brief respite from Latin. It is her earliest known piece of poetry, written at age eleven:

My dear papa tis very long,
Since I have had a vacation.
And now I write a little song,
To move your hearts compassion.
I'm tired to death of Latin,
As you no doubt do know.
I get on slow with practising,
Alas! Alas! how slow!
I think it is but fair,
That I should have *some* rest,
And tis my fervent prayer,
That you may think it best.
I'm but a child,
And rather wild,
As all the world doth know.
And this is why,
It seems so dry,
For me to study so.
That old brown book,
Has such a look,
It makes one sigh to see it.
And only think how long twill take,
For you to drag me through it.
Now if you'll grant a resting spell,
I think I then shall go on well.
I would write more but my thoughts are fled,
And mother says 'Now go to bed.'
I wish you'd answer this in rhyme,
If you can possibly find the time.
Your affectionate daughter, H. M. Fiske[43]

There is no evidence of Nathan's response to Helen's request, in verse or prose. Even if she did receive her desired respite, the following year she was again hard at work on her Latin, now as a boarding student at the Pittsfield Academy, studying under the Reverend E. Tyler, brother of the Amherst professor William S. Tyler. That spring she wrote to her mother, "Tell pa Mr. E. Tyler is as thorough in the Latin Grammar as he could desire."[44]

Nathan could be a severe critic when Helen did not perform according to his wishes. "I guess if you had seen me seated slate in hand," a defiant, wounded

Helen wrote to her father after one unknown altercation, "you would have retracted your *chosen* opinion 'that I cannot think.' "[45] Decades later, when she had become a professional writer, she acknowledged in two autobiographical essays for children that she had long lived in fear of displeasing her father. In "The First Time," she recounts the agony she once suffered upon lying to her parents about a bad report card. While thoughts of her "loving and sympathetic" mother made her continually wish to reveal and apologize for her lie, fear of her father's "stern" eyes and inevitable condemnation kept her quiet: "the terror of my father's suffering and displeasure sealed my lips." In "The Naughtiest Day of My Life, and What Came of It," she describes her father's verbal censure as the worst part of the punishment she received when her parents finally realized, a week after her early flight through the Amherst countryside, that she had no intentions of apologizing. "Helen, I would like to see you in my study a little while," her father said to her. "Oh, how my heart sank within me!" Jackson recalls. "As soon as I saw my father's face, I knew it was not a whipping I was to have, but something a great deal worse—a long talk."[46] Elsewhere, in an essay for adults in which Jackson argues that wounds inflicted by a parent are "certain to rankle and do harm," she uses her father's tendency toward harsh criticism as a case in point. "To this day," she writes, "the old tingling pain burns my cheeks as I recall certain rude and contemptuous words which were said to me when I was very young, and stamped on my memory forever. I was once called a 'stupid child' in the presence of strangers. I had brought the wrong book from my father's study. Nothing could be said to me today which would give me a tenth part of the hopeless sense of degradation which came from those words."[47]

Nathan was extreme in his demands because he wished Helen not only to fulfill her Christian obligation of active industry but also to develop the sort of earnest, focused view of the world that he himself possessed, and that he believed compatible with Christian submission. For his main intention in educating his daughter, like his main intention everywhere, was to evangelize.

Helen had a vivid imagination and from an early age took notable delight in hearing, reading, and inventing fanciful stories. When she was only twenty-seven months old, her mother told Aunt Vinal: "Helen is an 'everlasting talker' and has a great passion for stories—we can never satisfy her with telling her about you and uncle and uncle Vinals *horse*—she will say 'tell that adin Ma' a dozen times."[48] In 1841, when Helen was homesick in Hadley, she especially missed hearing family "anecdotes"; the following year, in discussing her studies with her mother, she explained, "I admire Natural History it is almost like a *story*."[49] Nathan disliked his daughter's tendency to waste time on "foolish dreams," however, and made every effort to have her concentrate instead on her obligations to God.[50] In his letters, he continually reminds her, just as he reminded young readers of *The Story of Aleck*, that God is always watching, and that she must therefore control her imagination. He urges her to read only educational and religious writings, which could "improve" both her "head" and her "heart," and tells her that if she must read fiction or poetry, she should give up her interest in such humanistic authors as Shakespeare—whom she had begun to admire at least by the fall of 1841—and focus instead on such moralists as Hannah More.[51] When Helen was ten years old, he advised her: "If you hope to live to old age & be happy then, you must lead until then a good & useful life, store your mind with important knowledge, & your imagination not with foolish fancies, but with beautiful pictures of truth & virtue."[52] Four years later, he offered similar advice, phrased in one of his trademark rhetorical questions: "How apt some persons are to mistake their own mere imaginations to be realities, so that they are scarcely able to distinguish between the conceptions which are accidentally awakened in their minds & reliable matters of fact. If you know any body who is too much given to indulge in flights of fancy & airy dreams & castle-building & story-making, what advice would you give to such an one?"[53]

By encouraging his daughter to be more sober-minded than was her natural inclination, Nathan hoped to help her attain a state of mind and soul in which she might undergo a conversion experience, the intense period of awakening to God that was a necessary rite of passage for every Calvinist. From an early age, Helen had resisted many of the tenets of Calvinism, finding them "very repulsive" to her feelings.[54] ("I was a skeptic before I could understand the plain English of the Scriptures which I doubted," she later explained to Julius Palmer.)[55] When she was six, her mother told a family relation: "she is quite inclined to question the authority of everything; the Bible she says she does not *feel* as if it was true."[56] Later, during her stay with the Vinals in Charlestown, she tried (unsuccessfully) to be excused from attending Sunday school. Steadily influenced by her father's efforts, however, she did eventually approach conversion on two occasions.

When she was thirteen, and boarding at the Pittsfield Academy, her father urged her to cultivate the friendship of Miss Lincoln, a pious teacher at the academy who was also Helen's roommate. Both he and Helen's mother corresponded with Miss Lincoln about the state of Helen's soul. Helen liked Miss Lincoln, and under the combined influence of this new teacher and her parents, she "obtained a hope" of conversion. As she later told Julius Palmer, she "made a *written* dedication" to God, "and for a short time was *happy*, as I have never been since." But when her mother died that winter, she saw "only too plainly" that her hope of faith had been unfounded: "I tremble sometimes now when I think of the bitterness and opposition which raged in my spirit, as I saw my dear mother's form laid under the cold wet ground," she told Palmer.[57]

The death of her mother plunged Helen back into her religious doubts, and forward into a period of prolonged mental anguish and depression. Her father, worried over her health and distressed by her abortive approach to conversion, removed her from the Pittsfield Academy and sent her to live in Falmouth with her mother's pious cousin, Martha Hooker, and Martha's husband the Reverend Henry Hooker, an austere Calvinist who had first introduced Helen's parents to each other. She spent more than two unhappy years in Falmouth. Her father became ever more adamant that she view her studies as ancillary to her religion. His letters to her from this period mimic exactly the central trope of his published writings: every discussion moves slowly but surely toward yet another assertion that the only truly important endeavor is to know God. Again and again, after discussing Helen's academic endeavors, Nathan reminds her that he desires no new accomplishment on her part "so much as to see you evincing a love for your Redeemer, & a conformity in temper & conduct to his requirements & example." He insists, "Especially I do hope, Helen, that you will improve your advantages for cultivating the fear of the Lord, & making attainments in true piety. I am far less anxious about your intellectual culture than respecting the training of your heart & dispositions."[58]

While Helen lived with the Hookers, Nathan expected her to train her dispositions, and demonstrate patient submission to her fate, by behaving with "constant self-control & prompt cheerful compliance with every regulation of the family."[59] This meant that she must faithfully attend Henry Hooker's church and yield to Martha Hooker's desire that she spend a good portion of her time in household chores, and less than she wished in studying for her classes at the local school or in reading—indeed, if she wished to read, she was to content herself with the religious works Martha selected for reading aloud. Nathan was no doubt pleased to have his skeptical daughter under the religious guidance of the pious Hookers. He was grateful, too, that Martha was willing to assume his deceased wife's place in directing Helen's domestic education: though he never explicitly mentions possible future occupations for Helen in his correspondence, not even matrimony, he occasionally alludes to a hope that she would one day return to manage his own Amherst home. But Helen was long accustomed to devoting herself to her studies, while servants did the cooking and cleaning. She developed a lasting hatred of Martha for forcing her to serve as the Hooker family's "maid of all work," for circumscribing her activities as if she were living in a "*prison*."[60]

She became adept at squirreling away every spare moment for study. By the summer of 1846, she was preparing so intensely for the entrance examinations to the new women's college at Mount Holyoke, for which she hoped to leave Falmouth in the fall, that the strain in her relations with the Hookers intensified. Her father interceded, reversing his original approval of Mount Holyoke and informing Helen that she must instead attend the Female Seminary at Ipswich, an institution that he believed would provide "less stimulus to intellectual effort."[61] This decision must have come as a great shock to Helen. Though her father had long urged her to be methodical and patient in her studies, never seeking to advance too quickly nor at the expense of maintaining a pious and obedient disposition, his sudden directive to refrain from making the most of herself intellectually went against all of his usual efforts to have her study well and diligently.

Distressed and anxious, her mind overwrought by the many demands being made upon it, Helen began her second approach to conversion. When a revival started in Henry Hooker's church, she was at first, as she would later tell Julius Palmer, "shocked at the depth of my hatred to the cause of Christ." But when Hooker discovered what she was feeling, "he talked with me hour after hour all to the affect that I was the most depraved of all sinners, was in the most ominous peril, &c, &c," until she was finally "fairly frightened into what I thought an actual submission of my own will and a resolution to be a Christian." But like her first approach to conversion, her new religion was not lasting. It quickly "wore off" when she left Falmouth for Ipswich, for it had been "merely an excitement fanned and stimulated to the highest pitch by external agonies, until from mere exhaustion, some rest must follow."[62]

That winter, as her father recorded his continued prayers for her conversion in his journal, Helen devoted her "whole soul" to study, making it her "idol."[63] Over the years, the main earthly reason Nathan had given her for doing well in school was the winning of his approval. Now, just before he set out for Palestine, he offered her an added incentive: he promised that upon his return, he would take her back home with him to Amherst and there personally supervise the completion of her education. "My heart beat high at the thought of it, and I took an instant resolve to strain every nerve during his absence," Helen later told Palmer. "I do not think that nine months were ever devoted to study with more miserly calculation of the exact amount of labor which could be accomplished in every moment than were those." She studied more than ever with the goal of pleasing her father, selecting many of her courses with his particular needs in mind:

I acquired a tolerable good knowledge of German (and as I knew that he had often occasion to refer to books in that language, I pleased myself with the idea that I might make my knowledge of it, useful to him). I read three new Latin authors. . . . I devoted a great deal of time to Intellectual Philosophy, which I knew to be one of his favorite studies. . . . I also . . . took lessons in perspective drawing, and took some dozen sketches from nature, because he had once told me that it would be very useful to him, could I do so.[64]

When Nathan died after Helen's first nine months at Ipswich, she lost her entire reason for studying. "No words can describe the sensations of loneliness, disappointment and discouragement which weighted down my spirit," she explained to Palmer. "I felt that I had now no motive to *do*, or even to *live*."[65] Immobilized by grief, she finally managed to recover herself and to continue with school only by deciding that her father would have wished her to do so. "To know that anything was or would be *his* wish will be sufficient to lead me unhesitatingly to do it," she determined at the time.[66]

Though Helen continued striving to please her father even after his death, she was never able to grant his greatest wish, that she undergo a heartfelt conversion to Calvinism. The day before her twenty-first birthday, she admitted to Julius Palmer in "the most *uncensored* outpouring" of her "most sacred thoughts & sorrows," that she considered herself unsuited ever to become a true Christian, for she was unwilling to make the sort of "entire, absolute, unconditional" commitment to "active exertion for the cause of Christ" that her father's example had made her believe necessary. "I love *dress;* I love *company;* I love *all* sorts of reading; I love *simple* intellectual exertion, without any view to an end," she confided. "I love, in short, the world: I *know* I am not willing to give it up."[67]

Unable to accept Calvinism, Helen was nonetheless "firmly resolved," as she entered adulthood, to "live in the daily observance of Christian duties; that even if I am never saved, I will exert as much of good influence in the world as I *can.*"[68] Like her father, she became a model of diligent submission in the face of adversity. Her diligence would allow her to accomplish much when she began to write professionally, even as her desire to do "good," and her deeply ingrained habit of seeking to please her father with her endeavors, would set somewhat restrictive parameters for her work.

While Helen's father was to have a profound influence on her literary career, her mother may largely be credited with making her career possible. For even as Nathan Fiske continually instructed Helen to give up her "foolish fancies" and direct all of her thoughts toward God, Deborah Fiske stoked the fires of her daughter's enthusiasm for storytelling and encouraged her to make the most of her active imagination. She wrote playful letters to Helen, examples of the fun that could be had with writing, and she urged her to develop a vivid, natural style in her correspondence and compositions.

Like her husband, Deborah Fiske had become a devoted Calvinist following an early conversion experience; like him, too, she lived in a world of moral absolutes in which all behavior could be judged according to laws laid down in the Bible and in which no endeavor was "of any consequence compared with securing the favor of God and a happy Eternity."[69] She believed it a Christian responsibility "to act under every circumstance from a conviction of duty rather than from momentary impulses," and she was given to making lists of her duties, with such titles as "Duties of Parents to Children" and "What Saith the Scriptures."[70]

In particular, she shared her husband's belief in the supreme importance of demonstrating Christian submission through constant diligence and cheerfulness. She often attended church four times on Sundays, for example, and she considered suffering an impetus for greater industriousness: upon the death of her baby boy Humphrey, she assured her father, "If this affliction should be the means of arousing us to prepare with more diligence for our own departure, we shall rejoice in Eternity that his precious spirit was called home so soon."[71] In her correspondence, the word "cheer" appears again and again, like a mantra: she is "cheerfully submissive" upon baby Humphrey's death; she struggles to be "cheerful always" during her own chronic illness; as her death approaches, she asks her husband to join her in placing "cheerful confidence in God."[72] Virtually every description of her ever written highlights her cheerful disposition. Unlike her husband, who was sanguine by force of will, Deborah Fiske possessed a natural, unforced brightness. "Mrs. Fiske was totally different from the Professor," said Edward Hitchcock, Jr., "a little woman, smiling, approaching you interestedly, but easily, with a kind remark always."[73] Upon Deborah's death, Heman Humphrey delivered a sermon, "The Woman That Feareth the Lord"; besides lauding her "meekness, humility, gentleness, charity, industry, fortitude," he praised her "perennial cheerfulness" nine times.[74]

Deborah Fiske not only embodied Christian submission but also worked earnestly to instill an attitude of submission in her children. Because she was always aware that she might die at any time, leaving her children motherless, she consciously fashioned temporary separations from them into training grounds for her impending permanent absence, using her letters to detail the necessity and advantages of obedience to God's will. She especially urged Helen to cultivate a cheerful and industrious disposition, knowing how important such a disposition would be if Helen were ever orphaned and forced to depend on the goodwill of others. Reminding Helen that she herself had lost her mother when she was very young, and had spent her own youth wandering from temporary home to temporary home, she repeatedly advised her daughter that the proper response to this situation was to "*be very obedient and pleasant and obliging wherever you go.*"[75] As early as 1836, when Helen was away with her father visiting Boston and Weston, where her paternal grandfather and aunt lived, Deborah told her that "every little girl should learn to love *work* while very young." She explained, "You must remember that you are *five* years old, and that if you try, there are a great many little things you can do to be useful."[76] In the following years, Deborah was no doubt gratified to receive reports, such as one from Martha Vinal in Charlestown, that Helen did try to make herself "uniformly pleasant and obedient" and "cheerful."[77]

After Deborah Fiske died, Nathan bound many of her letters to her children and to other relations into several letter books, which he gave to Helen and Ann before he departed for Palestine. He wrote prefatory notes for these books, advising his children of the appropriate way to read their mother's letters: he treats them as the writings of an exemplary Christian, thereby construing evangelism as their main purpose. To Helen, he explains that the letters should inspire her to "a suitable emulation" of her "dear mother's many virtues," so that she would "be prepared to meet her among the redeemed."[78]

When Helen perused the letters, she must indeed have been reminded of her departed mother's piety and sincere desire to advocate Christian submission. But at the same time, she would have been reminded with equal force of other qualities: her mother's imagination and creativity. In fact, unlike Helen's father, Deborah had never devoted her entire energies to proselytizing. She loved to read, and while she especially cherished certain pious authors, including Thomas à Kempis, Blaise Pascal, and William Cowper (whose poems and letters she cherished for their "heavenly spirit, full of gratitude and cheerful submission"),[79] she also read widely in history and travel. When directing Helen's reading, she urged study of the Bible and moralistic works like John Bunyan's *Pilgrim's Progress,* but she also encouraged her daughter to join in her own enthusiasm for travels and history. Unlike Helen's father, she did not object to Helen's early interest in Shakespeare. Moreover, Deborah's discussions of writing in her letters, and especially her own unique writerly voice, show her to be a woman of real literary feeling. She takes obvious joy in writing to Helen, and in the act of writing itself: she loves to "manufacture wonders," as she calls storytelling,[80] and to stimulate her daughter's imagination.

Like her husband, Deborah Fiske had a satirical sense of humor; unlike him, she made delightful, playful use of it. Thus, in a letter to Helen written after a visit with a cousin who believed in the power of mesmerism, or animal magnetism, Deborah lightly mocked such credulity, describing a dream in which she had the following conversation with an Amherst neighbor: "Mrs. Nelson asked me if I knew whether it was Mr. Fiske's opinion that *clams* could be *mesmerized.* I told her I did not know what *he* thought, but *my* opinion was they *could* be, because clams didn't *know enough* to *resist* the mesmeric influence."[81] Whereas Nathan Fiske ranged farthest from his usual didactic mode when he sent Helen a letter written in Latin, hoping by this means to promote her studies, Deborah Fiske sent her a letter written entirely in a kind of jabberwocky verse, titled "The jabberings of Helen Maria Fiske in her sleep, while she was dreaming about money, and kicking her cousin Sarah Hooker out of bed."[82] And in a letter illustrative of her gift for storytelling, Deborah asked Helen, "Wouldn't you like some Amherst news, and to see it dated from *our nursery window,* and written with my old pen?" She then offered a fanciful account of her own recent return to Amherst, accompanied by her father, David Vinal, and of the reception they received from Nathan Fiske:

> Last Monday afternoon, between the hours of three and four, a carriage entered the village drawn by four red horses, and drove up to the public house, where old and young were awaiting its arrival. It halted only long enough for salutations to be exchanged, and then proceeded on to the house of a private gentleman, who had

insisted that the travellers should at once become his guests. In a few moments the carriage was standing in front of a most rural residence. A most venerable looking old gentleman alighted, followed by an invalid daughter, and two attendants; their reception was most cordial; and so much do they seem to enjoy their delightful retreat that the probability is they will give up travelling for this season. In short, Helen, *we've got home*.[83]

In supervising Helen's progress in composition, Deborah encouraged imitation of her own inventive, pictorial manner of writing. She accomplished this task when Helen was away at school by reviewing the occasional school essay and especially by critiquing Helen's letters. Once, she criticized a letter in which Helen had merely listed her various activities "without a single incident connected with them, just like the bare *heads* of a sermon," and charged her to "send me a *graphic description* . . . so that we shall seem to see it ourselves, from your picture."[84] Another time, writing also on behalf of Ann, she asked Helen to "really tell us something to help us see where you are, and who you are with . . . and anything else that you think would be a good '*story*.'"[85] Helen soon adopted her mother's standards for composition, echoing her demands for entertaining and "very definite" letters and trying to write such letters herself.[86] From the beginning, she gave evidence of having inherited her mother's eye for the humorous in everyday life. "You would *laugh* to see her letter to me," Deborah Fiske wrote her husband when Helen was about ten years old, "a whole sheet filled, telling the whole about everything in a most amusing way."[87] Deborah rewarded her daughter's displays of humor, encouraging her to develop an easy, natural writing style: "When people don't write stiff primmed up letters, how much it is like a *real talk*. Such a talk, I was delighted to have from you this forenoon; and you will please to take notice that you have immediate attention in return, just such as the governor himself would have, should his highness send me letters—what do you suppose can be the reason he does not write?"[88]

While Deborah was playful and informal in her letters to Helen, and encouraged similar responses, she was careful to remind Helen never to write in a manner "not sufficiently refined" to people outside of the family: "things *said* may be forgotten," she warned her, "but things *written,* remain."[89] But in fact, Deborah herself was often far more whimsical than "refined" in her own correspondence with people outside her immediate family. She liked to assume new identities in her letters, for instance. Signing herself "Yours sincerely, One Night Cap," she once wrote to a needy acquaintance: "I am a poor lonesome creature, tired of my existence, and yet too conscientious to end it by suicide; therefore will good Mrs. Walker be kind enough to wear me out in her service, so that my life may be short and yet be the means of doing a little good."[90] She also liked to daydream, however much her husband was opposed to such self-indulgent behavior. "I *do* wish I could take a peep into Adeline's windpipe, Ellen's lungs and mine, and your joints that ache," she once wrote to Ann

Scholfield, one of her three beloved Scholfield cousins (these daughters of Martha Vinal's sister lived in Beacon Hill, Boston). "Like a thousand other gratified wishes, the result would bring nothing but vexation—the *pain* I shouldn't find in your poor knees—no dust that would explain Adeline's wheezing, nor apple cores or bits of flannel that would account for my cough or Ellen's."[91]

At times, Deborah's natural creativity was so powerful that it even threatened to obscure her firm sense of moral duty. In her letters to her Scholfield cousins, she sometimes indulged in a playful kind of "slandering and tattling," as she called it.[92] "I cannot describe to you how pleasant it is to me to see Adeline and Ellen," she wrote to cousin Ann during one visit to Boston:

> We talk about you, and everybody, and everything—praising or slandering just as we please after we have got through with making sport of all our friends' foibles, and wondering at the world at large. We have thought of penning a book to be called the black book in which a fine is to be charged for every instance of back biting to be paid over to some benevolent society. This idea was suggested by a *moral reform* publication sent by a good lady the other day to reform me,—such an experiment is in process with some of the contributors to that *purifying* periodical; but it is discouraging to try to do good or be good so many stand ready to pervert useful designs, now your Ellen, good as she is, insists upon it that the more we slander the better if the fine is to go to some good object. One thing I know no such account shall be opened while Adeline and Ellen stay—I'll have the full enjoyment of an unbridled tongue and save my coppers.[93]

For a woman as sincerely pious as Deborah Fiske, this letter is remarkably flippant on the subject of moral improvement. In fact, in another letter to Ann Scholfield, perhaps written while she was feeling anxious over her children's future, Deborah Fiske once questioned the effectiveness of her own efforts to do moral good: "As to doing good by letters, the moment I try to call up, out, or down, anything substantial, my head feels just like an egg-shell with the contents suddenly blown out."[94]

In early 1839, when she was thirty-two years old and had been married for more than ten years, Deborah Fiske tried a new way of effecting good with her writing: she wrote five pieces of children's fiction and published them anonymously in *Youth's Companion,* a children's magazine founded in 1827 as a Sunday school reader. Deborah tried to keep her work for *Youth's Companion* a secret from her family, and Helen seems never to have known of it. (Nor is there any record of her later reaction to the letter in her possession that revealed the secret.)[95] Still, Helen had been receiving *Youth's Companion* for several years when her mother's pieces appeared in the magazine; Deborah may well have directed her attention to these particular contributions, in which Deborah's protagonists are usually little girls just about the same age as eight-year-old Helen.

Deborah clearly intended her pieces as lessons in the importance of Christian diligence. Each of them is set up in the same way: Deborah writes of young people who are idle, inattentive, and unable to appreciate the advice of adults, with the hope that young readers will recognize whatever shortcomings they might share with these protagonists and dedicate themselves to becoming more industrious and obedient. But in fact, like her letters, her published writings are most remarkable not for their moral didacticism but for their wit. Deborah's natural zest for the ludicrous in everyday life continually leads her to betray sympathy for her boisterous protagonists. Thus, in "A Letter from a Little Girl Who Did Nothing but Play, to her Cousin Who Loved to Study," Deborah's fictional "Hannah," intended as a warning to children who neglect their studies, actually makes shirking seem a good option. "I hav lernte toe rede an rite and spel and thiss iz enuf phor mee," she says. "I pla orl most orl thee tyme. Kum and Pla with mee."[96] In another piece, titled "What a Useful Young Lady! Two Leaves from Her Journal, Picked Up in the Street a Few Days Ago," an indolent young diarist's description of her morning does more to amuse readers than to persuade them of the need for Christian diligence:

> Awoke early; a very cold morning; heard my mother and sisters getting breakfast; thought they would get along well enough without me; went to sleep again, and didn't wake till nine o'clock. Sat up in bed a while, looking at the frost upon the windows; screamed and screamed for somebody to come and make a fire in my room; nobody would hear. Suffered dreadfully from the cold putting on my clothes; knew I should actually perish if I stopped to comb my hair. Ran downstairs into the parlor; there was a good fire and my breakfast by it. The table cleared off, and the work all done, just as I thought it would be.[97]

Here, Deborah's comic sensibility and sympathy for children almost entirely overwhelm the moral lessons she wishes to impart. The same can be said of the drama of "Poor Susan," which played itself out in the pages of *Youth's Companion* for a month. In "Ten Questions That I Wish Nobody Would Ever Ask Me Again," Deborah's young Susan complains that she is incessantly "driven from one thing to another" by her Aunt Betsy's ten "why don't you's," demands for diligence and obedience that include such unreasonable requests as "why don't you keep still while others are talking." Poor Susan finds herself in need of commiseration:

> I really feel discouraged, and it is this feeling that makes me tell my troubles in the Youth's Companion. There is great comfort in sympathy; and will not some of my little mates write me a letter that will cheer up my spirits. It mustn't be a very long letter, for aunt Betsy, if it is, will be after me before I shall have read half of it, with some of her 'why don't you's.' Everything but absolute work and absolute study, she calls all nonsense that I am too big for. I am nine years old. I wish aunt Betsy was ninety-nine, but she is only thirty-seven.[98]

Within a few weeks, *Youth's Companion* received many responses to Susan, including letters from "C.N." and "S.P.G.," young readers who strove earnestly to assure Susan of her own culpability and to remind her of her duties.[99] The response of Deborah's "Aunt Betsy," on the other hand, is far less sober in effect. In "A Few Words to 'Poor Susan,'" Aunt Betsy intends to inform Susan that what she needs is not sympathy but a scolding. Yet in her righteous indignation, her eagerness to have the young readers of the *Youth's Companion* side with her, rather than with a clever child, Aunt Betsy makes herself ridiculous: "Aunt Betsy is not so easily imposed upon. To be sure she is more used to making puddings, than writing for the Youth's Companion; but she is not afraid to defend herself anywhere; and any little girl that comes out and tells but half of anything for the whole, needn't be surprised to see the other half from Aunt Betsy."[100]

Essentially, Deborah Fiske's sketches are not so much inducements to better behavior as they are comic portraits of behavioral battles in which children tend to act with a wisdom, albeit a naive wisdom, utterly lacking in their adult adversaries. Before publishing these pieces, Deborah had frequently alluded in her letters to a special interest in writing but had been unable to take her abilities seriously, always turning her interest into a joke. "It would prick my pride most grievously to know that you did not consider it a fine thing to receive such fine composition as I always 'make up' to put into letters," she teases her father in one letter; in another, playing with the idea of publication, she suggests that the two of them "make some books for others to read, you furnish the ideas and I will be your amanuensis."[101] In a letter to Ellen Scholfield, written during a period when Deborah's illness was making it difficult for her to do housework, she jokes about another writing project she never actually intends to undertake: "Of late my attention has been very much given to finding out the easiest way of doing things, and I have some hope of making discoveries that will be of great advantage to housekeepers and invalids; I will not specify them here, but if you see a work advertised with the title 'good news to hard workers' you may suspect that you know the author, and I advise you to buy a copy."[102]

Deborah could only joke about writing for publication in the years before her *Youth's Companion* pieces because she believed that her duty lay elsewhere, in her role as a wife and mother. Deborah's Calvinist faith taught her this, and her husband reinforced the notion. When the Fiskes were married, one of Nathan's friends sent Deborah a poem, "The Province of Woman," which specified the conventional, limited role that he, and by proxy Nathan himself, would "expect,—mark that word, *expect, confidently* expect" to see her fill. In the words of the poem, she was to withdraw her "modest head from public sight," "unknown to flourish, & unseen be great," so that she might "give domestic life its sweetest charm."[103] Deborah kept this letter and poem pressed into a scrapbook for reflection. Moreover, both she and her husband believed that all writers worthy of the name were engaged in the serious business of directing readers toward God. If it overtasked Nathan's energies to fulfill this obligation, how could Deborah, her days filled with domestic duties, conceive of becoming a writer? "How can *I* step into the perplexities that you with all your philosophy and firmness can hardly bear?" she once asked him.[104]

Though Deborah believed, and her husband insisted, that she should not stray from the domestic realm, she was sometimes frustrated within her limited role. As a student she had shined near the top of her class at a variety of boarding schools in Massachusetts and New Hampshire, but her illness made it impossible for her to excel as a housekeeper. In 1836, a particularly difficult year, she admitted to her husband that "it sometimes seems mysterious that when there is nothing in the world that I do not do better this should have been my employment."[105] Not long before she wrote her *Youth's Companion* pieces, she had begun to dream with new urgency of directing her efforts to something literary, perhaps for "the benefit of *little* children." In a letter to her cousin Martha Hooker, she explained: "*My life* is slipping away and I am doing nothing but taking care of my family. I know it is my *proper business,* but some do so much good besides."[106]

When Deborah finally did try writing for publication, making her attempt to "benefit" children in the pages of the *Youth's Companion,* she was ashamed of the results. She told Martha Hooker, who had somehow discovered her secret, that she had written fanciful pieces because she thought children might learn more readily from fiction than from narrow exhortation. But she believed that in the end she had produced only "silly things" and "nonsense," that she had been "a *fool*" to undertake writing for publication in the first place. "I have never been in the habit of writing anything but familiar letters about family matters or nothing at all and it is all I am fit for," she insisted. Deborah also admitted to Martha that she was worried about her husband's reaction to her secret endeavor, which he was soon to discover by reading her letter: "To make a bad matter *still* worse," she said, "Mr. Fiske must ask me to let him see this before it is sealed, so the cat will be out of the bag."[107] Indeed, Deborah's lengthy self-deprecations in this letter have the feel of being directed as much toward her husband as toward Martha. She never wrote for publication again.

Though Deborah was uncomfortable with her own irrepressible sense of humor, it seems to have been the very quality that most impressed Helen in her mother's writing. Early in her career she would find inspiration for several children's stories about the antics of cats in a rollicking series of letters her mother had sent to her in the summer of 1836, pretending to be her cat. And in 1879 she published *Letters from a Cat,* a revised version of her mother's actual letters.

Deborah Fiske's original cat letters are even more mischievous, more filled with sheer fun and frolic, than her other writings. The Fiske cat displays a literary sensibility in her letters, like Deborah herself; unlike Deborah, however, the cat revels in her talents, boasting of her ability to write better than other cats, who generally make "dreadful work . . . trying to print," and jealously guarding her reputation for erudition by telling Helen not to show her letters to anyone, "unless it may be to some cat who knows less than I do."[108] While Deborah mostly only dreamed about undertaking useful literary work, and was dissatisfied with the results when she did actually publish, the Fiske cat opens a school for other cats and candidly scorns females who confine themselves only to taking care of their own kittens. "The Judge's cat," she complains, "is very old and stupid, and so taken up with her six kittens (who are the ugliest I ever saw), that she does not take the least interest in her neighbor's affairs."[109]

In editing her mother's letters, Helen was careful to preserve their original charm. Take, for instance, a day when the cat is frightened by a spring house-cleaning, and bumps her nose against a window. In Deborah's original letter, the cat laments,

> My poor nose tingles yet from the sad thump it got against the glass and when I wash my face my nose feels as if it must have a very flat look. If it has such a look, I am sure I hope it will outgrow it for the beauty of any cats face is a handsome nose.[110]

In Helen's version, the cat is slightly more self-conscious, but still herself:

> But the worst of all is the condition of my nose. Everybody laughs who sees me, and I do not blame them; it is twice as large as it used to be, and I begin to be seriously afraid it will never return to its old shape. This will be a dreadful affliction: for who does not know that the nose is the chief beauty of a cat's face?[111]

In her introduction to *Letters from a Cat,* Helen describes Deborah Fiske as "the kindest human being I ever knew."[112] Surely this tribute was prompted not only by Deborah's cheerful good nature and constant desire to do "good," but also by the loving creativity that she poured into her relationship with her daughter. As a writer, Helen would find in her mother's comedic sensibility and interest in the idiosyncrasies of human character an important counterbalance to the sober legacy of her diligent, single-minded father—a man who, in a rare moment of self-pity, once complained, "I am obliged, if I use the pen at all, to do it in the capacity of a toilsome drudge."[113]

In the years immediately following the deaths of her parents, Helen acknowledged that they had both "left their teaching in the heart of their child."[114] Their lessons in Christian submission would help her carry on amid the many losses still in store for her, and fuel her early efforts to make good on her inherited literary disposition.

⌐ 3 ⌐

Literary Education

When I think of all that I have proposed, of all that I *would* and I
think, *might* be and do, my heart sighs, after some "lodge" where I
might flee—not to "*rest*," but to work.

JACKSON TO JULIUS PALMER, December 30, 1851, HHJ2

Helen's life was busy in the decade following her father's death. She completed
her formal education, worked for a short period as a teacher in a private school,
married, and had two children. Throughout this time, though not yet writing
for publication, she expressed a steady interest in literature and undertook a
number of literary projects. To some extent, her early literary endeavors were
little more than diversions—inspired by a Victorian taste for self-improvement,
commonly held notions of activities proper for a young lady, and the need to
be industrious that she had learned from her parents; like her mother, she
quickly gave up her endeavors when social or domestic duties beckoned. In her
more introspective moods, however, she longed almost desperately to accomplish something significant in writing—to really "work," as she says in the epigraph to this chapter—and her longing has the ring of true literary ambition.

For perhaps a year after her father died, Helen continued with her studies at
the Ipswich Female Seminary. As Nathan Fiske had hoped, the education offered there was not excessively stimulating but was unmistakably evangelical
in nature. The school's basic educational goal was "to make its pupils intelligent readers, easy writers, and companionable friends," and students were
"constantly pressed" to consider their every action in light of "the immutable
standard of right and wrong."[1] Helen found life at Ipswich almost as dreadfully
uncongenial as her time with the Hookers had been; in later years she would
refer to herself as a "survivor" of the "massacres" of Falmouth and Ipswich.[2]
She disliked Eunice Cowles, a former friend of her mother's who, along with
her husband John, was director of the school, and she believed the feeling was
mutual. She also disliked the quiet colonial town of Ipswich. "Nothing happens

here from morning till night, from one week end to the other," she wrote to Ann Scholfield, one of the Scholfield cousins from her own generation, not long after her arrival. Her letter foreshadows the descriptive powers and also the occasional mood of oppression that would mark her later regionalist writings on New England:

> Ipswich, you know, is an old town & if you did not know it before you would find it out before you had been here six hours. In some of the streets you see nothing but these gray & brown old houses, built with high slanting roofs & the upper story jutting out over the lower, while as you walk along by these specimens of antiquity, you see no one, in, around, or about them, but old men, old women, old *cats,* old *dogs,* old *hens,* (never the sign of a chicken) old trees, old fences, old stone walls. Every creature & thing looks as if it grew as old as it could grow two thousand years ago & has been *lasting* ever since.[3]

Bored by her surroundings, Helen continued to devote her energies to studying, both those subjects she had originally undertaken in order to please her father and her regular courses such as French and composition—indeed, she "particularly endeavored to improve in composition."[4] From as early as 1841, when she was studying in Hadley, she had felt an interest in English grammar; when she was later enrolled in Miss Austin's school in Charlestown, she had demonstrated such proficiency in composition that she had been allowed to choose her own topics for fortnightly exercises. Now at Ipswich she was careful to make time for extracurricular reading, including Dickens's *Dombey and Son* and the *Autobiography of Goethe,* and she turned her thoughts to the theory behind literary art, taking particular interest in Lord Kames's *Elements of Criticism* (1762).

In this book, which was widely read and studied in both the eighteenth and nineteenth centuries, Kames argues that aesthetic taste, like moral sense, is not "arbitrary" but rather "governed by principles common to all men," and therefore encompasses an understanding of "what is right and what is wrong." By cultivating an educated taste in the arts, says Kames, laymen can further the development of a "pure and untainted" morality, and writers can produce works capable of exerting a unique "influence" over "the heart," drawing readers out of their own "private" circumstances "to perform acts of generosity and benevolence."[5] Kames's focus on the moral ends of writing was eminently familiar to Helen from the teachings of her parents, of course, and it may have helped her accept her nascent literary impulses as compatible with those teachings. Years later, it would be one of the unspoken early influences behind her attempt to effect social change with her Indian reform writings.

By January 1849 Helen had moved to New York City to begin a final period of academic study at the Abbott Institute. She was happier there than she had been in years. A far cry from sleepy Ipswich, where everything seemed old and nothing ever happened, New York was the largest city in the country, with a population of more than half a million people and an ever increasing diversity made possible by the arrival of vast numbers of new immigrants, especially from Ireland, Germany, and other western and northern European countries. The city was fast on its way to eclipsing Boston as America's preeminent cultural center; Helen delighted in opportunities to see such famous international performers as the singer Jenny Lind. At the same time, on school outings to the Bowery and garment districts, her eyes were opened for the first time to the realities of tenement living and crushing poverty. "Never in my life did I see such misery, such degradation and wretchedness," she told her sister.[6]

Helen quickly came to love and admire the Reverend John Stevens Cabot Abbott, the well-known writer and educator who directed the Abbott Institute, in Manhattan, with his similarly gifted brother, the Reverend Jacob Abbott. John Abbott was a graduate of Bowdoin College's famous class of 1825, along with Nathaniel Hawthorne and Henry Wadsworth Longfellow; even as he worked at the institute he was well on his way to establishing what would prove a remarkably prolific career as the author of histories, biographies, educational manuals, and other nonfiction works. Helen lived with John Abbott's family in Lafayette Square during her time at his school, and she felt truly at home with him, his wife Jane, and his daughter Jennie, who became for a time her closest friend. Finally, she lost the sense of loneliness that had plagued her in each of her previous temporary residences. In the "genial light of Mr. John's good soul," in his daily manifestations of concern for her happiness, she found an antidote to the "doubting and gloomy misanthropy" that had threatened to overwhelm her upon the death of her father.[7] For many years, even after she was married, she would believe that John Abbott was the "*one* person" who had ever truly understood the depth of her need for "*love.*"[8]

John Abbott was the first of four clergymen who were to play important roles in Helen's literary development following the death of her father. In some respects, his teachings reinforced Nathan Fiske's. Both John and his older brother Jacob had attended Andover Theological Seminary. Indeed, Jacob had attended the seminary at the same time as Helen's father, and the two men were later colleagues at Amherst and coauthors of *The Bible Class Book,* the children's Sunday school pamphlet discussed in the previous chapter. John Abbott spelled out his own theories of children's education in a number of books, including one directed at girls: *The School-girl; or, The Principles of Christian Duty Familiarly Enforced* (1840). In this book, while reminding young readers that "to neglect mental improvement is a great sin," John Abbott especially emphasizes the importance of cheerful submission to God's will, just as Nathan Fiske had done in *The Bible Class Book* and his other writings. John argues that it is the schoolgirl's duty to "perseveringly and prayerfully" resist "every emotion of discontent" and to "cultivate the habit of looking upon the bright side of every object." He elaborates, "It is wicked to be melancholy. It is a duty to be happy. Gloom and despondency are not only the consequences of sin, but they are sinful states of the mind. They prove ingratitude, and want of submission to the government of God."[9]

John Abbott's emphasis on the necessity for cheerful Christian submission reinforced the teaching of Helen's father, but he was less narrow and dogmatic in his sectarian views. Helen admired his sermons. She quickly placed him alongside Julius Palmer (who served as a deacon in the Congregational Church, though he was by profession a lawyer) as the only two people who had ever urged religion on her "in a manner which did not in any respect, grate upon my feelings."[10] Moreover, unlike Helen's father, who wished her to bend all her intellectual efforts toward achieving a right attitude toward God, John Abbott encouraged her to consider a possible future in writing. According to the later testimony of a member of the Abbott family, Helen at this time was "a thinker" who "gave promise of future ability" in her "composition exercises," and John Abbott "often told her that God had given her a talent in this department which she was bound to use and to cultivate."[11] Indeed, even in *The School-girl,* where Abbott expresses an expectation that most young women will become homemakers, he nonetheless offers special praise to "distinguished" women writers like Germaine de Staël, who by "vivid imagination" and "the strength of their minds, have influenced the most powerful nations in the world."[12] He seems to have believed that Helen was capable of becoming distinguished in this way.

In the summer of 1849, when Helen had completed at least a semester of study at the Abbott Institute, she went to live in a lodging house in Charlestown, Massachusetts, with her grandfather David Vinal and her sister. As the rooms she was to share with Ann were being refurbished, she wrote to Julius Palmer, comparing her unsettled living situation to the frontier experience of the regionalist writer Caroline Kirkland. "We are living now in a fashion somewhat akin to that which new settlers at the West are obliged to adopt," Helen told Palmer, "and which Mrs. Kirkland humorously calls 'being anywhere, everywhere, and nowhere in particular.'"[13]

Helen's unsettled lodgings were not alone in making her feel like she was "nowhere in particular." After the excitement of New York, she found little to recommend "this little, tame, every day, do-nothing, know-nothing, hear-nothing, see-nothing of a place, Charlestown!"[14] Though nearby Boston was the nation's fourth-largest city, with almost 150,000 residents, and though three years later Helen would describe Boston as the cultural "centre of the universe,"[15] she had few opportunities to explore the city now. Moreover, she had grown accustomed to spending her days in the congenial company of the Abbott family, but now she had to spend most of her time alone. Her grandfather was usually engaged in business, her sister off at day school. Her only sources of stimulation were to "sew, read, write [letters] or practice [piano], by myself," a "routine" she "varied" on some afternoons "by a walk, a call at Aunt Vinal's, or if nothing else can be thought of, *by the breaking of a few lamp shades.*"[16]

Fortunately, within a matter of months John Abbott wrote to Helen, asking her to return to his New York home and to work as a teacher at the institute. She was eager to accept his offer. In seeking to convince her guardian of its merits, she revealed the extent to which, with Abbott's encouragement, she had begun to hope that she might have a literary future. She explained to Palmer that there were no "literary advantages" to her current living situation, for there was not "a single literary or even educated gentleman, in the place." If she were to resume life with the Abbotts, on the other hand, she felt that she would "of a necessity, improve by daily intercourse with persons of a highly elevated literary character, and varied attainments." She asked Palmer, "In an intellectual and literary point of view, what could be more desirable?" She assured him of her conviction that if she did not return to New York, "all hope of ever *being* or *doing* anything may as well be given up."[17]

Helen did return to the Abbott Institute, with her guardian's blessing, in January 1850. She spent a year and a half teaching there, achieving popularity and success with her students, earning an annual salary of $100, and finding ample opportunity to indulge her love for "solitary study."[18] She also carried out her first literary enterprise: the founding and editing of a school newsletter, the *Portfolio.* "I have the inspection, acceptation or rejection, correction, revision &c &c of all the matter good bad & indifferent, furnished by a class of some twelve in number," she playfully explained to Palmer. Following in her mother's footsteps, she looked with humor on her new literary endeavor, satirizing her own dilettantism. She spoke of herself as an "Editress" and boasted of her newsletter's "classical" title and "highly poetic" motto: "Portfolio leaves we offer here / Which chance has gathered far & near."[19] In volume 1 of the *Portfolio,* she sounds especially like her mother as she introduces an anonymous student's contribution to one of the newsletter's special departments, "Congressional News." "In pursuance of our design," Helen writes, "of making this periodical perfectly original in its character, we propose in each Number, to give some accounts of the proceedings in the various legislative bodies of the universe. Our news today, is of highly interesting character, being, as our readers will perceive, a report of the last business which was transacted in the . . . Senate Among the Fishes."[20] In volume 2 of her *Portfolio,* Helen features further "Congressional News" from "Piscatoria, the seat of finny government," and also informs her readers that she has "secured the services of a very graphic writer" for a department of "Foreign Correspondence." This writer, she says, will soon detail for the newsletter his "tour in those regions, which although the most interesting in the universe, are also the most seldom visited"—the regions of the moon.[21]

Just as Helen was settling into a happy routine at the institute, finding that she preferred working as a teacher, with a "quiet room, books and a pen, to this life that people lead who have to go to *sewing circles* &c &c &c,"[22] John and Jacob Abbott began making plans to close the school temporarily in the spring of 1851 so that they could transfer its directorship into the hands of their brother Gorham and devote themselves solely to writing. While Helen was saddened by these plans, which meant that she was to lose her job and her cherished home, the fact that John and Jacob Abbott were able to contemplate earning their living entirely by writing made a powerful impression on her. "The sale is really marvelous, of their books," she wrote to Julius Palmer. "The Harpers say that it is almost impossible for them to meet the orders for them, from *England* and the *Continent*." Full of admiration for the writer's life that John Abbott was about to lead, she told Palmer, "I am sure were I in his place, I should do just as he is doing."[23]

Briefly, Helen considered looking for another teaching position. She knew that she preferred "working hard" at a "stated employment" to "living in idleness," as she had recently done in Charlestown.[24] But while she had felt entirely comfortable taking a job with John Abbott, whom she knew and loved, she had trouble seeing herself as a "professional" teacher, forced to search for a position among strangers. Whenever she used the word "profession" in her letters from this period, she underlined it or enclosed it in quotation marks: in connection with herself, the word seemed incongruous, even ridiculous. Unable to resolve her conflicted feelings, she made visits to both of her grandfathers, in Charlestown and Weston, Massachusetts; then, in the fall of 1851, she went to stay with the family of her guardian's brother, the Reverend Ray Palmer, pastor of the First Congregational Church in Albany, New York.

Like Helen's father and John Abbott, Ray Palmer was a staunch advocate of the duty of cheerful submission—"We must not carry burdens" was his motto[25]—and he was also an author. He contributed essays to various periodicals of sectarian origin, including the Congregationalist *New York Independent,* which would later become Helen's main literary outlet. He was also a hymnodist of some repute, having written, among other popular pieces, "My Faith Looks Up to Thee," a hymn Helen considered "exquisite."[26] In 1851 he published *Closet Hours,* a new edition of his *Spiritual Improvements, or Aids to Growth in Grace* (1839). Upon first arriving in Albany, Helen shed some "foolish tears" over the many sorrows of her life to that point, but she soon came to love Ray Palmer and his wife Ann as much as she loved the Abbott family.[27] She stayed on with them for a year, forming a belief that their home at 157 Hamilton Street was "the pleasantest" she had "*ever* known."[28]

Helen's life in Albany was busy and full. When not helping Ann Palmer with her two young daughters, she had plenty of time to spend with new friends, like Mary Sprague, and she entered with mixed feelings into the rounds of formal society, with its regular calling hours and gossipy sewing circles. She took riding lessons, working to overcome a phobia that had taken possession of her after a recent fall. And she received the attention of at least two suitors: William B. Fox, whose occasional presence she endured only because his sister Jennie was among her closest friends, and Charles Clark. She also continued with her studies. She kept up with her languages and music, spending so much time in morning sessions at the piano that the Palmers had to rent a second instrument for her use. Every day after the midday meal, she and the Palmers read aloud together for an hour from such edifying works as Rev. James McCosh's *The Method of Divine Government* (1850). She often went to Ray Palmer's study to discuss books and authors, for her new guardian was well versed in literature, especially poetry. She also read a great deal on her own, devoting some time to canonical writers, including Bacon, Coleridge, and Tennyson, but mostly enjoying the latest in fiction and creative nonfiction. She liked writing that spoke to her of "poetry" and the ideal, such as *Dream Life* (1851) by Donald Grant Mitchell, alias "Ik Marvel"; she was also drawn to books that seemed to capture "reality" through their "life like-ness" and "graphic description, in characters and incidents."[29] In the latter category she included such works as Charles Kingsley's reforming novel *Yeast* (1850), William Starbuck Mayo's *Kaloolah, or Journeyings to the Djebel Kumri* (1849), and Susan Warner's fantastically popular *The Wide, Wide World* (1851). It was a somewhat guilty pleasure that she took in this last novel, a landmark in the genre today labeled "sentimentalism." "Were I forced to criticize it, I could not be enthusiastic in its praise," she admitted. "But the book is like some of my friends, I do not admire them, I would not be like them, I could not delight others by a detail of their character—but I do love dearly to be *with* them."[30]

As busy as Helen kept herself, as determined as she was not to be "discontented," she was nonetheless haunted by a frustration that had been at the back of her mind, "tossing there, in greater or less commotion for years." What had her education been "all *for*," she wondered, if she was to spend her days merely in leisure activities? She longed instead to put her writing skills "to work," and she dreamed of publication.[31] Sitting before her fire one day, she imagined it to be "after the same pattern as the one before which 'Ik Marvel' sat, while composing the 'Reveries of a Bachelor' " (another popular new book by Mitchell), and she joked in a letter to Julius Palmer that he "need not be surprised if in the course of a few months a work issues from the Albany press, bearing no name, but simply the title 'Reveries of an Old Maid'!"[32]

She was often solemn in confessing her frustrations and vague literary ambitions to Henry Root, an Amherst College student whom she had met during a brief visit to Amherst in August 1851, just before her move to Albany. Their acquaintanceship began among mutual friends during the festivities of commencement, with a memorable ride to Pelham Springs and a heart-to-heart talk that lasted until four o'clock one Saturday morning; it grew over the course of several years into a "best-friendship" that both cherished.[33] While there was speculation in Amherst that the attachment was romantic, and while on Henry's side, at least, there were phases in the relationship when this conjecture bore truth, it was in most respects what Helen termed "brotherly and sisterly,"[34] continuing nearly unchanged as both became interested in other people. Since they had few opportunities to see each other, their friendship took place primarily in letters. They wrote often, sometimes every fortnight, and they took pains with their letters, occasionally staying up late into the night to write by the light of an evocative moon, or selecting writing stations that were especially conducive to honest thought and unbridled fancy—in Helen's case, often a small rocking chair, covered in black haircloth, which had once belonged to her mother. Their correspondence survives today through a unique chain of sentiment. Henry's untimely death led Helen to preserve their letters, despite earlier worries that she should burn them. Long afterward, when she herself was dying and explicitly ordered William Jackson to burn the letters, he did not; instead, he passed them down to his descendants.

What Helen and Henry most appreciated in their relationship was its freedom from all need to posture. "I cannot write to you as I write to all my other friends, and as I speak to others—in a quite common way of common every day things," Helen once told Henry; "but all the deep, earnest, speculative notions, and thoughts and feelings which have lived restless in my brain for years, seem to find spontaneous utterance."[35] During Helen's year in Albany, which coincided with Henry's senior year at Amherst, both friends were plagued by worries that they were squandering their intellectual gifts: they feared they had been too "satisfied with a *consciousness of capability,* without *doing!*"[36] Henry was in fact so successful in his studies that he was near the top of his class, and he had already begun to publish literary reviews and deliver lyceum lectures, but he felt paralyzed by uncertainty over what he should do after college. (He would later decide to enter Harvard Law School, despite Helen's urging of the ministry.) As for Helen, she worried that she had become so accustomed in the course of her "wandering" life to a constant succession of "new scenery, new characters, new incidents" that she might never be able to settle down to accomplish anything.[37] "My nature seems to me a perfect compound of *nullifications,*" she told Henry.

> If I had not my love of dress and of society to interfere with my intellectual aims and pursuits, I might have been a scholar; if my intellect and reason did not continually make me ashamed of any thoughts of fashions, dress, &c, I might at least have been a *leader* of the *fashionables*—and *contemptible* as is that character,

it has supremacy in it, and that, in *anything,* I had very nearly said, even in *wickedness,* is better than quiescence;—and if I had had less absorbing interest in study, and more indifference to externals, I might at least have been a woman of heart—to win love from every body—but now—with an ever restless head—an intellect to conceive—and aim—but a want of *life-power* to execute—a heart which can love, if it could ever *stop* long enough, and whose deepest love is mingled ever with so many other things—Alas, what a life is mine.[38]

It was the intellectual life of the "scholar"—the literary life—that seemed to Helen most admirable among the several choices open to her. In her correspondence with Henry, she found a space in which to focus on attaining this life. Her letters from Albany are filled with allusions to authors—Harriet Beecher Stowe, Charles Lamb, Jane Austen, Goethe, and Shakespeare, among others. She sent Henry poems, novels, reviews, and sermons of special interest. And she often shared her thoughts on her current reading. "It is not very often that I am so completely 'book-mad' and 'word-crazy,'" she wrote after finishing Shelley's *Prometheus Unbound* (1820). "Oh, to have *conceived* a Prometheus, I would endure an eternity of tenfold his agony! . . . I *will* not let myself be turned into a young lady 'in society' who sleeps, goes to parties, receives and returns calls!"[39] Upon taking her first look into the writings and philosophy of Ralph Waldo Emerson, she seconded Henry's belief that Emerson's "view of life" was "*thrilling,* and *awakening,* even though it does not always prove . . . practical."[40] In one of her letters she enclosed an excerpt she had transcribed from the essay "Introductory Lecture on the Times," noting that she considered the essay "one of Emerson's best." "Our torment is Unbelief, the Uncertainty as to what we ought to do," Emerson writes in the quoted passage, giving voice to the very anxiety that plagued the two young friends.[41] Helen told Henry that she was giving a good deal of thought to Emerson, and also beginning to feel a new appreciation for "the Transcendental myths" set forth in Thomas Carlyle's *Sartor Resartus* (1833–34).[42]

Helen not only enjoyed discussing other authors with Henry, but she also used her letters as a forum for developing her own literary skills. When she made mistakes in grammar, she stopped to critique them. She often agonized over the inadequacy of words to express true emotion. She worked to create nice turns of phrase: one day, for instance, when she was half maddened by the "determinedly methodical patter" of the rain falling upon her roof, she grumbled, "I should think it must be some of the *very same* rain which fell in Noah's time, for it comes down as if it had been *so long used* to it!"[43] She offered vivid descriptions of scenes she encountered in Albany and of others she remembered longingly from her childhood, beginning to express what would prove a lasting interest in the influence of place. "How strange the link that binds our hearts to the external—the external of one spot, to that of another," she wrote after describing the scenery near her old Amherst home.[44] She also began thinking about the art of characterization. She and Henry often talked about "character," and delighted in making a "study" of the people they knew; Helen made plans to log her own observations in a "character book."[45] She was coming to depend on written expression, as writers do, as a means of both organizing and rectifying her experience: "Were it not for my ever-at-hand resource, in my pen, I should at once yield to a fit of melancholy contemplation," she told Henry one gloomy day.[46] Moreover, for perhaps the first time since her mother's death, she saw letter writing as an opportunity to indulge her imagination freely. Thus she once sent Henry a playful composition about clouds, titled "A Medley." Another time, on October 3, 1851, she sent him an anonymous poem, "Consecration" (since lost), which she would much later admit to having written herself. In his response, Henry commented on what was apparently the poem's depiction of romantic love, and guessed wrongly that the poem had been written by a man; he complied with Helen's wish that he return it, but asked her to please "copy, and send back" a "criticism" she had made of it on the same page.[47]

While it was in her letters to Henry Root that Helen most fully revealed her growing literary ambitions, it was at the prompting of Ray Palmer that she undertook her most ambitious literary endeavor of this period: the translation from French of a book apparently titled *Essays on the Difficulties of the Pentateuch.* By encouraging Helen to take on a project that he had originally planned to do himself, Palmer became the second clergyman of letters, after John Abbott, to further her literary development in the years following her father's death. Because Palmer had intended to publish his own translation of the *Essays,* he no doubt intended to help Helen publish hers.

After only a few months of effort, however, she lost interest in the undertaking. In December she was delighted to receive invitations from Molly Hunt, the wife of New York's Governor Washington Hunt, to two upcoming winter balls. These were "the great affairs of the season," Helen knew; and though she pooh-poohed them to Henry Root, complaining that she was not likely to find any "intellectual society, in *parties,*" to Julius Palmer she admitted that she looked forward to them not only as "a passport into Society" but also as her own "coming out," for she had never attended a "really large party" or even owned a "party dress."[48] As it happened, the first ball served as much more than a coming-out, for it was there that she first met the governor's youngest sibling, Edward Hunt.

Born in Livingstone County, New York, on June 15, 1822, to a family of farmers, Edward Hunt had graduated from West Point second in his class in 1845, then taught there for several years before assuming varied duties with the Army Corps of Engineers. When Helen met him, he had been posted since the spring of 1851 with the Coast Survey in Washington, D.C. He made a powerful impression on her at both of her winter parties. "You know you used to laugh sometimes, or *half* laugh, at my 'ideal' as you said, of manly perfection," she wrote to Henry Root.

> How much more would you laugh, if I should tell you that I had almost carried my simplicity so far as to believe that I have met the individual who actually *realizes* it? . . . He is very tall, very large, very dignified, *rather* cold in his manner at first, but *thaws* at once into most friendly earnestness: very intelligent, and I should judge highly intellectual in his tastes. He is said to take a very high position in his profession, and is universally spoken of as a man of remarkable information and reliability. But it is not any or all of these traits, that I admire. It is his evident seriousness—firmness—*heart*-fullness. . . . Now, my dear friend, do I not well to admire him?[49]

There would always remain a large measure of intellectual admiration in Helen's feelings for Edward: at this period in her life she felt a need "to reverence [her] husband's intellect—to entirely lean upon the better stronger head!"[50] Still, she was far from immune to the more visceral, heady rush of her "first love." "Mere intellect, however grand, would not fire my heart," she assured Henry Root, "let it win ever so great homage."[51] In some ways, Edward reminded her of both Henry and John Abbott. But as he began to call on her during his leaves from work, she developed a passion for him that was altogether new. Before long she was so distracted by happiness that she found herself daydreaming at the expense of all her usual studious endeavors. By early April, she could only joke about the possibility of someone "dragging out my *French translation* from underneath a pile of withered party flowers, and visiting cards, and manuscript editions of Sewing Circle gossip—(the only *press,* I fancy from which said translation will ever issue!)."[52]

In mid-April, Edward saw Helen off from New York City as she embarked on a lengthy pleasure trip with Julius and Lucy Palmer. Soon afterward she received his proposal in the mail. They were married six months later, on October 28, 1852, two weeks following Helen's twenty-second birthday. They spent their wedding night in a hotel room just adjacent to that of Ray Palmer and his wife. Helen later told Ann Palmer that she appreciated this circumstance, especially when she imagined the more frightening wedding nights of other brides: "I'd rather stay at a good Hotel in Springfield—and have a 'parson' and his wife in the next room, and the parson's wife to 'tuck me up'!"[53] For their wedding journey she and Edward made visits to their relations in Albany and in Edward's hometown of Portage, and they also went to Niagara Falls. In a letter to Henry Root, Helen complained about a large hotel that had recently been constructed there, expressing sentiments that would later mark her work as a professional travel writer. "There is one comfort though," she said. "Let civilization and fashion, and artificiality creep in as much as they may, many of the features of the place are intrinsically wild and grand beyond the power of man to alter."[54]

Edward proved a devoted husband. In the winter of 1856, during a period when he was working mostly with the Light House Board of Rhode Island, he once walked eighteen miles home to Newport from work, when carriages had stopped running in heavy snow, because he wanted to be sure Helen and their newborn son Rennie were safe. That fall, lonely and slightly ill, he wrote longingly at the end of a day to Helen, who was with Rennie on a trip away from home: "Good night, Helen, & when you feel that little nestler mousing around for you on one side, please indulge the wish for a moment that I was on the other instead of being here alone, weary & listless, but still your own Edward."[55]

Helen herself was "*more* than happy" with married life.[56] She believed that she and Edward were particularly close because both of them were orphans. She was also extremely proud of the success with which her husband carried out a variety of scientific pursuits in addition to his regular engineering duties with the army. Before their marriage, she had explained to Julius Palmer, "He has been engaged more or less for several years in some philosophical studies of a very scientific and profound nature—exactly *what* I could not attempt to tell you, for the very good reason that I don't more than half understand them myself:—but they are very abstruse, and yet tending to eminently practical results, and to a wide field of discovery and distinction."[57]

These "abstruse" studies were probably Edward's researches in molecular physics, which in subsequent years he worked on whenever time allowed. Hunt also wrote numerous articles for scientific journals, delivered papers at the annual meetings of the American Association for the Advancement of Science, wrote reports for the Coast Survey, and above all labored for years, as he said, "with all due diligence," to compile a massive "Alphabetical Index of the Ten Annual Coast Survey Reports."[58] By 1857 he had reviewed 7,000 books for this project and made 35,000 entries.

According to Hunt's friends and relatives, even as a child he "was never known to play" but was "ever ready to address himself with the greatest alacrity" to "work, of whatever description," finding "his chief interest" in "study." As an adult, he "was a man who let neither wife nor children nor personal interests interfere with his career."[59] Occasionally, Helen was frustrated and made lonely by her husband's "lack of capacity for recreation, or even for a remission of labor." For the most part, however, she was inspired by it. Like Helen's father, Hunt offered a strong example of "loft[y]" dedication to work.[60] During periods when the Hunts lived together, Edward often spent entire days "steadily writing," shaping his various scientific investigations into papers.[61] He read his works in progress aloud to Helen, and sometimes asked her to copy them out for him. When he was "up to his ears in another article," as Helen put it, he did not like to socialize. And although Helen had been eager upon marriage to participate in society, she felt "ashamed" to ask Edward to put aside his books for more frivolous activities.[62] Very soon, she developed her own lasting distaste for formal gatherings and large crowds. Only months after her wedding, she wrote humorously to Julius Palmer from her new home in Washington, D.C.: "I have the opportunity of seeing the kind of society for which I used to long, and shall I confess it to my dear guardian—in the midst of it all, I am tempted to exclaim—'fruits of Sodom'!"[63]

Because Hunt was preoccupied and often away from home, Helen found that married life afforded her ample free time to pursue her own interests. Of course, motherhood was demanding. She had severe morning sickness when pregnant with Murray. Later, she suffered long and terribly over his death. And her subsequent devotion to Rennie was consuming: "After mother-life and mother-love have once been known, nothing else can ever satisfy the heart," she said at the time.[64] But she had a servant to help her in the practical aspects of Rennie's care, and another to do most of the housekeeping and cooking, which she had disliked since her wretched days in Falmouth. Thus freed from most domestic obligations, she took lessons in painting and French, practiced the piano several times a day, attended concerts, and enjoyed seeing tableaux and performing in charades at the homes of friends. She loved to hear good singing, once going so far as to claim that she would be willing to "give up years and years and years of intellectual acquisition" to be able to sing as well as Lucy Palmer.[65]

Above all, she continued to pursue her interest in literature. For the first time in her life, she had no parent, foster parent, or teacher attempting in any way to influence what she should read, and she read widely—in history, accounts of travel, contemporary fiction including the novels of Charlotte Brontë and Elizabeth Gaskell, and poetry. During Edward's absences, she occasionally read all day, including during her meals. To her sister, who did all of her own housekeeping, Helen expressed feelings of guilt about all the time she spent idly reading, when she might instead have been doing something practical like catching up on her sewing and mending. "Those two hours of novel reading! Dear me! How much I might have done," she wrote Ann one day. "You have been dress making today. I suppose everything has gone nicely with your plans—as usual: but just think of poor me."[66] Still, she kept at her books, in the process beginning to formulate some of her enduring literary tastes. In particular, she developed a firm dislike of sentimental verse, or what she called "the 'bower and flower' 'love and above' 'rosy and posy' school of poetry," and a special admiration for the fiction of Harriet Beecher Stowe and Nathaniel Hawthorne.[67] According to a friend from this period, she believed that "she could test the intellect or heart of any acquaintance by inducing him or her to read one or another of Hawthorne's tales, and afterwards discovering what they thought of it." Thus, when a military colleague of Edward Hunt's professed "The Snow-Image" simply a "fairy-tale for a child," she quickly dismissed the man as "a gentlemanly blockhead."[68]

Unlike his unenlightened colleague, Edward Hunt did have some feeling for literary matters. When he was away from home, he wrote little stories for his son, and even in the midst of all his labors he enjoyed keeping up with current publications. Helen did not always share his tastes, but she respected his opinions, as when she found her own liking for the "peculiar *luxury*" of Robert Browning's *Men and Women* (1855) tempered by her husband's belief that an author should state his meaning "so clearly that it can be understood without groping after."[69] Furthermore, unlike Helen's father, Edward Hunt did not discourage Helen's active imagination. He himself had a number of "literary friends," and he was pleased to have Helen receive visits from such acquaintances as Katharine Wormeley—an "authoress," as Helen referred to her, who would later become known for her translations of Balzac's novels.[70]

Though her husband did not discourage her literary inclinations, Helen seems upon marriage to have given up any notion that she might actually write for publication. "It is a glorious thing to be a *man!*" she told Henry Root, noting that only men had the responsibility for carving out a "future" in their "own hands." She often wished her father were still alive, so that at least the goal of making him "proud" could have served as her "stimulating principle" for intellectual "progress."[71] Without that, however, she fell back, like her mother before her, on mere fantasies of publication. In early 1853, after copying a (now missing) extract from one of "the old poets" into a letter to Lucy Palmer, she joked about her literary proclivities, and delighted in imagining that the Palmer family might think she herself had written the poem:

> It will give my letter a highly literary bas-bleu sort of a look, which will not be at all lost on you! or upon the different members of your household, in case you chance to receive and read it at table: for if that is the case, of course you would be possessed of significant 'tact' to hold the *poetry* side in a conspicuous manner in sight of everybody—and moreover,—reply to all inquiries there-as-to, with a wise shake of the head and an all implying silence![72]

The following year, she wrote to Henry, "I hear new stories of one sort or another every day: if I hadn't a baby, I should certainly write a book! Lucky, isn't it, I *have?*"[73] Another time, when she was chafing at a period of separation from her husband, she dreamed of writing a novel based on her experiences as a lonely army wife. And on yet another occasion, when she had spent an exhausting day running about Newport to investigate a thieving servant while Edward sat "at home by the fire all day," only to declare upon her return "that he did really believe '*another such day would make him sick*,'" she told her sister, humorously, that she thought of "making an article for Putnams out of this scrap."[74]

There is some evidence that Helen not only dreamed of undertaking literary work during the decade of her marriage to Edward Hunt, but actually practiced writing poetry with some level of seriousness. Such practice would help to explain her sudden emergence as a skilled poet, capable of publication, in the summer of 1865.[75] Because no poems survive from this period, it is impossible to know with certainty whether she was writing anything other than private letters. Most commentators, including some who knew her at the time, have assumed that she was not. Yet Thomas Wentworth Higginson claimed that before beginning her career, Helen "had already written poems, and had shown them to her friends."[76] We know that she showed the poem titled "Consecration" to Henry Root in October 1851, and that after she married she at least continued to ponder her capabilities as a poet. In mid-1854 she reminded Henry of the "lines" she had sent him and finally revealed her authorship: "I was too timid to let you know & yet *so* anxious to see how they would strike the mind of a *man*," she admitted.[77] Higginson's claim would also seem to receive indirect support from the plots of two of Jackson's earliest, most autobiographical works of fiction, the novel *Mercy Philbrick's Choice* and the short story "Draxy Miller's Dowry"; both feature poet heroines who write privately for a significant time before seeking a wider audience.

Two circumstances of Helen's life during the period of her first marriage lend further credence to the notion that she was writing poetry at this time. First, she exhibited a growing distaste for writing personal letters, a distaste that would prove characteristic when she became a professional writer. In youth, she had viewed correspondence not simply as a means of communication but as a creative outlet. She happily wrote some thirty letters per month, often devoting entire mornings, afternoons, or evenings to the task. She was frustrated if she did not have ample time to write, and she creatively revised passages from one letter to another. In comparison with the letters of her friends and her sister, her early letters demonstrate a notable literary flair. During her marriage, to the contrary, she began to complain about her correspondence as a chore. "I *do* detest writing more & more," she told her sister in 1861, "& often give up telling something I would really like very much to tell just because I can't take the trouble to write it out."[78] When she became a professional writer, she would often explain to friends and family that it was her work on literary projects that made her dislike letter writing. "One of the (many) penalties which one pays for writing for the world of readers whom one does not know," she said, "is that the old handcraft which used to merely subserve affection, and be a pleasure, becomes a drudgery and a fatigue."[79] Perhaps letter writing first began to seem a drudgery after she married because she was directing her best writerly energies into poetry.

Another circumstance that suggests Helen was writing poetry during her marriage to Edward Hunt is the friendship she formed at this time with Anne Lynch Botta, a woman who made a habit of cultivating literary talent. Helen first met Botta in August 1855 at a meeting in Providence of the American Association for the Advancement of Science, where Edward was delivering a paper. Fifteen years Helen's senior, Botta had been writing and publishing for some twenty years: her nonfiction *Leaves from the Diary of a Recluse* appeared in 1838, a volume of poems in 1849. Although these were not works of great significance, Botta was quite knowledgeable about writers and writing: in 1860 she would publish an anthology of world literature. Moreover, by 1855 she was well embarked on a forty-year stint as hostess of one of the most active literary salons in the history of New York City. She and her salon had moved from Washington Square to West 37th Street upon her marriage to Vincenzo Botta, a former member of the Italian parliament who had become in America a well-known professor of Italian and translator of Dante.

At her evening gatherings and breakfasts, Botta welcomed the day's leading literary figures, including Edgar Allan Poe, William Cullen Bryant, Margaret Fuller, Alice and Phoebe Cary, Bayard Taylor, Catharine Sedgwick, Lydia Maria Child, Grace Greenwood, Julia Ward Howe, Richard and Elizabeth Stoddard, Edmund Clarence Stedman, and Ralph Waldo Emerson, who once called 25 West 37th Street the "house of the expanding doors."[80] From their first meeting, Helen began making visits to New York to stay with Botta, and she occasionally attended her salon and holiday parties. Eventually, she came to think of Botta's "dear hospitable house" as the place where "I have had all my best times, for so many years."[81] Among her literary circle, Botta was known for her desire to help "every young aspirant in whom she discovered talent, however unknown and friendless," and for taking an interest only in those "women whose lives were not the lives of toys and trinkets."[82] Helen herself found Botta an especially "kind & sympathetic" friend, the very definition of "incarnate philanthropy."[83] That she thought of Botta in this way, and was welcomed into her circle, suggests that she was a fledgling poet in the 1850s.

Helen's friendship with Botta, whom she sometimes playfully addressed as "Bottanie" in her letters, would last until her own death. During the years of her first marriage she also met other literary people who would play significant roles in her later life and career. Through Botta she first came to know a number of writers and editors who would ease her entry into print. And in 1856, while she was living temporarily in New Haven, she befriended a woman with whom she would come of age as a writer: Sarah Woolsey.

In their first years of friendship, she and "Sally," who was four years her junior, were at the same early stage of literary development. Together they worked to further their knowledge, reading the same books and discussing them, and seeking out the company of other intellectual women. Later, when they both became intent on professional work, they offered each other important moral support. In 1870 Woolsey even moved with her parents to Newport, in part so that she could be near Helen, who had by then made significant progress in establishing herself. That fall they traveled together to Bethlehem, New Hampshire, where Helen encouraged Sarah's work on a children's book, *The New Year's Bargain,* and tried to help her break into the prestigious pages of the *Atlantic Monthly,* where she herself had recently found entrée.

Helen thought *The New Year's Bargain* "delicious,"[84] and it is indeed a charming tale, featuring two children who steal some of Old Time's sand, then force every month of the year to come tell them a story in order to regain the treasure. Woolsey published the book in 1871 under her pseudonym "Susan Coolidge," and it received a great deal of positive attention, launching her on a long and successful career as a children's author. She also wrote poetry and travel sketches and edited many scholarly volumes, including an edition of Jane Austen's letters. Coolidge displayed less talent in her writing for adults, as Helen came to recognize over time, complaining to one mutual acquaintance about Woolsey's "careless, redundant and often inanimate" craftsmanship.[85] Whether because Helen had reservations about Woolsey's skill or for other unknown reasons, as time passed she ceased to confide her deepest literary preoccupations to her friend, nor did she turn to Woolsey when she needed help with her work.[86] But she always remained devoted to Woolsey—visiting her in Newport after moving to Colorado, lending her money, and, as the two writers settled into middle age, referring to her fondly as "one of my cronies."[87]

Though Woolsey would have little influence over Helen's writing at the conscious level, she made an important contribution to her personal development when, in the summer of 1862, she persuaded Helen to join in volunteer work at New Haven's Civil War hospital, thereby introducing her to social activism. For several months Helen worked in the linen room at the hospital, distributing supplies and mending old clothes. She also wrote letters for the soldiers three days a week. Her own correspondence from this period is mostly missing today, but two pieces of her later fiction allude to the impact of her hospital experience. In her short story "Joe Hale's Red Stockings," she lightly mocks her former female co-workers as dilettantes. But her story also reveals that her experience had the important effect of teaching her to distrust social distinctions, and to realize the need for people from different regions of the country to understand one another. In her unpublished novel "Elspeth Dynor," furthermore, she reveals how her volunteer experience may have influenced her decision to take up professional writing at the end of the war. She argues in this book that "very many" women who had worked during the war found, when this "most stimulating and ennobling motive for exertion . . . was suddenly withdrawn," that their former domestic occupations seemed "strangely inadequate and small."[88]

In joining with the approximately 20,000 other women who offered medical assistance to the Union during the Civil War, Helen acted mostly out of concern for the welfare of injured soldiers: her husband, after all, was in the Union Army. She was not motivated by any particular sympathy for the slaves whose fate was being decided by the war. Indeed, it would take the passage of time, and the accumulation of varied life experiences, for her to become sensitized to the suffering of racial minorities in America. In the meantime, marriage to Edward Hunt served to curtail the development of her race consciousness.

Hunt came from a socially conservative family. In 1862, perhaps at the very time Helen was working at the Civil War hospital, he wrote and published a sixty-one-page white supremacist monograph, *Union Foundations: A Study of American Nationality as a Fact of Science*. Seeking in this work to condemn secession and bolster Union optimism, Hunt argues that according to science, the proper answer to America's race problem is the forcible deportation of all black Americans, preferably to an "African empire of the Amazon."[89] Hunt believed slavery a sin; but, like many of his time, his personal dislike of the institution was based largely on the fact that slavery had allowed a black population to grow up in America. In *Union Foundations* he argues that God has arranged the world such that "[t]here are tropical races and there are temperate races, each thriving only in its own proper climate," and that the black "man of the tropics" therefore does not belong in the temperate American nation. He claims that during "the westward march of empire," North America had rightly been appropriated by Europe's "caucasian race, the most powerful and actively colonizing branch of the human family," and that this superior race needs all of America for its continued expansion. Caucasians thus rightly disapprove of any continued presence of blacks in the land, whether by "the perpetuation of the existing order of castes, or a resolution into free white and free black castes," or racial intermarriage.[90]

Helen seems not to have taken any special interest in her husband's pseudoscientific arguments for the exportation of African Americans, nor is there any evidence that she contradicted them. At the time of the Civil War, most American whites not only were emotionally opposed to the idea of full equality with blacks but had also come to believe that blacks were biologically inferior. Hunt was merely using his scientific training to elaborate a colonization scheme similar to those advocated by many of his northern white compatriots.[91] (In fact, *Union Foundations* received a strong endorsement from *Harper's New Monthly*, which summarized the pamphlet in its "Editor's Table" column of February 1863.) Because Helen, like most whites of her generation, had been raised to condescend toward people of different races, she was comfortable living with, and sharing in, her husband's racialist attitudes.

In the Fiske household, beliefs about race had been closely entwined with class prejudice, for it was only through their household "help" that the Fiske family came into close contact with people of different backgrounds, both African American and Irish—whom the Fiskes, like other Anglo-Americans of their time, considered a separate race of Catholics. In general, Deborah Fiske considered all household servants "provoking but sometimes amusing thunderheads."[92] She particularly disliked Irish servants, because she believed them to be lazy, and because in her view Catholics adhered to a religion that Nathan Fiske once denounced in a lecture as an "impious usurpation, with its whole disgusting history of imposture, craft, licentiousness, and persecution, and all its foolery and mummery, and its bigotry and cruelty and blasphemy."[93] On the other hand, Deborah and Nathan Fiske regarded poor people of any race who embraced, or might be converted to, Protestant Christianity as fit objects for their sympathy and charity. Thus, Nathan Fiske for many years provided financial support and advice to a boy in Persia named Moses, who eventually became a Protestant minister; and thus Deborah felt fondly toward some of her black servants, especially Sarah Ann, a black child from a poor Sturbridge family whom she hired in 1836 as a household helper and nurse for Ann. Sarah Ann lived with the Fiskes for almost eight years, much longer than any of their other servants, and Deborah grew very attached to her. By 1841 she had come to consider Sarah Ann a rare "comfort" in her life.[94] Shortly before her own death she sacrificed much of her limited strength in trying to nurse Sarah Ann through the severe, eight-week illness from which the girl finally died.

During childhood, encouraged by her mother's example, Helen was fond of Sarah Ann, thinking of her as a playmate and not merely a servant. "Ann [Fiske] the other day said something about a *nigger* in my presence," Deborah Fiske wrote to her husband during Sarah Ann's first year in the Fiske home. "I told her and told Helen they must not speak of negroes before Sarah—they both insisted that Sarah was *not* a negro that she was only *some* black and that they liked her better than if she was white."[95] Similarly, in 1841, when Helen was away in Hadley, she especially enjoyed playing with a black child who worked in Deacon Dickinson's household: "Most every night, we pop corn, and play button who's got the button," she reported to Rebecca Snell.[96] Despite these early friendships, the black children that Helen knew were invariably relegated to the role of household servant; she could scarcely escape adopting her parents' belief in the social inferiority of those races employed in their domestic service.

In her married life she expressed this prejudice. Like her mother, she particularly disliked Irish servants, even though after leaving Amherst she experienced life in ethnically diverse places such as New York and Boston—where, by the 1850s, more than one-fifth of all residents were Irish. In 1856, when the Hunts were living in Newport, an Irish employee named Bridget stole a lace collar and some other items from Helen, sealing her already formidable "dislike of [this] race."[97] After a long day of investigation, mentioned above, during which Helen had Bridget swear on a crucifix before the local priest that she had not stolen a dress that was also missing, Helen at first agreed to have Bridget stay on in her service, so long as she did not repeat her offense. Perhaps she did, however, for in May Helen wrote to her sister, "If ever another *Irish thing* darkens my door, it will be because I am reduced to the most direful extremity: I am more and more heartily sick of the *race:* I believe there is not more than one in a *thousand* you can depend on at all:—they are born liars."[98]

Helen was more fond of her African American servants. When she discovered in 1856 that it was actually Katy Willis, a black woman who had done some temporary work for her, who had stolen her dress, she was much more lenient with Katy than she had been with Bridget. Nonetheless, her kind feelings toward individual African Americans whom she knew were circumscribed by a broader prejudice, one that led her, on occasion, to use the words "darky" and "nigger" instead of the more respectful terms of the day, "negro" and "colored."[99] Moreover, in 1853, when the Hunts were newly married and living in Washington, D.C., one of the two black women whom they hired as servants was a slave. Though Helen had grown up in the shadow of Amherst College, which preached the evils of slavery, she seems to have felt few qualms about hiring Lucy's services from her owner. She praised Lucy fondly as a "gem" and "paragon," but also boasted in a letter to Ann Palmer of the cheap labor Lucy provided, and argued that slavery was a relatively good thing for her:

> I have grown stylish and keep my servant! Don't that sound grand? You would hardly believe that I hire the best, neatest, most respectful, *likeable* black girl I ever saw, and pay for her lodging out of the house for six dollars a month! She is a slave, and all that her master asks for her is $5.00 a month: she takes care of the rooms—sets the table—helps me dress—*puts away* everything that I leave out of place—in short, makes a fine lady of me—all in the quietest pleasantest way imaginable: and she looks so neat and nice that I am almost *proud* to have her around. This is one of the illustrations of the *bright* sides of slavery: her master is an old gentleman, and has made arrangements to have all his slaves freed at his death: but in the meantime, he takes care of them like a Christian: the other day he was here inquiring after '*his* Lucy'—He heard she wanted a pair of shoes, he said, and so he had come round to see!—It is a *great blessing,* for a negro, in this region to be a *slave*—strange as that sounds to northern ears, *if* they can have such masters as Lucy's. Lucy has occasionally a trouble in her eye, which I fear will ultimately destroy the sight—and some weeks ago, when she was suffering with it, she spoke of her own accord of the kindness of her master, and of her comfort in thinking that she should be taken care of in any event.[100]

Years later, some of Helen's early professional writings would reflect the racialist attitudes evident in this letter. Gradually, though, she would lose many of her prejudices, and her work would come to express an unusual level of appreciation for racial and ethnic diversity. Hints of the more sensitive woman she would become were present even during her marriage to Edward Hunt. For at that time, despite her employment of Lucy, she was sympathetic to abolitionism—a reform cause similar, in many ways, to her own later cause of Indian reform. In early 1854 Helen was filled with enthusiasm for Harriet Beecher Stowe's *Uncle Tom's Cabin* (1852). She persisted in expressing her enthusiasm even though her husband's army crowd was so opposed to the book's abolitionist views that Edward had "almost forbidden my talking on the subject," as she explained to Ann Palmer:

> You can't imagine how people here talk of Uncle Tom's Cabin and its author. I have much ado to hold my tongue—and indeed I have not sufficiently restrained it

at all times: only the other day, a gentleman, boarding here, and also, I am sorry to say, a member of this same Engineers Corps, to which my good man belongs—said to me after some discussion of the book—that he considered its authoress 'a talented *fiend* in human shape'!![101]

Helen told Ann Palmer that her admiration for *Uncle Tom's Cabin* had made Edward, who "abhor[red] abolitionists," "fear" that she was "a little infected" by the cause.[102] It seems that she was: she did not contradict Edward's suspicion in her letter to Palmer. Even more telling, she would soon form a very close friendship with a radical abolitionist, the Reverend Moncure Conway. In the years that followed, Conway would have a profound impact on her life, helping to shape not only her race views but also her literary and spiritual beliefs.

Helen first met Conway in late 1854 when he took over as pastor at the Unitarian church she and Edward had begun to attend in Washington. Born in Virginia in 1832, to a Methodist, slaveholding family, Conway had become a Unitarian abolitionist by the time the Hunts first heard him preach, though in the early 1850s he did not reveal the extent of his radicalism to his Washington congregation. In 1856, however—after the Hunts had moved away from Washington and had been living for more than six months in Newport—Conway began to make public the true nature of his views. They were revolutionary even among abolitionists. He believed, for instance, that intermarriage was a good solution to America's race problems. On January 27, 1856, Conway first preached abolitionism in Washington, a landmark sermon that called forth letters of support from distant fellow radical abolitionists (including Thomas Wentworth Higginson), but condemnation from Conway's own congregation. Members began to consider his dismissal; after he again preached against slavery in July, they took action, finally releasing him from their service in October. Neither Helen nor Edward seems to have agreed with this decision. They invited Conway to visit them in Newport in August 1856, at the height of his troubles in Washington. And it is likely that Helen expressed explicit support for Conway's abolitionist views during this visit, for years later, Conway would tell Mrs. Longfellow that Helen had been "the light of many a dark hour" during his Washington troubles.[103]

Helen never acted publicly on her sympathy for the abolitionist cause, perhaps out of respect for the opinions of her husband and perhaps also because at this time she believed women should eschew public life. In the future, though, when she did take up reform work, Moncure Conway's example of activism would be one of the early influences behind her efforts. Meanwhile, "Monk," as she affectionately called him, would affect her intellectual development in other, more direct ways. During the period of Helen's marriage to Edward Hunt, Conway became the third clergyman, after her father, to play an important role in her continuing literary education. Unlike her previous mentors, who were all Calvinists, he also enjoyed the satisfaction of seeing her convert to his religion, Unitarianism.

While a father-daughter dynamic had marked each of Helen's earlier relationships with her male literary role models, her relationship with Conway, who was slightly younger than she, was a spirited friendship between peers. From the beginning, Conway reminded her of Henry Root, in age, manner, and the "intellectual exhilaration" of his conversation;[104] as a literary companion, he would fill the void left in her life when Henry tragically succumbed to cancer in September 1855. She thought Conway a fascinating person, "wonderfully clever in wonderfully many ways."[105] He, in turn, once described her as "highly educated, brilliant, and sometimes satirical in conversation": "philosophical at one moment, merry and witty at another, and in whatever vein . . . engaging."[106] In the 1850s, young Conway was just beginning to branch out from his preaching duties to become an author, and he was befriending many of the famed writers of the day; these included Hawthorne, whom he encouraged Helen to continue reading, and Longfellow, whom he urged her to meet when she visited Cambridge. Helen was impressed that her new friend kept "*such* company," and she delighted in supporting his literary career.[107] "Only think, we *bought you,* in a store in Washington Street this spring," she wrote to him excitedly after one of his early efforts was published.[108]

Conway believed it a writer's duty to exert a positive moral influence over readers, but not by directing them to turn all their thoughts toward God. Rather, he believed that art should promote decent behavior on earth. Furthermore, like other Unitarian literati—and unlike Calvinist writers of Nathan Fiske's ilk, who were often suspicious of the arts—Conway believed that literature itself constituted a great moral good, didacticism aside, because it lent beauty to the world and inspired human emotions. These views, which Conway would go on to expound in such works as *The Earthward Pilgrimage* (1870) and *The Gospel of Art* (1883), were congenial to Helen given her need to reconcile the moral mandates of her upbringing with her own emerging sense of herself as an independent literary person.

Helen soon came to find that Conway's religion was also congenial to her. The Hunts had begun to search for a church to attend immediately following their marriage. Like many Americans of her time, Helen maintained a strong need for faith despite having rejected the Calvinist religion in which she had been raised; she had, as she once told Julius Palmer, been "too religiously brought up to find any repose, in deliberately giving up the subject."[109] She disliked "suspense and uncertainty," the idea that human life might be dictated by "only the inconsistent and ever varying caprice of chance," and she clung instead to a strong belief in God and his ordering of events on earth.[110] While she was mostly content to express her faith by trying to "live in the daily observance of Christian duties," in cheerful and diligent submission to God's will, she sometimes felt "a weariness and an unrest," particularly after Murray's death, that made her long for the solace of a confirmed belief in human immortality.[111] She hoped that attending church might lead her to clearer and firmer religious views, and at the very least provide her with a means of honoring the Sabbath. "I carry about with me the same old self tormenting *ideal* of what the Sabbath *should* be," she told Henry Root in January 1853. "I have ever present to my mind, the memory of my father's and mother's Sabbath—of the holy *joy* which I *know* they found in the things that I cannot endure—and the thought of it all makes my Sabbaths anything but days of *rest* to my spirit."[112] Edward Hunt shared his wife's desire to find an appropriate way to pass his Sundays, even though, as Helen once explained, he was "not what would be called, in common speech of the common religious world, a religious man."[113] Together they sampled the services of various denominations, discovering that they preferred the preaching of the Unitarian Church, first in upstate New York in early 1853, and later that same year in Washington.

Unitarianism was in origin a small, liberal branch of Congregationalism, one that had already been thriving at liberal institutions like Harvard when Helen's father was teaching at orthodox Amherst. While individual Unitarians held a variety of exact beliefs, centering on faith in God and hope in an afterlife, all stood opposed not only to orthodox, or Trinitarian, doctrines of a divine Christ but also to the orthodox beliefs that Adam's original sin had made all human nature depraved and that God had predetermined which people would and would not be saved from this depravity. Inspired by Enlightenment ideals of human progress, Unitarians believed people to be essentially good, and capable of improvement; they believed God to be loving and salvation to be attainable through the forging of good character. Morality became the essence of religion.

This positive view of human nature and fate appealed strongly to Helen. For although she sometimes joked that misfortune made her feel "Calvinist at core,—or fatalist," and that the bad behavior of others almost made her believe in the " 'total & original depravity' doctrine," in fact the doctrines of human depravity and predestination were what had always most disgusted her with Calvinism.[114] Her own early experience of learning to persevere in the face of the illnesses and deaths of her parents had taught her the importance and the power of the human will, and she would always celebrate and advocate individual willpower. Thus she would once tell a friend, when she was frustrated in executing some plans, "I believe in the total depravity of everything in life, except the human soul."[115] And in a published book review she would state her opposition to the "foreordination doctrine" as incompatible with her ideas of "justice and free will."[116]

Helen felt an immediate affinity for the Unitarian view of human nature, but she was slower in coming to a belief about Jesus' true nature. In late 1854 she told Henry Root that she had been studying the New Testament on this topic for a year, and that "the more I study, the more it seems to me *truly impossible* to draw the doctrine of the equal trinity from it."[117] She found herself sympathizing with the Unitarian minister and scholar Andrew Preston Peabody's concept of Jesus' divine mission, as opposed to Christ's essential divinity, as expressed in his *Lectures on Christian Doctrine* (1844). At church that Christmas, however, she was "shocked" by the lengths to which Moncure Conway went to prove Jesus a "*mere* man."[118] For the next several weeks, she was haunted by thoughts of how her parents would have abhorred such a notion. "I am not sure after all, but the main hindrance to my being openly & at once a Unitarian is the memory of my father & mother!" she told Henry Root in January 1855. "What perfect lives were theirs!—and how thoroughly did my father with his *clear* logical mind adhere to even the sternest Calvinism!" She wished that her father "had left some written exposition of his reasons," so that she could reconsider them. Yet she knew after all that she was "an *individual*," and must decide matters of conscience for herself.[119]

Before long, she decided in favor of Unitarianism. When she and Edward moved from Washington to Newport, they not only continued to attend Unitarian services but even participated in fund-raising for the local church, thereby offending the town's Congregational minister, an old friend of Helen's parents. Helen wished to believe that it was not any direct human influence, but rather her own feelings and study, that had led her to accept Unitarianism. Yet in truth Moncure Conway's influence was paramount. She was swept up by his "enthusiasm & fearlessness,"[120] even when he expressed beliefs that seemed too radical; and the intellectual excitement she felt in his presence confirmed the admiration she had long felt for the highly cultured, literate ethos of the Unitarian ministry in general. She was particularly inspired by the passion Conway, like many Unitarians, felt for the writings and philosophy of Ralph Waldo Emerson.

Conway was deeply under the influence of Emersonian Transcendentalism; he was first drawn to the Unitarian ministry by Emerson's books, and later formed a friendship with Emerson himself. (In 1883, the year after Emerson's death, Conway would publish a memoir of him.) A movement that had reached its peak back in the 1830s, Transcendentalism did not constitute a uniform body of beliefs; indeed, most people who espoused Transcendentalism were opposed to highly formal religion. In general, though, Transcendentalists believed in a God—or, in Emerson's words, an "Over-Soul"—to which all human beings were connected, but they did not agree with strict Unitarians or other Christians that true knowledge of God could be attained only through the revealed religion of the Bible. Instead, they believed that all people were born with an intuitive capacity for perceiving and understanding God. They approached the world and spiritual matters poetically, rather than by means of Lockean rationality, and they held art in great esteem as both a product and a promoter of spiritual intuition. They also revered nature as a source of spiritual inspiration and a worthy model for art.

Helen had been intrigued by Emerson's writings since her days in Albany. Now, under Conway's guidance, she enthusiastically embraced them. On March 27, 1857, she and Edward attended an evening lecture by Emerson in Newport. "I never looked in a face which so impressed me, or heard words which dwelt with me so long," she wrote to Conway two months later. "It was an *era* in my life—the next day I ordered a complete set of his works & *intended* to have read them *all* before this time—but I cannot get beyond his 'Nature'— as often as I take up the volume I turn in spite of myself to that & read it over again."[121] In *Nature,* an 1836 essay reissued to wide circulation in 1849, Emerson expounded his Transcendental philosophy, with its emphasis on human intuition and the spiritual essence of art and nature. Given her poetic sensibilities, love of nature, and strong belief in the power of the individual human will, Helen found these ideas rousing. She adopted them as her own, later going on to incorporate them in her poetry and prose.

As the decade of the 1850s slipped into the past, dragging in its wake the horrors of the Civil War, Helen's relatively peaceful phase of literary apprenticeship drew to a close. Edward Hunt died, followed by Rennie; and Moncure Conway, disgusted with the bloodshed of the war and the Union's weak stand on black rights, moved to London. Helen became more sporadic in her attendance of Unitarian church services. She would always consider herself a "good Unitarian" and claim to "love and trust the Unitarian faith" and "doctrines,"[122] but her attraction to intuitive, individual religion became more and more powerful. This increasing liberalism was so apparent it seems almost to have been written on her forehead. A Boston phrenologist once told her: "The development of your moral and religious faculties indicate a rigid orthodox education; but other faculties indicate a tendency to more liberal views as you advance in age."[123]

In 1868 Helen saw Monk in London during her first trip to Europe. Though for her the reunion called forth only her usual feelings of friendship and intellectual camaraderie, Conway was overcome by romantic longing.[124] He was now a married man, and devoted to his wife Ellen, but he poured out his heart in a passionate letter that has somehow escaped destruction. Near its close, he confessed:

> Dear Helen, I wonder if ever you will know all the abysses you trod near,—all the embers you stepped on—so long as you and I were together. Somehow I never think of you, but I feel an intimation that there must be another world, where we shall meet. Here and now, what were the use of our corresponding even? My voyage is by contract, and I must admit no warping magnet near the needle. . . . That you are happy, and have sunny outlooks, is to me a precious knowledge—I

should have been happier had I known it years ago. Let us not endanger the "well-enough" of our relation, which by contrast with our parting is almost joyful. The time may come when more shall be possible; so *I* hope at any rate. At present I must close this wild letter by saying that neither heart nor brain of mine, are equal to writing letters to you or receiving them from you. I know very well what I am saying in this. I can only trust that you will understand as I do; and I do not fear but that you will know how unbroken and unbreakable is my love for you.[125]

In fact, Conway did not insist on an end to their correspondence, despite some evidence that his feelings for Helen caused his wife anxiety. His passion cooled, and the two writers continued in their friendship, seemingly without interruption, to the end of Helen's life. They saw each other when their visits to New York coincided, and again in London in 1880. Then, Conway was still preaching and writing, and Helen had joined him in the professional world, having reinvented herself as one of the era's most successful authors.

PART THREE

"Very serious literary labor"
Doing Good and Making Good

✐ 4 ↰

Entering the Literary Marketplace

I always feel a little guilty in wishing for people that they may be happy:—it is so very doubtful a blessing. I myself never took an upward step, till I left happiness behind me.

JACKSON TO MARGARET CHANNING, niece of Mary Higginson, March 18, 1869, Harvard

On June 19, 1865, Jackson told a correspondent that she still felt such anguish over her son Rennie's recent death that she had no "courage to grope" toward any kind of exertion.[1] In fact, however, in the previous two weeks, while collecting her emotions at John Abbott's new home in New Haven, Connecticut, she had published her first two poems. Both were expressions of her grief and of Christian submission, and she signed them "Marah"—the Hebrew word for "bitter" and the name that the biblical Naomi assumes after the death of her own husband and two sons. "Call me Mara: for the Almighty hath dealt very bitterly with me," Naomi says in Ruth 1:20–21. "I went out full, and the LORD hath brought me home again empty."

Apparently gratified by publication, Jackson turned to other poetic topics in the fall of 1865, exchanging "Marah" for what would become her trademark signature: "H.H.," short for Helen Hunt. She also branched out from poetry that October, publishing her first piece of travel writing. The next year she published her first book review, and by 1867, when her first domestic advice essay appeared, she was publishing two pieces of poetry and nonfiction every month, mostly in the weekly literary newspaper the *New York Independent*. As the second anniversary of Rennie's death came and passed, she assured her sister that she was making both emotional and professional progress: "I do not see why you urge me so to take myself in hand. As if I had not done it!"[2]

Jackson never clearly explains in her existing correspondence why she suddenly began, at the relatively late age of thirty-four, to devote herself to professional writing. "It has been a great pleasure, and help to me, the little writing I have done," she told a friend in 1870. "I hardly know how it happened, almost by accident it seemed in the beginning; but now I have more purpose in it."[3] While Jackson's early writings no doubt did help her cope with her many personal losses, it was certainly not by accident but by very intentional labor that she managed to write so many pieces and to place them in prominent periodicals. She was not obliged to write out of financial necessity, for she received a quarterly income adequate to her needs from the estate left her by her grandfather David Vinal. Rather, as she hints in the words quoted at the head of this chapter, it was the loss of her "happiness"—her husband and child—that made it possible for her to take steps toward her own advancement. Without family life to occupy her, she finally acted on her long-standing interest in writing.

As for Jackson's claim that by 1870 she had developed "more purpose" in her writing, she seems to have meant, as she told another friend around this time, that her intention was to do her readers "a little good."[4] It was from her father that she had first learned to believe that writers should uplift their readers. She had also learned from him to direct her intellectual efforts toward winning approval, rather than toward discovering her own unique talents, and now she continued to feel more need to gain the approval of literary authorities than to map out her own literary terrain. As her career progressed, she sometimes claimed that being "so dependent on praise and recognition" caused her "pain."[5] At other times, though, she took solace in a belief that along with "the instinct of religious worship," the "love of approbation" was by nature one of "the two greatest passions of the human heart," and that it offered a useful motive for exertion.[6] She found reassurance in producing work that was readily accepted, and highly remunerated, by editors at the country's top periodicals; she was encouraged by the immediate critical praise won by her poetry. Above all, she took pride in working to meet the writing standards of Thomas Wentworth Higginson, who in 1866 became the fourth, final, and most important theologian to influence her literary development in the years following her father's death. Higginson was more concerned that Jackson devote her best energies to poetry than that she develop her own literary vision in prose. Thus, along with Nathan Fiske, he was partly responsible for her growing into her most distinctive, regionalist material only gradually during the first half of her career.

Both Jackson's first poem, "The Key of the Casket," and her first travel essay, "Mountain Life: The New Hampshire Town of Bethlehem," were accepted for publication by Parke Godwin of the *New York Evening Post,* an editor whom she had met through Anne Botta. Having managed to break into publishing by means of a personal connection, she shrewdly set about positioning herself to make more contacts. In February 1866 she went to spend the remainder of the winter in Newport, Rhode Island, a vibrant island town with a dense population of some 10,000 people, one-fifth of them foreign-born, and a growing reputation as the wealthiest resort in the East: every summer, fashionable seasonal residents and tourists invaded the local hotels; in the winter,

Newport was home to a large society of artists and writers. These included, at various times during the 1860s and 1870s, a number of people who would inspire or prove useful allies for Jackson: Thomas Wentworth Higginson; Sarah Woolsey; Kate Field, a journalist Jackson had befriended before she herself began to publish; Sara Dana Loring Greenough, a writer of fanciful stories and wife of the sculptor Richard S. Greenough; William Hunt, a painter; and Josiah Holland, a popular author and editor.

At the start of her career Jackson spent a total of six winters in Newport, always lodging at Hannah Dame's boardinghouse on the main residential thoroughfare of Broad Street. Participation in Newport's cultural life was liberating for her: surrounded by people who valued imagination and creativity, she was freed from her father's earlier interdictions against idle daydreaming and filled with enthusiasm for her new pursuit. She enjoyed coming together with like-minded acquaintances to study topics, such as astronomy, that were interesting simply because they afforded new knowledge; and she continued her habit of voracious reading, even meeting friends to read aloud while sewing. There was a playfulness to literary life in Newport that appealed to her. One year, for instance, before she had arrived in town for the winter, Higginson and other residents of Hannah Dame's (including Juliet Goodwin, a writer) sent her a jocular letter, designed collage-style from newspaper and magazine clippings. "DOCUMENT, YE DAME ROUND ROBIN TO H H THE GREAT AMERICAN OVERLAND TRAVELER WOMAN! CURE THAT HAY COLD COME TO NEWPORT," the outside of the collage reads, touting Newport, which was celebrated for its healthy climate, as the answer to Jackson's health problems. Inside, Jackson's housemates assure her that a return to their company will also be conducive to her writing: "O TIRED RAILWAY TRAVELER, welcome to port! Come and see our AMERICAN SEASIDE RESORT! Our GOLD and our CLOTHING we freely will lend you; THE 'LIGHT RUNNING' DOMESTIC named Rosa, will tend you; And when GEMS IN LITERATURE begin to grow ripe, you shall have for your breakfast a whole CASE OF TYPE."[7]

As this letter suggests, Jackson had many friends during her Newport years who were eager to support her nascent career. She received encouragement for her early efforts as a travel writer, in particular, from two women: Lucia Gilbert Calhoun Runkle and Kate Field. In 1868 she spent the summer exploring various Atlantic coastal and mountain retreats with Lucia Runkle ("Bertie"), a New York writer she had met through a mutual acquaintance at the *Independent*. In later years Runkle would work as a literary critic, but at this early date she was a journalist, contributing editorials and articles to periodicals including the *New York Tribune, Hearth and Home,* and *Harper's.* Jackson took delight in working alongside her friend, writing up accounts of their summer expeditions and publishing them simultaneously in different newspapers. At one point, when the two women had just completed a July trip to Block Island, Jackson began to describe the outing in a letter to her Newport friend Kate

Field, but then stopped herself short and, with obvious glee, directed Field's attention to the press: "For further particulars see Mrs. Calhoun's [later Runkle] letter & mine—which will shortly appear—Hers in the Chicago *Tribune* & mine in the *Post*. We must do our thunder in opposite quarters of the sky."[8]

This focus on the publication of travel experiences, as opposed to their private narration, was something that Kate Field endorsed. A literary woman who counted such eminent writers as Anthony Trollope and the Brownings among her familiars, and would later become famous as a lecturer, Field was publishing newspaper editorials and articles in the 1860s; these included, under the pseudonym "Straws, Jr.," regular travel essays in the *Boston Post*. Field had chosen this pseudonym to reflect the ephemeral, topical nature of her travel writing—"Straws merely show which way the wind blows," she explained to her readers—and she was eager to see Jackson make similar literary capital out of her daily wanderings and activities.[9] Indeed, in the summer of 1869, she made a lasting impression on Jackson when she accused her of being an "intellectual spendthrift" for sending long letters home to her friends from Europe, when she could have been more profitably turning her observations into articles for publication.[10] Jackson was insulted by Field's comment, which she considered evidence that Field did not value their correspondence, and their friendship was permanently strained. But upon her return to America in 1870 she quickly called in many of her letters and published extracts from them.

While Jackson's enthusiasm for travel writing was no doubt buoyed by the support she received from these friends, during her Newport years she considered poetry her primary art form and all other forms of writing secondary. Her judgment was corroborated by Thomas Wentworth Higginson, the person whose literary opinion meant most to her. Born in 1823 in Cambridge, Massachusetts, and educated as an undergraduate and divinity student at Harvard, the man Jackson knew as "Colonel" had begun his professional career as a Unitarian minister. Like Moncure Conway, he had been drawn to Unitarianism by Emerson's writings, and had afterward remained attached to Transcendentalism. Also like Conway, Higginson had been a radical abolitionist. In 1854 he registered his opposition to laws providing for the arrest of fugitive slaves by leading a mob against the Boston courthouse; later, during the Civil War, he served from 1862 until 1864 as commanding colonel of the Union's first regiment of freed slaves. After being wounded in the war, he settled in Newport to become a man of letters, giving up the ministry. While writing poetry, nonfiction, and eventually fiction, he devoted much of his time to civic affairs, as he worked to promote the rights of Newport's substantial African American population, and to various national reform movements.

Higginson would never reach great heights with his own creative writing, but when he and Jackson met he had an established and growing reputation as an intelligent social and literary critic. He soon recognized Jackson's talent; and though she had to "forgive him a little in the outset," as she told a friend, "for being such a radical radical,"[11] she quickly came to rely on him as both mentor and companion. Like most residents of their boardinghouse, except Higginson's wife Mary, whose rheumatism generally confined her to her room, Jackson and Higginson ate many of their meals together, gatherings that provided regular opportunities for conversation. They also shared in a variety of social activities, from rowing, sailing, and picnicking to attending the theater and literary readings. One night less than two months after Jackson first came to Hannah Dame's, while Mary was shut up in her room, they climbed together to the roof to watch a total eclipse of the moon.

In 1866 Higginson was at work on a translation of the writings of the first-century C.E. Stoic philosopher Epictetus, to be published that year. As Higginson explains in *The Works of Epictetus,* and no doubt frequently discussed with Jackson, Epictetus believed that people confronted with adversity should try to improve what they could in their lives, but should accept those circumstances that were beyond their control: "If uncontrollable, they are nothing to us, and we are merely to acquiesce, not with resignation alone, but joyously, knowing that an all-wise Father rules the whole. All success comes, according to Epictetus, from obedience to this rule; all failure proceeds from . . . trying to control what is uncontrollable, or from neglecting what is within our power."[12]

Inspired by Higginson's interest in these beliefs, Jackson developed her own lasting enthusiasm for Epictetus, finding in him a more palatable, because pre-Calvinist, version of the same doctrine of submission that she had already been taught to value by her parents and early teachers. In the years to come she would often allude to emotional stoicism as an ideal, especially when trying in her writings to exemplify or promote her own practical-minded code of cheerfulness and diligence. Indeed, in *Nelly's Silver Mine* (1878), her one full-length novel for children, she specifically instructs her young readers to heed the tenets of Epictetus, much as her father had preached Christian submission in his didactic writings for children. She quotes the philosopher:

> There are things which are within our power, and there are things which are beyond our power. Seek at once to be able to say to every unpleasing semblance: "You are but a semblance, and by no means the real thing." And then examine it by those rules which you have; and first and chiefly by this: whether it concerns the things which are within our own power, or those which are not; and if it concerns any thing beyond our power, be prepared to say that it is nothing to you.[13]

Jackson's early adoption of these ideas bolstered her efforts to overcome her many personal losses and to reinvent herself as a writer. Under Higginson's direction she also learned to stop merely joking and dreaming about a career, and to settle down to work. Higginson believed writers should care as much about delighting their readers as instructing them, and in his company Jackson began to place real value on imaginative writing. She also became increasingly comfortable with the idea that it was proper for women to establish public lives as authors, though she would always feel some ambivalence on this point. Unlike herself, Higginson was a suffragist and advocate of women's rights, and he frequently published articles in support of these causes. He not only believed, like John Abbott, that women could and should become writers, but he was committed to fostering their careers. Indeed, as he would most thoroughly explain in a collection of *Woman's Journal* essays published after the period of Jackson's literary apprenticeship, *Common Sense about Women* (1881), he believed that women deserved recognition for having already outdone men with much of their poetry and fiction. "It is amusing," Higginson says in *Common Sense,* "to read the criticism of languid and graceful masculine essayists on the want of vigorous intellect in the sex that wrote *Aurora Leigh* and *Middlemarch* and *Consuelo.*" Higginson favored the removal of "all legal or conventional obstacles" to women's entry into professional life, and hoped women would begin to ignore traditional pronouncements about what they should or should not do. "When authorship first came up among the women of America," he observes, "they not only claimed nothing more than the mere privilege of having brains, but they almost apologized for that." He encouraged the female author of his own day to break such restrictive bonds: she should cease trying "to work like a woman, or like a man, or unlike either, but . . . do her work thoroughly and well." In a radical move, he also urged literary women to consider their work a duty, one just as important as those duties (like motherhood) more commonly associated with female interests and capacities: "Usefulness is usefulness: there is no reason why it should be postponed from generation to generation, or why it is better to rear a serviceable human being than to be one in person."[14]

In the presence of such opinions, Jackson began to think of a literary career as a genuine possibility, one that she might attain through diligence and persistence. In youth she had learned from her father to make "a real intense *direct* effort" with her "entire energies" whenever she truly wanted to accomplish something;[15] this habit was later reinforced by Edward Hunt's example of dedication to work. Now she directed all her energies toward improving as a writer, striving to meet Higginson's standards for literary craftsmanship. It is impossible to know the exact guidance that he gave her, as no edited manuscripts or other private records of his assistance remain in existence. Still, Higginson's writings and published pieces of literary advice offer a good indication.

Throughout her life, Jackson claimed to regard Higginson's 1868 essay collection *Out-Door Papers* as her style manual for prose. These essays, which mostly concern the advantages of an active lifestyle and humane child-rearing practices, are written in clear and unadorned prose. In their style they aim to meet the Transcendental standards that some of them propound: namely, that art should pattern itself after "the simplicity and grace" of "natural beauty," and that "a finely organized sentence should throb and palpitate like the most delicate vibrations of the summer air."[16] They succeed fairly well, if unremarkably, in achieving this goal of naturalness—a modest accomplishment that Jackson considered perfect. The year *Out-Door Papers* appeared, she praised Higginson's writing, without naming him, in one of her pseudonymous travel essays. His "sentences are like nature's crystals," she says, "so transparent, so graceful, that our delight in their beauty is in danger of failing, at first, to recognize the subtle and patient laws by which their symmetrical harmony has grown."[17]

Higginson discussed what he considered the laws of effective prose in several *Atlantic Monthly* essays written during and shortly before Jackson's Newport years. In "Literature as Art," published in December 1867, he singles out Nathaniel Hawthorne and Washington Irving as America's best writers and outlines several hallmarks of masterly work. Such work, he says, demonstrates sound structure, meticulous word choice, and "thoroughness" in preparation and revision. Above all, it is characterized by "simplicity," or "smoothness and clearness," and also by "freshness." He calls this last quality "passion" in a later *Atlantic* essay, explaining that passion can be the product either of outside "inspiration" or of authorial "ardor, energy, depth of feeling or of thought."[18] While inspiration and ardor are impossible to teach, Higginson offers specific advice about how to achieve the more mundane attributes of good writing in his celebrated 1862 *Atlantic* essay, "A Letter to a Young Contributor." Here, he instructs novice writers to work carefully and slowly, aiming not for complexity but for clarity of expression, and he delivers two specific admonitions on style:

> Do not habitually prop your sentences on crutches, such as Italic-letters and exclamation-points, but make them stand without aid; if they cannot emphasize themselves, these devices are but a confession of helplessness. Do not leave loose ends as you go on, straggling things, to be caught up and dragged along uneasily in foot-notes; but work them all in neatly, as Biddy at her bread-pan gradually kneads in all the outlying bits of dough, till she has one round and comely mass.[19]

This is sound advice, and Jackson clearly benefited at the start of her career from private instruction in these and the other points Higginson stresses in his published essays. In the matters of sentence emphasis and organization, for example, her narrative prose demonstrates an increasing sophistication. While her early private letters reveal a special fondness for the "crutch" of underlining, her first Saxe Holm stories, published in the early 1870s, are not marked by excessive use of italics or exclamation points. In fact, a recent computer content analysis of Jackson's short stories and the fiction of many other nineteenth-century American writers has revealed that Jackson used such devices in her published work only about as often as did her peers, male and female. And while her earliest published travel essays are rather clumsy in expression and disorganized, those written only a few years later are marked by an elegant simplicity and clarity. Jackson's average sentence is far shorter in length, and less broken up by clauses, than that of her peers, especially her female peers, and she does not vary her sentence lengths extravagantly as did many other women writers of her time, who tended to write both very short and very long sentences. Today, when average sentence lengths are shorter than they were in the nineteenth century, yet only slightly shorter than Jackson's,[20] her style feels peculiarly modern.

Under Higginson's tutelage, Jackson became increasingly meticulous about polishing her prose and choosing precise diction. Though she was a facile writer who turned out private letters rapidly, she completed the first drafts of work intended for publication at a moderate rate of two to four pages per day, and she revised her work carefully. Examination of her manuscripts reveals extensive interlining, in general constituting alterations to about a quarter of her original writing. As she became established in her career, she often further revised her published periodical work before reprinting it in book form. Her commitment to exacting word choice is evident in her correspondence with various editors, where she sometimes argues over the use of particular words or expresses dismay when blunders are made in the printing of her work. In the early 1870s, in fact, she worried that her "insolent" stubbornness over a word in one of her European travel essays had earned her the enmity of William Dean Howells, just as he began his editorial tenure at the *Atlantic*. "In my Gastein article," she explained to a friend, "I said, 'Who cannot live without dining, would better stay away' from Gastein." In galley proofs of the article, Howells altered her "would better" to "had better," prompting Jackson to fume,

> Now if there is one barbarism which I hate with a phobia, it is "had better." I sharply cut off his correction, and restored the first form. After the proof left my hands, he altered it again over my correction, & made me say, twice in one paragraph, "had better."—I was so angry that I fear I misbehaved, in Mr. Fields office, and I sent word to Mr. Howells with Mrs. Hunt's compliments that she would be pleased to hear from him how he would parse the verb "had stay."[21]

While Jackson's perfectionism may have alienated some editors, it was good for her writing, and she was fortunate to have found at the start of her career a mentor who fostered such attention to detail. Higginson was extremely generous with his time. He not only edited a good deal of Jackson's early work, prose and poetry, but he was also willing to use his own growing reputation to ease her entry into print. He allowed her to use his name in submitting her work: "I send you another sonnet, about which I have little misgiving," Jackson writes in a typical early letter to an editor, "as my sternest critic, Col. Higginson, says it is the best I have ever written."[22] And he even submitted some of her pieces for her, an assistance Jackson did not hesitate to seek. While she was traveling in Europe in 1869, for example, she frequently sent him poems and travel articles to "forward" to various publications, imploring him not only to help her "get my way with Editors," but also to cast a final editorial glance over her work. "If you see a rent in any of the lines, you might perhaps patch it for me, dear Col. as you so often used to," she wrote when forwarding a poem from Rome. "Here I have nobody whose ear or sense I value higher than my own, & that is not good for so ignorant a worker as I am."[23]

As the somewhat obsequious tone of this last request suggests, the many advantages of Jackson's relationship with Higginson were in the end diminished by the very fact that she was able and inclined to rely so thoroughly upon him. For in her dependence she attached excessive importance to his opinions of her work, in particular to his belief that her greatest talent and "passion" as a writer was for poetry. Higginson had a strong personal and scholarly interest in poetry. His wife, Mary Channing, was the sister of the Concord poet William Ellery Channing. Higginson would eventually publish books on the New England poets Whittier and Longfellow and also on the fourteenth-century Italian poet Francesco Petrarca, whose work he first translated and praised in a September 1867 *Atlantic* essay, "Sunshine and Petrarch." He considered the Petrarchan sonnet form well suited to contemplative poetry, and he encouraged Jackson's early efforts in this area. He also thought highly of many of her poems on simple domestic topics, and especially on the topic of romantic love.

Higginson held a more exalted opinion of poetry than of prose, believing that poetry could touch the heart and soul in ways that prose could not. As he was only a mediocre poet himself, it was perhaps not surprising that he tended to overestimate his friend's immediate display of talent for this noblest of literary forms while overlooking what was actually most special in her early writing—the latent regionalist vision of her prose. He did recognize the importance of regionalism to American prose literature, writing on this topic as early as January 1870 in his *Atlantic* essay "Americanism in Literature." Over the course of his career he offered important critical support to the work of many emerging American realists. But he did not recognize Jackson's talent in this direction during her lifetime. In an 1879 *Literary World* essay about Jackson, which he included that year in his collection *Short Studies of American Authors,* he praised the "genius" of her poetry as surpassing Christina Rossetti's and rivaling Elizabeth Barrett Browning's. Yet he offered only a passing compliment to the special talent for "descriptive prose" evident in her western travel writing, because, as he said, he feared this work might imply a "shrinking from her full career" as a poet.[24]

Overall, Higginson encouraged Jackson toward ubiquity rather than depth of purpose in her prose writing. He taught her to view everything in her daily life as possible material for writing projects and to produce, as he later testified, a "wide variety of notes" in her work, with the aim of finding steady placement in the quality periodical press.[25] In his 1867 "Literature as Art," he argued that true artists must work above all to meet their personal standards of quality and meaning, not to gain money or fame, and must think of journalism only as an "outlet" for their "leisure time." Yet other factors made him advise Jackson to produce immediately marketable work. In the decades following the Civil War, publication in that era's newly prestigious, eastern literary magazines and newspapers was all but essential to the reputation of an American writer. Higginson viewed the contemporary literary marketplace as a difficult, highly competitive arena, and he knew that authors were often esteemed according to their ability to earn money for publishers. At the same time, like other Transcendentalists, he cared deeply about nurturing the whole person, as opposed to narrowly developing a talent. In 1873 he pasted a quotation from Emerson's lecture "Man the Reformer" inside the front cover of his diary: "Better that the book should not be quite so good, & the bookmaker abler & better, & not himself often a ludicrous contrast to all that he has written." Noting that perhaps "no sentence" had ever "influenced" his life as much as this one, he explained that it had taught him to work above all toward "personal development," rather than toward any "specific result" in his writing, for which he might have to "sacrifice" himself.[26] Given these beliefs, he was naturally inclined to encourage Jackson to explore a variety of topics and genres rather than to risk thwarting the development of her personality by too exclusive a focus on any one subject.

Jackson was disposed to accept Higginson's assessment of what was best for her not simply because she admired his work and respected his literary authority, but because their early relationship was in some manner romantic. Over the course of her life, Jackson had many warm, rather unconventional friendships with men, including Henry Root and Moncure Conway, but even when these friendships entailed some measure of mutual attraction, they still remained essentially friendships. Higginson also had many close friendships with women, especially those whom he mentored. But the relationship between the two of them was something more. As most of their mutual correspondence no longer exists, it is impossible to know the exact nature of their intimacy. Yet some of Jackson's published writings, and a number of her own and Higginson's private comments and actions, strongly suggest that they were romantically involved, though barred by Higginson's marriage and their own views of decency from acting on their feelings.

Jackson was not immediately attracted to Higginson. A month after first meeting him, she described him to Kate Field as lacking in "the truest flavor of manhood." Yet even then she excused his apparent weakness on the grounds that he was married to an invalid wife whom many believed to be imperious, despite her ready intelligence. "On the whole I think him an astonishing success under difficulties!" she told Field. "What would become of *you*, for instance, or me, to sleep where he sleeps—embrace what he embraces!"[27] During the following two winters, when she arrived in Newport in December and remained until May, she seems to have developed intense feelings for her mentor, feelings that Anna Mary Wells, the one Higginson biographer who has looked into this matter, believes were reciprocated.[28] For Higginson, association with Jackson seems to have provided some solace for the often difficult life he led with Mary, and for the loneliness he felt as a result of his wife's apparent disinclination to have children. "There was an utterly exotic and even tropical side of her nature, strangely mingled with the traits that came from her New England blood," he would later write of Jackson. "She was a person quite unique and utterly inexhaustible."[29] Jackson, in turn, found in her mentor a kindred spirit. She was inspired by their relationship to try to write well. But at the same time, as we will see later, some of her early poetry and fiction suggests that she suffered in caring for a man who was unavailable to her, and that she eventually came to believe he had been wrong to encourage her affections.

In the winter of 1868–69, Jackson did not return to Newport but instead went to Europe, where she traveled for more than a year. In May 1869 she made a possible allusion to her feelings for Higginson when she wrote from Venice to him and a group of other friends. "I am coming back here, another May, with I know whom, but you do not, to watch a pair of eyes looking at sunsets from the Lido," she said. "Then I shall not look at the sunsets so much as at the eyes."[30] She wrote more specifically, and less hopefully, about her relationship with Higginson in her correspondence with Charlotte Cushman, a woman then living in Europe who became her close friend sometime during this same trip.

When the two women met, Charlotte Cushman was America's most famous living actress. At a time when English men were earning the widest reputations in acting, Cushman had risen from a poverty-stricken Boston childhood to become a cosmopolitan, international superstar; as early as 1852, when she was only thirty-six, she had amassed a fortune large enough to support herself, her mother, and her siblings in perpetuity, and had gone into semiretirement. She emerged occasionally to make triumphal stage tours and to offer public readings from such authors as Shakespeare, Browning, and Tennyson. Cushman firmly believed that women artists must maintain control over their own destinies. She took it on herself to serve as Jackson's professional advisor, expressing strong opposition to the younger woman's romantic feelings for Higginson and to what she considered Jackson's excessive literary dependency.

From 1869 until Cushman's death in early 1876, Jackson and Cushman maintained an intense relationship of the sort Lillian Faderman and other scholars of the nineteenth century have discussed as "romantic friendship."[31] In their letters, they address each other as "Carissima Mia," "Carina," and "Darling," and continually express their love for each other. "It was a sweet pleasure to see you today," Cushman writes in a typical letter. "The perfume of you lingers still." "God bless you, sweet Sovrana! I kiss your hands—and love you with every single *bit* of me there is!!" Jackson closes one of hers.[32] For Charlotte Cushman, passionate feelings for women were the norm: she sustained her only long-term, committed relationships with women, including, from 1857 until the end of her life, the American sculptor Emma Stebbins, to whom Cushman considered herself "married" and to whom she referred in letters to Jackson as her "better half."[33] For Jackson, however, such emotional intensity with a woman was unusual, inspired by her deep admiration for Cushman's achievement and strength of character. "Oh you beloved glorious vital woman! How you triumph and conquer," she wrote to Cushman in 1870. "No wonder all who may, love you as we do—with the love we have for woman & the love we have for man, set into one love unlike all others." She made a special booklet of her poems for Cushman, telling her, "Never but once before have I done this thing—and that was for a man: for no woman in the world but you."[34] To other friends she declared herself Cushman's "worshipper," admitting that she loved her as she had "never loved any other woman in this world."[35] She wrote two poems for Cushman, odes to the "stimulus and lesson" she found in Cushman's life.[36] As late as 1883, she would claim that of all the women she had ever known, only Cushman and one other (Mary Trimble, a friend from New York) were strong enough that she would trust them in a crisis.

Jackson and Cushman had a great deal in common. During the six years of their friendship, they were both struggling by means of frequent relocation and patient submission to cope with chronic illness—in Cushman's case, advancing breast cancer. They were both professed Unitarians. They were both literary: Cushman prided herself on her unique interpretations of her tragic characters, and she had friends among the most celebrated writers of the day, including the Brownings and George Sand. Above all, they were both dedicated professionals. Jackson found in Cushman an exhilarating example of female commitment to craft and career at a time when she herself was becoming ever more devoted to her work.

In her letters to Jackson, Cushman frequently discussed work as the most important thing in her life, and in public she always insisted that success in the arts required single-minded devotion. "Art is an absolute mistress," she proclaimed in an 1874 speech before the Arcadian Club. "She will not be coquetted with or slighted; she requires the most entire self-devotion, and she repays with grand triumphs."[37] Jackson was so impressed by Cushman's achievement on the stage that she put aside her usual opposition to women performing in public, even despite Cushman's special fondness for playing male parts, and went to see her perform whenever possible. She traveled from Newport to Boston when Cushman was acting there in her two most famous roles, Lady Macbeth and Meg Merrilies, gypsy queen of *Guy Mannering*. She also attended several of Cushman's public readings. In 1872 Cushman read one of Jackson's poems in both Boston and Chicago. "I suppose I shall never feel again, in this life, as I did while hearing her read my 'Funeral March,' " Jackson wrote to Anne Botta after the Boston event. "Her readings are if possible grander than her acting. I never conceived of such reading."[38]

Cushman, in turn, did everything in her power to support Jackson's career. When Jackson was in Europe, Cushman tried to use her international literary connections to help Jackson meet Swinburne, Carlyle, and Eliot, though it does not appear that Jackson actually met any of the three. Cushman maintained a scrapbook of Jackson's poetry, asking Jackson to send her a copy of every new poem that she wrote. In 1871, when Jackson had not been sending much, Cushman tried to inspire her—"Imagine yourself a troubadour writing for the Queen of your soul"—and insisted that her own fame would ensure that any poems she received from Jackson would "live forever."[39] Early in their acquaintance, Jackson had told Cushman that her "words of praise" were especially "dear and helpful," so Cushman praised everything she read: in letter after letter, she tells Jackson how "sweet" and "lovely" and "fresh" and "exquisite" she finds Jackson's poems and travel sketches.[40]

On one matter, however, Cushman consistently disagreed with Jackson: she was entirely opposed to her friend's devotion to Thomas Wentworth Higginson. When Jackson was traveling in Europe, she missed Higginson and sometimes longed to return to Newport. Higginson missed her, too. "Two things I miss that gave me happiness a year ago," he noted in his diary after she had been gone a year. "One is *Malbone* [his recently published novel] is bad—the other was a dream."[41] Cushman believed that her friend was suffering under this impossible attachment, however. She repeatedly urged her to stay abroad, where there was "so much to see & to write about," and to stop "thinking of going back for what, after all, would disappoint you!"[42] When Jackson did return to America, in January 1870, she did not take up residence in Newport but instead spent the winter in New York and other places. Still, Cushman wrote admonishingly from Paris, "Your work was here & here you should have stayed. H— to the contrary notwithstanding."[43]

Cushman disliked Jackson's tendency to rely on Higginson as her literary agent, for she herself had long taken pride in being her "own business man."[44] When, after her return from Europe, Jackson asked both Higginson and Cushman to help her reconcile some difficulties she was having with James T. Fields over the publication of her *Verses* (1870), Cushman urged her to handle the matter herself. "It is only simple justice to yourself that you should transact your business yourself & not through a third person," she said. "You may do better for your book & your future, than you could in any other way."[45] Soon, Cushman began to conceive a personal dislike for Higginson and, perhaps jealously, to oppose Jackson's continued efforts to please him with her work.

In late 1870 Cushman returned from her sojourn in Europe to live in the United States, intending to spend a good deal of time in Newport. Jackson was eager that her two professional advisors should become friends. In September she wrote to Higginson from Bethlehem, New Hampshire, asking him to help Cushman find a house in Newport. She then wrote to Cushman, asking her to "keep ready to love him a little for my sake" and assuring her that, in time, Cushman would love him for "his own sake," as he was the "gentlest, and most loving of men."[46] In November Cushman reported to Jackson that she had "talked with 'he of Newport' & liked him very very much," though the presence of a third person had made it impossible for her to be "entirely at my ease as one is when one talks 'a due.' "[47] That same winter, as Jackson resumed her own habit of seasonal residence in Newport, Cushman sent her a note praising Higginson's poetry and *Out-Door Papers;* and Higginson recorded his delight in Cushman's company in his diary. By the late spring of 1871, however, Cushman had for unknown reasons begun to dislike Higginson, and was urging Jackson to move away from him and his influence. "Don't say it is not good for me to be here," Jackson wrote to Cushman in May.

> It hurts and troubles me, to have a point in all my thinking or living which is out of harmony with your wish or your judgment, my great grand darling! Some day when I see you more quietly, perhaps I can win you to see all as I see it:—most of all—to do justice to the sweetest patientest most self sacrificing human soul, that ever walked in chains! You can't tell me of any fault I do not see. I know some which you do not.
>
> > I see each failure he must make
> > Each step he cannot but mistake
> > And weeping for his soul's dear sake,
> > I set my faith with love's seal![48]

Cushman was not won over. She began to avoid social encounters with Higginson. By August 1871 friendly relations had ceased between the two. That month, Jackson became upset when Higginson apparently criticized as trifling a poem, "The Old Bell," that she had published in the August 3 *Independent* without first showing him. Cushman liked Jackson's simpler verses, including the one in question—a fairly amateurish elegy—and she urged Jackson to go on writing such poems, which offered "help, comfort & sympathy" to readers "which they could not find, in anything more high or grand!" She also pleaded with Jackson to stop attaching importance to Higginson's opinions of her work, for she was convinced the habit was making it impossible for Jackson to find her own way as a writer. "Why should *you*, who are able to criticize other people's thoughts," Cushman asked, "be subject to any mentor unless the *very* highest." She advised Jackson to "*create*—& then believe in your things, yourself," and not to trust "any eye in judgment but your own." And she criticized

Higginson as excessively controlling: "some minds are nothing if not critical—some, who have been honored by a submission to their judgment, would find their vanity a little mortified at anything's having been printed without their opinions having been asked."[49]

By 1874 Jackson's attachment to Higginson had placed a strain on her friendship with Cushman. That January, Cushman wrote to Jackson in her new residence of Colorado Springs, offering her usual praise of Jackson's work, and also seeking to assure Jackson that she did not love her "an atom less well than at the first," though she believed friends tended to "grow apart" when there was an "absorbing interest to one of two upon which they think dramatically opposite."[50] Still, when Cushman learned in July that she had done something in Newport to displease "T.W.H.," she made a point of reporting the fact to Jackson: "*That* pleases me. I don't care how much he is displeased with me, he can't beat my dislike of him."[51] Only Jackson's engagement to William Jackson the following year made it possible for the two friends to resume their old level of intimacy—as it turned out, only a few months before Cushman died. "It is better, so infinitely better, happier, wiser, gooder," Cushman wrote in July 1875 after receiving news of the impending marriage. "Believe me dear you will be in every way improved by this situation—you will work better & more after your own genius—after all work is all that is worth living for in this world!"[52]

Jackson did do better work after she shed her emotional dependence on Higginson. Upon marrying William Jackson she immediately began writing novels, and in both her fiction and nonfiction she began more thoroughly to explore the regionalist concerns that had long interested her. Still, she and Higginson would always remain friendly, and she would never entirely cease to rely on his patronage and support. Upon first arriving in Colorado, she referred to Higginson in a letter to a friend as "my mentor, my teacher—the one man to whom & to whose style I chiefly owe what little I have done in literature."[53] In January 1880, even as she was becoming swept up in advocacy work for Indians, she wrote to Higginson himself: "I shall never write a sentence, so long as I live, without studying it over from the standpoint of whether you would think it could be bettered."[54] That spring, exhausted from the hard work of writing *A Century of Dishonor* (1881), she set aside her usual meticulous concern for proofreading her own work and once again solicited Higginson's editorial assistance, asking him to review the galleys of her new book for her, so that she could rest in Europe.[55] Throughout these years, and later, she continued to benefit from his public expressions of support for her career.

Moreover, she always maintained the businesslike attitude toward writing, and the belief that she must publish continually in order to survive as a writer, that Higginson had first helped instill in her. "I envy you many things," she wrote to him in 1881, "but none more than the persistent tireless force which enables you to . . . treasure up every smallest bit of material for literary work."[56] Jackson never worked as a hack, writing on a topic only because she knew it would sell; she almost always decided for herself what she wished to write about and then looked for a suitable publisher. Yet she wrote always with the intention of immediate publication in the periodicals. Early in her career, she began to use her ability to publish as a gauge of her artistic success. She also devoted a good deal of energy to seeking the highest possible payment for her work, discovering in herself a taste for earning money that almost rivaled her desire to produce fine literature.

From the start, she relied on personal literary connections to enable her goal of frequent and advantageous publication. Especially in her Newport years, she had a passion for forming friendships with other literary people. In part, her enthusiasm was an outgrowth of the many personal losses she had suffered: having learned at the Abbott Institute and during her marriage to Edward Hunt that she liked the company of writers, she wished upon losing her husband and sons to reconstitute a "family" out of literary friends. (Thus, she claimed in the early 1870s that her ideal place to live would be populated by "all the leading magazine writers of New York & Boston.")[57] Her penchant for literary friendships also made good business sense. Throughout the nineteenth century, the American literary world was dominated and controlled by a close personal network of writers, editors, and publishers, and Jackson achieved prominence as quickly as she did because she was skilled at forming and maintaining important connections within this network.

At the same time that she was becoming established in Newport literary society, she also cultivated friendships with the literati of Boston and New York. In the Boston area, she found a forceful champion in Ralph Waldo Emerson, the most revered living writer in the country, and she was also friendly with the Alcotts, Lowell, Longfellow, Whittier, and Holmes, who particularly admired Jackson's "deep-toned contralto" poetic voice.[58] Among Boston editors, she had warm friendships with Edward Everett Hale, a Unitarian minister and writer who edited the journal *Old and New* before its 1875 absorption into *Scribner's Monthly,* and with Delano Goddard, the editor of Boston's *Daily Advertiser.* She was also close with Goddard's wife Martha, who wrote literary reviews for the paper.

She formed an early dislike of Boston's top publishing house, headed at various times by James T. Fields, J. R. Osgood, and Henry Oscar Houghton (and known today as Houghton Mifflin), perhaps because Fields cared little for the volume of *Verses* she published with him in 1870 and was slow in admitting much of her work to the publishing house's prestigious journal, the *Atlantic Monthly,* which he edited from 1861 until 1871. Given Fields's lack of enthusiasm, Jackson did not become part of the Boston literary coterie centered around his Charles Street home, though she maintained mostly friendly relations with his wife Annie, a poet and consummate hostess. She did, however, find an ally in the man who took over Fields's firm upon his death, Henry Oscar Houghton, often staying at Houghton's home during her visits to Boston. She also became friendly, after their rocky beginning, with Fields's successor as editor of the *Atlantic,* William Dean Howells, and especially with the poet Thomas Bailey Aldrich, formerly of New York, who succeeded Howells in 1881. She and Aldrich corresponded frequently, and not only about *Atlantic* business. "I believe it would be no exaggeration to say that I have written oftener to you, without 'having to,' than to any one else this winter," she told Aldrich in 1884.[59] She was occasionally his house guest in Boston. By the spring of 1880, when Jackson embarked from Boston on her second trip to Europe, she was so ensconced in the local literary society that she was escorted to the docks by "quite a galaxy of publishers," as she said, including H. O. Houghton and her good friend Thomas Niles of Roberts Brothers, the firm that published most of her books.[60] Founded in 1861, and acquired by Little, Brown within four decades, Roberts Brothers managed during its brief lifetime to rival Houghton's firm in its reputation for quality publications.

In New York City, Jackson established friendships with a number of important editors and writers, including Parke Godwin of the *Post;* George Ripley, longtime literary critic for the *Tribune;* and many of the poets then considered the best in America: Bayard Taylor, Richard Stoddard, Edmund Clarence Stedman, and Richard Watson Gilder. She was particularly close with Gilder, a highly influential editor and poet who did much to promote her career. From as early as 1869, when Gilder solicited Jackson's work for a journal he was then editing, *Hours at Home,* Jackson realized that he was her "ally" and determined to "fasten to him."[61] In the 1870s Gilder worked as assistant editor to Josiah Holland at the successor to *Hours at Home, Scribner's Monthly,* and helped Jackson publish her short fiction there. At the same time, he embarked on what would prove a prolific career as a poet, to which Jackson offered steady encouragement. Thrilled to have found in her an eminent "applauder, and sympathizer & friend," Gilder frequently sought her affirmation. "I hope you think I am a poet for I should like to be," he wrote to her in 1875. "I should like to look upon as much good work as you have done."[62] Once, filled with enthusiasm for his friendship with Jackson, he warned her that if she visited New York, he would impose heavily on her time:

> I'd make you tired of me. I'd go on like mad. I'd rave & tear my hair, in your
> room, & swear & argue & read sonnets and roll on the carpet. . . . I'd tease the life
> out of you. I'd write a poem in two seconds that would beat Bryant's Century of
> rhyme, and then I'd burlesque it and turn three somersaults backward on the floor,
> and fling it with my head in the fire, and upset the wash-bowl and the 19th century
> together.[63]

In 1881 Gilder became editor of *Scribner's* successor, *Century Magazine,* where he would use his position to further New York's eclipse of Boston as America's literary center. That year, fully aware of Gilder's power and all that he had done and was capable of doing for her career, Jackson admitted to a friend, "I would not have Gill my enemy for worlds."[64]

By means of her many literary connections and her own talent and industry, Jackson managed during her career to publish an average of almost three periodical pieces per month. She started out at a moderate pace, placing roughly a dozen pieces in each of her first two years as a writer, then quickly began to produce great quantities of work—as many as seventy items in the one year of 1870 alone. She slowed down temporarily only in 1873, when she was ill for most of the year. After 1876, when she began to work on books not based on previously published material, she reduced her output for the periodicals yet still published some twenty to thirty pieces a year.

She published most often in the *New York Independent,* where her friend Oliver Johnson, Jennie Abbott's husband, was responsible for "launching" her.[65] Founded in 1848 as a Congregationalist organ, the *Independent* had become by Jackson's time nonsectarian, but it remained morally didactic in tenor. Jackson's contact at the paper, William Hayes Ward, who was moving toward his eventual position as editor in chief, was a former Congregational minister who had attended Nathan Fiske's alma mater, Andover Theological Seminary. The *Independent* lacked the lofty reputation of the most prestigious magazines of the day, but many acclaimed prose writers, including Henry James and Louisa May Alcott, appeared in its pages; it was known in the 1870s for the quality of its poetry, including Jackson's. The paper was willing to publish almost anything Jackson offered, and throughout her career she used this ready entrée to maintain a loyal following among the *Independent*'s more than 200,000 readers.[66]

Among other newspapers, Jackson published significantly in the *New York Evening Post,* where she had been given her start as a poet and travel writer by her acquaintance Parke Godwin, and in the *New York Tribune.* The latter's managing editor, Whitelaw Reid, an acquaintance through Lucia Runkle and Anne Botta, printed some of her editorial work in the early 1870s and later gave singular support to her Indian reform effort. When Oliver Johnson left the *Independent* in 1873 to assume editorship of the *Christian Union,* a respected paper with a circulation of more than 100,000, Jackson also began to publish there.

In addition to publishing in newspapers, Jackson contributed regularly to the most prestigious magazines of the day, especially the highbrow *Atlantic Monthly,* where her friendly relations with Howells and Aldrich helped her gain frequent access. She also published often in the more middle-class *Scribner's Monthly* and its successor *Century Magazine,* where Gilder worked. She published occasionally in *Harper's Monthly* and in New York's *Galaxy,* before it was absorbed into the *Atlantic.* In the first years of her career she placed a good deal of poetry in the *Nation,* a New York journal that despite a small circulation of only about 10,000 readers carried great weight in the literary world. But by 1870 she had come to "hate" what she called "the Nation's arrogance,"[67] the journal's self-conscious elitism and bias against female authors. She began to write editorials criticizing the journal; and in 1871, when the *Nation* ran an unfair review of her *Verses,* charging that they lacked feminine "prettiness," she ceased to publish there.[68]

By focusing in the first half of her career on periodical publication primarily, and book publication only secondarily—during this period, before she began writing novels, her books were all compilations of previously published material—Jackson did much to promote her career. In the postbellum decades, American authors tended to make their critical reputations through the periodicals; they also tended to find more readers for their magazine work than for their books. While the *Atlantic* had a fairly small circulation of less than 20,000 throughout Jackson's career, the circulation of *Scribner's Monthly,* where she published most of her short stories, exceeded 100,000; its successor *Century,* where she published many pieces of western travel, had by 1885 reached a circulation of 200,000.[69] Like other authors of her time, Jackson earned more money from the periodical press than from her books. Though she often claimed that the loyal audience she had established among readers of the *Independent* could be counted on "to ensure a fair sale of any book I should publish," which in 1881 she estimated meant "at least 4000 or 5000" copies, the truth is that such sales figures were considered only "fair" by Jackson's publishers.[70] Her novels *Mercy Philbrick's Choice* and *Ramona* did by far the best, with *Mercy* selling 8,000 copies in just the four months following its 1876 publication, and *Ramona,* which alone among Jackson's novels was serialized before it was published in hardcover, reaching best-seller status with a sale of more than 20,000 copies in 1885.[71] According to Jackson's own estimation, *Bits of Travel* also did well over time, selling perhaps "15000 or 20000 copies" by 1880.[72] But some of Jackson's other books sold hardly at all. In 1880 executives at Scribner's told her that only 6,000 copies of her first collection of short stories, and 3,000 of her second collection, had sold. "The stories in the Magazine were a real 'hit,' but in book form they share the fate of all short stories," Gilder had earlier explained.[73] In late 1881 Jackson admitted that *A Century of Dishonor,* published earlier that year, had "not sold 2000 copies, outside of those I bought myself."[74] And as late as 1884, *Bits of Travel at Home* (1878) had sold fewer than 4,000 copies during six years in print.[75] Since most of Jackson's books cost $1 or $1.25, and earned royalties at the standard rate of 10 percent, such sales figures meant that Jackson earned little money from her books.

Yet Jackson received exceptionally high rates of pay for her periodical work, especially as her career progressed. Initially, in the 1860s, she was pleased to receive as little as $10 or sometimes $5 for a poem or page of prose. By the 1870s, however, *Scribner's* was paying her from $200 to $400 per Saxe Holm story. Even the *Independent,* which always paid her at lower rates than did other publications, was paying at least $15 for her short poems, $50 for longer poems, $40 for travel sketches, $25 for signed articles, and $20 for unsigned editorials. In the 1880s she received from $200 to $250 for articles in *Harper's* and *Century,* and her occasional pieces of children's writing brought in as much as $50 for short articles in *St. Nicholas* and on the order of $500 for one long *Youth's Companion* story.[76] In 1882 the *Atlantic* paid her $400 for two western travel articles, "A Midsummer Fete in the Pueblo of San Juan" and "Among the Skylines"—more than it paid any other writer in the decade except Thomas Hardy. (This was a rate of $28 per page, as compared, for example, to the $3 per page received by Sarah Orne Jewett, or the $10 given Annie Fields.)[77] That same year, Jackson told an acquaintance, "My own time is worth to me, on an average, $200 a month."[78] In fact, according to the account pages inside her date books, where she itemized both her payments from periodicals and her limited royalty earnings, it was worth even more. Each year in the early 1880s, a period when it was nearly impossible for most authors to earn a comfortable living of $2,000 per year, Jackson made almost $3,000.[79] Of course, there were some writers who actually became wealthy, but most of them either produced what Jackson and her peers considered inferior work or had wider reputations in the world of serious literature than did Jackson. "Nobody in this country has ever made a fortune by *good* work," Jackson once complained to Moncure Conway. She grumbled to her sister, "If I only knew how to write trashy novels like Mrs. [E. D. E. N.] Southworth, I could make money—or if I were a *genius,* like Mrs. [Frances Hodgson] Burnett. But my work is both too *good,* & too bad, to be profitable!"[80]

In some ways, she considered making as much money as possible from her writing a necessity. In October 1865, at the very start of her career, she told Parke Godwin that she needed money in order to help unnamed loved ones. "An unlooked for embarrassment falling more heavily upon those dear to me, than upon myself, has suggested to me the idea that I ought to be able to earn something," she said, explaining further that writing was "the only kind of digging, for which I discover in me, any sort of capacity."[81] It was probably her sister's family that she wished to help at this time, for Ann's attorney husband Everett Banfield was unable to earn a great deal of money, despite some significant career successes. For the next twenty years, Jackson did much to assist in the support of Ann's six children; for example, she helped put two of the girls through Vassar College. She also made financial gifts to a number of friends, including Jennie Abbott, Lucia Runkle, and especially Sarah Woolsey.

In addition to enabling her to help others, earning money bolstered Jackson's sense of independence and made it possible for her to live on a scale larger than the middle-class income from her trust fund would allow. "Think of me having actually earned every cent I have spent this summer!" she boasted to Charlotte Cushman from Bethlehem in 1870. "I feel as proud as a man or a peacock to think I could support myself for three months!"[82] She not only traveled constantly, which cost her about $10 per day when she was actually moving, but she also kept servants and maintained with exuberance the same predilection for nice clothing and personal effects that she had once guiltily confessed to Henry Root. In 1874, when a friend suggested that she might earn more for her books through the cheaper, less prestigious method of subscription sales than by continuing to publish with Thomas Niles of Roberts Brothers, she briefly considered the idea. "I like Mr. Niles heartily, but I like dollars better," she said. "I know I should turn faint whenever I saw my book, but $2000 or $3000 would buy so much Cologne I could recover."[83]

Her eagerness to earn money did not lessen after she married William Jackson, a well-to-do businessman who sometimes made thousands of dollars in mere months. William provided for the basic needs of their household by depositing between $175 and $200 per month in a bank account under Helen's name, for her to disperse. But he was a thrifty man, not given to spending money on himself, and both his Quaker upbringing and his experience as a self-made man—he had worked since the age of sixteen—made him wish to live simply in married life. "A very few mistakes would wipe out my small fortune & leave me to commence life again," he wrote to Helen during their engagement, a period when he was actually earning $5,000 per year as secretary of the Denver and Rio Grande Railroad in addition to his income from banking. "Respect this condition & curb your love of expenditures for pretty things that are not essential to our comfort."[84] Helen did indeed respect her husband's feelings about money. She thought him "*just,* to a wonderful degree—and generous in many ways," including in his monetary gifts to his mother and sisters.[85] But she could never bring herself to share his desire for plain living. Instead, she simply continued to buy her own clothes and assist her own relations, and she used her own money for many of her travel and household expenditures.

Taking care of her own expenses was agreeable to her, as it removed any shadow of a doubt that she had married her husband for money, at the same time enabling her to maintain her sense of independence. "If Mr. Jackson were a different sort of man," she told her sister, or if she had not begun "married life on such a totally distinct & independent basis in money matters," she might not have felt averse to asking him for money now and then.[86] As matters stood, however, she was eager to show William that she was capable of paying her own way. "I'd be a very proud woman, the day I could show Mr. Jackson an actual good business percentage on brains!" she told a friend in 1880.[87] She always made a point of paying him back whenever he gave her money in excess of the usual household fund. In 1880, for instance, when he paid for her to take a trip to Europe, she was determined to repay him, even though he repeatedly urged her to "spend whatever was necessary to make her trip a success."[88] Her letters home from abroad are filled with lists of the amounts of money she expects to earn from the periodical work she is doing and uncharacteristic references to her writing in purely monetary terms. From Paris, for instance, where she accidentally left her manuscript book of travel notes in an elevator for two hours before realizing it was missing, she reported to William, "I can tell you I was wretched—of course to lose *that* would be simply losing hundreds of dollars!"[89]

At least as important to Jackson as the financial independence that her earned income helped maintain were the psychological benefits that earning at a high rate provided her as a writer. For one thing, her idea that she must earn as much as possible enabled her to believe that in writing and publishing, she was being a good, diligent person, as her parents had taught her to be. Her efforts to earn money also helped her create a sense of urgency about her work, a feeling that she must avoid distractions and overcome inertia in order to get her writing done. As early as 1866, she confessed to Kate Field that she needed payment for her writing not only in order "to help those I love" but also because she was "a born spendthrift," and was simply "much too lazy" to write at all "unless each separate scramble was paid for."[90] Above all, given Higginson's early influence, she looked on the amounts of money editors paid her as a means of measuring her rank in the world of serious literature, and therefore worked to receive large sums. Throughout her career she used discussions of the amounts of money her writing was worth as a coded way of discussing and asserting her value as an artist. Indeed, she talks about money and her financial income in approximately one-fifth of her existing letters, more often than she discusses any other subject except her health.

As Jackson gained in reputation as a writer, she quickly showed herself to be a forceful and astute businesswoman, a savvy navigator of the literary marketplace. With editors, she expressed a capacity for successfully negotiating high pay for her work that might never have been anticipated from the young Abbott schoolteacher who could scarcely think of the word "profession" in association with herself. In truth, though, because she had been orphaned early in life, she had long been accustomed to looking out for her own financial interests. By monitoring the activities of her trustees, she had learned to be firm in asserting her financial desires, and to express this firmness in writing. As early as age twenty, when she wished Julius Palmer to send her more money than he had intended, she had admitted, "You know I am quite accustomed to doing business with you, by means of my pen as an interpreter, and indeed, there are some things of which I can easier write, than speak. . . . I refer to *money matters.*"[91]

In 1865 Jackson approached editors timidly, exuding deference—a manner that was common among nineteenth-century female authors, who generally felt impelled to mask their desires for money or else to justify them by assertions of real financial need. After publishing several poems in the *New York Evening Post,* for no payment, Jackson meekly asked Parke Godwin, begging him to be "patient" if her question seemed "presumptuous," "whether such odds & ends of verses as I have sent you, & as two or three similar things you may have chanced to see in the *Nation,* are worth any money?"[92] Within very few years, however, she had adopted a far less conventional approach, frankly admitting to all editors that although she did not "write for money" but "for love," she did "*print* for money."[93] With William Ward, the superintending editor of the *Independent,* she was particularly unabashed: "I make no pretence of not liking to earn money and finding plenty of use for all I earn."[94] Indeed, she came to demonstrate such unusual assertiveness in her financial negotiations that she earned quite a reputation among editors. In 1870, when she suggested to James T. Fields that he pay for her *Atlantic* contributions as much as Gilder paid her at *Scribner's Monthly*—$10 per page—Fields balked at her discussion of money, "a vile article," and asked her if Gilder "gilded" all of his contributors at such a "colossal rate." In response, Jackson assured Fields that even if Gilder's payments were high, she would take no less, and added, " 'cash *is* a vile article,' but there is one thing viler: and that is a purse without any cash in it."[95]

Often, in negotiating for high pay, Jackson claimed to be guided by scrupulous principles: she was opposed to "the so much per page plan" of payment because it placed a premium on quantity instead of quality, for instance; and she believed that an objective "market value" could be placed upon every piece of writing, to ignore which would constitute unfair business practice.[96] Her principles, while no doubt genuine, promoted her financial interests. Her concept of "market value" was particularly serviceable as a negotiating tool, since if she liked, she could claim that someone who did not set an adequate "market value" on her work was simply "ignorant of true literary standards & values."[97] In a typical negotiation, Jackson states what she considers the "market value" of the piece she is submitting and, noting that she could easily publish her piece elsewhere, but particularly wishes to place it with the editor she is addressing, asks him or her to return the piece if it is unwanted, as "nobody would be more unwilling than I should be to have an Editor pay for my work at my own valuation when his did not coincide with it."[98] She was especially fond of telling William Ward that the *Independent*'s larger audience made her prefer publication there, while at the same time assuring *Atlantic* editors, perhaps more truthfully, that the quality of their publication made her prefer having her work appear there than anywhere else. ("I don't want the *Atlantic* to go six whole months without mentioning me you know," she told Aldrich in 1882.)[99] Toward the end of her career, she negotiated with new editors by offering a more general statement: "I have the good fortune, or perhaps I ought not to call it fortune for it certainly has not come to me without very serious literary labor—to find an increasing demand for my work, and a steadily increasing market value to it, as my audience widens."[100]

Jackson was always especially assertive with the *Independent,* partly because she was confident that her work was in constant demand there, and partly because the *Independent'*s publisher, Henry Bowen, frequently balked at the prices she demanded. Indeed, from 1874, when Bowen instructed William Ward to pay Jackson less than a previously agreed-on rate, until a week before Jackson's death, when Jackson told Bowen where to send a final payment, Jackson battled constantly with Bowen, mostly through Ward. "Now for the money question. I am very sorry that your memory is at fault in this matter," she writes in a typical letter to Ward. "Never mind about 'begging ten thousand pardons,' " she says in another, "but do answer my questions!"[101] In 1875 disagreements were particularly sharp. "I am much disgusted with [Bowen's] repeated efforts to get good work—work which he must know has an established market value—at reduced rates," she told Ward in January.[102] That August she told Ward she did "not like to be as angry" as Bowen was making her: "The humiliation to a person of recognized and established position as a writer, of being forced to 'dicker' like a peddler of his wares, is intolerable; and if after fixed rates have been once laid down, insisted on, & accepted, there is yet no dependence to be placed on them, what is to be done. . . . I shall never write for any less."[103]

Jackson was fortunate in her ability to demand large sums of money for her work, and to place it with the most prominent periodicals and publishers of her day. The visibility she achieved from frequent publication, together with her talent, earned her a powerful reputation. In 1884 the strength of her position in the literary establishment was made clear when a respected literary journal called the *Critic*—run by Joseph and Jeanette Gilder, siblings of Richard—conducted a survey asking readers to submit the names of forty candidates who would most deserve inclusion if America were to establish an academy for its best living, male authors. Thomas Wentworth Higginson received the twenty-ninth most votes, placing him within the imagined academy; each of Jackson's earlier clergymen mentors also received mention: Moncure Conway and Ray Palmer were awarded places in the list of runners-up, while John Abbott headed a separate list compiled of responses from readers who had mistakenly submitted the names of dead male writers. Jackson herself was near the top of a list compiled from responses mistakenly advocating women, second only to Harriet Beecher Stowe.[104]

Though it served to make her famous in her time, Jackson's focus on constant, conspicuous publication slowed her ability to develop her own artistic vision. Instead of searching gradually and obsessively, as an artist must, to form a personal interpretation of the fundamental and enduring in human experience, whether or not that interpretation be popular, she was preoccupied in the first half of her career with earning the approbation of both her literary peers and the general public. Critical and popular approval came quickly for her poetry, as I discuss in the next chapter, and popular audiences also relished the comfort and advice that she offered in her simple essays on domestic topics.

Poetry and Domestic Essays

The verses you have written, come to me in every phase of my quiet life, heightening my joy, and often, often helping me to bear, bravely, and in silence, sorrow for trouble, which otherwise would be too heavy.

Oh, I wonder if you know how many *dear* friends you have, who have learned to love you through your writings! Some day, you will, and we can thank you for the comfort you have given to those who long, in vain, for sympathy and love.

JULIA H. MARVIN OF NEW YORK, letter to Jackson
in praise of her Verses, November 6, 1872, HHJ2

I have learned a good lesson, and acknowledge it gratefully. If your book is to others . . . what it is to me, you will have accomplished a good for which mothers & children shall rise up and call you blessed. I feel its moral purpose so deeply.

MARY E. BRADLEY OF NEW YORK CITY, letter to
Jackson in praise of her Bits of Talk about Home Matters,
March 13, 1873, HHJ2

As a poet and domestic essayist, Jackson worked with an underlying moral agenda: to promote honorable living, spiritual awareness, and contented perseverance among her readers. Essentially, her ultimate aims were those of the heroine of her autobiographical first novel, Mercy Philbrick, who writes poems in order "to do a little towards making people glad, towards making them kind to one another, towards opening their eyes to the omnipresent beauty."[1] Today, the didactic underpinnings of Jackson's poems and domestic essays tend to limit their appeal. But her contemporaries appreciated her efforts on their behalf, and many readers, especially women, sent her heartfelt letters of thanks.

Jackson's desire to uplift her readers was partly a product of her intensely religious upbringing. Though she delighted in aesthetic beauty and simple narrative entertainment, and wanted her writing to convey those pleasures, she emerged from youth with an imagination that was steadfastly moralistic, consistently exercised over gradations of right and wrong in human behavior. She tended frequently and almost unconsciously to quote from the Bible in her private correspondence, and to echo biblical diction and cadences in her creative work. Her father's early condemnation of her "foolish fancies" and "mere imaginations" meant that her first efforts at professional writing constituted an act of filial defiance. She managed this initial rebellion, and her subsequent literary career, only by making certain compromises with her past: by concentrating at the start of her career on spiritually uplifting poetry and educational nonfiction, the types of writing that her father had most approved, and by continuing to use her writing to celebrate cheerfulness and diligence, the personal virtues most valued by both her parents. Unlike them, she equated spiritual uplift not with Christian evangelism or narrow sectarianism but rather with moral injunctions of a softer sort, like those put forward by the Unitarian minister Edward Everett Hale in *Ten Times One Is Ten* (1871), a book Jackson admired: "Look up and not down. Look forward and not back. Look out and not in. And lend a hand."[2]

In her continuing preoccupation with morality and with offering moral guidance, Jackson was a product not merely of her own upbringing but also of the times in which she lived. As Walter Houghton and later scholars of the era have emphasized, many Victorians who rejected the Calvinism of their parents nonetheless remained zealously committed to moral earnestness, finding in the mandates of ethics a defense against epistemological doubt and the frightening implications of recent advances in science and historiography. Victorian readers tended to expect spiritual enlightenment from their writers, who in turn felt impelled to dogmatize, despite—or even because of—their own doubts.[3] Midway through her career, Jackson admitted to Moncure Conway that although she had always sought "the society and affection of the most heretical," she had never entirely abandoned her ties with traditional beliefs. "Mr. Jackson has again and again said to me, almost in the same words you used to use—'Oh you are not yet free from superstitions'—'There's a heap of orthodoxy left in you yet,'" she reported. "I suppose there is—and I don't believe it does me any harm either."[4]

Jackson was widely considered America's finest female poet during much of the late nineteenth century. At a time when only a few hundred women found a broad readership for their poetry, Jackson published some two poems per month in periodicals geared to national audiences. Her work was praised and promoted by the most influential editors at the most prestigious American magazines, which shaped the literary taste of America's educated class; it was also regularly featured on the front page of the less sophisticated *New York Independent,* where she garnered a large popular following.

Her first poems, written in the wake of Rennie's death, were fairly conventional exercises in the religious consolation of grief. She also made a few early translations from the French—codicils, of a sort, to her previous, aborted attempt at translation under Ray Palmer's tutelage: in 1866 she published two translations from Victor Hugo's *Les Chansons des rues et des bois* (1865); in 1867 she completed a translation of a long children's poem by the eighteenth-century fabulist Jean-Pierre Claris de Florian, which was published by Loring of Boston as *Bathmendi: A Persian Tale,* her first book. A veiled commentary on the elusive nature of happiness, *Bathmendi* was the first of several poems based on Persian legend or parable that Jackson would write during her career. For the most part, though, she took her inspiration from her own life and emotions. Publishing under the initials "H.H.," familiar to her as the monogram she had used on personal effects since marrying Edward Hunt, she composed on a wide variety of topics. She found her two main thematic concerns in spiritual and women's issues, and she produced two general types of work. Some was intellectually ambitious and some, aimed at her popular audience, was more direct and simple—what Jackson called "light verse."[5]

In 1870 Fields, Osgood and Company accepted her first collection of *Verses* for publication, though James T. Fields brought the book out with trepidation, insisting that Jackson pay for publication herself (she would receive one-half of retail earnings, or about sixty-two cents per copy sold) and confiding to his wife that he did not much like what he disdainfully called Jackson's "Pinch of Poetry," nor expect her to earn any money from it.[6] In fact, *Verses* established Jackson's reputation. The poems were widely praised as demonstrating rare wisdom, inventiveness, and skill; a typical notice claimed that in "breadth of imagination, elegance of expression, beauty of rhythm, and, beyond all, originality," they had "few superiors in the English language."[7] Fields's firm quickly brought out a second edition of the book. When Roberts Brothers became Jackson's main book publisher in 1873, they released an expanded *Verses* (with Jackson receiving the customary 10-percent royalties); later, after Jackson's poetic career came to an end with her death, they brought out a new collection titled *Sonnets and Lyrics* (1886), and finally a combination of the two previous collections, *Poems* (1892), which was reissued many times into the next century.

Jackson's poetry has a number of strengths. Her manner of expression is often elegant and rarely clichéd. Much of her work evinces a powerful intelligence. She experimented with a variety of formal stanzaic structures, and had more feeling for the relation between form and meaning than did many of her contemporaries. She produced interesting shifts in the final lines of many of her poems, often winnowing contemplation down to unexpected, crystallized assertion—an effect that cleverly anticipated what would become a standard practice of American poetry only in the twentieth century.[8] Her favorite form, like Higginson's, was the Petrarchan sonnet, and she was adept at sonnet turns. In "Dreams," after opening with an evocation of dreams as mysterious servants of the subconscious, then slipping into a second quatrain where dreams take on the power of prison guards, forcing humankind to remember past crimes and passions, she turns in the sestet to liken the grasp of the human unconscious to the inexorable pull of immortality and final judgment:

> Mysterious shapes, with wands of joy and pain,
> Which seize us unaware in helpless sleep
> And lead us to the houses where we keep
> Our secrets hid, well barred by every chain
> That we can forge and bind: the crime whose stain
> Is slowly fading 'neath the tears we weep;
> Dead bliss which, dead, can make our pulses leap—
> Oh, cruelty! To make these live again!
> They say that death is sleep, and heaven's rest
> Ends earth's short day, as, on the last faint gleam
> Of sun, our nights shut down, and we are blest.
> Let this, then, be of heaven's joy the test,
> The proof if heaven be, or only seem,
> That we forever choose what we will dream![9]

With its evocative imagery, effective conceit, and technically skilled turn, "Dreams" demonstrates the talent evident in Jackson's better poetry. Yet many of her poems are fatally marred by awkward and arrhythmic phrasing. (She herself knew that she was not "very musical.")[10] Other poems suffer from stilted or inappropriately archaic diction, or excessive imitativeness. Moreover, while Jackson produces an interesting meditation on a spiritual subject in "Dreams" and also in a few other poems—"In the Dark," "Resurgam," "Just out of Sight"—most of her poems on spiritual topics instead celebrate Christian submission or aspects of her own liberal Christian faith in ways that retain little power today, seeming either too didactic or else vague to the point of meaninglessness.

The ethos of Jackson's spiritual poetry is comprehensively Christian—able to accommodate her own Unitarianism and Transcendental leanings, as well as the lingering imperatives of her Calvinist upbringing and the expectations of the traditional editorship and audience of the *Independent,* where she published most of her poetry. Loyal readers there knew her to be a Unitarian—she was explicitly listed as such in a February 5, 1874, article on the religion of American authors—yet she intended her spiritual poetry to have a broader appeal. Like her heroine Mercy Philbrick, she offers "pleadings" in her poetry on behalf of "spiritual communion with things seen and unseen," a communion based on no exact "creed" but rather, as in Mercy's case, on the "realization of the solemn significance of the great fact of being alive[,] . . . of brotherhood to every human being, and . . . of the actual presence and near love of God."[11]

Jackson explicitly pays tribute to her faith in God and her liberal veneration for Jesus as a "brother" and guide in such poems as "Confession of Faith" and "My Legacy."[12] More often, she celebrates the spiritually optimistic vision at the heart of Christian submission, creating poetic testaments to her belief that God orders events on earth for a purpose, and that people should therefore strive for a state of cheerful "renunciation" and "content," as she says in poems by these titles—a state in which one "doubts not all that is is best."[13] Jackson here gives credit to the human will, but she praises God's will—which she equates with fate—as superior.

She often uses images of the loom, and of boats and voyages, to represent fate and submission to fate, as in her poems "Spinning," "Crossed Threads," "Bon Voyage," "My Ship," and "Emigravit." This last sonnet was probably Jackson's favorite among her own poems, for she not only uses it to close *Mercy Philbrick's Choice,* explaining that Mercy's friends have had the poem carved on Mercy's gravestone, but she also left instructions to have the word "Emigravit" engraved on her own tombstone. "Emigravit" is indeed among Jackson's more interesting contemplations of fate and submission. The poem opens with a scene of passengers setting out as emigrants on various ships, turns in the sestet to suggest that perhaps the fairest colonies for emigration lie not on earth but "Thick planted in the distant shining plains / Which we call sky because they lie so far," and then surprises with a final declarative couplet: "Oh, write of me, not 'Died in bitter pains,' / But 'Emigrated to another star!' "[14]

While "Emigravit" is among Jackson's better poems on the topic of submission, evocative because of its vague suggestiveness, "Spinning" is more representative: it is one of her many spiritual poems in which vagueness serves no thematic purpose but is only a flaw. Yet "Spinning" was one of Jackson's most popular poems, adored by the cosmopolite Charlotte Cushman and by impoverished western pioneers alike. It exemplifies her manner of promoting submission in her simpler poetry:

Like a blind spinner in the sun,
I tread my days;
I know that all the threads will run
Appointed ways;
I know each day will bring its task,
And, being blind, no more I ask.

I do not know the use or name
Of that I spin;
I only know that some one came,
And laid within
My hand the thread, and said, "Since you
Are blind, but one thing you can do."

Sometimes the threads so rough and fast
And tangled fly,
I know wild storms are sweeping past,

And fear that I
Shall fall; but dare not try to find
A safer place, since I am blind.

I know not why, but I am sure
That tint and place,
In some great fabric to endure
Past time and race
My threads will have; so from the first,
Though blind, I never felt accurst.

I think, perhaps, this trust has sprung
From one short word
Said over me when I was young,—
So young, I heard
It, knowing not that God's name signed
My brow, and sealed me his, though blind.

But whether this be seal or sign
Within, without,
It matters not. The bond divine
I never doubt.
I know he set me here, and still,
And glad, and blind, I wait His will;

But listen, listen, day by day,
To hear their tread
Who bear the finished web away,
And cut the thread,
And bring God's message in the sun,
"Thou poor blind spinner, work is done."[15]

Like Jackson herself, the narrator of "Spinning" is determinedly cheerful and diligent in her work, having been given when "young," as she surmises in the fifth stanza, a fortifying faith in God and his earthly plan. As in many of her poems, Jackson flirts here with moral doubt and dilemma—in the opening quatrains of the alternating second, fourth, and sixth stanzas—but she retreats so quickly into assertions of faith in God's will and contentment with her own weak, "blind" state that her assertions feel strained, as if she retreats simply because she is afraid to probe more deeply. In Jackson's time, critics were not troubled by such withdrawals, for they encountered religious ambivalence in a good deal of contemporary poetry; in comparison with the work of other women poets, where Christian submission was a major theme, Jackson's expressions of submission and faith seemed particularly unsentimental. Indeed, many reviewers found them not only "earnest" but admirably progressive.[16]

Jackson won a large, loyal following in her day much as other popular poets did: by writing in a manner that engaged her readers without too often shocking their moral or aesthetic sensibilities. Personally, she admired the poetry not only of acknowledged masters such as Shakespeare and Goethe but also of iconoclastic artists; among the latter were Dante Gabriel Rossetti and William Morris, who were members of the idealist, anti-industrialist Pre-Raphaelite school of poetry and art in England, and her friend Emily Dickinson. But she herself can best be considered the poetic peer of her more conventional friends Thomas Bailey Aldrich, Richard Watson Gilder, Richard Henry Stoddard, Edmund Clarence Stedman, and Bayard Taylor, core members of America's postbellum literary elite. These poets tended out of religious or social conservatism to cling to traditional pieties in their work, despite their interest in the new, Transcendentally inspired aestheticism of their age. Jackson sought their approval and enjoyed their poems—perhaps especially Gilder's "Laurel" and Taylor's "Prince Deukalion" and "Lars"—and her poetry was appreciated and solicited in return. In 1883 she quoted the final lines of "Lars" at the end of one of her travel essays, a quotation that reveals her attachment to moralistic poetry: "The healing of the world is in its nameless saints. Each separate star / Seems nothing, but a myriad scattered stars / Break up the night and make it beautiful."[17]

Moncure Conway, who once described the dilemma faced by nineteenth-century American Unitarian writers as "trying to hold on to the Christian fairy-tales after destroying the faith on which they rested,"[18] urged Jackson to abandon her conventional poetic vision for one less safe, less ordinary. "I find more than I like of tones I have heard before," he wrote to her upon reading some of her early poetry, in late 1868. He praised the "high, unsentimental vein, and the felicitous use of words" evident in much of her work, but he urged her to take a cue from Walt Whitman—"he has made spires of grass grow higher and finer than spires of churches"—and choose a more daring style and subject matter: "Anglosaxon law and morality, have reached their climax in New England, like a shining rocket: is it not time it should burst and sow the sky with new colours? A celebration of polygamy, of Mephistopheles, Nakedness, Illegitimacy, Miscegenation, Fire-Worship, would be refreshing. There are things the Mayflower was not big enough to hold, which America must recover."[19]

Jackson never went far in applying Conway's suggestions to her poetry; nor is there any evidence that she took much interest in Whitman, though toward the end of her life she kept a magazine portrait of him among her personal papers. Only in her prose would she attempt to "recover" a more diverse American history. She did, however, manage from the start of her career to please Conway with those of her spiritual poems which most clearly demonstrate her sympathy for Transcendentalism, especially her "tribute" to Ralph Waldo Emerson.

According to Conway, Jackson had her first personal encounter with Emerson, "the memory of which was treasured," sometime in the 1850s, when, finding herself in the same train car as the great man, she introduced herself in Conway's name.[20] Later, in July 1868, she and Emerson happened to spend four days together as guests at the Newport home of Sarah Clarke, a painter and sister to the Unitarian minister, Transcendentalist, and former abolitionist James Freeman Clarke. Of this sojourn in Newport, Emerson afterward wrote in his diary: "My chief acquisition was the acquaintance of Mrs. Helen Hunt . . . her poetry I could heartily praise. The sonnet 'Thought,' & 'Ariadne's Farewell,' were the best, but all had the merit of originality, elegance, & compression."[21] Jackson was nearly overwhelmed by the experience of spending time with Emerson and hearing him praise her work. It was, she told Kate Field, "the greatest pleasure on the whole, I have ever had: oh that wonderful man—the wisdom the gentleness—the humanity of him. And dear—he has said such things to me about my verses—I hardly dare again to write a word lest I fall short of what he said I might do."[22] In commemoration of Emerson's kindness on this occasion, and of her desire to continue writing in a manner worthy of his praise, she wrote her sonnet "Tribute: R.W.E.," which opens, "Midway in summer, face to face, a king / I met."[23]

Emerson remained one of Jackson's staunchest supporters, most admiring her denser and more cerebral poems, whether or not they specifically demonstrated any Transcendentalist influence. He kept a newspaper clipping of Jackson's poem "Coming Across" at the front of his journal for 1870, and he tried to call on her in October, apparently unsuccessfully.[24] He was very pleased with her collected *Verses* when they appeared that winter. In December Annie Fields noted in her diary that during a recent visit at her home, Emerson and his wife had expressed themselves "sincerely anxious to renew their intercourse" with Jackson, for they "liked her very much and her poems too, which are just out."[25] By 1872 Emerson had begun to include Jackson's poems "Thought" and "Joy" in some of his public readings. And in 1874 he paid her what poets of the time considered an honor of extreme importance, featuring five of her poems—"Thought," "Joy," "Ariadne's Farewell," "Coronation," and "My Legacy"—in his anthology of English-language poetry, *Parnassus*. In his preface to this volume, he draws attention to Jackson's work, along with that of only two other contributors, claiming that her poems have "rare merit of thought and expression, and will reward the reader for the careful attention which they require."[26] In 1879 Thomas Wentworth Higginson reported in his *Short Studies of American Authors*: "When some one asked Emerson a few years since whether he did not think 'H.H.' the best woman-poet on this continent, he answered in his meditative way, 'Perhaps we might as well omit the *woman*.'"[27]

This was all heady encouragement for a poet who, not so long before, had been discussing Emerson with Moncure Conway as a "great master spirit" above interaction with the "'commonality' of people."[28] Emerson's admiration for her work did a great deal to bolster Jackson's confidence, making her feel that the pains she took with her writing were worth the effort. "Emerson carried a sonnet of mine in his pocket for a time and used to read it to people," she told Richard Henry Stoddard in 1871. "That was the first reward for which I really cared a great deal in the bottom of my heart."[29] She delighted in her association with Emerson, occasionally meeting him in the Boston area and sending friends to Concord with letters of introduction, and continuing always until his death in 1882 to express "love and veneration" for him.[30]

Emerson's influence is clearly discernible in Jackson's poetry, not so much stylistically—though William Dean Howells, for one, did claim to detect the rhythms of Emerson's poetry in hers[31]—as thematically, in her many poems that reveal her continuing attachment to Emersonian Transcendentalism. Because Transcendentalists viewed faith as an intuitive, creative experience, they greatly prized creative artists, in particular poets, whom they considered uniquely suited to serve as spiritual guides because of their special intuitive powers. A number of Jackson's poems feature Transcendentalist representations of the poet as priest. In "The Singer's Hills," first published in *Scribner's Monthly* in January 1874, the poet is a Christ figure whose powerful visions, a far cry from the "mere imaginations" once derided by Jackson's father, are in league with divine creation itself. At the heart of this long poem, Jackson's inspired "Singer" pleads with the workaday world, but his message is only slightly comprehended:

> "Ho! tarry! tarry ye!
> Behold those purple mountains in the sea!"
> The people saw no mountains!
> "He is mad,"
> They careless said, and went their way and had
> No further thought of him.
> And so, among
> His fellows' noisy, idle, crossing throng,
> The Singer walked, as strangers walk who speak
> A foreign tongue and have no friend to seek.
> And yet the silent joy which filled his face
> Sometimes their wonder stirred a little space,
> And following his constant seaward look,
> One wistful gaze they also seaward took.[32]

Moreover, Jackson expresses her affinity for Emersonian Transcendentalism in some of her nature poetry. From the beginning of her career, moved by her love and knowledge of the outdoors and her long-standing admiration for the English Romantic poets, especially William Wordsworth, she wrote a wide variety of poems on nature topics; many were rather facile works, intended for a

popular audience. Her poem "October's Bright Blue Weather," a simple celebration of bumblebees, goldenrod, grapes, gentians, chestnuts, apples, wood-
bine, thirsty springs, and the fact that Jackson herself was twice married in October, ends in a final quatrain that schoolchildren around the country could
recite well into the twentieth century:

> O suns and skies and flowers of June,
> Count all your boasts together,
> Love loveth best of all the year
> October's bright blue weather.[33]

Yet Jackson also wrote many Transcendentalist nature poems, pieces not so
much about nature itself as about the spiritual implications of nature. In works
such as "Cheyenne Mountain" and "Sonnet, To One Who Complained of a
Poet for Not Writing about Nature," she celebrates what she calls in the latter
poem her "reverent" connection with nature.[34] In other classically Transcendentalist poems she contemplates nature as a physical manifestation, or "sign,"
of God's will, a manifestation of spirit that parallels, and can serve to inspire,
the human spirit. Thus the opening quatrain of her "Locusts and Wild
Honey":

> O hospitable wilderness,
> I know thy secret sign
> All human welcome seemeth less
> To me than thine.[35]

The one poem by another author that Jackson cherished above all others
was William Winter's "Golden Silence," a Transcendentalist meditation on the
spiritual significance of nature. In this poem Winter declares that nature
"speaks, in forms that cannot die," everything that humans "know of bliss or
grief," for nature is a "sign" of the divine spirit. Winter's poem ends with a
quatrain that could almost do service in Jackson's own "Locusts and Wild
Honey":

> The mountain peaks that shine afar,
> The silent stars, the pathless sea,
> Are living signs of all we are,
> And types of all we hope to be.[36]

In 1884 Jackson wrote an admiring letter to Winter—not her first, she claimed.
"Your verse, 'The Golden Silence,' goes with me, wherever I go, & has been
pinned on so many looking glass frames that it is hardly legible now," she told
him.[37]

Jackson told Winter that she also greatly admired his more recent poem
"The Sceptre," a celebration of the power of the individual human spirit that
Jackson claimed to believe "the sweetest strongest rarest note which has been

struck by any singer, on that theme." She explained that the new poem had taken its place on her dressing mirror beside "The Golden Silence," where she intended to "read them both every morning, as long as I live."[38] In "The Sceptre," humanity rules over misfortune by the dignifying staff of willpower. Though "torn by rock and whelmed by wave," the human will transcends even death: "She rears above her ocean grave / And sinks with every standard set."[39] In responding to Jackson's 1884 letter, Winter reiterated his poem's sentiments as his own: "Little by little everything else crumbles: the will alone—patient and without hope or fear—remains firm."[40]

Jackson shared Winter's belief in the power of the individual will. She had long despised the Calvinist doctrine of predestination as offering inadequate scope to free will, especially because her own experience of managing to succeed despite misfortune had taught her to believe that although God's power and plan for humanity were supreme—the belief she celebrated in her many poems of submission—there was still much that the human will was free to accomplish.[41] In Transcendentalism she found a spirituality that gave precedence to the individual spirit and its power for self-assertion. Over the course of her career she wrote many poems in celebration of that power, one of them, "A Woman's Battle," very similar in its use of naval battle imagery to Winter's "Sceptre." In Jackson's poem, her narrator knows that a superior will, ambiguously evoked as belonging to either God or a lover, is destined to triumph in the end, but by her own considerable willpower she maintains her dignity: "thou'lt not dream that I am dying, / As I sail by with colors flying!"[42]

Occasionally, Jackson's poems in celebration of the individual human spirit are animated by her growing interest in regionalism, an interest most apparent in her prose but also discernible in her poetry and poetic taste. As early as the fall of 1871, she praised the California regionalist poet Joaquin Miller in letters to several of her friends, arguing that Miller, a writer of Transcendentalist leanings who depicted true manhood as best achievable in nature, was one of America's few "indigenous" poets.[43] In the mid-1870s she claimed to "love" the poetry of the New England regionalist Celia Thaxter, and she offered hyperbolic praise to Robert Dwyer Joyce's poem *Deirdre* (1876), declaring herself "most delighted and proud that New England has done it—and New England published it."[44] In 1880, during her second trip to Europe, she made a solitary three-day "pilgrimage" to the old Ayrshire haunts of the Scottish regionalist poet Robert Burns, where she formed a belief that the poet's "delicious, rollicking" verse had bound his spirit forever to "the soil" upon which he once lived.[45]

In a number of her own poems, Jackson emphasizes humanity's spiritual connection to the natural environment—as she does in her regionalist prose— in order to protest the negative consequences of the rapidly expanding industrialism of her era. The narrator of "My Tenants" asserts ownership over a beloved piece of land by right of love alone, though the land is legally claimed by others. In "A Ballad of the Gold Country," which Jackson wrote after her first trip to California, a tender horticulturist outlasts a mining boom that destroys the land and the fortunes of lesser men. The 1878 poem "Border Lands" makes a statement against various forms of hegemony by conflating the "blissful, shadowy realms" occupied by diverse border dwellers with the landscape of new love; it opens:

> Oh, good the air of border lands;
> Oh, dangerous dear their subtle spell;
> Where thralldoms stretch uncertain hands,
> And careless, happy outlaws dwell.[46]

And in "The Shoshone Oath," written after Jackson became an activist for Native American rights, the Shoshones' poetic recognition of humanity's spiritual connection to nature is offered as a blueprint for leading a more genuine life.[47]

Along with her large and varied body of poetry on spiritual themes, Jackson wrote a significant number of poems on women's topics. Because she disdained the sentimental tradition in women's poetry and sympathized with Higginson's belief that a female author should not concern herself with her gender but should simply try to do good work, she wished to elude any restrictive classification of herself as a female poet working within strictly female poetic traditions. (She particularly admired the poetry of several contemporary English women who had managed to escape such categorization: George Eliot, Elizabeth Barrett Browning, and Christina Rossetti.)[48] For the most part, in her own day, she succeeded. Reviewers applauded her for eschewing the "tears," "morbid ringing of hands," and "languid sweetness" typical of such sentimental poets as Felicia Hemans and Lydia Sigourney, and for demonstrating instead an almost "masculine" sensibility of "fresh, strong beauty," "deep and sustaining joy," and "strength and terseness of expression."[49] Nevertheless, Jackson's poetry does exhibit many of the attributes that critics and readers of her era expected to find in female poets, including the heightened spirituality and reverence for nature discussed above. And she wrote many poems in celebration of the affections and capabilities of women, both personal friends and figures from biblical, classical, and popular legend.

She especially liked to read and to write poems on one theme that has been of continual interest to American women poets: thwarted love. In 1867 she told her sister she thought John Weiss's "Some Lover's Clear Day," a highly conventional poem in which the narrator longs for his absent lover on a beautiful day, "one of the sweetest poems I ever read."[50] Some fifteen years later, upon the publication of a new biography of the Italian Renaissance poet Gaspara Stampa, she wrote for the *Critic* of November 19, 1881, what she considered a "eulogy" for Stampa and her work.[51] In this appreciation, it is clear that while Jackson esteemed Stampa as one of Italy's greatest poets—the author of a significant body of lyric poetry that includes some two hundred poems in Jackson's favorite form, the Italian sonnet—Gaspara Stampa is most prized for both personally embodying and expressing in her poems the theme of tragically thwarted love. Indeed, in her review Jackson so lavishly praises Stampa's capacity for enduring and memorializing difficult love—for creating an entire "climate" of love and poetry that she laments is "foreign" to Puritanical America— that the *Springfield Republican* ridiculed her effusiveness as "illimitable gush."[52] Of Jackson's own poetry on the theme of thwarted love, her sonnet "Ariadne's Farewell," one of her poems that Emerson most admired, can serve as an example:

> The daughter of a king, how should I know
> That there were tinsels wearing face of gold,
> And worthless glass, which in the sunlight's hold
> Could shameless answer back my diamond's glow
> With cheat of kindred fire? The currents slow,
> And deep, and strong, and stainless, which had rolled
> Through royal veins for ages, what had told
> To them, that hasty heat and lie could show
> As quick and warm a red as theirs?
>   Go free!
> The sun is breaking on the sea's blue shield
> Its golden lances; by their gleam I see
> Thy ship's white sails. Go free, if scorn can yield
> Thee freedom!
>   Then, alone, my love and I,—
> We both are royal; we know how to die.[53]

Jackson's Ariadne is triumphant even in misery because of the supreme dignity of her will. The same may be said of the heroines of most of Jackson's poems on the theme of thwarted love, including "The Story of Boon," a long narrative piece that concerns not only thwarted love but also a common variation on that theme, forbidden love. Published both in the *Independent* and as a Roberts Brothers book in 1874, "The Story of Boon" apotheosizes a Thai woman who so loves her faithless husband that she willingly becomes the slave of his new mistress, a member of the king's harem, and later endures torture until death by order of the jealous king without ever revealing her husband's identity. This poem is Jackson's version of an incident first told by her friend Anna Leonowens, a former governess at the royal court in Thailand and the author of a memoir, *The English Governess at the Siamese Court* (1870).[54] In "Boon" Jackson employs a strategy common to women's poetry, the reworking of legend—in this case an emerging popular legend—as a screen for less conventional subject matter. The poem is unusually sensual, inscribing erotic fantasies of the harem and even of sadomasochism, allusions that are only thinly veiled by the poem's Orientalist references to foreign customs.

Jackson was drawn to explorations of passion outside the usual bounds of marriage from the very start of her poetic career. As early as April 1866, she published "Tryst," which concludes with the following entreaty to an errant lover (also a metaphor for death):

> O lover, whose lips chilling
> So many lips have kissed,
> Come, even if unwilling,
> And keep thy solemn tryst![55]

In the very next month she published "A Burial Service," which is an ode not to lost loved ones but to lost love, tragically thwarted yet still pure enough to merit future satisfaction in heaven.[56] Because Jackson demanded a fairly high level of conventional moral propriety from other writers—she once condemned Ella Wheeler Wilcox's *Poems of Passion* (1883) for containing "a few poems so immoral in their idea & wording, that I wonder any publisher would publish them"[57]—her more erotic poems of forbidden love are rather surprising. They can perhaps only be accounted for as reflections of Jackson's own unresolved feelings for Higginson during her Newport years. Take, for example, "Three Kisses of Farewell," which Jackson published as part of her 1871 Saxe Holm story "Esther Wynn's Love-Letters," the tale of a woman poet in love with her married mentor. As the poem's first stanza indicates, "Three Kisses" is about three melancholy kisses the poet gives her lover while taking final leave of him:

> Three, only three my darling,
> Separate, solemn, slow;
> Not like the swift and joyous ones
> We used to know
> When we kissed because we loved each other
> Simply to taste love's sweet,
> And lavished our kisses as the summer
> Lavishes heat,—
> But as they kiss whose hearts are wrung
> When hope and fear are spent,
> And nothing is left to give, except
> A sacrament![58]

Similarly, in "Vintage" another wistful narrator reminds an encumbered lover of the "[w]ine sweeter than first wine" that she has many times given him, and pleads, "darest thou still drink / Wine stronger than seal can sign?"[59] Charlotte Cushman recognized Higginson as the subject of "Vintage." In December 1870, when the poem appeared anonymously in *Old and*

New, she wrote to Jackson: "I know all about it, dear, & whereon it is poured."[60] Higginson himself seems to have been led by their private relationship to express excessive praise for Jackson's more daring poems of thwarted love. In a *Century* article composed upon Jackson's death and later reprinted in *Contemporaries* (1899), he would argue that Jackson's "love poems" demonstrated "extraordinary intensity and imaginative fullness."[61] In one of his late *Harper's* essays collected in *Concerning All of Us* (1892), he cited with approval a recent article in the *Nation* that had singled out Jackson's "Vintage" and Saxe Holm's "Three Kisses of Farewell" as among the only instances in which "women have reached in poetry the white-heat of passion."[62] And he strongly recommended "Vintage" and "Three Kisses" as among his favorite Jackson writings in a late private letter to Edmund Clarence Stedman. "The *fire* of her life was in its middle portion," he cryptically explained.[63]

Aside from her poems of forbidden love, most of Jackson's poems on women's themes remain well within the narrower bounds of the morality on display in her large body of spiritual poetry. Indeed, until the end of her career she continued to write many simple domestic poems on subjects then common in mainstream women's poetry, including the death of children and secret sorrow. "Dost know Grief well? Hast known her long?" Jackson asks in the opening line of one of her better poems on secret sorrow, "Acquainted with Grief." She elaborates on her opening question through several succeeding quatrains, including the second:

> So long, that with unflinching eyes
> Thou smilest to thyself apart,
> To watch each flimsy, fresh disguise
> She plans to stab anew thy heart?

Because Jackson wrote "Acquainted with Grief" as she lay dying, at the end of a life filled with trials, her concluding, routine insistence that grief can be overcome by stoic cheerfulness takes on special poignancy in the eighth stanza:

> She to the gazing world must bear
> Our crown of triumph, if we bid;
> Loyal and mute, our colors wear,
> Sign of her own forever hid.[64]

Jackson's main aim in her domestic women's poems, as in her spiritual poems, was to offer inspiration and encouragement to her readers, usually by reminding them of God's presence or, as in "Acquainted with Grief," of their capacity to persevere amid misfortune by the power of individual will. After Jackson's death, Higginson commented in his *Century* essay on the "distinct moral purpose" of her simpler poems, describing the joy she had felt whenever she received word that her efforts to help her readers had been successful: "she read with insatiable pleasure the letters that often came to her from lonely women or anxious schoolgirls who had found help in her simple domestic or religious poems, while her depths of passion would only have frightened them, and they would have listened bewildered to those sonnets which Emerson carried in his pocket-book and pulled out to show his friends."[65]

As in her popular poetry, Jackson aimed in her many domestic essays to uplift her readers by encouraging them to make the best of fate. She directed most of the essays at mothers, focusing on the topics of child rearing and home improvement. In the mid–nineteenth century, essays on these topics were among the "staple genres" of middle-class literature.[66] Jackson's were somewhat different from those of many other authors, though, because they were not so much about the practical details of housekeeping as about the importance of creating a nurturing and stimulating atmosphere in the home. From her miserable early experience in Falmouth after the death of her mother, when her aunt Martha Hooker had often forced her to cook and clean instead of study, Jackson had learned to hate the mundane aspects of "housework," once claiming in an adult letter to her cousin Ann Scholfield that while she had "the *greatest* respect" for good housekeeping "*at a distance,*" she found it mentally and physically exhausting; she declared that she would never "do again of my own free will & cheerfully one single one of the things she made me do in those two years!"[67] Instead, she left cooking and cleaning to servants, and devoted herself, and her domestic essays, to promoting those aspects of home life that she had found wanting in Falmouth— especially emotional warmth, aesthetic pleasure, and respect for the wishes and needs of children.

Writing under what was becoming her standard signature, "H.H.," Jackson began to publish advice articles in the periodical press, mostly the *Independent,* in 1867. In 1873 she published *Bits of Talk about Home Matters,* a collection of forty essays, many of them previously printed in the *Independent,* on the creation of home atmosphere and, more broadly, the establishment of harmonious human relations. Her essays on the latter topic, which never ceased to engage her energies in one form or another, range widely in their particular subjects, from pieces condemning gossip and the invasion of other people's privacy, such as "Glass Houses" and "Hysteria in Literature," to such exhortations as "The King's Friend," in which Jackson reminds readers to be kind to strangers, since their true merits may not be visible to casual observation.

Her essays on the creation of home atmosphere seek above all to defend the rights of children. She had first written on children's rights in the very year she began to dispense domestic advice, when, in a pseudonymous, pseudo-travel essay for the *New York Evening Post,* "A Visit to Borioboola Gha: The School

System There," she reported on a visit to a rural school where she had encountered two bright boys who appeared well on their way to dying of consumption. Horrified, she insisted that children everywhere should be allowed to spend less time in school and more in outdoor exercise: "until then we shall go on reading and piously lamenting that more than two-fifths of all the children born die before they are twelve years old."[68] In *Bits of Talk about Home Matters,* she makes the same argument in "Children in Nova Scotia" and "The Reign of Archelaus," in the latter article citing evidence from an earlier study by Thomas Wentworth Higginson.[69] In another essay in the collection, "The Republic of the Family," she promotes the rights of older unmarried daughters living at home, holding that they should be given greater freedom to direct their own lives than they usually are. And in the three essays that open the volume, all under the main title "The Inhumanities of Parents," she argues that young children deserve more respect from adults.

In two of these opening essays, Jackson draws directly on her own experiences as a child, though she usually avoided explicit autobiography. In one subtitled "Rudeness," she criticizes her father, as I noted earlier, for calling her a "stupid child" when she once brought the wrong book from his study. In contrast, she praises her "wise and tender mother" for teaching her, gently and through playacting, that she herself must not commit the "rudeness" of staring at strangers.[70] In another "Inhumanities of Parents" essay, subtitled "Corporal Punishment," she argues forcibly against the physical chastisement of children, a stance that was progressive for her time. When Jackson submitted the article to the *Independent* in 1871, William Ward refused to print it, as he disagreed with its premise. His rejection prompted Jackson to explain: "I myself was whipped; not immoderately—not half so often as I deserved *punishing* in some way—but I never lacked anything but the *power* to *kill* every human being that struck me. I had as keen a sense of the outrage of a blow, at ten, as I have at forty!"[71]

Bits of Talk about Home Matters received positive reviews upon its publication in 1873, with *Publishers Weekly* hailing it as an "excellent volume" marked by "graceful diction and poetic expression" and the *Boston Post* praising Jackson as the most "agreeable of essayists," her book filled with "practical good sense." The first edition sold out in only a few days.[72] Encouraged by this success, Jackson continued to write at least one domestic essay every year, even as she became increasingly busy with travel work and then fiction. In 1875 she published four domestic essays. In "Negative Selfishness," which ran in the *Independent* on February 11, 1875, she contends that the failure to give pleasure to others whenever an opportunity presents itself is selfish and wrong, and that "family life" would be much improved if every member would make an "active effort each day to give positive and distinct happiness to each other member." In "Fretting," published three months later in the *Independent* of

May 6, she claims that habitual worrying and complaining can destroy home life as surely as alcoholism does, and expounds the same duty of constant cheerfulness that she had early learned from her own father and other teachers. Fretting "is a sin," she says, because it constitutes "ingratitude to God," "unkindness and cruelty to our fellows," and simple foolishness. In making this last point, she draws on the science of evolution, thereby distinguishing herself from her early teachers: "Bigger if not better creatures have come and gone ahead of us, and bigger and better may be yet to come, who will study our inexplicable skeletons with as scientific and quenchless an interest as we study fossils to-day. We are not of the least consequence. It is a folly to fret."

Over the years Jackson took a growing interest in writing domestic essays designed for children themselves, just as she would also devote increasing attention to children's poetry, travel literature, and fiction. She published her children's work mostly in the juvenile section of the *Independent,* in the agricultural and literary miscellany *Hearth and Home,* and in several children's journals; these included the influential *St. Nicholas,* which was edited beginning in 1873 by a good friend of Jackson's from her Newport years, the New York writer and editor Mary Mapes Dodge ("Lizzie"). In 1876 Roberts Brothers brought out *Bits of Talk in Verse and Prose for Young Folks,* a collection of twenty-six pieces of Jackson's children's writing, many of them previously published. The domestic essays included in this volume concern topics Jackson also addressed in her adult compositions, such as "Cheery People" and "The Expression of Rooms." The latter essay offered suggestions on how to adorn rooms with flowers and plants, colored pieces of fabric, books, pictures, and fans, just as Jackson herself, who had a real passion for home décor, always outfitted each of her own lodgings. Jackson's ultimate goal in her children's essays, as in her adult domestic essays, was to uplift her readers. Thus, shortly before *Bits of Talk in Verse and Prose for Young Folks* was released, she explained to William Ward that she had long considered the writing of didactic essays for children a "field" in which she might be able to "do good," for she believed it "well to preach a little to the children," so long as one could "make the sermons jolly."[73]

After Jackson took up the cause of Native American rights in 1879 she lost some of her enthusiasm for domestic essays, as the moral energy that sustained her work in this field became absorbed in her new crusade. Still, she had time for simpler children's work, including, in the fall of 1880, the didactic piece "The Naughtiest Day of My Life, and What Came of It," her autobiographical account of her youthful flight from home with Mary Snell. In this essay Jackson explains that for a long time nothing could make her feel contrite over her transgression—neither seeing her father "lying on the sofa, utterly exhausted from anxiety and fatigue" at the end of her mischievous day, nor later being lectured, whipped, and shut up in the garret by him. (On that occasion, she simply entertained herself by poking holes through the plaster of the floor.) Only when her mother gave her an immense sewing project, telling her that she must work to repay the costs of a carriage that had been hired to search for her, was she gradually forced to realize her wrongdoing. As an adult, she believed that this slow, deliberate punishment had been "one of the very best things that ever happened to me."[74] She offered it as a lesson to her young readers, and an example to their parents.

In 1881 Jackson published several adult domestic essays in the *Christian Union,* which she then gathered in *The Training of Children* (1882), a short collection of four pieces. In these essays, Jackson's aim is to make parents more aware of their behavior, on the grounds that their actions will inevitably mold the moral character of their children. Thus, in "Occupation for Children," she urges mothers not to keep their children continually occupied, but rather to allow them to learn to entertain themselves; the result would be that instead of growing into adults "without individuality of purpose, without specialty of interest or aim, or even appreciation of interests and aims," they would develop a healthy enthusiasm for life, joining "the thinkers, and doers, and enjoyers of this world."[75] In "A Victory of Love," she recounts the story of a worthy mother who spends several inactive days in the nursery with her son, never leaving the room nor allowing her child to leave, as she waits patiently for him to pick up some papers he has scattered on the floor. When she finally begins to weep in frustration at her son's intransigence, he hurries to do his chore. Jackson uses this story to illustrate how to counter "willfulness" in a child without attempting to do what in her opinion must never be attempted: to break the child's "will." She had told similar tales to the same purpose several times before: in "The Naughtiest Day"; in "Breaking the Will," a *Home Matters* essay; and in "The First Time," published in *St. Nicholas* in May 1877.

In April 1884, shortly after finishing her novel *Ramona,* Jackson began making plans for another collection of domestic essays, to be called "Ethics of Home." When she offered the first serial rights of her six projected essays to the *Independent,* she told William Ward that the pieces would highlight what she considered "the four cardinal points of family happiness": "freedom" of "individual action," "system & punctuality," "habitual experience of goodwill affection etc.," and, of course, "cheerfulness."[76] As it happened, however, illness prevented her from realizing her plans. That December, fatally ill in California, she could offer no new pieces of domestic advice to some young friends who were about to be married, sending them instead a copy of her first collection. She explained, "In my *Bits of Talk on Home Matters* you will find the sum and substance of my notions about a home and about children. They will seem cranky to you, I dare say, but by the time you're as old as I am you'll be nearer my way of thinking."[77]

The "cranky," or traditional, ideas about domesticity that Jackson's early collection advocates, and that this letter from the end of her life indicates she never ceased to espouse, concern the role of women in the home. (In contrast, her opinions on child rearing were quite progressive.) Jackson expresses her feelings about women's home duties most directly in "Wanted: A Home," the concluding essay of *Bits of Talk about Home Matters* and the one that she always claimed to care most about. In this piece, Jackson works to refute the "evil fashion of speech which says it is a narrowing and narrow life that a woman leads who cares only, works only for her husband and children; that a higher, more imperative thing is that she herself be developed to the utmost." Instead, Jackson says, while a woman should certainly work to develop herself, she will find ample need for all the fruits of her development within her own home. It is "the true mission of women," she says, to make homes good places: "a woman who creates and sustains a home, and under whose hands children grow up to be strong and pure men and women, is a creator, second only to God." As such, the successful homemaker must be as "single-aimed" as any creative artist: "Never will the painter, sculptor, writer lose sight of his art. Even in the intervals of rest and diversion which are necessary to his health and growth, every thing he sees ministers to his passion. Consciously or unconsciously, he makes each shape, color, incident his own; sooner or later it will enter into his work. . . . So it must be with the woman who will create a home."[78]

In likening the single-minded obsession of the creative homemaker to that of the professional artist, Jackson ends by rendering these two callings mutually exclusive—a paradox, given that her own knowledge of the artist's obsession is based on her work as a writer, not a homemaker. The traditionalism of her statements on women's domestic duties is also highly paradoxical, as is the fact that she continued throughout her high-profile career to put such "very earnest and serious work," as she once described her efforts,[79] into domestic essays about the home and children. After all, her own children had both died before the age of ten, and in her adult life she herself had no permanent home until she was forty-five years old. Moreover, though she had become a writer only after she lost her family, and had been devoted to her husband and children while they lived, we have seen that even when she was a mother, she had longed to do something literary: "We can't *talk* with our babies," she complained to Anne Botta in 1855, "& although they do awaken such a new world in both heart & soul—there is another world, quite important & very interesting, from which we don't want to be *banished,* & to which babies *are no key!*"[80] When she did begin to write, her dedication to her career was at a level that could scarcely be maintained by a woman writing only for lack of better domestic occupation. After she remarried, she remained intensely absorbed in her work and travels, never limiting herself to the role of homemaker represented in her domestic essays.

To a certain extent, literary tradition and Jackson's conception of the audience for her domestic essays led her to preach in her domestic essays a mode of life that she herself transgressed. Those essays were part of a vast body of nineteenth-century literature on homemaking and child rearing, all of which advocated the home as woman's sphere. Her mother had read such books when raising her children; an 1831 edition of François Fénelon's *Treatise on the Education of Daughters* was in her library in 1832, two years after Jackson was born. Some of Jackson's own early acquaintances had made well-known contributions to the genre in America; for example, John Abbott had written *The School-girl,* and Heman Humphrey, the president of Amherst College, had advanced in many of his writings a rather bleak understanding of the home as a rigid patriarchy. In the years prior to Jackson's publication of *Home Matters,* women authors began to achieve prominence in the field. Catharine Beecher secured fame as a domestic authority with her 1869 *American Woman's Home,* a work that set forth many of the opinions soon to become central to Jackson's vision, including the notion that cheerfulness was of prime importance to home life. While Beecher and other midcentury authors stressed the importance and dignity of woman's role in the home, they nonetheless took for granted that home was the place for women; and the audience Jackson envisioned for her own domestic essays would have expected her to do the same. Her target audience for these essays was not the highly educated, limited group she hoped to address with her more intellectual poems, but rather the same broad audience of women who appreciated her simpler poetry. When *Bits of Talk about Home Matters* was published, she explained to two editor friends that the book was priced at only one dollar because she wished it to "go into the homes of the common people," to "the plain families where it will do good."[81]

Jackson no doubt expected most of her "common" women readers to be working in the home or perhaps on the home farm, uninterested in or incapable of attaining the sort of worldly success she had achieved. While their life path was not her own, she felt no qualms in proffering advice, for she was by nature outspoken in her opinions (privately, she often criticized her own sister's handling of family affairs rather sharply). In her desire to help unknown women through her writing, she set herself apart from them—above them—as one of the people whom she calls the "wise" in *Home Matters,* people who have a duty to offer "counsel" to those living in "ignorance."[82] She herself was able to combine domesticity and career after she remarried, taking great pains with the furnishings and decoration of her new home, and even managing such difficult feats as to appear the perfect domestic hostess in the midst of a workday: according to the journalist Alice Wellington Rollins, Jackson was careful when she had visitors to accomplish all of her writing "early in the day in the solitude of the lady's own chamber," so that she could later "emerge" simply as "the perfect housekeeper, the friend eager to hear what *you* are writing or doing."[83] Yet Jackson believed that few were capable of this sort of balancing act. Once, in offering congratulations upon a happy personal occasion to Kate Douglas Wiggin, a prominent educator and writer who would later publish *Rebecca of Sunnybrook Farm* (1903), she acknowledged, "You have a vista before you for work and happiness both—and that is not given to many women."[84] To the women she addressed in her domestic essays, she advised a more exclusive attention to home life. Despite her moral earnestness, she was comfortable with the idea that what one suggested in one's writings was not always exactly what one did in one's own life. As early as 1868, she had written convivially to Kate Field, "It was a good joke to think of you fleeing for your life from the Appledore, just after having chronicled it in the *Transcript*, as such a comfortable abode.—Which was true?—What you did, or what you said?"[85]

While literary custom and Jackson's conception of her audience were partly responsible for the more traditional opinions on women's duties that she expresses in her domestic essays, it was equally important that she actually held a number of traditional beliefs about what was best for women. Like most people, Jackson had complex, contradictory attitudes about the very things she cared most about. Though she was a professional of notable dedication, finding the greatest satisfactions of her life in her writing, she nonetheless looked back on her own time of motherhood as a period of ultimate happiness, never to be repeated. In 1869, after four years of professional writing, she could therefore admit to an acquaintance, "I myself never took an upward step, till I left happiness behind me," but still add, wistfully, "To be wife and mother is the best God has to give any woman."[86] She also still considered her own literary pursuits "very selfish" in comparison with the "hard burden of actual work" undertaken by her housewife sister.[87] And though she would devote a portion of her own income to seeing her sister's daughters through Vassar College, she later reversed her opinion on the new women's colleges when her niece Helen suffered a nervous breakdown. "Give a woman a good strong healthy body, to be a wife & mother, & bring forth healthy strong children—& you have done not only more for *her,* but more for the world, than if you give her all the languages, sciences, &c on the Vassar programme," she wrote to Ann.[88] As its very title would suggest, "Wanted: A Home"—written when she was still a wandering widow, before she had remarried—is predicated on her own longing for her lost, beloved husband and sons. And she was speaking of herself when she wrote of Mercy Philbrick, "The one grief above which she could not wholly rise, which at times smote her and bowed her down, was her sense of her loss in being childless."[89]

Like many women writers of her time, Jackson had conflicted feelings about her public identity, for public professions were widely considered of dubious propriety for women. She accepted many of the limitations of the "woman's sphere" as it was then conceived because she wished to be, and to appear, feminine and moral. She could feel more comfortable living as a dedicated professional if she discharged the traditional duty of maternity in her domestic essays. There, she could argue with the authority of her own yearning loss that "she is only half mother who does not see her own child in every child!—her own child's grief in every pain which makes another child weep!"[90] She could even stretch the truth, ignoring the fact that she actually experienced a wide variety of exuberant, original responses to life, in order to claim that "all things I see in life seem to me to have a voice either for or of children."[91]

Jackson's wish to maintain traditional feminine propriety, combined with her desire for personal privacy, accounted for her refusal to attach her own full name to her work until the very end of her life. After her early use of "Marah" and "Rip Van Winkle," she began to sign her poetry and nonfiction as "H.H." When editors asked her to use her entire name—or, like James T. Fields of the *Atlantic,* used her name without her permission—she insisted that she had a great "dislike" of seeing her full name in print and intended always to use only her initials, as a "shelter" from "publicity."[92] She never wavered in her efforts to avoid commercial exploitation of her private life, even though the public soon learned to recognize her initials as the signature of the person named Helen Hunt, and later Helen Jackson, and even though she herself worked to garner public attention for the work that appeared beneath her signature: as early as 1868, she told Horace Scudder that despite having come to dislike her own initials, ever since he had jokingly called her the "double aspirate," she would continue to use the signature because it had already garnered a "market value."[93] By writing under pseudonyms, Jackson was able to feel that she was personally separate from the very market she tried throughout her career to manipulate. Furthermore, she was able to distance herself from the feminist implications of being a public figure. Thus one late acquaintance claimed that Jackson "not only separated her individuality from her literary productions, but she even tried to ignore her instrumentality."[94]

Jackson's desire to separate her private, feminine self from her public persona and the outside world made itself felt in several other areas of her life as well. She always insisted that her correspondents, whether business associates or the closest of friends, follow the traditional custom of addressing envelopes to her in the name of her husband: she was first "Mrs. Edward B. Hunt," then "Mrs. William S. Jackson.[95] Whenever publishers were determined to make personal reference to her, she liked them to make it clear that she was not a spinster career woman.[96] And she refused ever to speak in public or to take part in any kind of public performance, even though general opposition to women on the platform had waned by the time of her career, and even though Higginson himself specifically urged women to give public lectures. In 1873 Jackson turned down an invitation to speak before the feminist New England Woman's

Club on subjects covered in *Bits of Talk about Home Matters,* claiming that she lacked the "courage" for public speaking, and adding:

> You would no doubt quite despise me if you had the least idea, how foreign to my instincts and tastes, such a thing would be.
>
> It is often almost more than I can bear the slight publicity which I have brought upon myself by saying—behind the shelter of initials, and in the crowded obscurity of print—a few of the things I have felt deeply.[97]

Given her traditional feelings about feminine propriety, it is hardly surprising that Jackson did not support the women's rights movement of her day. Indeed, not long before she turned down the Woman's Club's invitation to speak, she had told an editor friend that she intended *Bits of Talk about Home Matters* to represent "views of life which are incompatible with the 'Womans [sic] Rights Movement,' " and that her essay "Wanted: A Home," in particular, was her "protest against the Womans Rights people."[98] It was not that she believed women less intellectually capable than men: "Nobody sees the flimsy injustice of half the arguments against Woman's Suffrage &c, more clearly than I do, who hate and oppose it with all my soul," she insisted privately.[99] She often expressed hyperbolic enthusiasm for the intellects of her own female friends. Mary Mapes Dodge, for instance, so impressed Jackson with her children's writing and competent editorship of the children's magazine *St. Nicholas* that Jackson once declared her "the cleverest woman alive in America today."[100] Nor was Jackson opposed to women working for pay. She and almost all of her female friends worked, and she always wrote about working women with the utmost enthusiasm and respect. Rather, she believed that women had a special role to play in the family. This belief, together with the importance that she placed on submission and the individual human will, meant that until she finally joined the struggle for Indian rights, she considered it folly for women to join any organized, collective movement. If women wanted to better society, she believed they should confine their efforts to their own homes. "Home and private life," and "good just, loving, clear headed well educated mothers," she explained in rejecting the Woman's Club's invitation, together constituted "the one sublime point, from which the lever rightly poised, can move the whole world."[101]

Most of Jackson's countrywomen shared her negative opinions of the women's rights movement. Still, she took her opposition further than many, not only by offering "incompatible" views of life in *Bits of Talk about Home Matters* but also, in the years before publishing that volume, by writing several newspaper editorials in which she expressed her objection to particular members of the movement and its prime goal of women's suffrage. On May 30, 1870, she published her anonymous "Good-by, Leather Stockings!" in the *New York Tribune,* a piece that she intended as a "covert satire" on Elizabeth Cady Stanton and Susan B. Anthony[102]—the activists who led the more radical, New

York branch of the women's rights movement, which Jackson particularly disliked. In July of 1870 she published another critique: "American Women," contributed by "An American Woman." After being rejected elsewhere, it appeared in a popular New York newspaper, the *World*. "The woman of 1870 is about fourteen years old, goes to town school, and just now thinks she likes sliding down hill with the boys better than anything else," Jackson laments in this piece. "But she will outgrow all that; speak in a lower voice and be, ah, so beautiful at twenty-five!"[103] In 1871 she submitted an anti-suffragist essay for anonymous publication in the *Tribune*, but it was rejected. In response, she explained to the managing editor, Whitelaw Reid, how ardently she longed to "have at" the movement for suffrage; only the fact that some of her closest friends were "devoted to the Woman Suffrage cause" had been keeping her relatively silent. (Among Jackson's pro-suffrage friends were Higginson, her other activist male literary associates, and possibly also a few women friends, like Jeanne Carr, whom Jackson had first met among the wives at the 1855 meeting of the American Association for the Advancement of Science.) Perhaps, Jackson suggested to Reid, she could in the future contribute some "letters from a *country spinster* on the subject."[104] Whether she ever did so is unknown. In later years, she openly expressed her anti-suffrage opinions on at least one occasion, when she referred to herself, in an 1879 "H.H." *Atlantic Monthly* travel essay, as "not being a suffragist."[105]

Jackson thought of herself as an individual agent, as a writer and an artist. As such, she made her own way through a male-dominated publishing world, on its terms; like other female regionalists, she sought, and was granted, critical prestige in that male world. Apparently, because she managed to succeed in her chosen profession of writing, which was relatively open to women, she gave little thought to the legal prescriptions that prevented other women from exercising equally worthy talents. Expressing sentiments that were also Jackson's own, the novelist Elizabeth Stoddard once told Jackson that she considered the work of the "women's righters" "humiliating to our sex." She explained, "*I* can do all that is necessary in this world provided I have original power enough, and if I have not, of what use is it to attempt to bolster up imbecility?" Similarly, Jackson's friend Martha Goddard, a literary reviewer for the *Boston Daily Advertiser*, wrote to her, "I do think it would be a good plan for women to use the opportunities they have, before they make such a turmoil."[106]

While Jackson opposed the movement for women's rights, she always devoted a good deal of energy to promoting the career achievements of individual women. In doing so, she furthered the interests of women even as she explicitly denied any desire for change in their traditional social roles. In fact, as long as she found sufficient evidence of an attitude of Christian submission in a particular woman, she was open to supporting activities that were quite unconventional.[107] Her belief that Charlotte Cushman's "heart was as big as her head" allowed her to accept her friend's openly unconventional romances and famously masculine stage performances.[108] Similarly, her belief that Anna Leonowens, on whose observations in Thailand she had based her poem "Boon," was not only an "absolutely poor" widow working to support two children but also "warmhearted & lovable" and "charming and winning," led her to set aside her usual opposition to women's public speaking and help Leonowens organize a lecture tour in 1872.[109] She asked editor friends to publicize the tour in their newspapers, and set up and sold tickets to a Newport event. Two years later, the "gentle womanliness" and eloquence of one Mrs. Wilkes, who served for a short period as Unitarian minister in Colorado Springs, not only "softened" Jackson's usual "prejudices" against "womens preaching," as she admitted, but made her "want to help her," and she wrote to several publishers to solicit books for Wilkes's Sunday school.[110]

She even expressed support for the work of two notable women's rights activists with whom she had friendly personal dealings. After the suffragist Caroline Dall sent her the first of several pieces of fan mail in 1873, Jackson went so far as to compliment Dall on her own work. She continued to maintain cordial contact with Dall for a decade. She also offered some now unknown measure of support to Lucy Stone, head of the less radical, New England branch of the women's rights movement, whose suffragist *Woman's Journal* had favorably reviewed Jackson's work. According to Higginson, Jackson was first led to feel kindly toward Stone during her Newport years, when he took her to hear Stone speak at a woman's suffrage convention in New York. Though Jackson had contracted to write "a satirical report" on the convention, she gave up the assignment upon hearing Stone's "sweet voice." Years later, according to Higginson, Jackson even "hospitably entertained" Stone at her house in Colorado.[111]

Jackson was always particularly enamored of highly individualistic, intellectual women writers. She admired not only the famous women poets mentioned earlier, and many American women regionalists, as I will discuss later, but also the international feminist literary celebrities Harriet Martineau, Madame de Staël, and George Sand. Throughout her career, even though her own literary mentors were male, she considered it a duty to give special attention to the work of female authors. She sent brief congratulations when she came upon pieces that she especially admired by established women—"God bless you!" she exclaimed in a brief note of praise to Abby Morton Diaz[112]— and she wrote lengthy letters of encouragement to promising novices. "I want to tell you how much I like your little poem in the last Scribner," she wrote in 1882 to the fledgling poet Elizabeth Hutchinson. "I don't believe you will think it gratuitous in me to write & tell you this: for I know how it always does me good when anybody takes the trouble to tell me that something I have written has given him pleasure." Explaining that she took an "almost yearning interest" in "all the young singers who promise to take the next half century's places," she said it was always an especially "great pleasure to see any woman doing persistent, consistent praiseworthy work."[113]

She often exerted herself to find publishers for amateur women writers whom she considered gifted or capable of wide popularity. (Oddly enough, she usually advised these women to print under their own full names.) Among them, two went on to establish highly successful professional careers: her friend Sarah Woolsey, as discussed earlier, and the poet Edith M. Thomas. After Anne Botta convinced Jackson to read Edith Thomas's homespun scrapbook of poems in the winter of 1880–81, Jackson was so impressed that she recommended Thomas to *Scribner's Monthly,* the *Atlantic,* and Roberts Brothers. She never ceased to praise and to promote Thomas as her career blossomed, as Thomas appreciated immensely. Most important among the many amateur writers whom Jackson tried to help find publishers was Emily Dickinson. Of course, Dickinson mostly resisted those efforts. Though Dickinson knew some of the same prominent literary and publishing figures as Jackson, including Higginson, Josiah Holland, and Samuel Bowles, only ten of her poems are known to have been published during her lifetime—and those anonymously, not at her own request, and in many cases probably without her prior knowledge or consent.[114] Still, Jackson was the only person of letters to offer unstinting praise for Dickinson's poetry as she wrote it, and this enthusiasm meant a great deal to Dickinson.[115]

The two poets had known each other during their childhoods in Amherst, though their exact relationship is unclear. They were born within a few weeks of each other, their families were on friendly terms, and Helen's sister Ann played with Emily's sister Lavinia.[116] After Helen lost her family home, she and Henry Root frequently wrote to each other about the Dickinson children and other mutual Amherst acquaintances. For a time, Henry admired Sue Gilbert, who later married Emily's brother Austin: after an initial period of fondness for Sue, Helen came to dislike both members of this couple, and Austin, in turn, was not impressed with Edward Hunt. In 1854, when the Hunts were living in Washington, D.C., and Emily's father, Edward, had recently been elected to the House of Representatives, they invited Edward to spend an evening with them. Helen was not eager to take responsibility for entertaining Lavinia when she visited her father that same year, however: she admitted to Henry that she thought Vinnie "such a fat little country lassie!"[117] And the following year she somewhat guiltily refrained from calling on the Dickinson girls when both were in town with their father. The extant correspondence between Helen and Emily dates only from the period of Helen's second marriage, though it is known that they visited together in their adult lives at least as early as 1860, when Helen and Edward Hunt made a trip to Amherst. On that occasion, after the Hunts sat with the Dickinson family at church, they attended a reception at the Dickinson home; there, according to Higginson, Hunt made such an impression on Emily by his epigrammatic mode of speech that ten years later she claimed he had "interested her more than any man she ever saw." (According to Higginson, Hunt told Dickinson that her begging dog, who apparently was hoping that some scraps from the reception might fall, "understood gravitation"; and he made the promise that he would visit her again "in a year. If I say a shorter time it will be longer.")[118] Not long after 1866, when Higginson was advising both Jackson and Dickinson on their careers, he made them aware of each other's poetry. During the next few years they began a correspondence based on mutual admiration and support, which they continued sporadically until Jackson's death.[119]

Dickinson read Jackson's *Travel at Home, Verses,* and *Ramona,* praising the latter two works in her letters to Jackson and to mutual acquaintances. In 1871, for instance, she wrote to Higginson, "Mrs. Hunt's Poems are stronger than any written by Woman since Mrs.—Browning, with the exception of Mrs. Lewes."[120] She came to feel such strength of affection for Jackson that when Jackson died, she wrote with "fervor" to Higginson of her "love" for Jackson, and exclaimed to another friend, "Oh had that Keats a Severn!"[121] "[O]ne Day more I am deified, was the only impression she ever left on any Heart (House) she entered," she noted in a draft of a letter to the bereaved William Jackson.[122] The last two pieces of Dickinson's poetry for which the approximate dates of composition are known, April 1886, were enclosed in a letter to Higginson as homages to Jackson, one beginning "The Immortality she gave / We borrowed at her Grave," and the other, "Of Glory not a Beam is left / But her Eternal House."[123]

Because Jackson was during the time of her correspondence with Dickinson one of America's most famous poets, while her friend's poetry was very little known, their relationship was for the most part predicated on Jackson's eagerness to support Dickinson. Remarkably, Jackson was able not only to accept but even to relish the moral and aesthetic daring of Dickinson's innovative work, for she probably saw Dickinson as enacting the virtues of submission in many aspects of her life, if not her art, and she sympathized with Dickinson's poetic rebellion against a rigidly orthodox Calvinist upbringing, tied to Amherst College. Samuel Fowler Dickinson, Dickinson's grandfather, was a founder; her father, Edward, was a lawyer who served as the college's treasurer beginning in 1835. (Her brother Austin was to hold the same post from 1873 until his death in 1895.)

Dickinson sent Jackson a number of poems with her letters, and Higginson shared others, so that by 1876 Jackson had put together a manuscript volume of her friend's work. She often read the poems, and alluded to them positively in letters to Higginson and especially to Dickinson herself.[124] "You are a great poet," she wrote to Dickinson on March 20, 1876; and wishing to encourage her friend through enthusiastic patronage, much as Charlotte Cushman had once encouraged her, she asked Dickinson to "write to me now and then, when it did not bore you." She also began to urge Dickinson to publish, no doubt believing that Dickinson would receive stimulus from the recognition that accompanied publication, as she herself always had. In her efforts to overcome Dickinson's reluctance, she used the same reasoning by which she had conquered her own anxieties about publication—that it could serve to uplift people. "It is a wrong to the day you live in, that you will not sing aloud," she told Dickinson. "When you are what men call dead, you will be sorry you were so stingy."[125]

In particular, Jackson wished Dickinson to join her in making an anonymous contribution to *A Masque of Poets,* a volume of poems by seventy-five American and British authors to be published without attribution as an 1878 installment in Roberts Brothers' "No Name" series.[126] She wrote to Dickinson on the subject on August 20, 1876. She then attempted to persuade her in person on October 10, during a visit to Amherst. Dickinson reported their conversation of that day to Higginson:

> I told her I was unwilling, and she asked me why?—I said I was incapable and she seemed not to believe me and asked me not to decide for a few Days—meantime, she would write me—She was so sweetly noble, I would regret to estrange her, and if you would be willing to give me a note saying you disapproved it, and thought me unfit, she would believe you.[127]

When Jackson wrote to Dickinson as promised, she did continue to promote the Roberts Brothers volume: "You say you find great pleasure in reading my verses," she told her friend. "Let somebody somewhere whom you do not know have the same pleasure in reading yours." But she also made a point of asking to be forgiven if she had seemed too forward and meddlesome during her visit:

> I feel as if I had been very impertinent that day in speaking to you as I did,—accusing you of living away from the sunlight—and telling you that you looked ill . . . but really you looked so white and moth-like! Your hand felt like such a wisp in mine that you frightened me. I felt like a great ox talking to a white moth, and begging it to come and eat grass with me to see if it could not turn itself into beef! How stupid.[128]

Jackson took a break from her efforts to persuade Dickinson to publish. Then a year and a half later, on April 29, 1878, she revived the topic of the *Masque of Poets,* assuring Dickinson that she would copy any poem Dickinson agreed to contribute in her own handwriting, "and promise never to tell any one, not even the publishers," whose it was. ("I think you would have much amusement in seeing to whom the critics, those shrewd guessers would ascribe your verses," she told Dickinson.)[129] In October, during another autumnal visit to Amherst, Jackson called on Dickinson once again, this time accompanied by her second husband. It was a meeting Dickinson claimed to find "lovely" and "sweet."[130] "Now—will you send me the poem?" Jackson wrote to her afterward. As an alternative, she suggested that Dickinson allow her to send in a copy of Dickinson's poem "Success," which she knew by heart. "If you will, it will give me a great pleasure," Jackson said. "I ask it as a personal favor to myself—Can you refuse the only thing I perhaps shall ever ask at your hands?"[131]

Apparently, Dickinson could not refuse, for in December, Jackson wrote to her: "I suppose by this time you have seen the *Masque of Poets*. I hope you have not regretted giving me that choice bit of verse for it."[132] About the same time, Jackson wrote an anonymous review of the *Masque of Poets* for the Denver *Tribune*, in which she reprinted "Success," singling it out as "undoubtedly one of the strongest and finest wrought things in the book." She also explained that "all conjecture" over its authorship would be "wasted," as this information would "never be known to the public."[133]

During the following years, Jackson continued to encourage Dickinson to keep "at work" and to publish.[134] "What portfolios full of verses you must have," she wrote to her in late 1884, asking to be designated Dickinson's literary executor if she should outlive her, so that she could finally publish Dickinson's poetry. (In fact, Dickinson would outlive Jackson, though only by a matter of months.) Again, Jackson argued that publishing poems was a way of doing moral good. "It is a cruel wrong to your 'day & generation' that you will not give them light," she said. "I do not think we have a right to withhold from the world a word or a thought any more than a *deed,* which might help a single soul."[135]

Jackson's assumption that Dickinson, like herself, must at some deep level be impelled to "help" other people allowed her a vantage from which to appreciate Dickinson's powerfully unconventional art at a time when few might have—a notable act of sympathy, even if a rather myopic one. A similar sort of circumscribed yet nonetheless meaningful sympathy would motivate her travel essays. For as she moved about from place to place in her endless quest to find some "elixir" in the air, a "climate where throats *can't* ulcerate" and where her sorrows might disappear,[136] her habit of perceiving many of the people she encountered as cheerfully and diligently struggling, as she was, to persevere in the midst of difficulty, allowed her to identify with individuals who were otherwise quite different from herself.

"Eminent Women" composite photograph, 1886. Jackson is prominently featured at the center of this collage, an indication of her stature in her own time. Courtesy Schlesinger Library, Radcliffe Institute, Harvard University.

Helen Maria Fiske, ca. 1840s. Courtesy Special Collections, Tutt Library, Colorado College, Colorado Springs, Colorado.

The Fiske family home at 249 South Pleasant Street in Amherst, Massachusetts, ca. 1970s. Photo by Evelyn I. Banning, courtesy Special Collections, Tutt Library, Colorado College, Colorado Springs, Colorado.

Nathan Welby Fiske, Helen's father, ca. 1846, the year before he died. "I did almost worship my father," Helen admitted in 1850. "To win a word of praise, to see him smile as he often would when I had recited a lesson remarkably well, was my highest ambition, when a child." Portrait reprinted from Ruth Odell, *Helen Hunt Jackson (H.H.)*.

Deborah Waterman Vinal Fiske, Helen's mother, ca. 1843, the year before she died. As an adult, Jackson described her mother as "the kindest human being I ever knew," and claimed she had inherited her "mother's gift of cheer." Portrait reprinted from Ruth Odell, *Helen Hunt Jackson (H.H.)*.

Ann Scholfield Fiske ("Annie"), Helen's sister, ca.
1840s. Courtesy Special Collections, Tutt Library,
Colorado College, Colorado Springs, Colorado.

Edward Hunt, Helen's first husband, ca. 1860. "He was an unusually handsome man, very tall and of stately, soldierly presence. His movements were deliberate, and so, in a way, were the workings of his mind; but he was endowed with much scientific ability and a nature just, temperate, and kindly," wrote Jackson's friend Sarah Woolsey in an introduction to *Ramona*. Courtesy Special Collections, Tutt Library, Colorado College, Colorado Springs, Colorado.

Helen Hunt with her son Murray,
who was born in 1853 and lived
less than a year. Courtesy Special
Collections, Tutt Library,
Colorado College, Colorado
Springs, Colorado.

Helen's son Warren Horsford Hunt, called "Rennie,"
not long before he died in April 1865, age nine. "She is
only half mother who does not see her own child in
every child! her own child's grief in every pain which
makes another child weep!" Jackson insisted in her
domestic essays. Courtesy Colorado Springs Pioneers
Museum, Starsmore Center for Local History.

Helen Hunt, ca. 1865. Courtesy Colorado Springs Pioneers Museum, Starsmore Center for Local History.

Writer and social activist Thomas Wentworth Higginson, ca. 1870s. In 1873 Jackson described Higginson as "my mentor, my teacher— the one man to whom & to whose style I chiefly owe what little I have done in literature." Courtesy Special Collections, Tutt Library, Colorado College, Colorado Springs, Colorado.

Above: Actress Charlotte Cushman. Upon Cushman's death in 1876, Jackson lamented, "I have known her well for six years and loved her as I never loved any other woman in this world." Courtesy Special Collections, Tutt Library, Colorado College, Colorado Springs, Colorado.

Left: Caroline Hahlreiner, the subject of Jackson's 1870 *Atlantic Monthly* travel essay "A German Landlady." After this essay received acclaim, Jackson continued to focus in her travel essays and fiction on sympathetic, regionalist character portrayal. Courtesy Special Collections, Tutt Library, Colorado College, Colorado Springs, Colorado.

William Sharpless Jackson, Helen's second husband, in the 1870s. "A man of excellent business
reputation and ability, possessed of sound, clear
judgment and a particularly sunny, kindly temper,"
wrote Sarah Woolsey. "Their marriage was exceptionally happy." William Jackson's wish to see his
wife "despise & utterly condemn any & every thing
that borders on cast or exclusiveness" helped in-
crease her appreciation for ethnic and racial diversity. Courtesy Special Collections, Tutt Library,
Colorado College, Colorado Springs, Colorado.

The Jackson home at 228 East Kiowa Street, corner of Weber, in Colorado Springs, ca. 1890s. Courtesy Special Collections, Tutt Library, Colorado College, Colorado Springs, Colorado.

North Cheyenne Canyon, outside Colorado Springs, ca. 1882–96. Jackson loved Colorado's natural beauty and protested its destruction by careless U.S. miners and developers. "Helen Hunt Falls" was named in her honor during her lifetime by a friend, Mrs. Mary Tenney Hatch. In 1966 the parks department of Colorado Springs made the name official. Today there is a visitor center at the spot, where key rings, T-shirts, and postcards are for sale. Courtesy Special Collections, Tutt Library, Colorado College, Colorado Springs, Colorado.

Top: Mexican houses near Walsenburg, Colorado, ca. 1888. Jackson visited a Mexican home during her 1877 visit to Walsenburg. Afterward, she watched with mixed emotions in a field outside the town as a plowshare cut the first furrow for a new terminus of the Denver and Rio Grand Railroad. Courtesy Colorado Historical Society, F-13,974, O.T. Davis photo.

Bottom: Chest Street, Leadville, in 1879, the year Jackson wrote of this silver mining boomtown in her *Atlantic Monthly* essay "To Leadville." Leadville represented the epitome of the spread of United States industrialism, which Jackson both protested and unintentionally promoted in her travel essays. Courtesy Special Collections, Tutt Library, Colorado College, Colorado Springs, Colorado.

Activist Susette La Flesche and her brother Francis, at the
time of their 1879–80 tour of eastern cities with Ponca
Chief Standing Bear. Susette La Flesche's charm and com-
mitment to obtaining legal rights for Indians helped inspire
Jackson to take up advocacy work. Courtesy Nebraska
State Historical Society.

Helen Jackson at her writing desk in Colorado Springs, with an unidentified guest, ca. 1881. The room is decorated after Jackson's trademark fashion, with vines and leaves gathered on her nature outings. Courtesy Special Collections, Tutt Library, Colorado College, Colorado Springs, Colorado.

An Indian home in San Gabriel, Southern California, probably January 17, 1882. In a letter dated this day, Jackson told her friend Thomas Bailey Aldrich that she had been "reveling in the society" of "two old women, Laura, and Benjaminia," 102 and 117 years old. "117 repeated the Lords Prayer—Hail Mary, & Creed, & sang a psalm in Indian. 102 was popping corn in an iron pot over a few embers. Today, I had them photographed, squatting in front of their straw hut." Quotation, Harvard; photo courtesy Special Collections, Tutt Library, Colorado College, Colorado Springs, Colorado.

Top: Antonio and Mariana Coronel, Jackson's closest friends in Southern California, at "El Recreo," their home in Los Angeles, ca. 1888. The Coronels are demonstrating an old Mexican dance. Jackson's romantic view of Southern California's Hispanic past, and negative view of the American oppression of local Indians, owed a great deal to the opinions of Antonio Coronel. Courtesy the Ramona Pageant Association.

Bottom: The nascent American wine industry in Southern California, 1882. This photograph, which Jackson owned, is titled "Vintage. Recorking & Disgorging . . . Year After Bottling." For Jackson, new agricultural enterprises represented the most benevolent type of American expansion. Courtesy Special Collections, Tutt Library, Colorado College, Colorado Springs, Colorado.

First page of the manuscript of *Ramona*. Jackson has crossed out her original title for the book, "In the Name of the Law," and written in the new title. She has also revised the book's first sentence, renaming "Widow Moreno" as "Señora Moreno." Pieces of the *Ramona* manuscript are now scattered across the country. Most of the manuscript is in Colorado Springs at the Tutt Library; the first page of chapter 16 is in Amherst at the Jones Library; most of chapters 10 through 14 are at the Lilly Library of Indiana University in Bloomington, a place unknown to Jackson; and some twenty pages are missing. Courtesy Special Collections, Tutt Library, Colorado College, Colorado Springs, Colorado.

The site of Jackson's first grave, on Cheyenne Mountain near her beloved South Cheyenne Canyon, outside Colorado Springs, ca. 1890. For many years, fans paid tribute to her by piling up stones and other mementos at this site. "There is a constant procession of visitors to her resting-place," noted one local newspaper. "An extraordinary mania possesses some of these admirers, and they leave on the grave visiting cards and scraps of newspapers on which their names are written." Today, tourists who have paid the required entrance fee at Seven Falls below can still hike to the pile of stones, where an apocryphal plaque claims that Jackson wrote parts of *Ramona* at the spot. Quotation from " 'H.H.' and Her Admirers," unidentified newspaper clipping in HHJ1, box 6, fd. 24; photo courtesy The Denver Public Library, Western History Collection.

The Ramona Pageant in Hemet, California, ca. 1928, five years after annual pro-
duction began. The pageant is now the longest-running outdoor play in America.
Ironically enough, given Jackson's criticism in *Ramona* of the American conquest
of California, it is also the state of California's "official" outdoor play. The Hemet
Chamber of Commerce originally conceived of the pageant as a tourist draw,
commissioning the pageanteer Garnet Holme to write the script. Courtesy the
Ramona Pageant Association.

PART FOUR

"A Protest against the Spread of Civilization"

Jackson as Regionalist and Reformer

6

Travel Writing

"How many boarders are there in the hotel?" said I, at [the coach driver's] first pause.

"Oh, nigh on to a hundred, and a hundred more coming and going every day. Next year, Mr. Sinclair, he's going to put up an addition to accommodate three hundred and fifty people, and he's just sent off to buy ten more horses. We get one dollar an hour now for a saddle horse, and two dollars for a single team to go to Littleton, and there's lots of folks every day that wants to ride and can't."

For a mile or more he ran on in this strain, undeterred by my silence, or by the look of dismay which I think must have been on my face. At last he stopped, and I fell into a dreamy reverie over the unhappy fate of the North American Indian. It seemed to me that I had never before realized his miseries, the injustice with which he had been treated, and the utter hopelessness of any effort on his part to resist the fatal march of civilization.

JACKSON, "A Protest against the Spread of Civilization" (1867)

Only six months following Rennie's death and four months after Jackson began writing poetry for publication, she published her first travel essay, in the *New York Evening Post*: "Mountain Life: The New Hampshire Town of Bethlehem—Where It Is, What It Is, and All about It," a celebration of the rural town that remained her favorite warm-weather escape from hay fever throughout the years she wintered in Newport. At this early date in her career, she was eager to make a name for herself as a poet and disdained as a "form of literary suicide" the gossipy women's "letters" from various cities that were then appearing as popular columns in many newspapers.[1] Yet in her observations of the regional customs and natural environments of rural New England she began to find material not only for descriptive travel sketches but also for what would become her own regionalist vision of embattled rural America. With her very first travel essay she initiated a lasting practice of setting most of her creative prose writing in rural or newly developing places, often ones that she visited during her seasonal wanderings; the eastern cities where she conducted her literary business and lived during the winters would almost never figure in her travel work or fiction except as places to be avoided, or as unnamed forces behind the urban industrialization threatening rural America.

By writing about her many wanderings, Jackson found a means of digesting them and adding to their enjoyment. She had felt an impulse in this direction as early as 1852, when she took a long, hurried journey with Julius and Lucy Palmer: "Traveling must be indeed bewitching if one can take it leisurely enough to stop every other day, and write the record of the preceding," she had mused then in a letter to Henry Root.[2] As a professional, she found that recording her travel observations also afforded other psychological benefits. For one thing, the act of writing turned her constant travels for health and leisure, which might otherwise have troubled her as self-indulgent, into an exercise in diligence, thereby meeting familial expectations. Her parents had held educational nonfiction in high esteem; as early as age eleven she had enjoyed reading records of travel with her mother. Now she would not simply be a wanderer and poet, the sort of daydreamer her father would have scorned, but a methodical literary worker, scrupulously writing up informative accounts of her every movement.

The extent to which she felt driven by her familial inheritance when she was starting out as a travel writer is evident in one of two essays that she wrote about Boston in the fall of 1867, at the request of Parke Godwin of the *New York Evening Post,* just before she decided to eschew writing about cities. In a column titled "Boston Gossip," she claims that her purpose is to "investigate the present state of Boston Congregationalism," but she also has an unstated goal: to prove to herself that the state of Congregationalism is not good, and that she can therefore feel justified in turning her attention away from religious to secular matters (including, in this case, an exhibit of pictures of California, a region to which she here refers for the first time in print). Seeking to prove Calvinism defunct, the narrator of "Boston Gossip" visits the "ugly," "unadorned" Park Street Church, and finds it completely empty except for a pair of chattering old ladies.[3] Jackson does not tell her readers that this church was the site of her own mother's conversion to Calvinism some forty years earlier and also the site of her parents' Calvinist wedding ceremony. Yet her essay is written in prose so uncharacteristically scattered and tortured, even taking into consideration that she was still only learning to write effectively, that her psychological burden is unconsciously revealed.

In later years, some of the societal constraints placed on nineteenth-century women encouraged her to continue writing assiduously about all of her travels. Though in her early New England wanderings she was often accompanied by friends—including Lucia Runkle, Sarah Woolsey, Priscilla Stearns, and

Sarah and Lilian Clarke, sister and daughter of James Freeman Clarke—in 1869, during her first trip to Europe, she started making short trips by herself. At that time, solitary travel was only just becoming socially acceptable for middle-class American women. The sorts of journeys Jackson soon embarked on to and within America's Far West were still considered of dubious propriety for unaccompanied women, as they entailed long train rides, difficult terrain, and nights in remote, ramshackle accommodations. Jackson had no wish to buck prevailing standards of femininity. Like many of the professional and would-be professional female writers who, like their male counterparts, sent sketches home to East Coast periodicals from Europe and the West during the decades following the Civil War, she wrote about her travels not simply to create literary art but also to recast her unconventional behavior as earnest and productive labor.

One year after she published "Mountain Life," she wrote her second travel essay, "In the White Mountains," for the September 13, 1866, *Independent.* In both of these first two travel pieces, which she signed "H.H.," she describes quiet Bethlehem, New Hampshire, as the best of all towns in the White Mountains, a region then gaining reputation as a popular summer resort. She lauds Bethlehem's scenery as the prettiest and Bethlehem's people as the friendliest in the area, and predicts in "Mountain Life" that it is the town's "destiny" to draw "a crowd" of visitors: "Bethlehem is not yet ready for strangers, but Bethlehem means to be," she says.[4] By the time Jackson published her third travel essay a year later, on August 29, 1867, in the *New York Evening Post,* a crowd of strangers had indeed discovered Bethlehem. She titled her reaction to their presence "A Protest against the Spread of Civilization" and published the essay under the pseudonym "Rip Van Winkle," after the genial, dreamy hero of Washington Irving's famous early story, first recounted in his landmark collection of tales and travel, *The Sketch Book of Geoffrey Crayon, Gent.* (1819–20). Jackson had probably read this book by the mid-1850s, when she made references to Irving in her letters; she no doubt studied *The Sketch Book* again during these first years of her career at the prompting of Higginson, who revered Irving. In his original incarnation, Irving's Rip imbibes a magic liquor that makes him sleep for twenty years, finally awakening to find himself in entirely changed surroundings. In "A Protest," Jackson's own latter-day Rip claims he fell asleep a year ago, just after spending a wonderful fall season in isolated, beautiful Bethlehem, only to discover upon recently coming to his senses that Bethlehem has been overrun by tourists, who are destroying the town's peace and driving up prices.

With "A Protest against the Spread of Civilization," the first of twelve early *Post* essays that Jackson would publish as Rip Van Winkle, she began to explore the themes and literary techniques that would continue to preoccupy her in all her regionalist writing. Most obviously, this essay reveals her burgeoning interest in the topic of American industrial expansion and her ambivalent relationship to that expansion. On the one hand, she expresses a wish in "A Protest" that Bethlehem might be preserved as a sort of rural backwater—what she calls "An Out of the Way Place" in the title of one 1868 Rip Van Winkle essay—an enclave reminiscent of the Amherst of her youth, where traditional lifeways and nature's beauty endure. Jackson would always seek out such places in her travels, and she became known for writing about them. On the other hand, even as she appreciated and wished to protect America's rural havens, she herself was part of the very "spread of civilization" she disdained, a fact that renders her "Protest" paradoxical. She took up temporary residence in rural towns, helping to transform them by her own urbane presence; and through writings such as "Mountain Life" and "In the White Mountains," she encouraged other urbanites to do the same. In fact, as Sarah Woolsey would later testify, Jackson's "enthusiastic" essays about Bethlehem were largely responsible for turning a town that had been sleepy and little known when Jackson first visited into a thriving vacation resort.[5]

Jackson realized the effect her articles were having: in 1874 she returned to Bethlehem after her first sojourn in Colorado to find that her old hideaway had become "simply a town of boarding houses," as she told her sister.[6] To a certain extent, she had consciously worked to produce this transformation. After using Bethlehem as the subject of her first travel writings, she wrote about the town again and again—five times in 1870 alone. In one of the three Bethlehem pieces she published that year in the *Independent*, "A Bethlehem of Today," she muses on the town's ineffable appeal: "of places, as of people, the subtlest charm can never be told, let the catalogue of their qualities be ever so faithful and minute. There is a personal magnetism in a hill or a valley, individual atmosphere in a grove or a meadow, which no words can render."[7] While such quintessentially regionalist musings are a key aspect of "A Bethlehem of Today," this essay also explicitly encourages tourists and allergy sufferers to come to the town, offering practical information on several local boardinghouses and on the most comfortable means of reaching Bethlehem from New York City. Jackson knew that this sort of information was promotional. On July 1, 1870, the day after "A Bethlehem of Today" appeared in print, she wrote to Whitelaw Reid of the *New York Tribune* asking him to copy the piece, explaining, "I want to exalt the blessed and beloved little town far and wide."[8] In response, on August 13 Reid instead ran a new Jackson essay, "An Afternoon's Chances in Bethlehem," in his paper's "Summer Letters" column, a regular feature that explicitly served to promote various vacation destinations.

Given the active role she would play in popularizing tourism to Bethlehem, Jackson's initial "Protest against the Spread of Civilization" can seem false and self-serving, or at best intentionally ironic. Yet to consider it only in this light would be to miss Jackson's main point. For with her first "Protest" she began a lasting project of criticizing not expansion per se but what she saw as the wrong sorts of urban industrial expansion into rural America, and also the wrong attitudes toward expansion. In particular, she did not wish to criticize newcomers for entering country places—she considered the intermingling of different sorts of people a very positive thing, one of the great boons of travel and relocation—but rather desired to encourage them to respect local environments and the preeminent rights of native residents.

An early example of Jackson's differential judgments of industrial expansion can be found in her various comments on a new cog train that was sent up Mount Washington, sixteen miles from Bethlehem, in the late 1860s. In "A Protest," Jackson's Rip is disgruntled when, leaving Bethlehem for Mount Washington in order to get "further away from civilization," he ends up simply finding new evidence of civilization in this railroad.[9] Similarly, in a private letter to a city friend, Jackson once called the Mount Washington train an "abomination" amid Bethlehem's remote charms.[10] Yet on a fall day in 1870, just a few months after she wrote that critical letter, she learned that the train could actually add to the region's magic if one approached it with the right attitude. As she reports in "A Second Celestial Railroad," by looking "brave and willful" and chatting amiably with the conductor, she was allowed to ride up Mount Washington on the outside of the train's engine, a vantage that afforded her new depths of appreciation for the area's natural beauty.[11] A year later, in "Mt. Washington in September," she explicitly discusses her developing belief that there are both good and bad ways of being involved with the new train. Riding outside the train's engine, she notes, can offer a dazzling opportunity for communion with nature to Transcendentally awakened people for "whom the nearness of the upper world, the wine of the upper air, the revelation of the solemn greatness of one little corner of God's universe, are an uplifting and a joy." But this special opportunity is lost on bustling expansionists who make no effort to fit in with local ways, nor to set aside their usual prejudices and preoccupations when encountering new situations. Jackson feels "like throwing overboard men and women who in such moments talk of 'dried-apple pie,' and 'carbolic soap,' and the 'hasps' to their 'trunks.' "[12]

In the passage from "A Protest against the Spread of Civilization" excerpted at the head of this chapter, Jackson's Rip Van Winkle places himself in league with American Indians, as joint sufferers of "miseries" and "injustices" inflicted by insensitive industrial expansionists. Of course, Rip's frustration at being surrounded by tourists can scarcely be equated with the life struggles of Native Americans. In this passage Jackson adopts a fallacious view, prevalent among Anglo-Americans of her time, that Indian survival was a "hopeless" cause over which a well-meaning white person could do nothing but sigh. Before long, increased contact with actual Indians would change her outlook. But in her first years as a travel writer, even as she often decried culturally insensitive behavior, she was still under the influence of the prejudicial ideas about race (and in this case specifically about Native Americans) that she had learned in childhood.

Although Jackson's father had joined Amherst College in expressing support for the Cherokee Indians during Jackson's youth, as I will discuss later, for the most part her parents had taught her to think of Native Americans as people who had little to do with everyday life in America. Because no Indians worked as servants in the Fiske household, Helen was never given the distinct impression that they belonged, like the family's African American and Irish help, to a lower, servant class. Yet she was led to think of them as beings from another time and place. According to Edward Hitchcock, during one early Amherst celebration, Jackson's father delighted his listeners with stories about former local Indians, "transporting his hearers back to other times, and reminding them of another race which then inhabited this beautiful Valley, and other scenes quite unlike those which are now occurring."[13] On this occasion, at least, Nathan Fiske professed the Indians of New England to be the exotic stuff of history and legend, no longer a vital part of ordinary life. Jackson's "Protest" portrays Indians in the same light, as do two of her other Rip Van Winkle essays, "A New Sleepy Hollow" and "A Morning in a Vermont Graveyard." In the latter, she investigates an eighteenth-century captivity case, making a sensationalistic beginning to the more sober local research and personal interviewing that would later become integral to her travel writing.[14]

While Jackson's father may have considered Indians a people of the past, her mother seems to have held a related view of living Indians as cultural curiosities, anomalies in nineteenth-century America. At age eleven, when Helen was staying in Charlestown, she saw some Indians, an experience she related matter-of-factly in a detailed letter to her mother:

> Monday night Sarah, May, and myself walked over behind Medford Hill to see the indians. I wished very much Anne [sic] was there. There were four tents in one of them was a woman with a little baby or *pappoose*. . . . They were all as busy as bees making baskets. I had no money with me or I would have bought Anne one some of them were very handsome they were dressed very curiously. . . . When we were coming home we met four Indian women that had been out to sell their baskets . . . one woman had on a sort of habit of blue woolen cloth the whole front of her waist was covered with little tin plates larger than half a dollar with a little hole in the middle and a very gay handkerchief about her neck and a great deal of red about her person.[15]

Helen explained to her mother that this "*description*" was written more for the benefit of Annie, to whom her mother would read her letter, than for Deborah herself, whom Helen did not expect to be "much interested in it." The description is simply expository, not pejorative; it is less carefully punctuated, and more breathless, than Helen's usual correspondence, and appears to have been written with a good deal of excitement. Soon, however, Helen received an answer from her mother of a very different kind. "Saturday it was rumoured about within Ann's hearing that there were Indians to be seen in Amherst, that they were over in Dr. Humphrey's lot," Deborah said, explaining that Ann had insisted upon going to see them, "*just* as *Helen* did." When they arrived upon the scene, though, they found "*not* indians, but rather dark indian looking folks." Deborah considered the impoverished living conditions of these people "*disgusting,*" and so fixed her attention instead on the "decent people that were there to see them."[16] In this account of her failed outing, Deborah reveals a preconceived notion of the Indians she had hoped to see as outcasts whom she expected to be if not "disgusting," like some other itinerant people, then at least so powerless as to be easily gazed on and objectified. Jackson would express a similar prejudice in several of her early travel essays from her first trip to California. Furthermore, while she would later cease to exoticize or negatively objectify her Indian subjects, and begin instead to insist on their place in present-day America, she would nonetheless continue in her regionalist work to make ethnic comparisons based implicitly on a sense of her own ethnic hegemony. In an early 1867 "Rip Van Winkle" essay, "Notes of Travel," she subtly establishes her ethnic standpoint when her Rip rattles off a list of the beggars who walk the aisles of his New England train. Rip ascribes no ethnicity to a "one-armed soldier" who is apparently, like Rip's Dutch prototype and Jackson herself, of European Protestant extraction. (Jackson's father's and mother's ancestors had both emigrated to New England from England in the seventeenth century.) But he does detail the ethnicities of those passengers belonging to immigrant groups more recently established in America:

One one-armed soldier with a pamphlet to sell, price twenty-five cents;
One one-armed Irish boy with a card of appeal;
One grimy, tattered Italian boy with a harp of more than a thousand strings, and all cracked;
One long-haired grinning German boy with a very bad fiddle.[17]

Jackson would continue throughout her career as a travel writer to position herself as a white Anglo-American of Protestant extraction not so much by direct statement as by her habit of most explicitly characterizing ethnic, racial, religious, and class traits different from her own. In "Notes of Travel," she uses her ethnic comparison as a means of criticizing what she describes as the widespread narrow-mindedness and selfishness of her own ethnic group: Rip upbraids the "selfishness and vulgarity" of his fellow Yankee passengers, who offer nothing to help the beggars on their train, while he praises one "coarse untidy Irish woman with three children" who, least able to afford charity, is the only person to offer it. Jackson would make similar criticisms of her ethnic peers in many of her subsequent travel essays, including "A Bethlehem of Today," where she links the rigidity of the New England personality to the harshness of the New England landscape: "New England is lovely only along her river courses; she needs their help to keep her landscapes green and gracious, just as the stern uprightness and alarming well-educatedness of her men and women need (and do not always have) especial graces of behavior to make them pleasant to see."[18]

With "A Protest against the Spread of Civilization," Jackson began not only to write as a regionalist, with a focus on the issues of industrial expansion and ethnic diversity, but also to establish the particular literary sensibility and voice that would animate much of her prose. To a degree, her decision to assume the name of Rip Van Winkle in this and many of her other earliest travel essays was simply a form of whimsy: printed in the "Correspondence" columns of the *Post,* these essays are distinctly reminiscent of the "Foreign Correspondence" from the moon and special dispatches from "Piscatoria, the seat of finny government," that a younger Helen Fiske once featured in her Abbott School *Portfolio.* Yet her allusions to Irving's work during her formative years as a travel writer were extensive and significant. She not only built her literary persona as Rip Van Winkle on Irving's fictional creation but in addition liked to claim that her Rip lived in the town made famous by another *Sketch Book* story, "The Legend of Sleepy Hollow."[19] With the *Sketch Book,* Irving had pioneered the sort of descriptive, distinctively regionalist travel "sketch" Jackson wished to write as she set out in her career. Her work shows the influence of Irving's focus on the regional picturesque and also his informal, urbane, sometimes gently satirical narrative voice. Like the original Rip Van Winkle, full of wonderment at life in post-Revolution America, the narrators of Jackson's travel essays wander through post–Civil War America, marveling at its diverse people and places.[20] In "A Protest," as in many of her later essays, Jackson's transcription of idiosyncratic local dialects stands in marked contrast to her own educated, grammatically standardized Yankee narrative voice. Jackson may have been inspired as well by Irving's manner of interspersing fiction and nonfiction in his *Sketch Book* pieces to incorporate fictional techniques in her travel essays. Her early experiments with the persona of Rip were a type of fictionalization, of course, as was her burgeoning habit of portraying the people she encountered in her travels as "characters": she offered stylized descriptions and biographical sketches of them and recorded their conversations after the fashion of fictional dialogue, when in reality she could never have captured their words and pronunciations exactly, even when she took notes.[21]

It was in one of her "H.H." essays about her first trip to Europe that Jackson firmly established her lasting manner of focusing on character portraiture in her travel writing. Seeking diversion and artistic education, she set out for Europe on November 5, 1868. Before she returned home more than a year later, on January 22, 1870, she made lengthy visits to England, Paris, Italy, Germany, and Austria, accompanied at various times by Nelly and Priscilla Stearns of Boston, and by Sarah and Lilian Clarke. She wrote up numerous accounts of her experiences, sending a series of nine essays to the *New York Independent* and mailing home a special private series of fourteen monthly travelogues to a circle of friends and relations that included her sister Ann, her sister-in-law Molly Hunt, Higginson, Sarah Woolsey, and other Newport and New York literary associates. She wrote these special letters more carefully and deliberately than her usual personal correspondence, often working on them over the course of several days. She and her friends called them "Encyclicals," as she later explained to James T. Fields, because "they began from Rome; and were sent to all the faithful."[22] After Jackson returned home, she sent Fields several of her encyclicals and essays about Europe, and was delighted when he accepted them for publication in the *Atlantic Monthly*—hitherto he had accepted only two of her poems. He also began to welcome her travel essays on America at this time.

Jackson's writings on Europe are in many ways fairly conventional. Most of the prominent American authors of her era visited Europe, as did a great many lesser-known writers, and it was customary to publish essays and letters about the trip. While Jackson was among the more talented writers to follow this pattern, she nonetheless brought to the task more of a journalist's than an artist's sensibility. The essays she wrote for the periodical press lack overall artistic coherence. They also fail to encompass that sense of travel as a journey into self-awareness and identity that animates the best literary, as opposed to journalistic, travel writing. Even her encyclicals are impersonal in this sense, though they were originally composed for private friends, because she excised their more intimate passages before publication. Like many of today's columnists for newspaper travel sections, Jackson never explicitly discusses or describes herself in her travel writing, despite the obvious significance to her cultural opinions of her own personal background. From Europe she writes variously in the first-person singular, first-person plural, and declarative second person, revealing herself only in scattered, tantalizing hints: she and her travel companions are "women, good friends, good travellers" "of the self-asserting sort," "with no hats on their heads, alone," whose "independent" manner leaves at least "one stuffy old Englishman" almost "frightened to death."[23]

Furthermore, though Jackson does occasionally offer up brief, aphoristic comments on life and human nature in her European essays, she seldom considers how her opinion of herself as an American, or her opinion of America itself, might develop in relation to her experience of various cultures—subjects that, like self-exploration, form an important component of much good literary travel writing, and that Jackson does address in her American travel essays and in some of her more personal, unpublished letters from Europe. In one such letter, dated from Rome on January 31, 1869, she alludes in a beguiling way to her own Puritanical upbringing and the way it colored, and was also challenged by, her experience of Italy:

> The men carry little canes, in their yellow & lavender fingers, & stick eye glasses up when some girl goes by, with more than usual black hair down her shoulders; and they all have that indescribable atmosphere about them, which if I were the Apostle Paul, I should call, "a name of living while they are really dead"—but being only a fellow woman with a great preference for French clothes at the bottom of my own heart, and a kind of sneaking respect for the gigantic enterprise with which they carry the thing out, I shall only call, the technical "society" atmosphere.[24]

Unfortunately, Jackson mostly eschews such personally revealing cultural commentaries in her published writings on Europe, concentrating instead on creating a scrupulous, chronological record of her movements and activities. In fact, in her very first published encyclical, she explicitly declares her intention to curtail all unnecessary digressions. "I shall never get through at this rate," she says after an encounter with an orderly London railway station leads her to wonder in print whether foreigners dread New York's more chaotic terminals. "I must lay down the rule in the outset not to say what I *think*."[25]

Though Jackson's decision not to draw personal inferences from her experiences abroad weakens her European travel essays, the essays nonetheless possess descriptive strengths that elevate them above the mediocrity of common travel journalism. Jackson was a skilled reporter, possessed of uncommon powers of observation and intuition. She was capable of grasping and expertly conveying both general scenes and their most telling details. Like many good travelers, she was an advocate of leisurely journeying, knowing that "ways are so sure to be nicer than any places you set out to reach,"[26] and she described the things she saw during her meanderings vividly and feelingly. In Europe's cities, which she did not avoid in her travel writing as she did America's, she invites her readers to "study old stones inch by inch" with her, "to lounge on doorsteps, and peer into shadowy places."[27] And she approaches Europe's rural places with reverence, offering compelling descriptions of fields, mountains, and flowers, and apt reflections on their Transcendental significances.[28] In one of her essays from Italy, "A May-Day in Albano," she muses: "We are not ashamed to spend summer after summer face to face with flowers and trees and stones, and never so much as know them by name. I wonder they treat us so well as they do, provide us with food and beauty so often, poison us so seldom. It must be only out of the pity they feel, being diviner than we."[29]

Jackson's essays from Europe are also frequently enlivened by a winning sense of humor. Like Mark Twain's "innocents abroad," she and her traveling companions make ludicrous, high-spirited efforts to sneak into forbidden cloisters and bring home relics, greeting the hallowed sites of European tourism with playful skepticism. In her essay from Albano, for instance, she teases: "We climbed round the convent on a narrow rocky path overhanging the lake, to see an old tomb 'supposed to be that of Cneius Cornelius Scipio Hispallus.' We saw no reason to doubt its being his."[30] From Badgastein, Austria, she even jokes about her own problematic determination to squeeze all of her observations into marketable pieces for the periodical press, a habit that in this instance has created an awkward gap in one of her encyclicals: "Now you see there is nothing left of that waterfall, for since August 11th, when I began this letter, I've cooked it for a newspaper! It fitted and slipped in so naturally into [an essay] I was writing I could not resist the temptation to serve it hot *à la carte* to those customers, and this is all you'll get of it, unless you look up the waiter who carried it off."[31]

This sort of exuberant, confiding humor is rarely to be found in Jackson's published writing after her 1872 trip to California; it is present here in part because many of her public comments on Europe were first made privately, in encyclicals that she claimed were "unstudied," "wholly informal and familiar."[32] The wit of these earlier essays also owes a good deal to her determination "never to do guide-book," as she says in one encyclical[33]—that is, never to belabor the sorts of factual travel details that her readers could easily find elsewhere, in Murray or Baedeker guidebooks. Finally, it owes something to the impious tone of much American travel writing at the time, and to the humorous classics of short prose that were then inspiring her: in addition to Irving's genial *Sketch Book* pieces on Europe, she admired what she called the "mirthful" essays of the early-nineteenth-century English writer Charles Lamb.[34] She does not seem to have been particularly influenced by Twain's *Innocents Abroad* (1869) or by his other writing, despite the similar tenor of some of their scrambles abroad.[35]

While many of Jackson's essays about Europe demonstrate her talent for description and narration, essential gifts for any regionalist writer, her single most important essay from this period was "A German Landlady," where she first demonstrated her capacity for regionalist character portraiture. Originally titled "Fräulein Hahlreiner," this essay was accepted for publication after Jackson returned from Europe by Edward Everett Hale at *Old and New;* but when he delayed in publishing it, she withdrew the piece and managed to place it with the *Atlantic Monthly.* It appeared there in October 1870 as "A German Landlady," Jackson's debut in the magazine's prestigious travel pages. Throughout her time in Europe, Jackson had studied the people she encountered as if they were literary characters—especially seventeen-year-old Marianina, who cared for her rooms in Rome and traveled with her to Albano, and Dr. Proell in Badgastein. But it was with "A German Landlady" that she developed what was to become her standard working method of identifying personally with the female subjects of her travel essays, usually on the grounds of a shared determination to persevere. She also established a habit of trying to capture their personalities in writing through phonetic transcription of their vernacular speech.[36]

The original for Jackson's "German Landlady" was Mrs. Caroline Hahlreiner, in whose boardinghouse Jackson stayed while in Munich and who afterward served as Jackson's maid on a trip to Nuremberg, the Rhine, and Rotterdam. In part 1 of her thirty-three-page essay, Jackson works to capture "the charm of atmosphere that there was about our dear Fräulein and everything she did or said," especially her sly talent for imitating the people they encountered on their joint travels: "never off the stage, and rarely on it, have I seen such power of mimicry as had this wonderful old Fräulein," Jackson says. Jackson also shares her delight in Hahlreiner's "broken English," a "deliciously comic and effectively eloquent language" that Jackson attempts to reproduce in her essay. "O my dear lady, you make me go to be like fool, to think of so nice journey," Hahlreiner responds when Jackson first invites her on the trip, "clapping one hand to her head, snapping the fingers of the other, and pirouetting on her fat legs."[37] Though some of Jackson's later transcriptions of local dialects would prove awkward, her representation of Hahlreiner's halting English, and of the warm friendship that developed between them, rings true. (It also accords well with the phrasing and tenor of a message the actual Hahlreiner once wrote to Jackson on the back of a photo of herself, reproduced in the photo section of this book: "Mrs. Hellen Hund [sic] my love and remember from your Caroline.")[38]

In part 2 of "A German Landlady," Jackson outlines Hahlreiner's life history, in the process revealing that she was able to enjoy her landlady's company so thoroughly because she did not simply look on her as a literary subject but in fact identified with her on personal grounds. With her talent for acting, Hahlreiner was something of an artist, like Jackson herself. Moreover, she had endured many of the same trials in life as Jackson—she had been orphaned, forced for a time to serve as housemaid for an unsympathetic aunt, and later deprived of a loved one by tuberculosis. Yet she had remained always cheerful, diligent, and independent-minded, the sort of person for whom Jackson felt most sympathy and respect. Because of her sympathetic identification with Hahlreiner, Jackson was able to tolerate, even to appreciate, their differences. Above all, though she had been raised to abhor Catholicism, she came to respect Hahlreiner's practice of that religion. Earlier in her career, she had on occasion allowed her dislike of Irish Catholics to make itself felt in her work for the *Independent,* a circumstance that led one Irish reader to rebuke her, "I think you the meanest creature on earth."[39] During her travels in Europe, however, her prejudices began to soften. In Italy she shared the sentiments of many literary American travelers of her time in being both repulsed and enthralled by Roman Catholicism—she considered the religion idolatrous, but was drawn to its artistic ethos. Once settled in Germany, lingering in the Bavarian Alps, she met "honest, earnest, solemn country people" who made her feel for the first time that she could understand "what the Roman Catholic religion was intended to be."[40] Her intimacy with Hahlreiner sealed this new understanding. Hahlreiner was practical and good, not at all the Puritan stereotype of a superstitious idolater; she even held some of the same progressive ideas about religion as Jackson. In particular, the two women discovered that they both admired the books of the French biographer of Jesus and relativist Ernest Renan, a scholar who was taking the bold step of reading the Bible as history and literature.

With "A German Landlady" Jackson began to demonstrate an increasing interest in promoting religious tolerance in her writing, not only in her essays, as we will see, but also in such poems as "The Abbot Paphnutius," first published two months after "A German Landlady" in the December 1870 *Scribner's Monthly*.[41] Moreover, she began in all her regionalist writing to work by the same process of sympathetic identification that had allowed her to appreciate Hahlreiner. By selecting or creating subjects possessed of the virtues of cheerful submission and diligence, and often artistic sensibilities, she was able to identify personally with women from a wide variety of class and ethnic backgrounds. She was encouraged in these directions by the enthusiastic popular response to "A German Landlady" immediately upon its appearance in the *Atlantic*. "I have received five letters about the 'German Landlady'!" Jackson wrote to Fields in early October. "I never dreamed of the old darling's making such a triumphant debut in her old age, but I don't wonder after all, for she tells her own story. It is none of mine."[42] Soon afterward, when Jackson gathered ten of her European *Atlantic* and *Independent* essays and excerpts from her encyclicals for a collection to be published by J. R. Osgood, *Bits of Travel* (1872), she selected "A German Landlady" to open the volume.

Upon returning to New England from her sojourn in Europe, Jackson also returned to her work in American regionalism, incorporating her new methods of character portraiture. In her first year back, 1870, she published five essays about Bethlehem, New Hampshire; in one of these—her *New York Tribune* essay "An Afternoon's Chances in Bethlehem," subtitled "A Farmer and His Wife"—her new focus on character is especially apparent. Yet while Jackson would always consider herself a "good patriotic New Englander" at heart,[43] and would continue often to write about New England in both occasional travel pieces and fiction, her trip to Europe marked the beginning of a series of far-ranging journeys that would eventually lead her to take up residence in Colorado Territory and to think of New England as only one among her several literary provenances. Her European *Bits of Travel* received such positive reviews upon publication that she felt confident in her ability to write meaningfully of new places. Some reviewers hailed her as America's most promising new writer. "It is long since anyone has imparted such freshness, beauty, and pleasantness to anything from the well-worn field of European travel," declared one.

Many praised her for her "vivacious" humor and "natural language," marveling that the essays possessed "no less honest secular flavor than if the writer were not a poetess of high mystic intuitions."[44]

In May 1872, just three years after the transcontinental railroad was completed, Jackson set out with Sarah Woolsey for two and a half months in Northern California, a place where her native knowledge of New England could serve only as a point of comparison. She had long been drawn in imagination to the West. In 1852, when she was about to embark on her pleasure trip with Julius and Lucy Palmer, she could scarcely contain her excitement over the "glorious" romance of a "journey to the West"—they were to travel in a clockwise loop from Massachusetts to Philadelphia, Baltimore, Washington, Louisville, Cincinnati, Columbus, St. Louis, Chicago, Detroit, and Buffalo.[45] At that early date, the war with Mexico and the California gold rush had ensured that points even farther west were also present to the minds of most easterners; later, during the years of Jackson's career, San Francisco's brief spell as an important literary center meant that literary people—particularly those of a regionalist bent, like Jackson—were often reminded of California's most populous city. By 1870 Jackson was using the word "California" in her private correspondence as a synonym for supreme pleasure. When she finally arrived there, both she and Sarah Woolsey were thrilled with what they found. "I don't believe any two people ever had a better time or made more out of ten weeks than we have done," Woolsey wrote to William Ward at trip's end.[46] Both women published accounts of their trip, Jackson having arranged in advance to write about her journey for the *New York Independent*. The first of her fifteen California essays for that journal appeared in June 1872.

Jackson and Woolsey devoted their time in California to visiting places in the Bay Area and the Sierras that a number of writers from the East had visited before them, though certainly far fewer than had preceded Jackson to Europe, since only the recent joining of the Union and Central Pacific railroads had made regular tourism to California possible. In California, as earlier in Europe, Jackson used guidebooks and personal travel narratives to familiarize herself with the new places she was visiting. She mentions two of these explicitly, Bancroft's guide to San Francisco and Eliza Farnham's *California, In-doors and Out* (1856). She writes with special approval of the latter, today something of a feminist touchstone, in her essay "Holy Cross Village and Mrs. Pope's," where she acquaints her readers with Farnham's early success in establishing a farm at Santa Cruz.[47] While she relied on guidebooks in her own travels, Jackson still wished not to dwell too much on the usual sites and subjects in her travel essays. In the Sierras she preferred to seek out "sweet and unexpected revealings in level places and valleys, secrets of near woods, and glories of everyday paths,"[48] instead of the grand vistas recommended by her guidebooks. And she expressed humorous disdain for most things about San Francisco, a city that epitomized America's rapid urban industrial expansion, having grown up almost overnight during the gold rush. Even the city's natural attractions did not escape her satire. "It is so much the fashion to be tender, not to say sentimental, over the seals of the Cliff House rocks," Jackson scoffs.

> I make bold to declare that, if there be in the whole animal kingdom any creature of size and sound less adapted than a seal for a public pet, . . . I do not know such creature's name. Shapeless, boneless, limbless, and featureless; neither fish nor flesh; of the color and consistency of India-rubber diluted with mucilage; slipping, clinging, sticking, like gigantic leeches[.] . . . Let them be sold, and their skins given to the poor.[49]

Before long, sadly, Jackson would forgo such comedy in the interests of her increasingly earnest endeavor to document regional lifeways. In her essays on her first trip to California, her growing commitment to regionalism is most evident in her many brief descriptions of westerners of different ethnicities and races. These are merely sketches, not thorough portraits like "A German Landlady," and some are marred by Jackson's lingering adherence to the prejudices of her time and of her upbringing. Still, many demonstrate her new tendency to sympathize with individuals, however humble and of whatever ethnicity or race, in whom she recognizes familiar values and experiences. In "From Chicago to Ogden" and "From Ogden to San Francisco," two essays about the course of her journey on the Union Pacific, she marvels at the persevering European emigrants who are helping to bring about what she calls "the whole grand movement of the vast continent" westward. "Now we see for the first time the distinctive expression of American overland travel," she writes of an early stop along the way, where passenger luggage is being sorted and rechecked:

> Side by side with the rich and flurried New-Yorker stands the poor and flurried emigrant. Equality rules. Big bundles of feather-beds, tied up in blue check, red chests, corded with rope, get ahead of Saratoga trunks. Many languages are spoken. German, Irish, French, Spanish, a little English, and all varieties of American, I heard during thirty minutes in that luggage-shed. Inside the wall was a pathetic sight,—a poor German woman on her knees before a chest which had burst open on the journey. . . . [I]t was evidently all she owned; it was the home she had brought with her from the Fatherland, and would be the home she would set up in the prairie. The railroad-men were good to her, and were helping her with ropes and nails. This comforted me somewhat; but it seemed almost a sin to be journeying luxuriously on the same day and train with that poor soul.[50]

Jackson writes sympathetically of other women struggling valiantly to persevere in "Salt Lake City," an essay in which she discusses her stopover in a city then the object of a national outcry against Mormon polygamy. She has nothing positive to say about the leaders of the Mormon church, describing one with disgust: "His eyes were small, light, and watery, but sharp and cruel. His face was bloated, coarse, sensual: I have never seen a more repulsive man." Her personal opposition to polygamy even leads her, uncharacteristically, to express approval of the culturally nullifying effects of American industrial expansion: "Polygamy is as sure to disappear before civilization as flails are to go down before steam-threshers," she predicts. But when she notices to her great surprise that local women seem not miserable but happy and healthy, she not only expresses a good deal of sympathy for them—arguing, for example, that they should be permitted to maintain control of their own property—but also begins to feel more respect for the Mormon people and religion as a whole:

> These are the Mormons, of whom we have heard such terrible tales of cruelty and crime. . . . [T]hese are the down-trodden and heart-broken women for whom we have wept! The problem grows more and more perplexing with every hour that you spend in the city, and with every word that you hear. Men, not Mormons, who have lived here for years, bear the strongest testimony to the uprightness, honesty, industry, purity of Mormon lives, and to their charity also.[51]

Like the Mormons of Salt Lake City, the Chinese of California both repelled Jackson with the foreignness of some of their customs and won her over to sympathy by their industry and perseverance in the face of mounting, widespread prejudice. In "The Chinese Empire," an essay about San Francisco's Chinatown, Jackson explains that before coming to this place, she had known Chinese people only through painted images (even cosmopolitan New York City then had only about five hundred Chinese residents). Her essay reveals her lack of exposure, as when she describes the local Chinese opera as "incomprehensibly childish" and refers pejoratively to Chinese people in the singular as "Chow Chong." It also reveals the transformative power of her first encounter with large numbers of Chinese, particularly of her realization that they owned much of San Francisco: hence the pointed title of her essay. Jackson explains that as a child, she had set off Chinese firecrackers on the Fourth of July, "to celebrate our superiority as a nation." But once in Chinatown, she "did not feel so sure of our superiority." In fact, she says, not only are the residents of Chinatown singularly "neat" and "clean" for westerners, but they also demonstrate amazing "patience under the insulting and curious gaze of many strangers." As she walks through the streets taking notes, she is aware that even as she considers many Chinese habits ridiculous, the people she meets feel the same way about her. This circumstance appeals to both her sense of justice and her sense of the ludicrous:

> The men of China looked at me, observantly; now and then, they exchanged significant glances with each other. . . . I looked up into their faces and smiled, and said: "I never saw Chinese shops before. Very good, very good." And they laughed, and moved on,—no doubt inwardly moved with compassion for my ignorance.

Now and then, a woman would brush by me, turn half round, and give me a quick look of such contempt that I winced a little. Judged by her standard, I must sink very low, indeed. She herself did not venture to walk thus, in open daylight among her countrymen, until she had lost all sense of decency, as her race hold it. What must I be, then,—a white woman who had not come to buy, but simply to look at, to lift, to taste, or to smell the extraordinary commodities offered for sale in the empire? No wonder she despised me! I avenge myself by describing her hair. It was all drawn back from her forehead, twisted tight from the nape of the neck to the crown of the head, stiffened with glue, glistening with oil, and made into four huge double wings, which stood out beyond her ears on either side. It looked a little like two gigantic black satin bats, pinned to the back of her head, or still more like a windmill gone into mourning. . . . Could she be uglier? . . . But pass on, sister! In the sunless recesses of Quong Tuck Lane, I trust thou hast had many a laugh with thy comrades over the gown and hat I wore on Dupont Street that day.[52]

Jackson approached the West's Native American population with a similar mixture of ethnocentrism and relativism—sometimes describing Indians pejoratively, like her parents before her, as cultural relics or oddities; at other times presenting them more sympathetically, through the eyes of personal identification. When she first sees an Indian woman on her train during the journey west, she believes "it" to be "the most abject, loathly living thing I ever saw." But her impression changes when she realizes the woman is a mother, possessed of strong maternal instincts: "Idle and thoughtless passengers jeered the squaw, saying: 'Sell us the pappoose.' 'Give you greenbacks for the pappoose.' Then, and not till then, I saw a human look in the India-rubber face. The eyes could flash, and the mouth could show scorn, as well as animal greed. The expression was almost malignant, but it bettered the face; for it made it the face of a woman, of a mother."[53]

Similarly, in her nine essays about Yosemite, where she spent eight days, Jackson overcomes an initial impression of local Indians as "loathsome," "vicious," and "soulless" when she discovers their veneration for the area's pristine beauty. She expresses particular respect for the "poets among them" who have given lovely names to the land's natural features. She uses these names in her essays, believing them superior to more recent American designations. Indeed, she discusses the Americans who have renamed Yosemite's lakes and rivers as crass materialists, expansionists of the worst sort. Lake "Ah-wi-yah," she explains facetiously, is "known now, thanks to some American importer of looking-glasses, as Mirror Lake." And she accounts thus for the title of her essay "Pi-wy-ack and Yo-wi-he": "In the language of the Ah-wah-ne-chee, who always spoke truth, 'Pi-wy-ack' means 'white water' or 'shower of shining crystals,' and 'Yo-wi-he' means 'the twisting' or 'the meandering.' These were the names of the two great falls by which the Merced (River of Mercy) leaps into Ah-wah-ne. Then came the white men, liars; they called the upper fall 'Nevada,' and the lower one 'Vernal;' and the lies prevailed; being, as lies are apt to be, easier said than the truth."[54]

Such was Jackson's delight in Yosemite that she began to identify with local Indians on the grounds of their mutual affection for the land. By 1872 Yosemite had become perhaps the major tourist destination in California—Jackson's friends Ralph Waldo Emerson and Lucia Runkle had already visited—but it was still quite rustic, having only begun to welcome visitors in 1855. Like other female tourists to the area, Jackson reveled in the opportunities for unconventional behavior and adventure that exploration of the park's wild trails and rivers afforded. Her experiences roused her to sympathy for the area's original inhabitants. In one of her Yosemite essays, she recounts the story of a six-year-old local Indian boy who, having been kidnapped by white men, subsequently stole two horses and escaped: " 'to illustrate the folly of attempting to civilize the race,' says the biographer of the poor Ah-wah-ne-chee; 'to illustrate the spell of Ah-wah-ne,' say I." In another Yosemite essay, she imagines herself one of the local Indians. Unable to press on with her guide John Murphy and the rest of his party one day, she insists that they leave her behind. When they come back several hours later, they are surprised to find her unafraid:

> "Oh! Has not the time seemed long to you?" exclaimed everybody, in sympathizing tones, as the party rode up. Murphy looked observantly into my face, a twinkle came into his eye, and, as he mounted me once more on that mule, he said, in a low tone:
> "I reckon ye like bein' alone; don't yer?"
> "Yes, Mr. Murphy," said I. "As well as if I were a woman of the Ah-wah-ne-chee."[55]

Shortly after Jackson returned to the East from California, she jokingly told a friend that her experiences "in the saddle" in Yosemite had been "as good as a quarter of a century of pioneering."[56] While she was referring to the arduousness of her trip—she disliked riding horses and mules—there was a broader truth to her statement: her powers of observation had allowed her to witness much in a short time, and what she had seen had affected her profoundly. Only a year later, she actually became a pioneer. In the spring of 1873, unable to shake off a bout of diphtheria that had taken hold of her that winter and left her so sick she was mostly unable to write, she began feeling "irresistibly impelled" to visit Colorado Territory.[57] Colorado was then becoming famous as a healthful sanctuary for people with respiratory infections and also as a tourist destination. Jackson hoped to recover there and to find fresh subjects for a new collection of travel essays. At first she tried to convince various friends, including May Alcott (Louisa May's sister) and Jessy Bross of Chicago, to make a brief trip with her. But in November, when she still had not found an available friend and her illness still had not lifted, she set out for a prolonged, solitary stay, accompanied on the train by her Amherst homeopathist Dr. Cate and a nurse.

When she first arrived in the new town of Colorado Springs, sixty-eight miles south of Denver, she was dejected. "I shall never forget my sudden sense of hopeless disappointment at the moment when I first looked on the town," she writes in her essay "Colorado Springs," published in the *Independent* on August 13, 1874.

> I had crossed the continent, ill, disheartened, to find a climate which would not kill. There stretched before me, to the east, a bleak, bare, unrelieved, desolate plain. There rose behind me, to the west, a dark range of mountains, snow-topped, rocky-walled, stern, cruel, relentless. Between lay the town—small, straight, new, treeless.
> "One might die of such a place alone," I said bitterly. "Death by disease would be more natural."[58]

Despite these early misgivings, Jackson quickly recovered from her illness in Colorado, reveling in what she described to Kate Field as "the divinest air I ever breathed."[59] She also quickly came to love Colorado Springs and the surrounding landscape. Founded in 1871 by General William Jackson Palmer as the "Fountain Colony," one of the private landholding companies attached to his Denver and Rio Grande Railroad, the renamed Colorado Springs had grown by the time Jackson arrived to a bustling place of 3,000 pioneers. "Already there are in the town, bakeries, laundries, livery stables, billiard halls, restaurants, mills, shops, hotels, and churches," Jackson writes in "Colorado Springs." "In all these respects, the town is far better provided than the average New England town of the same population. Remoteness from centres of supplies compels towns, as it compels individuals, to take care of themselves."[60]

Before departing for Colorado, Jackson had been given some twenty letters of introduction to local residents from two eastern literary acquaintances who had previously visited the region: Sara Lippincott, a popular journalist who wrote under the pseudonym "Grace Greenwood," and Samuel Bowles, the editor of the *Springfield Republican*. One of her letters from Bowles introduced her to William Sharpless Jackson, a resident of her own Colorado Springs Hotel. Born in 1836 in Pennsylvania, and raised a Quaker, William Jackson had been working in St. Paul, Minnesota, as treasurer of the Lake Superior and Mississippi Railroad before coming to Colorado in 1871 to join in the administration of the Denver and Rio Grande. By the time Helen met him in 1873, he had also bought into Colorado Springs and started the El Paso County Bank, having acquired its failing precursor during that year's financial panic.

Along with other guests of their hotel, Helen and William took most of their meals together, and Helen greatly enjoyed his "agreeable talk," as she told Anne Botta.[61] They began venturing out on carriage rides, coming to know each other at the same time that they explored the wonders of the surrounding region: the Garden of the Gods, a sprawling assemblage of unusual red rock formations; Manitou Springs, a neighboring town where the hot springs for which Colorado Springs was named are actually located; and the majestic Rocky Mountains, where Helen discovered quiet, beloved retreats at Cheyenne Mountain and South Cheyenne Canyon. She took to calling her new companion "Will," and he, for unknown reasons, nicknamed her "Peggy." Sometime in 1874, when Helen moved into an unpleasant two-room apartment in a boardinghouse on Kiowa Street, between Cascade and Tejon—an area known as "Dead Man's Row" for the large number of invalids living there—she and William began, as she would later explain, to feel *"almost as if we were married."*[62] By the time she returned to the East Coast that fall, she had an actual marriage proposal to consider. She was not displeased to have her doctors pronounce her in imminent need of more recuperation in the West.

That winter in Colorado Springs, as her attachment to William grew, she wrestled with the question of remarriage. William was a thoroughly practical person, little given to dwelling on either emotional or aesthetic issues, and she had "mighty misgivings" about marrying a man who shared none of her literary passions. At the same time, however, with the success of her career she had grown beyond her old need for intellectual mentorship. She seems also to have tired of the strain of caring for Thomas Wentworth Higginson, though until this point she had not been much moved by the attentions she had received from other men. (In Colorado, her suitors apparently included Colonel Robert H. Lamborn, a medical doctor and high-ranking official of the Denver and Rio Grande.)[63] She found herself more and more powerfully drawn to the simple goodness she detected in William. "It is a strange thing in the life of a woman organized as I am, and who has had the experience that I have,—that the only man who has compelled her seriously to think of marrying, should be a plain unvarnished, comparatively uneducated business man," she wrote to Charlotte Cushman. "But so it is: and when I go away from him in the spring, I shall miss his simple-hearted, quiet, patient devotion out of my life, more than I have ever yet missed anything a man had to give me!"[64] When she wrote again to Cushman that July from the East, it was to thank her friend for congratulations on her engagement. "He rests me: and I trust him to the *core*, which is what I have seldom felt of any man," she said.

> I know perfectly well that there will be moments when he will jar on my taste, or my prejudices or conventional customs, so that I shall turn red:—*but*—of all the

men I have known who would never have jarred me, that way, there has not been *one* of whom I should be so sure of never having to blush at *heart,* for a meanness or a falsity which *I* alone knew! He is truth, and uprightness itself—& as sunny as sunshine:—and he has won me to care for him by so slow a winning, that I am persuaded it must last.[65]

They were married in October in a Quaker ceremony at Annie's house in Wolfboro, New Hampshire.

The Jackson marriage was happy, especially in its early years. As Sarah Woolsey would later claim, Helen's letters from this period express "a content and satisfaction such as she never before had tasted in her life."[66] William's letters also convey great happiness. "We are both well and very happy. I think we have not made a mistake," Helen wrote to Annie from Colorado Springs a few weeks after the marriage. "I cannot but wonder at the strange fates which kept us so long unmarried, & then brought us together in this remote spot."[67] In February 1876 the Jacksons together wrote a playful note to Samuel Bowles, thanking him for introducing them and asking him to visit them in their new home, a small house they were renting while making plans to remodel another that William owned, at 228 East Kiowa Street, on the corner of Weber. "I want Mrs. Jackson to be here when you make your visit," William told Bowles, "that you may judge whether you did well or ill by me. Come and see." To which Helen gleefully appended: "That is a truly masculine way of putting things! Come and judge whether you did well or ill by *me.* I say! Come and see!"[68] That spring William Ward wrote to congratulate the couple, joking that Mr. Jackson "could not find a wife on earth & had to go to Helen Hunt for one." Will soon replied: "Fallen Angels are very loveable—I advise every man to go to the same place in search."[69]

In May, Helen wrote a joyous long letter to her new sister-in-law Hannah, in response to a request for news of Will. "I have had a hearty laugh over your suggestion that I should write an account of a 'Model Home' for the *Independent,* and thereby let you know something about him," she said. "He looks splendidly well—has grown stout—and is as happy in his house as if he were a boy. I really believe he likes me on the whole much better than he thought he should; we both of us regret only one thing and that is that we were so foolish as to wait nearly two years for all this happiness." Helen told Hannah that their rented house was small, but she had managed to make it cozy and picturesque by decorating it after her usual fashion, with unique furnishings, vines, flowers, fans, paintings, and various objects of local craftsmanship. She described for Hannah the satisfying home life she and William had established:

We breakfast at half past seven, dine at half past one, and take tea at half past six. Will draws the water (which has to be brought from a well in the next yard & put in a barrel by the back door)—chops kindlings, and breaks up the coal, every morning. Think of that! I dust my sitting room and dining room before breakfast every morning. The dusting of my sitting room is something I never allow a servant to do. They disarrange books & papers so, and do not dust well either. After breakfast, I make Will's bed and mine[.] . . . —From ten to twelve, every morning, I write.—Between twelve and one, I walk down town—often walk home with Will to dinner.—After dinner, I always take a drive, if it is pleasant, and it usually is; last month I drove every day but four;—once in a great while Will goes with me—but usually he is too busy to do anything more than take a little turn when I get back, just before supper. But on Sunday we usually go off for the whole day out of doors . . . after tea, we read the newspapers, or play backgammon, or make a call—or chat with our neighbors who often drop in.—We have friends to tea and to dinner very often—but never give large parties; our life is really exactly what I like and enjoy.[70]

As Jackson mentions in this letter, she maintained regular daily hours for writing even in the midst of her newly married, western life. Indeed, by this time she was so committed to her career that she allowed nothing except illness or real crisis to alter her working habits. She was usually awake by 5:45, and her writing day often began sooner, and continued longer, than the two-hour mid-morning session she mentions to Hannah. When she was at her desk, she scrupulously avoided all interruptions. She did most of her writing for the press in pencil on large yellow sheets of low-gloss post office paper, having learned from occasional attempts to work while lying ill in bed that she could write most neatly and quickly with these implements. Both at home and when she was away on travels, she took care to make her work area aesthetically pleasing and comfortable, decorating the walls around her desk with vines or leaves and keeping a fire burning nearby. On her afternoon carriage rides in the area surrounding Colorado Springs, and on longer train expeditions, she carried blank manuscript books in which she recorded notes for her travel essays. She thought nothing of writing in moving vehicles; she also carried a portable camp stool for when she wished to work in the open field. Though she was not as intrepid as some pioneers, being a poor horseback rider, during her outings she enjoyed hiking or riding mules to the most out-of-the-way places she could find, sometimes staying overnight in rough lodgings: "I can sleep anywhere for two nights," she said.[71] In Crystal Park, near Manitou Springs, she and Will once camped for several nights on the floor of an empty toll booth in order to secure a good view of the local sunrise.[72]

The essays she wrote about her observations in and around Colorado, many of them never collected, retain substantial historical interest today. The first one appeared in print in March 1874 in the *Independent,* and seven more were published there that year. During each of the following years before she took up the cause of Indian rights, she published from two to six Colorado essays. She believed readers of the *Independent* liked her travel essays best among the many types of writing she published in those pages. They were certainly more welcome than her other work at the *Atlantic,* where the editors James T. Fields and his successor William Dean Howells were both eager proponents of American regionalism and of writing that grappled with the effects of postwar industrial expansion. In fact, Howells featured so much of Jackson's travel writing that he once assured her he would have trouble "getting on without" it.[73] In 1878 Jackson collected eighteen of her Colorado essays, together with four of her old pieces on New England and sixteen about her 1872 trip to California, in a book called *Bits of Travel at Home,* published by Roberts Brothers.[74] While this second "H.H." travel collection received more mixed reviews than had her first, European volume—some thought it monotonous—her powers of description and characterization were widely praised. "No writer has given so vividly, brilliantly, and yet without exaggeration, the characteristic features of the great west," the *Hartford Courant* claimed. With a measure of proprietary self-congratulation, the *Atlantic* boasted, "Her accounts of the people she meets are always clever and entertaining, and it is pleasant to find so bold and imperturbably cheerful a traveler setting down her experience in strange parts."[75]

Jackson's Colorado essays rarely exhibit the comic flair that had enlivened her essays on Europe and Northern California. Her 1878 *Independent* piece "Down the Arkansas River to New York" is a delightful exception. In it, she satirizes the cattle roundup so romanticized by people living in the East. "To a 'round-up,'" she says, "as to so many other things in this world, enchantment is lent of distance." She offers in its place a more realistic, though far less glamorous, symbol for the rusticity of western life:

> The ubiquitousness of the Western pig is something to which no writer, so far as I know, has done justice. He rambles about in a leisurely fashion everywhere, like a distinguished guest, to whom the freedom of the city has been extended. He casts an oblique and contemptuous leer on strangers who turn out for him. . . . He has an abominably knowing look. It would hardly astonish one if he were presently to take out a cigar and sit down to smoke. He looks as much at ease as if he owned every pork-packing establishment west of Boston.[76]

While most of Jackson's essays on the West are more sober-minded, they are no less compelling, for with her move to Colorado she began to produce increasingly distinctive regionalist work. Not surprisingly, she wrote frequently about the grandeur of western nature and of life carried out in harmony with it. In this same essay apotheosizing the western pig, for example, she contrasts "the repose and rapture of the wilderness" seen from her window on a train headed east with what strikes her, upon her arrival in New York, as the "terrible and fierce" aspect of existence in the city: "While my eyes were lingering compassionately on the tired, listless, or desperate faces near me, I was seeing with a strange vividness such pictures as these: A strip of grass bleached white, silvery as silver or spun glass, between a belt of yellow sun flowers and a bit of green meadow; an oak tree, bright, dark green, rising behind a huge stack of yellow straw; a shining meadow."

Jackson never tired of trying to capture in words Colorado's mountains, canyons, waterfalls, plants, flowers, and birds. As usual, she discovered Transcendental significances in nature's bounty; more than ever, she focused on the power of place to shape, and to mirror, the inner lives of local people. In "A Symphony in Yellow and Red," the Garden of the Gods is a living entity, possessed even of its own ethnic dialect: "I have fancied that its speech was to the speech of ordinary nature what the Romany is among the dialects of the civilized,—fierce, wild, free, defiantly tender."[77] In "The Cradle of Peace," an alpine valley exerts an indomitable influence over all who know it well:

> There are some spots on earth which seem to have a strong personality about them, . . . a charm which charms like the beauty of a human face, and a spell which lasts like the bond of a human relation. In such spots we can live alone without being lonely. We go away from them with the same sort of sorrow with which we part from friends, and we recall their looks with the yearning tenderness with which we look on the photographs of beloved absent faces.[78]

During Jackson's residency, Colorado was in the midst of a mining and development boom that was threatening the existence of such bucolic havens. With Will, she visited mining settlements and railroad terminuses, often just at the point when these places were mushrooming into cities. She went down a gold mine in Central City and a silver mine in Georgetown, and she toured such bustling mining towns as Fair Play, Rosita, and Leadville. When she visited Leadville in 1879, it was experiencing an amazing growth spurt begun only two years earlier when the land began to yield vast quantities of silver under new smelting techniques. The town's population, which had jumped from fewer than 200 residents to almost 14,000, was a motley assortment of emigrants from the East Coast and places much farther afield, especially Cornwall, Ireland, and Germany. Newcomers made their way to the mines every day. In her *Atlantic* essay "To Leadville," Jackson describes passing some of these pilgrims on her own way to the town:

> Families—fathers, mothers, with crowds of little children, bedsteads, iron pots, comforters, chairs, tables, cooking-stoves, cradles—wedged into small wagons, toiling slowly up the long hills and across the long stretches of plain, all going to Leadville to seek that fortune which had so evidently eluded their efforts hitherto; solitary adventurers, whose worldly possessions consisted of a pack-mule, a bundle,

and a pick-axe; and adventurers still more solitary, with only the bundle and pick-axe, and no mule; dozens of these we passed.

"Going to Leadville?" was our usual greeting.[79]

Here and elsewhere in her western travel essays, Jackson writes with sympathy of humble pioneers struggling, like herself, to establish new lives in the West; along with nature, these miners, farmers, innkeepers, wives, and small-scale entrepreneurs are the main focus of her Colorado essays. Yet she also expresses concern over the harm done to the local environment by the new emigrants—especially the miners, who hurry from one location to another in search of fortune, trailing tin cans, slapdash towns, and permanent railroad infrastructures in their wake. In her 1878 *Independent* essay "Alamosa," she laments one old town's sacrifices to industrialization:

> Whatever it gains in material success, it will have lost something when the whistle of railroad trains and the noisy bustle of many people's living shall have driven off the antelope and the deer, which now come down to the river to drink, and shall have frightened away forever the great flocks of wild geese and ducks and fans, which look so majestic now as they slowly soar overhead at twilight.[80]

Jackson worried, too, over the many changes being forced on the region's original inhabitants by the ascendant American hegemony. Before 1879 she said little in print about Colorado's Native Americans, but she did occasionally express sympathetic interest in the lives of local Hispanic residents and in the well-being of their principal religion, Catholicism. In her 1877 essay "Wa-ha-toy-a; or, Before the Graders," she describes the small Mexican town of Walsenburg, at the foot of the Spanish Peaks, or "Wa-ha-toy-a." This town consists of some fifty, mostly mud homes, Jackson says, "not as uncomfortable as one would suppose, and by no means as ugly." She is given a tour through one of these homes by an elderly woman, whose graciousness makes a strong impression:

> When I took leave of her I said through my interpreter, "I am greatly obliged to you for showing me your house."
> With rapid gestures and shrugs of the shoulders she poured forth sentence after sentence, all the while looking into my face with smiles and taking my hand in hers.
> "What does she say?" I asked.
> "She says," replied my guide, "that her poor house is not worth looking at, and she is the one who is obliged that so beautiful a lady should enter it." And this was a poverty-stricken old woman in a single garment of tattered calico, living in a mud hut, without a chair or a bed![81]

Only a few days after receiving this warm welcome, Jackson drove with her husband to a meadow outside Walsenburg, where local residents were gathered to await the arrival of the "graders," workers who would prepare the ground for a new track of the Denver and Rio Grande Railroad. "We had arrived at an important moment in the history of the little town," Jackson explains: "the railroad was about to begin." She narrates this event with a sense of foreboding, as if it implies an enormity of changes that the Mexican residents of Walsenburg scarcely realize:

> Just as we drove up, a man advanced from the crowd, dragging a ploughshare. Nobody took any special note of him. He bent himself sturdily to the handles of the plough, and in a moment more soft ridges of upturned earth, and a line of rich dark brown, marked a narrow furrow. Swiftly he walked westward, the slender, significant dark-brown furrow lengthening rod by rod as he walked. His shadow lengthened until it became a slenderer line than the furrow in the distance, and was lost at last in the great purple shadow of Wa-ha-toy-a. The railroad was begun; the wilderness had surrendered.[82]

Jackson's concern for the preservation of Colorado's early lifeways sets her essays apart from the work of several other famous travel writers who visited the region around this same time: Grace Greenwood, Bayard Taylor, and the Englishwoman Isabella Bird Bishop. Like Samuel Bowles, whose *Our New West* (1869) documented his journey through America's newly won territories as part of a political entourage, these authors all expressed overriding approval of the American development of Colorado. They gathered their information on local race matters from prominent American pioneers; those pioneers included William Byers, the editor and publisher of the *Rocky Mountain News,* whose derogatory view of local Indians would later lead him into a public dispute with Jackson. Greenwood's *New Life in New Lands* (1873), Taylor's *Colorado: A Summer Trip* (1867), and Bishop's *Lady's Life in the Rocky Mountains* (1879) all present Colorado as a primitive, difficult place, filled with "savage" Indians who deserve to be displaced by the American empire. Jackson's essays, in contrast, demonstrate sympathy for the plight of Colorado's early residents, and she writes of the region surrounding her new home matter-of-factly, without sensationalizing the hardships of western existence. She knew from painful personal experience that hardship was to be expected in life, and that what was most remarkable was the ability to carry on in spite of it. Her writings are based on her personal interviews with ordinary people of different races, not with prominent whites only, and also on her own experiences as a committed pioneer, not simply a transient visitor. In October 1877 she and William moved into their permanent home on Kiowa Street, after she had overseen the transformation of its kitchen into a living room (because that location afforded the best view of Pike's Peak) and the creation of a new entryway.

That Jackson's western travel writings demonstrate more race tolerance than those of her peers owes a good deal to her relationship with her husband. Whereas Edward Hunt had been, like herself, the descendant of English, Protestant emigrants to colonial Massachusetts, and had shared in her inherited race, class, and religious prejudices, William Jackson was of Irish Quaker ancestry, the descendant of eighteenth-century emigrants. He had grown up in Pennsylvania in a family of antislavery activists. "Mr. Jackson recollects your name," Helen told Moncure Conway after her remarriage. "When he was a boy, he used to be waked up at night to drive fugitive slaves across country to some Quakers house for hiding."[83] Helen was impressed by her husband's youthful valor, as she reveals in the following passage from her unpublished novel "Elspeth Dynor":

> There were many Friends' houses in Pennsylvania at this time which were houses of shelter for fugitive slaves making their way to the north. Many a poor hunted creature, starved and footsore, was taken in, hidden, fed, clothed and carried his way by these compassionate people. Stealthily, on bypaths, and at night the fugitives were passed along from house to house, until they were out of danger. Very heroic were these noncombatants, in their own fashion of combating. Many a Friend has driven, alone, twenty, thirty, fifty miles with a black man hidden under the straw of his wagon, through districts where he was liable to be shot at sight, if his errand were discovered.[84]

As an adult, William continued to express solidarity with people of different backgrounds, though his statements became less dramatic. "I despise & utterly condemn any & every thing that borders on cast or exclusiveness," he told Helen in a letter shortly before they were married. In the same letter, though he rarely commented explicitly on her work, he endorsed her habit of writing about humble, persevering people by commending one of her poems, "Pheonixiana," for "revealing so clearly the injustice of cast in any and all its forms, how it melts away before sore trials & the outcasts often come to the surface as the real characters, possessing the true courage & strength."[85] In the years to come, William acted on his belief in the inward nature of true character by trying to live simply and without financial pretension, even though he was gradually amassing a substantial fortune, and by frequently imploring Helen to unite with him in this effort. He also lent support to her mounting religious liberalism and tolerance. Though he had been raised a Quaker, he attended Unitarian services with her during the brief period that they were held in Colorado Springs; when the Unitarian Church folded, he joined her in eschewing church altogether in favor of spending their Sundays outdoors. (On one of these heretical Sundays, the Jacksons' elderly cook, Jane, reportedly dipped into William's whiskey, threw open the scullery window, and wailed, "Oh Lord Lord Lord—Mr & Mrs Jackson they've gone off on a pleasure trip on the Lords day & they'll never go to Heaven's sure's anything! Oh! Oh! Oh!")[86] By 1880 he was professing a keen interest in the theories of Christian communism expounded by the English agnostic writer Eliza Lynn Linton in *The True History of Joshua Davidson* (1872). "It is odd how with my old superstitions still clinging to me I perpetually drift into the society and affection of the most heretical," Helen marveled in a letter to Moncure Conway.[87]

In William's company, Helen gradually moved away from her early tendency to view people of different races and religions as belonging to a lower, servant class, and toward a notable appreciation for diversity. The extent of her husband's influence, evident in her Colorado essays, can perhaps best be understood elsewhere, in the changing tenor of her feelings about African Americans. Back in 1869, when she was still under the influence of Fiske and Hunt family conceptions of race and caste, she had told friends in a private letter from Rome that she thought the celebrated expatriate American sculptor Edmonia Lewis looked "just like a little shiny brown toad stool, with a black velvet smoking cap on," and smirked, "I think she can't possibly help believing that my smile & shake of the hand mean a great deal more than they do—& I feel as if it were not honest to let her suppose I shouldn't just the least bit in the world mind breakfasting with her!"[88] Later, when she began to write fiction, she sometimes relied on racial and ethnic stereotypes in the development of her minor characters as a means of attempting comic relief. In 1875, in contrast, she wrote a sonnet inspired by the plight of blacks under Reconstruction, "Freedom," which William Jackson commended as "a just & proper defense of the poor Negroes."[89] And in an 1879 travel essay about Mount Desert, Maine, titled "Eden, Formerly on the Euphrates," she lauds a local marriage between a black sea captain and a Yankee white girl, including their happy union among the evidences that make Mount Desert a new "Eden." This metaphor has rather remarkable implications, for if Mount Desert is Eden, this man and woman are its Adam and Eve, destined to bring forth a new people.[90] By 1880 Jackson was not only willing to "breakfast" with a black woman but once, in making preparations for a trip to Washington, D.C., particularly sought out a room in a black woman's boardinghouse, having heard good things of the establishment.[91]

Even as Jackson grew in racial and religious tolerance during her years with William Jackson, her association with him also heightened the paradox that was always present in her literary protests against industrial development. William Jackson was a railroad executive and enthusiastic leader in the American development of Colorado; his connection to the expanding Denver and Rio Grande Railroad was the very reason Helen was on hand in Walsenburg and other towns as they first faced the threat of industrialization. In her early essay "Colorado Springs," she had specifically stated her intention to eschew in her own work the boosterism evident in much contemporary American writing on the West. But after her marriage she wrote many glowing accounts of her travels on the Denver and Rio Grande as it expanded south toward El Paso, Texas, and then west from Pueblo up the Arkansas River, through Leadville, and eventually on to Salt Lake City. In effect, these accounts were every bit as promotional as the relatively few essays in which she explicitly advertised American life in Colorado, such as "The Kansas & Colorado Building at the Centennial Exposition" and "A State without a Debt."[92] In her essay "Alamosa," for example, even as she laments one town's sacrifices in becoming the latest terminus of the Denver and Rio Grande, she sings the praises of "the plucky little narrow-gauge road of whose progress in the last four years Colorado has such reason to be proud."[93]

Jackson further promoted the American development of Colorado by working to advance local American cultural institutions. She solicited books for a local miner's library from readers of the *Independent;* ran "Our Book Table," a literary review column for the Denver *Tribune;* and, in her travel essays, expressed special approval of local residents, of whatever race or ethnicity, who conducted their domestic lives according to her pet virtues of cheerfulness and diligence. In all of these endeavors, she might be seen as promoting a type of cultural manifest destiny. Privately, in fact, she sometimes expressed a belief that the vicinity of her "little frontier town" was entirely lacking in culture and even history, as if its native Indian and Hispanic cultures were of no consequence.[94] "There is something to me grander in the stupendous waiting of this wilderness for its history than in any Old World thing I ever saw," she wrote to an eastern friend in 1874. "The spaces, the silences, the colossal strengths, the ineffable beauties—all waiting!" (On a related note, she once joked that she was "four fifths barbarian" because she liked Mexican towns such as Santa Fe and Paso Del Norte.)[95] Publicly, in her essay "Colorado Springs," she predicted that in the future—with the advent of American culture—there would "be born of these plains and mountains, all along the great central plateaus of our continent, the very best life, physical and mental, of the coming centuries."[96]

Jackson's references to the West as an empty land, "waiting" to be developed by Americans, are linked to a commonplace, pernicious Anglo-American viewpoint of her time, later known as the "Black Legend." Ever since the Spanish colonial period in what is now the American Southwest, American writers had helped justify American interest in taking over the region by describing local Hispanic residents as lazy and lacking in culture. In the mid–nineteenth century, well-meaning white Americans like Jackson no longer condemned Hispanics for this supposed backwardness; but in a new twist on an old prejudice, which the historian George Fredrickson labeled "romantic racialism" in his influential book *The Black Image in the White Mind* (1971), they built on pseudoscientific theories of inherent racial difference in order to praise racial minorities for their perceived simplicity and indolence, traits seen as sadly lacking in the Caucasian gene pool. Jackson's 1879 essay "A Day in Trinidad," about a trading town twelve miles north of the New Mexican border, offers a classic example of this attitude:

I think I saw in the streets three Mexicans for one American. A most picturesque race they are, too, like all the gay, idle, southern peoples. Their rich brown skins, their shining dark eyes and coal-black hair, their smiles and their white teeth, their movement, their attitudes, and their rags, all are picturesque and full of beauty. And as for their atmosphere of reposeful leisure, it is a perpetual lesson and rebuke to the bustling, nervous Anglo-Saxon.[97]

To a certain degree, Jackson knew there was prejudice inherent in this sort of observation. In several of her travel essays from her Colorado period, as in her earlier piece on San Francisco's Chinatown, she deliberately raises the issue of cultural relativism by allowing individuals for whom she expresses contempt to express their mutual scorn for her. In "Alamosa," when she asks some Mexican men to dance for her because they remind her of merry Italian peasants, they mock her request, offering to dance only for pay. And during her "Day in Trinidad," she is busy wondering over the fate of a local impoverished couple, when she notices that she herself is an object of derisive speculation: "A group of Mexican men, seeing me watching these beggars, said something among themselves, and all burst into a laugh."

Jackson was also at least intermittently aware of the ambivalence of her position in regard to the American development of the West. Toward the end of her career, in an 1883 *Atlantic* travel piece, "By Horse Cars into Mexico," she would ponder the opposing standpoints of those who built, and those who were forced to welcome, America's new railroads, referring to herself as one of "those unfortunately constituted persons who are born with a worse than second sight; that sort of double sight which persists in seeing both sides of a thing."[98] In her Colorado essays, she reconciled her conflicting desires to both promote and protest the industrialization of the region, insofar as she did reconcile them, much as she had done earlier in New England: by paying tribute to gentler, more respectful ways of taking part in change. In her 1876 *Atlantic* essay "A Colorado Road," about a new toll road over Cheyenne Mountain, she makes the same point she had made years before about the new cog train up Mount Washington: that appreciation for a place's native beauty should be more important to the newcomer than exploitation.[99] Similarly, in "O-Be-Joyful Creek and Poverty Gulch," published in the *Atlantic* in 1883, she reminds her readers that "there are many sorts of 'claims,' 'prospectors,' and 'prospecting,'" and that people who cherish Colorado's natural splendors are actually better off than the crass materialists who fill the region's mining towns:

There is a field of purple asters two miles west of Crested Butte that some people would rather possess for the rest of the summers of their lives than the coal bank opposite it. . . . The men who are digging, coking, selling the coal opposite the aster field, do not see the asters; the prospectors hammering away high up above the foaming, splashing, sparkling torrent of the O-Be-Joyful water do not know where it is amber and where it is white, or care for it unless they need drink. . . . There is one comfort: the market in which stock in aster fields and brooks is bought is always strong. Margins are safe, and dividends are sure.[100]

In writing of individual Colorado residents, whether native or more newly arrived, Jackson expresses most approval of those who forge quiet, decent lives in the region, persevering with diligence and good cheer in the midst of the many changes occurring all around them at the hands of more powerful and unscrupulous developers. She takes special interest in the lives of local women, as she explains in "To Leadville":

> The ordinary visitor to Leadville listens to the talk of men, and busies himself with the statistics of the nearly-made fortunes. . . . But to me the whole thing resolved itself, after all, into the same old story: so many men getting rich of a sudden; so many men getting poor; crowds pouring in to snatch at chances. . . . One who wishes to know the real atmosphere of a place lingers in suburbs, chats on doorsteps, and does not concern himself about town records. By far the most vivid impressions I brought away from Leadville are of conversations which I had with women whom I met accidentally, and who never dreamed that they were telling history.[101]

The women Jackson features in her Leadville essay include Canadian and English launderers, a German shopkeeper, and an innkeeper from Kansas. In another essay about Colorado's mining boom, "A New Anvil Chorus," she devotes as much attention to her encounter with an impoverished old Frenchwoman known as "Grandma" as she does to her description of newly created Garland City. "Finding me so sympathetic a listener, she told me bit by bit the whole history of her emigration from Missouri to Colorado," Jackson explains. It is a sad tale, featuring family losses to consumption and the Civil War that echo Jackson's own, and a doggedly cheerful perseverance that awakens her admiration:

> "Grandma," said I, "you have had a great deal of trouble in your life; yet you look happier than most people do."
> "Oh, no! I ain't never suffered," she said. "I've always had plenty. I've always been took care of. God's always taken care of me."[102]

Jackson describes a woman of similar bravery in her 1882 *Atlantic* essay, "Aunty Lane," about the proprietress of a lodge for summer travelers, high up in the mountains outside Colorado Springs, where Jackson once spent a night. Although Aunty Lane's life has been full of difficulties, from the time of her earliest, terrible years as an orphan in the East, to her present lonely exile, she has persevered by means of a "remarkable temperament," Jackson says, which "nothing could daunt or cast down." Jackson argues that in America's remote places there are "hundreds and thousands of American women leading just such lives; working side by side with men, uncomplaining, unknown; doing the hardest part of the work." For Jackson, these women demonstrate a "heroism" that is "far greater than most of the heroisms which are accounted as such by the world."[103] It is this sort of heroism, the valor of ordinary people carving out dignity from a world full of trouble and change, that Jackson commemorates in her travel writing, and also, as we are about to see, in her fiction.

7

Short Stories and Early Novels

"Let me make the songs of the community, and I care not who makes its laws," was well said. It was song which Draxy supplied to these people's lives. Not often in verse, in sound, in any shape that could be measured, but in spirit. She vivified their every sense of beauty, moral and physical. She opened their eyes to joy; she revealed to them the sacredness and delight of common things; she made their hearts sing.

JACKSON, "The Elder's Wife" (1873)

If there be a pitiless community in this world, it is a small New England village. Calvinism, in its sternest aspects, broods over it; narrowness and monotony make rigid the hearts which theology has chilled; and a grim Pharisaism, born of a certain sort of intellectual keen-wittedness, completes the cruel inhumanity.

JACKSON, *Hetty's Strange History* (1877)

Jackson once believed herself entirely incapable of writing fiction. "As for writing stories, I could as soon turn architect & build churches!" she told Kate Field in March 1866. "It always has been & always will be, a profound mystery to me, how they do it!"[1] A year later, though, apparently inspired by the early example of her mother's playful cat letters, she began trying to write partly fictional children's stories about cats. By January 1868 she had placed one, "A Christmas Tree for Cats," in the *Riverside Magazine for Young People*. Over the next several years, as she became increasingly adept within her travel essays at character portrayal and regional description—and as she watched Thomas Wentworth Higginson and other Newport friends, like Sara Greenough, begin to write short stories for adults—she prepared to try her own hand. In September 1871 she published the story "Whose Wife Was She?" in the new *Scribner's Monthly* magazine, under the elusive pseudonym "Saxe Holm."

This and the other lengthy Saxe Holm stories she would soon publish in

Scribner's were very popular with readers, and curiosity about their hidden authorship—which the literary scholar Susan Coultrap-McQuin has called "the best kept literary secret of the nineteenth century"[2]—fueled a great deal of speculation in the newspapers. When in late 1873 Scribner published a collection of the first six Saxe Holm stories, *Saxe Holm's Stories, First Series,* it met with startling success in some quarters: the review in *Publisher's Weekly* was one of many that found the stories "among the most brilliant ever written in America."[3] All of this enthusiasm bolstered the reputation of *Scribner's Monthly* but had a less salutary effect on Jackson, who was encouraged by public demand and ready payment to produce rather formulaic work as a sidelight to her more earnest career as a poet and essayist. Only when she began to write novels, in 1876, did she truly begin to grow as a fiction writer.

Like her travel writing, Jackson's fiction explores the same regions that she came to know in the course of her own wandering life; it initially set forth life in the small towns and rural hamlets of New England, with brief forays into Canada, New York, and Europe, then later moved on to an increasing preoccupation with the rustic West. During the decades of Jackson's career, while most Americans still lived in the countryside, rural places not only were being threatened with gradual development and industrialization but also were steadily losing national influence to the large cities. By focusing on admirable characters who lead full lives in America's increasingly marginalized rural locations, Jackson made her fiction an inexplicit yet important component in the same "protest against the spread of civilization" that she waged more directly in her travel writing.

Her Saxe Holm stories, which she began to write when she was still dividing her time between Newport and various northeastern summer resorts, reflect the strength of her imaginative bond with her native region. One review of her first collection, which contains "Whose Wife Was She?" and five other stories—"Draxy Miller's Dowry" and its sequel "The Elder's Wife," "The One-Legged Dancers," "How One Woman Kept Her Husband," and "Esther Wynn's Love-Letters"—aptly labeled Saxe Holm "A New England Writer of New England Fiction."[4] Even after she moved to Colorado, Jackson continued to set most of her Saxe Holm fiction in the New England she had known since youth, as is evident in the five stories gathered in her second collection, *Saxe Holm's Stories, Second Series* (1878): "Susan Lawton's Escape," "A Four-Leaved Clover," "Joe Hale's Red Stockings," "Farmer Bassett's Romance," and "My Tourmaline." In 1877, the year before that collection was published, Jackson discussed her continued attachment to the landscape and domestic life of New England in one of her domestic essays for the *New York Independent,* "Wanted, in New England, An Apostle for Sunshine." She wrote this essay after a return visit to New England, undertaken in part as research for a travel book that never came to fruition. "In the course of last summer and fall I was in some twenty or thirty

New England towns—in Massachusetts, in New Hampshire, in Vermont," she explains.

> I drove every day from twelve to eighteen miles, up and down the hills, through the beautiful valleys, along the dancing watercourses. I know all the different types of the New England rural home, from the neat, precise, and often ornate house of the well-to-do man in the manufacturing town, to the gray, weather-beaten, lichen-grown old house of the poorest farmer among the hills. I know them all. I love them all with that loyalty to the soil which I sometimes think is stronger in the New Englander than in any other American.[5]

In Jackson's very first Saxe Holm story, "Whose Wife Was She?," a first-person narrator named Helen describes the bizarre effects of typhus fever on her cousin, Annie Ware; in the process she gradually reveals her own persistent attachment to the domestic customs of one unnamed New England town. Annie awakens from her delirium having lost all memory of her standing engagement to her doting older cousin George; soon, she marries a young, more cosmopolitan suitor, Edward Neal, who is fresh on the scene from European travels. Helen satirizes the clannishness of her Yankee relations, for their failure to sympathize with people outside their own kith and kin has been partly to blame for Annie's illness in the first place. "For weeks a malignant typhus fever had been slowly creeping about in the lower part of our village, in all the streets which had been under water in the spring freshet," she recounts. But families like her own had felt such smug confidence in their separation from the "lower" inhabitants that they had taken no precautions against the disease:

> These streets were occupied chiefly by laboring people, either mill-operatives, or shopkeepers of the poorer class. It was part of the cruel "calamity" of their "poverty" that they could not afford to have homesteads on the high plateau, which lifted itself quite suddenly from the river meadow, and made our village a by-word of beauty all through New England.
> Upon this plateau were laid out streets of great regularity, shaded by grand elms, many of which had been planted by hands that had handled the ropes of the *Mayflower*. Under the shade of these elms stood large old-fashioned houses, in that sort of sleepy dignity peculiar to old New England. We who lived in these houses were also sleepy and dignified. We knew that "under the hill," as it was called, lived many hundreds of men and women, who were stifled in summer for want of the breezes which swept across our heights, cold in winter because the wall of our plateau shut down upon them the icy airs from the frozen river, and cut off the afternoon sun. We were sorry for them, and we sent them cold meat and flannels sometimes; but their life was as remote from our life as if they never crossed our paths.[6]

Helen's subtle criticism of her own social group sounds a good deal like that of Jackson's "Rip Van Winkle," who bemoaned the selfishness of the Yankee passengers on his train in "Notes of Travel." Also like Rip, though, Helen is actually very much one of her own class. Even more than Annie's own parents, she dislikes the fever-induced turn in Annie's affections, for she is convinced that Annie would have been more deeply content and comfortable, even if not more gay, if she had settled down at home with sober cousin George instead of marrying an outsider. Indeed, when Annie suddenly regains the memory of her old commitment, after giving birth to a baby, Helen agrees with her that it is "better" she should die than live with the knowledge of her infidelity to George.[7]

Jackson's second Saxe Holm collection includes another cautionary tale about the perils of disloyalty to rural family origins, "Farmer Bassett's Romance." This story is something of an anomaly within Jackson's larger body of fiction, for it is the only piece in which she explicitly contrasts the integrity of New England country life with the more flashy and dangerous temptations of the city. In two other stories in the same volume, "A Four-Leaved Clover" and "Joe Hale's Red Stockings," she moves beyond issues of regional loyalty to examine the need for regional and national reconciliation in the wake of the Civil War. Both of these narratives celebrate the harmonious uniting of various parts of the country in the marriages of New England girls with Union veterans from different regional and ethnic backgrounds. In "A Four-Leaved Clover," actually set in Chicago, the New England schoolteacher Margaret Warren finally accepts the marriage proposal of Karl Reutner, a Bavarian immigrant and member of the working class. Jackson foreshadows Margaret's capacity for embodying ethnic and regional reconciliation early in the story, when Margaret and Karl's twin brother, Wilhelm, read an erroneous report of Karl's death at Gettysburg. Wilhelm is angry that his brother has died for a new country, which is not his "Fatherland." But when he tells Margaret, "We are Germans; we are not of your blood," she responds pointedly, "All men are of one blood, when the fight is that all men may be free, my friend."[8]

In "Joe Hale's Red Stockings," the Union veteran Joe Hale, from western New York, ends by marrying Matilda Bennet, a New England woman who has grown up in Provincetown, Massachusetts, where she was the daughter of the local lighthouse keeper. Joe and Matilda meet through the auspices of Netty and Sarah, two of the society ladies who have taken over daily operations at the veterans' hospital in "Menthaven," Connecticut—a thinly disguised allusion to New Haven, Connecticut, where Jackson and Sarah Woolsey did their own Civil War volunteer work in the summer of 1862. By selecting Joe to receive a pair of hand-knit red socks that Matilda has donated, and later quietly abetting the correspondence that develops between them, Netty and Sarah demonstrate what Jackson represents as the best characteristics of the New England personality: intelligence, good cheer, and unassuming industriousness. They watch with a mixture of humor and indignation as their more sanctimonious colleagues undertake work that is beyond them, ministering ineptly to the wounded soldiers:

> [W]hen they saw Clara Winthrop, who had never in her life cooked anything more nutritious than sponge-cake, and who was used, in her father's house, to having four servants at her command, gravely assuming the entire control of the diet kitchen; and flighty Mrs. Kate Seely, who could not even be trusted with her own baby when it had croup, installed as head nurse in one of the largest wards, Sarah and Netty looked at each other, and said, in the expressive New England vernacular,—
> "Did you ever!"[9]

Jackson's invocation here of the "New England vernacular" attests to the effort she made in much of her fiction, as in her travel writing, to reproduce the spoken dialects of the places she explored in print. In "Joe Hale's Red Stockings," the result is simple and effective. Elsewhere, however, she sometimes adopts bizarre spelling and phrasing in her quest for phonetic accuracy, with the result that her sentences written in dialect can seem amateurish. In "The Elder's Wife," for instance, the sequel to one of Jackson's first Saxe Holm stories, "Draxy Miller's Dowry," the otherwise mature Elder Kinney speaks in a strangely childish Yankee twang. "It's only my bein' a minister that makes her think anythin' o' me," he says upon first realizing that the heroine Draxy Miller cares for him.[10]

The awkwardness of Elder Kinney's folksy dialect is amplified by its juxtaposition in the Draxy Miller stories to a good deal of incongruously heightened narrative language. When foreshadowing an important change in store for Draxy, for instance, Jackson slips into clichéd, biblical diction. "It came, as the great consecrations of life are apt to come, suddenly, without warning," she writes. "While we are patiently and faithfully keeping sheep in the wilderness, the messenger is journeying toward us with the vial of sacred oil, to make us kings."[11] This sentimental language is intended to make Draxy exceptional. In the end, however, it works not only to confound Jackson's simultaneous attempts at phonetic realism but also to overshadow her basic concern for regional realism in these stories, for it functions along with other details of plot and character development to idealize Draxy. When just a girl, Draxy saves her ineffectual parents after they lose their farm in western New York, whisking them off to stay with relatives on the Atlantic seaboard. There she undertakes to support the family by working as a seamstress even as she continues to cheer them and to attend to her own inner growth by reading Epictetus and studying the art of poetry. She eventually manages to regain possession of a piece of her father's land from a creditor, in the process inspiring that miserly man to change his ways. She then takes her parents to their land in "Clairvend," in the northeast corner of New Hampshire, where she marries the local minister, Elder Kinney. It soon becomes clear that with her ready sympathies and poetic talents, she can minister to the needs of the congregation at least as effectively as her husband. When he dies, the local people ask her to take over his position.

Draxy is a woman whose role in life, as noted in this chapter's first epigraph, is to reveal to everyone she meets "the sacredness and delight of common things"—that is, of ordinary, real life. At the same time, though, as also noted above, the guiding concept behind the Draxy Miller stories is that an ideal, artistic view of life is more important than the everyday realities of life itself: thus the narrator invokes the aphorism "Let me make the songs of the community, and I care not who makes its laws."[12] Jackson would never again create a heroine quite so otherworldly. Yet Draxy Miller did become the basic model for her later protagonists, with the result that most of her fiction demonstrates some confusion between the literary mandates of realism and sentimentalism. This confusion is most detrimental to her Saxe Holm stories, which almost all fall into a similar pattern. Even as she aims in them to depict regional existence, her protagonists, who are usually female, are very much alike, regardless of the details of their regional or ethnic backgrounds. Embodiments of cheerful and diligent perseverance, and possessed of exceptional intuitive powers in matters both artistic and spiritual, these Saxe Holm heroines all serve as unfailing inspirations for their fellow characters. Any one of them might have dreamed up Jackson's popular poem "Spinning" (1869), or taken the place of "Aunty Lane" in that lonesome Colorado lodge, enlightening travelers by a quiet heroism superior to the sort usually recognized by the world.[13]

The confusion between sentimentalism and realism evident in Jackson's short fiction was endemic to her era. Many writers of this period were gradually moving away from Romanticism to realism, at the very same time that they were beginning to hope a viable alternative to the otherworldly inspirations once found in established religion might somehow be established in literature. Jackson wanted her work to encompass not only a concern for regional life but also her own Unitarian and Transcendental leanings, and she looked for similar qualities in the work of other authors. She was after "passion" and "poetic quality," as she said, in addition to local color and flavor.[14] What she meant by "poetic quality" was an intimation of ideal essences to be found beyond surface realities, together with the striving toward universal human truths that she considered necessary to the highest art. By "passion," she meant the same quality that her mentor Thomas Wentworth Higginson had valued: authorial ardor. She believed authors should demonstrate a sense of sympathetic engagement with their subject matter and characters. In 1872 she published an anonymous editorial in the *Independent*, "A Good Word for 'Gush,'" in which she argued that true authorial "enthusiasm"—not its "wordy pretense, made by heartless, brainless people"—was a form of sincerity essential to good art.[15]

Many of the fiction writers who most appealed to Jackson were New England or western regionalists. She was very impressed with Bret Harte's seminal stories of early California. She had begun in girlhood to admire two of the founders of the female tradition in American regionalism, Caroline Kirkland and Harriet Beecher Stowe. From as early as 1849, she was quoting in her letters from Kirkland, whose three books about Michigan frontier life—especially her first, *A New Home: Who'll Follow?* (1839)—went far toward establishing the norms of western regionalism. Jackson also began in youth to express enthusiasm for Stowe, who in 1843 published one of the founding works of New England regionalism, *The Mayflower; or, Sketches of Scenes and Characters among the Descendents of the Pilgrims.* Jackson was never to know either of these two women personally, though their circles overlapped, and though her parents had been friendly with the Beechers: Nathan and Deborah were married by Harriet's brother Edward, and Deborah also knew Harriet's brother Lyman, who later stayed with the Palmers during Jackson's year in Albany and earned Jackson's lasting goodwill. Jackson did know other regionalists. In 1870 she enjoyed a brief, intense, and ultimately disappointing period of friendship with Elizabeth Stoddard, the author of emotionally powerful, idiosyncratic novels of Massachusetts life and the wife of the poet Richard Henry Stoddard, Jackson's friend. Jackson was acquainted with two of the New England regionalists who are best remembered today, Sarah Orne Jewett and Elizabeth Stuart Phelps. And in 1879, when she visited Leadville, she paid a friendly, supportive call on the emerging western regionalist Mary Hallock Foote, a temporary resident there.

While Jackson appreciated the regional specificity in the work of these authors, she also looked to them and other writers to uphold her values of idealism. This double-sided critical agenda both reflected and served to reinforce the confusion between realism and Romanticism evident in her own fiction. In the early 1870s, just as she was beginning to delineate her own fictional territory, she made a number of telling remarks in this regard. In March 1871, six months before she published her first short story, she told the publisher Thomas Niles, of Roberts Brothers, that she considered the pioneering Scottish regionalist George MacDonald "certainly the foremost storyteller today," and that she particularly liked his novel *Alec Forbes of Howglen* (1865), with its extensive phonetic replication of lowland Scots dialect.[16] That same month, she praised Harriet Waters Preston's New England novel *Aspendale* in a review for *Scribner's Monthly.* One year later, though, in February 1872, she offered her incongruous laudatory reviews to both John De Forest's regionalist novel *Overland* and William Hunt's Romantic paintings (discussed in the introduction), in the very same issue of *Scribner's* in which her own third Saxe Holm story appeared. She also wrote a third review for that issue of the magazine, of Harriet Beecher Stowe's *My Wife and I,* in which she indirectly admitted her dual allegiance to both realism and idealism. Applauding Stowe's novel as possessing the necessary "color," she criticized it for lacking the "idealization of persons, places, or incidents" that she had come to expect in Stowe.

Because Jackson required idealization and a sense of sympathetic involvement from herself and other fiction writers, she disliked the work of some of the most important realists of her day. She was particularly opposed to work that, in her opinion, reeked of "vulgarity" and "indecency," such as Émile Zola's "nasty" classic of early naturalism, *Nana* (1880).[17] She was less scandalized by, but still fairly dismissive of, the work of the pioneering realists Henry James and William Dean Howells. She had personal grudges with both of these men that added to her initial literary disaffection. She believed that Henry James, who gave a negative review to her first novel, held his fictional characters at arm's length, like "psychological marionettes," rather than taking a passionate, sympathetic interest in them.[18] When she was just beginning to write fiction, she not only got into a dispute with William Dean Howells over the grammar in one of her *Atlantic* travel essays but also took offense when he apparently referred to her as a "lady-writer." She retaliated by maligning him in a letter to a friend as "a much overrated 'gentleman writer,' " whose "shallow" work impressed readers by a "fine trick of wording."[19] Later, as Howells began to depend on her travel writing for his magazine, they developed a friendship; once, she even sent him an idea for a story she thought suitable for a writer interested "in Boston character painting."[20] Still, she never gained much appreciation for his fiction. As late as 1885, she argued cunningly in a letter to a friend that Howells's most recent stories had "less flavor than his earlier ones"[21]—which she had never much liked in the first place. And that same year, in a letter to the new editor of the *Atlantic,* Thomas Bailey Aldrich, she praised the fiction of the southern regionalist Mary Noailles Murfree for possessing "the ring of passion which Howells and James so woefully lack."[22]

Jackson's search for poetry and passion in the work of other writers did not incline her toward the work of contemporary sentimentalists, as it sometimes had in her youth and young adulthood. Yet it did lead her to admire and sometimes attempt to emulate the work of several major authors who combined Romantic tendencies with an abiding concern for place: Washington Irving, Nathaniel Hawthorne, and George Eliot. As we have seen, Jackson's interest in Irving had salutary effects on her travel writing, helping her to formulate her theme of rural protest and to take interesting fictional liberties with her non-fiction essays. Her enthusiasm for Hawthorne and Eliot was less beneficial; working under their influence, she was inclined to enlarge on the very aspects of Romanticism that are most out of place in her early fiction.

Throughout Jackson's professional life, Hawthorne was widely considered the greatest fiction writer America had yet produced. Jackson had admired him at least since the period of her first marriage; later, Higginson's enthusiasm reinforced her own, and she expressed her veneration openly in two of her early travel essays, "In the White Mountains" (1866) and "A Second Celestial Railroad" (1870). When she began to write fiction, though, she occasionally made more subtle attempts to incorporate elements of Hawthornesque supernaturalism in her own work, with generally poor results. (In this respect, she resembled many of her literary contemporaries.) She was most successful in borrowing from Hawthorne when she managed, like him, to link the supernatural events in her fiction with the psychology of her characters. Both Annie of "Whose Wife Was She?" and a character named Rachel in Jackson's second novel, *Hetty's Strange History* (1877), have interesting otherworldly experiences that stem from the passions of forbidden love. But other stories founder whenever Hawthorne makes his shadowy appearance. Jackson's Civil War tale "A Four-Leaved Clover," for instance, suffers from Margaret Warren's ill-conceived ability to receive communications from Karl's dead first love. And Jackson's longest Saxe Holm story, the 125-page "My Tourmaline," is entirely deformed by a bizarre supernaturalism. The story opens with a realistic, rather charming account of a young man's being sent away from college to rusticate for a term in Maine. Quickly, however, Jackson interrupts her regional narrative with the appearance of an orphan girl named Ally, who is able to see things happening at great distances when she touches tourmaline stones. When the otherwise practical-minded college boy finally accepts the reality of Ally's clairvoyance, they marry and live happily ever after. Jackson intends her tale to re-create the moral of Hawthorne's story "The Snow-Image": common sense is sometimes inadequate to the very important business of recognizing uncommon sense and beauty. But unlike Hawthorne, she never manages in "My Tourmaline" to create another realm beyond the real, where the supernatural might seem natural, nor any powerful psychological reality to which the supernatural might be linked. Instead, her story is simply absurd, a true example of that childishness with which Edward Hunt's "blockhead" friend once charged Hawthorne's original tale.[23]

Jackson's admiration for the novels of George Eliot was nearly inevitable. Given her early training in the doctrine of submission and the need for didacticism in literature, she tended to believe that fiction should be inspirational, and naturally shared Eliot's penchant for heroines who embody the ideals of Christian love and duty. She also shared Eliot's realistic interest in the rural community. The first book review she ever wrote, for the *Independent* of September 13, 1866, was in praise of Eliot's *Felix Holt*. "Your book has done me good," she told Eliot in this piece, expressing delight in Eliot's sense of humor and especially in her capacity for creating characters who represent both "hearty, flesh-and-blood" realities and also "pure" ideals. In the coming years, Jackson continued to read and reread Eliot's novels, becoming so familiar with them that she sometimes fancied herself encountering Eliot's characters during her travels. And she always considered Eliot herself a shining example of womanhood, despite Eliot's decades-long cohabitation with the married George Henry Lewes.[24]

While Jackson's admiration for Eliot's novels was not in itself problematic, her manner of putting to use the inspiration she found in Eliot's heroines often was. Draxy Miller, for instance, is a Yankee incarnation of *Adam Bede*'s Dinah Morris, her very name seemingly chosen in tribute to Eliot's earlier creation, her character intended to illustrate the same ideal spirit of Christianity. But unlike Eliot, Jackson provides no adequate psychological or social counterbalance to the idealized perfection of Draxy or her other Saxe Holm heroines. Very few of the characters in her short stories are evil or even untoward, yet her heroines still manage to be better than everyone around them: they are more practical and diligent, more artistic, more feminine, or some combination of these qualities, and they are invariably more cheerful.

The Saxe Holm heroine's lack of psychological depth stems in part from a weakness inherent in Jackson's use of autobiographical material. Almost all of Jackson's fiction is based on her own life, whether she modeled a particular story closely on her own experience or instead found her inspiration in the newspaper, for it is her own concern for cheerful perseverance that her protagonists inevitably display. As in her travel writing, this tendency to grant her own cherished values to her literary subjects was in some ways advantageous to her work, but in other ways detrimental. Through personal identification she was able to sympathize with individuals from a variety of ethnic, regional, and class backgrounds, a fact indicated textually by her frequent use of first-person narration and her habit of giving her characters her own name; close substitutes for her name, such as Nell and Henrietta; or the names of loved ones, such as Ann and Sarah. Moreover, the indomitable cheerfulness and industriousness of her heroines often serve interesting subversive purposes: these qualities are intended to make her heroines so winning that readers will continue to sympathize with them even when they do unconventional things, such as taking up public preaching, as Draxy Miller does. Thus Moncure Conway once described Draxy's tale as "worth all the woman's rights movements & appeals put together."[25]

At the same time, however, because Jackson grants her heroines the virtues she cherished but none of her own worldliness or complexity of character, her portraits of them can seem superficial, even patronizing. This is particularly true in her delineation of their work lives. Many of the Saxe Holm heroines are lauded professionals, whether nurses, teachers, farmers, preachers, or poets, and most are possessed of artistic "natures" and "sensibilities." But Jackson describes them all as somehow simply falling into their various jobs and avocations, and maintaining their stature by natural pluck and force of personality. They do not struggle for position in the world, nor are they very ambitious; they are uncomplicated, placid people who never gain much in the way of sophistication from all their years at work. In short, they are entirely unlike Jackson herself, or most real people.

A similarly warped use of autobiographical material mars Jackson's depiction of the romantic lives of many of her heroines. Jackson's plots almost invariably center on love between a man and a woman who either come together under peculiar circumstances or have peculiar experiences when together. In time, she would learn to write with some skill of the shifting relations between couples. In her Saxe Holm stories, though, she finds exalted romantic ideals in situations that would hardly seem to merit the honor. Like Jackson herself, for example, a number of her female characters have adored fathers or father figures, often ministers, who offer them their closest intellectual companionship. Filial or romantic relationships between childlike women and paternalistic men were commonly depicted in the fiction of Jackson's day, yet Jackson sometimes combined the romantic with the filial in an effort to heighten their beauty, with strange results. In her early story "Esther Wynn's Love-Letters," for example, the young narrator Nell and her beloved Uncle Joe call each other "pet," "dear," and "darling," and keep secrets from Joe's wife. "I understood him far better than his wife did," Nell explains, and Uncle Joe is given to declaring, "Nell, my girl, you'll never have another lover like me!"[26] In essence, Nell and Uncle Joe are belated partners. Their erotically charged, almost incestuous relationship is shadowed in "Esther Wynn's Love-Letters" by another unconventional, oddly idealized relationship—this one between a poet named Esther Wynn and her married mentor. The latter illustrates a second common flaw in Jackson's approach to creating autobiographical romantic ideals. All three of her very first Saxe Holm stories—"Esther Wynn's Love-Letters," "Whose Wife Was She?" and "How One Woman Kept Her Husband"—are about soul mates who meet after one of them is already married. Like Jackson's poems of forbidden love, these stories are founded in her own early relationship with Higginson. They demonstrate a sense of compassion for extramarital love that was somewhat unusual for the time. Yet they are oddly sanitized, for Jackson's eagerness to lend "poetry" to her stories, along with her concern for conventional literary propriety, prevented her from depicting any of the crueler realities of illicit love. When, in "Esther Wynn's Love-Letters," Nell and Joe discover a hidden stash of old letters written by the now-deceased Esther Wynn to her mentor, they consider the letters evidence of lofty romantic devotion: because their sympathies are all with Esther, they give little thought to the painfulness of the mentor's situation, or that of his wife.

Many of Jackson's contemporaries appreciated her efforts to imbue her regional stories with a sense of idealism and to create inspirational heroines. "Everything is true to the life, but all is more or less idealized," wrote a critic for the *World,* declaring that this rare "combination of truth and poetry" placed "Saxe Holm" at the forefront of American writers.[27] Saxe Holm received a good deal of fan mail from readers who found strength in the example of her heroines, the typical letter being, as Jackson explained to her publishers at Scribner's, an "earnest expression of gratitude, and desire to ask help and sympathy."[28] Nevertheless, the reviews of Jackson's second Saxe Holm collection were generally less enthusiastic than those of her first. The *New York Times* explicitly condemned the uniform "virtue and comeliness" of the heroines, and was harsh in its appraisal of what another paper condemned as Saxe Holm's "mystical burden." "This story of 'Tourmaline' affects one as if recited by a person laboring under a mild form of hysteria, so incongruous with New England and New England life are all its personages," the *Times* scoffed.[29] The incongruous elements of idealism and sentimentalism in the Saxe Holm stories and the lack of psychological complexity of their heroines go far toward rendering them outdated by today's standards.

"Sax" is an abbreviation for "Saxon," a person of English descent, and "holm" is an English word meaning an island in a river. Jackson's reasons for selecting this particular pseudonym are not known, but her reasons for wishing to publish her short fiction under a separate, unrecognizable name are fairly clear. Initially, she was eager to distance herself from the autobiographical material in her stories; later, a variety of circumstances, including her own growing doubts over the quality of the stories, led her to continue trying to mask her authorship. So determined was she in this effort that she even refused to admit her identity as Saxe Holm to many publishers and friends, including Sarah Woolsey.

Her first three tales, all about forbidden love and all partly autobiographical, were written when she was still living in the same boardinghouse as Thomas Wentworth Higginson and his wife. According to Jackson, Higginson even "helped write" these stories, including her personal favorite, "Esther Wynn's Love-Letters."[30] Understandably enough, she was desperate to have her authorship and Higginson's editorship of these incriminating narratives escape the notice of Mary Higginson. Yet when she confessed her secret to Charlotte Cushman, saying that she would stop writing Saxe Holm stories if her identity ever became public knowledge, her friend chided her for inconsistency. "You have virtually drawn it upon yourself," Cushman wrote to her in January 1874. She told Jackson that many people already suspected the hand of "H.H." in the stories, and that there was no logical reason for Jackson's concern:

> By only one person will anything be suspected—& for her you do not care. I think you were imprudent—may I say foolish—to so advertise matters to those who know anything or have any suspicions. But you choose to do it—you are no child to act from impulse—& you have doubtless calculated the consequences—so—being defiant once why not go on—you need write no *more just such*.[31]

In a letter written the following month, after "H.H." had published a denial of her authorship of the Saxe Holm stories in the *Woman's Journal,* Cushman told

Jackson that she believed no number of denials would long "convince *her*" that Jackson was not Saxe Holm.[32]

Jackson was particularly worried about being discovered in early 1874 because her first story collection had just been published and many critics were speculating about Saxe Holm's identity. She was mortified when Samuel Bowles wrote a review for the *Springfield Republican* in which he argued from evidence within the Saxe Holm stories that Helen Hunt was Saxe Holm, and that she denied her authorship because her stories were autobiographical. "She perhaps shrinks from appearing before the world as the originator of characters which recall so vividly the life of the past," Bowles suggested.[33] Without delay, inquiring friends forwarded nine copies of the *Republican* article to Jackson at the Colorado Springs Hotel. Not surprisingly, she was temporarily enraged with Bowles. "To have the insight to recognize that the writer of those stories wished to remain unknown *because* the stories touched her own life so closely, and then to do all in one's power to drag her into notoriety—is a species of inconsistency not to say brutality," she fumed in a letter to Edward Seymour, the publisher of *Scribner's*.[34] Immediately, she redoubled her efforts to guard her anonymity. When William Ward of the *Independent* sent her a postcard that made reference to Saxe Holm's work, she chastised him angrily. "I am not the author of the stories to which I suppose you refer," she told him. "And please don't ever send me on postal cards allusions to matters which might be supposed to be private! I have no doubt that every one I receive is read by the clerk of this Hotel and I heartily wish that the man who invented postal cards was smothered under a ton of them."[35] Now, when she wrote new Saxe Holm stories, she was more careful about her use of autobiographical material. "The S.H. story came to a sudden halt," she reported to Edward Seymour on one occasion in late 1874. "I was dissatisfied with it. It was growing in spite of me so true to an actual experience, that it would have been recognized."[36]

Even as Jackson struggled to disassociate herself from her short fiction, a number of unknown, aspiring authors began coming forward eagerly to proclaim themselves the true Saxe Holm. On February 7, 1874, the *Woman's Journal* ran a letter from a woman named Celia Burleigh, who argued that her friend Ruth Ellis, a teacher from central New York, was the real Saxe Holm. Jackson was at first pleased and amused by this false claim, as it helped draw speculation away from herself. "God bless Celia Burleigh!" she wrote to Edward Seymour. "Nothing could have happened which would so have delighted me and helped me in my wish to be unknown."[37] Still, she disliked seeing credit for her work going to another, and on February 23, 1874, the real "Saxe Holm" wrote an open letter to Burleigh for publication in the *Woman's Journal*. She was sorry that Burleigh's friend Ruth Ellis "should have been tempted by ambition to tell such a falsehood," she said, and she suggested to Burleigh that it would "be an act of true friendship for you to prevent her continuing to make this misrepresentation, which must sooner or later cover her with embarrassment and disgrace."[38] Jackson also wrote directly to Burleigh, signing her letter Saxe Holm and sending it through Scribner's with their endorsement of authenticity. Her efforts had little effect, however, and soon Jackson began "growing rather indignant" at Ellis's "repeated lies."[39] Over the next several years, this imposter enlisted in her cause not only Celia Burleigh but also a respected gentleman from Chicago named Mr. Lewis, who once, during a visit to Colorado Springs, actually insisted on Ellis's claim at Jackson's own dinner table. Other false Saxe Holms also began to clamor for attention. These "claimants," as Jackson called them, included an unnamed young woman from New York City, whose pathetic tale of wronged authorship was repeatedly brought forward by a jeweler from the Bowery named Mr. Johnston, and a teacher from Pennsylvania named Alma Calder. In 1878 the announcement of the marriage of Alma Calder to a New York man who happened to have the last name of Johnston led the *Springfield Republican* to speculate, humorously, that "Mr. Johnston has yielded to a terrible mania, and is making a collection of Saxe Holms."[40]

"It surely is a psychological phenomenon, that any human being can invent and persist in such monstrous deceits," Jackson wrote to the publisher John B. Scribner shortly after her second collection came out and the Saxe Holm pretenders began asserting their claims with renewed vigor. "If I have any share of responsibility for all these falsehoods, on the part of people who say they did when they didn't, in addition to the responsibility of the true Saxe Holm who says she didn't when she did, shall I not have a big account to settle?"[41] Yet the truth is that Jackson successfully repressed any guilt she might have felt over her own "monstrous deceits." In 1875 she had asked Moncure Conway, with whom she had shared the secret of her authorship, to contradict any false rumors of Saxe Holm's identity that he overheard, but never to give her name as the actual Saxe Holm: "That you must withhold—even by a lie, if need be—as I do myself." Conway had disapproved of this falsity on moral grounds. "Won't your rosy cloud grow moister and even clammy," he asked her, "when you look earthward and see somewhere the epitaph: 'H.H. Poetess and Humbug. She said she wasn't Saxe Holm and she was.' Or perhaps it will begin with a 'Here LIES.'" Speaking more seriously, he urged her to "make a clear breast of it."[42] But Jackson was unmoved. By this point, she had already settled it within herself that the help she had received from Higginson on the stories gathered in her first collection made it possible for her honestly to deny being Saxe Holm. "There are circumstances connected with the writing of the stories, which make it possible for me to say with strict letter of truth, that I am not their author," she had told Edward Seymour. "There is not really one of which I have written the whole."[43]

Jackson's belief that she was justified in denying her identity as Saxe Holm was put to the test in May 1877, when she made the mistake of publishing under the Saxe Holm signature a highly autobiographical children's essay, "The First Time," in the children's magazine *St. Nicholas*. Seizing on this essay's close depiction of Amherst and Jackson's early home life, the *New York Tribune* immediately published an article titled "Who Saxe-Holm Is," correctly identifying Jackson as Saxe Holm. In reply, "Saxe Holm" sent through her intermediaries at Scribner's a carefully worded refutation:

> I have seen with much surprise an article in the *Tribune* arguing from some of the statements in my story "The First Time," in *St. Nicholas* for May, that it must have been written by Mrs. Helen Jackson (H.H.).
> Accidental coincidences of names and places are sometimes inexplicable[.]

The editor of the *Tribune* published this statement, but not without attaching the following sharp paragraph:

> The proper disposition of the above would have been to return it to the eminent publishing house through which it was received, with the statement that the *Tribune* never accepts anonymous contributions. This, however, in spite of its seeming denials, is hardly anonymous. The "coincidences of names and places" are not at all "inexplicable"—they explain themselves so conclusively that no card on the subject is needed.[44]

This interchange in the *Tribune* and Jackson's story in *St. Nicholas* convinced some critics and readers that Jackson was Saxe Holm, while for others their consanguinity remained only a possibility, not a surety. After the second Saxe Holm volume was published, the *Springfield Republican* ran an article titled "Saxe Holm Evolved," in which an anonymous commentator argued that Jackson's denials of her involvement in the stories should be taken seriously.[45] In previous years, various newspapers had occasionally backed other established artists as possible Saxe Holms, including Sarah Woolsey, Helena de Kay, and even Mark Twain, who, according to one report, not only denied the charge, but added, "all other denials are bogus."[46] Now the writer for the *Republican* drew on various details in the stories, including their allusions to Amherst, to put forth a vision of Saxe Holm that sounds peculiarly like Emily Dickinson. "We may imagine her to be a member of one of those 'sleepy and dignified' New England families whom she has so vividly described; of a timid nature; separated from the outside world, devoted to literature and flowers. We cannot refrain, also, from picturing her robed in white, like Draxy Miller," the critic said. "Two persons capable of literary expression may have lived in the same town, and, therefore, we suggest that we take 'H.H' at her word and *hunt* up her neighbors."[47] For some readers, no doubt, this suggestion must have served as an effective decoy. Still, there would soon be new reason to suspect that Jackson was Saxe Holm. In 1879 Thomas Wentworth Higginson himself described the recent Saxe Holm controversy in terms that made the truth fairly obvious, in his essay about Jackson in *Short Studies of American Authors*.

"The more Mrs. Jackson denied the authorship," he said, "the more resolutely the public mind intrenched itself in the belief that she had something to do with the stories."[48]

Later, when Higginson wrote about Jackson after her death, he would be more careful not to comment on her connection with the Saxe Holm stories. For by the end of her life, Jackson had determined to do all that she could to keep her Saxe Holm stories forever separated from her main body of work. Back in 1875 she had told Moncure Conway, "I *intend* to deny it, till I die. *Then* I wish it to be known."[49] In subsequent years, though, her initial determination to keep up her subterfuge because of the autobiographical content of her stories was reinforced, as she told John B. Scribner, by "a great many reasons," including her understanding "that the market value of the work is much enhanced by the mystery, and by the conflicting of claimants."[50] She also enjoyed hearing how her stories impressed critics and acquaintances who were not aware of their authorship: she wanted the shelter of anonymity for her early fiction, much as, when an aspiring poet, she had wished to hear Henry Root's reaction to her early poem "Consecration" before she revealed to him that the poem was hers. Finally, when public knowledge of the shared identity of "H.H." and Saxe Holm had become fairly widespread, she decided that she must nevertheless continue to insist on their difference in order to safeguard her established reputation.

From the start, she had considered her short stories simply "light fiction," and she had been surprised by all the praise they received: "I have all along felt great doubts of the work's really being so good as some of the critics have seemed to consider it," she confessed to Edward Seymour early in 1874.[51] Her doubts increased that year when an article in the *Nation* apparently accused her of being a sentimentalist. By writing under an unrecognizable pseudonym, she still felt comfortable continuing to publish her popular stories. But when her second collection came out to less enthusiastic reviews than had greeted her first, she began to fear that if the stories were known to be hers, they would harm her standing as a poet and essayist. At least one critic warned of such an outcome: "The 'Saxe Holm' stories are trash, and would lower rather than raise 'H.H.'s permanent reputation."[52] In 1882, therefore, Jackson told Thomas Bailey Aldrich that all the stories she had "ever written" had been published "under fictitious signatures, never acknowledged, and never to be acknowledged," and that she was "especially anxious that no suggestion of any possibility of 'short story' work should ever be associated with my name."[53] And just before she died, she earnestly charged both Thomas Niles and her husband with the task of continuing to safeguard her secret. For this reason, reprints of the Saxe Holm work did not bear Jackson's name until the influence of these two men had waned.

Like her Saxe Holm stories, Jackson's novels are autobiographical and feature idealized heroines, but they surmount the problems that overwhelm her short fiction and thus remain of considerable interest today. Jackson had five years of experience as a fiction writer behind her when she became a novelist in 1876, and she was more aware of the need to contextualize the exemplary virtues of her heroines. In particular, she began to counterbalance their brightness with depictions of some of the more complex and occasionally unpleasant social constraints of regional life, as seen in her description, excerpted at the head of this chapter, of the cold Calvinism pervading one small New England village.

Jackson's ability to avoid in her novels some of the pitfalls of her short fiction was also abetted by the distance she achieved from both Thomas Wentworth Higginson and her *Scribner's* editor Josiah Holland upon her move to Colorado Springs in 1873. These two men had been partly responsible for steering her toward the morally and psychologically simplistic in her early Saxe Holm stories. In theory, Higginson was in favor of realistic social fiction. But in reality, like Jackson herself, he yearned after idealism. In his own fiction, he tended to slip despite himself into sentimentalism; his own short stories and novel, *Malbone* (1869), were undistinguished. Given his own unconscious tendencies, he must naturally have influenced Jackson toward sentimentalism when he edited her first fiction. He would long consider the feeble "Draxy Miller" her best short story, even praising it as one of "the very best stories yet written in America" in his *Short Studies of American Authors*.[54]

Josiah Holland was a clergyman, sentimental poet, and popular prose writer. Jackson had first met him in Newport. When she began to write for his magazine, his ability to satisfy upper-middle-class standards of moral and literary propriety was on its way to making him one of the most successful editors of his time. Because Jackson partly shared his suspicion of thoroughgoing realism, and was eager to maintain the prominent position he awarded her first fiction in the magazine, she was pleased to meet his standards for moral respectability in literature. She also accepted his career guidance without rancor. After her first collection of stories was published, Holland asked her to send him more fiction as fast as she could write it, and to remember that she could not in good conscience publish stories elsewhere, as *Scribner's* had "nurtured" Saxe Holm in her "youth."[55] For a time, she willingly met these demands. When she began writing novels, however, Holland objected to the content of both of her first two books. Whatever the bases for these disagreements, which extant letters do not reveal, they led Holland to reject the books—an act that especially angered Jackson because the publishers of *Scribner's* had for several years been urging her to write novels for them. In private, she began to distance herself from Holland's ideas about literature. She disparaged his writing as sentimental, and told William that she agreed with a *Nation* article of June 21, 1877, that lambasted Holland for pandering in all of his work to the saccharine tastes of unsophisticated readers.[56]

Jackson could afford to admit her grievances with Holland in 1877 because by then she had a new literary sponsor, Thomas Niles, whom she could count on to publish her fiction without trying to influence it. Niles was the chief editor at Roberts Brothers, which became Jackson's main book publisher with the 1873 release of *Bits of Talk about Home Matters*. Jackson thought Niles "the ideal of publishers."[57] He was known for his skill in obtaining and promoting the work of women: under his guidance Roberts Brothers successfully published the children's books of Louisa May Alcott and Jackson's friend Sarah Woolsey, the first American editions of George Sand's novels, and poetry collections by Christina Rossetti, Jean Ingelow, and, after her death, Emily Dickinson. Niles was so loyal to Jackson that she gave out his firm's name as her forwarding address at least as often as she gave out the address of her Boston financial trustees or of her own home in Colorado Springs—she kept Roberts Brothers continually informed by telegraph of her movements. Niles published her work in all genres, but was especially supportive of her novels. He picked up both her first, *Mercy Philbrick's Choice* (1876), and her second, *Hetty's Strange History* (1877), after Holland rejected them. Niles also published all of Jackson's subsequent novels. He made special efforts to bring each one of them to the attention of the public, with the result that they sold better than most of her other books. His enthusiasm gave Jackson the confidence to write novels on her own schedule, without advance contracts, certain that they would find their way into print.

At the same time that Jackson moved to Colorado Springs and began to publish with Thomas Niles, in 1873, she also began deriving important support for her fiction writing from two other new sources: the writer Charles Dudley Warner and William Jackson. She first made the acquaintance of Warner in January 1871 after she reviewed his new essay collection, *My Summer in a Garden* (1870), for *Scribner's*. Just one year younger than Jackson, Warner was an essayist after the fashion of Washington Irving and Charles Lamb—his tenor genial, mellow, sometimes playfully bordering on the irreverent. In her review Jackson praised his "mirthfulness" as possessing a "tenderness and passion" that elevated it above mere humor. She also wrote personally to Warner to tell him "how heartily, how tenderly" she had enjoyed his book.[58] Her letter served to initiate a friendship that was to grow ever closer in the following years, flourishing mostly in letters but also in Jackson's occasional visits to Warner and his wife Susan Lee at their Hartford home. Perhaps because their feelings for each other contained no hint on either side of the personal attractions that complicated Jackson's relationships with both Higginson and Conway, Jackson expressed her literary views with unique candor in her letters to Warner, giving vent to her own native comic bent and to some of her more pointed opinions of other writers.

Though he was frequently condescending toward literary women, Warner thought Jackson uniquely brilliant. And unlike her other friends, he most admired her as a fiction writer, not a poet. In 1873 he himself coauthored a novel, *The Gilded Age,* with his friend Mark Twain; in later years, he would dedicate himself to writing more novels. During Jackson's lifetime, though, he encouraged her to focus on fiction, while he continued to write essays on domestic life, literature, and travel, and to keep up his regular day job as editor of the *Hartford Courant.* He knew that Jackson was Saxe Holm, and despite her playful denials of the fact in her letters to him, he often complimented her on her stories. After her first collection came out, he began urging her to write longer fiction. On December 21, 1873, he entreated Saxe Holm to write a novel in his review of her book for the *Courant.* He also began asking Jackson personally whether she had yet attempted "the great American novel."[59] When her first two novels did come out, he praised them both privately and in the pages of the *Courant.*

Warner's enthusiasm meant a great deal to Jackson. In fact, under his influence she was emboldened not only to begin writing novels but also to take some entirely new steps in her later career as a fiction writer. On December 3, 1879, she and Warner sat side by side at the head table at the *Atlantic Monthly*'s gala birthday breakfast in honor of Oliver Wendell Holmes, in Boston. For once, she temporarily renounced her secrecy on the Saxe Holm stories and allowed Warner to allude to her authorship: as Warner stood to read aloud a poem Jackson had written for Holmes, he declared that he had been "authorized" to "announce publicly that H.H. is really the author of certain words of fact and fiction,—I hope I am saying nothing indiscreet,—the maternity of which has been much discussed."[60] In the succeeding months, Jackson also made another move in her fiction that she assured Warner she "would not have ventured alone" to undertake: she began to write a play.[61] It was to be a collaborative effort, based on a recent incident at the Boston Public Library, when a local girl had won the heart of an English aristocrat. The plan, apparently, was that Jackson would provide most of the ideas, Warner would "sketch it out," and then the two of them would jointly "finish it up."[62] In the end, neither of them made much progress on the play, though they returned to the idea intermittently throughout the early 1880s. Still, Jackson always delighted in the thought that they might one day take their work to the stage, and this vision helped her maintain her enthusiasm for fiction in years when she was mostly absorbed in her new crusade for Indian rights.

Among the several new relationships that fostered Jackson's ability to undertake the difficult work of writing long fiction in the second half of her career, that with her second husband was by far the most important. After their initial months of giddy joy together, the Jacksons did begin to chafe occasionally at the differences in personality that had so worried Helen before they were married. Several of the short stories in her second collection, which she wrote after becoming involved with William—including "A Four-Leaved Clover,"

"My Tourmaline," and "Susan Lawton's Escape"—concern the romantic negotiations of artistic women who find themselves coupled with thoroughly practical men. While these heroines manage to delight their mates by their efforts to share their own refined aesthetic tastes, in real life Helen's efforts to improve her husband's spelling and convince him to keep up with the latest publications served only to frustrate them both. Still, the Jacksons' marriage remained at bottom solid and loving. Marriage to William brought Helen the immeasurable benefit of emotional stability. She was able to concentrate longer and with greater purpose, and her writing improved. Moreover, William not only accepted the fact that she was already a well-known and committed professional when they met, but he also did everything in his power to encourage her career.

Though he could not, like Higginson, offer specific critiques of her work, William read many of her writings, or listened to her read them aloud, and he gave her business advice and broad career suggestions, such as urging her to write more for children. Almost invariably, he expressed enthusiasm for each one of her literary endeavors: when she first became interested in writing a play, for instance, he expressed "great faith" in her ability to write a good one.[63] His steadfast support buoyed Helen in her work. And because he understood the importance of writing to his wife's well-being, and shared her work ethic and Stoic philosophy, he made a special point of urging industry on her in times of crisis. Like Helen's father, William was convinced of the virtue of cheerful diligence in the face of adversity; unlike Fiske, though, he urged Helen to demonstrate it in creative writing—to "dream away," as he put it.[64] During the long period when Helen was trying to decide whether to accept his marriage proposal, for instance, and often finding herself "worried nearly sick" over the question, William repeatedly insisted that the issue did not merit her destroying her ability to be productive. "My Philosophy is do the best you can under the circumstances & then avoid fretting," he said, reminding her that she should not dwell too long upon personal issues but focus instead on her "higher" calling of work.[65]

William's support for Helen's career was all the more remarkable given that she was not always entirely supportive of his work in return. At the start of their second year of marriage, in the fall of 1876, William made a bid on behalf of the Republican Party for one of the first seats in the U.S. Senate to be held from the new state of Colorado. Helen did not want to see her husband enter politics, however, and hoped fervently for his defeat, as she admitted to many. When William Ward expressed surprise at her lack of support, she explained,

> Human nature being what it is, I believe that our "institutions" will always bring to the surface of political power the scum of the land:—now I know these are

unpopular beliefs—and I rarely air them:—but you have forced me to declare myself. To see my husband in that crew of liars and pickpockets will almost kill me: and to breathe the air myself will be a perpetual moral typhoid fever.[66]

She was frankly elated when William lost the election. "Congratulate me on one thing—Mr. Jackson is defeated," she wrote excitedly to Ward. "I feel like a new woman," she told her sister.[67] From this point forward, she did everything in her power to keep William from falling again into politics. Of his own accord, he devoted his attention to his bank and to civic enterprises, even while remaining involved with the Denver and Rio Grande and a number of the railroad's ancillary contract and land development companies. Yet she was sometimes almost as frustrated with her husband's business endeavors as she might have been with a political career, for his many responsibilities meant that he could neither remain at home nor leave the area in accord with mere personal preference. The Jacksons always tried hard to arrange meetings when one of them had to travel, and Helen sometimes enjoyed the pleasure of accompanying William on interesting trips. More often, though, she was plagued by the loneliness of missing him and annoyed that he was unable to travel exactly when and where she wanted. "The bank holds the banker year in & year out," she complained to Moncure Conway.[68] And to an old acquaintance who had known Edward Hunt's commitment to work, she explained, "While he is always ready for a 'lark' of any kind, if business does not interfere, when business does interfere, no power under Heaven can divert him from it. He is as bad as an *Engineer* about that."[69]

Because William was always busy with his work, Helen had little choice but to continue in her steady devotion to her own. In fact, she began the absorbing project of writing her first novel in February 1876, almost immediately after she and William were married and settled into their newly rented home. She worked on this book in the same way that she worked on her short fiction: first making notes on her projected narrative, then writing out an outline and sketching in certain scenes, and finally settling down to write out the story in consecutive morning sessions and occasional longer stints that sometimes lasted all day. *Mercy Philbrick's Choice,* which Jackson finished in June 1876 and published later that year, is of unique, enduring interest because it is a veiled portrait of her own coming of age as an artist; as such, it is a rarity in literature, a female writer's *Künstlerroman.*[70] Jackson drew on the painful subterfuges of her relationship with Higginson and her later emotional separation from him in writing of her poet heroine Mercy. The "choice" facing her is between continuing to love a man who, though similar to her in aesthetic refinement and artistic tastes, is unavailable to her and striking out on her own to make her way as a professional writer. Jackson admitted that she had thought about the story "for a long time" before committing it to paper, and both she and her husband believed it the "best" she had yet written.[71] While Jackson's manipulation of autobiographical material is imperfect, and her novel is also marred by redundancies, small inconsistencies, and unwarranted digressions into the histories of minor characters, it is a solid book, for the most part well written, in a simple and polished style and understated tone.

With *Mercy Philbrick's Choice,* which she originally considered naming "The Lady of Ensworth County," Jackson began a regular habit in her novels of presenting the usual cheer, diligence, and artistry of her heroines as virtues that, while originating in their firm loyalty to the natural and spiritual wonders of their local regions, can finally be maintained only by removal from these regions and their less enlightened inhabitants. From the novel's opening pages, Jackson's narrator, occasionally present in the first person, provides a foil for the gleaming portrait she is about to draw of Mercy by describing the normal human behavior in small New England towns as entirely stultifying: "In the ordinary New England town, neighborhood never means much: there is a dismal lack of cohesion to the relations between people. The community is loosely held together by a few accidental points of contact or common interest. The individuality of individuals is, by a strange sort of paradox, at once respected and ignored. This is indifference rather than consideration, selfishness rather than generosity."[72]

The story that transpires in dreary "Penfield" is set in a vaguely defined recent past, as all Jackson's novels would be. Newly widowed, eighteen-year-old Mercy Carr Philbrick moves from Cape Cod to Penfield with her helpless invalid mother, hoping that the inland climate will alleviate Mrs. Carr's nascent consumption. In Penfield the two women rent rooms in the home of a man named Stephen White, himself the loyal child of an invalid mother. Both Stephen's and Mercy's mothers, and also some minor local characters like the charming eccentric "Old Man Wheeler," speak in distinctive Yankee dialects, often to intended comic effect. Mercy herself is more refined, however, speaking like a lady and expressing a sensitive appreciation for nature and art. Her perpetual cheer is noticed by all who meet her, and she often remarks on the virtues of submission. "I am not sure that it is right to let ourselves be unhappy about anything, even the worst of troubles," she says (65).

Mercy is just starting out as a professional poet, having published a few poems in periodicals, when she takes up residence in the same house as Stephen White. Recognizing in each other "the artistic temperament" (6), they quickly fall in love. Yet Stephen insists that they keep their love secret, because his difficult invalid mother is jealous of any person who interests him. Mercy justifies her acceptance of this arrangement on the grounds of Mrs. White's neediness and harsh temper. She loses her "first feeling of impatience" with Stephen's "seeming want of manliness" and comes to sympathize with him "in his renunciation; in his self-sacrifice; in his loyalty of reticence; in his humility of uncomplainingness" (200, 165). Jackson's narrator explains, "If any one had said to Mercy at this time: 'It was not honorable in this man, knowing or feeling that he could not marry you, to tell you of his love, and to allow you to show him yours for him. He is putting you in a false position, and may be blighting your whole life,' Mercy would have repelled the accusation most indignantly" (168–69).

An invalid mother makes a weak stand-in for an unwanted wife, and Stephen's obedience to his mother's whim seems rather too unnecessary to be compelling. Still, Jackson uses this awkward adaptation of her own early situation with Higginson to branch out into more interesting fictional territory. As time passes, and the daily deceptions involved in Mercy's hidden love affair begin to offend her "firm moral rectitude" (193), her charitable opinion of Stephen darkens. She pulls away from him emotionally, though he does not realize it, and begins devoting herself increasingly to poetry. She finds a literary mentor and personal admirer in Parson Dorrance, an intellectual older man whose own wife—described, rather absurdly, as yet another invalid—is deceased, and who now spends his free time preaching to former slaves. Showing a combination of traits drawn from both Higginson and William Jackson, Parson Dorrance patiently supports Mercy's decision, upon her mother's death, to move away from himself, Stephen, and the town of Penfield in order to forge a literary career in the city.

When Mercy leaves rural life behind her, she carries with her the best fruits of her regional inheritance: her solid sense of herself, which has been sharpened through her artistic struggles amid the mostly uncomprehending residents of Penfield, and her sensitive appreciation for nature and beauty. Her dignity, firmly rooted in the land of rural New England, is solidly impervious to change. And though she sometimes feels lonely in the city, with her "intense individuality" and "creative faculty" making "a certain amount of isolation . . . inevitable, all through her life," she finds that "her art" becomes "more and more to her every day" (87, 88, 238). Her poems, like Jackson's own, "surprise" readers "by their beauty, and still more by their condensation of thought," which seems to some "almost more masculine than feminine" (185). She delights in earning money for her work. She enjoys a "constantly broadening" life of new friends and travel. And as she becomes increasingly well known, she begins to receive fan letters— "sometimes a word of gratitude for help, sometimes a word of hearty praise"— which make her realize that she has "her own circle of listeners, unknown friends, who were always ready to hear her when she spoke" (238–39).

Mercy corresponds with Stephen for a time after she moves to the city, but he soon gives her reason to abandon him in favor of the solitary pursuit of her art. In one of his letters, he informs her that he has discovered some money hidden in his house. Though he knows the money belongs to the woman who originally owned the house, a crazy old widow named Mrs. Jacobs, he says he intends to keep it rather than return it, for he wishes to provide a better life for his mother. Mercy considers Stephen's decision immoral and suddenly views him in a whole new light: he no longer seems an upright man, forced into keeping their own relationship a secret, but instead a person capable of any number of deceptions. She immediately breaks off their affair. From this point on, she lives her life in her poetry, regretting her childlessness but filled with the "inward joy" of her successful career. She exerts great "influence" with her writing, making it her ambition "to do a little towards making people glad, towards making them kind to one another, towards opening their eyes to the omnipresent beauty" (283–84). Eventually, after Parson Dorrance's death, she comes to believe that her old tutor would have made the perfect husband, and she eagerly anticipates meeting him in heaven. Stephen, on the other hand, lives out the remainder of his life alone, with no compensatory hopes or pleasures; he dies a heartbroken man, never having ceased to love Mercy.

Jackson's book endorses the strict moralism that leads Mercy to reject Stephen. "What a terrible thing is the power which human beings have of deceiving each other!" Jackson writes. "Woe to any soul which trusts itself to any thing less than an organic integrity of nature, to which a lie is impossible!" (238). Many readers were moved by Mercy's firm integrity. "Something of her I am glad I feel akin to; but she is more honest than any woman I know *always* is; and so she lifts and inspires one," a young fan named Henrietta Hardy wrote to Jackson in 1877.[73] Yet Jackson did not intend her approval of Mercy to be without qualification. Stephen is presented as always well-meaning, his love for Mercy sincere; her abrupt dismissal of him is rather hard. Indeed, Jackson's novel raises complex questions about the meaning of sincerity and deception. How condemnable are Stephen's lies, if they are made in the name of love? And is Mercy herself even capable of love, if she can turn off her emotions so willfully? As in some of her domestic essays and poems, Jackson suggests that no person can ever entirely know another, however intimate the connection.

Jackson would continue to explore the ethics of sincerity and deception in all her future novels. Various personal issues sustained her interest in this topic. In writing *Mercy*, of course, she was seeking to come to terms with her old clandestine relationship with Higginson. She was also on some level grappling with the dubious morality of her ongoing public and private denials of her identity as Saxe Holm, and of her standing habit of presenting a cheerful façade to the world even when she was secretly suffering. While she believed that cheerful submission was a virtue and duty, and found ways to justify her secrecy on the Saxe Holm matter, she nonetheless wondered at a world in which people could so easily keep important matters hidden. She was especially curious about secrets among loved ones and the damage they could cause. She had first developed this concern in childhood, as she explained not long after *Mercy* was published in her May 1877 *St. Nicholas* children's essay, "The First Time." (Ironically, this was the same autobiographical essay, published under her Saxe

Holm signature, that she would later falsely deny as her own.) "I don't believe anybody can ever forget the misery of having told a lie," she writes in this piece, recounting the story of her own first lie, to her parents, about a bad report card. Right away, she learned that her lie itself was far worse torture than any physical chastisement might have been, for she felt terribly guilty about her transgression and was for a long time nagged by the consciousness that she should at least tell the truth to her mother. But she waits too long. "I remember that when I looked on her face in her coffin, I thought about that lie and wished I had confessed it to her before she died," Jackson writes. She explains that she has written her essay in an effort "to atone" for her old sin, and in hopes that her story will make her readers realize "what a wicked, mean, cowardly, sneaking thing it is to tell a lie, and what dreadful misery all liars live in." To some extent, *Mercy* was written for the same purpose.

In exploring the nature and consequences of sincerity and deception, and in presenting Penfield as a difficult place that Mercy must finally leave in order to realize her full artistic potential, Jackson aimed in her first novel to break away from the simpler vision of her Saxe Holm stories even as she continued to present her heroine as a moral paragon. Like many other nineteenth-century American women writers, Jackson had ambivalent feelings about her role as a professional and felt impelled to justify her work before a male-dominated, moralistic society. She was particularly burdened by the memory of her father's moral opposition to purely imaginative, nondidactic literature. In her own life, her habit of conceiving cheerfulness and industriousness as supreme moral duties, as her parents had taught her to do, enabled her to maintain a sense of herself as a good woman even as she abandoned Calvinism and became a Unitarian, with Transcendentally inspired beliefs about spiritual, artistic, and personal fulfillment, and even as she directed her industriousness toward a writing career and constant traveling, rather than conventional home duties. In her novels and some of her short stories, her heroines demonstrate submission to much the same purpose. Their virtues enabled Jackson to feel that writing about them was virtuous. At the same time, their virtues are intended to make them sympathetic to readers even when they make unusual choices. For Jackson's heroines, as for Jackson herself, earnest labor serves as a screen for unconventional behavior, and worldly compensations are often the reward for unworldly renunciations.

Thomas Niles was excited about Jackson's new departure in fiction. Teasing her that *Mercy Philbrick's Choice* might be "the Great American Novelette,"[74] he issued the book toward the end of 1876 as the first number in Roberts Brothers' much-publicized "No Name" series of hardcover anonymous novels. Shortly thereafter, he made *Mercy* the first book published by the firm in cheaper paperback. In this way, Jackson's first novel managed to garner substantial sales: some 11,000 copies of the paperback edition of *Mercy* had sold by November 1877.[75] Jackson had originally hoped to publish her book in *Scribner's Monthly,* where she had a large loyal following for her fiction and could benefit from the financial rewards of serial publication. But Niles's special efforts made up entirely for her initial frustration over Holland's rejection.

Many readers recognized the hand of "H.H." in the anonymous *Mercy Philbrick's Choice,* and the general reaction to Jackson's first novel was quite positive. Yet reviews in several of America's most important periodicals unknowingly punished her for taking a new course in her fiction, for they condemned the bleakness of her regional vision and especially what they perceived as the lack of womanliness implied in Mercy's choice of work over love. "We venture to believe that, had she been married to some sensible and honest man, and had a few little children to nurse and educate, she would have made more of her life than she was able to make now with all her poems," proclaimed the *Saturday Review.*[76] The *Literary World* condemned the book in an article filled with factual errors. When Jackson's friend Martha Goddard pointed out these errors, anonymously, in the *Boston Daily Advertiser,* the *World* publicly defended its original pronunciation against any "feminine literary cabal."[77] Even Henry James, who wrote a negative review for the *Nation* that was otherwise fair, argued that Mercy was "decidedly too angular and pedantic a young woman," finding the idea of her "poetical contributions to the magazines" merely ridiculous. "New England life is not the most picturesque in the world," he noted wryly, "but there is something regrettable in this pale, unlighted representation of a dry and bloodless population, and a style of manners farther removed from the spectacular than a cranberry-bog from a vineyard."[78]

Today, the biased assumptions of these negative reviews seem obvious, even outrageous. At the time, however, such literary sexism was nothing unusual. Though Elizabeth Barrett Browning had allowed her poet heroine to succeed in both love and literature in *Aurora Leigh* (1857), and in the process had written in verse perhaps the most important Victorian *Künstlerroman,* Puritanical nineteenth-century American reviewers continually pressured American writers to have their heroines give up their careers for domesticity. Combined with the conservatism of most publishers, their censure essentially prohibited women authors from writing about their actual struggles as artists. Jackson was well aware of the extreme disapproval that had been directed at Sara Willis Parton ("Fanny Fern") and her autobiographical novel *Ruth Hall* (1854), in which the heroine forgoes marriage in order to pursue a successful literary career. Back in the days of her correspondence with Henry Root, she herself had even blamed Parton for inviting public excoriation by daring to challenge common notions of propriety in the first place. Jackson also knew that in Augusta Jane Evans's hugely popular novel *St. Elmo* (1867), the artist heroine gives up her career for domesticity. She responded to this critical climate by granting the heroines of her short fiction and novels only one sort of fulfillment, either personal or professional, even though she herself managed to combine both work and domesticity in the final decade of her life. In *Mercy Philbrick's Choice,* she took the brave step of allowing her heroine to choose literature over love. Yet she still tried in many ways to ensure Mercy's essential womanliness, even pairing her off at book's end with the beatified Parson Dorrance. Given her discretion, she had trouble understanding that Mercy's "choice" could still elicit such hostility among reviewers. "I am quite at sea about the book," she wrote anxiously to Moncure Conway in January 1877.

> I honestly tried my best to write a good story—I honestly thought it was fairly good work;—but the Saturday Review—the Nation—& the Literary World all abuse it unmeasuredly. . . . [O]f course there has been a great wave of adulation of it—but from inferior sources—Warner & [George William] Curtis are the only men of standing who have praised it:—and I have an unfortunate but unconquerable tendency, always to doubt the praise—and believe the blame.[79]

Nonetheless, she was not entirely daunted. She told Conway that she was soon going to try writing another novel. Without intending to, she also hinted in her letter at what would become its subject: a woman who allows herself to be duped by false standards of feminine desirability. Apparently, Conway had recently claimed in a published letter that while George Henry Lewes grew better looking with age, "the same could not be said" of George Eliot. Jackson now sternly reprimanded him, explaining that such ideas made aging very difficult for women; she herself had to "try not to think whenever I begin to remember how old I am, and how I shall look in about five years more."[80]

Though Jackson did not tell Conway, her own advancing years were weighing heavily on her at this time because she was beginning to realize, at age forty-six, that she was probably not going to be able to have any children with William. She had been hopeful a year earlier, when they were first married, because her periods were still regular. (She would not go through menopause until 1884.) But as month after month passed without result, she began to experience a "very great disappointment—especially on Will's account," as she explained to her sister in March 1877, shortly after writing to Conway. She compensated for her own sorrow by increasing her level of involvement with Annie's children, sending them money and offering them career advice. For William's sake, she told herself that with all her health troubles, she would surely die in time for him to marry another woman who could bear him children. He was quite happy with her for the present, she told Annie, and would be "for six or eight years" more, at which point she would "get out of the way (I trust!) in time for him to have his babies by a second wife—after he has made his fortune & is ready to take his leisure."[81] This fancy seems to have given Jackson real comfort: she wished the best for William, and she herself had long insisted that she neither wanted nor expected to live into old age. Even so, it was painful to think of her husband happy with another woman. She needed some surety that he would never forget their own love. And she needed to convince herself that he would never regret having once married an older, independent woman. In the opening months of 1877, she struggled to come to terms with these issues by writing *Hetty's Strange History.* "I know Hetty Williams," she would acknowledge in the book's final line, making a sly reference to her autobiographical connection with her heroine.[82]

While Jackson's second novel does not retain for today's reader the special interest of her earlier *Künstlerroman,* it is a more polished work, not marred by the prolonged digressions, loose ends, redundancies, and contradictions that weaken *Mercy.* The book opens in the fictional town of Welbury, Massachusetts, as thirty-five-year-old Hetty Gunn comes into possession of her family's five-hundred-acre farm upon the deaths of her parents. Hetty has always lived at home, and she is deeply pained by the loss of her parents, especially her father. But she has inherited valuable traits of persistence and resolute cheerfulness from her grandfather, now deceased, a farmer and veteran of the Revolutionary War modeled loosely after Jackson's grandfather Fiske. Hetty believes it "a sin, if one can possibly help it," to give way to misery (222). With good cheer and great common sense she begins to manage the farm herself, making such a success that her efforts belie the community's generally "accepted theory" about the proper "sphere of woman's activities and manifestations" (10).

Hetty both loves and hates her New England home. When she is asked soon after the death of her parents if she intends to move away from Welbury, she replies, "I wouldn't go for anything in the world. What should I go away for?" And when asked if she wants to sell the family farm, she says, "I'd as soon sell myself" (25). Yet Welbury is in many ways a stifling community. As Jackson writes in the passage quoted as an epigraph to this chapter, the people of the town have been reared on a "pitiless" Calvinism (38), and many of them are more concerned with the letter of religious law than its spirit. Hetty makes a stand against this sanctimoniousness as soon as she gains her independence. Right away, she hires two community outcasts, Sally and Jim Little, to help her run her farm. Years earlier, Sally became pregnant before she and Jim were married. And though their child soon died, and they expressed constant contrition after their marriage, they were never forgiven by the population of Welbury. Hetty insists that "it is the Lord's business to punish people, not ours" (33), however, and makes Jim overseer of her farm. The Littles soon reveal themselves to be truly good and honest people, and Hetty is delighted when Sally gives birth to a baby boy at her home. The black servants in Hetty's establishment, Caesar and Nan, also demonstrate a truer spirituality than most residents of Welbury.

When Sally becomes temporarily ill after the birth of her baby, Hetty and Dr. Eben Williams take her and the baby to the seaside to convalesce. There Hetty and Dr. Eben fall in love, recognizing that they share a sturdy, commonsense outlook on life and a mutual admiration for the Stoic teachings of Epictetus. They soon marry, and Hetty becomes a "changed woman in the habits and motives of her whole life" (147). Once entirely dedicated to her own pursuits, she now turns the management of her farm over to Jim Little and begins to spend her time accompanying her husband on his house calls. They have eight years of matrimonial happiness. Then, one day, they call on a sick, beautiful young woman named Rachel. This stranger looks at Eben with such transparent admiration that Hetty begins to doubt her own relation to her husband. "Much as Hetty loved Dr. Eben, passionately as her whole life centred around him," Jackson's narrator explains, "there had never been such a feeling as this: they were the heartiest of comrades, but each life was on a plane of absolute independence" (173). Hetty broods on this fact, gradually becoming obsessed with the idea that "youth is beautiful, and old age is ugly" (231). Because her practical husband is "not given to words or demonstrations of affection" (155), she comes to believe that his thoughts are secretly turning toward Rachel, that he would be happier if she were dead so that he could marry the girl. She keeps her suspicion cloaked behind her ever-cheerful demeanor. But in secret she devises a plan for freeing her husband: one day, when she is out rowing on Welbury Lake, she deliberately capsizes her boat and leaves behind a few items to suggest that she has drowned. She then steals away on a train to Canada.

She goes to live in St. Mary's, Canada, where she assumes the unlikely name of Mrs. Hibba Smailli and becomes friendly with a local priest named Father Antoine. This man demonstrates true Christianity, in "spite of his arbitrary Romanism" (216), by helping her to secure a job as a nurse in a Catholic charity hospital. In her new life, Hetty gains an appreciation for Catholicism because she sees that it is able to "teach joy," while her own New England Protestantism begins to seem in contrast "pretty much all terror" (225). She also finds the "*abandon* and unthinkingness" of her French Canadian townspeople delightful "after the grim composure" of her old Welbury neighbors (224). Hetty is forty-six years old when she takes up residence in St. Mary's, but because she goes "cheerfully" about her nursing work, putting all "sufferings" at Eben's loss "away from her with an unflinching resolution," she begins to look "better and younger every day" (230, 242).

A decade passes, and she is still young at fifty-six, when Eben arrives one day by chance in St. Mary's, en route to Europe. Unlike Hetty, he has "grown old fast" (245) since the day of her supposed drowning. He never had any interest in Rachel, and was heartbroken by his wife's disappearance. Now he is retired from his career and seeking solace in travel. When he and Hetty meet, they recognize each other immediately. His worn face instantly proves to Hetty the grave error of her long-ago decision. After their initial shock, they gratefully resume life as husband and wife. But their reunion is not free from tension and sorrow. They have the sense not to return to Welbury, for they know the town would never forgive Hetty, yet Hetty is still forced to do penance for her folly for the rest of her life. She cannot forgive herself. And although Eben forgives her, he cannot forget what she has done and sometimes speaks to her with "great anger" (278).

The reader is left to ponder the nature of Hetty's burden. Is she atoning for having deceived and abandoned her husband? If so, do her good intentions nullify her sin? Or was her selfless act actually a form of selfishness, as twisted an interpretation of true Christianity, in its way, as any of the false pieties of her Welbury neighbors? In that case, Hetty may be atoning for having deceived herself, not Eben, in ever believing that she had only his interests in mind when she left him. Her early decision to give up the management of her farm upon marriage may have gone against her nature, for she was surprisingly happy with her new profession in St. Mary's. Eben senses this in their reunion. "A strange feeling was creeping over him, that, by Hetty's removal of herself from him, by her new life, her new name, new duties, she had really ceased to be his," Jackson writes. "He felt weak and helpless" (268). Much as in Jackson's first novel, Hetty's concealments raise complex questions about the nature of sincerity and deception. Early on, Jackson foreshadows the moral dilemmas that will ensue from Hetty's disappearance on the local lake. "It was believed that Welbury Lake was unfathomable," she writes, "but this notion probably had its foundation in the limited facilities in that region for sounding deep waters" (180).

Thomas Niles published Jackson's second novel, like her first, in the No Name series, which by the fall of 1877 was popular enough to almost guarantee decent sales. He advised Jackson on the title of her book, which he believed would attract readers by its mysteriousness, and he advertised it as "by the author of *Mercy Philbrick's Choice*." *Hetty's Strange History* received a fairly warm welcome in the press. Reviewers differed in their opinions of whether Hetty's deceptions could be justified morally, but many shared the opinion that the book's anonymous author had grown significantly in her craft between her first and second novels. Mary Abigail Dodge ("Gail Hamilton"), for instance, wrote a long piece for the *Independent* in which she humorously criticized the inconsistencies of *Mercy Philbrick's Choice*, rightly guessing that they stemmed from a faulty use of autobiographical material, but praised the growth evident in *Hetty's Strange History* as auguring a major new talent.[83] Her generosity earned Jackson's lasting goodwill, though Jackson would never care for Dodge's blunt manner of expression.

Almost immediately after finishing her second novel, in the spring of 1877, Jackson turned her attention to plans for a children's book, *Nelly's Silver Mine*. She had only recently published her *Bits of Talk in Verse and Prose for Young Folks* (1876), a collection that included some fiction, often of a moralistic bent, in addition to its offerings in poetry, travel, and domestic improvement. She had long admired good children's fiction, especially the work of Mary Mapes Dodge, Louisa May Alcott, Lewis Carroll, Flora Shaw, and Margaret Oliphant. But she had never devoted much sustained energy to her own juvenile work, instead coming up with ideas for children simply as afterthoughts to other projects. Now, buoyed by William's interest, she decided to write a lengthy story for children. In June she traveled alone to the Colorado mining boom town of Rosita (population 2,000) in order to undertake local research. On the twenty-eighth, she complained in a letter to William that Rosita was "the dirtiest place I ever saw," and that bedbugs were keeping her awake at night. She also shared the good news that she had begun her new novel.[84] Indeed, she was fascinated by her surroundings, and used them effectively as one of the settings in her book. Today, when the town of Rosita no longer exists, her portrait takes on special interest. Her descriptions of various Coloradans and their hardscrabble professions are also compelling.

Nelly's Silver Mine is more solidly regionalist, less permeated by incongruous idealism, than Jackson's other fiction. The novel opens at Christmastime in the town of "Mayfield," in "one of the pleasantest counties in Massachusetts," as the March family begins making plans to move away to Colorado. Mr. March is a preacher, modeled after Nathan Fiske. He is suffering from severe asthma, which the family hopes might be cured by a western climate and a newly active outdoor life in ranching. Mrs. March, originally from England, is a cheerful and competent woman who has a natural appreciation for the tenets of Epictetus, her mottoes being: "First. If you don't like a thing, try with all your might to make it as you do like it. Second. If you can't possibly make it as you like it, stop thinking about it: let it go." The heroine of the novel, Nelly, is a twelve-year-old aspiring poet, who reads voraciously. She is based on Jackson herself, her name being a version of Jackson's own schoolgirl nickname, "Nellie." Jackson is also the model for Nelly's twin brother Rob, who suffers from chronic sore throats but has a native restlessness and the "the longing of a born traveller" in his eyes.[85] Nelly and Rob are delighted at the prospect of moving to Colorado, and the whole family is reassured about their decision when eccentric old Deacon and Mrs. Plummer decide to join in the adventure, for unlike the Marches they are experienced farmers.

Narrating her story in a charming, intimate first-person voice, as if she were simply speaking to a circle of children, Jackson describes the train trip to Colorado in vivid detail. Nelly and Rob meet emigrants from many places and learn the pleasures and hardships of nights in sleeping cars. When the Marches and Plummers finally arrive in Denver, they board the Denver and Rio Grande Railroad south, the children expressing surprise at the small proportions of the narrow-gauge road. As their train approaches Colorado Springs, Mrs. March speaks with a woman who reassures her about the health benefits of Colorado. "I came out here three years ago on a mattress, with my doctor and nurse, and thought it very doubtful if I lived to get here; and I have been perfectly well ever since," the lady explains, sounding a good deal like Jackson herself. Not only has her "throat trouble" been contained, she says, but she has been in every way improved by her new home. She particularly revels in the area's natural beauty. "I love these mountains so that, whenever I go away from them, I miss them all the time," she says. "I keep seeing them before me all the while, just as you see the face of a dear friend you are separated from."[86]

In Colorado the Marches meet ranchers, teamsters, shopkeepers, miners, and wealthy health seekers. Nelly glimpses the rough side of western life, the occasional drunks and ruffians, but she also experiences the friendly sympathy and camaraderie of pioneers from around the world. She thinks Pike's Peak majestic, and enjoys exploring local canyons and woods. During the first year of their new life, the Marches and Plummers live up in the hills of Ute Pass, not far outside Colorado Springs, on some land Mr. March purchased back in Massachusetts. But they quickly discover the spot to be unsuitable for farming. In their second year they move south to a grassy canyon in Wet Mountain Valley, five miles away from Rosita. The Plummers decide to return to Massachusetts at the time of this move, as the high altitude of Colorado has been straining old Mrs. Plummer's heart. But the Marches are all entirely renewed in health. With the help of the teamster Long Billy and his fiancée Lucinda Harkiss, who are welcomed on egalitarian terms as working members of the family, they make a promising start with their new farm. But before summer, grasshoppers eat their entire crop. When the same thing happens again the following year, the Marches are suddenly plunged into poverty.

At this point, Nelly's true character begins to reveal itself. She insists on helping to support her family by selling eggs and butter in Rosita several days a week, making the long five-mile trip into town by foot. Soon, she inspires Rob to do his part by accompanying her and selling trout that he catches in a local stream. In Rosita, Nelly makes many new friends, including Swedish Jan and his wife Ulrica, a washerwoman; and Mr. Kleesman, an old German who works as an assayer of silver. One day, as Nelly is watching Mr. Kleesman at work, a prospector comes in to show him a sampling of ordinary stones that, as Mr. Kleesman explains, generally indicate the presence of buried silver. Suddenly, Nelly remembers that she herself has recently seen a number of similar stones on one of her rambles through the woods. The next day she shows the spot to Mr. March and one of his mining acquaintances, and the whole family is thrown into a frenzy of hope and expectation. They start up in the mining business. Before long, however, Mr. Kleesman makes an assay that proves the "Good Luck Mine" to be worthless. Nelly is sorely disappointed. Even in the midst of her sorrow, though, she demonstrates her usual steadfast good humor, thereby enabling Jackson to extrapolate the moral of her story. While Nelly's silver mine was deceptive, seeming valuable according to surface appearances but actually worthless inside, Nelly herself possesses true inner riches. At the very end of the novel, as Nelly heads off happily to spend a summer in the East, Mr. Kleesman exclaims, "[S]he haf better than any silver mine in her own self. She haf such goot-vill, such patient, such true, she haf always 'goot luck.' She are 'Goot Luck mine' her own self.'"[87]

While *Nelly's Silver Mine* suffers from a few inconsistencies, including the fact that Nelly seems much younger than her supposed fifteen years at story's end, the charm of Jackson's narrative style and her lively depictions of pioneer life in Colorado outweigh any minor defects. In 1878 Niles garnered special attention for Jackson's new book by bringing it out as the first installment in his new children's western series and publishing it under Jackson's acknowledged "H.H." signature. In December 1878 a reviewer for the *Atlantic* recognized the book's best qualities: "What we especially like in it, and what seems to interest the writer most, is the characterization of a few types of border life, less swaggering and riotous than usually find their way into print."[88] Children also liked the novel. Although it sold fewer than 5,000 copies before Jackson's death, it afterward maintained a small, steady sale of some 100 books per year straight through the 1950s.[89]

By the time Jackson finished *Nelly's Silver Mine,* she had gained considerably in her skills as a fiction writer. Not only had she produced several creditable novels at a swift pace, but she was also about to write several unusually interesting short stories. In early 1877, Josiah Holland began to make what would prove to be a series of rejections of her efforts to arrange for the publication of a new novel, "Elspeth Dynor," in his magazine. She therefore abandoned her earlier willingness to publish her short fiction only in *Scribner's* and began to explore other literary outlets and manners of writing. On June 19 and 26, 1879, she published "The Story of Clotilde Danarosch" in the *Independent* under her recognizable "H.H." signature, which except in the case of *Nelly's Silver Mine* she had hitherto reserved only for nonfiction and poetry.[90] In this story she temporarily set aside her commitment to American regionalism to write of Germany and Italy, in the process creating an evocative portrait of the complexities of European social life.

In July of the same year, and again in November, she returned to the fictional territory of New England in two stories for the *Atlantic Monthly,* "Massy Sprague's Daughter" and "Sister Mary's Story." She published these stories under the pseudonym "Jane Silsbee." In choosing this new, Yankee-sounding name, she seems to have been guided by a desire to prevent her Saxe Holm pseudonym from becoming overused. "I have a great dislike to the practice so many writers have, of having their names in all the papers and magazines," she had told William Ward back in 1875.[91] She also enjoyed the simple fun of using many names. "It is entertaining to keep a little cupboard full of literary dominoes," she would later tell Thomas Bailey Aldrich when explaining her use of various literary signatures.[92] She was not intent on keeping her authorship of the Jane Silsbee stories hidden, as she was with her Saxe Holm stories, for she apparently approved Jane Silsbee's listing as a pseudonym for Helen Jackson in the 1880 *Atlantic Index.*

In "Massy Sprague's Daughter," Jackson for the first time makes "a protest against the spread of civilization" the overt subject of a piece of her fiction, something she would not do again until *Ramona.* In this narrative, Toinette, the "rarely beautiful" and "sensitive" daughter of a somewhat bigoted East Indian woman named Massy Sprague, is lured away from her wholesome small town life on Block Island, Rhode Island, and her love for her black boyfriend, Ramby, by a capricious visiting tourist; the capricious woman hires Toinette to work as a servant in her own elegant home in Newport. There Toinette is seduced by an evil white man. She returns home in shame with her child to die under the faithful Ramby's final ministrations, her tale a sad illustration of the perils of advancing civilization. In "Sister Mary's Story," published in the November 1879 *Atlantic,* an outwardly typical New England spinster, Mary, who works as a nurse in a Catholic charity hospital, is revealed to have depths of passion that difficult life experiences have forced her to repress.

Less than two years after publishing these quintessential pieces of New England regionalism, Jackson wrote a story that made lighthearted fun of the conventions of the genre, "Mrs. Millington and Her Librarian." Based partly on the same subject matter that Jackson was then planning to use in her collaborative play with Charles Dudley Warner, this story appeared under her Saxe Holm signature in *Harper's Magazine* of June 1881, after *Scribner's* had rejected it for being not "*Scribner-y*" and the *Atlantic* for being too closely based on a real Boston incident.[93] One of the main characters of this tale, the librarian Jerusha, has the sort of "straightforward, strong, loyal, affectionate nature" that Jackson celebrates in all her Saxe Holm heroines, and is rewarded for her goodness by a fairy-tale marriage to an English aristocrat. Her employer Mrs. Millington, however, is a comic representative of her region, a New England version of *Adam Bede*'s Mrs. Poyser. A good person but lacking in the usual Saxe Holm heroine's self-restraint, Mrs. Millington cannot abide the quiet retirement in the country that is imposed on her after her husband's death. Her decision to return to Boston to run a library is not an altogether fitting one, however. "If I couldn't talk, I'd die," she explains. "That's what Mr. M. said when he took me to Paris. . . . Says he, 'Little woman, you've got to a place now where you've got to hold your tongue; d'ye think it'll kill ye?' an' I 'most thought 'twould." Mrs. Millington ends up married to her deceased husband's ungainly brother, working behind the counter of an old wig shop, where she spends her days measuring heads, mixing hair dyes, and chatting.

At least for a time, Jackson thought the novel she had begun to work on before writing these later short stories, "Elspeth Dynor," was her best novel to date. She had made intermittent progress on the manuscript between 1877 and 1879, completing at least 566 pages before she set it aside in the summer of 1879. She intended to return to it but never did, as she soon became unwilling to spend large amounts of time away from her work on behalf of Indian rights. Before she died, however, she had the incomplete existing manuscript, which had been languishing at Scribner's, sent to Roberts Brothers for possible posthumous publication. Thomas Niles thought it showed "remarkable vigor and promise" and considered asking Sarah Woolsey to complete it.[94] Finally, though, he settled on publishing three chapters from the manuscript as a short story titled "The Inn of the Golden Pear" in a posthumous collection of Jackson's final short stories, *Between Whiles* (1887), with Woolsey supplying a concluding paragraph for the excerpt.

Today, the existing manuscript of "Elspeth Dynor" is housed in the New York Public Library, absent chapters two through four, which Niles published.[95] Read together with the published excerpt, the manuscript is clearly an unfinished product, marred by insufficient development of many scenes and an awkward handling of flashbacks and character background information. But it does show real promise. It is not blatantly autobiographical like Jackson's earlier novels; yet, for the first time, it makes use of Jackson's actual experiences as an artist and worldly woman in its probing analysis of the dashing, yet "cynical, contemptuous" sculptor Ned Blake, a man as inherently deceptive and cunning in nature as the novel's heroine Elspeth Dynor is upright and honest.[96] Here Jackson's usual interest in the ethics of sincerity and deception makes itself felt in complex questions about the moral nature of the artist. What can account for immorality in a person capable of creating works of great beauty? Are beautiful works by disingenuous artists also somehow deceptive? Does great art excuse immorality in an artist?

Most of the present action of "Elspeth Dynor" takes place on a steamer bound from New York to Europe, shortly after the close of the Civil War. Even before the ship embarks, Ned Blake finds his attention drawn to an old man and an attractive young woman who are traveling together: he wants to use the old man as a model for his sculpting, and to know the woman. The old man is General Walter Dynor, a Quaker who during the war had set aside the pacifism of his creed in order to take up arms. He is accompanied by his grandniece Elspeth, who embodies the intuitive artistry, cheer, and diligence typical of Jackson's heroines. Ned determines to insinuate himself into the company of the Dynors. He gets his opportunity when, shortly after the ship leaves shore, General Dynor suffers a stroke that confines him to his bed, leaving Elspeth without supervision. Immediately, Ned joins the ship's young doctor in proclaiming himself Elspeth's protector. Unknown to her, however, Ned is entirely unlike the "pure, steadfast" Dr. Linnell, for he comes from a family that holds nothing sacred (49). "In the days when New England was only a group of thinly settled wilderness called 'provinces,' . . . far up in the North, near the Canada line," both Ned's grandfather and father had married wild, unprincipled French Catholic women, for they had not sympathized with the hardworking, self-denying ways of their Puritanical neighbors.[97] Upon the death of Ned's father, his mother, the fiery Victorine Dubois Blaycke, left the town of "St. Urbans" to take up a wandering life in Europe, dragging Ned and his brothers along on her dishonorable escapades. His character thus ill-formed, Ned has since continued to spend most of his time in dissipated European travels. His only anchor to a more honorable, rooted life is his one sister, Rebecca. "Bonnie" lives a quietly "content" and "industrious" life in St. Urbans, finding comfort for her loneliness in her love for her native region, "the old stone house, the lake, the pine groves, the mountains" (233, 235, 265).

Elspeth Dynor, like Bonnie Blake and unlike Ned, is a woman firmly connected to her regional origins. She and her beloved uncle, who has taken care of her since the deaths of her parents, are Pennsylvania Friends, their early experiences partly modeled after those of William Jackson. Prior to the Civil War, Elspeth helped her uncle smuggle fugitive slaves along the Underground Railroad; when the war came, and Walter Dynor entered the army, Elspeth worked for the Sanitary Commission. The Dynors are now on their way to Europe to find some rest from their labors in the diversions of "a new soil" (330). When Elspeth crosses paths with Ned Blake, he is returning to Europe after visiting his sister, who has upset him by suggesting that his art is suffering because of his degenerate lifestyle. Though "nobody could be more brilliantly eloquent than Ned Blake on the palpable absurdity of the theory that there could be any possible relation between a man's moral character and his artistic capacity" (286), he is beginning to fear that there might be something to it after all. He is powerfully attracted by Elspeth's goodness, even as she is attracted by his reputation as a great artist. Like most passengers on the ship, she has long known and appreciated Ned's work, especially his most famous piece, an often-reproduced, glorious head of Psyche.

Elspeth and Ned begin to fall in love, engaging in long conversations about art and the state of art criticism in America. In these conversations, Ned serves as a mouthpiece for some of Jackson's own opinions. Jackson herself never developed any stable criteria as a literary reviewer; like many writers, she was disposed to think well of books written by her acquaintances and published by her publisher. But she held professional critics to a higher standard, and was rarely impressed by their work. Just as Elspeth and Ned are growing closer through their exchange of ideas, Dr. Linnell one day catches Ned spying on Elspeth in her sleep, and warns the girl that his own mother had once criticized Ned's famous Psyche as representing "the climax of sensuousness: and not of spirituality" (417–18). But Elspeth is smitten by Ned's outward charm and his desire to become a better person in her company, and is therefore unable to see "the evil forces that were in his blood, the evil influences of his bad mother, the reckless habits of his life" (550). She is not alone in being deceived by Ned. He charms all of the ship's passengers with entertaining stories and gestures of friendship, even as he secretly sneers at them.

In writing of Ned's dualistic personality, Jackson explores personal character as the product of early family and regional environment, as well as heredity and "race." To some extent, she imputes Ned's unruliness to his French Canadian blood, though in *Hetty's Strange History* she had portrayed the freedom of her French Canadian characters in a much more positive light. She also explains Ned's behavior as animalistic and organic, in a manner that reflects the emerging literary naturalism of her era. "Many things were to be forgiven in Ned Blake, by reason of his organization," she writes. "He was built for swift and unthinking conduct, as surely as the ostrich is built to run and the eagle to fly" (36). When Ned is engaged in his art, he comes "as nearly to leading a purely spiritual existence, as a soul fettered with a body can" (380)—immediately after spying on Elspeth in her sleep, for instance, he goes to his cabin to work on a bust of her, rising "for the time being, above all that is petty, all that is groveling" (379). But at other times he is a debased liar and voluptuary, an evil tempter whom several characters aptly compare to Mephistopheles. Jackson muses:

> If there are plants whose law of flowering includes the unsightly drying and shriveling of the stalks, which must lie prone on the ground, black, and blighted, till a new impulse draws new currents from the still living root, and a new spring sees new blossoms, as pure and beautiful as the old, who shall say that there may not be souls, whose organic life is as complex, whose seasons are as fixed, and whose actions are as unlike, as inconsistent, as opposed to each other, as bloom and blight, verdure and barrenness? And the more exquisite the flower, the sharper will be the contrast of the succeeding desolation. (381–82)

When their boat reaches Europe and Ned must depart from the Dynors, he impulsively decides to test the strength of his affection for Elspeth by seeking out one of his former lovers, Marishka. Two years earlier, at Marishka's home in Camogli, Italy, Ned had deceived both her and her Hungarian immigrant father, entering closely into their most intimate family life only to abandon Marishka when he tired of her company. Now he returns to Camogli, where he is by chance discovered one night—when he is out rowing in the moonlight with Marishka and their illegitimate baby—by a horrified Elspeth Dynor.

Jackson's manuscript ends at this point, so we cannot know what she had in store for Ned and Elspeth and her other characters. Her intended final pronouncement on the connection between morality and art is not hard to ascertain, however. She believed that good art could not justify bad behavior. In the novel, she argues that "no man may dare to say" "how far moral responsibility enters into the balancing of the deeds of such natures" as Ned Blake's (381).

Later she even hints that duplicity may in fact be inherent to art, which is, after all, only a simulacrum of life: near the end of the manuscript, we learn that Ned actually modeled his wonderful Psyche on Marishka, and that it does depict "the climax of sensuousness: and not of spirituality," as Dr. Linnell's mother had suspected. Still, Jackson had been taught by all her literary mentors, from her father straight through to Thomas Wentworth Higginson, that the personal morality of writers was at bottom more important than the work they produced. And though she believed that heredity, biology, morality, and intellect were all connected, she did not believe that their connection could be used as an excuse for any current misbehavior. Earlier, in a June 1871 *Scribner's* review of Oliver Wendell Holmes's *Mechanism in Thought and Morals,* she had stated this belief specifically. "It would be a very comfortable thing to ascribe all our sins, big and little, to a sudden shifting of molecules in our left leg, and our great-grandfather responsible for it, at that!" she wrote. "But earnest souls find in it no justification of moral inertia."

Jackson stopped working on her new novel in the summer of 1879 because she was beginning to descend into one of her worst depressions. The past winter had been difficult. Josiah Holland had finally agreed to read the first portions of "Elspeth Dynor" and to consider making an advance payment on it, but had then enraged her by offering only $1,000. She had suffered attack after attack of bronchitis. And on February 6, Thomas Wentworth Higginson, whose first wife Mary had died only a year and a half before, married a young poet named Mary Thacher. By the time warm weather arrived, Jackson was in poor health both mentally and physically, and she was nearly prostrated when a sudden, forty-two-day dry spell sent temperatures soaring above eighty degrees inside the Jackson home and ninety degrees outside. While she had once loved the Colorado climate, she now began to feel that the summers were too hot, the winters too cold and dry, and the altitude altogether too high. She was also growing disenchanted with some of her neighbors. In her first years in Colorado Springs she had relished the easy friendliness of the townspeople and made a number of new friends, including Fanny Parish, Virginia King Pearson, Mrs. Gerald de Coursey, and Abbie Sage Richardson. In more recent years, however, many local residents had begun to consider her haughty and to gossip about her fame, her earnings, her unusually liberal religious beliefs, and her frank enjoyment of champagne, wine, and sherry, which flew in the face of the Colorado Springs Company's original mandate of temperance. She began feeling bored by her surroundings and unable to concentrate well on her work. Her old restlessness returned. She wished that she and William could leave Colorado Springs and travel together, perhaps for several years. But William's business interests made it impossible for him to consider the idea. His immovability on this subject, together with the fact that he had never been much given to romantic words, hurt her now when she was feeling needy, and heightened her anxieties about their temperamental differences and childlessness.

Finally, despite her wish to remain near to William, she decided that her health could not tolerate another winter or summer season in Colorado. For a time it looked as though William's work would necessitate a trip to New York, and they made plans to travel there together. The awaited order never came, however, so Helen determined to go east without her husband, possibly for an entire year. She and William would spend time together when work finally did bring him to New York. She might also make a return visit to Europe. With William's wholehearted support, she set out in early August. He wrote to her while she was still on the train, imploring her to trust in their relationship and to look for fulfillment in her writing. "If you make the effort you promise yourself to make you will get out of any rut you are now in & I will certainly, my dear girl, do all I can to aid you," he said.

> There is a brighter day coming for us if we are true to ourselves. We are both going to be happy & contented.—You will lead your life in your work & in which you are doing good. I will lead mine in a business line. . . . You will come back to me, in September next, with a new mucous membrane & with all the old cobweb washed away—Only a clean sunlight of love & trust left in their stead. I promise you you will find me meeting you even more than half way. . . . Keep good courage & make the most of your self.[98]

⤳ 8 ↩

Indian Reform Work,
Late Travel Writing, and *Ramona*

All the beauty and perfection of art, all the song and music and
loveliness and good in which I have hitherto taken delight, on which
I have hitherto had my eyes fixed, as only poor blind poet's eyes
could be!—I see now that all these things are so small so fleeting so
few so powerless by side of the huge sin and wrong, that I wonder
we know they exist at all. They are no more than one poor little
flower blossoming for a moment on the edge of a volcano, into
which it must fall.

JACKSON TO WILLIAM JACKSON,
August 18, 1879, WSJ1

After Jackson became depressed in the summer of 1879 she found herself not
only unable to complete "Elspeth Dynor" but also doubting her very purposes
as an artist. Writing to William on August 18 upon her arrival in New York
from Colorado, she agonized over the insufficiency of art in a world filled with
pain and trouble. Suddenly, it seemed to her that art was nearly insignificant
"by side of the huge sin and wrong." Her own efforts to promote honorable living among her readers also seemed unimportant. These were new feelings, yet
she had been working up to them for nearly two years, ever since she had begun in her new novel to ponder the moral value of art. In fact, in one of her
1877 domestic essays, "Wanted, in New England, An Apostle for Sunshine,"
she had written, "It is a trite quotation, the saying of the poet, who boasted: 'Let
me make songs for the people, and I care not who makes their laws.' "[1] Earlier,
she had espoused this same "trite" quotation as the guiding concept behind her
"Draxy Miller" stories. But by 1877 the idea that art and artistic sensibility
were more important than the practical matters of life no longer seemed ten-
able. People could not make poetry, she had come to realize, unless they first
had their freedom and their health. Now, in the summer of 1879, she struggled
to find a more concrete moral purpose for her writing.

She succeeded that fall, when during a visit to Boston she was moved to join in local agitation over the plight of the Ponca Indians. On October 29, it seems, she attended a public reception at Boston's Horticultural Hall for Ponca Chief Standing Bear.[2] Accompanied by his interpreter, Omaha Indian Susette La Flesche (also known as Inshta Theumba, or "Bright Eyes"), her brother Francis, and the activist Thomas Henry Tibbles, a former assistant editor at the *Omaha Herald,* Standing Bear was making a six-month consciousness-raising tour of eastern cities (a tour organized by Tibbles). His objective was to publicize the miseries and deaths his tribe had recently suffered upon being forcibly removed by the federal government from Dakota Territory to Indian Territory. He and his supporters were raising money for Ponca repatriation and also for a proposed suit in the Supreme Court, where they hoped to secure legal status for Indians by drawing on a recent landmark decision in Nebraska district court by Judge Elmer S. Dundy. In arguing that Ponca Indians who chose to leave Indian Territory could not be forcibly detained, Dundy had held that Indians, who were usually given no standing in American courts, were in fact "persons" with legal rights.

Jackson was naturally drawn in imagination to the plight of the agricultural Ponca tribe. Their efforts to secure their lands from the rapacious advance of American civilization represented a supreme example of the very "protest" that she had been waging for years in her travel essays and fiction. Their present homelessness recalled her own early sorrows as a homeless wanderer, sorrows out of which she had written countless domestic essays about the sanctity of the home. Their embattled plight also appealed to her interest in the meaning and consequences of sincerity and deception. From the beginning of her involvement in Indian reform work until the end of her life, she would condemn the United States government and many of its representatives and citizens as "wicked, insincere, & hypocritical" in their dealings with Native Americans,[3] while praising Native Americans as sincere and justified in their efforts to secure their lands and legal rights. In her single-minded quest for justice, she would shed her initial low spirits and redouble the time and energy that she poured into her work. Like her father before her, her increasing devotion to her cause would lead her to forgo some of the simpler pleasures of social and family life: in the coming years, she would accomplish much of her best work not at home but away in eastern hotels, where she was far from the difficult weather of Colorado Springs and her usual domestic responsibilities, and where she could easily use her fragile health as an excuse for avoiding social interruptions to her writing.

Several specific factors in the Ponca case inclined her to move beyond mere feelings of sympathy to make the cause of Indian rights her own. She believed that the treaties the American government had made with the Poncas were more exact than many others, so that ignoring them was a graver crime. She thought that the Poncas had demonstrated remarkable character and forbearance in responding to the outrages committed against them without violence. She was also immensely impressed by the perseverance and personal charisma of Standing Bear and especially of his translator, Susette La Flesche. In one of her first Indian reform essays, "Standing Bear and Bright Eyes," published in the *New York Independent* on November 20, 1879, Jackson profiled these activists in the hope that her readers would be similarly impressed, and therefore reject tired notions that "Indians are devils, and the sooner the country rids itself of them the better, no matter by what means." She described Standing Bear as dignified but despairing, his face "stamped with unutterable sadness" at the loss of his land, and longing for the comforts of home as much as any domestic American. She described La Flesche as equally dignified and domestic. "She is a well educated, graceful, winning, lovely girl," Jackson says, "and speaks English so quaint, so simple, and yet so stately in its very simplicity, that one is lost in wonder until he learns that the only book of value this Indian girl owns is a little edition of Shakespeare, which she won as a prize at school and knows well nigh by heart."

La Flesche was to have an important influence on Jackson's basic reform objectives, helping to shape her belief that legal rights were what all Indians, not only the Poncas, most needed, and what the American people must demand for them. The daughter of Omaha Chief Joseph La Flesche, himself the son of a French trader and an Indian woman, and Mary Gale, also of mixed Indian and white parentage, La Flesche had been a teacher on the Omaha Reservation before embracing activism with the Poncas. She was increasingly interested in writing; when Jackson met her, she had just completed an introduction for Thomas Henry Tibbles's account of the Ponca affair, *The Ponca Chiefs: An Indian's Attempt to Appeal from the Tomahawk to the Courts* (1879).[4] This introduction had a powerful impact on Jackson. La Flesche argued that it was in America's "homes" that the power existed "to remedy the evil" done to Indians, for ordinary Americans could demand that the courts grant them legal rights. "It is a little thing, a simple thing, which my people ask of a nation whose watchword is liberty; but it is endless in its consequences," La Flesche wrote. "They ask for their liberty, and law is liberty."[5] Jackson considered this last sentence especially wise and eloquent and would often quote it in her own reform writings. She would also labor to rouse public sentiment in favor of securing legal rights for Indians, including the right to remain on ancestral lands, the right of citizenship, the right to testify in court, and the many varied and specific rights enumerated in existing treaties. In these aims, Jackson promoted a pluralistic vision of American society that was progressive for her time.

"I have become what I have said a thousand times was the most odious thing in life, 'a woman with a hobby,'" Jackson wrote to Thomas Wentworth Higginson in January 1880. "But I cannot help it. I think I feel as you must have felt in the old abolition days. I cannot think of anything else from night to morning and from morning to night."[6] Jackson knew that in taking up reform work, she was drawing closer in spirit to activist friends such as Higginson and Moncure Conway and was rejecting her earlier belief that women should limit their desires to improve society to the confines of their own homes. As she hinted to one acquaintance, both changing times and broadened personal experience had contributed to this transformation: she believed that the reason her longtime friend Molly Hunt, her sister-in-law from her first marriage, did not sympathize with her concern for Indian rights was that Molly still held "the conservative views" of the Hunt family, having lived cut off from "the force of events" since her husband's death.[7] Jackson, in contrast, had gained a great deal of worldly experience since the years of her first marriage. In her many travels, she had met and learned to appreciate individuals from a variety of ethnic backgrounds. With William Jackson's encouragement, she had shed many, though not all, of her race and class prejudices.

During the Civil War, when social activists such as Higginson and Conway had been absorbed in the cause of abolition, Edward Hunt had not only promoted a colonization scheme for African Americans in his *Union Foundations* but had also attempted in that pamphlet to justify American dispossession of Native American lands. "Caucasian civilization has an overmastering vitality and reality, which not only gives it superior power, but a higher right to expand and assert itself," he wrote. "The Indian title has rightly been swept away before the colonizing demands of the highest earthly civilization, and no inferior race is privileged to bar its progress over the New World."[8] By the time Jackson took up reform work, she was no longer willing to stand by in silence while such views were expressed. "There are people—and their number seems increasing in our country every day—who hold that the Indian's 'right of occupancy' was never any 'right' at all—was nothing that he had the power to sell, or white men need have troubled themselves to buy," she declares in "The Wards of the United States Government," published in *Scribner's Monthly* in March 1880. (She uses the words "wards" and "guardian" satirically in this essay, arguing, as she often would, against white efforts to infantilize or assume a possessive relation toward Indians.) In fact, she says, the American government has recognized Indian rights of occupancy in hundreds of treaties, and Americans have ignored these rights only because they have been led by false information to believe themselves morally superior to Indians. "Too often the tale is told from the white man's side, and not from the Indian's," she insists.

Like so many of her beliefs, Jackson's sense that it was appropriate for her, an outsider, to try to tell the Indian's side of the story was at bottom rooted in her childhood. Her early contact with actual individual Indians had been limited; indeed, she marveled to Charles Dudley Warner that during her youth her reading of "the accounts of massacres" had given her a "childish terror" that "Indians would come in the night, & kill us!"[9] Her own parents had taught her to think of Indians as historical relics or cultural oddities, views that she conveyed in her early travel writing and also in the few references she made to Indians in her domestic essays and fiction from the 1870s. At the same time, however, the Fiskes had considered any people who either practiced or might be converted to Protestant Christianity as worthy beneficiaries of their assistance, and they included Indians in this category. As a child, the only book about Indians Helen owned was William Andrus Alcott's *Stories of Eliot and the Indians* (1838), which suggested that Indians were by nature not murderers but candidates for Christianity. Moreover, though Amherst was generally conservative in religious and political matters, the college stood opposed to mistreatment of Indians, much as it opposed slavery. Not long before Helen was born, in fact, her father joined with other faculty in expressing support for the Cherokees, who were living in imminent danger of being driven from their Georgia homelands by Andrew Jackson's administration.

In December 1829 Nathan reported in a letter to Helen's mother that Heman Humphrey, the president of Amherst College, had delivered an "eloquent" sermon on the plight of the Cherokees, which had so "waked up" up the college that the students were "half ready to *fight*" on their behalf.[10] Because the Cherokees were not actually forced to Indian Territory until 1838, it is likely that Helen heard her father express continued support for them at various times during her childhood. She was probably even familiar with the specific sorts of arguments contained in Humphrey's sermon, "Indian Rights and Our Duties," which was published after Humphrey had delivered it in several towns. She would make many of the same arguments in her own reform work. For example, Humphrey offered special praise to the Cherokees for what he considered their advancement "under the influence of industrious habits, of education, of religion, and of efficient laws," just as Jackson would always express most sympathy for those Indian tribes, including the Cherokees, whom she considered industrious and upright. Humphrey also argued in terms very similar to Jackson's that the American nation had a special duty to its Native tribes, having entered into official treaties with them as sovereign nations, and that it was the responsibility of individual Americans to demand fulfillment of this duty or else risk moral humiliation. "I am but an humble individual. . . . But as yet, I am free," Humphrey declared, urging individuals to realize the power of the awakened conscience: "I bless God, that I have a heart which cannot help being distressed for the poor persecuted Indians. I have a voice, feeble though it be, and no man, without the scimitar or bow string, shall hinder my pleading for the oppressed. I have a right to petition, to remonstrate, to implore, and God forbid that I should be silent."[11]

The first phase of Jackson's own pleading for the rights of Indians extended from her initial espousal of the cause of the Poncas in the fall of 1879 through the 1881 publication of *A Century of Dishonor.* During this period, she helped organize the Boston Indian Citizenship Committee and became loosely affiliated with the Women's National Indian Association, twice gathering signatures among her acquaintances for WNIA petitions to the federal government. For the most part, though, she worked alone, as an individual writer. She wrote private letters to prominent literary connections, including Henry Wadsworth Longfellow, James Russell Lowell, Oliver Wendell Holmes, John Greenleaf Whittier, William Dean Howells, and Henry Oscar Houghton, explaining the situation of the Poncas as she saw it and soliciting support for their cause. She wrote to politicians, seeking to influence the composition of a government committee that was being formed to visit the Poncas in Indian Territory. She asked influential editor friends, including Charles Dudley Warner at the *Hartford Courant* and Noah Brooks at the *New York Times,* to write editorials in support of the Poncas. Above all, she herself wrote many articles and open letters to newspapers, including the *New York Evening Post,* the *New York Times,* the *New York Herald,* the *Springfield Republican,* and especially the *New York Tribune,* whose editor, Whitelaw Reid, was open to her insistence that it was "the function of a great and powerful newspaper" to rouse public sentiment over important moral issues.[12] In these newspaper pieces, which she signed openly as "H.H.," she wrote on a number of contemporary issues in Indian affairs, but caused public commotions with two of her subjects in particular.

Beginning in December 1879, she engaged in a contentious exchange of letters about the Ponca case with Carl Schurz, secretary of the interior from 1877 to 1881. Some of these letters were published at the time in the *New York Tribune* and *Boston Daily Advertiser,* and later reprinted as an appendix, "The Ponca Case," in Jackson's *Century of Dishonor.* Although there were Americans who believed that Schurz, a liberal Republican, was working to halt governmental abuse of Native Americans, Jackson and a number of other reformers were increasingly infuriated with him because he had blocked all efforts to have Judge Dundy's decision brought before the Supreme Court and was refusing to allow Ponca repatriation. Jackson was "profoundly flattered" that Schurz felt it necessary to respond to her accusations on these topics. "I have hardly dared to hope that I could do anything for the Indians," she told Whitelaw Reid, "but now I begin to hope I can, and I do not mean to 'let go' so long as there is a stone left to turn."[13] In private, she castigated Schurz in letters to Charles Dudley Warner and Senator Dawes as an "Arch Hypocrite," an "Arch Villain," and "a very stupid man."[14]

In late January 1880, as her correspondence with Schurz drew to a close, Jackson caused another public stir when she began focusing attention on the plight of the White River Utes of Colorado. The Department of the Interior was denying rations to this tribe because a small number of them had murdered an Indian agent, Nathan C. Meeker, the previous September. In several articles,

Jackson argued that the Utes had been provoked to murder by years of mistreatment by the federal government and by many of Colorado's white settlers, who since statehood in 1876 had been prospecting on Indian lands and agitating for mass expulsions to Indian Territory. She insisted, moreover, that if the entire Ute tribe was to be punished for the deeds of a few men, then every white American in Colorado should be punished for the Sand Creek Massacre of November 29, 1864, when Colonel John Chivington and his volunteers had attacked and murdered several hundred peaceable Cheyenne and Arapaho men, women, and children. Her description of the Sand Creek Massacre elicited an angry response from William N. Byers of Washington, D.C., a former resident of Colorado and editor of the *Rocky Mountain News,* which in 1864 had praised Chivington and his men for having "covered themselves with glory" in the massacre. Jackson now entered into a contentious open exchange of letters about the massacre with Byers in the pages of the *New York Tribune* (reprinted as an appendix in *A Century of Dishonor*). At the end of this debate, in March, she felt satisfied that she had vanquished her foe by quoting from official court testimonies about the atrocities committed by whites at Sand Creek. Still, she remained disgusted at Byers's "lies," which she believed had "been more astounding even" than Schurz's.[15]

At the same time that she was becoming involved in these heated public battles, in early January 1880, Jackson relocated from Boston to New York to start research for a book about the history of the U.S. government's conduct toward Indians. It was to be "simply & *curtly* a record of our broken Treaties," she explained to Charles Dudley Warner, with "no sentiment—no prattle of suggestion—a bare record of facts in fewest possible words." She believed mere knowledge of the historical facts would be enough to persuade many readers to join her in a crusade to which she was now passionately devoted. "I shall be found with 'Indians' engraved on my brain, when I am dead," she told Warner. "A fire has been kindled within me, which will never go out."[16] Over the next several months, she spent seven hours a day at New York's Astor Library, writing and studying the official reports of the War Department and the Department of the Interior.

She was joined in New York during much of this period by William Jackson, who had intermittent business in the city. Back in December, William had expressed reservations about her new concern for Indian rights. He had criticized the personal nature of her attacks against Carl Schurz, warned her against sentimentalism, and urged her to avoid writing about the Utes and Agent Meeker. "The Indian will never get my sympathy, until he will work honestly & industriously for a living, which I have but little faith of his ever doing," he had told her.[17] His stance was not altogether surprising, though it flew in the face of both his usual support for his wife's work and his own longtime opposition to racial oppression: he was entirely dependent in his banking and railroad interests on the goodwill of his white Colorado neighbors. None of these neighbors cared "a straw" about local Indians, as Helen herself knew; their desire to rid the area of Indians was not merely "brutal," she believed, but "fiendish."[18] Neither of the Jacksons considered it worthwhile even to talk about Indian matters among their Colorado Springs acquaintances. Helen had nonetheless argued strenuously against her husband's prejudices, imploring him to examine his conscience on the matter. "Dear heart—by virtue of your organization, you ought to be as strong for *justice* to the Indian as you were for *justice* to the Negro," she insisted. "I can't write a word, or work with any heart, if you are not going to feel with me in it all—& I do feel as earnest & solemn a 'call' as ever a human being felt to work for this cause."[19] By the time she and William were reunited in New York, he had regained most of his usual interest in supporting her work, no doubt happy to find her lifted out of her earlier melancholy. He advised her to write and publish without reservation. He told her that he hoped her new book would serve to awaken the country's leaders "to some sense of the degradation that we as a nation should feel in the true history of our dealings with a comparatively defenseless race."[20] And he even encouraged some of her work on Colorado Indian affairs, passing along a number of her articles to newspaper men he knew there and privately praising one of her controversial Sand Creek articles. Still, he would remain for an indefinite period "only *half* converted" to his wife's cause, as she would admit to a friend in 1881.[21]

Jackson had felt "superstitious" about the "irresistible impulse" she felt "to say especial words & phrases," and about the speed with which she was able to accomplish her work, since first beginning to write about Indian affairs. "I write these sentences—which would ordinarily cost me much thought & work, to get them so condensed—as *fast* as I can write the words," she had told William in December 1879.[22] It seemed to her that she was "in the hands of powers & events" that she "could neither resist nor understand," and she wondered whether she were "being wrought upon, for some purpose." Now she made remarkably rapid progress on her book, finishing it by early May. She gave it the title *A Century of Dishonor*, words that, as she washed one morning during the past December, had come to her all at once, "as if someone spoke them aloud in the room."[23] She told William that she had not experienced a similar instance of spontaneous inspiration since her earliest days as a poet. In fact, she now began to experience a type of subconscious absorption in her work that was in many ways altogether new, and that would enable her to accomplish some of the best work of her career.

A Century of Dishonor: A Sketch of the United States Government's Dealings with Some of the Indian Tribes, published by Harper and Brothers in 1881 after Scribner's and even Roberts Brothers turned it down, is both something less and something more than the record of broken treaties Jackson had initially envisioned. It does not profess to offer a full history of the relationship between the federal government and the Indian tribes; instead it summarizes the history of the government's interactions with seven tribes—the Poncas, Cherokees, Delawares, Cheyennes, Nez Percés, Sioux, and Winnebagoes—relying heavily on extracts from official government documents.[24] In an opening "author's note," Jackson explains that her aim has been "simply to show our causes for national shame in the matter of our treatment of the Indians," so that "the American people" might "rise up and demand" justice for them. ("What the people demand, Congress will do," she insists elsewhere in the volume.) She achieves an impact greater than that produced by the few comparable books of the era by going beyond the scope of her original intention, buttressing her arraignment of American mistreatment of Native Americans with a variety of supplementary materials. She provides an "introductory" chapter summarizing international laws on the rights of prior occupancy, arguing that they must be applied to Native Americans even when "ultimate sovereignty" is ceded to the "civilized discoverer."[25] In a chapter on "massacres of Indians by whites," she seeks to prove that Indian violence against whites is almost invariably provoked by white mistreatment. And she includes many appendixes, in which she offers evidence of Indian "character" and of various "outrages committed on Indians by Whites." Among these is a letter written by Sarah Winnemucca, a Nevada Piute writer and activist. Winnemucca argues that her tribe wishes not to live on any distant reservation but rather to be secured in their rights to their native lands, a stance that Jackson eagerly supported.

In the spring of 1880, exhausted from her hard labor on *A Century of Dishonor* and in need of a rest, Jackson yearned to take the European vacation that she had been pondering for almost a year. Her husband was still bound by his work, unfortunately, but it happened that one of her closest, most trusted old friends from the years of her first marriage, the Harvard chemistry professor Eben Horsford, was just then preparing to take his daughters Kate and Cornelia on a tour of England, Scotland, Norway, Denmark, the Bavarian Alps, and Paris. When he invited Helen to join them, and William gave the idea his wholehearted support, she jumped at the opportunity. They set out on May 29 for a journey that would last more than four months. During a good portion of that time, Jackson traveled separately from the Horsfords on trips of special interest to herself. In Norway, for instance, she engaged the services of Mrs. Susanna Steen ("Sanna"), who had been recommended by Moncure Conway, to accompany her on a short trip through the fjords later described in her essay "Four Days with Sanna." By placing an advertisement she also hired another Norwegian woman, named Katrina, who traveled with her for a month overland to Christiania, a joyful adventure that Jackson afterward recounted in "The Katrina Saga." In Germany she went to Munich to visit the dear old friend whose memory was now, as ever, serving to inspire her in her affectionate portraits of local women—her old "German landlady," Mrs. Hahlreiner.

Jackson had contracted in advance to write a number of essays about her trip, and while she was abroad she worked harder than ever to make literary capital out of her travels. She had each of her hotel rooms furnished with a table for her books and papers and also a desk, where she often spent the whole day writing. During some of these writings sessions she worked on her actual essays, while in others she wrote detailed "encyclicals" home to a small group that now included only William, Molly Hunt, Sarah Woolsey, and Annie; or she simply made extensive notes to be worked into essays in the months and years following her return to the United States. In the end, she produced three lengthy pieces about Scotland and England, three about Scandinavia, and two about Oberammergau, where she and the Horsfords witnessed the Passion Play as performed every ten years since the seventeenth century in celebration of the end of the Black Death. These essays all appeared in the *Atlantic* or *Century* between 1881 and 1884, and they were later published by Roberts Brothers in a posthumous volume titled *Glimpses of Three Coasts* (1886). This collection also includes three encyclicals about Scandinavia that Jackson had saved for initial publication in book form.

Jackson's essays from her second trip abroad are less interesting than most of her other travel essays. Only a vague presence in her first collection of European pieces, *Bits of Travel,* in her new essays she is a still stranger entity whom the people she meets occasionally address as "sir." Her descriptions of local places are also rather nondescript and sadly lacking in the old comic flair. Before she set out with the Horsfords, she had intended to "strike for out of the way places—remote country districts, and individual people, types among the peasantry, islands off the coast, etc.," and to produce work that "would not be in the conventional and worn out vein."[26] When she actually set foot abroad, though, she broke with her earlier practice and became focused on seeing and describing the region's famous tourist attractions.

Still, her tendency to identify and sympathize with a variety of local women did enable her to produce some interesting brief portraits of particular individuals. In Chester, England, for example, she met a local marketwoman whom she would later describe in print. As it happens, it is possible here to trace the process of her sympathetic identification because the manuscript notebook in which she recorded her first reaction to the marketwoman—alone among the countless manuscript notebooks she must have filled over the course of her career—still exists today. In this instance, she used the consecutive right-hand pages of her notebook for detailed notes on her travels and the consecutive left-hand pages for jotting down rough drafts of poems, story ideas, and general thoughts. On one left-hand page, she has written in a hurried, unusually dark hand: "Grief & joy are the only things that never change shape!—love & love's losses & hurts the same yesterday today & forever!"[27] This sentiment appears by itself in the notebook, with no indication of which outing might have inspired it. The answer is revealed in Jackson's essay "Chester Streets," which appeared in the *Atlantic* in January 1884. At the marketplace in Chester, she had been drawn to the beauty of some flowers for sale in an impoverished old woman's stall. Yet when she asked the woman the name of the flowers, the woman was unable to recall it: she had no " 'eart to take pains with the flowers" because her family had recently suffered the death of a child. The woman's words "smote like a sudden bell-note echo from a far past," Jackson admits in her essay, "an echo that never ceases for hearts that have once known how bell-notes sound when bells toll for beloved dead!" She concludes her essay with a revised version of her original reaction to meeting the marketwoman: "Grief and joy do not alter shape or sort. Love and love's losses and hurts are the same yesterday, to-day, and forever."[28]

Jackson's 1880 manuscript book reveals that she did not forget her ongoing concern with American regionalism while she was in Europe, nor cease trying to assuage the anxieties she had been feeling at home over the temperamental differences between herself and William, their childlessness, and William's happiness. On the left-hand pages of the manuscript book she jotted down a revealing outline for a never-realized theatrical play, "The Cook of the Buckeye Mine."[29] This play was to be set mostly in Leadville, Colorado, and to touch on the lives of a variety of immigrants to that place—especially one eastern, presumably Protestant woman and her "rich" Quaker husband, a farmer. The couple begin to suffer needlessly because the husband's religion "teaches him not to express any fondness," despite his genuine love for his wife, while the wife "yearns" and "pines" and "begs" for explicit words of love. Jackson found the details for this portion of her play, which she sketched out at some length in her notebook, in a series of letters that she and William exchanged while she was abroad. She had long known that William was opposed to expressing passion in his letters: a year before they were married, he had warned her "not to look for the ordinary demonstrative kind of letters from me, that I can't write them & don't want to write them."[30] While in Europe, though, she tried to teach him effusiveness by example, reminding him repeatedly that she missed him and was kissing his photograph and letters every night. "Goodbye & goodbye & goodbye my precious one," she signed off on one occasion. "Remember always that you are the whole world & more than the world to your faithful loving Peggy."[31] She also directly implored him to be more demonstrative in his letters:

Why have you this false shame my beloved one? All the great men of the world have been great lovers—passion is as great as action—there never was a strong great man or woman born who did not love with fire and ardor, and glory in loving! Oh what you lose in your silence!—no other world can make it up to you!—How shall I win you to come into the true land of true loving, my one precious darling—![32]

William was often affectionately playful in response to his wife's cajoling. Upon receiving a letter in which she had enclosed a piece of her hair and a daisy that she had kissed, asking him to send her a piece of his own hair in return, he did as she requested but reminded her, "Now my precious Peggy don't you know that I have no hair to spare & can't make fair exchanges on that basis even with you who have no great surplus."[33] He also reminded her that her emotions could be hard to keep up with:

> The quality of 'too muchness' predominates in your nature, in everything almost. I should think a thousand times since I have known my Peggy she has had the best time in her life or she never suffered so in her life before, or it was the most horrid experience she had ever had & so on through the list—entirely true I think for the time being—but an extravagance of speech as well as feeling.[34]

More soberly, William restated his disinterest in epistolary effusions. "I have repeatedly written you that I cannot write, cannot even talk much & you know these things full well you must accept me as I am—quiet & reticent but none the less affectionate at heart," he said. "You can't expect to change my whole plan of life any more than I can change yours. We are what we are & no requests no urging can change us."[35]

In "The Cook of the Buckeye Mine," the husband "resents" his wife's repeated demands for verbal affection. "If you don't believe I love you nothing I could *say* would make you," he says. The wife cannot understand his reticence and becomes convinced that he would be happier without her. Just like Hetty in Jackson's second novel, she feigns death in order to free him: she "gallops off on her pony—into the mountains—turns the pony loose to go home by itself & let him think she has been thrown & killed." She then runs away to Leadville, where she takes work as a cook in a boardinghouse for miners. There, the proprietor of the mine, "an old Mormon," falls in love with her and tries to persuade her to join his religion and run away with him to Utah. This man is so practiced with deceitful words that he easily covers up his numerous existing marriages and begins to win the wife over "with his arguments and with words of love."[36] At last, however, the Quaker husband shows up and exposes the Mormon's polygamy. Because the husband's hair has turned white from worrying that his wife might be dead, he now instantly convinces her, without any words, of the depth of the love he has always felt for her.

Just as Jackson did not entirely set aside the concerns of home while she was traveling in Europe, neither did she entirely forgo her passionate involvement in the cause of Native American rights. In Copenhagen she visited the Ethnographic Museum, where she found a large and important collection of Native American artifacts. She felt that this collection revealed more appreciation for the "noble qualities" of American Indians than did any monument in her own country. "My eyes filled with tears, I confess, to find at last in little Denmark one spot in the world where there will be kept a complete pictorial record of the race of men that we have done our best to wipe out from the face of the earth," she wrote in one of her encyclicals. Here, at least, "historical justice" would be given to them, she said, "as a race of splendid possibilities, and attainments marvelous."[37] Privately, Jackson told her husband that she knew her comments on the Ethnographic Museum would "make the Colorado people madder than ever."[38] William had already assured her that he would pay no attention to their opinions. Still, he remained dependent on their goodwill for his success in business, and so he also told her, somewhat testily, that if she wanted to keep abreast of American sentiment on Indian matters while she was abroad she should turn not to him but instead to her "Eastern 'sentimental' friends that are constantly looking outside of their homes their towns & their state for some wrong to correct."[39]

Upon her return to the United States on October 9, Jackson quickly resumed writing articles and letters on Indian affairs, submitting them to newspapers from her Boston and New York hotel rooms. William soon came east to meet her, and in early February they traveled together to Washington, D.C., where congressional hearings on the Ponca situation were under way. Jackson watched some of the proceedings in the company of her new friend and correspondent Amelia Stone Quinton, one of the two founders of the WNIA. Her indignation was roused when she witnessed Carl Schurz serving as chief speaker in the Senate hearings, a scenario that seemed as terrible to her as "Pharaoh masquerading in Moses' clothing."[40] She sought revenge for the outrage by attempting to persuade a number of prominent friends not to attend a Boston dinner that was soon to be given in Schurz's honor. In her quest to help the Poncas, she spoke privately with several members of Congress, seeking to remind them of their duty. And according to Thomas Wentworth Higginson, she gave a copy of *A Century of Dishonor,* which had just been released in January, to every senator and representative at her own expense.[41] (She also sent the book to many influential clergymen.) The brown cloth cover of this first edition was embossed in gold with a pointed epigraph: "When one of the Spartan kings pronounced that commonwealth happy which was bounded by the sword and spear, Pompey, correcting him, said: 'Yea, rather that commonwealth is truly happy which is on every side bounded with justice.'" At last, on March 31, 1881, a bill passed that provided the Poncas $165,000 in reparations for their disastrous removal to Indian Territory and allowed them to choose for themselves which reservation they wanted to live on. Soon, Jackson enjoyed the pleasure of seeing Schurz's term in office come to an end. President Chester Arthur's new secretary of the interior was Henry Teller, one of the Colorado senators who had defeated William Jackson in the 1876 elections, and a man whom both of the Jacksons knew and respected.

Jackson hoped that the book reviews of *A Century of Dishonor* would help garner publicity for her cause. She was therefore eager to see critics draw attention not to the book's literary attributes but to its contents. Before the book was published, she had made her wish known to well-positioned friends and acquaintances. She had written to Moncure Conway and Charles Dudley Warner, of course, and also to other writers whom she knew less well but believed to be sympathetic to her interests. "The thing I want most is that the notices of the book shall help to circulate the real knowledge on the Indian Question," she told Rebecca Harding Davis, who had earlier taken Jackson's side against Carl Schurz in articles for the *New York Tribune*.[42] Davis proved unable to write a review, but Jackson had better luck with her activist friend Caroline Dall, who published a piece that met Jackson's specifications perfectly, "The Story of Indian Wrongs," in the February 13, 1881, *Courier*.

As it happened, in fact, most of the reviews of *A Century of Dishonor* were better than Jackson might have hoped for, since they both discussed the content of the book and praised her writing. "Harpers sent me 75 the other day, all long—all complimentary & earnest & sympathetic," she wrote excitedly to Charles Dudley Warner in March.[43] She was especially "delighted" with Martha Goddard's review for the *Atlantic,* and no doubt very pleasantly surprised when even her old nemesis the *Nation* called the book "intelligent and sympathetic."[44] In April 1881 the noted historian Francis Parkman wrote to her, "Your book is an honest and valuable record of a scandalous and shameful page in the history of the American people—for the blame lies with them in the last resort. I am glad it is written, and think it likely to do good."[45]

Buoyed by all this positive feedback, Jackson was filled with hope that she might succeed in rousing the public to action. But she soon came to the sad realization that very few members of the public were actually buying her book, and that only people who "did not need" to read it were actually doing so.[46] "I confess I am greatly disheartened, by the entire failure of my book. It has not sold 2000 copies, outside of those I bought myself," she wrote to Amelia Stone Quinton in August. "Even my own audience, on whom I can count with certainty for at least 4000 or 5000, for any book I publish, refuse to buy even a book of mine, simply because it is about Indians."[47]

While Jackson was worrying in the spring of 1881 about the impact of *A Century of Dishonor* and also battling an attack of bronchitis, she received an invitation from *Harper's* to write a series of travel essays about Southern California. "I have not much more idea of Southern California than I have of Patagonia," she admitted to an acquaintance at the time, but the project appealed to her.[48] She became especially excited about it when William said that he would at last take a vacation and go with her. On April 2, however, he suddenly informed her by telegraph that important bank business had called him away to Leadville; upon his return to Colorado Springs, he would no longer be able to make the journey. Greatly disappointed, Jackson went home to be with him. Her frustration soon waned as she began to explore the local area with an eye to writing new travel essays. Kate Horsford came out for a long visit, and together they made a number of week-long journeys, including a trip with William south to Colorado's San Luis Park and on to New Mexico. The previous year, when she had been busy with her reform work and European travel essays, Jackson had written about Colorado only for *Youth's Companion.* Now she found a new venue for her travel work, the *Christian Union,* and also wrote several Colorado pieces for the *Atlantic,* three of which appeared in 1882. In one of these, "Aunty Lane," she made a point of again denouncing Colorado's Sand Creek Massacre.

In the fall of 1881, a second opportunity to visit Southern California presented itself: an invitation to write four topical essays for the new *Century Magazine,* successor to *Scribner's Monthly.* Jackson eagerly accepted, as she had decided that she could never pass another winter in Colorado's harsh climate. Before heading west, she returned east to Boston and New York to undertake research for her journey. In New York's Astor Library she read several books that had been recommended to her by Edward Everett Hale, who was something of an expert on California history. Some of these books were available only in Spanish and she had to work her way through them slowly, relying on her early knowledge of French and Latin. They included the eighteenth-century classic *Noticia de la California* (Madrid, 1757) by the Mexican Jesuit Miguèl Venegas, who celebrated the role of his order in early Baja California; *Historia de la Compañia de Jesus en Nueva-España* (Mexico, 1841–42) by the Jesuit historian Francisco Javier Alegre, who recorded his order's undertakings in the Americas; and *Personal Narrative of Explorations and Incidents in Texas, New Mexico, California, Sonora, and Chihuahua* (1854) by the American J. Russell Bartlett, one of the founders of the American Ethnological Society and commissioner of the United States–Mexican Boundary Survey of 1850 to 1853. In this last book, which served for some time as a guide for Americans visiting the areas he described, Bartlett expressed a good deal of esteem for many of the Indian tribes of California. His opinions stood in marked contrast to the more prejudice-laced accounts of western Indians with which Jackson was already familiar, in Parkman's *Oregon Trail* (1849) and John Charles Frémont's *Report of the Exploring Expedition to the Rocky Mountains in the Year 1842, and to Oregon and North California in the Years 1843–'44* (1845).

Hale also recommended that Jackson read an essay in his own collection *His Level Best and Other Stories* (1872), "The Queen of California," which had originally been published in the *Atlantic* of March 1864. In it, he made the important historical contribution of locating the probable origins of the name of California in the character Calafia, the Amazon-like queen of a mythical island featured in *Las Sergas de Esplandiàn* (1510), a popular Spanish romance by Garcia Ordonez de Montalvo. Hale also sent Jackson copies of his contributions to William Cullen Bryant's *Popular History of the United States* (1876–80), in which he had written of the early history of the West.

This advance research sparked an interest in California history that would become passionate during Jackson's travels in Southern California. She arrived in Los Angeles from New York on December 18, 1881, having taken the new, direct Southern Pacific line west through Arizona, thereby avoiding the detour through San Francisco that all train passengers had previously made. (In 1883 and 1885, Jackson would publish essays about traveling west on the Southern Pacific's new line, "A Pot of Gold" and "A Short Cut from Icicles to Oranges.")[49] At first, she settled in Los Angeles at the fancy Pico House, built in 1869 by Pío Pico, the last Mexican governor. Within ten days, though, she had moved to a genteel boardinghouse on New High Street, the Kimball Mansion.

Los Angeles had been founded exactly one hundred years earlier, in 1781, the twelfth year of the Spanish rule of California; it remained merely a village during the succeeding period of Mexican rule, from 1822 to 1846. In 1830, the year Jackson was born, Los Angeles was far smaller than the town of Amherst, with a population of some 650 residents. Fifty years later, the population was still only about 12,000 and many residents were continuing their preindustrial lifeways. Nevertheless, there were signs of escalating development everywhere. The local economy, which had made the transition from cattle ranching to sheep farming in the 1860s, was now dominated by large American agricultural interests. Some residents of Los Angeles were even beginning to enjoy the luxuries of electricity, cement sidewalks, and the newly invented telephone. In her essay "Echoes in the City of the Angels," Jackson described the city as she first encountered it in 1881:

> The City of the Angels is a prosperous city now. It has business thoroughfares, blocks of fine stone buildings, hotels, shops, banks, and is growing daily. Its outlying regions are a great circuit of gardens, orchards, vineyards, and corn-fields, and its suburbs are fast filling up with houses of a showy though cheap architecture. But it has not yet shaken off its past. A certain indefinable, delicious aroma from the old, ignorant, picturesque times lingers still, not only in byways and corners, but in the very centres of its newest activities.[50]

As in all of her American travels, Jackson's main interest in Southern California lay in searching out traditional ways of life amid the changes being wrought by the spread of American industrialization. Given her commitment to promoting the rights of Native Americans, she was especially interested in the living conditions of the local "Mission" Indians, whose struggles to secure their lands from grasping white settlers led her toward advocacy on their behalf. In taking up their cause, she entered on the second phase of her Indian reform work. At the same time, she became powerfully attracted to what she called the "Mexican element" of Southern California. "This is the picturesque side of the continent," she wrote to Thomas Bailey Aldrich a few months after her arrival, "red tiles, brown faces, shawls over heads—dark eyes and soft voice, and the Spanish tongue: and once in thirty miles, for a seven hundred mile line of coast, a grand old ruin of a Franciscan Mission."[51]

Before coming to Southern California, Jackson had solicited letters of introduction to prominent local people from several of her acquaintances who knew the area. One of these letters introduced her in Los Angeles to Bishop Francis Mora, who in turn introduced her to Antonio F. Coronel. Coronel and his wife Mariana soon become Jackson's closest friends in California. Born in Mexico in 1817, Coronel had come to Los Angeles as a colonist with his parents in 1834. In midlife he was influential in both the Mexican and American governments of the city, serving in a variety of positions including inspector of the missions under Mexican rule; he was elected mayor under American rule in 1853. He was knowledgeable about the history and current living conditions of Southern California's Hispanic and Native American residents. He shared his knowledge and opinions with Jackson during her many visits to his house, and he helped her plan a travel itinerary that focused mainly on the region's Hispanic homes and Native American villages.

On January 22, 1882, Jackson traveled north from Los Angeles to Santa Barbara. At Coronel's suggestion, she stopped during the journey at Rancho Camulos. This estate of the prominent del Valle family was located forty-five miles northwest of Los Angeles, near Piru in Ventura County. Jackson spent only the morning there, not finding Señora del Valle at home. Still, Camulos made a powerful impression on her. "It was a most interesting place," she wrote to Kinney afterward, "all as Mexican & un-American as heart could wish."[52] Two years later she would rely on her memories of Camulos in inventing the Moreno estate in her novel *Ramona*.[53] Once arrived in Santa Barbara, she checked into the Arlington Hotel and began to explore the area. She disliked the city's climate and considered most of the town's American population uninteresting, if uncommonly intelligent for westerners. But she was delighted by the Santa Barbara mission, the only mission then still in the hands of the Franciscan founders. There she made the acquaintance of Father O'Keefe and Father Francisco de Jesús Sanchez and read books from the Franciscan College library on the history of the order in California. She admired the library's portrait of Father Junipero Serra, founder of the Franciscan missions, and began to take a strong interest in Serra's life.

She left Santa Barbara by steamer in early March and headed south to San Diego, where she took up residence at the Horton House. There she established a general routine of writing in the mornings and exploring the surrounding region in the afternoons. She thought San Diego "a dreary little town,"[54] but she loved the local climate, as it was both sunny and free from the dust and dry heat that sometimes bothered her in Los Angeles. On March 8, 1882, she visited the city's second annual citrus fair, where she was dazzled by the produce and the rapid growth of the local citrus industry. "Oranges—6 years ago only 2 trees in the county—605 acres & upwards orchards on one ranch alone," she marveled in her date book.[55] As in Santa Barbara, though, she was most interested not in new American activities but in the lives of the region's earlier inhabitants. Through a letter of introduction to David Cronyn, a Unitarian minister, she met the Spanish priest Anthony Ubach, who helped her visit many Indian villages in San Diego and Riverside Counties. In Temecula, a village once connected with Mission San Luis Rey, she stayed at the combined hostelry and trading post of Louis and Ramona Wolf. Ramona accompanied her on some of her visits to nearby Indian homes. On March 16 she visited Tijuana, Mexico, for the day.

Jackson returned to Los Angeles in April to await the arrival of the Canadian artist Henry Sandham, who was to illustrate her *Century* articles.[56] Between April 22 and 29, they traveled together to Mission San Juan Capistrano, Mission San Luis Rey and its outlying chapel at Pala, and also Temecula. At the end of the month they settled back in Los Angeles. There Jackson grew closer to Abbot Kinney, a resident of San Gabriel who sometimes stayed at the Kimball Mansion when he had business in the city. When Jackson had first met Kinney, during her initial weeks in Los Angeles, she had been prepared to dislike him; her old friend Jeanne Carr, who now lived in Pasadena, had driven her past Kinney's large, white hillside house, Kinneloa, which Jackson had considered distasteful. Upon further acquaintance, though, Jackson discovered that Kinney was a fledgling writer, contributing articles to various periodicals, and that he shared her concern for the early inhabitants of California. She tried to help him with his writing, and he agreed to help her with her local research. They soon became fast friends. "She found out that I spoke Spanish, and as she was anxious to talk with Indians and Mexicans, and also to call upon some of the Spanish families at the old ranch-houses, she gently intimated that it would be a great favor to her if I would go and interpret for her," Kinney would later explain. "My natural sympathies being largely in tune with her own you can well understand how she interested me."[57]

Early in May, Kinney helped Jackson visit the Santa Anita ranch. He then traveled north with her, Sandham, and William Jackson, who after a series of delays occasioned by his business and financial interests had come out to meet his wife; the group visited the missions between Santa Barbara and Monterey. In mid-June, the Jacksons left alone by boat from San Francisco—a city that Jackson now heartily disliked—for a two-week excursion to Washington and Oregon. After they returned to San Francisco, on July 6, William made his way home to Colorado, while Helen remained behind at the Palace Hotel until the end of the month. There she made the acquaintance of Mary Trimble, a Quaker widow from New York "of keen literary perceptions and judgment,"[58] who immediately became a valued friend. And she researched the history of California's missions and ranchos at Hubert Howe Bancroft's library of western Americana, then located at 1538 Valencia Street. Before she and William had set out for Oregon, she had written to Secretary of the Interior Henry Teller suggesting that she might be made an official commissioner to the Mission Indians of Southern California, in charge of investigating their condition and needs. While conducting her research in San Francisco, she received word from federal Indian Commissioner Hiram Price that he and Teller had approved her request.

Back in Colorado Springs for the late summer and fall of 1882, Jackson made arrangements for Abbot Kinney to serve as her official co-commissioner on her next, government-sponsored trip to Southern California. In September she and William took an interesting trip together, traveling south on a new extension of the Atchison, Topeka, and Santa Fe Railroad toward Paso del Norte (now Juarez), Mexico. Jackson recounted this journey in a travel essay titled "By Horse Cars into Mexico," which was published in the *Atlantic* in March 1883. She also began writing up her *Century* essays on Southern California for initial publication in 1883, a year in which more than twenty of her travel pieces would appear in print. Her four *Century* essays are "Outdoor Industries in Southern California," "Echoes in the City of the Angels," "Father Junipero and His Work," and "The Present Condition of the Mission Indians in Southern California." Many of the topics Jackson covered in these pieces had never before been so fully addressed in the English language; after Roberts Brothers included them in the posthumous collection *Glimpses of Three Coasts,* they would be reprinted and widely read well into the early twentieth century. Today some of the views Jackson expresses have been discredited, but the essays nonetheless retain considerable historical interest. They are also excellent examples of Jackson's later, more factual brand of regionalist writing.

In "Outdoor Industries in Southern California," the ambivalent nature of her long-standing determination to "protest against the spread of civilization" in America is readily apparent. She frames the essay with an insistence that the way of living most suitable to Southern California is best understood not by newcomers but by the region's longer-established inhabitants. "Climate is to a country what temperament is to a man,—Fate," she writes in the essay's opening line. At the end of the essay, she claims that the sunny climate of Southern California has led local Hispanic residents to adopt a generous, carefree lifestyle, and she expresses a hope that this same sunny climate will one day lead "the restless, inquisitive, insatiable, close-reckoning Yankee" to "a slacking, a toning down, and a readjusting of standards and habits by a scale in which money and work will not be the highest values."[59] In the body of her essay, though, she favorably discusses, and thereby promotes, American enterprise in California.

In part, this focus was dictated by the demands of *Century Magazine,* which had requested some "industrial & picturesque narrative for illustration."[60] Before Jackson wrote the article, she told Kinney she thought its subject "appalling,"[61] and she later depended on his assistance in the unsavory tasks of planning it out and double-checking its facts before it was published. Yet Jackson was inclined to support certain types of increased American influence in Southern California, for she believed the region was sadly lacking in culture. "Anything that helps educate, enlighten, train, soften, civilize this side of our continent, is of interest to the other, and should be helped by the other," she would later write from Los Angeles to Thomas Bailey Aldrich.[62] Moreover, she knew that Americans were in the region to stay—that California was in effect America's "empire."[63] She therefore made it her ambition not to protest the American presence in California per se, but to advocate for a gentler, more sensitive sort of presence. This was a stance very similar to that seen in her protests against the industrialization of rural New England and Colorado. In "Outdoor Industries in Southern California," she celebrates the enterprise then dominating the region's economy, agriculture, as a model for responsible development. Describing the sun-drenched counties of San Diego, Los Angeles, San Bernardino, Ventura, and Santa Barbara as "climatically insulated,—a sort of island on land," she predicts that they are destined under American initiative to become "the Garden of the world."[64] She portrays various Anglo farms in glowing terms, providing a detailed accounting of their different agricultural products. She especially praises new grape and wine enterprises as picturesque and appropriate to the region.

Jackson's other *Century* essays on Southern California are more thoroughly devoted to discussion of the region's earlier inhabitants. She explores the Hispanic heritage of Southern California in "Echoes in the City of the Angels" and "Father Junipero and His Work." In the first, she describes her encounters with a number of dignified, persevering Mexican and Spanish residents of Los Angeles. After experiencing "the good fortune to win past the barrier of proud, sensitive, tender reserve" of several elderly women, for instance, she finds in their homes "stintless hospitality and immeasurable courtesy," "an atmosphere of simple-hearted joyousness and generosity never known by any other communities on the American continent." She also offers a lengthy, affectionate portrait of her friend Antonio Coronel, complete with a recounting of some of his "graphic narratives of the olden time."[65]

Jackson presents Coronel as a man nostalgic for the days before the 1846 American invasion of California. In her personal encounters with him, he apparently gave her the impression that despite his long years of life and work under the American government, he was still the embodiment of the aristocratic Mexican don. He was indeed a fairly wealthy man, though he had lost a good deal of land in the postwar adjudications of the United States Land Commission. When Jackson met him he was eagerly attempting to preserve in his own life and home the Mexican cultural values of the region. He owned an extensive antiquarian library, which he shared with Jackson. He and his young wife Mariana enjoyed performing old Mexican dances. And Mariana translated his comments to Jackson in English inflected by a picturesque Spanish accent, though she had in fact been born Mary Burton Williamson, the biracial daughter of a Yankee father and Mexican mother, and probably had ample experience in speaking English. In talking to Jackson, Coronel seems to have expressed a sense of longing for the old days in California similar to that which he had voiced five years earlier, in 1877, when he was interviewed by Thomas Savage. Savage, an assistant of the historian Hubert Howe Bancroft, was helping Bancroft in his endeavor to record the personal *testimonios* of early Hispanic Californians. In "Cosas de California," which records his own words more directly than does Jackson's essay, Coronel paints a gracious picture of the lifestyles of the early *Californios*. He describes the missions as bastions of culture that, although guilty of treating Indians like children, were nonetheless far kinder to them than were the later Americans. He also discusses with pride his own armed resistance to the United States during the Mexican War.[66]

In general, the sense of nostalgia pervading Coronel's *testimonio*—as well as, apparently, his home life as Jackson witnessed it—seems to have constituted a veiled form of resistance to the American occupation of California. As the literary scholar Genaro M. Padillo has explained, many Hispanic Californians of this era used expressions of nostalgia "not [as] a non-critical reaction to loss, but [as] an oppositional response to displacement, albeit a response often deeply mediated by a language of accommodation."[67] But in "Echoes in the City of the Angels," Jackson depicts Coronel's nostalgia as lacking in nuance and agency. To her, it appeared that California's Hispanic population was experiencing a fatal decline. During the 1870s Americans took possession of many Hispanic ranches, even though America had promised the *Californios* secure possession of their property upon the conclusion of the Mexican War; during the 1880s American settlers were pouring into Los Angeles, so that by 1887, less than 10 percent of the city's population would be Hispanic. Jackson did not guess that twentieth-century Hispanic immigration to California would later serve to shift the state's balance of power yet again. Her unfortunate tendency toward romantic racialism—the idea that Mexican and Spanish cultures were somehow backward, albeit charmingly so—also colored her portrait of Coronel:

> Full of sentiment, of an intense and poetic nature, he looks back to the lost empire of his race and people on the California shores with a sorrow far too proud for any antagonisms or complaints. He recognizes the inexorableness of the laws under whose workings his nation is slowly, surely giving place to one more representative of the age. Intellectually he is in sympathy with progress, with reform, with civilization at its utmost; he would not have had them stayed, or changed, because

his people could not keep up, and were not ready. But his heart is none the less saddened and lonely.[68]

In her lengthy, two-part essay "Father Junipero and His Work: A Sketch of the Foundation, Prosperity, and Ruin of the Franciscan Missions in California," Jackson sharply criticizes the United States government for having allowed its citizens to usurp the lands of many Mexican Californians like Antonio Coronel. Her main purpose, however, is to extol the history of the Franciscan missions in California—a subject she found of "inexhaustible interest"[69]—and especially the vision of their founder, Father Junípero Serra. Jackson's appreciation for the Franciscan missions, which represented the culmination of the steadily increasing interest in Catholicism evident in her previous travel writing and fiction, was unusual for her time. During the early 1880s, many Protestant Americans were still very suspicious of Catholicism; few had any deep interest in California's Catholic missions. *Century Magazine,* recognizing these facts, gave Jackson permission only for a " 'popular' treatment" of the subject. She insisted nonetheless on writing a "historical" treatment, intended solely for the magazine's more "thoughtful & serious readers."[70] She worked harder and longer on this piece than she ever had on a travel essay, even taking the uncharacteristic step of seeking advice on early drafts not only from Thomas Wentworth Higginson but also from the *Century* editor Richard Watson Gilder and the writers Sarah Orne Jewett and Annie Fields. In the end, she produced an essay that possessed, to her mind, "more real value & substance than anything merely 'descriptive' I have ever done."[71]

Because she had grown up the daughter of an evangelical minister, Jackson felt a natural respect for the spiritual dedication of the Franciscans, who took over as missionaries in California when the Jesuits were expelled by King Charles III of Spain in 1767; they ultimately founded twenty-one missions in Alta California. In one of her essays from her first trip to California, in 1872, she had praised the Franciscan missions and missionaries: "Sacred for ever and everywhere on earth are the places whose first founders and builders were men who went simply to carry the news of their Christ and who sought no personal gain."[72] In "Father Junipero and His Work," she argues that "only narrow-minded bigotry" could fail to view the missions as proof "of a spiritual enthusiasm and exaltation of self-sacrifice which are rarely paralleled in the world's history."[73] Jackson surely knew that the Catholic religion was alive and thriving in California and America at large, having vastly more adherents than her own Unitarianism or her father's old brand of Congregationalism; yet she believed that the type of old-style, Catholic fervor that had once inspired and supported the Franciscan missions was a thing of the past.

Jackson's main premise in "Father Junipero and His Work," that the Franciscans had been throughout their history in California the "benefactors of men," is problematic.[74] Today, we know that the Franciscan missionary system was based on the forcible subjugation and servitude of local Indians, who were decimated by their contact with foreign diseases. Within fifty years, California's Indian population decreased from approximately 300,000 at the start of the Spanish colonial period to only 200,000 when Mexican rule began. Jackson argues in her essay against what she calls the "scanty evidence" that Indian converts were often brought into the missions by force, however; and she also argues that while "individual instances of cruelty" must have occurred in the missions, "seeds of it being indigenous in human nature," the Franciscans must have been on the whole "both wise and humane" in their dealings with the Indians, or more of them would have actively revolted. Oddly, Jackson uses examples of practices that today seem clearly cruel and inhumane to support her arguments: "The rule of the friars was in the main a kindly one. The vice of drunkenness was severely punished by flogging. Quarrelling between husbands and wives was also dealt with summarily, the offending parties being chained together by the leg until they were glad to promise to keep peace."[75]

Along with the opinions of her friend Antonio Coronel, the historical sources Jackson studied while preparing her California essays influenced her excessively positive view of the Franciscan missions. Two of the books that Edward Everett Hale had recommended before her trip were written by Jesuit missionaries and were therefore sympathetic in a general sense toward Catholic missionary enterprises, though they did not touch on the work of the Franciscans. Many of the sources that Jackson studied in California at the Franciscan College library of the Santa Barbara mission and at Hubert Howe Bancroft's library in San Francisco were overtly sympathetic toward the work of the Franciscans. Among the works that she cites in "Father Junipero and His Work" are several written by early Franciscan missionaries, including *La Vida de Junípero Serra* (Mexico, 1787) by Junípero Serra's friend and fellow missionary Francisco Paloú, as well as the diaries of Father Juan Crespí. Three other books were influential in shaping her belief, expressed in her essay, that the Franciscans had treated California's Indians better than any other whites had ever done: Duflot de Mofras's *Exploration du Territoire de L'Orégon, des Californies et de la Mer Vermeille, executée pendant les années 1840, 1841 et 1842* (Paris, 1844); B. D. Wilson's official 1852 report on the conditions of Southern California's Indians (serialized in the Los Angeles *Star* in 1868); and John Whipple Dwinelle's *Colonial History of the City of San Francisco* (4th ed.; San Francisco, 1867). Jackson also supported her arguments for the exemplary behavior of the Franciscans with quotations from the Englishman Alexander Forbes's well-known *California: A History of Upper and Lower California from Their First Discovery to the Present Time* (London, 1839), glossing over Forbes's forceful condemnation of the mission system in favor of his admission that the Franciscans had doubtless undertaken their work with pure motives and treated their Indian subjects kindly enough to win great devotion from many of them.

Jackson was at such pains to represent the Franciscans as benefactors of California's Indians for several reasons. In general, she believed that "civilized" life could be superior to the sort of life California's Indians had led prior to the advent of colonialism. Thus, she praised the Franciscans for having transformed the local Indian "from the naked savage with his one stone tool, grinding acorn-meal in a rock bowl, to the industrious tiller of soil, weaver of cloth, worker in metals, and singer of sacred hymns." She was also impressed by the priority Spain and its missionaries had given to spiritual matters, which seemed to stand in marked contrast to what she saw as the insatiable financial greed and personal selfishness exhibited by more recent American settlers. (She quotes a devout Portuguese guard at the San Carlos mission: " 'Dem work for civilize,' he said, 'not work for money. Dey work to religion.' ") In addition, she was powerfully attracted to what she envisioned as the romance and color of mission life. "There was a strange difference, fifty years ago, between the atmosphere of life on the east and west sides of the American continent," she writes of the time when she herself was three years old in Amherst. "On the Atlantic shore, the descendants of the Puritans, weighed down by serious purpose, half grudging the time for their one staid yearly Thanksgiving, and . . . on the sunny Pacific shore, the merry people of Mexican and Spanish blood, troubling themselves about nothing, dancing away whole days and nights like children."[76] This vision of California's past, tainted by romantic racialism, led Jackson to depict the mission period as a pastoral ideal, a golden era from which dehumanizing American industrialization had later fallen.

Above all, Jackson praised the Franciscans because she recognized that Americans had treated the native population of the continent far worse than the Franciscans ever had. When she compared the two sides of the continent at the time of the Spanish colonization of California, she envisioned the descendants of the Puritans "driving the Indians farther and farther into the wilderness every year, fighting and killing them," while in California "priests were gathering the Indians by thousands into communities, and feeding and teaching them."[77] In a private letter to Amelia Stone Quinton, she insisted: "If their rule had been left undisturbed, there would be today a large Indian population on this coast, intelligent and self supporting."[78] During the decade of the 1850s, though, immediately following the American conquest of California, California's Indian population decreased 80 percent, from 150,000 to 30,000. In her own travels in Southern California, Jackson met both Indian and Hispanic residents who insisted that life had been far better for Indians under Spanish rule. Many former Mission Indians, impoverished and dispossessed of their lands by Americans, naturally expressed a desire for a return to days when they had at least had enough to eat. "I asked if he had a good time in the mission," Jackson writes elsewhere of one very old Indian man whom she interviewed via an interpreter. " 'Yes, yes,' he said, turning his sightless eyes up to the sky; 'much good time,' 'plenty to eat,' *'atole,' 'pozzole,'* 'meat;' now, 'no meat;' 'all the time to beg, beg;' 'all the time hungry.' "[79] Antonio Coronel told Jackson that while the Spanish "used to treat the Indians like animals, decimating them under forced labor," still they "could not destroy everything, because in the end the Indian culture became mixed with the Spanish religion and culture." But the Americans, he said, had accomplished near total destruction of the population with "ease," and with the support of American law.[80]

By depicting Southern California's Indians as longing for the days of mission rule, and by focusing her attention in "Father Junipero" on which colonial government in California had been least cruel to them, Jackson placed undue emphasis on the supposed helplessness of local Indians—what she called in one private letter their "patient suffering" and "gentleness and meekness"—rather than on the strength and ingenuity they had displayed in surviving their oppression.[81] She seems to have taken this stance because she wished to counter traditional American narratives of Indian aggression: she knew that many Americans used the supposed barbarism of Indians as justification for their annihilation. At the same time, however, what initially drew her to the cause of Indian rights, and what impressed her about many of the Indians she met in Southern California, was their determined perseverance in the face of adversity. In her final *Century* essay, "The Present Condition of the Mission Indians in Southern California," she highlights this perseverance.

During her 1882 travels in California, Jackson visited Luiseño, Cahuilla, Cupeño, Ipai, and Serrano Indian villages.[82] In "The Present Condition of the Mission Indians," she relates her conversations with many of the Indians she met in these villages. She describes a night she passed in a hospitable Luiseño home near the village of Pala, where her hostess gave up her own bed for her and treated her with unrivaled "thoughtfulness and delicacy." And she condemns unscrupulous whites who have stolen Indian lands, explaining that these lands had been cultivated by Indians for decades and secured to them under Mexican law. She particularly focuses on the earlier wholesale dispossession of the settled, agricultural villages at San Pasqual, in 1871, and Temecula, in 1875. Upon being evicted from San Pasqual, she says, most former residents "fled into secret lairs like hunted wild beasts," attempting to eke out meager livings "hidden away in the cañons and rifts of the near hills." When the sheriff and his men arrived to evict the village of Temecula, "The Indians' first impulse was as determined as it could have been if they had been white, to resist the outrage."[83] But after friends convinced them that they would only be shot down if they resisted, they sat on the ground, refusing to take part in the travesty, and watched as the whites raided their good adobe homes and piled all their possessions onto wagons. (Later, many Temecula refugees resettled in Pechanga.) Jackson explains that a similar eviction suit is currently threatening the Indian village at Soboba, and she reprints a May 29, 1882, letter from José Jesus Castillo to Secretary of the Interior Henry Teller, in which Castillo appeals for some safeguarding of the lands upon which his tribe has lived for more than a hundred years.[84] In summing up, Jackson writes bitterly: "The combination of cruelty and unprincipled greed on the part of the American settlers, with culpable ignorance, indifference, and neglect on the part of the Government at Washington has resulted in an aggregate of monstrous injustice."[85]

Jackson would soon undertake personally to ameliorate this injustice. After spending much of the winter in Boston and New York (she now avoided Newport on her trips east, having lost her good opinion of the town's climate), she arrived in Los Angeles on February 25, 1883, for her second visit to Southern California. As a "special agent" reporting to Hiram Price, the commissioner of Indian affairs, she was to ascertain the location and condition of Indians in California's three southernmost counties and to determine whether government lands should be set aside, or new lands purchased, as reservations for them. The reservations that had been created in the 1870s were inadequate, because most Indian lands had by then already been usurped by white settlers. Jackson was one of the first women ever to hold such a position. She requested no pay for her work; both she and her co-commissioner Abbot Kinney would be reimbursed only for their living and travel expenses. In mid-March, they made brief visits to Indian bands around San Bernardino and Riverside, met with Indian Agent S. S. Lawson, and first learned in a letter from Mary J. Ticknor, the government schoolteacher at the Cahuilla village, of the recent murder of a Cahuilla Indian, Juan Diego, at the hands of a white settler. (Jackson would later make use of this incident in *Ramona*.) After returning to Los Angeles, they set out again, on April 4, for a one-month tour of eighteen Indian villages, many of which Jackson had already visited the year before. They were accompanied in their travels by an agency interpreter, Jesús López, who assisted them when Kinney's Spanish proved inadequate; their carriage driver also sometimes served as an interpreter. Kinney took to calling Jackson "General," in playful recognition of her authority, while she called him "Comrade" or, in an apparent reference to his many previous travels, "Sailing Master." Far from finding Jackson truly dictatorial, Kinney was amazed by her capacity to empathize with the people they met on their journey. "Her sympathies and knowledge were so broad," he would later recall. "She seemed to have intuitions that were more than human. She could go up to utter strangers, people of the most diverse kind,—diverse in nature, social position, work, education, ideals,—and in a few minutes, without any leading or prompting, they seemed to pour out their inmost ideas to her."[86]

Six months earlier Jackson had told Charles Dudley Warner, "There is not in all the Century of Dishonor, so black a chapter as the history of these Mission Indians—peaceable farmers for a hundred years—driven off their lands like foxes & wolves—driven *out* of good adobe houses & the white men who had driven them out, settling down, calm & comfortable in the houses!"[87] Now, on May 4, 1883, the day she and Kinney returned to Los Angeles from their official tour of Southern California Indian villages, she wrote a sad letter to Thomas Bailey Aldrich. "My opinion of human nature has gone down 100 per ct. in the last thirty days," she said. "Such heart sickening fraud, violence, cruelty as we have unearthed here—I did not believe could exist in civilized communities."[88] She began soliciting the assistance of Secretary Teller and Commissioner Price in resolving several local problems and was for a time delighted by their quick responses. She worked to protect threatened Indian villages in San Ysidro Canyon and Soboba; to restore the salary of Mary Sheriff, the government schoolteacher at Soboba; to have the Los Angeles law firm of Brunson and Wells appointed as official U.S. attorneys in charge of handling land disputes for local Indians; and to bring about the replacement of Indian Agent Lawson, whom she had grown to distrust. Before long, her efforts in each of these areas bore fruit.

On May 20 Jackson left Los Angeles for San Francisco by steamer, and five days later she and Abbot Kinney returned to Colorado Springs. Kinney stayed with the Jacksons until June 4, apparently making his final contributions to the report. Jackson then wrote up the thirty-five-page official document, finishing it in July. In *Report on the Condition and Needs of the Mission Indians of California,* she argues that "atonement" should be made to Southern California's Indians for all that they have continued to suffer at the hands of white American settlers. She offers eleven specific recommendations, her main point being that the government should wherever possible "uphold and defend" the "right" of local Indians "to remain where they are."[89] As early as October 31, 1882, when she was planning her trip, she had told Hiram Price that forming new reservations would be only a poor second choice to allowing Southern California's Indians to remain on their ancestral lands. "I am entirely sure that to propose to those self supporting farmers, to submit themselves to the usual reservation laws and restrictions would be futile," she wrote. "It would be also, insulting. There is no more right or reason in an Indian Agent with the usual Indian Agent's authority, being set over them, than there would be in attempting to bring the white farmers of Anaheim or Riverside under such an authoritative control."[90] In her *Report,* she emphasizes that local Indians have long been cultivating their lands. Nonetheless, she explains, "From tract after tract of such lands they have been driven out, year by year, by the white settlers of the country, until they can retreat no farther; some of their villages being literally in . . . mountain fastnesses." She discusses individual cases of unjust theft and impending theft of Indian lands, including the situation of an exceedingly industrious and "intelligent" man named Alessandro, who was living in imminent danger of his unmarked "eight acres in grain, vine, and fruit trees" being stolen by neighboring whites.[91] Jackson insists that there is a great need for "some legal protection for the Indians in Southern California"; as evidence of this need, she cites in one of the eighteen "exhibits" at the end of the *Report* the case of the unpunished murder of the Cahuilla Indian Juan Diego. Noting details that she would later incorporate in the denouement of *Ramona,* she describes Diego as a "locoed" but harmless man, who "had built for himself a house and cultivated a small patch of ground on a high mountain ledge a few miles north of the (Cahuilla) village," where he lived peaceably, "alone with his wife and baby," until he was one day murdered under false accusations of horse thievery by a white man named Sam Temple.[92]

In the months after completing her *Report,* Jackson turned her attention back to travel writing. Following her first trip to Southern California, she had written several travel essays for publications other than *Century Magazine,* and these were now appearing in the periodicals. Two of them, children's pieces for *St. Nicholas* about the Chinese populations of Santa Barbara and Monterey, revealed that she had not entirely outgrown her early race prejudices. Both are shot through with ethnocentrism, despite Jackson's insistence in them that Chinese children deserve kind treatment. Yet other essays demonstrated her significant growth in tolerance. More than a decade earlier, during her first trip to Europe, she had written for the *Independent* an extremely prejudiced piece, "An Afternoon in the Ghetto of Rome," in which she had expressed overt repugnance for Italian Jews. In Southern California, though, she stayed in an inn run by a Polish Jew, and in a *Christian Union* piece titled "Breakfast in San Juan Capistrano" she not only wrote of this man sympathetically but also expressed a keen sense of identification with him as a fellow "exile" from a beloved home.[93] She demonstrated an especially high level of appreciation for racial diversity in her essays concerning local Indians. In "Queen Eumesia," published in the *Christian Union,* she described her encounter in Monterey with a 122-year-old Indian woman. Though she first saw Eumesia standing "on a mound of ashes and refuse of every conceivable sort, rummaging it with a stick," "her expression was not without dignity," Jackson says.[94] In "Three Pennsylvania Women," which also appeared in the *Christian Union,* Jackson celebrated, without naming them, three white emigrants to Southern California who treated local Indians with fairness: Emaline Jordan, Mary Ticknor, and Mary Sheriff. And in one of two essays that she published in the *Atlantic* about her trip to the Northwest with her husband, "Chance Days in Oregon," she briefly insisted, in the words of an old Oregon settler, that that region's Indians had always been "Jest 's civil 's any people in the world." Any "troubles" between them and local whites, this settler said, were "the white people's fault every time.' "[95] The *Atlantic* chose not to publish any of Jackson's writings that dealt directly with Indian affairs. In the early 1880s, even as Jackson and the editor Thomas Bailey Aldrich developed a close friendship, Aldrich was beginning to move the magazine away from its previous tradition of social engagement. "What I want for the magazine is *story*," he told Jackson, asking her not to send too many essays.[96]

During each of her first two visits to Southern California, Jackson had hunted eagerly for "old relics," as she often called Indian and Hispanic cultural artifacts. Yet her essays based on her second visit, which she wrote in the late summer of 1883, reveal just how far she had come from her early view of Indians themselves as cultural relics. On September 3, 1883 she sent William Ward a series of essays for the *Independent,* all of them containing arguments in favor of granting a more prominent and secure place to Southern California's present Indian population. In "Justifiable Homicide in Southern California," printed in the *Independent* on September 27, she tells the story of Juan Diego, the Cahuilla Indian murdered by Sam Temple. Temple's act of "barbaric" violence was condoned by a San Jacinto justice of the peace, who ruled that no trial was necessary in the case. Jackson explains that the incident "gives a fair and actual showing, in the first place, of the helpless and unprotected condition of Indians in Southern California; in the second place, of the nature of public sentiment there." In "A Day with the Cahuillas," published on October 11, she recounts a visit to a Cahuilla village. Jackson finds in the Cahuilla Indians virtues of industrious perseverance that would "have astonished persons in the habit of regarding all Indians not only as barbarians, but as lazy idlers, unwilling to work." She also praises a local white man who, unlike most, "has had conscience enough to give the position of lawful wife to the Indian mother of his half-breed children." "He need not be ashamed of them," she says, for his daughter is "as gracious and courteous a hostess as one need wish to meet." "Captain Pablo's Story," which appeared on October 25, recounts Jackson's meeting with the head of a local band of Indians; this man's scorn of injustice and particular "contour" of face remind Jackson of Abraham Lincoln. "The Temecula Exiles," printed on November 29, describes the 1875 eviction of the Indians at Temecula, offering praise to their former chief Pablo Apis as "a man of character and force." And, finally, "The Fate of Saboba [*sic*]," published on December 13, warns of the threat against Soboba; it includes transcripts of two letters from Indian youths seeking help in preserving their village.

In January 1884, after Jackson's official *Report* had been published by the Government Printing Office, she sent two hundred copies to various prominent friends and acquaintances; she hoped that they might be able to influence public opinion in favor of an impending congressional bill on the *Report*'s findings. In fact, however, while the substance of this bill would one day be enacted into law, "An Act for the Relief of the Mission Indians in the State of California" would not be passed until 1891, six years after Jackson's death.

Jackson was bitterly disappointed over the lack of immediate response to her *Report,* but she had learned from her earlier disappointment over *A Century of Dishonor* that she could never count on rousing public sentiment in favor of Indian rights by means of even the most scrupulous factual presentation of American misdeeds. Indeed, at the time her *Report* was first published, she had already begun to switch tactics. From the beginning of her involvement in reform work, she had wondered whether she might best be able to reach the public through a fictional "story that should 'tell' on the Indian question."[97] Many years earlier, during her schoolgirl days at Ipswich, she had read in Lord Kames's *Elements of Criticism* that works of fiction could often move hearts more effectively than nonfiction; she had come across the same idea expressed within Edward Bulwer-Lytton's *My Novel* (1853), which for a time in young adulthood she considered "the *best* novel I *ever* read."[98] Harriet Beecher Stowe's immensely effective reform novel, *Uncle Tom's Cabin* (1851–52), had made a powerful impression on her during the years of her first marriage. When she herself became a writer, she had quickly learned to incorporate portraits of individual people in all of her nonfiction, for she knew readers were naturally drawn to personal stories. "Of any new or exceptional life the narrative of one individual home will give a far better history than volumes of statistics and general descriptions," she explained in one of her travel essays.[99]

Shortly after she began reform work, she was several times reminded of the potential power of socially engaged fiction. In November 1879, just as she was becoming involved in the Ponca case, she was on hand at the publisher Henry Houghton's home in Boston when Henry Wadsworth Longfellow was first introduced to Susette La Flesche. "The author of 'Hiawatha' seemed no stranger to Bright Eyes; and, when he paid her the courteous compliment of calling her 'Minnehaha,' she received it with exquisite grace and pleasure," Jackson recalled in her essay "Standing Bear and Bright Eyes."[100] Two weeks later, she was present at the *Atlantic*'s December 3 birthday celebration for Oliver Wendell Holmes when Houghton singled out Longfellow, among all his guests, in his welcome address, praising the author's "sweet, sad story of Evangeline" as "an immortal protest against wrong." In discoursing on the present state of American literature, moreover, Houghton happened to predict that among those fiction writers gathered in the room were some who would one day "sing of the wrongs and heroism of the Indian" with new vigor.[101] Jackson had never liked the crude meter of Longfellow's famed Indian poem, *Hiawatha* (1857), but she had long admired *Evangeline* (1847), his mythic poem of the dispossession and long-suffering vagrancy of a group of Catholic Acadians. At the beginning of her career, in 1867, she had spent two weeks exploring the "old Evangeline district" of Nova Scotia; afterward, in her travel essay "The Basin of Minas, and Evangeline's home," she had expressed compassion for the fictional heroine Evangeline's loss of her home to Protestant "tyrants."[102] Encountering Longfellow just as she became involved in Indian reform work, and being reminded then of the popular currency that powerful works of protest fiction could sometimes attain, she no doubt was struck—perhaps for the first time—by the idea that she herself might one day "sing of the wrongs and heroism of the Indian."

Other promptings quickly followed. In the spring of 1880, just after she finished writing A Century of Dishonor, William Jackson happened to meet the regionalist writer Albion Tourgée, who had recently made a stir with A Fool's Errand (1879), his novel condemning the failure of Reconstruction. The encounter convinced William, as he told his wife, that a writer might "more certainly" "reach a people," and thereby do "great good," through a made-up story "than by any direct statement of fact—however accurately & graphically put."[103] In early 1881 Jackson herself published a laudatory anonymous review of William Justin Harsha's new Indian reform novel, Ploughed Under. Privately, she admitted to the Critic editor J. B. Gilder that she believed the book very poorly written. But in her review for Gilder's magazine she defended Harsha's novel on the grounds that such a piece of fiction, "backed by an array of facts, and incidents drawn from actual life," might manage to reach readers "who would never be reached in any other way," helping to open their "eyes to truth, and making them think rightly."[104]

Jackson had recognized the possibilities for setting a novel in Southern California immediately upon her first arrival there. "Whoever will come & live a year on this coast, can make a book of romance which will live: it is a tropic of color and song," she had written to Thomas Bailey Aldrich on January 17, 1882.[105] As she later told the Coronels, she had no specific "plan" to write a story during either of her first two visits to the region.[106] Gradually, though, as she became more and more familiar with Southern California and its people, the idea of using them in a novel concerning Indian rights gained strength at the back of her mind. She finally felt that she possessed sufficient knowledge of the region's "local color" to attempt such a novel after completing her last, official tour of Indian villages.[107] "I have never before felt that I could write an Indian story. I had not got the background. Now I have, and sooner or later, I shall write the story," she told Aldrich on May 4, 1883. "If I could write a story that would do for the Indian a thousandth part what Uncle Tom's Cabin did for the Negro, I would be thankful the rest of my life."[108]

Five months later, she was back in Colorado Springs. Early on an October morning before she was entirely awake, the "whole plot" for the novel she had been considering "flashed" into her mind, much as the words "A Century of Dishonor" had suggested themselves several years before. As she later explained to Thomas Wentworth Higginson, the new story idea came to her "in less than five minutes, as if someone spoke it," and over the following days became "more and more vivid." In late November, still "haunted" by this plot, she traveled to New York.[109] There she checked into the Berkeley Hotel, making arrangements for the exclusive permanent rental of an apartment on the sixth floor. She settled down immediately for a period of intensive work. "My story is all planned: in fact, it is so thought out it is practically half written," she wrote to Aldrich on November 24. "It is chiefly Indian—but the scene is in Southern California, and the Mexican life will enter it largely. I hope it will be a telling book—and will reach people who would not read my Century of Dishonor."[110]

Jackson wrote the first words of *Ramona* on December 1, 1883. Later that month, William joined her for several weeks over the holidays; but for the remainder of her stay she secreted herself away in her rooms, avoiding most social interaction and making it a rule never to go outside in the evenings, when she feared she might contract bronchitis and be kept from her writing. Outside her windows, "snow after snow, after snow" fell on New York, making her "sigh for San Gabriel sunshine."[111] She had surrounded herself with Indian baskets purchased in Southern California, though, and her thoughts were entirely on her story. Within only three days of beginning the novel, she was shocked to find that it was "all so predestined" in her mind that she composed it as quickly as she would a letter.[112] Several times she found it necessary to write to friends in Southern California seeking specific information, and on two separate occasions she became so run down from her feverish labor that she suffered week-long bouts of incapacitating exhaustion.[113] At these junctures, and every afternoon when she had finished her regular daily writing session, she found it almost excruciating to be in the same room as her manuscript but not working on it. "It is like keeping away from a lover, whose hand I can reach," she told Higginson in early February. "It racks me like a struggle with an outside power. . . . Am I possessed of a demon? Is it a freak of mental disturbance?" She told Higginson that although she was working at lightning speed, she believed she was writing the best "English" of her life.[114] By the middle of February, the book was already more than half finished. On March 9, at eleven in the evening, she penciled the final words. The whole project had taken her only three months.

"I wrote the whole of Ramona, at the rate of 2000 to 3000 words a morning—faster than I can write an ordinary letter—& I altered hardly a word to a chapter, on revising it," she would later marvel to Aldrich. "It was an extraordinary experience, and I am not without my superstition about it."[115] In expressing a sense of superstitious awe at her accomplishment, and suggesting that her actions might have been dictated by some outside force, Jackson placed herself squarely within the inspired tradition of Transcendentalism. She also positioned herself as the latest in a long line of American women artists, including Harriet Beecher Stowe, who used claims of outside inspiration as a means of both excusing and shrewdly consecrating their own responsibility for work that challenged social norms. Yet however much Jackson may have felt inspired to write *Ramona,* or wished to ascribe its message to outside inspiration, there was little mystery about the unprecedented power that she demonstrated in writing her new novel. She had some fifteen years of experience in regionalist description and character portraiture behind her, and she had spent longer mulling over this particular project than any in her past. *Ramona* was the culminating expression of her career both as a regionalist writer and as a reformer. Many of her most powerful preoccupations came together in this book, from her long-standing interest in celebrating perseverance and protesting "the spread of civilization," to her lingering tendency toward both idealism and moralism, to the many difficult experiences of her own early life—the orphanhood, loss of her children and first husband, and wandering homelessness— which until this point she had kept hidden even in her fiction behind her determined ethic of cheer.

Like all Jackson's novels, *Ramona* takes place in a vaguely defined recent past. Various incidents link the book's present action to two periods following the American takeover of California, the 1850s/early 1860s and the 1870s.[116] From *Ramona*'s first sentence, Jackson hints that normal life has been disrupted in Southern California: "It was sheep-shearing time in Southern California; but sheep-shearing was late at the Señora Moreno's." Sheepshearing has been delayed at the Moreno estate because Father Salvierderra, one of the few Franciscan priests remaining in California, is weeks late in arriving to bless the undertaking. Jackson seems to have based her portrait of Father Salvierderra partly on Father Francisco de Jesús Sanchez, whom she had met at the Santa Barbara mission; many of the people and situations she encountered in preparing her Southern California travel essays and official *Report* would broadly serve to inspire the fictional characters and events in her novel.[117] When Father Salvierderra finally does make his appearance, Jackson briefly revels in the splendid local color of the region, vividly describing the priest's approach on foot through tall fields of wild mustard weed. But Father Salvierderra is decrepit and downhearted. The Americans have stripped all glory from California's traditional Franciscan priesthood, completing a process of diminution begun in the 1830s with the Mexican government's secularization of mission lands. Father Salvierderra is now a man without a country.

He is not alone in his suffering. All the principal characters of *Ramona* are soon to be deprived by the American government and people of their regional birthright of connection to the land. In "Elspeth Dynor" Jackson had attempted to create a protagonist, Ned Blake, who was raised to feel no wholesome connection to any region, and therefore suffered spiritually. In *Ramona* her characters are forced by circumstances outside their control to give up their ardent attachment to their native soil.

As the book opens, Señora Moreno, the proprietress of the Moreno estate, is caught in the maws of American rapaciousness. A proud and stately woman born in Seville and raised in Southern California, she has seen control of the region pass away from the hands of men like her deceased father, onetime commandante of the Santa Barbara presidio, and her deceased husband, an important Mexican general. (Jackson seems to have borrowed Señora Moreno's name from one of the several elderly women she described in "Echoes in the City of the Angels," a granddaughter of the Moreno who was one of the first Spanish soldiers to arrive in Los Angeles.) In recent years Americans have stolen much of the Moreno estate, which once spanned "all the land within a radius of forty miles"; now, "after all the claims, counter-claims, petitions, appeals, and adjudications" of the United States Land Commission, it seems despite its remaining grandeur but "a pitiful fragment" to "the despoiled and indignant Señora" (12–13). Though she has fond memories of a "picturesque" early life of "gayety" and "romance," when homes like her own dominated the landscape, only a faint "aroma" of these old times "lingers" amid the new era of American "industries and inventions" (12). Señora Moreno is miserable at being ruled by a nation of "English-speaking people" whom she had known in her youth as mere "traders" and "pedlers," and now despises as "thieves" and "hounds." She is certain that her husband "would have chosen to die rather than to have been forced to see his country in the hands of the enemy" (22–23, 12), and this knowledge has served to vanquish her grief over his death in the war against them. She is pleased that the Americans have constructed a new road along the backside of her house, rather than the front: "whatever she, by policy or in business, might be forced to do, the old house, at any rate, would always keep the attitude of contempt,—its face turned away." Prompted by both "religious devotion and race antagonism," she has also taken pleasure in having large wooden crosses erected on all the hills surrounding her house, so that passing Americans will know they are "on the estate of a good Catholic" (13–14).

Though the Señora was once a "gay, tender, sentimental girl," the war and her subsequent sufferings have made her "the silent, reserved, stern, implacable woman" she is at age sixty (23). Authoritarian and industrious, in this respect belying common stereotypes, Señora Moreno is perhaps the most complex figure in all Jackson's fiction. Since her husband's death, she alone has managed the Moreno lands, staff, and sheep business, and raised two children to young adulthood—her beloved, indolent son Felipe and an orphan girl named Ramona. The Señora is talented, elegant, and warmly devoted to her religion. But like Ned Blake of "Elspeth Dynor," she also possesses a formidable capacity for cruelty and deception. "So quiet, so reserved, so gentle an exterior never was known to veil such an imperious and passionate nature, brimful of storm, always passing through stress; never thwarted, except at peril of those who did it; adored and hated by turns, and each at the hottest," Jackson writes

(1). Señora Moreno manipulates her adored Felipe, controlling and dictating his every action even while contriving to hide her machinations from him; and she deceives Ramona, long refusing to inform the girl of her actual parentage.

Ramona's outward appearance has always allowed her to pass as a member of the Hispanic elite, despite "her straight, massive black eyebrows," which stand in marked contrast to "Felipe's, arched and delicately pencilled" (40). Yet Ramona is actually the daughter of a never-named Native American woman from San Gabriel and a Scottish man named Angus Phail.[118] Before marrying his Indian wife, Angus Phail had loved Señora Moreno's sister. Shortly before dying, he gave his new baby, Ramona, to this sister, who in turn, upon her own death, gave the child to Señora Moreno. Compared to the Señora, Ramona is on the surface a flat character, as determinedly cheerful and diligent—and as monotonously sensitive, nature-loving, and morally inspiring—as any Saxe Holm heroine. In fact, Ramona is more "simple" and "clinging" (34) than Jackson's other heroines, and therefore more closely allied to the many motherless young girls of traditional American domestic fiction. She is also more highly idealized: her Hispanic upbringing and Scottish and Indian heritage make themselves felt in her character only in fairly generalized ways. (According to Sarah Woolsey, Jackson was inspired in her portrait of Ramona by a Dante Gabriel Rossetti print of a white woman's and a man's heads "set in a nimbus of clouds, with a strange beautiful regard and meaning in their eyes.")[119] In part, Jackson whitewashed Ramona's character because she intended her person and attitudes to express to white readers an appeal for help, one that could transcend and eradicate their race prejudices. She also wished, as usual, to make her heroine so morally unobjectionable that readers would sympathize with her whatever she might do. Fortunately, unlike Jackson's earlier heroines, Ramona demonstrates her uniform goodness before other characters who are not simply weaker versions of her own virtuous self, but are complex and in some cases evil; she also acts in the face of an encroaching American industrialization that is not merely implied, but is specific and terrible. As time passes, Ramona is revealed to be as stoic and stalwart beneath her placid exterior as any of Jackson's persevering heroines.

While Jackson's heroines tend to be in some degree autobiographical, Ramona most closely shares in the tragedies of Jackson's own early life. To begin with, she endures a difficult orphanhood. Although Señora Moreno does her Catholic duty in sheltering and feeding her, and even puts her through two years of school at the Convent of the Sacred Heart in Los Angeles, she dislikes Ramona. Indeed, the Señora is repulsed by the sad family history her ward embodies, and especially by her mixed racial heritage. Ramona survives this lack of parental love only by embracing the Christian mandate of submission. She also takes some comfort in the loving support of her foster brother, Felipe. Shortly after the novel opens, moreover, she falls in love with a Luiseño Indian named Alessandro, who comes to the Moreno estate from Temecula as the head of a hired band of sheepshearers. She and Alessandro soon decide to marry. Señora Moreno violently opposes the plan, however, even though Alessandro's "skin was not a shade darker than Felipe's" (75) and Ramona herself is half Indian, as the Señora now suddenly reveals to her.

In most respects, Alessandro's character is very similar to Ramona's. After the closing of Mission San Luis Rey, his father, whom Jackson conceives as the actual Chief Pablo, taught his people to become industrious farmers in Temecula; he also passed on many of his personal characteristics and skills to Alessandro. Alessandro always follows the "path of duty," being "by nature full of veneration and the religious instinct" (69, 74); he is uniquely pure and beloved by everyone; and he has an artistic sensibility, possessing great talent for the violin and also, like Ramona, for singing. But in one key respect, Alessandro is very different from Ramona: he does not consider it his duty to be cheerful. Unlike Ramona, he is critical of the earlier rule of the Franciscans, insisting that they forced many Indians to enter the missions. "Some of them preferred to stay in the woods, and live as they always had lived; and I think they had a right to do that if they preferred," he tells Ramona (231). He especially despises his new American oppressors. Shortly after the Señora opposes his marriage to Ramona, he learns that Temecula has been violently overtaken by white settlers from the United States and that his father has died of the shock. Homeless, he no longer thinks he deserves Ramona as his wife, and he determines to return to his tribe and share in their fate. But Ramona, passionately in love, begs him to take her away with him, crying, "I would rather die than have you leave me!" (182).

From the time Ramona and Alessandro leave the Moreno estate, a juncture that occurs almost exactly in the middle of the novel, their story becomes one of wandering exile. They make their way furtively to Temecula, where, while Ramona waits at a safe distance, Alessandro approaches his old house, now occupied by white settlers. "His blood seemed turning to fire," Jackson writes. "Ramona would not have recognized the face of her Alessandro now. It was full of implacable vengeance" (215). In this instance, and several to come, Alessandro manages to restrain his murderous impulses toward whites only by remembering Ramona's gentle presence. He makes a brief stop at a shop run by the Hartsels, where he asks Mrs. Hartsel, a Mexican, to sell his father's violin for him; he and Ramona then set out for San Diego. There, they are married by the local priest, Father Gaspara, a character Jackson modeled in part after the San Diego priest Anthony Ubach. Finally, Ramona and Alessandro set up home in the Indian village at San Pasquale [sic], where, before long, Ramona gives birth to a baby girl. After only eighteen months, however, the village is overrun by white settlers just as Temecula had been.[120] Ramona and Alessandro have little choice but to take their baby and move to another Indian village, at Saboba [sic], even though Saboba is also in imminent danger of being overrun.

Through these and other trials, Ramona suffers and becomes more sober, but still contrives to keep up her spirits. Life improves in Saboba. Ramona and Alessandro both enjoy the friendship of the Hyers, a poor white family from Tennessee, the first truly decent Americans they have ever met. And though the eviction from San Pasquale has permanently changed Alessandro, making him moody and pessimistic, his "sense of home," which is his "strongest passion" aside from his love for his wife, begins to revive (289). Soon, though, Ramona and Alessandro's troubles resume. Their baby becomes ill, and dies when an American government doctor refuses her treatment. This incident seals Alessandro's fate. He now begins to experience periodic bouts of insanity, and persuades Ramona to flee with him away from the company of white people to an isolated spot on San Jacinto mountain, high above the nearest Indian village. There, they have another baby girl; and an old woman, who offers Ramona a glimpse of what her own mother might have been like, comes to live with them for a time. But the family's stalwart efforts to begin life anew are once again thwarted. One day, when Alessandro is off making arrangements to shear a white man's sheep, he has one of his spells and mistakenly exchanges his own pony for a horse owned by a rough American named Jim Farrar. Like everybody else in the vicinity, Farrar knows that Alessandro's mind is disordered, and that "Alessandro in his sense was as incapable of stealing a horse as any white man in the valley" (322). Nonetheless, Farrar is furious. He hurries up the mountain, becoming more and more enraged as he makes the steep climb, and kills Alessandro before Ramona's eyes. Farrar is never brought to justice. And because Ramona has no rights before U.S. courts, she is incapable of doing anything about it.

Ramona finally succumbs to illness, having struggled desperately against despair for the sake of both religion and her daughter. Fortunately, Felipe has been searching for her and Alessandro ever since Señora Moreno's recent death, and he now finds her just in time. He takes Ramona and her baby home with him to the Moreno estate. Yet Felipe has come to despise life in California, much like his mother before him: "The methods, aims, standards of the fast incoming Americans were to him odious. Their boasted successes, the crowding of colonies, schemes of settlement and development,—all were disagreeable and irritating. The passion for money and reckless spending of it, the great fortunes made in one hour, thrown away in another, savored to Felipe's mind more of brigandage and gambling than of the occupations of gentlemen. He loathed them" (359).

Felipe wishes to move to Mexico, "which he had never seen, yet yearned for like an exile." There, he believes, "he might yet live among men of his own race and degree, and of congenial beliefs and occupations." Yet he is determined never to leave without Ramona, for he now understands that he has always loved her. "Could it be that she felt a bond to this land, in which she had known nothing but suffering?" he wonders (359). In fact, even Ramona can no longer endure life in Southern California. She hates the American government and wishes to spare her daughter the race oppression she has suffered. She therefore accompanies Felipe to Mexico, where, feeling emotionally "dead" but grateful for his help and unwilling to cause him pain, she accepts his marriage proposal (361).

This is not a happy ending. Felipe does not understand the difference between Ramona's sisterly affection for him and the strength of the romantic passion she had once felt for Alessandro. Nor does he realize that it is only Ramona's everlasting commitment to "the duty of joyfulness" (358) that allows her to keep up appearances as his wife. In having Ramona and Felipe leave their native region for Mexico, moreover, Jackson implies that California is on a road to self-destruction. The heroines of all her novels eventually decide that they must leave once-beloved lands, and their departures are always intended as some form of indictment of the people they leave behind. In *Mercy Philbrick's Choice* and *Hetty's Strange History,* local prejudices impel worthy heroines to flee. In *Ramona,* local prejudices are coupled for the first time in Jackson's fiction with the violent advance of American civilization to create a surprisingly bleak vision of a once magnificent region.

Jackson intended her readers to be ashamed of their nation for inspiring the hatred of a good woman like Ramona. *Ramona* functions as what the literary scholar Sacvan Bercovitch has termed an "American jeremiad."[121] Like the Hebrew prophet Jeremiah, who foretold doom for his people if they did not adhere to their original covenant with God, Jackson attempts in *Ramona* to recall Americans to their original commitment to human equality and justice, first articulated in the Declaration of Independence. Because she believed *A Century of Dishonor* had been too overtly didactic to be successful, she masked her reform purpose in *Ramona.* "Every incident in Ramona (ie of the Indian History) is true," she assured Thomas Bailey Aldrich shortly after the novel was published. Yet she did not want her readers to dwell on that point until their sympathies were entirely with her. She therefore focused in the first half of the book not on Indian affairs but on romantic descriptions of early *Californio* life, the colorful antics of many of the workers living at the Moreno estate, and the love story of her protagonists. "What I wanted to do," she told Aldrich, "was to draw a picture so winning and alluring in the beginning of the story, that the reader would become thoroughly interested in the characters before he dreamed of what was before him:—and would have swallowed a big dose of information on the Indian question, without knowing it."[122]

Jackson's desire to reach a wide audience and stimulate social reform with her novel dictated the choices she made in its publication. Originally, she had intended to call the book "In the Name of the Law"; but when friends expressed concern that this title might repel some readers, she selected a new, more innocuous name, one more in keeping with the titles of her previous novels. She also arranged to have her novel serialized in the *Christian Union* before Roberts Brothers published it in book form. As she considered *Ramona* a type of veiled "tract," written to inspire "conversion" to her cause, she was particularly desirous of reaching what she called "the religious element" with her novel.[123] And she respected the *Christian Union*, believing it had lately come to surpass the *Independent* in quality. *Ramona* appeared in the paper in weekly installments between May 15 and November 6, 1884. It was printed under her own name, Helen Jackson, with her "H.H." signature attached. Previously, she had used her own name only in the publication of her official *Report* and some of her articles on Indian affairs. From this point forward, though, she began to use it often. Ever since remarrying, she had wondered whether she should give up the old "H.H."; but as she explained to Thomas Bailey Aldrich, it was only the appearance of imposter "H.H."s, who suddenly began "contributing sketches of travel on the Rhine, verses etc. to newspapers & magazines," that finally convinced her to take the step.[124] The appearance of imposter Saxe Holms earlier in her career never induced her to take a similar step and reveal her identity as the author of short stories; she thus seems to have felt especially confident about having her own name associated with her Indian reform work.

After Roberts Brothers published *Ramona* in November 1884, Jackson eagerly studied the reviews. She was delighted to find that most praised her writing very highly; Horace Scudder's laudatory piece in the *Atlantic*, in particular, gave her such intense satisfaction that she confessed to Aldrich, "I am silly enough to shut my eyes sometimes with pleasure at recalling it."[125] She was as angry as ever when her old nemesis, the *Nation*, offered the book one of its few negative notices. Yet what she hoped above all was that the reviews would call attention to her intended reform message. "I care more for making one soul burn with indignation and protest against our wrongs to the Indian," she told Aldrich, "than I do *even* for having you praise the quality of my work as work."[126] In the end, she was "much cast down" to realize that most critics had paid little heed to the actual Indian history in *Ramona*.[127] Instead, they focused on the novel's love story and idealized evocation of early *Californio* lifeways.

The literary models Jackson had drawn on in writing *Ramona* were partly responsible for the way in which critics, and after them the general public, tended to view the book.[128] The model Jackson mentioned most often in her private letters, Stowe's *Uncle Tom's Cabin*, inspired her to create a heroine who, like Uncle Tom, is so saintly, and so familiar to white readers, that she has the potential to win them over to her cause; at the same time, however, Ramona's perfections give her story an air of unreality, of myth. This feeling is compounded by Jackson's focus in the first half of the novel on fading *Californio* lifeways, and the vague definition of the period in which all the events in her book, including the American dispossession of local Indians, take place. Its lack of historical specificity gives the novel an elegiac feeling, like that of Longfellow's *Evangeline:* Jackson seems to be describing events buried solidly in the past rather than ongoing travesties that demand present intervention. Jackson's final model for *Ramona,* Charles Dudley Warner's 1878 short story "A-Hunting of the Deer,"[129] also inclined her toward presenting her reform message in a manner too veiled to command any action from most of her readers. Warner's story offers a long and painful account of a deer hunt from a nursing doe's point of view, stopping at two points to compare the delight that many Americans take in the slaughter of innocent animals to the American military's brutal massacres of Indians. When she was just beginning reform work, Jackson had asked Warner himself to write an actual Indian story modeled after "A-Hunting of the Deer," with no results. Later, after she had met Indians in Southern California who were being forced to live like "hunted wild beasts,"[130] she was reminded of Warner's story. "Do you remember, of course you do, Warner's story of the Doe?" she asked Thomas Bailey Aldrich in November 1883 as she was preparing to write *Ramona.* "Do you think the story of two human beings, husband and wife, fleeing from place to place, seeking a chance of life and a home, and never finding it, could be told as *simply* and unsupportedly as that was, and be effective? I think so. That is what I am going to try to do."[131] In the end, though, her account of the American dispossession of Indian lands was both too personalized and too vague to suggest to many readers that there were still Indians in Southern California who were suffering as Ramona and Alessandro had.

Although the idealized tone of *Ramona* allowed many early readers to overlook the book's reform message, the message is there. Indeed, *Ramona* more clearly and unequivocally advocates the rights of Native Americans than any other nineteenth-century novel written by a European American.[132] (Novels by Native American authors concerning Native American life did not begin to appear until well after Jackson's death.)[133] *Ramona* also expresses an opposition to American imperialism, and a hope for a more equitable, multicultural America, that was advanced for its time and that resonates with the desires expressed in the California writings of Jackson's Hispanic contemporaries, including María Amparo Ruiz de Burton.[134] Even the sense of nostalgia for earlier times that pervades *Ramona,* and in some respects draws attention away from Jackson's reform objective, is related to the oppositional nostalgia that some contemporary Hispanics, including Antonio Coronel, were given to expressing. Near the opening of *Ramona,* Jackson expands on Señora Moreno's longing for earlier times and her hatred of America and Americans:

The people of the United States have never in the least realized that the taking possession of California was not only a conquering of Mexico, but a conquering of California as well; that the real bitterness of the surrender was not so much to the empire which gave up the country, as to the country itself which was given up. Provinces passed back and forth in that way, helpless in the hands of great powers, have all the ignominy and humiliation of defeat, with none of the dignities or compensations of the transaction. (12–13)

Jackson validates the bitterness felt by Señora Moreno and the other Hispanic and Indian characters in her novel by constructing them, not the American colonialists who oppress them, as the regional "norm." She accomplishes this by inverting her usual methods for transcribing regionalist dialect. All the Native American and Hispanic characters in *Ramona* speak a heightened, formal English, one perhaps modeled after the English of Susette La Flesche, which Jackson once described as "so quaint, so simple, and yet so stately in its very simplicity."[135] All the white Americans, on the other hand, speak in dialects they have learned in their regions of origin, not in California. Their linguistic foreignness indicates that they do not naturally belong in the land they have conquered. Jackson does not mean to suggest that they should not stay there; instead, as in all of her regionalist writing, she is urging that they should respect the preeminent rights of the region's earlier inhabitants.

Jackson hoped that California's diverse residents might one day learn to live in neighborly proximity, rather than in hegemonic opposition. In *Ramona* she offers several examples of relatively harmonious integration. The "half shop, half farm, half tavern" run by the Hartsels, which Alessandro visits upon his return with Ramona to Temecula, is a "mongrel establishment" that "gathered up to itself all the threads of the life of the whole region," Jackson explains. "Indians, ranchmen, travellers of all sorts, traded at Hartsel's, drank at Hartsel's, slept at Hartsel's. It was the only place of its kind within a radius of twenty miles; and it was the least bad place of its kind within a much wider radius" (217). *Ramona* prominently features several racial intermarriages: between Ramona's parents, Ramona and Alessandro, and finally Ramona and Felipe. In a sense, Jackson was simply being true to local reality in portraying so many intermarriages, for while she was in California she met many intermarried couples, including the Coronels and the Wolfs, the Temecula proprietors who helped inspire her fictional portrait of the Hartsels: Ramona Wolf was part Native American and part African American; her husband was Alsatian. At the same time, however, Jackson's focus on intermarriage was quite daring, for in 1884 this subject was still widely considered taboo in America and American literature.[136] As in her two earlier Civil War stories, Jackson's depictions in *Ramona* of marriage between people of different backgrounds are intended to promote not only regional but national reconciliation. In *Ramona,* as in all her writing, Jackson constructs family and home as life's most desirable objects.

The people she depicts as most deserving a good home, Ramona and Alessandro, are in a racially mixed marriage. And that they are never allowed to establish a home, despite all of their earnest efforts, is intended as a negative commentary on the moral health of the American nation.

Several characters in *Ramona* serve as models for how a reader might learn to grow in race tolerance. Ramona herself, the most exemplary character in the book and the one with whom readers are most intended to sympathize, is one such model. Ramona chooses to identify as Indian, rather than as a member of the European or Hispanic elites; as she gradually enters the Indian world, she discovers that it is filled with ordinary, worthy people who are being unjustly persecuted. Several minor characters, including Young Merrill, Judge Wells, and an American man who buys Alessandro's home in San Pasquale, make similar discoveries. Perhaps the most important model for racial tolerance presented in the book is "Aunt" Ri Hyer, a poor American pioneer from Tennessee, who together with her ineffectual husband and invalid son becomes a good friend to Ramona and Alessandro. Based partly on a pioneer woman named Emaline Jordan, with whom Jackson and Abbot Kinney had stayed while visiting San Jacinto, Aunt Ri serves in many ways as Jackson's mouthpiece: her very name is a nickname for Maria, Jackson's own middle name.

In early life, Aunt Ri's "ideas of Indians" had not been very positive. Like Jackson's own, they "had been drawn from newspapers, and from a book or two of narratives of massacres, and from an occasional sight of vagabond bands or families" (286). But upon meeting Ramona, Alessandro, and other Southern California Indians, all of her prejudices gradually disappear. She is immediately impressed by Ramona's homemaking skills and the strength of her maternal feelings. "She's fond uv her baby's enny white woman! I kin see thet," Aunt Ri says (283). She also comes to appreciate the "kindness and goodness of the Cahuilla people," near whom she lives. Indeed, "the last vestige of her prejudice against Indians" eventually disappears "in the presence of their simplehearted friendliness" (347). She begins to criticize the American government's dealings with local Indians, and to insist that just as personal contact has eliminated her own prejudices, so personal familiarity with actual Indians would eliminate the prejudices of all Americans. " 'Pears like there cudn't nobody b'leeve ennythin' 'n this world 'thout seein' 't theirselves," she says. "I wuz thet way tew; I allow I hain't got no call ter talk; but I jest wish the hull world could see what I've seen!" (348). Aunt Ri insists that if more Americans knew about the injustices taking place in California, they would never permit them. "I tell you, naow, the Ummeriken people don't want any o' this cheatin' done," she says. "Why, it's a burnin' shame to any country!" (291). Jackson hoped her novel might vicariously afford her readers the same personal experience that had transformed Aunt Ri.

In her own life, Aunt Ri works to promote racial tolerance. When she first meets Felipe, as he arrives to rescue Ramona, she asks him to call her "aunt," and tells her son, " 'Pears like I'd known him all my days, jest ez 't did with her, arter the fust. I'm free to confess I take more ter these Mexicans than I do ter these low-down, driven Yankees, ennyhow" (335). Aunt Ri takes special pride in making beautiful rag carpets that feature "no set stripes or regular alternation of colors, but ball after ball of the indiscriminately mixed tints, woven back and forth," for she believes that "the constant variety" and "unexpectedly harmonious blending of the colors" of these rugs afford an important subject for "not unphilosophical reflection" (349). Her reflections give rise to an unrestricted, pluralistic vision of America that still resonates today:

> "Wall," she said, "it's called ther 'hit-er-miss' pattren; but it's 'hit' oftener 'n 't is 'miss.' Thar ain't enny accountin' fur ther way ther breadths 'll come, sometimes; 'pears like 't wuz kind er magic, when they air sewed tergether; 'n' I allow thet's ther way it's gwine ter be with heaps er things in this life. It's jest a kind er 'hit-er-miss' pattren we air all on us livin' on; 't ain't much use tryin' ter reckon how 't'll come aout; but the breadths does fit heaps better 'n yer'd think; come ter sew 'em, 't aint never no sech colors ez yer thought 't wuz gwine ter be, but it's allers pooty, allers; never see a 'hit-er-miss' pattren 'n my life yit, thet wa'n't pooty." (349–50)[137]

Though Jackson hoped that the many peoples of California and the American nation might one day live in harmony, she had grave doubts as to the sincerity of the American government's commitment to bringing such a future about. These doubts came to a head in the months following *Ramona*'s publication and led her to devote the final year of her life to writings that were adamant in their opposition to race, class, and even gender inequality.

⌐ 9 ⌐

Last Words

I am heartily, honestly, and cheerfully ready to go. In fact, I am glad
to go. You have never fully realized how for the last four years my
whole heart has been full of the Indian cause—how I have felt, as the
Quakers say, 'a concern' to work for it. My "Century of Dishonor"
and "Ramona" are the only things I have done of which I am glad
now. The rest is of no moment. They will live, and they will bear
fruit. . . . I want you to know that I am looking with an almost eager
interest into the 'undiscovered country,' and leaving this earth with
no regret except that I have not accomplished more work; especially
that it was so late in the day when I began to work in real earnest.
But I do not doubt that we shall keep on working. . . . Any other
conception of existence is to me monstrous.

JACKSON TO THOMAS WENTWORTH HIGGINSON,
July 27, 1885, in Higginson, "Helen Jackson"

Just three months after she finished writing *Ramona,* on June 28, 1884, Jackson suffered a terrible accident, falling down an entire flight of stairs in her Colorado Springs home and breaking her lower left leg in three places. She became bedridden for months. As usual, she accepted her condition without rancor, calling on the habits of submission she had been cultivating for more than fifty years. She assured eastern correspondents that she deserved no special attention, and she tried not to complain when William's recent appointment as receiver for the financially troubled Denver and Rio Grand often kept him away from home. A handful of local friends—Hatty, Alise, Mrs. Hamp, and Mrs. Mary Tenney Hatch—attempted to cheer her lonely confinement. Yet her fall marked the onset of a general physical decline.

As winter approached, she was still walking very little, and then only with two crutches. She decided she would not travel east at the first warning of snow, as had become her custom, but instead would go to Southern California, where she hoped the mild climate might aid in her convalescence. In mid-November, she set out with her maid Effie McLeod and a personal nurse for her third visit in as many years to Los Angeles. There she took up residence at a promising new boardinghouse run by Mrs. D. J. Whipple. Soon, however, she became seriously ill. Fearing she had contracted malaria, she resolved to move. She could no longer consider making the long trip east, though, or even home to Colorado Springs. On March 13, 1885, she took the train for San Francisco.

Jackson had been planning many new writing projects before she broke her leg. At one point, she had expected to earn as much as $1,000 for her work in the summer of 1884 alone. But she found it difficult to work as her health deteriorated, and often bemoaned "the irreparable loss of time" for writing as "the worst thing about illness."[1] She was forced to abandon a recent intention to write a novel about Quaker life: when her sister-in-law Margaret sent her some books she had requested on the topic, Jackson admitted that she did not have the strength to study them. Still, she accomplished a good deal in the year after her fall. Working mostly in bed, often suffering, she produced poems, a number of short stories, and the beginnings of a new Colorado novel. "It's astonishing what way there is, when there's a will," she told Charles Dudley Warner in October 1884.[2]

Much of Jackson's final work reveals a concern for social justice that includes, but also transcends, the single issue of Indian rights. Jackson had always admired the American nation for being founded on "the new basis of liberty and equality,"[3] but she had long mistrusted the politicians who made it their business to ensure the enactment of those values. After she became an activist, her distrust of the American political leadership increased as she uncovered countless incidents of governmental misconduct in Indian affairs. She was especially demoralized by the government's lack of response to her efforts on behalf of Southern California's Indians. In the autumn of 1884, she complained to Moncure Conway that those Indians had "had *nothing* done for them yet," but were "being driven off their lands just the same." This neglect, combined with other national events that included the starvation of a group of Piegan Indians on a reservation in Montana at the same time that wheat was being stockpiled in the Midwest, led her almost to despise her country. "If I were the Lord I'd rain fire & brimstone on these United States," she told Conway. "Treasury running over with money—*last year's* wheat piled up in Chicago—*kept* for a rise—& bands of Indians that we *promised to feed,* dying of starvation, north & south—Sometimes I wish I were dead, I am so ashamed."[4]

The cruel contrast between the abundance in Chicago and the suffering in Montana prompted her to write a poem, "Too Much Wheat," which was published in the *Independent* on November 6, 1884. Like many of Jackson's final writings, this poem is essentially an early piece of muckraking journalism; Jackson hoped it would "strike home to people's consciences."[5] In the second stanza, she laments that "Hundreds of men lie dying, dead, / Brothers of ours, though their skins are red." And in the third stanza, she blames the American nation for this travesty:

O, dastard Nation! dastard deed!
They starve like beasts in pens and fold,
While we hoard wheat to sell for gold.
"Too much wheat!" Men's lives are dross!
"How shall the farmers be saved from loss?"

"Too Much Wheat" reveals not only the strength of Jackson's anger over American mistreatment of Indians but also her increasing sensitivity to issues of class. Two years earlier she had been profoundly affected by an article in the *Atlantic Monthly* by the nascent muckraker Henry Demarest Lloyd, "The Political Economy of Seventy-Three Million Dollars," about corruption in the railroads. "When I came to the end I choked & it was all I could do to read the last paragraphs," she told Lloyd's wife, Jessy Bross, an old friend. "I am not sure that I think anything so splendid as that paper has ever been done in America!" The paragraphs that Jackson could scarcely read described how the Wabash railroad was paying handsome dividends to its stockholders even as the laboring men of the road all reported themselves to be "on the edge of starvation."[6] In "Too Much Wheat" and another late poem, "The Mill Has Shut Down," Jackson highlights what she considered the "terrible antithesis" between the lives of the rich and the poor, blaming the problems of the poor on widespread human insensitivity and corruption in government and big business.[7] As with many of her last writings, she published these poems under her own name, with her old "H.H." signature appended.

Jackson's "highest ambition" during the year after her fall remained the writing of a long "Indian (& Mexican) story for the *Youth's Companion*,"[8] a sort of children's version of *Ramona*. In recent years she had been writing a good deal for *Youth's Companion*. No longer directed chiefly at Sunday schools, as it had been when Jackson's mother secretly published there, the magazine had gradually attained an enormous circulation of some 400,000 readers.[9] Jackson was eager to advocate the rights of Indians before this huge audience of children and their parents, but she was determined never to compromise her principles just to win the approval of the magazine's editor, William H. Rideing. In the spring of 1884, when she first approached Rideing about contributing an Indian story and also another about the Underground Railroad, Rideing rejected the latter proposal on the grounds that such a story might offend his Southern readers. "It would of course be offensive to a large portion of your Southern audience," Jackson replied indignantly. "So might the Indian story to some of your Californian and Western readers. Had you thought of that?"[10] In the end, much to her chagrin, Jackson's illness prevented her from making much progress on her Indian story. She did, however, complete a number of less ambitious works for children. She wrote several didactic, regionalist stories for *Wide Awake* about a Tennessee girl named "Popsy" and another girl growing up in a Scottish immigrant milieu, "Pansy Billings." And with *The Hunter Cats of Connorloa* (1884) she brought to a culmination her playful series of cat books for children, which already included her revision of her mother's letters, *Letters from a Cat* (1879), and *Mammy Tittleback and Her Family: A True Story of Seventeen Cats* (1881). *The Hunter Cats of Connorloa* is set in a San Gabriel house resembling Abbot Kinney's, and its events are based on a local Indian eviction.

Jackson also wrote a number of late short stories for adults. She intended several of them to be Saxe Holm or Jane Silsbee tales; and though "The Mystery of Wilhelm Rutter," "The Captain of the 'Heather Bell,'" and "Little Bel's Supplement" were eventually published posthumously under her own name in *Century* and *Harper's* magazines, and afterward in the collection *Between Whiles* (1887), they all suffer from the usual weaknesses of her Saxe Holm fiction. Much more interesting are an Adirondacks story, "Dandy Steve," which was published only in *Between Whiles,* and a charming New England tale, "Farmer Worrall's Case," which appeared as a Saxe Holm story in *Harper's* while Jackson was still alive, in December 1884. Perhaps best of all Jackson's final fictional work was "The Prince's Little Sweetheart," a story she wrote in Colorado Springs shortly after breaking her leg. She published it under her own name in May 1885, in *Century,* and it was later included in *Between Whiles.* In this short piece, which is entirely unlike Jackson's other fiction, a common girl is whisked off to a palace to marry a prince. There she enjoys a rapturous night of dancing, riches, and passion, only to awaken the next morning to find herself stripped of her fancy new clothes and returned to her old brown stuff gown. Desperate, she searches through the empty palace, finally stumbling on a whole crowd of young women in homely dresses, all of them busy "sweeping spiders" in the corners of a dark room. They assure her they were all "Prince's Sweethearts" one day. Overwhelmed by this bleak vision of her future, the girl asks plaintively:

> "Is it only for one day, then?"
> "Only for one day," they all replied.
> "And always after that do you have to kill spiders?" she cried.
> "Yes; that or nothing," they said.

It is an oddly powerful, surreal vision. According to Flora Haynes Apponyi, a fledgling California writer who became a frequent visitor to Jackson's bedside in San Francisco, Jackson received more fan mail for "The Prince's Little Sweetheart" than for any short story she had ever written. When Apponyi told Jackson she suspected that the story was an allegory of women's plight upon marriage, however, Jackson insisted it had no special meaning but had simply come to her in a dream. "I dreamed it all out, every detail, just as I afterward wrote it," she said.[11] While Jackson may have wished to downplay her intentions, Apponyi was clearly right. According to Thomas Wentworth Higginson, Jackson even admitted to a mutual acquaintance around this time that she was at last becoming interested in writing about "the legal and other disabilities of women."[12]

Jackson's final fictional undertaking, a novel called *Zeph,* supports the notion that she was becoming interested in promoting the rights of women, perhaps especially a woman's right to leave an unhappy marriage without being stigmatized. Zeph Riker is a carpenter in "Pendar Basin," Colorado. A passive and endlessly forgiving man, he clings to his drunken wife Rusha though she continually ridicules and betrays him. At close range, he is admirable, even Christlike in his martyrdom. Yet his peers consider him unmanly; to their way of thinking, only women are intended by nature to submit to cruel spouses. By pointing out this common double standard, and at the same time vividly depicting Zeph's misery and degradation, Jackson cunningly suggests that it is unfair to expect women, any more than men, to remain locked in unhappy marriages. When Rusha finally runs off with a mining cook, taking her and Zeph's two children with her, Zeph falls into the healing company of thirty-five-year-old Sophy Burr, a typically sensible, cheerful, and industrious Jackson heroine. At last, Zeph realizes that he has suffered long enough, and he divorces Rusha to marry Sophy. Jackson never completed the novel. Yet in her outline for its conclusion, which Thomas Niles would later publish with Jackson's unfinished manuscript after her death, it is clear that she intended Zeph and Sophy to lead a happy and productive life, and to eventually gain custody of Zeph's children. The wholesomeness of their marriage, especially in contrast to Zeph's previous marriage, suggests that divorce can sometimes be the right course of action. A decade earlier, in 1876, Jackson had told her niece Helen that she believed "men and women who have made a mistake in marrying, and are perfectly wretched together, and cannot therefore build up a happy home, or be really good parents to their children," should be allowed to divorce "without feeling that they have committed a sin, and without being disgraced."[13]

Although Jackson had hoped her health would improve after she relocated to San Francisco, she enjoyed only one brief period of recovery there before her condition returned to worsening. She was afflicted with diarrhea and nausea so incessant that eventually she found relief only in injections of morphine. Repulsed by food and unable to keep it down, she actually began to experience her worst fear—wasting away as her parents had done so many years before. "The flesh has rained off me," she told Abbot Kinney in April 1885. "I must have lost at least forty pounds, and I am wan and yellow in the face. Nothing ever before so utterly upset me."[14] Resorting once again to her usual strategy, she moved, this time from her boardinghouse at the corner of Leavenworth and Sutter to another house at 1600 Taylor Street. The change was of no use. By June she had lost her powers of concentration and memory, and she began to suspect that in addition to malaria she was suffering from "cerebral exhaustion" or "nervous prostration."[15] Still, her attitude of Christian submission never faltered: visitors to her bedside invariably found her cheerful, "a hero in her suffering," according to her young homeopathic doctor, A. T. Boericke.[16]

"If I were foolish enough to want to escape dying, I would go to the Yo Semite," Jackson had once told Charles Dudley Warner, in 1872, after her first trip to Northern California.[17] Now she briefly considered the idea of a camping excursion, writing to the naturalist John Muir for his advice. It soon became clear that she would not be able to leave her bed, however. She took what comfort she could from her various callers, who included, in addition to her kind doctor, a precious new friend named Sara Thibault, Abbot Kinney, and Flora Haynes Apponyi. Jackson considered Apponyi, like most of the local California writers whose work she knew, merely an apprentice. She urged her to study her craft diligently, recommending her own early model for composition, Thomas Wentworth Higginson's *Out-Door Papers* (1868). She also wrote many letters in support of other women writers whose work she wished to promote. During the previous winter, she had been greatly impressed by the new short story collection by the regionalist writer Mary Noailles Murfree, *In the Tennessee Mountains* (1884), and also by two regionalist stories in the *Christian Union* by the British expatriate Amelia Edith Barr. She had written to Thomas Bailey Aldrich at the *Atlantic* and to Millicent Shinn, the editor of the new *Overland Monthly,* in praise of these two writers. Now she sent a personal letter to Amelia Barr. She also wrote several encouraging notes for other women writers and mailed them to Hamilton Wright Mabie, the editor of the *Christian Union,* to be forwarded. According to Mabie, these notes all contained "words of generous praise, of unstinted admiration, of stimulus and hope for the future."[18]

Far more painful were the letters she wrote to her husband. He had been named temporary president of the Denver and Rio Grande and was so busy with his work that he could scarcely consider leaving Colorado. She did not encourage him to come to her, apparently preferring, as she had often claimed when she first broke her leg, that he not see her in her suffering. Yet she was becoming convinced that she would never recover from this illness. Not surprisingly, there were many things that she wanted to settle with William. Back in March, she had taken advantage of a period of lucidity to write a long farewell letter to him. In it, she had expressed pride in her *Century of Dishonor* (1881) and her best-selling novel *Ramona* (1884), and a hope, much like the one she would later express to Thomas Wentworth Higginson in the letter excerpted in this chapter's epigraph, that these two books would "tell, in the long run" on the state of Indian affairs. More soberly, she had confessed to her husband, "The thought of this is my only consolation as I look back over the last ten years & realize how I have failed to be to you what I longed & hoped to be."[19]

At last, she had determined to admit her long worries over their temperamental differences and childlessness, and to encourage William to begin a new family after she died. In 1877 she had written to her sister, "Pretty soon after I am fifty, I shall pass on & make room for my successor!"[20] By March 1885 she believed that her prophecy was soon to be fulfilled. She urged William to consider marrying her favorite niece, Helen Banfield, who had spent much of the previous winter with William in Colorado Springs, recuperating from a nervous breakdown, while Jackson herself was writing *Ramona* in New York. She explained that she had drawn up a will leaving much of her estate to Helen, since her grandfather had wished his property to descend through his female offspring, and since William himself had no want of money.[21] If William did not find himself drawn to Helen, she implored him to marry someone else, and quickly, but to "be *sure,* this time, dearest, to marry some one whose tastes & standards in all matters of living are like your own.—Don't make a second mistake love." Her counsel was sincere, and no doubt cost her a great deal in the writing. In the concluding portion of her letter, though, as in the conclusions to *Hetty's Strange History* (1877) and her outline for "The Cook of the Buckeye Mine," she could not resist expressing a hope that William would never find a love more powerful than theirs:

> Will—you have never known how deep my realization has been of the fact that I was not the right wife for you:—much as I have loved you:—with a different woman & with children at your knees, you would have been a different man—& a happier one.—God will give it to you yet—& it was time! I am glad to go for your sake, my beloved one. Forgive every pain & vexation I have ever given you, & only remember that I loved you as few men are ever loved, in this world. *Nobody* will ever love you so well;—that you will feel, as the years go on—& I shall perhaps hear you say it to yourself, some day as I am watching you—Your Peggy.[22]

As her health deteriorated in the summer of 1885, Jackson sent her husband careful letters of instruction on the disbursement of her personal possessions. If William were to have a daughter in the future, she wanted the girl to have her wedding ring. "Her mother will not object I am sure," she wrote. "Perhaps she would even be willing that you should name her Margaret & call her Peggy which is one of the nicknames for Margaret!"[23] She asked William to burn every piece of manuscript she had left in the house. The materials she had been gathering for a projected novel about Quaker life were to be sent to Sarah Woolsey, in hopes her friend might one day undertake the project. Remembrances of Rennie that she had kept in a box on her dresser ever since his death should be destroyed; a trunk of his old clothes, which she had "never had courage to open," should be sent to her niece Helen.[24] (She had already mailed a photograph of Rennie, "the most precious thing I possess," to her cousin Ann Scholfield.)[25] In separate letters to William and to Helen, she arranged for the distribution and future use of her clothing, linen, silver, rugs, and decorative items from various parts of world. Her instructions were remarkably detailed and precise, an indication of how heartfelt had been her many articles on home décor and management. She asked both William and Helen to be sure always to keep the large writing desk upon which she had written *Ramona;* the other furniture in her New York apartment they might do with as they liked.

She also provided them with very specific directives for how to handle her death and funeral. "Don't one of you put on a shred of black for me. This is my earnest request," she wrote to Helen.[26] She told William that she wished to be buried on Cheyenne Mountain, "the spot I love best of the whole world," explaining that her first choice for a gravesite would be *"behind* the big rock where we used to camp in the *winter,* in the olden days—near where the black-smith's tent was." She wanted to be carried up in an open wagon with kin-nikinick vines strewn over her, not in a hearse, and she wanted the proceedings to be kept as secret and simple as possible. On a plain slab of granite, she wished to have written, "Helen, / Wife of Wm S. Jackson," with only the word *EMI-GRAVIT,* title to her old poem, and the date of her death below.[27] If William wanted, a local friend named Mr. Gregg might accompany him up the mountain to read aloud a poem she had published in 1881, "Last Words."

Sometime in July, Dr. Boericke began to realize that while his patient might have arrived from Los Angeles with malaria, she was suffering primarily from cancer. Though he did not reveal this information to Jackson, she eventually began to suspect it but kept her suspicions from her husband. Finally, though, Dr. Boericke contacted him. William arrived in San Francisco on August 2. On first seeing him, Helen momentarily lost her composure and wept. William was also overcome. "The hardest thing I have had to do in my life is to be forced to watch & see this wasting away of a beautiful & useful life without being able to do one single thing to save her," he wrote to his sister Margaret on the fifth. "It is only within the last few days that I have had my eyes opened to it as the Doctors have heretofore expressed the most confident assurances." To Helen Banfield he admitted, "I am broken to pieces by the alarming prospect."[28]

On the seventh and eighth, which would prove her last lucid days, Jackson made several final arrangements. She wrote to Thomas Niles, expressing her desire for the posthumous publication of new volumes of her poetry, travel writing, and short fiction, and perhaps also of her unfinished novels, *Zeph* and "Elspeth Dynor." As always, Niles carried out her wishes exactly. She wrote to Helen Banfield, asking her to be sure to give her two servants, Effie McLeod and Katy, $5 for Christmas every year as a present from her. She told her mother-in-law that it was "hard to leave Will . . . with all my intense love for him," but she also expressed assurances that he had a "more completely rounded" future ahead of him.[29] And she wrote to President Grover Cleveland, begging him, from her "death bed," to read *A Century of Dishonor,* and claiming that she was "dying happier for the belief" that he might work to redress "the wrongs of the Indian race."[30] During the previous weeks, she had managed to write a handful of poems. Two of them, "The Song He Never Wrote" and "A Last

Prayer," were poignant expressions of regret that she had not begun earlier in her career to write about issues of social justice. Now she wrote one last poem, "Habeas Corpus," in which she expressed a sense of calm resignation to death. She admitted, however, that she did "grudge" the loss of her writing hand.[31]

On the night of August 8, Dr. Boericke administered a heavy dose of morphine, and she was seldom conscious afterward. On the eleventh, William telegraphed to Annie: "Helen is gradually sinking to final rest nothing can be done but accept the fate disease soft cancer of stomach."[32] She died the following day at 4 P.M. Curiously, Dr. Boericke's postmortem analysis echoed his patient's lifelong belief that she must constantly move in order to stave off the disease that had killed her parents. Writing to Jackson's niece Edith Banfield, Dr. Boericke declared his belief that Jackson's stomach cancer, whenever it might first have formed, had been aggravated by the long bed rest she had been forced to endure after breaking her leg—a confinement especially deleterious "to one so active before"—and that it was in essence the final result of a "latent disease tendency" originating "in her hereditary tag of consumption."[33]

A quiet Unitarian service was held at Jackson's boardinghouse on August 14. Her body was then carried out of the house to be temporarily interred, and Sara Thibault and Effie McLeod spent the next four hours burning every piece of writing she had left behind, as she had instructed them to do. In October her body was transferred to a gravesite on Cheyenne Mountain, as close as proved possible to the place she had requested. Her "Last Words" were read during the simple service. This poem, which expresses a desire for a grave washed by the ordinary flow of nature, concludes:

And when, remembering me, you come some day
And stand there, speak no praise, but only say,
"How she loved us! 'T was that which made her dear!"
Those are the words that I shall joy to hear.[34]

While Jackson had hoped that her gravesite would be a humble one, it was not long before countless fans began making pilgrimages to the spot, piling up a great mound of stones and mementos to their beloved author, and taking away branches and twigs to remember her by. In 1891 William had her body removed to Evergreen Cemetery in town.

William had been prostrated with grief for many days following his wife's death. Before long, though, he regained his composure by means that would have made perfect sense to her: he went "straight to work," keeping himself "very very busy." Pausing for a moment at the end of August to console a grieving Helen Banfield, he emphasized the value of diligence. "What a blessing work is. It is the salt that saves the world," he told her. "Idle people must have a horrible time. Your Auntie never could be idle & will not be in the new life if the new order contemplates her being busy."[35] Several years later, William

Jackson and Helen Banfield were married. Together they had seven children. But perhaps their family grew too rapidly, for Helen Banfield did not possess her aunt's remarkable ability to overcome adversity. When her third daughter—Margaret—died in infancy in 1899, she killed herself.

In the weeks following his first wife's death, William had been flooded with letters of condolence from family and friends. Members of the Banfield family wrote, as did Molly Hunt and William's own sisters. Many of Jackson's old literary friends and associates expressed the love and admiration they had felt for her: letters arrived from Charles Dudley Warner, Sarah Woolsey, Kate Field, Richard Watson Gilder, Edward Everett Hale, Mary Mapes Dodge, Lucia Runkle, Martha Goddard, Edith Thomas, Thomas Niles, Jenny Abbott Johnson, Hubert Howe Bancroft, and even the journalist Alice Wellington Rollins, whose recent biographical portrait had so offended Jackson. Emily Dickinson wrote begging for some news of Jackson's final hours. "Helen of Troy will die, but Helen of Colorado, never," she would later exclaim in a draft for another letter to William. "Dear friend, can you walk, were the last words that I wrote her. Dear friend, I can fly—her immortal (soaring) reply."[36] On the day Jackson died, Thomas Wentworth Higginson had scribbled in his diary, "A strange sensation!"[37] He now sent William a copy of a sketch he had written about Jackson for the *Nation,* along with a perfunctory note of sympathy.

Elsewhere, Higginson was more effusive. He wrote a poem in memory of Jackson; and in addition to his article for the *Nation,* he wrote glowing retrospectives of her career for the *New York Evening Post,* the *Critic,* and *Century Magazine.* In this last piece, which he would later revise and include in his *Contemporaries* (1899), and also in his revised essay on Jackson for a new edition of *Short Studies of American Authors* (1883), he finally expressed some recognition that it was Jackson's prose, rather than her poetry, that most deserved attention. Still, he always continued to prize her poems; in 1890 he included four of them, as many as he allotted to any author, in his collection of *American Sonnets.* Other writers also published tributes to Jackson in the months and years following her death. Sarah Woolsey, the California writer Ina Coolbrith, Edith Thomas, Richard Watson Gilder, and Elizabeth Stuart Phelps all wrote poems about her. Charles Dudley Warner, whose later published writings about his travels in California would evince an American boosterism never seen in Jackson's writings, retraced some of his old friend's steps in "'H.H.' in Southern California," published in the *Critic* on May 14, 1887. In his 1896 multivolume *Library of the World's Best Literature,* he praised *Ramona* as ranking "among the half dozen best distinctively American stories."[38] Joaquin Miller also expressed great admiration for *Ramona,* arguing that California's regional majesty had inspired Jackson to greatness in the novel. Albion Tourgée considered *Ramona* "unquestionably the best novel yet produced by an American woman," and praised the novel's anti-imperialist intent.[39] In 1887 José

Martí, the Cuban poet, prosodist, and revolutionary, published a Spanish translation of *Ramona*. In his admiring prologue, he hinted that the novel might serve as a model for his notion of "Our America": an egalitarian, *mestizo* Latin America that might stand in opposition to the expansion and domination of Anglo-American industrial capitalism.[40] In time, Mexican and Mexican American playwrights and screenwriters would produce their own Spanish-language versions of *Ramona*.

Jackson was for many years considered a fine stylist whose poetry and prose aspiring authors would do well to imitate. At present, we give little thought to the early writers whose work most directly demonstrates her influence: the southwestern author Mary Austin, who variously praised and disparaged her predecessor;[41] the California regionalists Charles Fletcher Lummis and Gertrude Atherton; and Elaine Goodale, the poet, activist, and eventual wife of the Native American writer Charles Eastman. For several decades following her death, Jackson was lionized by critics. Beginning in the 1930s, however, as pure realism became prized in literature, she was consigned to a lowly place in literary history—condemned, as it were, to "sweeping spiders" in back rooms with other neglected authors. She was even given the wrong name, "Helen Hunt Jackson." Ever since her second marriage, when some personal friends, publishers, and critics had taken to calling her by this amalgamated name, Jackson had declared that she detested the practice. "It is not proper to keep one's first *married* name, after a second marriage," she had explained to Moncure Conway. "The name 'Hunt' no longer exists for me."[42] Later she had complained to Caroline Dall, "I am positively waging war as well as I can against peoples' habit of calling me Helen Hunt Jackson, & I hope to succeed finally in putting an end to it."[43]

Jackson would not have been pleased, either, with the way her novel *Ramona* was misinterpreted in California. At first the book's excoriation of American oppression of local Indians had caused a great deal of resentment among white settlers, as Jackson herself had been "glad" to learn.[44] In short order, though, white readers in Southern California began to dote on *Ramona*— chiefly for its love story, which gave their region a unique romantic legend, and for its mythic evocation of a glorious Hispanic colonial past. Variously labeled the "Ramona Myth" and the "fantasy heritage," a term coined by the historian Carey McWilliams in *North from Mexico* (1949), this tendency to romanticize the region's "Spanish" history provided American newcomers to California with a ready-made, usable past, one with which they could more easily identify than with the region's actual history of Native American tenure and still troubled colonial occupation. As the historian Kevin Starr has noted, "No other act of symbolic expression affected the imagination of nineteenth-century Southern California so forcibly" as *Ramona*.[45]

In March 1885 the Atchison, Topeka, and Santa Fe Railroad arrived in Southern California. A rate war with the established Southern Pacific ensued, prompting more and more Americans to migrate to the region. During the eighties, Los Angeles's population grew fivefold, reaching 50,000 by the end of the decade. In this heady atmosphere, *Ramona* was exploited by local entrepreneurs and civic organizations as a tourist draw, for newcomers and visitors who adored Jackson's best-seller were eager to pay homage at local sites rendered sacred by real or trumped-up association with the novel. And white Southern Californians were not the only people interested in profiting from *Ramona*. Señor del Valle, the owner of Rancho Camulos, was at first disgusted by the tourists who came to see the "real" Moreno estate. Before long, however, he began taking pride in his association with the romantic Ramona Myth, even commissioning "Home of Ramona" labels for the citrus fruits produced on his ranch. Some local Indians also asserted their right to a share in the profits from Jackson's novel. Ramona Lubo, the widow of Juan Diego, the murdered Cahuilla Indian whose death had inspired the death of Jackson's hero Alessandro, allowed tourists to photograph her for a fee and several times posed as an exhibit at local fairs.[46] Obviously, such an outcome could not have been farther from Jackson's original intention in writing *Ramona*. Yet in the end, her one novel to offer an explicit protest against the spread of American civilization had the same paradoxical effect as much of her travel writing: *Ramona* drew outsiders to Southern California to further endanger and exploit the very people and places she had wished to protect.

There are more positive reasons to remember Jackson. Her reform writings were progressive for their time, and they did help lead the American government and people toward a better awareness of the struggles of Native Americans. They also had some practical results: in 1891 the passage of the Act for the Relief of the Mission Indians, which was based on Jackson's 1883 official report, led to the setting aside of vast tracts of land in reservations that still exist today. *A Century of Dishonor* is now in print again and receiving recognition for its groundbreaking attempt to document American mistreatment of Indians. Many of Jackson's other writings are also of continued interest. Because her tendency toward idealism and her concern for cheerful perseverance make much of her poetry and short fiction seem dated, it is unlikely that her work in those genres will ever again have any broad appeal. Still, Jackson, as Higginson himself once publicly insisted, was not simply "a conventional Sunday-school saint."[47] Her confidence in asserting her professional rights, and the prominent position she achieved in her time, should be remembered by readers and writers interested in American literary history and women's literary history. Her first novel, *Mercy Philbrick's Choice* (1876), offers rare testimony to a woman's coming-of-age as an artist. Much of her travel writing, especially her writing on the American West, is of real historic value.

Ramona is an especially powerful book. Even while it is Jackson's most typically "sentimental" work, it offers a vision for multicultural America that still resonates today. It also initiated a long line of dystopian fiction about Southern California. Jackson believed that California had been created a kind of paradise on earth, a place that would always inspire new people to seek their fortunes there. Yet she also believed that no amount of personal dignity and perseverance on the part of California's Indians could succeed alone in maintaining this paradise in the face of American rapacity. Displaced, disillusioned, and increasingly alone, her heroes Alessandro and Ramona wander helplessly through Southern California, longing for a past golden age, for connection to the land, to community, to history. So many subsequent writers have created dystopian portraits of Southern California that their combined efforts might well constitute an archetypal vision of the place. Witness, for example, the classic depictions of disappointment in California that appeared in a single decade, in Nathanael West's *Day of the Locust* (1939), F. Scott Fitzgerald's *Last Tycoon* (1941), John Steinbeck's *Grapes of Wrath* (1939), and Evelyn Waugh's *Loved One* (1948). In *Ramona,* as in all of her regionalist writing, Jackson began a struggle to come to terms with an America undergoing rapid change and development, a concern that will no doubt continue to command the attention of readers far into the future.

Acknowledgments

This book originated in my doctoral dissertation. I wish to thank my dissertation advisor, Sacvan Bercovitch, and my second reader, Werner Sollors, for offering me kind instruction throughout my graduate years, for reading and rereading this book, and for continuing to inspire me with the example of their superior work. I am grateful to Harvard University and the program in the History of American Civilization for providing me with the opportunity and financial support to pursue graduate studies. And I thank Christine McFadden, the program administrator, for her guidance and heartening good cheer.

Monica McCormick, my editor at the University of California Press, has sustained this project with her insight and enthusiasm. I have also valued the assistance of my copyeditor, Alice Falk; my project editor, Sue Heinemann; and my publicist, Lorraine Weston.

I am deeply indebted to Anne Borchardt, my literary agent, for all of her work on my behalf and for her patient interest in my writing.

Ginny Kiefer, who recently retired from her position as curator of Special Collections at the Tutt Library of Colorado College, welcomed me to Colorado Springs in 1993 when I first began research for my dissertation; she greeted me again years later as I gathered illustrations for this book. Her gracious, expert archival assistance has made my work possible. I also very much appreciate the efforts of her successor, Jessy Randall, and of the dozens of other librarians and archivists who facilitated my research in their collections or mailed me photocopies of Jackson materials. Although space limitations prevent me from mentioning each of them by name, I offer each my sincere thanks.

The pleasure of friendship with Bill Jackson—grandson of Helen's second husband William Jackson and his second wife, who was Helen's niece—and Bill's wife, Patricia, has enlivened and enriched my undertaking. Bill grew up in the Jackson home in Colorado Springs. During his childhood many of Helen Jackson's possessions remained in place in the house, including some of the dried plants with which she had decorated, a bust of her son Rennie, and a corner room of bookcases, which she had dubbed "flirtation corner." When the Jackson house was demolished in 1961, four of its rooms were reconstructed inside the local Pioneers Museum, including this corner book nook containing over 600 of Jackson's old books. I am grateful for all Bill has done to help me with this project.

Valerie Sherer Mathes, Susan Gillman, Susan Coultrap-McQuinn, Carole Schmudde, and Georgiana Strickland, all of whom have written about aspects of Jackson's career, have offered friendly replies to my inquiries and provided me with insight through their work. Phil Brigandi—historian, expert on *Ramona* and Jackson's activities in Southern California, and curator of the Ramona Pageant Museum in Hemet, California—has done even more. He twice read this book in manuscript, offering useful suggestions, he devoted an entire day to showing me places Jackson knew in Riverside and San Diego Counties, and he has many times helped me immensely by sharing his knowledge and opinions. His passion and sense of fun about Jackson studies are contagious.

I am obliged to Stanford University's history department, and in particular to George Fredrickson, for accepting me as a visiting scholar in 1998. While revising this book, I found the advice and writings of Gerald Vizenor particularly helpful in my effort to evaluate Jackson's interest in Native American perseverance, and Anne Goldman's perceptive comments on my manuscript helped me envision new contexts for Jackson's writings on the West.

I am always thankful for the love and support of my parents, Joan and Richard Phillips, my newer parents, Phyllis and Fred Ross, my sisters Sarah and Liz, and grandmothers Adele Phillips and Frances Pomer. Trista Conger has enchanted me with her theatrical play about Jackson. Many other friends have given me suggestions for this project and willingly tolerated my long obsession with it, especially Nicole Huang, Alexis McCrossen, Margot Livesey, Bethany Rogers, Cynthia Wachtell, Becky Soglin, Celia Bloomfield, Lina Lee, Alex Regan, Serena Algozer, Kristen Steck, Jennifer Portillo, Becky Bjork, Lena Deevy, and Charley Haley. Jessica Dorman, after helping me make it through graduate school, has now helped me finish this book. I owe her a great deal and I cherish our friendship. Olga Carolina Toval, Alma Gonzalez, and my cousin Mary Rozance have helped me enormously by offering loving care to my children during my hours at my desk. Sam and Jonathan, the delight of my life, did their own part for this book by finally learning to sleep through the night. My husband Michael Ross has for many years endured the formidable presence of Helen Jackson in our home. Thank you, Mike, for making it possible for me to get my work done, and for the joy you've given me outside of working hours.

Notes

PROLOGUE

1. In 1869 Jackson claimed that although she had tried on various occasions to keep a diary, she had never succeeded. Years later, in 1881, she lamented this failure for the loss that it meant to her stores of literary material, admitting to her mentor Thomas Wentworth Higginson, "Every now and then I get spasms of remorse that I do not keep diaries" (see Jackson to circle of friends, May 22, 1869, Yale; Jackson to Higginson, July 22, 1881, Harvard).

2. The Tutt Library, collection HHJ1, houses eight of Jackson's pocket date books, one from 1852 and others from 1876 to 1878 and 1880 to 1883. The date book from 1852, before Jackson became a professional writer, comes closest to approximating a journal. But even in it, Jackson mostly records her doings; she writes little about her feelings, observations, or opinions. In the later date books she simply dashes off brief and often cryptic notes on some, but not all, of her days: her comings and goings, the weather, the names of people with whom she dines or visits, her pleasure outings, her sore throats and colds, and, occasionally, the name of a piece of writing she has completed or mailed off to a publisher. Here is a typical entry, from a Colorado day in 1876: "Reached Pueblo—Horrible cold—Mrs. Malbone's" (Jackson, December 22, 1876, 1876 date book, HHJ1).

3. Jackson to Ann Banfield, April 12, 1869, HHJ2.

4. Jackson to William Jackson, August 16, 1880, WSJ1.

5. Jackson to Charles Dudley Warner, January 10, [1883], Trinity. Jackson refers to Whittier's concern about the "new terrors added to death."

6. Jackson, instructions to William Jackson about the final dispersal of her goods, [1885], HHJ4.

7. Thomas Wentworth Higginson, quoted in Millicent Todd Bingham, *Ancestors' Brocades: The Literary Debut of Emily Dickinson* (1945; reprint, New York: Dover, 1967), 237.

8. Jackson to Ann Banfield, July 25, 1878, HHJ5.

9. Jackson, "Glass Houses" and "The Old-Clothes Monger in Journalism," in *Bits of Talk about Home Matters* (Boston: Roberts Brothers, 1873), 212, 218. Here and in subsequent notes I do not indicate the specific signatures under which Jackson published her various writings, as these may be found in the bibliography.

10. Jackson to William Jackson, [1880], WSJ1; Jackson to Joseph Gilder, May 20, 1885, NYP.

11. Jackson to Whitelaw Reid, June 25, 1879, Congress.

12. Jackson to Joseph Gilder, June 3, 1885, NYP.

13. Helen Bartlett, "A Famous Literary Woman," *Journalist* (New York), January 3, 1885. Jackson refutes Bartlett's claims in a letter to Charles Dudley Warner, February 8, 1885, Trinity.

14. Jackson to Joseph Gilder, June 3 and May 20, 1885, NYP; see also Alice Wellington Rollins, "Authors at Home: Mrs. Jackson ('H.H.') at Colorado Springs," *Critic,* April 25, 1885. Jackson succeeded in convincing Gilder not to include Rollins's piece in a projected volume of author portraits.

15. Jackson to Charles Dudley Warner, February 8, 1885, Trinity.

16. Jackson, "A Burns Pilgrimage," in *Glimpses of Three Coasts* (1886; reprint, Boston: Roberts Brothers, 1891), 153–74.

Chapter 1. Staying Power

1. Upon Jackson's birth, her father wrote a letter stating that she had arrived at 11:30 in the evening on October 14, 1830 (Nathan Fiske to Martha Vinal, October 15, 1830, HHJ1). Jackson always celebrated her birthday on October 15, however. Later, for reasons that remain unclear, she did much to obfuscate her date of birth and age, including allowing many intimate friends to believe that she had been born in 1831.

2. I am indebted to Sheila M. Rothman, the author of *Living in the Shadow of Death: Tuberculosis and the Social Experience of Illness in American History* (New York: HarperCollins, 1994), for her important discovery that Jackson's mother secretly wrote and published fiction. Rothman uses Deborah Fiske as a case study for her chapter titled "The Female Invalid."

3. Nathan Fiske to Deborah Fiske, December 6, 1829, HHJ1; Deborah Fiske to Nathan Fiske, [1833], HHJ1.

4. Jackson, "A Christmas Tree for Cats," in *Bits of Talk in Verse and Prose for Young Folks* (Boston: Roberts Brothers, 1876), 21–22.

5. Heman Humphrey, *The Woman That Feareth the Lord, a Discourse Delivered at the Funeral of Mrs. D. W. V. Fiske, 21 February 1844* (Amherst, Mass.: J. S. and C. Adams, 1844), 33.

6. Deborah Fiske to Ann Scholfield, [November 1843], HHJ1; Nathan Fiske, journal, HHJ1.

7. Jackson to Nathan Fiske, November 18, 1841, HHJ1.

8. Jackson to Deborah Fiske, [1841], HHJ1.

9. Jackson to Deborah Fiske, [May 1843], HHJ1.

10. Nathan Fiske, journal, HHJ1.

11. Jackson to Henry Root, n.d., HHJ6.

12. Deborah Fiske to Ellen Scholfield, n.d., HHJ1.

13. Deborah Fiske to Jackson, [May 1843], HHJ1.

14. In adult life, Jackson apparently charged friends touring Palestine with the task of visiting her father's grave, as both Charles Dudley Warner and Robert H. Lamborn sent her flowers gathered at the site.

15. Jackson to Julius Palmer, December 16, 1849 and October 13, 1851, HHJ2.

16. I have been able to locate only Jackson's letters to Julius Palmer dated through 1856, none from the final fifteen years of Palmer's life.

17. Jackson to Julius Palmer, March 8, 1850, HHJ2.

18. Jackson to Hannah Shepard Terry, December 2, 1851, Jones.

19. Jackson to Lucy Palmer, n.d., HHJ2.

20. Jackson to Lucy Palmer, n.d., HHJ2.

21. Jackson to Lucy Palmer, December 23, 1852, HHJ2.

22. Jackson to Ann Banfield, n.d., transcript, WSJ2.

23. Edward Hunt to Alexander Dallas Bache, June 13, 1857, Congress.

24. Jackson to Lucy Palmer, n.d., fragment, HHJ2.

25. Jackson to William Church, March 20, 1864, NYP.

26. Jackson to Julius Palmer, March 26, 1850, HHJ2.

27. Jackson to William Church, March 20, 1864, NYP. According to Valerie Sherer Mathes, the scientists Alexander Twining and William Trowbridge did attempt to carry on Hunt's work; see Jackson, *The Indian Reform Letters of Helen Hunt Jackson: 1879–1885*, ed. Mathes (Norman: University of Oklahoma Press, 1998), 162.

28. Jackson to Eliot McCormick, March 14, 1882, in McCormick, "H.H.: A Reminiscence," *Christian Union*, September 17, 1885.

29. Jackson quoting Deborah Fiske, in Jackson to Deborah Fiske, October 6, [1841], HHJ1.

30. Edward Hitchcock, Jr., quoted in Jay Leyda, *The Years and Hours of Emily Dickinson* (New Haven, Conn.: Yale University Press, 1960), 1:xlvi.

31. Jackson, "The Naughtiest Day of My Life, and What Came of It," *St. Nicholas*, September and October 1880.

32. Jackson to Ann Banfield, March 22, 1849, transcript, WSJ2.

33. Jackson to Julius Palmer, July 5, 1849, BP (this and all subsequent BP letters courtesy of the Trustees); Jackson to Julius Palmer, n.d., HHJ2.

34. Jackson to Ann Banfield, April 30, 1867, HHJ2.

35. Jackson to Kate Field, September 6, 1868, BP.

36. Susan Coolidge [Sarah Woolsey], introduction to *Ramona*, by Jackson, illustrated by Henry Sandham, Monterey ed. (Boston: Little, Brown, 1900), vi, xiv, x.

37. Jackson to Abbot Kinney, September 28, 1884, in James, p. 339.

38. Jackson to Ann Banfield, April 8, 1872, WSJ2; Jackson to Jenny Fox, July 3, 1870, AAS.

39. Jackson to Susan Lee Warner, July 19, 1884, Trinity.

40. Jackson to Kate Field, July 11, 1866, BP; Jackson to Ann Banfield, January 20, 1879, HHJ5.

41. Jackson, "Friends of the Prisoners," in *Bits of Talk about Home Matters* (Boston: Roberts Brothers, 1873), 120. This essay first appeared in the *New York Independent*, March 10, 1870.

42. Jackson to Mary Sprague, March 23, 1872, Huntington.

43. Jackson to Dr. Nichols, December 30, 1873, Princeton.

44. Jackson to Ann Banfield, May 7, 1872, WSJ2.

45. Jackson to Ann Scholfield, January 14, 1856, WSJ2.

46. Jackson to Sarah Orne Jewett, April 21, 1867, Huntington.

47. Jackson to Dr. Nichols, December 30, 1873, Princeton; Jackson to William Jackson, July 24, 1880, WSJ1; Jackson to Kate Field, April 23, 1874, BP.

48. Jackson to Julius Palmer, n.d., HHJ2.

49. Jackson to Joseph Benson Gilder, November 7, 1881, NYP.

50. Jackson to William Jackson, July 1, 1880, WSJ1; Jackson to Ray and Ann Palmer, June 16, 1861, NYU; Jackson to Charlotte Cushman, May 17, 1871, Congress.

51. Although Jackson once visited spas in Badgastein, Austria, and Great Malvern, England, she was highly skeptical of the water cures favored by many invalids during the nineteenth century. She never even tried the popular waters at Manitou Springs, Colorado. "I would die before I touched a drop," she told a friend. "I am a homeopathist" (Jackson to Kate Field, April 23, 1874, BP).

52. Commenting on "the mysterious interdependence of soul and body in the artist nature," Jackson once told a friend, "I, my whole *self,* can cease to exist, in a twenty four hours time, if the rascally mucous membrane in which I am sheathed, sees fit to swell up a millionth of an inch, or turn red, a shade or two!" (Jackson to Charlotte Cushman, n.d., fragment, Congress).

53. Jackson to Edward Seymour, [October 1873], BYU.

54. Jackson to Charlotte Cushman, October 28, 1874, Congress; Jackson to Ann Palmer, August 8, 1852, Huntington; Jackson to Julius Palmer, May 14, 1851, HHJ2; Jackson to Lucy Palmer, July 3, 1852, HHJ2.

55. Jackson to Moncure Conway, October 28, 1884, Columbia.

56. Jackson, "A Parable," in *Bits of Talk for Young Folks* (1876), 158–59.

57. Susan Coolidge, "H.H.," *New York Independent,* September 3, 1885.

58. Jackson to William Jackson, [August 1879], WSJ1.

59. Jackson, "The Naughtiest Day of My Life, and What Came of It," *St. Nicholas,* September 1880.

60. Coolidge, introduction to *Ramona,* xv.

61. Jackson to James T. Fields, October 11, 1870, Huntington; Jackson to Charles Dudley Warner, July 29, 1874, Trinity.

62. Jackson to Elizabeth Benham, July 7, 1856, Congress.

63. Jackson to Hannah Shepard Terry, December 2, 1851, Jones; and Jackson, Our Book Table, "William P. Atkinson's 'On the Right Use of Books' " and "The Family Library of British Poetry," *Denver Tribune,* March 9 and February 23, 1879. "A Protest against the Spread of Civilization" appeared in the *New York Evening Post,* August 29, 1867.

64. Jackson to Thomas Bailey Aldrich, January 25, 1884, Harvard.

65. Jackson to Edward Seymour, [October 1873], BYU.

66. That Jackson's heroines are exemplary because they behave well, even though most of them eschew traditional religion, reflects Jackson's participation in a shift in contemporary American values, away from widespread Calvinist belief in salvation by grace alone toward belief in salvation by good works. Josephine Donovan describes this transformation as one of the "philosophical issues endemic to American local color literature" (*New England Local Color Literature: A Women's Tradition* [New York: Frederick Ungar, 1983], 8).

67. Jackson to Abigail Williams May, August 17, 1873, Schlesinger.

68. Jackson, review of *Ploughed Under,* by William Justin Harsha, *Critic,* February 26, 1881.

69. Jackson to Henry Dawes, December 10, 1880, Congress.

70. "Mission Indians" was the general term applied by Americans to the surviving native peoples of Southern California in the late nineteenth century. Many of their villages had come under the influence of the Franciscan missions established along the coast in the late eighteenth century. In keeping with Jackson's habit, in this book I designate some of Southern California's tribes and bands by the missions with which they were once associated. For more accurate designations of these tribes, and a helpful map, see Malcolm Margolin, ed., *The Way We Lived: California Indian Stories, Songs, and Reminiscences,* rev. ed. (Berkeley: California Historical Society and Heyday Books, 1993).

71. Valerie Sherer Mathes discusses the atypical nature of Jackson's reform work in her commentary in *The Indian Reform Letters of Helen Hunt Jackson,* and especially *Helen Hunt Jackson and Her Indian Reform Legacy* (1990; reprint, Norman: University of Oklahoma Press, 1997). In one late private letter, Jackson did express approval of Indian boarding schools (Jackson to Mary Sheriff, January 20, 1884, Huntington), and she was pleased with the early activities of the Women's National Indian Association. In general, though, any desire on her part to see Indians behave more like white Americans seems to have stemmed not so much from assimilationism as from her belief that Americans would treat Indians more fairly if they could only be made to understand, as she once explained to a Cahuilla child, that Indians could "do all things as well as the Americans do" (Jackson to Leonicio Lugo, July 1, 1883, in "Indian Has Letter Penned in 1883 by Author of Ramona," *Hemet News,* April 15, 1932).

72. Jackson to Amelia Stone Quinton, October 17, 1883, Bancroft.

73. Jackson to Whitelaw Reid, December 1, 1880, Congress. Jackson told Secretary of the Interior Henry Teller that the agricultural Soboba Indians of Southern California's San Jacinto Valley did not "want a land title in common with their tribe, any more than you would want a title in common with the Central City people, or Mr. Jackson with those of Colorado Springs" (Jackson to Teller, June 11, 1882, transcript, NatArch, #11429-[11701]-1882, Special Case 31). In fact, most Southern California Indians did desire individual ownership of their lands, and allotment had more positive results there than in many other places. See Florence Connolly Shipek, *Pushed into the Rocks: Southern California Indian Land Tenure, 1769–1986* (Lincoln: University of Nebraska Press, 1987), esp. 152.

74. Jackson to Antonio and Mariana Coronel, September 4, 1884, in Lindley, p. 206.

75. Jackson, "The Indian Problem: How Secretary Schurz Would Solve It," *New York Tribune,* February 12, 1880.

76. Carlyle Channing Davis and William A. Alderson, *The True Story of Ramona* (New York: Dodge, 1914), 10–11.

77. Governor Peter Burnett, "Message to the California State Legislature," January 7, 1851, *California State Senate Journal,* 1851, 15; quoted in Albert L. Hurtado, *Indian Survival on the California Frontier* (New Haven: Yale University Press, 1988), 135.

78. "The Indian Agency," *San Luis Rey Star,* August 4, 1883. Jackson was also attacked by "Q." in "An Indian Commission," *San Diego Union,* June 1, 1883; and in "Trouble in the Indian Service," *San Bernardino Times,* date unknown, which Jackson enclosed in a letter to Hiram Price, July 27, 1883, NatArch, #14177-1883. The previous year, a reporter for the *Los Angeles Times* had shown more sympathy for her and her reform work in "Helen Hunt's Last Book," *Los Angeles Times,* January 15, 1882.

79. Mary H. Wills, *A Winter in California* (Norristown, Pa.: the author, 1889), 54-55.

80. The terms *Californio* and *Californiana* are sometimes used to refer strictly to nineteenth-century persons of Mexican or Spanish descent *born* in California, and sometimes applied (as here) to any relatively wealthy nineteenth-century Hispanic Californians.

81. Jackson to unknown recipient, January 22, 1885, in "Helen Jackson," *Literary World,* May 29, 1886.

82. Elizabeth B. Custer, "Ramona's Land: Camulos, the Home of Ramona, as Seen by the Widow of General Custer," *Boston Evening Transcript,* May 14, 1887. Twenty years later, public prejudice was still such that George Wharton James, writing about Jackson's novel, felt compelled to prove that real Indians could be as "honest" and "loving" as Ramona and Alessandro (see *Through Ramona's Country* [1908; reprint, Boston: Little, Brown, 1913], 83-93).

83. Jackson to unknown recipient, January 13, 1885, Princeton.

84. Thomas Wentworth Higginson, "Helen Jackson," *Nation,* August 20, 1885.

85. Flora Haynes Apponyi, "The Last Days of Mrs. Helen Hunt Jackson," and Millicent Shinn, "The Verse and Prose of 'H.H.,' " *Overland Monthly Magazine,* September 1885.

86. James D. Hart, *The Popular Book: A History of America's Literary Taste* (New York: Oxford University Press, 1950), 183.

87. Herbert Jenkins to William Jackson, September 25, 1936, WSJ1.

88. Before the 1930s Jackson's work was occasionally dismissed as unrealistic, but such interpretations did not then represent a consensus of critical opinion. For example, in seeking to discredit Jackson's *Century of Dishonor,* Theodore Roosevelt argued that it had been written by a "sentimentalist" (*The Winning of the West* [New York: G. P. Putnam's Sons, 1889], 1:288-90).

89. Original dust-jacket copy for Ruth Odell, *Helen Hunt Jackson (H.H.)* (New York: D. Appleton-Century, 1939).

90. Howard Mumford Jones, review of *Helen Hunt Jackson (H.H.),* by Ruth Odell, *Boston Evening Transcript,* April 22, 1939. *Ramona*'s quality, Jones claimed, had nothing to do with Jackson, but was "miraculous." As evidence for the miracle, he noted that Jackson "was never to do anything as good again." Given that Jackson was ill when *Ramona* was published, and died within a year, it would have been "miraculous" indeed had she produced another major work. Other midcentury critics, including Ludwig Lewisohn, Wallace Stegner, and Richard Chase, were similarly dismissive of Jackson's career, though Stegner, himself a western novelist, offered genuine praise for *Ramona* in Robert E. Spiller et al., eds., *Literary History of the United States,* rev. ed. (New York: Macmillan, 1953), 869.

91. In the 1970s Ann Douglas echoed earlier complaints against women's domestic fiction as evincing a debased mentality in *The Feminization of American Cul-*

ture (New York: Knopf, 1978), but other scholars—such as Nina Baym, in *Woman's Fiction: A Guide to Novels by and about Women in America, 1820–1870* (New York: Knopf, 1978)—began to argue that nineteenth-century women's fiction, so often dismissed as all of a kind, was in fact diverse and thematically complex.

92. Shirley Samuels, introduction to *The Culture of Sentiment: Race, Gender, and Sentimentality in Nineteenth-Century America,* ed. Samuels (New York: Oxford University Press, 1992), 6, 4. See also Jane Tompkins, *Sensational Designs: The Cultural Work of American Fiction, 1790–1860* (New York: Oxford University Press, 1985).

93. Jackson, "Hysteria in Literature," in *Bits of Talk about Home Matters* (1873), 194, 198, 196.

94. In 1884 Jackson was temporarily enraged with Annie Fields, a poet and the wife of Boston publisher James T. Fields, for publishing an article that mentioned Emerson's admiration for both Jackson and Felicia Hemans. Though Hemans exerted an undeniable influence on women's poetry in the nineteenth century, and though Jackson herself had kept a two-volume copy of Hemans's *Poems* in her personal library as a child, she considered Fields's coupling "as deft a blow as could well be dealt" to her own reputation. When the *Atlantic* editor Thomas Bailey Aldrich interceded, claiming Fields had meant only to "illustrate Emerson's whimsical taste," Jackson replied indignantly: "I am so egregiously vain, that I dislike sharing with Mrs. Felicia Hemans the conspicuous honor of illustrating that whimsical taste!" (Jackson to Aldrich, February 23 and March 10, 1884, Harvard).

95. Jackson to William Jackson, December 29, 1879, WSJ1; Jackson to Mary Mapes Dodge, June 5, 1874, Princeton; Jackson to William Church, May 9, 1868, NYP.

96. Jackson to William Jackson, December 19, 1879, WSJ1; Jackson, "American Women," *New York World,* July 17, 1870.

97. Jackson, "A Calendar of Sunrises in Colorado," in *Bits of Travel at Home* (1878; reprint, Boston: Roberts Brothers, 1880), 413. For a study of more conventional views of domesticity, see Barbara Welter, *Dimity Convictions: The American Woman in the Nineteenth Century* (Athens: Ohio University Press, 1976).

98. Eric Sundquist has noted that "those in power (say, white urban males) have more often been judged 'realists,' while those removed from the seats of power (say, Midwesterners, blacks, immigrants, or women) have been categorized as regionalists" ("Realism and Regionalism," in *Columbia Literary History of the United States,* ed. Emory Elliott [New York: Columbia University Press, 1988], 503). Cathy N. Davidson and Linda Wagner-Martin make a similar point about the pejorative uses of both "regionalism" and "sentimentalism" in their *Oxford Companion to Women's Writing in the United States* (New York: Oxford University Press, 1995), 752, 786–88.

99. Richard H. Brodhead, *Cultures of Letters: Scenes of Reading and Writing in Nineteenth-Century America* (Chicago: University of Chicago Press, 1993), 119, 116.

100. For a good discussion of the roots of regionalism in the realistic components of early women's writing and in the frontier humor tradition, and for an overview of recent scholarship on regionalism, see Donna M. Campbell, *Resisting Regionalism: Gender and Naturalism in American Fiction, 1885–1915* (Athens:

Ohio University Press, 1997). For further information on regionalism as a women's tradition, see Donovan, *New England Local Color Literature.*

101. On the new artistic prestige accorded to women regionalists, and not to female writers considered "sentimental," see, among other sources, Elaine Showalter, *Sister's Choice: Tradition and Change in American Women's Writing* (Oxford: Clarendon Press, 1991), esp. 67.

102. Jackson to Thomas Bailey Aldrich, November 29, 1882, Harvard.

103. Jackson to Charles Dudley Warner, August 13, 1883, Trinity.

104. Jackson to Thomas Wentworth Higginson, February 5, 1884, in Higginson, "How Ramona Was Written," *Atlantic Monthly,* November 1900.

105. See Jackson to Thomas Bailey Aldrich, February 9, 1885, Harvard; and Jackson, *Bits of Travel* (Boston: J. R. Osgood, 1872), 273.

106. Jackson, review of *Overland,* by John De Forest, *Scribner's Monthly,* February 1872.

107. Jackson, review of "William Hunt's Pictures," *Scribner's Monthly,* February 1872. Jackson's praise of Hunt's idealism appeared in the same issue of *Scribner's Monthly* as her commendation of De Forest's "sectional" realism.

108. Jackson to Thomas Bailey Aldrich, July 16, 1881, Harvard. As it happens, the essay under consideration is not an American regional essay but a European one: "The Katrina Saga," published in the *Atlantic Monthly* of September and October 1881, and reprinted in the posthumous *Glimpses of Three Coasts* (Boston: Roberts Brothers, 1886).

109. Both "Joe Hale's Red Stockings" and "A Four Leaved Clover," discussed in chapter 7, are collected in Jackson, *Saxe Holm's Stories, Second Series* (1878; reprint, New York: Charles Scribner's Sons, 1899).

110. In their anthology *American Women Regionalists, 1850–1910* (New York: W. W. Norton, 1992), and elsewhere, Judith Fetterley and Marjorie Pryse have recommended that the term "regionalist" be applied only to writers who express sympathetic identification with their local subjects, and that the term "local color" be used for writers who express a more distanced, condescending attitude. While I appreciate the important contributions Fetterley and Pryse have made to regionalist scholarship, I believe the distinction they make is too subjective. Not all readers will agree on whether a particular writer demonstrates "correct" forms of empathy, and focusing on such criteria can degenerate into essentialist efforts to determine which writers have the authority to write about which places. Moreover, the focus on sympathy precludes other authorial attitudes toward region (such as ironic distance) that are just as legitimate for not being strictly adulatory. Indeed, complex reactions to a place often indicate a continued involvement more intense than simple fondness, as in Jackson's New England novels, where she writes with a mixture of sympathy and hatred for the local culture she knew in youth. See also Donovan, *New England Local Color Literature,* and Sherrie A. Inness and Diana Royer, eds., *Breaking Boundaries: New Perspectives on Women's Regional Writing* (Iowa City: University of Iowa Press, 1997).

111. Nancy Glazener, *Reading for Realism: The History of a U.S. Literary Institution, 1850–1910* (Durham: Duke University Press, 1997).

112. Brodhead, *Cultures of Letters,* 120, 177, 144, 134; on the "supersession of local cultures," see Richard H. Brodhead, "Literature and Culture," in Elliott, *Columbia Literary History of the United States,* 474. Brodhead identifies Jackson

as a regionalist in *Cultures of Letters*. See also Benedict Anderson, *Imagined Communities: Reflections on the Origin and Spread of Nationalism,* rev. ed. (London: Verso, 1991).

113. Sundquist, "Realism and Regionalism," 503; Amy Kaplan, "Nation, Region, and Empire," in *The Columbia History of the American Novel,* ed. Emory Elliott (New York: Columbia University Press, 1991), 251. Kaplan identifies Jackson as a regionalist in this essay. Elsewhere, she has described all realism, not simply regionalism, as a "strategy for imagining and managing the threats of social change" (Kaplan, *The Social Construction of American Realism* [Chicago: University of Chicago Press, 1988], 10).

114. In a study of the forces responsible for the surge in dialect literature following the Civil War, which included new developments in the field of linguistics, Gavin Jones has argued that all nineteenth-century dialect literature represented an "ambivalent power," capable of both bolstering and undermining linguistic, and therefore social, hierarchies. He also explains, however, that in the latter half of the century, "there was an overall movement away from demeaning appropriations of vernacular voices" on the part of authors. Critics of this period likewise viewed vernacular literature "as part of a sincere, democratic interest in recording the speechways of subaltern cultural groups" (Jones, *Strange Talk: The Politics of Dialect Literature in Gilded Age America* [Berkeley: University of California Press, 1999], 13, 211, 8).

115. I do not have space to elaborate on recent developments in the theory of travel literature, where the complex issues of race, class, gender, and nation that implicate both writers and subjects of travel literature have been analyzed. For theories of travel writing as a tool of imperialism, see esp. Renato Rosaldo's chapter on "imperialist nostalgia" in *Culture and Truth: The Remaking of Social Analysis* (Boston: Beacon Press, 1989), and Mary Louise Pratt, *Imperial Eyes: Travel Writing and Transculturation* (London: Routledge, 1992).

116. Jackson to Thomas Bailey Aldrich, May 13, 1882, Harvard.

117. Thomas Wentworth Higginson, *Short Studies of American Authors,* rev. ed. (Boston: Lee and Shepard, 1888), 45.

118. On January 31, 1882, Jackson writes from Santa Barbara: "Interesting people in hovel at top of Pass—had the 'Blind Spinner' pasted in a scrapbook." On March 24, 1882, she records her visit to an "adobe shanty" in the countryside surrounding Riverside, where "four lonely children—3 girls & a boy . . . underfed faces . . . had all read my books" (HHJ1).

119. Jackson to William Jackson, August 18, 1879, WSJ1.

CHAPTER 2. LESSONS FROM FATHER AND MOTHER

1. Nathan Fiske had earned only between $800 and $1,000 per year, and he left behind little savings. Before her first marriage, Jackson received through her guardian Julius Palmer some $100 per year, which apparently came from her father's estate. At the same time, David Vinal provided for her board and expenses with some $400 dollars every year. When Vinal died, he left Jackson property in Boston's South End valued at approximately $32,000 (most of it mortgaged) and more than $20,000 in cash. Throughout her life, Jackson received quarterly interest payments on this inheritance, along with other personal banking services, from a succession of Boston-based financial trustees: first from her guardian Julius Palmer; next, upon Palmer's death in 1872, from his son Julius, Jr., and an associ-

ate, Mr. Poor; then, when she and Ann became dissatisfied with Julius, Jr.'s handling of their investments, from Charles Tufts; and finally, beginning in 1879, from Charles Fiske, a paternal relative. During her marriage to Hunt, she received some $400 per year as a supplement to Edward Hunt's annual income of $1,400. Following Hunt's death in 1863, she and Rennie lived on her trust income alone. It was not until after the Civil War ended that she began to write for publication; she was then also given a lump military widow's payment of $500 along with a monthly "widow's claim" of $25. During Julius Palmer, Jr.'s tenure as trustee, she received between $2,000 and $2,600 in interest per year, and during the tenure of Charles Fiske, she continued to receive an average of $2,000 per year—amounts that allowed for comfortable living. (Letters and other documents providing information on Jackson's finances are housed in the Tutt Library.)

2. The earlier Nathan Fiske, who was born in 1733 and died in 1799, anticipated his great-nephew in his orthodoxy, his belief in the importance of cheerfulness and industry, and many of his literary tastes. One hundred fifty-one of his newspaper essays, originally published under a variety of pseudonyms, are gathered in a two-volume publication titled *The Moral Monitor; or a Collection of Essays on Various Subjects* (Worcester, Mass.: Isaiah Thomas, 1801). In these essays, the elder Fiske sounds like the younger in his desire to promote what he calls "the union of piety and poetry." He insists that all good writing, indeed everything worth knowing, leads to "just ideas of God," and that any writer who gives "loose reins to an unhallowed imagination" is to be rejected (1:99, 2:124, 1:154). It is not known whether Jackson ever read *The Moral Monitor*.

3. Elias Cornelius, *Sermon, Delivered in the Tabernacle Church, Salem, Mass., Sept. 25, 1823* . . . (Boston: Crocker and Brewster, 1823), 3.

4. According to Cynthia Griffin Wolff, Amherst's population "increased by only 575 persons, from 2,631 to 3,206," from the year of Jackson's birth until 1860, even as "neighboring Northampton, which boasted a number of local industries and factories, nearly doubled in size" (*Emily Dickinson* [1986; reprint, Reading, Mass.: Addison-Wesley, 1988], 557 n. 3).

5. Heman Humphrey, *Memoir of Rev. Nathan W. Fiske, Professor of Intellectual and Moral Philosophy in Amherst College; Together with Selections from His Sermons and Other Writings* (Amherst, Mass.: J. S. & C. Adams, 1850), 83. Along with his remembrances of Fiske, Humphrey's *Memoir* includes a selection of Fiske's sermons, two of his lectures, and excerpts from the private journals Fiske kept with some regularity beginning in college. Three of Fiske's actual journals are housed in HHJ1.

6. Ibid., 83, 76–78.

7. Edward Hitchcock, *Reminiscences of Amherst College, Historical, Scientific, Biographical, and Autobiographical: Also, of Other and Wider Life Experiences* (Northampton, Mass.: Bridgman & Childs, 1863), 30–31.

8. On Fiske's nickname among his students, "Kai Gar" (formed from two Greek particles), see William Gardiner Hammond, *Remembrance of Amherst, An Undergraduate's Diary, 1846–1848*, ed. George F. Whicher (New York: Columbia University Press, 1946), 29, 289 n. 5; Claude Moore Fuess, *Amherst: The Story of a New England College* (Boston: Little, Brown, 1935), 101 n. 4.

9. Anonymous student, quoted in Humphrey, *Memoir of Rev. Nathan W. Fiske*, 85.

10. Anonymous student, quoted in ibid., 89.

11. Edward Hitchcock, Jr., quoted in Jay Leyda, *Years and Hours of Emily Dickinson* (New Haven: Yale University Press, 1960), 1:xlvi.

12. Nathan Fiske to Deborah Fiske, December 22, 1829, HHJ1.

13. Nathan Fiske to Deborah Fiske, January 17, [1831], HHJ1.

14. Deborah Fiske to Nathan Fiske, [October 1841], HHJ1.

15. Nathan Fiske to David Vinal, February 17, 1832, HHJ1.

16. Nathan Fiske, *Obituary Address at the Funeral of the Rev. Royal Washburn, Amherst, Mass., January 4, 1833* (Amherst, Mass.: J. S. & C. Adams, 1833), 24–26.

17. Nathan Fiske, journal, in Humphrey, *Memoir of Rev. Nathan W. Fiske*, 56.

18. Deborah Fiske to Nathan Fiske, [1836], HHJ1.

19. Nathan Fiske to Deborah Fiske, [1832], HHJ1.

20. Humphrey, *Memoir of Rev. Nathan W. Fiske*, iv.

21. Ibid., 88. See also William S. Tyler, *A History of Amherst College during the Administrations of Its First Five Presidents from 1821 to 1891* (New York: Frederick H. Hitchcock, 1895), 135.

22. Nathan Fiske, "Spiritual Liberty," in Humphrey, *Memoir of Rev. Nathan W. Fiske*, 106.

23. Tyler, *A History of Amherst College*, 135, 277.

24. Jackson to Henry Root, March 28, 1852, HHJ5.

25. In addition to the works I discuss, Fiske published *Outlines of Mental Philosophy* (n.d.); a *Memoir* of Philip Doddridge, which Fiske mentions in his journal, but which I have been unable to locate; an edition of *The Course of Time*, by Robert Pollok (1828); and perhaps a children's book called *Young Peter's Voyage around the World*, which Ruth Odell mentions in her biography of Jackson, but which neither she nor I succeeded in locating.

26. Johann Joachim Eschenburg (1743–1820) was a German literary critic, historian, and poet. His own *Handbuch der klassischen Literatur* was published in 1783. Fiske's version of the *Manual* was used as a textbook at Amherst and Harvard, among other colleges, and some 12,000 copies had been purchased by the time of its fourth edition.

27. Nathan Fiske, trans. and comp., *Manual of Classical Literature*, by Johann Joachim Eschenburg, 4th ed., with additions (Philadelphia: E. C. & J. Biddle, 1854), 85, xii.

28. Ibid., 542.

29. Humphrey, *Memoir of Rev. Nathan W. Fiske*, 83.

30. Nathan Fiske, May 29, 1844, journal, HHJ1. Fiske's entry for this day offers a retrospect of the previous ten years.

31. Deborah Fiske to Jackson, [1842] and [1842], HHJ1.

32. By age nine, Helen had a personal library of eighty-six books, including, in addition to *The Story of Aleck*, such titles as *Temperance Tales*, in five volumes; *The Reformation; The Young Lady's Guide* and *The Young Lady's Friend*; Kempis's *Imitation of Christ*; and *Am I a Christian?* (see listing of books in Helen's library, HHJ1). Ten of young Helen's actual books are stored in HHJ1; all are pious volumes, including two Bibles—one given to her by her father, the other by her mother.

33. Nathan Fiske, *The Story of Aleck: or, Pitcairn's Island. Being a True Account of a Very Singular and Interesting Colony* (Amherst, Mass.: J. S. & C. Adams, 1829), 6, 20–21, 47.

34. Nathan Fiske and Jacob Abbott, *The Bible Class Book; Designed for Bible Classes, Sabbath Schools, and Families,* Scripture Duties No. 2 (Boston: T. R. Marvin, 1829), 9. This series was sponsored by the Massachusetts Sabbath School Union.

35. Ibid., 31–32, 29.

36. Ann Fiske Banfield to Helen Jackson (Ann Banfield's granddaughter), April 24, 1906, HHJ2.

37. Jackson to Deborah Fiske, [1841], HHJ1.

38. Jackson to Deborah Fiske, [1841], HHJ1.

39. Cousin Martha to Deborah Fiske, [1842], HHJ1.

40. Jackson to Deborah Fiske, [1842], HHJ1.

41. Nathan Fiske to Jackson, October 24, 1844, HHJ1.

42. Jackson to Deborah Fiske, [1841], HHJ1.

43. Jackson to Nathan Fiske, [1842], HHJ1.

44. Jackson to Deborah Fiske, [May 1843], HHJ1.

45. Jackson to Nathan Fiske, November 14, 1841, HHJ1.

46. Jackson, "The First Time," *St. Nicholas,* May 1877; "The Naughtiest Day of My Life, and What Came of It," *St. Nicholas,* October 1880.

47. Jackson, "The Inhumanities of Parents—Rudeness," in *Bits of Talk about Home Matters* (Boston: Roberts Brothers, 1873), 36–37.

48. Deborah Fiske to Martha Vinal, February 7, 1833; quoted in Leyda, *Years and Hours of Emily Dickinson,* 1:19.

49. Jackson to Deborah Fiske, [1841] and [1842], HHJ1.

50. Nathan Fiske to Jackson, September 15, 1844, HHJ1.

51. Nathan Fiske to Jackson, September 30, 1844, HHJ1. "In the evening I read Shakespeare," Helen had told her mother when she was in Hadley in 1841 (HHJ1).

52. Nathan Fiske to Jackson, December 17, 1840, HHJ1.

53. Nathan Fiske to Jackson, January 21, 1845, HHJ1.

54. Jackson to Julius Palmer, October 6, 1850, HHJ2.

55. Jackson to Julius Palmer, March 8, 1850, HHJ2.

56. Deborah Fiske to Martha Hooker, April 28, 1837; quoted in Leyda, *Years and Hours of Emily Dickinson,* 1:36.

57. Jackson to Julius Palmer, March 8, 1850, HHJ2. "That was a great many years ago, but I remember it as if it were yesterday," Jackson would later write of her mother's funeral ("The First Time," *St. Nicholas,* May 1877).

58. Nathan Fiske to Jackson, September 15 and November 23, 1844, HHJ1.

59. Nathan Fiske to Jackson, November 23, 1844, HHJ1.

60. Jackson to Ann Scholfield, January 14, 1856, transcript, WSJ2.

61. Nathan Fiske to Jackson, July 10, 1846, HHJ1.

62. Jackson to Julius Palmer, March 8, 1850, HHJ2.

63. Ibid. See also Fiske's journal, January 30, 1847, HHJ1.

64. Jackson to Julius Palmer, March 8, 1850, HHJ2.

65. Ibid.

66. Jackson to Ann Scholfield, July 29, 1847, transcript, WSJ2.

67. Jackson to Julius Palmer, October 13, 1851, HHJ2.

68. Jackson to Julius Palmer, December 15, 1850, HHJ2.

69. Deborah Fiske to Jackson, [June 1843], HHJ1.

70. Deborah Fiske to Elizabeth Holmes Washburn, n.d., HHJ1; Deborah Fiske, duty lists, HHJ1.

71. Deborah Fiske to David Vinal, n.d., HHJ1.

72. Deborah Fiske to David Vinal, n.d., HHJ1; Deborah Fiske to Nathan Fiske, [1833] and n.d., HHJ1.

73. Edward Hitchcock, Jr., quoted in Leyda, *Years and Hours of Emily Dickinson*, 1:xlvi.

74. Heman Humphrey, *The Woman That Feareth the Lord, a Discourse Delivered at the Funeral of Mrs. D. W. V. Fiske, February 21, 1844* (Amherst, Mass.: J. S. & C. Adams, 1844), 12–13, 36. Humphrey's sermon is based on Proverbs 31:10 and 30.

75. Deborah Fiske to Jackson, [summer 1836], HHJ1.

76. Deborah Fiske to Jackson, [summer 1836], HHJ1.

77. Martha Vinal to Deborah Fiske, [1842], HHJ1.

78. Nathan Fiske, prefatory note to letter book 1 (correspondence of Deborah and Helen Fiske, 1835–43), June 25, 1846, HHJ1.

79. Deborah Fiske to Ann Scholfield, [1841], HHJ1.

80. Deborah Fiske to Jackson, [September 1841], HHJ1.

81. Deborah Fiske to Jackson, n.d., HHJ1.

82. Deborah Fiske to Jackson, [1842], HHJ1.

83. Deborah Fiske to Jackson, [1843], HHJ1.

84. Deborah Fiske to Jackson, October 4, 1841, HHJ1.

85. Deborah Fiske to Jackson, [May 1843], HHJ1.

86. Jackson to Deborah Fiske, [May 1843], HHJ1.

87. Deborah Fiske to Nathan Fiske, n.d., HHJ1.

88. Deborah Fiske to Jackson, [October 1841], HHJ1.

89. Deborah Fiske to Jackson, [1842], HHJ1.

90. Deborah Fiske to Mrs. Walker, n.d., HHJ1.

91. Deborah Fiske to Ann Scholfield, n.d., HHJ1.

92. Deborah Fiske to Ann Scholfield, [1841], HHJ1.

93. Deborah Fiske to Ann Scholfield, n.d., HHJ1.

94. Deborah Fiske to Ann Scholfield, [1841], HHJ1.

95. Deborah claims in a letter to Martha Hooker to have published, in addition to those I discuss, a *Youth's Companion* piece called "One of Grandma's Bible Stories" (see Deborah Fiske to Hooker, April 14, 1839, HHJ1). I have been unable to locate it.

96. Deborah Fiske, "A Letter from a Little Girl Who Did Nothing but Play, to Her Cousin Who Loved to Study," *Youth's Companion,* February 1, 1839.

97. Deborah Fiske, "What a Useful Young Lady! Two Leaves from Her Journal, Picked Up in the Street a Few Days Ago," *Youth's Companion,* February 22, 1839.

98. Deborah Fiske, "Ten Questions That I Wish Nobody Would Ever Ask Me Again," *Youth's Companion,* February 1, 1839. At this time, Deborah Fiske was only thirty-two years old, not thirty-seven.

99. See "To the Editor of the Youth's Companion" and "The Ten Questions," *Youth's Companion,* February 22 and March 1, 1839.

100. Deborah Fiske, "A Few Words to 'Poor Susan,'" *Youth's Companion,* February 22, 1839.

101. Deborah Fiske to David Vinal, December 11, 1823 and March 16, 1828, HHJ1.

102. Deborah Fiske to Ellen Scholfield, n.d., in Sheila M. Rothman, *Living in the Shadow of Death: Tuberculosis and the Social Experience of Illness in American History* (New York: HarperCollins, 1994), 96.

103. W.S. to Deborah Fiske, including copy of poem "The Province of Woman," October 21, 1828, HHJ1.

104. Deborah Fiske to Nathan Fiske, [1836], HHJ1.

105. Deborah Fiske to Nathan Fiske, [September 1836], HHJ1.

106. Deborah Fiske to Martha Hooker, [1838 or early 1839]; in Rothman, *Living in the Shadow of Death,* 97.

107. Deborah Fiske to Martha Hooker, April 14, 1839, HHJ1.

108. Deborah Fiske to Jackson, [summer 1836], HHJ1.

109. Jackson, *Letters from a Cat: Published by Her Mistress* (1879; reprint, Boston: Little, Brown, 1902), 42–43.

110. Deborah Fiske to Jackson, [summer 1836], HHJ1.

111. Jackson, *Letters from a Cat* (1879), 56–57.

112. Ibid., 19.

113. Nathan Fiske to Henry Hooker, April 14, 1839, HHJ1.

114. Jackson to Julius Palmer, December 15, 1850, HHJ2.

CHAPTER 3. LITERARY EDUCATION

1. Edward Hitchcock et al., *The Power of Christian Benevolence Illustrated in the Life and Labors of Mary Lyon* (Northampton, Mass.: Bridgman & Childs, 1860), 136–38.

2. Jackson to Julius Palmer, April 6, 1852, HHJ2.

3. Jackson to Ann Scholfield, February 1, 1847, transcript, WSJ2.

4. Jackson to Julius Palmer, March 8, 1850, HHJ2.

5. Henry Home, Lord Kames, *Elements of Criticism,* 6th ed. (1785; reprint, London: Routledge, 1993), 1:6, 100.

6. Jackson to Ann Banfield, March 22, 1849, transcript, WSJ2.

7. Jackson to Henry Root, March 13, 1852, HHJ5.

8. Jackson to Henry Root, May 25, 1855, HHJ5. Some of Jackson's letters from early adulthood indicate that she corresponded frequently with John Abbott, but I have not located any of this correspondence.

9. John S.C. Abbott, *The School-girl; or, The Principles of Christian Duty Familiarly Enforced* (Boston: Crocker & Brewster, 1840), 141, 45, 41–43.

10. Jackson to Julius Palmer, March 26, 1850, HHJ2.

11. J., "Helen Jackson: A Recollection," *Literary World,* May 29, 1886. The identity of the author of this article is uncertain.

12. Abbott, *The School-girl,* 147, 130.

13. Jackson to Julius Palmer, August 9, 1849, HHJ2.

14. Jackson to Henry Root, [1851], HHJ5.

15. Jackson to Lucy Palmer, February 6, 1853, HHJ2.

16. Jackson to Julius Palmer, December 16, 1849, HHJ2. While Jackson may well have been frustrated enough to want to break something, she had in fact accidentally broken a lampshade in recent weeks, and in an earlier letter had asked her guardian about a replacement.

17. Jackson to Julius Palmer, December 16, 1849, HHJ2.

18. Jackson to Julius Palmer, February 25, 1851, HHJ2.

19. Jackson to Julius Palmer, n.d., HHJ2.

20. *Portfolio* of the Abbott Institute, vol. 1, 1850, HHJ2.

21. *Portfolio* of the Abbott Institute, vol. 2, 1850, HHJ2.

22. Jackson to Lucy Palmer, n.d., HHJ2.

23. Jackson to Julius Palmer, November 20, 1850, HHJ2.

24. Jackson to Julius Palmer, February 25, 1851, HHJ2.

25. See obituary for Ray Palmer, *New York Independent,* April 14, 1887.

26. Jackson to Henry Root, October 16, 1851, HHJ5.

27. Jackson to Henry Root, October 3, 1851, HHJ5.

28. Jackson to Ann Palmer, [1853], Huntington.

29. Jackson to Henry Root, February 16 and January 22, 1852, October 3, 1851, HHJ5.

30. Jackson to Henry Root, January 22, 1852, HHJ5.

31. Jackson to Henry Root, October 16, 1851, HHJ5; Jackson to Julius Palmer, October 13 and December 30, 1851, HHJ2.

32. Jackson to Julius Palmer, January 14, 1852, HHJ2.

33. Jackson to Henry Root, June 7, 1855, HHJ5.

34. Jackson to Ann Palmer, August 8, 1852, Huntington.

35. Jackson to Henry Root, November 7, 1851, HHJ5.

36. Jackson to Julius Palmer, April 6, 1852, HHJ2. In this letter to her guardian, Helen discusses the anxiety she and Henry Root share.

37. Jackson to Henry Root, October 3, 1851, HHJ5.

38. Jackson to Henry Root, October 16, 1851, HHJ5.

39. Jackson to Henry Root, February 16, 1852, HHJ5.

40. Henry Root to Jackson, [1851], HHJ5.

41. Jackson to [Henry Root], n.d., fragment, HHJ6. Emerson's essay "Introductory Lecture on the Times" was published in *Nature; Addresses and Lectures* (Boston: James Munroe, 1849).

42. Jackson to Henry Root, January 22, 1852, HHJ5.

43. Jackson to Henry Root, March 13, 1852, HHJ5.

44. Jackson to Henry Root, November 7, 1851, HHJ5.

45. Jackson to Henry Root, October 3, 1851, HHJ5. Helen mentions "character" in many of her letters to Root.

46. Ibid.

47. Henry Root to Jackson, [October 1851], HHJ6.

48. Jackson to Julius Palmer, December 12, 1851, HHJ2; Jackson to Henry Root, January 22, 1852, HHJ5.

49. Jackson to Henry Root, February 16, 1852, HHJ5.

50. Jackson to Henry Root, [March 1854], HHJ6.

51. Jackson to Henry Root, [1854] and July 3, 1852, HHJ6.

52. Jackson to Julius Palmer, April 6, 1852, HHJ2. This letter might imply that Helen was editing or at least contributing to a newsletter sent to members of a sewing circle, but no copies of any such newsletter survive.

53. Jackson to Ann Palmer, [1853], Huntington.

54. Jackson to Henry Root, [1852], HHJ5.

55. Edward Hunt to Jackson, October 9, 1856, Wisconsin.

56. Jackson to Henry Root, July 12, 1853, HHJ5.

57. Jackson to Julius Palmer, [July 1852], HHJ2.

58. Edward Hunt to Alexander Bache, June 13, 1857, Congress.

59. F. A. P. Barnard, "Memoir of Edward B. Hunt, 1822–1863," *Biographical Memoirs* 3, no. 3 (1895): 31; William S. Hunt, grandnephew of Edward Hunt, quoted in Ruth Odell, *Helen Hunt Jackson (H.H.)* (New York: D. Appleton-Century, 1939), 59.

60. Jackson, quoted in Barnard, "Memoir of Edward B. Hunt," 32; Jackson to Julius Palmer, April 6, 1852, HHJ2.

61. Edward Hunt to Everett Banfield, December 14, 1855, WSJ2.

62. Jackson to Everett Banfield, November 24, 1855, transcript, WSJ2; Jackson to Lucy Palmer, January 14, 1853, HHJ2.

63. Jackson to Julius Palmer, January 9, 1853, HHJ2.

64. Jackson to Ann Scholfield, July 21, 1855, transcript, WSJ2.

65. Jackson to Julius Palmer, n.d., HHJ2.

66. Jackson to Ann Banfield, n.d., HHJ2.

67. Jackson to Lucy Palmer, January 14, 1853, HHJ2.

68. Jackson, quoted in Moncure Daniel Conway, *Autobiography, Memories and Experiences of Moncure Daniel Conway* (Boston: Houghton, Mifflin, 1904), 1:202.

69. Jackson quoting Edward Hunt to Moncure Conway, April 6, 1856, Columbia.

70. Jackson to Julius Palmer, July 1852, HHJ5; Jackson to Ann Banfield, February 8, 1856, HHJ2. Wormeley would also become known for her work with the United States Sanitary Commission during the Civil War.

71. Jackson to Henry Root, September 2, 1852 and July 12, 1853, HHJ5.

72. Jackson to Lucy Palmer, January 14, 1853, HHJ2.

73. Jackson to Henry Root, [1854], HHJ6.

74. Jackson to Ann Banfield, March 31, 1856, Wisconsin.

75. We know exactly when Jackson began to write and publish stories and travel essays: in 1867 and 1865, respectively. But although we know that she wrote poetry as a schoolgirl, we do not know exactly when she began to write more seriously, of her own volition. Thomas Wentworth Higginson claims that she "published some girlish verses in the Boston *Press and Post*" in her teens (*Contemporaries* [Boston: Houghton, Mifflin, 1899], 148); Allan Nevins says she published poems in the *New York Evening Post* before the end of the Civil War (*The "Evening Post": A Century of Journalism* [1922; reprint, New York: Russell & Russell, 1968], 325); and some bibliographic sources list Jackson as the author of "A Charade," published by one "H.H." in Brooklyn's *Daily Morning Drum-Beat*, March 1, 1864. I have found no proof of Jackson's authorship of any poems published before the summer of 1865.

76. Higginson, *Contemporaries*, 148.

77. Jackson to Henry Root, [1854], HHJ5.

78. Jackson to Ann Banfield, July 29, 1861, HHJ2.

79. Jackson to Moncure Conway, January 14, 1877, Columbia.

80. Emerson, quoted in Anne C. Lynch Botta, *Memoirs of Anne C. L. Botta, Written by Her Friends . . .*, ed. Vincenzo Botta (New York: J. S. Tait & Sons, 1893), 177.

81. Jackson to Anne Botta, n.d., BANC MSS 88/37c, Bancroft. Later, Jackson would praise the "gracious freedom" of Botta's house in the tribute "To A.C.L.B.," printed in Jackson, *Poems* (1892; reprint, Boston: Little, Brown, 1906), 118.

82. Grace Greenwood and Lucia Runkle, contributions to Botta, *Memoirs of Anne C. L. Botta,* 86, 87.

83. Jackson to Anne Botta, October 11, 1855 and January 26, 1872, Jones.

84. Jackson to Charlotte Cushman, n.d., fragment, Congress.

85. Jackson to William Ward, February 28, 1874, Jones. Though Jackson was critical of Woolsey's later work, she expressed admiration for her friend's poetic tribute to Emerson, "Concord, May 31, 1882," published in the *Atlantic Monthly,* July 1882.

86. It is impossible to know exactly how the friendship between Jackson and Woolsey developed, because their correspondence is missing. Ruth Odell was able to review ten letters from Jackson to Woolsey, eight written in the final summer of Jackson's life and two in the summer of 1862. Odell cites these letters as belonging to Ruth Davenport, but they are not to be found in the Tutt Library, where portions of Davenport's collection are housed today. (The Tutt does hold one letter from "Sally" to Jackson, July 10, 1882, HHJ2.) I infer that Jackson did not reveal her deepest literary concerns to Woolsey from two facts. First, she did not admit her authorship of the "Saxe Holm" stories to Woolsey, explaining to a mutual acquaintance, "She is not one I could trust with the secret" (Jackson to Charlotte Cushman, n.d., Congress). Second, in 1880, when she needed a friend to read the proofs of *A Century of Dishonor,* she asked Thomas Wentworth Higginson, not Woolsey, telling her husband, "I can trust him implicitly and I can't trust Sally in all matters" (Jackson to William Jackson, [1880], WSJ1).

87. Jackson to Thomas Bailey Aldrich, December 9, 1882, Harvard.

88. Jackson, "Joe Hale's Red Stockings," in *Saxe Holm's Stories, Second Series* (1878; reprint, New York: Charles Scribner's Sons, 1899); "Elspeth Dynor," unpublished MS, in NYP, 328.

89. Edward B. Hunt, *Union Foundations: A Study of American Nationality as a Fact of Science* (New York: D. Van Nostrand, 1863), 53.

90. Ibid., 48–49, 53.

91. For a seminal discussion of nineteenth-century colonization efforts and norms of white feeling about blacks, see George M. Fredrickson, *The Black Image in the White Mind: The Debate on Afro-American Character and Destiny, 1817–1914* (New York: Harper & Row, 1971).

92. Deborah Fiske to Ann Scholfield, n.d., HHJ1.

93. Nathan Fiske, "On the Unity and History of Providence," in *Memoir of Rev. Nathan W. Fiske, Professor of Intellectual and Moral Philosophy in Amherst College; Together with Selections from His Sermons and Other Writings,* by Humphrey Heman (Amherst, Mass.: J. S. & C. Adams, 1850), 375.

94. Deborah Fiske to Nathan Fiske, [1841], HHJ1.

95. Deborah Fiske to Nathan Fiske, [1836], HHJ1.

96. Jackson to Rebecca Snell, October 7, [1841], Amherst.

97. Jackson to Julius Palmer, January 30, 1856, HHJ2.

98. Jackson to Ann Banfield, May 10, 1856, HHJ2.

99. See, for example, Jackson to Ray and Ann Palmer, June 16, 1861, NYU; Jackson to Lucy Palmer, February 27, 1853, HHJ2.

100. Jackson to Lucy Palmer, February 27, 1853, HHJ2; Jackson to Harriet Palmer, September 9, 1853, BP; Jackson to Ann Palmer, [1853], #HM13917, Huntington.

101. Jackson to Ann Palmer, January 2, 1854, Huntington.

102. Ibid.

103. Moncure Conway to Mrs. Henry Wadsworth Longfellow, February 16, 1859, HHJ1.

104. Jackson to Henry Root, [1854], HHJ5.

105. Jackson to Charles Dudley Warner, November 11, 1880, Trinity.

106. Conway, *Autobiography of Moncure Daniel Conway,* 1:202.

107. Jackson to Henry Root, May 25, 1855, HHJ5.

108. Jackson to Moncure Conway, June 1, 1857, Columbia.

109. Jackson to Julius Palmer, March 8, 1850, HHJ2.

110. Jackson to Julius Palmer, February 25, 1851 and January 17, 1850, HHJ2.

111. Jackson to Julius Palmer, December 15, 1850, HHJ2; Jackson to Henry Root, July 12, 1853, HHJ5.

112. Jackson to Henry Root, January 16, 1853, HHJ5.

113. Jackson, quoted in Barnard, "Memoir of Edward B. Hunt," 40.

114. Jackson to Charles Dudley Warner, July 7, 1884, Trinity; Jackson to Moncure Conway, April 6, 1856, Columbia.

115. Jackson to Charles Dudley Warner, November 28, 1882, Trinity.

116. Jackson, Our Book Table, review of *Spiritual Manifestations,* by Charles Beecher, *Denver Tribune,* date unknown, housed in HHJ1.

117. Jackson to Henry Root, December 3, 1854, HHJ5.

118. Jackson to Henry Root, December 29, 1854, HHJ5.

119. Jackson to Henry Root, [January 1855], HHJ5.

120. Ibid.

121. Jackson to Moncure Conway, June 1, 1857, Columbia.

122. Jackson to Jabez Sunderland, December 3, 1884, Michigan.

123. Dr. Butler, "Phrenological Character of Mrs. Hunt," HHJ1. Dr. Butler, detecting Helen's "intense imagination" and talent with language, also predicted her success in "Poetry."

124. In the 1850s Helen had felt that she must "look & behave my 'prettiest'" whenever Conway visited the Hunts, but as she expressed this feeling openly, it cannot be interpreted as having any great significance (Jackson to Ann Banfield, n.d., Wisconsin).

125. Moncure Conway to Jackson, December 29, 1868, HHJ2.

CHAPTER 4. ENTERING THE LITERARY MARKETPLACE

1. Jackson to Kate Field, June 19, 1865, BP.

2. Jackson to Ann Banfield, April 30, 1867, HHJ2.

3. Jackson to Jenny Fox, July 3, 1870, AAS.

4. Jackson to Mary Sprague, March 23, 1872, Huntington.

5. Jackson to Charlotte Cushman, n.d., fragment, Congress.

6. Jackson, "The Passion Play at Oberammergau," in *Glimpses of Three Coasts* (Boston: Roberts Brothers, 1886), 407.

7. This collage is held in HHJ1, box 9, fd. 10.

8. Jackson to Kate Field, July 23, 1868, BP.

9. Kate Field, "From Newport," *Boston Post,* August 16, 1865.

10. Kate Field, quoted by Jackson in a letter to a circle of friends, July 14, 1869, Yale.

11. Jackson to Charlotte Cushman, September 4, 1870, Congress.

12. Thomas Wentworth Higginson, *The Works of Epictetus* . . . , a translation from the Greek based on that of Elizabeth Carter (Boston: Little, Brown, 1866), vi.

13. Jackson, *Nelly's Silver Mine* (1878; reprint, Boston: Roberts Brothers, 1885), 50.

14. Thomas Wentworth Higginson, *Common Sense about Women* (Boston: Lee & Shepard, 1881), 17, 40, 328–29, 62, 137.

15. Jackson to Julius Palmer, October 13, 1851, HHJ2.

16. Thomas Wentworth Higginson, *Out-Door Papers* (1868; reprint, Boston: Lee & Shepard, 1886), 254.

17. Jackson, "A New Sleepy Hollow," *New York Evening Post,* January 13, 1868.

18. Thomas Wentworth Higginson, "Americanism in Literature," *Atlantic Monthly,* January 1870.

19. Thomas Wentworth Higginson, "A Letter to a Young Contributor," *Atlantic Monthly,* April 1862; later included in *Hints on Writing and Speech Making* (Boston: Lee & Shepard, 1887), 18, 35–36.

20. See Mary P. Hiatt, *Style and the "Scribbling Women": An Empirical Analysis of Nineteenth-Century American Fiction* (Westport, Conn.: Greenwood Press, 1993). According to Hiatt, Jackson's average sentence length is 19 words, compared to an average of 24.5 words for both her female and male contemporaries; Jackson's longest sentence contains 53 words, while her female peers often wrote sentences of 61 words or more. Today the average sentence length is 16.5 words.

21. Jackson to Charles Dudley Warner, July 21, 1872, Trinity.

22. Jackson to William Church, May 16, 1867, NYP.

23. Jackson's comments to Higginson appear in two letters to a circle of friends, January 11 and August 22, 1869, Yale.

24. Thomas Wentworth Higginson, *Short Studies of American Authors,* rev. ed. (Boston: Lee & Shepard, 1888), 41, 49.

25. Thomas Wentworth Higginson, *Contemporaries* (Boston: Houghton, Mifflin, 1899), 148.

26. Thomas Wentworth Higginson, 1873 diary, bMS AM 1162, Thomas Wentworth Higginson Papers, Harvard.

27. Jackson to Kate Field, March 7, 1866, BP.

28. See Anna Mary Wells, *Dear Preceptor: The Life and Times of Thomas Wentworth Higginson* (Boston: Houghton Mifflin, 1963), esp. 200–212, 268.

29. Higginson, *Contemporaries,* 164, 165.

30. Jackson to circle of friends, May 22, 1869, Yale.

31. See Lillian Faderman, *Surpassing the Love of Men: Romantic Friendship and Love between Women from the Renaissance to the Present* (New York: Morrow, 1981). In 1975 Carroll Smith-Rosenberg offered the first influential discussion of passionate friendship between nineteenth-century American women in "The Female World of Love and Ritual," reprinted in *Disorderly Conduct: Visions of Gender in Victorian America* (New York: Alfred A. Knopf, 1985).

32. Charlotte Cushman to Jackson, [1870?], HHJ2; Jackson to Cushman, May 17, 1871, Congress.

33. Jackson understood the serious nature of Cushman's commitment to Emma Stebbins and was not in the least troubled by it. Once, after Jackson had apparently

referred to Stebbins as Cushman's "wife," Cushman felt comfortable admitting the pain she felt over some recent troubles with Stebbins. "You are wrong dear in your term *'wife* Emma.' *'Friend* Emma' is the *more* correct state of things," she said. "I am not even the leastest [?] beloved—just but unkind—The largest sorrow & mortification of my life" (Charlotte Cushman to Jackson, December 6, 1869, HHJ2).

34. Jackson to Charlotte Cushman, September 4, 1870 and n.d., Congress.

35. Jackson to "Dear Souls" [Mary Mapes Dodge and Lucia Runkle], September 7, 1871, NYP; Jackson to William Ward, February 21, 1876, Huntington.

36. Jackson to William Ward, February 21, 1876, Huntington. Jackson's elegy "Charlotte Cushman" appeared in the *New York Independent* on March 9, 1876, and is reprinted in *Poems* (1892; reprint, Boston: Little, Brown, 1906), 250–51. In 1870 Jackson wrote the poem "Welcome" for Cushman; it is also in *Poems,* 161.

37. Charlotte Cushman, quoted in Emma Stebbins, ed., *Charlotte Cushman: Her Letters and Memories of Her Life* (1879; reprint, New York: Benjamin Bloom, 1972), 264.

38. Jackson to Anne Botta, January 14, 1872, Jones. "A Funeral March" is printed in *Poems* (1892), 26–31.

39. Charlotte Cushman to Jackson, March 12, 1871, HHJ2.

40. Jackson to Charlotte Cushman, n.d., Congress; Cushman to Jackson, n.d., July 28, 1869, and October 13, 1870, HHJ2.

41. Thomas Wentworth Higginson, quoted in Wells, *Dear Preceptor,* 204.

42. Charlotte Cushman to Jackson, November 28, 1869, HHJ2.

43. Charlotte Cushman to Jackson, June 7, 1870, HHJ2.

44. Charlotte Cushman to Jackson, June 11, 1871, HHJ2.

45. Charlotte Cushman to Jackson, n.d., HHJ2.

46. Jackson to Charlotte Cushman, September 4, 1870, Congress.

47. Charlotte Cushman to Jackson, November 19, 1870, HHJ2.

48. Jackson to Charlotte Cushman, May 17, 1871, Congress. The verse Jackson quotes in her letter is an excerpt from her poem "Two Loves," included in *Poems* (1892), 102–5.

49. Charlotte Cushman to Jackson, August 18, 1871, HHJ2.

50. Charlotte Cushman to Jackson, January 6, 1874, HHJ2.

51. Charlotte Cushman to Jackson, July 29, 1874, HHJ2.

52. Charlotte Cushman to Jackson, July 24, 1875, HHJ2.

53. Jackson to Charles Dudley Warner, December 22, 1873, Trinity.

54. Jackson to Thomas Wentworth Higginson, January 17, 1880; quoted in Higginson, *Contemporaries,* 156.

55. Jackson made a similar request to only one other person, when, ill with diphtheria in 1873, she asked Rev. C. A. L. Richards of Providence, Rhode Island, to proofread her *Saxe Holm Stories, First Series.*

56. Jackson to Thomas Wentworth Higginson, July 27, 1881, Harvard.

57. Jackson to Charles Dudley Warner, December 22, 1873, Trinity.

58. Oliver Wendell Holmes to Jackson, December 13, 1879, HHJ2.

59. Jackson to Thomas Bailey Aldrich, March 10, 1884, Harvard.

60. Jackson to William Jackson, May 28, 1880, WSJ1.

61. Jackson to circle of friends, September 28, 1869, Yale.

62. Richard Watson Gilder to Jackson, October 4, 1873 and August 26, 1875, HHJ2.

63. Richard Watson Gilder to Jackson, September 24, 1873, HHJ2.

64. Jackson to Charles Dudley Warner, April 13, 1881, Trinity.

65. Jackson to William Ward, April 18, 1873, Huntington.

66. This and all succeeding circulation figures, unless otherwise noted, are based on estimates made by Frank Luther Mott, *A History of American Magazines,* vol. 3, *1865–1885* (Cambridge, Mass.: Harvard University Press, 1957), esp. 7. Different sources diverge widely in circulation numbers for nineteenth-century periodicals; the figures I give should be considered rough estimates.

67. Jackson to Whitelaw Reid, September 26, 1870, Congress.

68. Review of *Verses, Nation,* March 16, 1871. Jackson first tried to print an editorial critical of the *Nation* in the *New York Tribune* in 1870, with unknown results. The following year she succeeded in placing an unsigned criticism, "The Moral 'Zone of Calms,' " in the *New York Independent* of January 26, 1871. The year after that, she sent the *Tribune* another editorial, titled "Laodician," in which she condemned the *Nation*'s critical standards. Reid rejected the submission.

69. For the *Atlantic*'s circulation figures, see Ellen Ballou, *The Building of the House: Houghton Mifflin's Formative Years* (Boston: Houghton Mifflin, 1870), 375.

70. Jackson to Josiah Holland, September 28, 1870, UVA; Jackson to Amelia Stone Quinton, August 19, 1881, Bancroft; Thomas Niles to Jackson, January 19, 1877, HHJ1. Jackson did have a loyal following at the *New York Independent,* even if these readers did not always buy her books in large numbers. In 1875, when she solicited books for a Colorado library in one of her articles, three hundred readers responded. The following year, Jackson ascribed her continued loyalty to the *Independent* to her pleasure in writing to this loyal audience, and to her having written there early in her career (see Jackson to William Ward, November 1, 1876, Huntington).

71. Ruth Odell, *Helen Hunt Jackson (H.H.)* (New York: D. Appleton-Century, 1939), 141; Michele Moylan, "Materiality as Performance: The Forming of Helen Hunt Jackson's *Ramona,*" in *Reading Books: Essays on the Material Text and Literature in America,* ed. Moylan and Lane Stiles (Boston: University of Massachusetts Press, 1997), 225. Moylan claims that *Ramona*'s sale of 20,000 books in 1885 made it a best-seller. In Frank Luther Mott's estimation, though, a novel had to sell 500,000 copies to be a "best" seller in any year of the 1880s, meaning *Ramona* was only a "better" seller (*Golden Multitudes: The Story of Best Sellers in the United States* [New York: Macmillan, 1947], 323).

72. Jackson to William Jackson, August 16, 1880, WSJ1.

73. Richard Watson Gilder to Jackson, January 7, 1874, HHJ2. Scribner's gives the quoted sales figures in Charles Scribner to Jackson, February 13, 1880, Princeton; and in a letter to Roberts Brothers, [March 1879], Princeton.

74. Jackson to Amelia Stone Quinton, August 19, 1881, Bancroft.

75. Roberts Brothers account statements, HHJ1.

76. Jackson's rates of pay for various types of periodical work are culled from her correspondence with editors.

77. Ballou, *The Building of the House,* 377. Jackson told the *Atlantic* editor Thomas Bailey Aldrich that she had felt a little guilty earning so much for these two articles, but that "Mr. Jackson took a business view of the situation, & laughed me out of it" (Jackson to Aldrich, October 16, 1882, Harvard).

78. Jackson to Henry Teller, September 16, 1882, transcript, NatArch, #18905-1882.

79. See "Cash Account" pages from Jackson's date books for 1881, 1882, and 1883, HHJ1.

80. Jackson to Moncure Conway, January 14, 1877, Columbia; Jackson to Ann Banfield, March 3, 1879, HHJ5.

81. Jackson to Parke Godwin, October 10, 1865, NYP.

82. Jackson to Charlotte Cushman, September 4, 1870, Congress.

83. Jackson to Charles Dudley Warner, July 7 and September 22, 1874, Trinity.

84. William Jackson to Jackson, September 5, 1875, WSJ1.

85. Jackson to Ann Banfield, January 20, 1879, HHJ5.

86. Ibid.

87. Jackson to Charles Dudley Warner, April 24, 1880, Trinity.

88. William Jackson to Jackson, n.d., WSJ1.

89. Jackson to William Jackson, September 11, 1880, WSJ2.

90. Jackson to Kate Field, March 7, 1866, BP. Once, when Jackson was experiencing a creative lull after an illness, she admitted to an editor: "I have sometimes wished that I were really compelled to earn my bread (as I am, my butter!)—and then I should rise above these fits of indisposition to put pen to paper" (Jackson to Edward Seymour, April 30, 1875, BYU).

91. Jackson to Julius Palmer, September 20, 1851, HHJ2.

92. Jackson to Parke Godwin, October 10, 1865, NYP.

93. Jackson to James T. Fields, December 26, 1870, Huntington; emphasis Jackson's.

94. Jackson to William Ward, November 1, 1876, Huntington.

95. Jackson to James T. Fields, December 26, 1870, Huntington.

96. For Jackson's comments on "the so much per page plan," see her letter to Thomas Bailey Aldrich, February 22, 1883, Harvard. She mentions "market value" in many of her letters to editors and publishers, including, for instance, Jackson to William Ward, July 13, 1873, Huntington.

97. Jackson to William Ward, April 16, 1884, Huntington.

98. Jackson to William Ward, February 4, 1874, Huntington.

99. Jackson to Thomas Bailey Aldrich, May 8, 1882, Harvard.

100. Jackson to Henry Bowen, April 16, 1884, UVA.

101. Jackson to William Ward, February 4, 1874 and April 10, 1879, Huntington. See also Jackson to William Ward, January 19, 1875, Huntington; Jackson to Henry Bowen, August 6, 1885, Huntington.

102. Jackson to William Ward, January 19, 1875, Huntington.

103. Jackson to William Ward, August 22, 1875, Huntington. In 1877 Jackson wrote for the *New York Independent* less frequently than usual, partly because she was still perturbed.

104. "Our 'Forty Immortals,' " *Critic,* April 12, 1884.

CHAPTER 5. POETRY AND DOMESTIC ESSAYS

1. Jackson, *Mercy Philbrick's Choice,* No Name Series (Boston: Roberts Brothers, 1876), 284.

2. Edward Everett Hale, quoted by Jackson in her anonymous appreciation of his *Ten Times One Is Ten* (1871), Our Book Table, *Denver Tribune,* [1879?], HHJ1. Jackson tried to praise Hale's book shortly after its initial publication in both the

New York Independent and the New York Tribune, but her pieces apparently were not accepted.

3. On the topic of continuing Victorian earnestness, see among other studies Walter Houghton, The Victorian Frame of Mind, 1830–1870 (New Haven: Yale University Press, 1957).

4. Jackson to Moncure Conway, January 14, 1877, Columbia.

5. Jackson to Mary Booth, January 17, 1884, NYP.

6. James T. Fields, quoted in Annie Fields's diary, in Jay Leyda, Years and Hours of Emily Dickinson (New Haven: Yale University Press, 1960), 2:159. Though Jackson paid for the publication of the first edition of Verses out of her trust fund, Fields mistakenly believed that she was "earning her livelihood at the point of her pen," and thought it "silly beyond expression" for her to "put 520 good hard dollars into printing a fanciful little volume of her own poems." Jackson claims that she earns sixty-two cents for every copy sold of the second edition of Verses in a letter to William Ward, May 6, 1871, CCRoom.

7. From a collection of anonymous, unidentified newspaper articles in HHJ1, box 6, fd. 24.

8. See Cheryl Walker, The Nightingale's Burden: Women Poets and American Culture before 1900 (Bloomington: Indiana University Press, 1982), 99. In addition to her astute comments on Jackson's final lines, Walker's discussion of the secret sorrow and forbidden love as themes in American women's poetry has been very helpful in my analysis of Jackson's poems.

9. Jackson, "Dreams," in Poems (1892; reprint, Boston: Little, Brown, 1906), 252–53. Unless otherwise indicated, all poems that I mention can be found in this same volume.

10. Jackson to Thomas Bailey Aldrich, February 23, 1884, Harvard.

11. Jackson, Mercy Philbrick's Choice (1876), 284–85.

12. Jackson's "Confession of Faith," like most of her more didactic testaments to her beliefs, appeared in the New York Independent (March 31, 1870) and was never collected in book form; see also, in the Independent, "The Shadow" (October 22, 1868), "Shape" (December 29, 1870), and "The Pilgrim Forefathers" (March 27, 1879). "My Legacy" is included in Poems (1892), 15–16.

13. Jackson, "Content," New York Independent, November 14, 1867.

14. Jackson, "Emigravit," in Poems (1892), 218, and Mercy Philbrick's Choice (1876), 296.

15. Jackson, "Spinning," in Poems (1892), 13–14.

16. See anonymous, mostly unidentified articles in HHJ1, box 6, fd. 24, especially the Boston Daily Advertiser of December 22, 1873, which compares Jackson's "deep" and "earnest" "religious feeling" to that of Cowper—an honor that would have pleased Jackson's mother.

17. Bayard Taylor, "Lars," quoted in Jackson's "Three Pennsylvania Women," part 2, Christian Union, January 4, 1883.

18. Moncure Conway, Emerson at Home and Abroad (London: Trubner, 1883), 74.

19. Moncure Conway to Jackson, December 29, 1868, HHJ2.

20. Moncure Daniel Conway, Autobiography, Memories and Experiences of Moncure Daniel Conway (Boston: Houghton, Mifflin, 1904), 1:202.

21. Ralph Waldo Emerson, entry for "July 13," in The Journals and Miscella-

neous Notebooks of Ralph Waldo Emerson, vol. 16, 1866–1882, ed. Ronald A. Bosco and Glen M. Johnson (Cambridge, Mass.: Harvard University Press, 1982), 105. The poems Emerson admired had only recently been published when he and Jackson met in Newport: "Ariadne's Farewell" in the *Nation,* February 1868, and "Thought" in *Galaxy,* July 1868 (see also *Poems* [1892], 108, 109).

22. Jackson to Kate Field, July 23, 1868, BP.

23. Jackson, "Tribute: R.W.E.," in *Poems* (1892), 97.

24. See Emerson, *Journals and Miscellaneous Notebooks,* 16:98. On October 5, 1870, Emerson left his calling card with Jackson: "For Mrs. Hunt. Mr R W Emerson at 4 o'clock will call with good hope" (HHJ2).

25. Annie Fields records Emerson's comments on Jackson in her diary for December 6, 1870, quoted in Leyda, *Years and Hours of Emily Dickinson,* 2:159.

26. Ralph Waldo Emerson, ed., *Parnassus* (1874; reprint, Boston: Houghton, Mifflin, 1881), x.

27. Thomas Wentworth Higginson, *Short Studies of American Authors,* rev. ed. (Boston: Lee & Shepard, 1888), 41.

28. Jackson to Moncure Conway, June 1, 1857, Columbia.

29. Jackson to Richard Henry Stoddard, August 30, 1871, Copley.

30. Jackson to Edward Abbott, March 20, 1880, Bowdoin. Jackson wrote a memorial poem upon Emerson's death; see her letter to Henry Oscar Houghton, July 3, 1882, Harvard.

31. See William Dean Howells to Jackson, November 6, 1876, HHJ2.

32. Jackson, "The Singer's Hills," *Scribner's Monthly,* January 1874; in *Poems* (1892), 58–59.

33. Jackson, "October's Bright Blue Weather," in *Poems* (1892), 255.

34. Jackson, "Sonnet, To One Who Complained of a Poet for Not Writing about Nature," *Scribner's Monthly,* May 1875.

35. Jackson, "Locusts and Wild Honey," in *Poems* (1892), 110.

36. William Winter, "The Golden Silence," in *Wanderers: The Poems of William Winter,* new ed. (New York: Macmillan, 1893), 139–40. In this poem Winter also comments obliquely on the poet as one destined, like nature, to bring forth manifestations of divine spirit: "What nature wishes should be said / She'll find the rightful voice to say!" Jackson's own meditation on this theme appears in "The Way to Sing," one of her few early poems accepted by James T. Fields for the *Atlantic Monthly* (and reprinted in *Poems* [1892], 37–38). In this poem, she depicts the true poet as one of nature's children, disdaining the pressures of the public market—a stance that can seem disingenuous, given her own sharp commercial negotiating, if her Transcendental beliefs (and perhaps the conventional expectations then placed on female poets) are not taken into consideration.

37. Jackson to William Winter, March 19, 1884, UVA.

38. Ibid.

39. William Winter, "The Sceptre," in *Wanderers,* 115.

40. William Winter to Jackson, March 21, 1884, HHJ2.

41. In her children's novel, *Nelly's Silver Mine,* Jackson illustrates her thinking on predestination and free will in the words of Mr. March, who tells his son that God's control over humanity is similar to his own control over his garden: "I know when it is time to have the corn hoed; and I know, when there hasn't been any rain for a long time, that I must water it. But I don't think about each particular carrot

or parsnip in the bed" (*Nelly's Silver Mine* [1878; reprint, Boston: Roberts Brothers, 1885], 74).

42. Jackson, "A Woman's Battle," in *Poems* (1892), 179.

43. Jackson to "Dear Souls," September 7, 1871, NYP. Jackson did not like the work of another California regionalist poet who, like Miller, was attracting much attention at the time: Charles Warren Stoddard. In 1873 she claimed to feel about reading Stoddard's work as she felt about eating a banana: "I like the smell of it & the color of it so much. I'd give anything to eat a whole banana at once, and I always try; but I never get beyond the first half of the second mouthful" (Jackson to Charles Dudley Warner, December 22, 1873, Trinity).

44. Jackson to Horace Scudder, July 9, 1874, NYP; Jackson to William Ward, [1876], Huntington. No evidence exists of Jackson's opinion of Thaxter's regionalist prose, though *Among the Isles of Shoals* (1873), Thaxter's nonfiction piece about her home in the islands off the coast of Maine, was published the year before Jackson claimed to love her poetry and is superior work.

45. Jackson, "A Burns Pilgrimage," in *Glimpses of Three Coasts* (Boston: Roberts Brothers, 1886), 153, 168.

46. Jackson, "Border Lands," *Atlantic Monthly*, June 1878.

47. Jackson, "The Shoshone Oath," *Critic*, May 21, 1881.

48. Jackson tried to convince Emerson to admire George Eliot's 1868 poem *The Spanish Gypsy* during their sojourn together in Newport, and later praised her "Choir Invisible" to Emily Dickinson. She sometimes found inspiration to write by reading Elizabeth Barrett Browning's poetry, and she occasionally lapsed into imitation of Barrett Browning's sonnets, despite believing herself incapable of writing in that vein. She began to admire Christina Rossetti as early as 1868, when, on her first trip to Europe, she searched twelve London bookshops for a copy of one of Rossetti's volumes before finally going directly to Rossetti's publisher to buy it. A decade later, she wrote a variation on Rossetti's "Goblin Market" as a chapter epigraph for her never-published novel "Elspeth Dynor": "Who buys? Who buys? 'T is like a market-fair," Jackson's poem opens. It was published posthumously, out of place, in an excerpt from "Elspeth Dynor" in *Between Whiles* (1887; reprint, Boston: Roberts Brothers, 1898), 7.

49. See anonymous article from the *Index*, February 5, 1874; Mrs. C. J. Baker, unidentified newspaper article from Sioux City, Iowa, June 6, 1878, in HHJ1, box 6, fd. 24; and other anonymous, unidentified newspaper articles held in this folder.

50. Jackson to Ann Banfield, May 15, 1867, HHJ2. John Weiss (1818–79) was a Transcendentalist and a Unitarian minister, though his father was a German Jew. His "Some Lover's Clear Day" appeared in the *Galaxy* of May 1867.

51. Jackson to Joseph Gilder, November 27, 1881, NYP.

52. Jackson, review of *Gaspara Stampa*, by Eugene Benson, *Critic*, November 19, 1881; Frank Sanborn, author of anonymous editorial on Jackson's review of *Gaspara Stampa* in "Nature, Arts, and Letters," *Springfield Republican*, November 20, 1881.

53. Jackson, "Ariadne's Farewell," in *Poems* (1892), 108.

54. Anna Leonowens's writings and lectures about her observations in Thailand were garnering a good deal of publicity in the early 1870s. *The English Governess at the Siamese Court* would enjoy countless reincarnations even into the twenty-first century, especially as the basis for the popular Rodgers and Hammerstein musical *The King and I*.

55. Jackson, "Tryst," *Nation,* April 12, 1866; and in *Poems* (1892), 144.

56. Jackson, "A Burial Service," *Nation,* May 22, 1866; and in *Poems* (1892), 131–32.

57. Jackson to Millicent Shinn, February 10, 1885, CHS.

58. "Three Kisses of Farewell" appears in "Esther Wynn's Love-Letters," in *Saxe Holm's Stories, First Series* (1873; reprint, New York: Charles Scribner's Sons, 1898), 345–46.

59. Jackson, "Vintage," in *Poems* (1892), 173.

60. Charlotte Cushman to Jackson, December 29, 1870, HHJ2.

61. Thomas Wentworth Higginson, *Contemporaries* (Boston: Houghton, Mifflin, 1899), 162.

62. Thomas Wentworth Higginson, "Repression at Long Range," in *Concerning All of Us* (New York: Harper & Brothers, 1892), 204.

63. Thomas Wentworth Higginson to Edmund Clarence Stedman, August 19, 1888, Columbia.

64. "Acquainted with Grief" was first published among the "Last Poems of Helen Jackson ('H.H.')" in *Century Magazine,* December 1885; see also *Poems* (1892), 209–11.

65. Higginson, *Contemporaries,* 157.

66. See Richard Brodhead, *Cultures of Letters: Scenes of Reading and Writing in Nineteenth-Century America* (Chicago: University of Chicago Press, 1993), 125.

67. Jackson to Ann Scholfield, January 14, 1856, transcript, WSJ2.

68. Jackson [Rip Van Winkle, pseud.], "A Visit to Borioboola Gha: The School System There," *New York Evening Post,* November 18, 1867. "Borioboola Gha" alludes to Dickens's Mrs. Jellyby, the character in *Bleak House* who is so obsessed with schemes to improve Borioboola-Gha, in Africa, that she neglects her own children.

69. Jackson, "The Reign of Archelaus," in *Bits of Talk about Home Matters* (Boston: Roberts Brothers, 1873), 51.

70. Jackson, "The Inhumanities of Parents—Rudeness," in ibid., 37, 36.

71. Jackson to William Ward, July 19, 1871, Huntington.

72. See *Publishers Weekly,* March 8, 1873; undated, anonymous *Boston Post* article; and unidentified clipping; all gathered with other reviews in HHJ1, box 6, fd. 12.

73. Jackson to William Ward, April 4, 1876, Huntington.

74. Jackson, "The Naughtiest Day of My Life, and What Came of It," *St. Nicholas,* September and October 1880.

75. Jackson, "Occupation for Children," in *The Training of Children* (New York: New York and Brooklyn Publishing, 1882), 32.

76. Jackson to William Ward, April 14, 1884, Huntington.

77. Jackson to Abbot Kinney, December 8, 1884, in James, p. 347.

78. Jackson, "Wanted: A Home," in *Home Matters* (1873), 235–37.

79. Jackson to Henry Bowen, April 15, 1884, UVA.

80. Jackson to Anne Lynch Botta, October 11, 1855, Jones.

81. Jackson to Charles Dudley Warner, March 3, 1873, Trinity; Jackson to William Ward, January 23, 1873, NYP.

82. Jackson, "The Inhumanities of Parents—Rudeness," 37.

83. Alice Wellington Rollins, "Authors at Home: Mrs Jackson ('H.H.') at Colorado Springs," *Critic,* April 25, 1885.

84. Jackson to Kate Douglas Wiggin, n.d., Bowdoin.

85. Jackson to Kate Field, September 6, 1868, BP.

86. Jackson to Margaret Channing, March 18, 1869, Harvard.

87. Jackson to Ann Banfield, June 9, 1869, HHJ2.

88. Jackson to Ann Banfield, November 6, 1883, HHJ5.

89. Jackson, *Mercy Philbrick's Choice* (1876), 286.

90. Jackson, "In a Railway Station," in *Home Matters* (1873), 104.

91. Jackson, "Wet the Clay," in ibid., 145.

92. Jackson to James T. Fields, July 29, 1870, Huntington; Jackson to Horace Scudder, April 5, 1868, NYP; Jackson to William Church, February 20, 1867, NYP.

93. Jackson to Horace Scudder, August 20, 1868, NYP.

94. Flora Haynes Apponyi, "The Last Days of Mrs. Helen Hunt Jackson," *Overland Monthly Magazine,* September 1885.

95. When Charles Dudley Warner once teased her for insisting on this propriety, saying, "if you want to be called William instead of Helen I am agreeable," she took up the joke, signing some of her letters, "Yours always, William Jackson." But when Warner actually forgot her mandate, she sent him a serious scolding: "You forget, this time, that my first name is William, outside of a letter!—Don't! I hate it" (Warner to Jackson, April 27, 1880, HHJ2; Jackson to Warner, October 19, 1882 and July 19, 1884, Trinity).

96. In 1870 Jackson requested that "the disagreeable but inevitable advertising" for her soon-to-be-published *Verses* refer to her as Helen Hunt, "widow of the late Major Edward B. Hunt, U.S. Engineer Corps" (Jackson to James T. Fields, October 30, 1870, Huntington). Fifteen years later, when the *Critic* published Alice Wellington Rollins's article on Jackson's home life in Colorado, she was particularly horrified to find that it made no reference to William Jackson. She raged to the editor Joseph Gilder: "The cruel idiotic hurt of this picture of me & my life there without any allusion to my husband, is something which it passes my patience to bear, or my utmost thinking to understand!" (Jackson to Gilder, May 6, 1885, NYP).

97. Jackson to Abigail Williams May, August 17, 1873, Schlesinger.

98. Jackson to Charles Dudley Warner, March 3, 1873, Trinity.

99. Jackson to Whitelaw Reid, n.d., Congress. In her early "Rip Van Winkle" travel article "A Protest against the Spread of Civilization" (*New York Evening Post,* August 29, 1867), Jackson hints that arguments about women's native inferiority almost make her want to support suffrage.

100. Jackson to Edward Seymour, January 30, 1874, BYU.

101. Jackson to Abigail Williams May, August 17, 1873, Schlesinger.

102. Jackson to Whitelaw Reid, May 26, 1870, Congress.

103. Jackson, "American Women," *World,* July 17, 1870. Jackson published her piece as a satirical response to the British writer Justin McCarthy's "American Women and English Women" (*Galaxy,* July 1870).

104. Jackson to Whitelaw Reid, August 4, 1871, Congress.

105. Jackson, "To Leadville," *Atlantic Monthly,* May 1879.

106. Elizabeth Stoddard to Jackson, April 7, 1870, HHJ2; Martha Goddard to Jackson, July 17, 1874, HHJ2.

107. Conversely, Jackson always expressed disdain for the public activities of women who in her opinion promoted sexual immorality, or with whom she had personal grievances. In 1869, because of what she perceived as Kate Field's insulting ad-

vice that she not waste her time in writing Field private letters from Europe, she scorned Field's decision to take up public lecturing. She continued to express contemptuous pity for Field's lectures for the rest of her life. While in Europe in 1869, Jackson also ridiculed news of a lecture to be given by the writer and suffragist Lillie Devereux Blake, explaining to friends that Blake had once written such an "immoral & vulgar book"—probably a reference to *Southwold* (1859)—that Blake's "own cousins the Woolseys, do not speak to her" (Jackson to circle of friends, September 28, 1869, Yale). Though Sarah Woolsey may not have spoken to Blake, she did not scruple to satirize her in the character of "Nippy Nutcracker" the squirrel, who fights "the Wrongs of Squirrelesses" in chapter 10 of *The New Year's Bargain* (Boston: Roberts Brothers, 1872).

108. Jackson to William Ward, February 21, 1876, Huntington.

109. Jackson to Frank Sanborn, February 13, 1872, Dartmouth; Jackson to Charles Dudley Warner, March 12, 1872, Trinity. Jackson also tried to publish a review of the *English Governess* in the *Atlantic* (see Jackson to James T. Fields, December 21, 1870, Huntington).

110. Jackson to Edward Seymour, February 18, 1874, BYU.

111. Higginson, *Contemporaries,* 158. For possible further evidence that Jackson was supportive of Lucy Stone, see a letter from an unknown person to Jackson, July 14, 1873, HHJ2; and the two photos of Stone that Jackson kept among other photos of friends, HHJ1. Jackson also kept two photos of the writer Julia Ward Howe, one of the country's most prominent suffragists, whom she may have met during her Newport years.

112. Jackson to Abby Morton Diaz, October 12, 1874, UVA.

113. Jackson to Elizabeth Hutchinson, October 29, 1882, Yale.

114. For a listing of Dickinson's poems published in her lifetime, see R. W. Franklin, appendix 1, in *The Poems of Emily Dickinson,* by Emily Dickinson, ed. Franklin, variorum ed. (Cambridge, Mass.: Harvard University Press, Belknap Press, 1998), vol. 3.

115. Dickinson's biographers Thomas Johnson and Cynthia Griffin Wolff have both noted the unique importance to her of Jackson's appreciation for her poetry. "Helen Jackson had given Emily Dickinson, as no other person ever did, a sense that her poems were of first importance. Nothing ever touched her more deeply than the recognition thus bestowed upon her art—and by another poet, one whom the best critics of the day acclaimed as a leading, if not the leading, writer of verse in America," says Johnson (*Emily Dickinson: An Interpretive Biography* [Cambridge, Mass.: Belknap Press, 1955]), 179. See also Wolff, *Emily Dickinson* (1986; reprint, Reading, Mass.: Addison-Wesley, 1988), 509.

116. As late as 1885, for unknown reasons, Emily Dickinson identified Jackson herself as Lavinia's friend. See Dickinson's comment in *The Letters of Emily Dickinson,* ed. Thomas H. Johnson (Cambridge, Mass.: Harvard University Press, Belknap Press, 1958), 3:890.

117. Jackson to Henry Root, [1854], HHJ6. In general, this information about Jackson and the Dickinsons in the 1850s is culled from the letters of Jackson and Henry Root in HHJ5 and HHJ6; for Austin's opinion of Hunt, see Austin Dickinson to Sue Gilbert, [July 1852]; quoted in Leyda, *Years and Hours of Emily Dickinson,* 1:253.

118. Thomas Wentworth Higginson to Mary Higginson, [August 17, 1870], in Dickinson, *Letters of Emily Dickinson,* 2:475–76. Dickinson's reputed fondness for

Hunt led some early Dickinson scholars to conjecture, wrongly, that Hunt might have been her secret lover.

119. Jackson and Dickinson are not known to have seen each other in person between 1860 and the period of Jackson's second marriage. In 1873 Jackson asked Dickinson to recommend a boardinghouse in Amherst, but the two women apparently did not meet during Jackson's ensuing visit, for she thought the house unhealthy and left town earlier than planned (see Jackson to Ann Banfield, n.d., HHJ2).

120. Emily Dickinson to Thomas Wentworth Higginson, [November 1871], in Dickinson, *Letters of Emily Dickinson*, 2:491. While most scholars, like myself, believe that Dickinson genuinely appreciated Jackson's work, a few have questioned the sincerity of her praise. See, for example, Betsey Erkkila, *The Wicked Sisters: Women Poets, Literary History, and Discord* (New York: Oxford University Press, 1992), esp. 87, 97.

121. Emily Dickinson to Thomas Wentworth Higginson, [spring 1886], and Emily Dickinson to Forrest F. Emerson, [late September 1885], in Dickinson, *Letters of Emily Dickinson*, 3:903, 890. Severn was with the poet John Keats when Keats died, and recorded his final words.

122. Emily Dickinson to William Jackson, draft, in ibid., 3:889.

123. See Dickinson, *The Poems of Emily Dickinson*, 3:1474–75.

124. Jackson refers to the poetry of "E.D." in a letter to Thomas Wentworth Higginson, July 22, 1881, Harvard; and she sometimes forwarded to Higginson poems that Dickinson sent her. Over the course of their correspondence, Dickinson included the following poems, or lines from them, in letters to Jackson: "Upon a Lilac Sea," "Spurn the temerity," "Before you thought of Spring," "One of the ones that Midas touched," "A Route of Evanescence," "To be forgot by thee," "Upon his Saddle sprung a Bird," "In other Motes," "The farthest Thunder that I heard," "Take all away from me, but leave me Ecstasy" (unsent), "Of God we ask one favor" (unsent), and perhaps "How happy is the little stone" (see Dickinson, *The Poems of Emily Dickinson*, 3:1553–54, 1299).

125. Jackson to Emily Dickinson, March 20, 1876, in Dickinson, *Letters of Emily Dickinson*, 2:545.

126. Jackson's own contributions to *A Masque of Poets*, ed. George Parsons Lathrop (Boston: Roberts Brothers, 1878), included "A Woman's Death Wound," mentioned earlier; "Horizon"; and "Quatrains—The Money-Seeker; The Lover," which also appears in *Poems* (1892), 216.

127. Emily Dickinson to Thomas Wentworth Higginson, [October 1876], in Dickinson, *Letters of Emily Dickinson*, 2:563.

128. Jackson to Emily Dickinson, [October 1876], in ibid., 2:565.

129. Jackson to Emily Dickinson, April 29, 1878, in ibid., 2:624–25. As it happened, many readers of *A Masque of Poets* believed Emerson to have written the Dickinson poem that finally appeared in the volume, "Success."

130. Emily Dickinson to Maria Whitney, [late 1878], in ibid., 2:623; and Dickinson to Thomas Wentworth Higginson, [November 1878], in ibid., 2:627.

131. Jackson to Emily Dickinson, October 25, 1878, in ibid., 2:625.

132. Jackson to Emily Dickinson, December 8, 1878, in ibid., 2:626.

133. Jackson, Our Book Table, "A Critical Opinion of the Last Literary Venture," *Denver Tribune*, date unknown, stored in HHJ1.

134. This particular quotation is from Jackson to Emily Dickinson, February 3, 1885, in Dickinson, *Letters of Emily Dickinson*, 3:869. In 1882 Thomas Niles of Roberts Brothers wrote to Dickinson: " 'H.H.' once told me that she wished you could be induced to publish a volume of poems. I should not want to say how highly she praised them, but to such an extent that I wish also that you could" (Niles to Dickinson, April 24, 1882, in ibid., 3:726). For Dickinson's response to "the kind but incredible opinion of 'H.H.,' " see her letter to Niles, [late April 1882], in ibid., 3:725.

135. Jackson to Emily Dickinson, September 5, 1884, in ibid., 3:841–42.

136. Jackson to Thomas Bailey Aldrich, February 22, 1883, Harvard; Jackson to Horace Scudder, July 9, 1874, NYP.

Chapter 6. Travel Writing

1. Jackson to Parke Godwin, October 15, 1865, NYP.

2. Jackson to Henry Root, May 17, 1852, HHJ5.

3. Jackson, "Boston Gossip," *New York Evening Post*, October 9, 1867.

4. Jackson, "Mountain Life: The New Hampshire Town of Bethlehem—Where It Is, What It Is, and All about It," *New York Evening Post*, October 18, 1865.

5. Susan Coolidge [Sarah Woolsey], introduction to *Ramona*, by Jackson, Monterey edition (Boston: Little, Brown, 1900), xiii.

6. Jackson to Ann Banfield, October 11, 1874, Wisconsin.

7. Jackson, "A Bethlehem of Today," *New York Independent*, June 30, 1870.

8. Jackson to Whitelaw Reid, July 1, 1870, Congress.

9. Jackson, "A Protest against the Spread of Civilization," *New York Evening Post*, August 29, 1867.

10. Jackson to Edward Everett Hale, June 19, 1870, Penn.

11. Jackson, "A Second Celestial Railroad," *New York Independent*, October 13, 1870.

12. Jackson, "Mt. Washington in September," *New York Independent*, September 28, 1871.

13. Edward Hitchcock, *Reminiscences of Amherst College, Historical, Scientific, Biographical, and Autobiographical: Also, of Other and Wider Life Experiences* (Northampton, Mass.: Bridgman & Childs, 1863), 224–25.

14. Jackson, "A New Sleepy Hollow: Letter from Rip Van Winkle," *New York Evening Post*, January 13, 1868, and "A Morning in a Vermont Graveyard," *New York Evening Post*, November 14, 1867 (also collected in *Bits of Travel at Home* [1878; reprint, Boston: Roberts Brothers, 1880], 201–7). See also Jackson's later "Hide and Seek Town," where she reports reading in "some old, tattered leather-bound books behind the counter of 'the store' " about the fears colonists in Princeton, Massachusetts, had of "hostile Indians" (*Scribner's Monthly*, August 1877; also collected in *Travel at Home* [1878], 175–90).

15. Jackson to Deborah Fiske, [September 1842], HHJ1.

16. Deborah Fiske to Jackson, [1842], HHJ1.

17. Jackson, "Notes of Travel: Letter from Rip Van Winkle," *New York Evening Post*, November 27, 1867.

18. Jackson, "A Bethlehem of Today" (1870).

19. Jackson uses "Sleepy Hollow" as a sly reference to Newport, a place full of

Van Winkle "artists," "for whose work there must first be a dream" ("A New Sleepy Hollow" [1868]).

20. Many American writers of Jackson's era worked under Irving's influence, and many called Rip Van Winkle to mind as they surveyed their changing country. Irving meant the most to Jackson at the start of her career; but even as late as 1882, when she visited Oregon, she alluded to his 1836 *Astoria* (see "Chance Days in Oregon," in *Glimpses of Three Coasts* [Boston: Roberts Brothers, 1886], 130).

21. Given the growing emphasis on characters in Jackson's travel essays, it is not surprising that when she actually began to write fiction, she found material for two short stories among her early Rip Van Winkle essays. Her story "Massy Sprague's Daughter" (*Atlantic Monthly,* July 1879) draws on her travel essay "An Out of the Way Place: From Sleepy Hollow to Block Island" (*New York Evening Post,* August 18, 1868), and her story "Esther Wynn's Love-Letters" (*Scribner's Monthly,* December 1871; reprinted in *Saxe Holm's Stories, First Series* [1873; reprint, New York: Charles Scribner's Sons, 1898], 313–50) is based on an incident first related in "A Turkish Bath and a Parcel of Old Love Letters" (*New York Evening Post,* December 19, 1867).

22. Jackson to James T. Fields, November 16, 1870, Huntington.

23. Jackson, "Encyclicals," in *Bits of Travel* (Boston: J. R. Osgood, 1872), 193, 233, 168.

24. Jackson to circle of friends, January 31, 1869, Yale.

25. Jackson, "Encyclicals," 134.

26. This particular quotation is from a later travel essay, "Holy Cross Village and Mrs. Pope's," in *Travel at Home* (1878), 53.

27. Jackson, "A German Landlady," in *Bits of Travel* (1872), 5.

28. In the summer of 1869, Jackson spent several weeks alone in the Bavarian Alps and Badgastein, Austria, studying the classic works of Transcendentalism: Emerson's essays and Henry David Thoreau's published letters and *A Week on the Concord and Merrimack Rivers* (1849). While she often publicly mentioned her appreciation for Emerson, in her encyclicals from Europe as elsewhere, she expressed her admiration for Thoreau less frequently; see her early travel essay "In the White Mountains" (*New York Independent,* September 13, 1866) and her later unsigned review for the *Denver Tribune,* Our Book Table, "A Critical Opinion of the Last Literary Venture" (HHJ1, box 6, fd. 3).

29. Jackson, "A May-Day in Albano," in *Bits of Travel* (1872), 85.

30. Ibid., 87.

31. Jackson, "Encyclicals," 244.

32. Jackson to James T. Fields, March 10, 1871, Huntington.

33. Jackson, "Encyclicals," 206. In the case of Venice, Jackson also wished not to sound like the famed literary figures who had preceded her to that place, William D. Howells and John Ruskin. She initially admired Howells's *Venetian Life* (1866) and Ruskin's *Stones of Venice* (1851–53), and in her professional capacity continued to offer these books praise; but in her private correspondence from Europe she admitted that she had grown to detest them both.

34. Jackson, review of *My Summer in a Garden,* by Charles Dudley Warner, *Scribner's Monthly,* March 1871. Later in her career, Jackson seems to have enjoyed Robert Louis Stevenson's comic travel book, *Travels with a Donkey in the Cévennes* (1879). Her copy of the book, with Stevenson's card, is housed today in the Pioneers Museum of Colorado Springs.

35. Twain's *Innocents Abroad* began to appear in the *New York Tribune* before Jackson left for Europe. Her only reference to it or any of Twain's work in her extant letters is an insistence that Sarah Woolsey had drawn *not* on *The Innocents Abroad* in one of her children's stories, but instead verbatim from the diary of Jackson's own deceased son, Rennie (see Jackson to Charles Dudley Warner, January 14, 1873, Trinity).

36. In one of her earlier European travel essays, "A Glimpse of the Queen of England" (*New York Independent*, December 16, 1869), Jackson had identified personally with Queen Victoria in her efforts to survive widowhood, but she did not develop her standard regionalist manner of describing her subjects until "A German Landlady."

37. Jackson, "A German Landlady," 3, 11, 2.

38. Caroline Hahlreiner, inscription on back of photo, HHJ1.

39. Anonymous to Jackson, n.d., HHJ2, box 2, fd. 28. I have been unable to locate the offending essay or essays.

40. Jackson, "Encyclicals," 233.

41. Jackson's "Abbot Paphnutius" is also reprinted in *Poems* (1892; reprint, Boston: Little, Brown, 1906), 78–82.

42. Jackson to James T. Fields, October 11, 1870, Huntington.

43. Jackson to Charles Dudley Warner, July 18, 1878, Trinity.

44. See anonymous article in the *Weekly Trade Circular,* February 1, 1872, and other articles gathered in HHJ1, box 6, fd. 11.

45. Jackson to Julius Palmer, March 1852, HHJ2.

46. Sarah Woolsey to William Ward, July 18, 1872, Morgan.

47. When Jackson and Woolsey visited Santa Cruz, Eliza Farnham was dead, but her friend Georgia Bruce (Kirby), of whom Farnham had written in *California, In-doors and Out,* was still alive and resident in the town. Like Farnham, Kirby was a writer in addition to a pioneer and farmer. Jackson was delighted to meet her. Jackson's essay "Holy Cross Village and Mrs. Pope's" is collected in *Travel at Home* (1878), 53–61.

48. Jackson, "The Geysers," in *Travel at Home* (1878), 46.

49. Jackson, "San Francisco," in ibid., 84.

50. Jackson, "From Ogden to San Francisco" and "From Chicago to Ogden," in ibid., 40, 6–7.

51. Jackson, "Salt Lake City," in ibid., 17, 27, 22. Years later, Jackson would again write sympathetically of Mormon women and their convictions in "Women of the Beehive," *Century,* May 1884.

52. Jackson, "The Chinese Empire," in *Travel at Home* (1878), 74, 62–64.

53. Jackson, "From Chicago to Ogden," 9–10.

54. Jackson, "The Way to Ah-Wah-Ne," "Ah-wah-ne Days," and "Pi-wy-ack and Yo-wi-he," in *Travel at Home* (1878), 91, 107, 108, 115.

55. Jackson, "My Day in the Wilderness" and "Ah-wah-ne Days," in ibid., 157, 114.

56. Jackson to Charles Dudley Warner, September 23, 1872, Trinity.

57. Jackson to William Ward, May 11, 1873, Huntington. Jackson first publicly mentioned Colorado, more explicitly Pike's Peak, in an early travel essay, "In the White Mountains" (1866).

58. Jackson, "Colorado Springs," in *Travel at Home* (1878), 224.

59. Jackson to Kate Field, April 23, 1874, BPL.

60. Jackson, "Colorado Springs," 226.

61. Jackson to Anne Lynch Botta, January 28, 1874, Jones.

62. Jackson to Ann Banfield, December 13, 1875, HHJ6.

63. See Robert Lamborn to Jackson, April 24 and May 9, 1875, HHJ2.

64. Jackson to Charlotte Cushman, n.d., fragment, Congress.

65. Jackson to Charlotte Cushman, July 29, 1875, Congress.

66. Coolidge, introduction to *Ramona,* xix.

67. Jackson to Ann Banfield, November 12, 1875, HHJ5.

68. William and Helen Jackson to Samuel Bowles, February 27, 1876, YS.

69. William Jackson [with explanatory note added by William Ward] to Ward, May 2, 1876, Huntington.

70. Jackson to Hannah Jackson Price, May 22, 1876, WSJ3.

71. Jackson to Ann Banfield, August 28, 1872, HHJ6.

72. Jackson hints at these rustic accommodations in "The Stone-Mason's Garden of Eden," *Christian Union,* November 23, 1881. They are also described in a rare eyewitness account by Mrs. Emma Brown, of Golden, Colorado, in "A Day with Helen Hunt Jackson" (typescript in Bancroft, BANC MSS 93/18c). As a child, Brown camped with her parents near the Jacksons in Crystal Park. Though the Jacksons' "accommodations were far from luxurious," Brown says, "Mrs. Jackson's enthusiasm more than sufficed for all deficiency." Jackson delighted the girl by inviting her for a carriage ride and then, after finishing some writing, jumping out with her to explore a gulf.

73. William Dean Howells to Jackson, April 18, 1880, HHJ2.

74. Among the New England essays included in *Bits of Travel at Home* is Jackson's 1867 Rip Van Winkle piece, "A Morning in a Vermont Graveyard." Perhaps Jackson was not averse to discerning readers' discovering the joint identity of "Rip Van Winkle" and "H.H."

75. Anonymous (probably by Charles Dudley Warner), article from the *Hartford Courant,* date unknown, held in HHJ1; T. S. Perry, review of *Bits of Travel at Home,* by Jackson, *Atlantic Monthly,* December 1878.

76. Jackson, "Down the Arkansas River to New York," *New York Independent,* October 3 and 17, 1878.

77. Jackson, "A Symphony in Yellow and Red," in *Travel at Home* (1878), 219.

78. Jackson, "The Cradle of Peace," in ibid., 314–15.

79. Jackson, "To Leadville," *Atlantic Monthly,* May 1879.

80. Jackson, "Alamosa," *New York Independent,* June 6 and 13, 1878.

81. Jackson, "Wa-ha-toy-a; or, Before the Graders," in *Travel at Home* (1878), 356–58.

82. Ibid., 362.

83. Jackson to Moncure Conway, n.d., fragment, Columbia.

84. Jackson, "Elspeth Dynor," unpublished MS, in NYP, 299–300.

85. William Jackson to Jackson, July 18, 1875, WSJ1. I have been unable to locate Jackson's poem "Pheonixiana."

86. Jackson to Ann Banfield, November 22, 1877, HHJ5.

87. Jackson to Moncure Conway, January 14, 1877, Columbia.

88. Jackson to circle of friends, January 11, 1869, Yale.

89. William Jackson to Jackson, July 18, 1875, WSJ1. Jackson's "Freedom" appears in *Poems* (1892), 175–76.

90. See part 3 of Jackson's "Eden, Formerly on the Euphrates," *New York Independent*, October 9, 16, and 23, 1879. This essay, one of the few New England pieces Jackson wrote after becoming an experienced fiction writer, is also of special interest because it is in some ways more typical of New England regionalist writing than are her earliest pieces. It features lonely old women who have been left behind in the countryside by their urbanized offspring.

91. See Jackson to Henry Dawes, December 10, 1880, Congress.

92. Jackson, "The Kansas & Colorado Building at the Centennial Exposition," *New York Independent*, October 12, 1876; and "A State without a Debt," *Christian Union*, November 22, 1883.

93. Jackson, "Alamosa" (1878).

94. Jackson to Moncure Conway, January 14, 1877, Columbia.

95. Jackson to Charles Dudley Warner, July 29, 1874 and October 31, 1882, Trinity.

96. Jackson, "Colorado Springs," 233. As early as 1852, Jackson had envisioned the West as "the field of action, for the next fifty years." "I can conceive it a glorious mission to plunge into the midst of the crude elements there, and hasten on the fulfillment," she told Henry Root: "still it would be a mission, bearing the life long character of martyrdom" (Jackson to Root, July 3, 1852, HHJ6).

97. Jackson, "A Day in Trinidad," *New York Independent*, June 5, 1879. On "romantic racialism," see George M. Fredrickson, *The Black Image in the White Mind: The Debate on Afro-American Character and Destiny, 1817–1914* (New York: Harper & Row, 1971).

98. Jackson, "By Horse Cars into Mexico," *Atlantic Monthly*, March 1883.

99. Jackson's "A Colorado Road" appears as "Our New Road" in *Travel at Home* (1878), 331–44.

100. Jackson, "O-Be-Joyful Creek and Poverty Gulch," *Atlantic Monthly*, December 1883.

101. Jackson, "To Leadville" (1879).

102. Jackson, "A New Anvil Chorus," in *Travel at Home* (1878), 402, 400.

103. Jackson, "Aunty Lane," *Atlantic Monthly*, May 1882.

Chapter 7. Short Stories and Early Novels

1. Jackson to Kate Field, March 7, 1866, BP.

2. Susan Coultrap-McQuin, " 'Very Serious Literary Labor': The Career of Helen Hunt Jackson," in *Doing Literary Business: American Women Writers in the Nineteenth Century* (Chapel Hill: University of North Carolina Press, 1990), 161.

3. Review of *Saxe Holm's Stories, First Series,* by Jackson, *Publisher's Weekly,* October 25, 1873.

4. [Samuel Bowles], "Saxe Holm's Stories: A New England Writer of New England Fiction," *Springfield Republican*, January 1, 1874.

5. Jackson, "Wanted, in New England, An Apostle for Sunshine," *New York Independent*, July 5, 1877.

6. Jackson, "Whose Wife Was She?" in *Saxe Holm's Stories, First Series* (1873; reprint, New York: Charles Scribner's Sons, 1898), 166–67.

7. Ibid., 204. See also "Notes of Travel: Letter from Rip Van Winkle," *New York Evening Post*, November 27, 1867.

8. Jackson, "A Four-Leaved Clover," in *Saxe Holm's Stories, Second Series* (1878; reprint, New York: Charles Scribner's Sons, 1899), 23.

9. Jackson, "Joe Hale's Red Stockings," in ibid., 268.

10. Jackson, "The Elder's Wife," in *Saxe Holm's Stories, First Series* (1873), 91.

11. Ibid., 123.

12. Ibid.

13. Jackson, "Aunty Lane," *Atlantic Monthly,* May 1882.

14. Jackson to William Ward, February 28, 1874, Jones.

15. Jackson, "A Good Word for 'Gush,'" *New York Independent,* January 18, 1872.

16. Jackson to Thomas Niles, March 2, 1871, UVA.

17. In a review in *Scribner's Monthly,* October 1871, Jackson condemns *A Terrible Temptation* by the popular English writer Charles Reade for "vulgarity" and "indecency"; she lambastes *Nana* in a letter to William Jackson, [1879], WSJ1.

18. Jackson to Charles Dudley Warner, February 8, 1885, Trinity.

19. Jackson to Charles Dudley Warner, July 21, 1872, Trinity.

20. Jackson to William Dean Howells, July 31, 1876, Hayes.

21. Jackson to Charles Dudley Warner, February 8, 1885, Trinity.

22. Jackson to Thomas Bailey Aldrich, January 10, 1885, Harvard.

23. See Moncure Daniel Conway, *Autobiography, Memories and Experiences of Moncure Daniel Conway* (Boston: Houghton, Mifflin, 1904), 1:202.

24. Jackson's acceptance of Eliot's relationship with Lewes may have been influenced by idealized notions of her own early involvement with Thomas Wentworth Higginson. She was far less charitable with both Charles Dickens and William Hunt when she came to believe that they were guilty of adultery.

25. Moncure Conway to Jackson, December 24 [no year], HHJ2.

26. Jackson, "Esther Wynn's Love-Letters," in *Saxe Holm's Stories, First Series* (1873), 318, 315.

27. Anonymous article, *New York World,* title and date unknown, HHJ1, box 6, fd. 13.

28. Jackson to Messrs. Charles Scribner's Sons, March 1, 1879, Princeton. Fan letters to Saxe Holm, which support Jackson's claim, are held in HHJ2, box 2.

29. "The Unknown Story-Teller," *New York Times,* date unknown, HHJ1, box 6, fd. 13; the "mystical burden" is described in "Books, Authors, and Art," *Springfield Republican,* July 26, 1878.

30. Jackson to Edward Seymour, January 2, 1874, BYU.

31. Charlotte Cushman to Jackson, January 6, 1874, HHJ2.

32. Charlotte Cushman to Jackson, [February 1874], HHJ2.

33. [Bowles], "Saxe Holm's Stories."

34. Jackson to Edward Seymour, January 30, 1874, BYU.

35. Jackson to William Ward, February 4, 1874, Huntington.

36. Jackson to Edward Seymour, November 18, 1874, BYU.

37. Jackson to Edward Seymour, February 18, 1874, BYU.

38. Jackson, "Saxe Holm Rises to Explain," *Woman's Journal,* April 4, 1874.

39. Jackson to Edward Seymour, August 10, 1875, BYU.

40. "Books, Authors, and Art." For a selection of contemporary newspaper articles about the identity of Saxe Holm and the Saxe Holm claimants, see holdings in Helen Hunt Jackson "miscellaneous clippings," NYP; and HHJ1, box 6, fd. 13.

41. Jackson to John B. Scribner, June 25, 1878, Princeton.

42. Jackson to Moncure Conway, November 16, 1875, Columbia; Conway to Jackson, December 24 [no year], HHJ2.

43. Jackson to Edward Seymour, January 30, 1874, BYU.

44. Jackson et al., "A Card from Saxe Holm," *New York Tribune,* June 1, 1877. "Who Saxe-Holm Is" appeared in the *Tribune* on May 12, 1877.

45. This anonymous piece makes several negative insinuations about Jackson. The editor Samuel Bowles, who had written the review of *Saxe Holm Stories, First Series* that so enraged Jackson, died in 1878. By that point, friendly relations had been fully restored between them. The Jacksons were grateful to Samuel Bowles for having introduced them, as noted in chapter 6; and according to Emily Dickinson, "love of Mr Bowles" led them to visit his bereaved wife during their October 1878 travels in Massachusetts (Dickinson to Maria Whitney, [late 1878], in *The Letters of Emily Dickinson,* ed. Thomas H. Johnson [Cambridge, Mass.: Harvard University Press, Belknap Press, 1958], 2:623).

46. See paragraph by anonymous editor attached to a reprinting of Saxe Holm's letter to Celia Burleigh titled "Letter from 'Saxe Holme' [sic]," no citation information, HHJ1, box 6, fd. 13.

47. "Saxe Holm Evolved," *Springfield Republican,* May 25, 1878.

48. Thomas Wentworth Higginson, *Short Studies of American Authors,* rev. ed. (Boston: Lee & Shepard, 1888), 47.

49. Jackson to Moncure Conway, November 16, 1875, Columbia.

50. Jackson to John B. Scribner, July 11, 1878, Princeton.

51. Jackson to Edward Seymour, [October 1873] and January 2, 1874, BYU.

52. Anonymous article about the Saxe Holm stories, *Travelers Record,* date unknown, in HHJ1, box 6, fd. 24.

53. Jackson to Thomas Bailey Aldrich, October 16, 1882, Harvard.

54. Higginson, *Short Studies of American Authors,* 46.

55. Josiah Holland, quoted in Richard Watson Gilder to Jackson, March 21, 1874, HHJ2.

56. See the anonymous review of *Everyday Topics,* by Josiah Holland, *Nation,* June 21, 1877; and Jackson to William Jackson, June 28, 1877, WSJ1.

57. Jackson to Charles Dudley Warner, December 22, 1873, Trinity.

58. Jackson, review of *My Summer in a Garden,* by Charles Dudley Warner, *Scribner's Monthly,* March 1871; Jackson to Warner, January 17, 1871, Trinity.

59. Jackson quotes Charles Dudley Warner in a letter to him, December 22, 1873, Trinity.

60. Charles Dudley Warner, quoted in "The Holmes Breakfast," *Atlantic Monthly,* supplement, February 1880.

61. Jackson to Charles Dudley Warner, April 24, 1880, Trinity.

62. Jackson to Charles Dudley Warner, [1880], Trinity.

63. William Jackson to Jackson, June 6, 1880, WSJ1.

64. William Jackson to Jackson, June 25, 1880, WSJ1.

65. William Jackson to Jackson, including his quotation of her words, November 9, 1874, WSJ1; William Jackson to Jackson, August 15, 1875, WSJ1.

66. Jackson to William Ward, November 1, 1876, Huntington.

67. Jackson to William Ward, [1876], Huntington; Jackson to Ann Banfield, November 16, 1876, HHJ5.

68. Jackson to Moncure Conway, n.d., fragment, Columbia.

69. Jackson to Elizabeth Benham, January 30, [1880], NHHS.

70. Some literary historians and critics, knowing little about Jackson and interested not in her but in her friend Emily Dickinson, have erroneously argued or been persuaded by arguments that Jackson intended Mercy Philbrick to be a portrait not of herself but of Emily Dickinson, because Mercy is a poet who dresses in white. In fact, not only is Jackson's first novel palpably autobiographical, but it is worth noting that even if Jackson did make fictional use of Dickinson's dressing habits, she also had her own interest in the symbolic meanings of white clothing, having spent many years of her own life in black mourning dress. As early as 1873, when her adult relationship with Dickinson was just beginning, she depicted her Saxe Holm heroine Draxy Miller as wearing only white clothing following her husband's death, under a belief that gloomy mourning clothes were unchristian. And when Jackson saw her own death approaching, she specifically requested that nobody ever wear mourning clothes on her behalf. Similarly erroneous are any claims that the poems included in Jackson's early Saxe Holm story "Esther Wynn's Love-Letters" are poor imitations of Dickinson's. In fact, they are characteristic of her own work.

71. Jackson to Edward Seymour, June 1, 1876, in unattributed transcript, HHJ6.

72. Jackson, *Mercy Philbrick's Choice*, No Name Series (Boston: Roberts Brothers, 1876), 13; this edition is hereafter cited parenthetically in the text.

73. Henrietta Hardy, Brooklyn, to Jackson, July 13, 1877, HHJ2.

74. Thomas Niles to Jackson, July 6, 1876, WSJ1.

75. Raymond L. Kilgour, *Messrs. Roberts Brothers Publishers* (Ann Arbor: University of Michigan Press, 1952), 151.

76. Review of *Mercy Philbrick's Choice*, by Jackson, *Saturday Review*, November 4, 1876.

77. Mr. Crocker, "A Re-Review of a Review," *Literary World*, stored together with *Boston Daily Advertiser* piece, dates unknown, in HHJ1, box 6, fd. 14. The *Literary World*'s original review was published on November 1, 1876.

78. Henry James, "An American and an English Novel," *Nation*, December 21, 1876.

79. Jackson to Moncure Conway, January 14, 1877, Columbia.

80. Ibid. Jackson quotes Conway's "printed" words in this letter.

81. Jackson to Ann Banfield, March 20, 1877, HHJ5.

82. Jackson, *Hetty's Strange History*, No Name Series (Boston: Roberts Brothers, 1877), 291; this edition is hereafter cited parenthetically in the text.

83. Gail Hamilton, "A Pair of Novels," *New York Independent*, October 11, 1877. See also other reviews of *Hetty's Strange History* in HHJ1, box 6, fd. 14.

84. Jackson to William Jackson, June 28, 1877, WSJ1.

85. Jackson, *Nelly's Silver Mine* (1878; reprint, Boston: Roberts Brothers, 1885), 45, 50, 288.

86. Ibid., 119.

87. Ibid., 379.

88. Review of *Nelly's Silver Mine*, by Jackson, *Atlantic Monthly*, December 1878.

89. See Kilgour, *Messrs. Roberts Brothers Publishers*, 161, 297 n. 161; and records of Little, Brown in WSJ1.

90. Some contemporary newspaper articles suggest that Jackson may have published earlier pieces of short fiction as "H.H.," but I have not been able to locate any.

91. Jackson to William Ward, January 19, 1875, Huntington.

92. Jackson to Thomas Bailey Aldrich, April 3, 1884, Harvard. In this letter Jackson says that in addition to the two stories I mention, Jane Silsbee has "masqueraded in some other places also, & will have a volume out some day." I have not been able to locate any other Jane Silsbee stories.

93. Jackson to Charles Dudley Warner, November 9, 1880, Trinity.

94. Thomas Niles, in Jackson, *Between Whiles* (1887; reprint, Boston: Roberts Brothers, 1898), 115.

95. The existing manuscript of "Elspeth Dynor" includes pages 1–50, 220–406, and 408–566. By 1932 it had somehow made its way to a Connecticut bookstore, and was brought to the attention of Ruth Odell, Jackson's biographer, by Gilbert Doane of the University of Wisconsin. Odell later transferred the novel along with her other Jackson papers to the New York Public Library.

96. Jackson, "Elspeth Dynor," 31; the manuscript is hereafter quoted parenthetically in the text.

97. Jackson, "The Inn of the Golden Pear," in *Between Whiles* (1887), 7–8.

98. William Jackson to Jackson, [August 1879], WSJ1.

CHAPTER 8. INDIAN REFORM WORK, LATE TRAVEL WRITING, AND *RAMONA*

1. Jackson, "Wanted, in New England, An Apostle for Sunshine," *New York Independent,* July 5, 1877.

2. In a letter to Miss Clarke, April 14, 1880, Smith, Jackson claims she began Indian reform work the previous October. In a letter to William Ward (October 25, 1879), Huntington, she makes no mention of such work, which suggests that she first heard Standing Bear at the October 29 event.

3. Jackson, writing about Carl Schurz, to William Ward, March 23, 1881, Huntington.

4. In January 1881, perhaps with Jackson's encouragement, La Flesche published her first piece of fiction, "Nedawi," in *St. Nicholas.* In later years, married to Thomas Henry Tibbles, she would do some work as a journalist, including a stint as a war correspondent from the battle of Wounded Knee.

5. Susette La Flesche, introduction to *Standing Bear and the Ponca Chiefs* (1879), by Thomas Henry Tibbles, ed. Kay Graber (Lincoln: University of Nebraska Press, 1995), 3.

6. Jackson to Thomas Wentworth Higginson, January 17, 1880, in Higginson, *Contemporaries* (Boston: Houghton, Mifflin, 1899), 155.

7. Jackson to Bishop Whipple, October 29, 1880, MNHS.

8. Edward Bissell Hunt, *Union Foundations: A Study of American Nationality as a Fact of Science* (New York: D. Van Nostrand, 1863), 49.

9. Jackson to Charles Dudley Warner, October 2, 1884, Trinity.

10. Nathan Fiske to Deborah Fiske, December 22, 1829, HHJ1.

11. Heman Humphrey, *Indian Rights and Our Duties: An Address Delivered at Amherst, Hartford, etc., December 1829* (Amherst, Mass.: J. S. & C. Adams, 1830), 13, 16.

12. Jackson to Whitelaw Reid, December 1, 1880, Congress.

13. Jackson to Whitelaw Reid, December 20, 1879, Congress.

14. Jackson to Charles Dudley Warner, December 3, 1880 and February 12, 1881, Trinity; Jackson to Henry Dawes, December 10, 1880, Congress.

15. Jackson to Thomas Henry Tibbles, March 4, 1880, UVA.

16. Jackson to Charles Dudley Warner, December 21, 1879, Trinity.

17. Jackson quoting William Jackson in a letter to him, December 26, 1879, WSJ1.

18. Jackson to Amelia Stone Quinton, August 19, 1881, Bancroft.

19. Jackson to William Jackson, December 26, 1879, WSJ1.

20. William Jackson to Jackson, [1880], WSJ1.

21. Jackson to Amelia Stone Quinton, August 19, 1881, Bancroft.

22. Jackson to William Jackson, December 16, 1879, WSJ1.

23. Jackson to William Jackson, December 19, 1879, WSJ1.

24. For a more complete overview of relations between the federal government and Indian tribes than Jackson offers, see Francis Paul Prucha, *The Great Father: The United States Government and the American Indians,* abridged ed. (Lincoln: University of Nebraska Press, 1984).

25. Jackson, *A Century of Dishonor: A Sketch of the United States Government's Dealings with Some of the Indian Tribes* (New York: Harper & Brothers, 1881), 7, 30, 10.

26. Jackson to Whitelaw Reid, June 25, 1879, Congress.

27. Jackson's 1880 manuscript book (not to be confused with her 1880 date book) is stored in HHJ1, box 3.

28. Jackson, "Chester Streets," in *Glimpses of Three Coasts* (Boston: Roberts Brothers, 1886), 218.

29. Jackson refers to the outline of "The Cook of the Buckeye Mine" as a projected play in a letter to William Jackson, July 26, 1880, WSJ1.

30. William Jackson to Jackson, November 9, 1874, WSJ1. Indeed, William apparently disliked writing letters of any sort. "He hates to write a letter," Helen explained in 1877 to her mother-in-law Mary Ann, who had been hearing little from her son. "The only way I get any out of him, myself, when we are separated, is by giving him a package of envelopes all addressed and stamped, ready to mail, so that he has only to slip in a bit of paper with a few words written on it" (Jackson to Mary Ann Jackson, November 17, 1877, fragment, HHJ6).

31. Jackson to William Jackson, July 24, 1880, WSJ1.

32. Jackson to William Jackson, July 1, 1880, WSJ1.

33. William Jackson to Jackson, June 25, 1880, WSJ1.

34. William Jackson to Jackson, [1880], WSJ1.

35. William Jackson to Jackson, May 30, 1880, WSJ1.

36. Jackson, 1880 manuscript book, HHJ1.

37. Jackson, "Encyclicals of a Traveller," in *Glimpses of Three Coasts* (1886), 355.

38. Jackson to William Jackson, September 11, 1880, WSJ2.

39. William Jackson to Jackson, September 10, 1880, WSJ1.

40. Jackson to Oliver Wendell Holmes, March 19, 1881, Congress.

41. See Thomas Wentworth Higginson, "How Ramona Was Written," *Atlantic Monthly,* November 1900.

42. Jackson to Rebecca Harding Davis, December 30, 1880, UVA.

43. Jackson to Charles Dudley Warner, March 3, 1881, Trinity.

44. Jackson to Henry Houghton, March 20, 1881, Harvard; review of *A Century of Dishonor,* by Jackson, *Nation,* March 3, 1881.

45. Francis Parkman to Jackson, April 15, 1881, HHJ2.

46. Jackson to unknown recipient, January 13, 1885, Princeton.

47. Jackson to Amelia Stone Quinton, August 19, 1881, Bancroft.

48. Jackson to Lilly [Elizabeth Dwight Woolsey] Gilman, March 4 [1881], Hopkins.

49. Jackson, "A Pot of Gold," *New York Independent,* July 26, 1883, and "A Short Cut from Icicles to Oranges," *Christian Union,* February 19, 1885.

50. Jackson, "Echoes in the City of the Angels," in *Glimpses of Three Coasts* (1886), 110.

51. Jackson to Thomas Bailey Aldrich, April 12, 1882, Harvard.

52. Jackson to Abbot Kinney, February 4, 1882, Bancroft.

53. She may also have drawn on Rancho Guajome, in San Diego County, but there is no firm evidence of her having visited that estate.

54. Jackson to Ann Banfield, March 11, 1882, HHJ6.

55. Jackson, entries for March 8–11, 1882 date book, HHJ1.

56. After Jackson's death, Sandham also illustrated the 1900 Monterey edition of *Ramona* (Boston: Little, Brown).

57. Abbott Kinney, quoted in George Wharton James, *Through Ramona's Country* (1908; reprint, Boston: Little, Brown, 1913), 317.

58. Jackson to Thomas Wentworth Higginson, February 5, 1884; in Higginson, "How Ramona Was Written."

59. Jackson, "Outdoor Industries in Southern California," in *Glimpses of Three Coasts* (1886), 3, 29.

60. Jackson to Thomas Bailey Aldrich, April 21, 1882, Harvard.

61. Jackson to Abbot Kinney, January 29, 1882, Bancroft.

62. Jackson to Thomas Bailey Aldrich, May 4, 1883, Harvard.

63. See, for example, Jackson to William Ward, April 10, 1882, Huntington.

64. Jackson, "Outdoor Industries in Southern California," 4, 9.

65. Jackson, "Echoes in the City of the Angels," 112–13, 124.

66. Antonio Coronel's original *testimonio* is housed along with the other testimonials gathered by Hubert Bancroft in the Bancroft Library at the University of California. It is also available in English in an abridged translation, *Tales of Mexican California,* ed. Doyce B. Nunis, Jr., trans. Diane de Avalle-Arce (Santa Barbara, Calif.: Bellerophon Books, 1994).

67. Genaro M. Padillo, *My History, Not Yours: The Formation of Mexican American Autobiography* (Madison: University of Wisconsin Press, 1993), x.

68. Jackson, "Echoes in the City of the Angels," 120. At the turn of the twenty-first century, "borderlands" historians, who focus on those areas of the United States that were once part of the Spanish empire, and especially Chicano and Chicana scholars, have made available many more accurate and complete assessments of early Hispanic culture in California.

69. Jackson to William Ward, April 10, 1882, Huntington.

70. Jackson to Annie Fields, January 5, 1883, Huntington; Jackson to Robert Underwood Johnson, October 28, 1882, Columbia.

71. Jackson to Robert Underwood Johnson, October 28, 1882, Columbia.

72. Jackson, "Holy Cross Village and Mrs. Pope's," in *Bits of Travel at Home* (1878; reprint, Boston: Roberts Brothers, 1880), 53.

73. Jackson, "Father Junipero and His Work," in *Glimpses of Three Coasts* (1886), 38–39.

74. Ibid., 31. For more realistic accounts of Indian life during the California mission period, see among other works Luiseño Indian Pablo Tac's own written account of his experiences at Mission San Luis Rey, Julio César's *testimonio* to Bancroft about his experiences there, and other sources, some of which document Indian resistance to the mission system, in Edward D. Castillo, ed., *Native American Perspectives on the Hispanic Colonization of Alta California,* Spanish Borderlands Sourcebooks 26 (New York: Garland Publishing, 1991). See also Ramón Gutiérrez and Richard J. Orsi, eds., *Contested Eden* (Berkeley: University of California Press, 1998); Edward Castillo and Robert H. Jackson, *Indians, Franciscans, and Spanish Colonization: The Impact of the Mission System on California Indians* (Albuquerque: University of New Mexico Press, 1995); and Douglas Monroy, *Thrown among Strangers: The Making of Mexican Culture in Frontier California* (Berkeley: University of California Press, 1990).

75. Jackson, "Father Junipero and His Work," 54, 46.

76. Ibid., 45, 50, 56–57.

77. Ibid., 56–57.

78. Jackson to Amelia Stone Quinton, March 19, 1882, Bancroft.

79. Jackson, "The Present Condition of the Mission Indians in Southern California," in *Glimpses of Three Coasts* (1886), 89–90. Also see Jackson's private description of this same interview in her letter to Amelia Stone Quinton, March 19, 1882, Bancroft.

80. See fragments of Antonio Coronel's letter to Jackson, #404 and #405, December 1882, LACMNH. Professor Victor M. Rodriguez of Pacific University kindly helped me translate Coronel's Spanish-language letters to Jackson.

81. Jackson to Thomas Bailey Aldrich, April 1, 1883, Harvard. Recent scholars, including Gerald Vizenor, Jack Forbes, George Harwood Phillips, and Albert L. Hurtado, have done much to refocus attention on Indian autonomy and survival.

82. See Valerie Sherer Mathes, *Helen Hunt Jackson and Her Indian Reform Legacy* (1990; reprint, Norman: University of Oklahoma Press, 1997), xi, 40, for a map of the Indian villages Jackson visited and for background information on their history. When Jackson visited San Pasqual she unwittingly upset local Indians by wearing a Paris bonnet that had an owl attached to it.

83. Jackson, "The Present Condition of the Mission Indians," 99, 89, 84.

84. José Jesus Castillo's original letter to Henry Teller is stored with Jackson's June 11, 1882 letter to him, transcript, NatArch, #11429-[11701]-1882, Special Case 31.

85. Jackson, "The Present Condition of the Mission Indians," 88. For a history of Indian landholding in Southern California at this time, and information on the subsequent situation of local Indian bands, see Florence Connolly Shipek, *Pushed into the Rocks: Southern California Indian Land Tenure, 1769–1986* (Lincoln: University of Nebraska Press, 1987).

86. Abbot Kinney, quoted in James, *Through Ramona's Country,* 319.

87. Jackson to Charles Dudley Warner, October 31, 1882, Trinity.

88. Jackson to Thomas Bailey Aldrich, May 4, 1883, Harvard.

89. Helen Jackson and Abbot Kinney, *Report on the Condition and Needs of the Mission Indians of California* (Washington, D.C.: Government Printing Office, 1883), 7, 8. Jackson's *Report* is included in editions of *A Century of Dishonor* published after 1885.

90. Jackson to Hiram Price, October 31, 1882, NatArch, #19910-1882.

91. Jackson and Kinney, *Report on the Condition and Needs of the Mission Indians*, 4, 9. The individual Jackson identifies in her *Report* as "Alessandro," an Italian name she would later use for the hero of *Ramona*, may actually have been named Alejandro. It is probable that Jackson used an *s* in the name so that American readers would at least pronounce it euphoniously, rather than with a hard *j*. In her earlier Colorado essay "Alamosa," printed in the *New York Independent* of June 6 and 13, 1878, she explained that she especially delighted in Spanish names that featured the letter *s,* because Americans so often botched the pronunciation of more unfamiliar Spanish letters.

92. Jackson and Kinney, *Report on the Condition and Needs of the Mission Indians*, 19.

93. Jackson, "Breakfast in San Juan Capistrano," *Christian Union,* October 18, 1883. See also "A Chinese New Year's Day in Santa Barbara," *St. Nicholas,* January 1883; "A Brave Chinese Baby," *St. Nicholas,* April 1883; and "An Afternoon in the Ghetto of Rome," *New York Independent,* August 5, 1869.

94. Jackson, "Queen Eumesia," *Christian Union,* December 20, 1883.

95. Jackson, "Chance Days in Oregon," *Atlantic Monthly,* January 1883; and in *Glimpses of Three Coasts* (1886), 139–40. See also "Three Pennsylvania Women," *Christian Union,* December 28, 1882 and January 4, 1883.

96. Thomas Bailey Aldrich to Jackson, November 20, 1882, HHJ2.

97. Jackson to Thomas Wentworth Higginson, February 5, 1884, in Higginson, "How Ramona Was Written." In this letter, Jackson reminds Higginson that she has "longed" to write an Indian story "for three or four years."

98. Jackson to Henry Root, [1853], fragment, HHJ5.

99. Jackson, "To Leadville," *Atlantic Monthly,* May 1879.

100. Jackson, "Standing Bear and Bright Eyes," *New York Independent,* November 20, 1879.

101. H. O. Houghton, quoted in "The Holmes Breakfast," *Atlantic Monthly,* supplement, February 1880.

102. Jackson to Ann Banfield, May 15, 1867, HHJ2; Jackson, "The Basin of Minas, and Evangeline's Home," *New York Independent,* July 2, 1868.

103. William Jackson to Jackson, May 30, 1880, WSJ1.

104. Jackson, review of *Ploughed Under,* by William Justin Harsha, *Critic,* February 26, 1881.

105. Jackson to Thomas Bailey Aldrich, January 17, 1882, Harvard.

106. Jackson to Antonio and Mariana Coronel, November 8, 1883, in James, p. 21.

107. Jackson to Thomas Wentworth Higginson, February 5, 1884, in Higginson, "How Ramona Was Written"; Jackson to Samuel Chapman Armstrong, May 14, 1885, Hampton.

108. Jackson to Thomas Bailey Aldrich, May 4, 1883, Harvard.

109. Jackson to Thomas Wentworth Higginson, February 5, 1884, in Higginson, "How Ramona Was Written."

110. Jackson to Thomas Bailey Aldrich, November 24, 1883, Harvard.

111. Jackson to Abbot Kinney, January 17 (completed February 2), 1884 and February 20, 1884, in James, pp. 329, 337.

112. Jackson to Thomas Bailey Aldrich, December 4, 1883, Harvard.

113. Jackson sought information on the Temecula eviction from Ephraim W. Morse of San Diego, from the law firm of Brunson and Wells, and from the Coronels. She asked Mary Sheriff to obtain information from the rancher Will Webster about Sam Temple's hearing. And she asked Richard Egan for help with an Indian equivalent for the words "Wild Wood Dove," which he told her was "Majel"; she used it, changed slightly to "Majella," as Alessandro's nickname for Ramona in her book.

114. Jackson to Thomas Wentworth Higginson, February 5, 1884, in Higginson, "How Ramona Was Written."

115. Jackson to Thomas Bailey Aldrich, December 1, 1884, Harvard.

116. Jackson suggests that her novel takes place in the 1850s or early 1860s by claiming that the sixty-year-old Señora Moreno was first married, at age twenty, while the missions were still in their heyday, through the 1820s; and that twenty-one-year-old Alessandro had been a "little fellow" before the secularization of the missions, which took place in the early 1830s. Elsewhere, she hints that her book is intended to take place in the 1870s: she notes that Felipe once put on the uniform "which his father had worn twenty-five years before." Since Señor Moreno wore his uniform during the Mexican War, in the mid-1840s, Felipe would have donned it around 1870. The evictions at San Pasqual and Temecula, which feature prominently in the book, also took place in the 1870s. See Jackson, *Ramona* (1884; reprint, New York: Penguin, 1988), 19–21, 65, 8; this edition is hereafter cited parenthetically in the text.

117. Among the many early books that attempt to pinpoint which actual Southern California people and places Jackson may have had in mind when writing *Ramona,* the best is George Wharton James's *Through Ramona's Country* (1908). Among later authors, Ruth Odell offers reliable information on this topic (in *Helen Hunt Jackson (H.H.)* [New York: D. Appleton-Century, 1939]), as does Dydia De-Lyser in "Ramona Memories—Constructing the Landscape in Southern California through a Fictional Text" (master's thesis, Syracuse University, 1996).

118. Jackson's Angus Phail is partly modeled after Hugo Reid, an early settler of California. Reid, a Scottish immigrant, married a Gabrieliño woman and in 1852 published a series of twenty-two letters in the *Los Angeles Star* about the life his wife's people had led at the San Gabriel mission. Jackson mentions Reid in the back "Memoranda" pages of her 1882 date book as a source to obtain for study.

119. Susan Coolidge [Sarah Woolsey], introduction to *Ramona,* by Jackson, Monterey ed. (Boston: Little, Brown, 1900), xx–xxi.

120. "For dramatic purposes I have put the Temecula ejectment *before* the first troubles in San Pasquale," Jackson explained to Abbot Kinney as she was writing *Ramona.* "Will anybody be idiot enough to make a point of that?" (Jackson to Kinney, February 20, 1884, in James, p. 336).

121. See Sacvan Bercovitch, *The American Jeremiad* (Madison: University of Wisconsin Press, 1978).

122. Jackson to Thomas Bailey Aldrich, December 1, 1884, Harvard.

123. Jackson to William Ward, December 17, 1883, Huntington; Jackson to

unknown recipient, January 22, 1885, in J., "Helen Jackson: A Recollection," *Literary World,* May 29, 1886; Jackson to Amelia Stone Quinton, April 2, 1884, Morgan.

124. Jackson to Thomas Bailey Aldrich, April 22, 1885, Harvard.

125. Jackson to Thomas Bailey Aldrich, February 9, 1885, Harvard.

126. Jackson to Thomas Bailey Aldrich, January 10, 1885, Harvard.

127. Jackson to Charles Dudley Warner, December 25, 1884, Trinity.

128. I discuss only those literary works that Jackson clearly had in mind when writing *Ramona.* Though she admired Joaquin Miller's poetry, there is no evidence that she ever read his engaging piece of autobiographical protest literature, *Life amongst the Modocs: Unwritten History* (1873). Nor did she draw directly on familiar white invocations of the "noble" Indian and his supposed demise, such as those presented in the novels of James Fenimore Cooper. In 1879, in order to publicize her then-nascent cause, Jackson had commented favorably in the *Evening Post* on Thomas Tibbles's *Ponca Chiefs: An Indian's Attempt to Appeal from the Tomahawk to the Courts* (1879); but in 1885, upon the publication of Tibbles's novel *Hidden Power,* she admitted that she thought Tibbles a "crude" writer (Jackson to Samuel Chapman Armstrong, May 14, 1885, Hampton).

129. Charles Dudley Warner's story "A-Hunting of the Deer" is included in his collection *In the Wilderness* (Boston: Houghton, Mifflin, 1878).

130. Jackson, "The Present Condition of the Mission Indians," 89.

131. Jackson to Thomas Bailey Aldrich, November 24, 1883, Harvard.

132. Historical overviews of the image of Native Americans in the Euro-American imagination include Robert F. Berkhofer, Jr., *The White Man's Indian: Images of the American Indian from Columbus to the Present* (New York: Alfred A. Knopf, 1978), and James J. Rawls, *Indians of California: The Changing Image* (Norman: University of Oklahoma Press, 1984). Recent doctoral dissertations, and also Roberto Fernández Retamar's "Sobre 'Ramona' de Helen Hunt Jackson y José Martí," in vol. 2 of *Mélanges à la mémoire d'André Joucla-Ruau* (Aix-en-Provence: Éditions de l'Université de Provence, 1978), tend to compare *Ramona* favorably with the "Indian" novels of other white nineteenth-century authors. Some Native American writers and scholars have commented favorably on *Ramona:* see Michael Dorris's introduction to the Penguin edition of *Ramona* (1988) and William Oandasan's "Ramona: Reflected through Indigenous Eyes," *California Historical Courier* 28 (February/March 1986): 7. Rebecca Tsosie is more critical in "Changing Women: The Crosscurrents of American Indian Feminine Identity," in *Unequal Sisters: A Multi-Cultural Reader in U.S. Women's History,* ed. Vicki L. Ruiz and Ellen Carol DuBois, 2d ed. (New York: Routledge, 1994).

133. The first novel by a Native American author, which happened to be set in California, was published during Jackson's lifetime. In *The Life and Adventures of Joaquin Murietta* (1854), the prolific Cherokee writer John Rollin Ridge seems to have dealt indirectly with American injustice to Indians by portraying the race struggles of California's Hispanic population. There is no evidence that Jackson knew of Rollins's work, however. She did probably know of Sarah Winnemucca's more accomplished nonfiction jeremiad, *Life among the Piutes: Their Wrongs and Claims* (1883), the first autobiography published by an Indian woman, for Jackson had reprinted a letter written by Winnemucca in *A Century of Dishonor.* Unfortunately, Jackson's extant writings offer no comment on Winnemucca's book.

134. Jackson died before she could become aware of María Amparo Ruiz de Burton's *The Squatter and the Don* (1885), the earliest known Southern California novel published by a Hispanic author. This novel takes place in the early 1870s, the same years in which much of *Ramona* is set. While it suffers, like *Ramona,* from some of the prejudices of its time, and also from its author's relatively limited literary experience, it makes some of the same key points as Jackson's book: it excoriates the American government, American monopoly capitalism, and the American people for oppressing the *Californios.*

135. Jackson, "Standing Bear and Bright Eyes" (1879).

136. For an overview of literary depictions of intermarriage between Indians and whites, see William J. Scheick, *The Half-Blood: A Cultural Symbol in Nineteenth-Century American Fiction* (Lexington: University Press of Kentucky, 1979).

137. Jackson had first expressed her admiration for rag carpets woven at random, in "a sort of weird, irregular . . . pattern, much more effective than the blocks of ordinary rag carpets," in "An Afternoon's Chances in Bethlehem: A Farmer and His Wife," *New York Tribune,* August 13, 1870. In the autumn of 1883, shortly before she began work on *Ramona,* she wrote to Abbot Kinney from Colorado Springs that she had "made the acquaintance of an old carpet-weaver—most interesting woman in town!" (Jackson to Kinney, October 19, 1883, Bancroft).

CHAPTER 9. LAST WORDS

1. Jackson to Horatio Nelson Rust, April 29, 1885, Huntington.
2. Jackson to Charles Dudley Warner, October 2, 1884, Trinity.
3. Jackson, "American Women," *New York World,* July 17, 1870.
4. Jackson to Moncure Conway, October 28, 1884, Columbia.
5. Jackson to Henry Bowen, October 15, 1884, UVA.
6. Jackson to Jessy Bross Lloyd, July 3, 1882, WSHS; Henry D. Lloyd, "The Political Economy of Seventy-Three Million Dollars," *Atlantic Monthly,* July 1882.
7. Jackson to Henry Bowen, October 15, 1884, UVA; "The Mill Has Shut Down" appeared in the *New York Independent,* December 11, 1884.
8. Jackson to Thomas Bailey Aldrich, December 1, 1884, Harvard.
9. Richard Cutts, *Index to the Youth's Companion, 1871–1929* (Metuchen, N.J.: Scarecrow Press, 1972), viii.
10. Jackson to William Rideing, May 28, 1884, Jones.
11. Jackson, quoted in Flora Haynes Apponyi, "The Last Days of Mrs. Helen Hunt Jackson," *Overland Monthly Magazine,* September 1885.
12. Thomas Wentworth Higginson, citing the opinion of an unnamed acquaintance, in *Contemporaries* (Boston: Houghton, Mifflin, 1899), 159.
13. Jackson to Helen Banfield, May 14, 1876, HHJ2.
14. Jackson to Abbot Kinney, April 1, 1885, in James, p. 343.
15. Jackson to Jeanne Carr, June 14, 1885, Huntington; Jackson to Thomas Bailey Aldrich, April 22, 1885, Harvard.
16. A. T. Boericke to Edith Colby Banfield ("Kitty"), October 27, 1885, WSJ2.
17. Jackson to Charles Dudley Warner, July 21, 1872, Trinity.
18. Hamilton Mabie, "Helen Jackson," *Christian Union,* August 20, 1885.
19. Jackson to William Jackson, March 29, 1885, WSJ1.

20. Jackson to Ann Banfield, March 20, 1877, HHJ5.

21. Jackson left her inheritance to Helen Banfield and to Helen's sisters, Ann, Mary, and Edith. She left the royalties from her writings to William Jackson's two sisters, Margaret and Hannah Jackson Price. She also gave each of these two women and their widowed mother $1,000 from her savings. She gave $3,000 to Jenny Abbott Johnson, $500 to Juliet Goodwin, $500 to her aunt Maria Fiske of Weston, and $100 for every year of her employment to her maid Effie McCleod. Jackson's will is stored in WSJ1; see also the explanation of her bequests in her letter to Helen Banfield, May 20, 1885, WSJ1.

22. Jackson to William Jackson, March 29, 1885, WSJ1.

23. Jackson to William Jackson, June 9, 1885, HHJ4.

24. Jackson, "Directions" for William Jackson, HHJ4.

25. Jackson to Ann Scholfield, May 25 [1885], HHJ6.

26. Jackson to Helen Banfield, [summer 1885], HHJ4.

27. Jackson to William Jackson, "Directions" and June 10, 1885, HHJ4.

28. William Jackson to Margaret Jackson, August 5, 1885, HHJ6; William Jackson to Helen Banfield, [August 1885], WSJ1.

29. Jackson to Mary Ann Jackson, August 7, 1885, HHJ6. See also Jackson to Helen Banfield, August 7, 1885, HHJ4.

30. Jackson to President Grover Cleveland, August 8, 1885, Princeton.

31. The manuscript of "Habeas Corpus," dated August 7, 1885, is held in the Jones Library. It is printed in Poems (1892; reprint, Boston: Little, Brown, 1906), 261–63.

32. William Jackson to Ann Banfield, telegram, August 11, 1885, WSJ1.

33. A. T. Boericke to Edith Banfield, October 27 and November 16, 1885, WSJ2.

34. Jackson, "Last Words," Century, December 1881; and in Poems (1892), 173.

35. William Jackson to Helen Banfield, August 30 and September 17, 1885, WSJ1.

36. Emily Dickinson to William Jackson, draft, in The Letters of Emily Dickinson, ed. Thomas H. Johnson (Cambridge, Mass.: Harvard University Press, Belknap Press, 1958), 3:889. See also Dickinson to William Jackson, [mid-August 1885], in ibid., 885.

37. Higginson, quoted in Anna Mary Wells, Dear Preceptor: The Life and Times of Thomas Wentworth Higginson (Boston: Houghton Mifflin, 1963), 268.

38. Charles Dudley Warner, ed., A Library of the World's Best Literature, Ancient and Modern, Hamilton Wright Mabie, Lucia Gilbert Runkle, and George Henry Warner, associate editors (New York: International Society, 1896), 20:8058.

39. See Joaquin Miller, "The Life Work of Helen Hunt Jackson," San Francisco Morning Call, September 18, 1892; Albion Tourgée, "Study in Civilization," North American Review, September 1886.

40. See José Martí, prologue to Ramona: Novela Americana por Helen Hunt Jackson, trans. Martí (1887; reprint, Havana: Rambla, Bouza, 1915), 37–40.

41. See Mary Austin, "An Old Favorite Takes on New Meaning," New York Herald Tribune Books, November 13, 1932; Earth Horizon: Autobiography (1932; reprint, Albuquerque: University of New Mexico Press, 1991); and "Regionalism in American Fiction," English Journal 21 (February 1932): 97–107.

42. Jackson to Moncure Conway, November 16, 1875, Columbia.

43. Jackson to Caroline Dall, February 23, 1881, MHS.

44. Jackson to Mary Sheriff, July 17, 1885, Huntington.

45. Kevin Starr, *Inventing the Dream: California through the Progressive Era* (1985; reprint, New York: Oxford University Press, 1986), 55. On the "fantasy heritage," see Carey McWilliams, *North from Mexico: The Spanish-Speaking People of the United States,* ed. Louis Adamic (Philadelphia: J. B. Lippincott, 1948).

46. Jackson did not use Ramona Lubo as a model for her heroine: she did not learn that Juan Diego's wife was actually named Ramona until she had written half of her novel. She may have borrowed her heroine's name from the Temecula proprietor Ramona Wolf or some other local woman.

47. Higginson, *Contemporaries,* 142.

Bibliography

ABBREVIATIONS OF MANUSCRIPT COLLECTIONS AND BOOKS

AAS	American Antiquarian Society
Amherst	Amherst College Library
Bancroft	University of California, Berkeley, Bancroft Library
Bowdoin	Bowdoin College Library
BP	Boston Public Library
BYU	Brigham Young University, Harold B. Lee Library
CCRoom	Colorado College, Tutt Library; separate accession, Colorado Room
CHS	California Historical Society, North Baker Library
Columbia	Columbia University, Rare Book and Manuscript Library
Congress	Library of Congress
Copley	James S. Copley Library
Dartmouth	Dartmouth College Library
Hampton	Hampton University
Harvard	Harvard University, Houghton Library
Hayes	Rutherford B. Hayes Presidential Center, Research Division
HHJ1–6	Colorado College, Tutt Library; Helen Hunt Jackson Papers, Parts 1–6
Hopkins	Johns Hopkins University, Milton S. Eisenhower Library

Huntington	Huntington Library
James	George Wharton James, *Through Ramona's Country*
Jones	Jones Library
LACMNH	Los Angeles County Museum of Natural History
Lindley	Walter Lindley and J. P. Widney, *California of the South*
MHS	Massachusetts Historical Society
Michigan	University of Michigan, Bentley Historical Library
MNHS	Minnesota Historical Society
Morgan	Pierpont Morgan Library
NatArch	National Archives
NHHS	New Hampshire Historical Society
NYP	New York Public Library
NYU	New York University, Fales Library
Penn	University of Pennsylvania Library
Princeton	Princeton University Library
Schlesinger	Harvard University, Schlesinger Library
Smith	Smith College Library
Trinity	Trinity College, Watkinson Library
Tutt Library	Colorado College, Tutt Library
UVA	University of Virginia, Alderman Library
Wisconsin	University of Wisconsin–Madison, Memorial Library
WSHS	Wisconsin State Historical Society
WSJ1–3	Colorado College, Tutt Library; William S. Jackson Collection, Parts 1–3
Yale	Yale University, Beinecke Rare Book and Manuscript Library
YS	Yale University, Sterling Memorial Library

HELEN JACKSON'S WRITINGS
(Arranged Chronologically)

Books

[H.H.]. *Bathmendi: A Persian Tale.* Boston: Loring, 1867. Republished in *St. Nicholas,* May 1885.
[H.H.]. *Verses.* Boston: Fields, Osgood, 1870. Expanded ed., Boston: Roberts Brothers, 1873.
[H.H.]. *Bits of Travel.* Boston: J. R. Osgood, 1872.
[H.H.]. *Bits of Talk about Home Matters.* Boston: Roberts Brothers, 1873.

[Saxe Holm]. *Saxe Holm's Stories, First Series*. New York: Scribner, Armstrong, 1873. Reprint, New York: Charles Scribner's Sons, 1898.

[H.H.]. *The Story of Boon*. Boston: Roberts Brothers, 1874.

[H.H.]. *Bits of Talk in Verse and Prose for Young Folks*. Boston: Roberts Brothers, 1876.

[Anonymous]. *Mercy Philbrick's Choice*. No Name Series. Boston: Roberts Brothers, 1876.

[Anonymous, "by the author of *Mercy Philbrick's Choice*"]. *Hetty's Strange History*. No Name Series. Boston: Roberts Brothers, 1877.

[H.H.]. *Nelly's Silver Mine*. 1878. Reprint, Boston: Roberts Brothers, 1885.

[Saxe Holm]. *Saxe Holm's Stories, Second Series*. 1878. Reprint, New York: Charles Scribner's Sons, 1899.

[H.H.]. *Bits of Travel at Home*. 1878. Reprint, Boston: Roberts Brothers, 1880.

[H.H.]. *Letters from a Cat: Published by Her Mistress*. Boston: Roberts Brothers, 1879. Reprint, Boston: Little, Brown, 1902.

[H.H.]. *A Century of Dishonor: A Sketch of the United States Government's Dealings with Some of the Indian Tribes*. New York: Harper & Brothers, 1881.

[H.H.]. *Mammy Tittleback and Her Family: A Story of Seventeen Cats*. Boston: Roberts Brothers, 1881.

[H.H.]. *The Training of Children*. New York: New York and Brooklyn Publishing, 1882.

[Mrs. Helen Jackson] and Abbot Kinney. *Report on the Condition and Needs of the Mission Indians*. Washington, D.C.: Government Printing Office, 1883.

[Helen Jackson (H.H.)]. *Ramona*. Boston: Roberts Brothers, 1884. Reprint, with an introduction by Michael Dorris, New York: Penguin, 1988.

[Helen Jackson (H.H.)]. *The Hunter Cats of Connorloa*. Boston: Roberts Brothers, 1884.

[Helen Jackson (H.H.)]. *Zeph*. Boston: Roberts Brothers, 1885.

[Helen Jackson (H.H.)]. *Glimpses of Three Coasts*. 1886. Reprint, Boston: Roberts Brothers, 1891.

[Helen Jackson (H.H.)]. *Sonnets and Lyrics*. Boston: Roberts Brothers, 1886.

[Helen Jackson (H.H.)]. *Between Whiles*. 1887. Reprint, Boston: Roberts Brothers, 1898.

[Helen Jackson]. *Poems*. Boston: Roberts Brothers, 1892. Reprint, Boston: Little, Brown, 1906. Includes poems from *Verses* (1873) and *Sonnets and Lyrics* (1886).

[H.H. (Helen Hunt Jackson)]. *Pansy Billings and Popsy: Two Stories of Girl Life*. Boston: Lothrop, 1898.

[Helen Hunt Jackson]. *Glimpses of California and the Missions*. Boston: Little, Brown, 1902.

"Elspeth Dynor." Unpublished, incomplete novel; manuscript in NYP.

Uncollected Publications

The best bibliography of Jackson's many uncollected writings is to be found in Ruth Odell, *Helen Hunt Jackson (H.H.)*, 250–79. Here I list only those uncollected pieces that have been of most use to me, or that Odell does not mention. Unless otherwise noted, all pieces appeared originally under the signature "H.H."

Review of *Felix Holt,* by George Eliot. *New York Independent,* September 13, 1866.

"West Point Poetry." *New York Independent,* June 6, 1867.

"The Art Exposition at Munich." *New York Independent,* November 25, 1869.

"The Highest Possible Standard of Journalism." *New York Independent,* April 21, 1870.

[An American Woman]. "American Women." *New York World,* July 17, 1870. (Jackson claims this piece in two letters to Whitelaw Reid, July 1 and 24, 1870, Congress.)

[Anonymous]. "The Moral 'Zone of Calms.'" *New York Independent,* January 26, 1871. (Jackson claims this piece in a letter to Whitelaw Reid, January 29, 1871, Congress.)

[Anonymous]. Reviews of *Aspendale,* by Harriet W. Preston; *My Summer in a Garden,* by Charles Dudley Warner; "Konewka's Silhouettes"; and possibly others. *Scribner's Monthly,* March 1871. (Jackson claims these pieces in letters to Thomas Niles, March 2, 1871, UVA, and Charles Dudley Warner, January 17, 1871, Trinity.)

[Anonymous]. Reviews of *Reginald Archer,* by Anne Seemuller; *The Silent Partner,* by Elizabeth Stuart Phelps; *The Children's Crusade,* by George Gray; *Mechanism in Thought and Morals,* by Oliver Wendell Holmes; *Body and Mind,* by Dr. Maudsley; and possibly others, including *Three Proverb Stories,* by Louisa May Alcott. *Scribner's Monthly,* June 1871. (Jackson claims these pieces in a letter to Richard Henry Stoddard, August 30, 1871, Copley.)

[Anonymous]. Review of *A Terrible Temptation,* by Charles Reade. *Scribner's Monthly,* October 1871.

[Anonymous]. "A Good Word for 'Gush.'" *New York Independent,* January 18, 1872. (Jackson claims this piece in a letter to Charles Dudley Warner, March 12, 1872, Trinity.)

[Anonymous]. Reviews of *Overland,* by John De Forest; *My Wife and I,* by Harriet Beecher Stowe; and "William Hunt's Pictures." *Scribner's Monthly,* February 1872. (Jackson claims these pieces in a letter to William Ward, January 22, 1872, NYP.)

Denial of being Saxe Holm. *Woman's Journal,* January 17, 1874.

[Saxe Holm]. "Saxe Holm Rises to Explain." *Woman's Journal,* April 4, 1874.

"In Memoriam: The Dear Old Adjectives." *New York Independent,* July 29, 1875.

"Mrs. Maxwell's Museum." *New York Independent,* September 23, 1875.

[Anonymous]. "Heap Fool, Freeze Keeping Warm." *New York Independent,* August 24, 1876.

"The Kansas and Colorado Building at the Centennial Exposition." *New York Independent,* October 12, 1876.

"Literary Pemmican." *New York Independent,* November 2, 1876.

Review of *Deirdre,* by Robert Dwyer Joyce. *New York Independent,* January 11, 1877.

[Saxe Holm et al.]. "A Card from Saxe Holm." *New York Tribune,* June 1, 1877.

[Anonymous]. Reviews in "Our Book Table," a column Jackson occasionally wrote for the *Denver Tribune,* of *Ten Times One Is Ten,* by Edward Everett Hale; "The Poems of Richard Watson Gilder"; *A Masque of Poets* (1878), in an article titled "A Critical Opinion of the Last Literary Venture"; *Meg: A Pastoral* and other poems by Zadel Barnes Gustafson; *The Family Library of British Poetry,* edited by James T. Fields and Edwin P. Whipple; "Two Good Cook Books"; *Spiritual Manifestations,* by Charles Beecher, March 2, 1879; and *On the Right Use of Books,* by William P. Atkinson, March 9, 1879. (Where dates are not given, see Jackson's saved, undated copies of her reviews in HHJ1, box 6, fd. 3. Jackson discusses "Our Book Table" and mentions some of the reviews she wrote for her column in a letter to Scribner's, February 26, 1879, Princeton.)

"Standing Bear and Bright Eyes." *New York Independent,* November 20, 1879.

"The Story of the Poncas: A Vigorous Rehearsal of a Shameful Tale." Letter to the editor, *New York Evening Post,* December 17, 1879.

"The Letters of Charles Dickens. A Second Notice." *Literary World,* December 20, 1879.

"The Indian Problem: How Secretary Schurz Would Solve It." *New York Tribune,* February 12, 1880.

"The Wards of the United States Government." *Scribner's Monthly,* March 1880.

"One of the Early Indian Removals." *New York Independent,* May 20, 1880.

"Bright Eyes and Her People." Letter to the editor, *New York Evening Post,* December 29, 1880.

[Anonymous]. Review of *Ploughed Under,* by William J. Harsha. *Critic,* February 26, 1881.

Review of *Gaspara Stampa,* by Eugene Benson. *Critic,* November 19, 1881.

[Anonymous]. Review of *Hector,* by Flora L. Shaw. *Critic,* November 19, 1881.

POETRY

[Marah]. "The Key of the Casket." *New York Evening Post,* June 7, 1865.

[Marah]. "It Is Not All of Life to Live." *New York Evening Post,* June 16, 1865.

"An Alcove to the East," translated from Victor Hugo. *New York Evening Post,* March 17, 1866.

"Saison des Semailles, Le Soir," translated from Victor Hugo. *Nation,* April 26, 1866.

"Content." *New York Independent,* November 14, 1867.

"The Shadow." *New York Independent,* October 22, 1868.

"Confession of Faith." *New York Independent,* March 31, 1870.

[Anonymous]. "Vintage." *Old and New,* December 1870.

"Shape." *New York Independent,* December 29, 1870.

"The Story of Boon." *New York Independent,* December 3 and 10, 1874.

"Sonnet. To One Who Complained of a Poet for Not Writing about Nature." *Scribner's Monthly,* May 1875.

"Deeds and Words." *New York Independent,* June 24, 1875.

"The Old Homestead." *New York Independent,* August 5, 1875.

"Border Lands." *Atlantic Monthly,* June 1878.

"Bayard Taylor." *New York Independent,* January 2, 1879.

"The Pilgrim Forefathers." *New York Independent,* March 27, 1879.

"The Shoshone Oath." *Critic,* May 21, 1881.

[Helen Jackson (H.H.)]. "Too Much Wheat." *New York Independent,* November 6, 1884.

[Helen Jackson (H.H.)]. "The Mill Has Shut Down." *New York Independent,* December 11, 1884.
["The late Helen Jackson ('H.H.')"]. "An Unknown Man Respectably Dressed." *New York Independent,* August 20, 1885.
["The late Helen Jackson. ('H.H.')"]. "The Cruise of the Ship 'Happy.'" *New York Independent,* October 29, 1885.

DOMESTIC ESSAYS

[Rip Van Winkle]. "A Visit to Borioboola Gha: The School System There." *New York Evening Post,* November 18, 1867.
"Chum Yum." *New York Independent,* December 17, 1868.
"Boarding-House Levites." *New York Independent,* January 1, 1874.
"Negative Selfishness." *New York Independent,* February 11, 1875.
"Fretting." *New York Independent,* May 6, 1875.
"Wanted, in New England, An Apostle for Sunshine." *New York Independent,* July 5, 1877.
"Map of the Battlefield." *Christian Union,* March 2, 1882.

TRAVEL WRITING

"Mountain Life: The New Hampshire Town of Bethlehem—Where It Is, What It Is, and All about It." *New York Evening Post,* October 18, 1865.
"In the White Mountains." *New York Independent,* September 13, 1866.
[Rip Van Winkle]. "A Protest against the Spread of Civilization." *New York Evening Post,* August 29, 1867.
[Rip Van Winkle]. "A Morning's Chances in Boston: Another Letter from Rip Van Winkle." *New York Evening Post,* September 24, 1867.
[Rip Van Winkle]. "Boston Gossip." *New York Evening Post,* October 9, 1867.
"The Great Bore in Nova Scotia: A Chase after a Norman Kirtle." *New York Evening Post,* November 4, 1867.
[Rip Van Winkle]. "Notes of Travel: Letter from Rip Van Winkle." *New York Evening Post,* November 27, 1867.
[Rip Van Winkle]. "A Turkish Bath and a Parcel of Old Love Letters: Letter from Rip Van Winkle." *New York Evening Post,* December 19, 1867.
[Rip Van Winkle]. "A New Sleepy Hollow: Letter from Rip Van Winkle." *New York Evening Post,* January 13, 1868.
"The Basin of Minas, and Evangeline's Home." *New York Independent,* July 2, 1868.
[Rip Van Winkle]. "An Out of the Way Place: From Sleepy Hollow to Block Island." *New York Evening Post,* August 18, 1868.
[Rip Van Winkle]. "In and Out of Boston." *New York Evening Post,* August 27, 1868.
[Rip Van Winkle]. "Academy of Sciences." *New York Evening Post,* August 28, 1868.
"An Afternoon in the Ghetto of Rome." *New York Independent,* August 5, 1869.
[Rip Van Winkle]. "Germany: Roadside Incidents—Zell am See—Cupid and Psyche—Mistress and Maid—Reichenhail." *New York Evening Post,* November 2, 1869.

"A Glimpse of the Queen of England." *New York Independent*, December 16, 1869.

"The Foundling Hospital of London." *New York Independent*, February 17, 1870.

"A Bethlehem of Today." *New York Independent*, June 30, 1870.

"An Afternoon's Chances in Bethlehem: A Farmer and His Wife." *New York Tribune*, August 13, 1870.

"Stamped by Stubbs." *New York Independent*, October 6, 1870.

"A Second Celestial Railroad." *New York Independent*, October 13, 1870.

"A Sermon among the Mountains." *New York Independent*, September 21, 1871.

"Mt. Washington in September." *New York Independent*, September 28, 1871.

"The Brownville Lyceum." *New York Independent*, August 12, 1875.

"Alamosa." *New York Independent*, June 6 and 13, 1878.

"Down the Arkansas River to New York." *New York Independent*, October 3 and 17, 1878.

"To Leadville." *Atlantic Monthly*, May 1879.

"Our Seven Lakes." *New York Independent*, May 1, 1879.

"A Day in Trinidad." *New York Independent*, June 5, 1879.

"Finding Fern Canyon." *New York Independent*, September 14, 1879.

"Eden, Formerly on the Euphrates." *New York Independent*, October 9, 16, and 23, 1879.

"The Stone-Mason's Garden of Eden." *Christian Union*, November 23, 1881.

"A Trip into the Gunisson Country." *New York Independent*, December 29, 1881, January 12 and March 23, 1882.

"A Midsummer Fete in the Pueblo of San Juan." *Atlantic Monthly*, January 1882.

"Brother Stolz's Beat." *Century Magazine*, February 1882.

"Aunty Lane." *Atlantic Monthly*, May 1882.

"Estes Park." *Christian Union*, June 29, July 6 and 13, 1882.

"Three Pennsylvania Women." *Christian Union*, December 28, 1882 and January 4, 1883.

"By Horse Cars into Mexico." *Atlantic Monthly*, March 1883.

"A Chance Afternoon in California." *New York Independent*, April 5, 1883.

"A Night at Pala." *New York Independent*, April 19, 1883.

"A Pot of Gold." *New York Independent*, July 26, 1883.

"Justifiable Homicide in Southern California." *New York Independent*, September 27, 1883.

"A Day with the Cahuillas." *New York Independent*, October 11, 1883.

"Breakfast in San Juan Capistrano." *Christian Union*, October 18, 1883.

"Captain Pablo's Story." *New York Independent*, October 25, 1883.

"A State without a Debt." *Christian Union*, November 22, 1883.

"The Temecula Exiles." *New York Independent*, November 29, 1883.

"O-Be-Joyful Creek and Poverty Gulch." *Atlantic Monthly*, December 1883.

"The Fate of Saboba." *New York Independent*, December 13, 1883.

"Queen Eumesia." *Christian Union*, December 20, 1883.

[Helen Jackson (H.H.)]. "Women of the Beehive." *Century Magazine*, May 1884.

[Helen Jackson]. "A Short Cut from Icicles to Oranges." *Christian Union*, February 19, 1885.

[Helen Jackson (H.H.)]. "One Thirty-Six Hours on the Denver and Rio Grande Railroad." *Christian Union*, November 26, 1885.

SHORT FICTION

"The Story of Clotilde Danarosch." *New York Independent,* June 19 and 26, 1879.
[Jane Silsbee]. "Massy Sprague's Daughter." *Atlantic Monthly,* July 1879.
[Jane Silsbee]. "Sister Mary's Story." *Atlantic Monthly,* November 1879.
[Saxe Holm]. "Mrs. Millington and Her Librarian: A Love Story." *Harper's Magazine,* June 1881.
[Saxe Holm]. "Farmer Worrall's Case." *Harper's Magazine,* December 1884.

CHILDREN'S WRITING

"A Christmas Tree for Cats." *Riverside Magazine for Young People,* January 1868.
[Saxe Holm]. "The First Time." *St. Nicholas,* May 1877.
"The Naughtiest Day of My Life, and What Came of It." *St. Nicholas,* September and October 1880.
"A Chinese New Year's Day in Santa Barbara." *St. Nicholas,* January 1883.
"A Brave Chinese Baby." *St. Nicholas,* April 1883.
"Mr. Any-Time the Spaniard." *Wide Awake,* August 1883. [Also collected in *We Young Folks: Original Stories for Boys and Girls,* by Harriet Beecher Stowe et al. (Boston: D. Lothrop, 1886).]
[Helen Jackson ("H.H.")]. "An Indian Girl's Definition." *Youth's Companion,* February 5, 1885.

Private Letters

For this book I examined more than 1,300 letters written by Jackson, now to be found in the following libraries, collections, and printed sources. I have specified the number of Jackson letters in each location in brackets, and also the names of letter recipients; for exact information on each letter's recipient, date, place of composition, and whether or not a particular letter is complete, see my list on deposit with the Tutt Library of Colorado College. Abbreviations used to cite letters in my endnotes are indicated here in parentheses. All quotations in the text of my book appear by permission of the relevant libraries and of William S. Jackson III, heir to the Jackson estate. While I have also read a great many letters written to Jackson, and many others concerning her, because of space limitations I cite these only when I refer to them, in my endnotes. The Tutt Library houses an especially large collection of letters written by Jackson's friends and families of birth and marriage.

MANUSCRIPT LETTERS

American Antiquarian Society (AAS), Worcester, Mass. [2]. Miscellaneous Manuscripts "J" Collection. To Jenny Fox; Mrs. Francis.
Amherst College Library (Amherst), Archives and Special Collections, Amherst, Mass. [5]. Miscellaneous manuscripts: To Mr. Clarke; Mr. Frisbie; Mary Snell and Rebecca Snell. Chopin-Kiley Manuscript Collection: To Lyman Abbott.

Barnard College, Wollman Library, Columbia University, New York, N.Y. [2]. To Edward Everett Hale; William Hayes Ward.

Boston Public Library (BP), Rare Books Department, Boston, Mass. [16]. To Kate Field; James T. Fields; Mr. Lothrop; James Osgood; Harriet Palmer; Julius Palmer.

Bowdoin College Library (Bowdoin), Special Collections, Brunswick, Me. [9]. Abbott Memorial Collection, Lyman Abbott Autograph Collection. To Edward Abbott; Kate Douglas Wiggin.

Brigham Young University (BYU), Harold B. Lee Library, L. Tom Perry Special Collections, Provo, Utah [16]. Vault Collection, #664. To Edward Seymour.

Brown University Library, Providence, R.I. [1]. To Henry Bowen.

California Historical Society (CHS), North Baker Research Library, Manuscript Collection, San Francisco, Calif. [1]. Millicent Washburn Shinn Papers, 1880–1925, MS 1960. To Millicent Shinn.

Colby College, Miller Library, Special Collections, Waterville, Me. [3]. To William Dean Howells; Hamilton Mabie.

Colorado College, Tutt Library, Special Collections, Colorado Springs, Colo. [473].

> Note: Some Fiske family letters previously held in the private collection of Ruth Davenport, a granddaughter of Jackson's sister Ann, are now available only in transcript at the Tutt Library. (Some other letters from the Davenport collection are currently unlocated.)

> Helen Hunt Jackson Papers Part 1, Ms #0020 (HHJ1) [34]. To Deborah Fiske; Nathan Welby Fiske; Chauncey Hayes (draft); S. S. Lawson (drafts); Capt. J. Q. A. Stanley (draft); Henry Teller (draft); Aunt Martha Vinal.

> Helen Hunt Jackson Papers Part 2, Ms #0156 (HHJ2) [130]. To Augustus Bachelder; Ann Fiske Banfield ("Annie"); Everett Banfield; Helen Banfield; Richard Watson Gilder (draft); Julius Palmer; Mr. and Mrs. Julius Palmer; Lucy Palmer; Ann Scholfield.

> Helen Hunt Jackson Papers Part 4, Ms #0348 (HHJ4) [7]. To Helen Banfield; William S. Jackson.

> Helen Hunt Jackson Papers Part 5, Ms #0351 (HHJ5) [162]. To Annie; Helen Banfield; Henry Root.

> Helen Hunt Jackson Papers Part 6, Ms #0353 (HHJ6) [32]. To Annie; Josiah Holland, in unattributed transcript; Margaret Jackson ("Maggie" and "Maggy"); Mrs. Mary Ann Jackson; Julius Palmer; Lucy Palmer; Henry Root; Ann Scholfield; Edward Seymour, in unattributed transcript.

> William S. Jackson Collection Part 1 (WSJ1) [35]. To Annie; Helen Banfield; Betty (a housemaid); William S. Jackson.

> William S. Jackson Collection Part 2 (WSJ2) [67]. To Annie; Annie, in Davenport transcript; Everett Banfield; William S. Jackson; Ann Scholfield; Ann Scholfield, in Davenport transcript.

> William S. Jackson Collection Part 3 (WSJ3) [1]. To Hannah Jackson.

> Separate accession, #0126, Mf 0126 [1]. To Mrs. E. C. Stedman.

> Separate accession, Colorado Room (with *Century of Dishonor,* 1885) (CC-Room) [1]. To William Ward.

Separate accession, Autograph Collection of Prominent 19th Century Americans (Ms #0005) [1]. To Kilpatrick & Brown.

Columbia University (Columbia), Rare Book and Manuscript Library, New York, N.Y. [20]. Moncure Conway Papers: To Ellen Conway; M.D. Conway. Robert Underwood Johnson Papers: To R.U. Johnson. Hitchcock Papers: To Richard Henry Stoddard.

Dartmouth College Library (Dartmouth), Hanover, N.H. [1]. To Frank Sanborn.

Forbes Library, Northampton, Mass. [1]. Clifford H. Lyman Autograph Collection. To Mary Mapes Dodge.

Hampton University Archives (Hampton), Hampton, Va. [1]. To Gen. Samuel Chapman Armstrong.

Harvard University, Houghton Library (Harvard), Cambridge, Mass. [79]. Autograph File: To Miss Emerson; Thomas Wentworth Higginson; H.W. Longfellow; James Osgood; William Hayes Ward. bMS Am 1648 (509): To Henry Oscar Houghton. bMS Am 1429 (2479–2545): To Thomas Bailey Aldrich. bMS Am 1429: To Mrs. Aldrich. bMS Am 1610 (36): To Margaret Fuller Channing Loring. bMS Am 1232: To Edward Abbott. bMS Am 1569.8 (213): To Anna Clarke. bMS Am 1784: To William Dean Howells. bMS Am 1241.1: To Oliver W. Holmes. bMS Am 1429 (2502–2503): To Horace Elisha Scudder. According to Thomas Johnson in *Letters of Emily Dickinson,* 9 manuscript letters from Jackson to Dickinson are housed at Houghton. They are listed there in the Dickinson Family Papers, box 8, but could not be found as of the date of this book's publication.

Harvard University, Schlesinger Library (Schlesinger), Radcliffe Institute, Cambridge, Mass. [1]. May-Goddard Family Papers. To Abigail Williams May.

Haverford College Library, Special Collections, Haverford, Pa. [3]. The Quaker Collection: To William Hayes Ward. Charles Roberts Autograph Collection: To James T. Fields; Osgood & Co.

Huntington Library (Huntington), San Marino, Calif. [158]. Helen Hunt Jackson Collection: To Henry Bowen; Richard Egan; Sarah Orne Jewett; Ann Palmer; Ray Palmer; Ray and Ann Palmer; Mary Sprague; Theodore Tilton; William Hayes Ward; Mrs. D.J. Whipple. James T. Fields Collection: To Mrs. Annie Fields; Mr. James T. Fields. Jeanne Carr Collection: To Jeanne Carr. Mary Sheriff (Fowler) Collection: To Mary Sheriff. Horatio Nelson Rust Papers: To H.N. Rust.

Indiana University, Lilly Library, Manuscripts Department, Bloomington, Ind. [1]. To Mrs. Roberts.

James S. Copley Library (Copley), La Jolla, Calif. [3]. To Mr. Laughlin; Roswell Smith; Richard Henry Stoddard.

Johns Hopkins University (Hopkins), Milton S. Eisenhower Library, Special Collections, Baltimore, Md. [3]. Daniel Coit Gilman Papers, Ms. 1. To D.C. Gilman; Elizabeth Dwight Woolsey ("Lilly") Gilman.

Jones Library (Jones), Inc., Amherst, Mass. [26]. To Anne Lynch Botta; C.W. Chase; Mr. Clarke; Coates & Co.; Cross's Pens; Estes & Lauriat; Mr. Fairbanks; Miss Gilder; Mr. Marion; Mr. Nims; Lizzie Ordway; Elizabeth Stuart Phelps; William Rideing; Hannah Shepard Terry; William Hayes Ward; Mr. Welch; Mr. Wilkinson.

Knox College, Seymour Library, Galesburg, Ill. [2]. Bookfellow Collection. To Mary Mapes Dodge; Scribner's.

Library of Congress (Congress), Washington, D.C. [78]. Charlotte Cushman Papers: To Charlotte Cushman. Benham-McNeil Family Papers Collection: To Elizabeth McNeil Benham. Henry L. Dawes Collection: To Henry Dawes. Separate accession: To unknown recipient. Oliver Wendell Holmes Collection: To O. W. Holmes. Whitelaw Reid Papers: To Whitelaw Reid.

Los Angeles County Museum of Natural History (LACMNH), Seaver Center for Western History Research, Los Angeles, Calif. [6]. To Antonio Coronel (including one photocopy); Antonio and Mariana Coronel (including two photocopies of missing originals).

Massachusetts Historical Society (MHS), Boston, Mass. [6]. Caroline Wells Healey Dall Papers. To Caroline Dall.

Minnesota Historical Society (MNHS), St. Paul, Minn. [4]. Henry B. Whipple Papers. To Henry Whipple.

National Archives (NatArch), Washington, D.C. [29]. Record Group 75. Records of the Bureau of Indian Affairs. Office of Indian Affairs, Letters Received. To Hiram Price; Henry Teller (including four transcripts).

New Hampshire Historical Society (NHHS), Concord, N.H. [5]. To Mrs. Elizabeth McNeil Benham.

New Haven Colony Historical Society, The Whitney Library, New Haven, Conn. [1]. To Alexander Twining.

New York Public Library (NYP), Astor, Lenox and Tilden Foundations, New York, N.Y. [74]. Berg Collection of English and American Literature: To Mary Booth; Mr. Payne. Manuscripts and Archives Division. Personal Miscellaneous Papers—Helen Hunt Jackson: To Anne Lynch Botta; William Church; Joseph Benson Gilder; Anna Leonowens; *New York Tribune;* John G. Piatt; Horace Scudder; Theodore Tilton; General Wallin; William Ward. Anthony Collection: To Mary Mapes Dodge and Lucia Runkle ("Dear Souls"). Bryant-Godwin Collection: To Parke Godwin. William Conant Church Papers: To William Conant Church. Joseph Benson Gilder Papers: To J. B. Gilder. David McNeely Stauffer Collection: To Mr. Ruggles.

New York University (NYU), Fales Library, New York, N.Y. [4]. To Mr. Abbott; Mrs. Ellen Conway; Mr. Mason; Ray and Ann Palmer.

Pasadena Public Library, Pasadena, Calif. [1]. To Charles Dudley Warner.

Pennsylvania Historical Society, Manuscripts and Archives Department, Philadelphia, Pa. [3]. To "Old Mary"; Edmund C. Stedman; Mr. Welch.

Pierpont Morgan Library (Morgan), New York, N.Y. [1]. MA 4571. To Amelia Stone Quinton.

Princeton University Library (Princeton), Manuscripts Division, Department of Rare Books and Special Collections, Princeton, N.J. [32]. General Manuscript Collection and Frank Jewett Mather Autograph Collection: To Grover Cleveland; Jean Gilder; Thomas Wentworth Higginson; "Madam" (an anthologizer); Dr. Nichols; unknown recipient. Donald and Robert M. Dodge Collection, and Wilkinson Collection of Mary Mapes Dodge: To Mary Mapes Dodge ("Lizzy"). Charles Scribner's Sons Collection: To Messrs. Scribner Armstrong & Co.; Charles Scribner; John Blair Scribner; Messrs. Charles Scribner's Sons; Edward Seymour.

Rutherford B. Hayes Presidential Center (Hayes), Research Division, Fremont, Ohio [2]. William Dean Howells Collection: To W. D. Howells. William Claflin Collection: To Mrs. Mary Claflin.

San Diego Historical Society, Balboa Park, San Diego, Calif. [3]. To Ephraim Morse; Mary Sheriff; Mrs. D. J. Whipple.

San Francisco Public Library, Special Collections Department, San Francisco, Calif. [4]. Phelan Collection. To Ephraim Morse.

Paul J. Scheips, personal collection [3]. To Anne Lynch Botta.

Smith College Library (Smith), Special Collections, Northampton, Mass. [3]. Sophia Smith Collection. To Miss Clarke; Kate Morris; Osgood & Co.

Staten Island Institute of Arts and Sciences. Staten Island, N.Y. [1]. To George William Curtis.

Temecula Valley Museum, Temecula, Calif. [2]. To Ramona Place Wolf.

Trinity College (Trinity), Watkinson Library, Hartford, Conn. [73]. Charles Dudley Warner Collection. To Mr. and Mrs. C. D. Warner; Mrs. C. D. Warner; Charles Dudley Warner.

United States Department of the Interior, Morristown National Historical Park, Morristown, N.J. [2]. LWS 1179: To Henry Mills Alden. LWS 2563: To Mrs. Pratt.

University of California, Berkeley (Bancroft), Bancroft Library, Berkeley, Calif. [27]. Helen Hunt Jackson Letters: To Henry Mills Alden; Anne Lynch Botta; Jeannette Gilder; Thomas Niles. William Alvord Papers: To William Alvord. Henry Lebbeus Oak Papers: To Henry Oak. BANC MSS 99/279 C2: To Abbot Kinney; Amelia Stone Quinton; Messrs. Rogers and Kinney.

University of California, Los Angeles, Special Collections, Los Angeles, Calif. [1]. Collection 100, box 64. To Amelia Stone Quinton.

University of Michigan (Michigan), Bentley Historical Library, Ann Arbor, Mich. [1]. Jabez Thomas Sunderland Collection. To Jabez Sunderland.

University of Pennsylvania Library (Penn), Rare Book and Manuscript Library, Philadelphia, Pa. [5]. Elsa Noble Collection. To Edward Everett Hale.

University of Rochester, Rush Rhees Library, Department of Rare Books and Special Collections, Rochester, N.Y. [1]. To Mr. Coan.

University of the Pacific Libraries, Holt-Atherton Department of Special Collections, Stockton, Calif. [2]. John Muir Papers. To John Muir.

University of Virginia (UVA), Clifton Waller Barrett Library, The Albert H. Small Special Collections Library, Charlottesville, Va. [25]. Helen Hunt Jackson Collection (#7080): To Edward Abbott; Henry Bowen; Moncure D. Conway; Abby Morton Diaz; Mr. Drake; Mr. Gardner; Josiah Holland; Miss Houghton; Henry Oscar Houghton; Robert Underwood Johnson; Thomas Niles; Messrs. J. R. Osgood & Co.; Mr. Payne; Mr. Perry; Thomas Henry Tibbles; William Hayes Ward (including final two pages of a letter in the Huntington Library, dated "1-23-1877"); William Winter. Richard Harding Davis Collection (#6109-A): To Rebecca Harding Davis.

University of Wisconsin–Madison (Wisconsin), Memorial Library, Department of Special Collections, Madison, Wis. [15]. Cairns Collection. To Henry Mills Alden; Annie; Everett Banfield; Messrs. Osgood; William Ward.

Wellesley College, Margaret Clapp Library, Special Collections, Wellesley, Mass. [2]. To Edward Abbott; Margaret Jackson.

Wisconsin State Historical Society (WSHS), Madison, Wis. [2]. Reel #2, Henry Demarest Lloyd microfilm. To Henry D. Lloyd; Mrs. Jessy Lloyd.

Yale University, Beinecke Rare Book and Manuscript Library (Yale), Collection of American Literature, New Haven, Conn. [15]. To "Dear Souls" and "Dear People" (a circle of friends); Elizabeth Hutchinson.

Yale University, Sterling Memorial Library (YS), New Haven, Conn. [5]. To Samuel Bowles (including two notes inside letters from William Jackson to Bowles).

LETTERS APPEARING ONLY IN PERIODICALS

Atlantic Monthly, November 1900 [1]. In Thomas Wentworth Higginson, "How Ramona Was Written." To Higginson.

Christian Union, September 17, 1885 [1]. In Eliot McCormick, "H.H.: A Reminiscence." To McCormick.

Hemet News, April 15, 1932 [1]. In "Indian Has Letter Penned in 1883 by Author of Ramona." To Leonicio Lugo.

Literary World, May 29, 1886 [1]. In "Helen Jackson." To unknown recipient.

Nation, August 20, 1885 [1]. In Thomas Wentworth Higginson, "Helen Jackson." To Higginson. (Also excerpted at less length in Higginson, *Contemporaries*, 166–67.)

LETTERS APPEARING ONLY IN BOOKS

Dickinson, Emily, *The Letters of Emily Dickinson*, edited by Thomas H. Johnson [9]. To Emily Dickinson.

Higginson, Thomas Wentworth, *Contemporaries* [1]. This letter was first printed in Higginson's essay in *Century Magazine*, "Mrs. Helen Jackson ('H.H.')," December 1885.

Jackson, *A Century of Dishonor* [2]. To Carl Schurz.

————, *The Indian Reform Letters of Helen Hunt Jackson, 1879–1885*, edited by Valerie Sherer Mathes. Mathes annotates some 200 letters from the final six years of Jackson's life, including private letters from the above collections and also previously published letters to the editors of the *New York Tribune, New York Evening Post, New York Times, New York Herald, Springfield Republican*, and *Harper's*.

James, George Wharton, *Through Ramona's Country* (James) [10]. To Antonio and Mariana Coronel; Abbot Kinney.

Lindley, Walter, and J.P. Widney, *California of the South* (Lindley) [3]. To Antonio and Mariana Coronel. This book contains a fourth letter to the Coronels, which is also printed in James.

Odell, Ruth, *Helen Hunt Jackson (H.H.)* [1]. To Sarah Woolsey. Excerpt.

Smith, Wallace E., *This Land Was Ours: The Del Valles and Camulos* [2]. To Abbot Kinney; Amelia Stone Quinton. This book contains seven other letters to Kinney and Quinton, but their originals are available at the Bancroft Library.

Unpublished Manuscripts Cited

[Helen Fiske, ed.]. *Portfolio* of the Abbott Institute, vols. 1 and 2, 1850, HHJ2.

[Helen Jackson]. Pocket date books, 1852, 1876–78, and 1880–83, HHJ1.

[Helen Jackson]. 1880 MS book, HHJ1.

SECONDARY WORKS CITED

Abbott, John Stevens Cabot. *The School-girl; or, The Principles of Christian Duty Familiarly Enforced.* Boston: Crocker & Brewster, 1840.

Anderson, Benedict. *Imagined Communities: Reflections on the Origin and Spread of Nationalism.* Rev. ed. London: Verso, 1991.

Apponyi, Flora Haynes. "The Last Days of Mrs. Helen Hunt Jackson." *Overland Monthly Magazine,* September 1885.

Austin, Mary. *Earth Horizon: Autobiography.* 1932. Reprint, Albuquerque: University of New Mexico Press, 1991.

———. "An Old Favorite Takes on New Meaning." *New York Herald Tribune Books,* November 13, 1932.

———. "Regionalism in American Fiction." *English Journal* 21 (February 1932): 97–107.

Ballou, Ellen B. *The Building of the House: Houghton Mifflin's Formative Years.* Boston: Houghton Mifflin, 1970.

Barnard, F. A. P. "Memoir of Edward B. Hunt, 1822–1863." Read before the National Academy of Sciences, August 1864. *Biographical Memoirs* 3, no. 3 (1895): 31–40.

Bartlett, Helen. "A Famous Literary Woman." *New York Journalist* (New York), January 3, 1885.

Baym, Nina. *Woman's Fiction: A Guide to Novels by and about Women in America, 1820–1870.* Ithaca, N.Y.: Cornell University Press, 1978.

Bercovitch, Sacvan. *The American Jeremiad.* Madison: University of Wisconsin Press, 1978.

Berkhofer, Robert F., Jr. *The White Man's Indian: Images of the American Indian from Columbus to the Present.* New York: Alfred A. Knopf, 1978.

Bingham, Millicent Todd. *Ancestors' Brocades: The Literary Debut of Emily Dickinson.* 1945. Reprint, New York: Dover, 1967.

"Books, Authors, and Art." *Springfield Republican,* July 26, 1878.

Botta, Anne C. Lynch. *Memoirs of Anne C. L. Botta, Written by Her Friends. With Selections from Her Correspondence, and from Her Writings in Prose and Poetry.* Edited by Vincenzo Botta. New York: J. S. Tait & Sons, 1893.

[Bowles, Samuel]. "Saxe Holm's Stories: A New England Writer of New England Fiction." *Springfield Republican,* January 1, 1874.

Brodhead, Richard H. *Cultures of Letters: Scenes of Reading and Writing in Nineteenth-Century America.* Chicago: University of Chicago Press, 1993.

———. "Literature and Culture." In *Columbia Literary History of the United States,* edited by Emory Elliott. New York: Columbia University Press, 1988.

Campbell, Donna M. *Resisting Regionalism: Gender and Naturalism in American Fiction, 1885–1915.* Athens: Ohio University Press, 1997.

Castillo, Edward D., ed. *Native American Perspectives on the Hispanic Colonization of Alta California.* Spanish Borderlands Sourcebooks 26. New York: Garland Publishing, 1991.

Castillo, Edward, and Robert H. Jackson. *Indians, Franciscans, and Spanish Colonization: The Impact of the Mission System on California Indians.* Albuquerque: University of New Mexico Press, 1995.

Comment on Ralph Waldo Emerson. *Index,* February 5, 1874.

Conway, Moncure Daniel. *Autobiography, Memories and Experiences of Moncure Daniel Conway.* 2 vols. Boston: Houghton, Mifflin, 1904.

———. *Emerson at Home and Abroad.* London: Trubner, 1883.

Coolidge, Susan [Sarah Woolsey]. "Concord, May 31, 1882." *Atlantic Monthly,* July 1882.

———. "H.H." *New York Independent,* September 3, 1885.

———. Introduction to *Ramona,* by Jackson. Illustrated by Henry Sandham. Monterey ed. Boston: Little, Brown, 1900.

———. *The New-Year's Bargain.* Boston: Roberts Brothers, 1872.

Cornelius, Elias. *Sermon, Delivered in the Tabernacle Church, Salem, Mass., Sept. 25, 1823, at the Ordination of the Rev. Edmund Frost as a Missionary to the Heathen; and the Rev. Messrs. Aaron W. Warner, Ansel D. Eddy, Nathan W. Fiske, Isaac Oakes, and George Sheldon, as Evangelists.* Boston: Crocker & Brewster, 1823.

Coronel, Antonio. *Tales of Mexican California.* Edited by Doyce B. Nunis, Jr. Translated by Diane de Avalle-Arce. Santa Barbara, Calif.: Bellerophon Books, 1994. Originally dictated to Thomas Savage in 1877 and titled "Cosas de California" (MS in Bancroft).

Coultrap-McQuin, Susan. " 'Very Serious Literary Labor': The Career of Helen Hunt Jackson." In *Doing Literary Business: American Women Writers in the Nineteenth Century.* Chapel Hill: University of North Carolina Press, 1990.

Custer, Elizabeth B. "Ramona's Land: Comulos, the Home of Ramona, as Seen by the Widow of General Custer." *Boston Evening Transcript,* May 14, 1887.

Cutts, Richard. *Index to the Youth's Companion, 1871–1929.* Metuchen, N.J.: Scarecrow Press, 1972.

Dall, Caroline. "The Story of Indian Wrongs." Review of *A Century of Dishonor,* by Jackson. *Courier,* February 13, 1881, in HHJ1, box 6, fd. 16.

Davidson, Cathy N., and Linda Wagner-Martin, eds. *Oxford Companion to Women's Writing in the United States.* New York: Oxford University Press, 1995.

Davis, Carlyle Channing, and William A. Alderson. *The True Story of Ramona.* New York: Dodge, 1914.

DeLyser, Dydia. "Ramona Memories—Constructing the Landscape in Southern California through a Fictional Text." Master's thesis, Syracuse University, 1996.

Dickinson, Emily. *The Letters of Emily Dickinson.* Edited by Thomas H. Johnson. 3 vols. Cambridge, Mass.: Harvard University Press, Belknap Press, 1958.

———. *The Poems of Emily Dickinson.* Edited by R. W. Franklin. 3 vols. Variorum ed. Cambridge, Mass.: Harvard University Press, Belknap Press, 1998.

Donovan, Josephine. *New England Local Color Literature: A Women's Tradition.* New York: Frederick Ungar, 1983.

Dorris, Michael. Introduction to *Ramona,* by Jackson. New York: Penguin, 1988.

Douglas, Ann. *The Feminization of American Culture.* New York: Knopf, 1977.

Emerson, Ralph Waldo. "Introductory Lecture on the Times." In *Nature; Addresses and Lectures.* Boston: James Munroe, 1849.

———. *The Journals and Miscellaneous Notebooks of Ralph Waldo Emerson.* Vol. 16, *1866–1882.* Edited by Ronald A. Bosco and Glen M. Johnson. Cambridge, Mass.: Harvard University Press, 1982.

———, ed. *Parnassus.* 1874. Reprint, Boston: Houghton, Mifflin, 1881.

Erkkila, Betsey. *The Wicked Sisters: Women Poets, Literary History, and Discord.* New York: Oxford University Press, 1992.

Faderman, Lillian. *Surpassing the Love of Men: Romantic Friendships and Love between Women from the Renaissance to the Present.* New York: Morrow, 1981.

Fernández Retamar, Roberto. "Sobre 'Ramona' de Helen Hunt Jackson y José Martí." In *Mélanges à la Mémoire d'André Joucla-Ruau,* vol. 2. Aix-en-Provence: Éditions de l'Université de Provence, 1978.

Fetterley, Judith, and Marjorie Pryse, eds. *American Women Regionalists, 1850–1910.* New York: W. W. Norton, 1992.

Field, Kate ["Straws, Jr."]. "From Newport." *Boston Post,* August 16, 1865.

Fiske, Deborah [Anonymous]. "A Few Words to 'Poor Susan.'" *Youth's Companion,* February 22, 1839.

———. "A Letter from a Little Girl Who Did Nothing but Play, to Her Cousin Who Loved to Study." *Youth's Companion,* February 1, 1839.

———. "Ten Questions That I Wish Nobody Would Ever Ask Me Again." *Youth's Companion,* February 1, 1839.

———. "What a Useful Young Lady! Two Leaves from Her Journal, Picked Up in the Street a Few Days Ago." *Youth's Companion,* February 22, 1839.

Fiske, Nathan. *The Moral Monitor; or a Collection of Essays on Various Subjects.* 2 vols. Worcester, Mass.: Isaiah Thomas, 1801.

Fiske, Nathan Welby. *Obituary Address at the Funeral of the Rev. Royal Washburn, Amherst, Mass., January 4, 1833.* Amherst, Mass.: J. S. & C. Adams, 1833.

———. *The Story of Aleck: or, Pitcairn's Island. Being a True Account of a Very Singular and Interesting Colony.* Amherst, Mass.: J. S. & C. Adams, 1829.

———, trans. and comp. *Manual of Classical Literature,* by Johann Joachim Eschenburg. 4th ed., with additions. Philadelphia: E. C. & J. Biddle, 1854.

Fiske, Nathan Welby, and Jacob Abbott. *The Bible Class Book; Designed for Bible Classes, Sabbath Schools, and Families.* Scripture Duties No. 2. Boston: T. R. Marvin, 1829.

Franklin, R. W. Appendix 1 in *The Poems of Emily Dickinson,* vol. 3. By Emily Dickinson, edited by Franklin. 3 vols. Variorum ed. Cambridge, Mass.: Harvard University Press, Belknap Press, 1998.

Fredrickson, George M. *The Black Image in the White Mind: The Debate on Afro-American Character and Destiny, 1817–1914.* New York: Harper & Row, 1971.

Fuess, Claude Moore. *Amherst: The Story of a New England College.* Boston: Little, Brown, 1935.

Glazener, Nancy. *Reading for Realism: The History of a U.S. Literary Institution, 1850–1910.* Durham: Duke University Press, 1997.

Gutiérrez, Ramón A., and Richard J. Orsi, eds. *Contested Eden: California before the Gold Rush.* Berkeley: University of California Press, 1998.

Hamilton, Gail. "A Pair of Novels." *New York Independent,* October 11, 1877.

Hammond, William Gardiner. *Remembrance of Amherst, An Undergraduate's Diary, 1846–1848.* Edited by George F. Whicher. New York: Columbia University Press, 1946.

Hart, James D. *The Popular Book: A History of America's Literary Taste.* New York: Oxford University Press, 1951.

"Helen Hunt's Last Book. A Work on the North American Indian. What She Intends to Do Here. She Defends the Poor Indian and Shows Plainly That He Has Not Been Treated Right." *Los Angeles Times,* January 15, 1882.

"H.H." [identity of author unknown]. "A Charade." *Brooklyn Daily Morning Drum-Beat,* March 1, 1864.

" 'H.H.' and Her Admirers." Unidentified newspaper clipping about visitors to Jackson's grave, HHJ1, box 6, fd. 24.

Hiatt, Mary P. *Style and the "Scribbling Women": An Empirical Analysis of Nineteenth-Century American Fiction.* Westport, Conn.: Greenwood Press, 1993.

Higginson, Thomas Wentworth. "Americanism in Literature." *Atlantic Monthly,* January 1870.

———. *Common Sense about Women.* Boston: Lee & Shepard, 1881.

———. *Concerning All of Us.* New York: Harper & Brothers, 1892.

———. *Contemporaries.* Boston: Houghton, Mifflin, 1899.

———. "Helen Jackson." *Nation,* August 20, 1885.

———. *Hints on Writing and Speech Making.* Boston: Lee & Shepard, 1887.

———. "How Ramona Was Written." *Atlantic,* November 1900.

———. "Literature as Art." *Atlantic Monthly,* December 1867.

———. *Out-Door Papers.* 1868. Reprint, Boston: Lee & Shepard, 1886.

———. *Short Studies of American Authors.* Rev. ed. Boston: Lee and Shepard, 1888. (First published in 1879.)

———, trans. *The Works of Epictetus. Consisting of His Discourses, in Four Books, The Enchiridion, and Fragments.* A translation from the Greek based on that of Elizabeth Carter. Boston: Little, Brown, 1866.

Higginson, T. W., and E. H. Bigelow, eds. *American Sonnets.* Boston: Houghton, Mifflin, 1890.

Hitchcock, Edward. *Reminiscences of Amherst College, Historical, Scientific, Biographical, and Autobiographical: Also, of Other and Wider Life Experiences.* Northampton, Mass.: Bridgman & Childs, 1863.

Hitchcock, Edward, et al. *The Power of Christian Benevolence Illustrated in the Life and Labors of Mary Lyon.* Northampton, Mass.: Bridgman & Childs, 1860.

"The Holmes Breakfast." *Atlantic Monthly,* supplement, February 1880.

Houghton, Walter. *The Victorian Frame of Mind, 1830–1870.* New Haven: Yale University Press, 1957.

Humphrey, Heman. *Indian Rights and Our Duties: An Address Delivered at Amherst, Hartford, etc., December 1829.* Amherst, Mass.: J. S. & C. Adams, 1830.

———. *Memoir of Rev. Nathan W. Fiske, Professor of Intellectual and Moral Philosophy in Amherst College; Together with Selections from His Sermons and Other Writings.* Amherst, Mass.: J. S. & C. Adams, 1850.

———. *The Woman That Feareth the Lord, a Discourse Delivered at the Funeral of Mrs. D. W. V. Fiske, February 21, 1844.* Amherst, Mass.: J. S. & C. Adams, 1844.

Hunt, Edward Bissell. *Union Foundations: A Study of American Nationality as a Fact of Science.* New York: D. Van Nostrand, 1863.

Hurtado, Albert L. *Indian Survival on the California Frontier.* New Haven: Yale University Press, 1988.

"The Indian Agency." *San Luis Rey Star,* August 4, 1883.

Inness, Sherrie A., and Diana Royer, eds. *Breaking Boundaries: New Perspectives on Women's Regional Writing.* Iowa City: University of Iowa Press, 1997.

J. "Helen Jackson: A Recollection." *Literary World,* May 29, 1886.

Jackson, Helen Hunt. *The Indian Reform Letters of Helen Hunt Jackson, 1879–1885.* Edited by Valerie Sherer Mathes. Norman: University of Oklahoma Press, 1998.

James, George Wharton. *Through Ramona's Country.* 1908. Reprint, Boston: Little, Brown, 1913.

James, Henry. "An American and an English Novel." *Nation,* December 21, 1876.

Johnson, Thomas H. *Emily Dickinson: An Interpretive Biography.* Cambridge, Mass.: Belknap Press, 1955.

Jones, Gavin. *Strange Talk: The Politics of Dialect Literature in Gilded Age America.* Berkeley: University of California Press, 1999.

Jones, Howard Mumford. Review of *Helen Hunt Jackson (H.H.),* by Ruth Odell. *Boston Evening Transcript,* April 22, 1939.

Kames, Henry Home, Lord. *Elements of Criticism.* 6th ed. 2 vols. 1785. Reprint, London: Routledge, 1993.

Kaplan, Amy. "Nation, Region, and Empire." In *The Columbia History of the American Novel,* edited by Emory Elliott. New York: Columbia University Press, 1991.

———. *The Social Construction of American Realism.* Chicago: University of Chicago Press, 1988.

Kilgour, Raymond L. *Messrs. Roberts Brothers Publishers.* Ann Arbor: University of Michigan Press, 1952.

"Letter from 'Saxe Holme' [*sic*]." HHJ1, box 6, fd. 13.

Leyda, Jay. *The Years and Hours of Emily Dickinson.* 2 vols. New Haven: Yale University Press, 1960.

Lloyd, Henry D. "The Political Economy of Seventy-Three Million Dollars." *Atlantic Monthly,* July 1882.

Mabie, Hamilton. "Helen Hunt Jackson." *Christian Union,* August 20, 1885.

Margolin, Malcolm, ed. *The Way We Lived: California Indian Stories, Songs, and Reminiscences.* Rev. ed. Berkeley: California Historical Society and Heyday Books, 1993.

Martí, José. Prologue to *Ramona: Novela Americana por Helen Hunt Jackson.* Translated by Martí. 1887. Reprint, Havana: Rambla, Bouza, 1915.

Mathes, Valerie Sherer. *Helen Hunt Jackson and Her Indian Reform Legacy.* 1990. Reprint, Norman: University of Oklahoma Press, 1997.

McCarthy, Justin. "American Women and English Women." *Galaxy,* July 1870.

McWilliams, Carey. *North from Mexico: The Spanish-Speaking People of the United States.* Edited by Louis Adamic. Philadelphia: J. B. Lippincott, 1948.

Miller, Joaquin. "The Life Work of Helen Hunt Jackson." *San Francisco Morning Call,* September 18, 1892.

Monroy, Douglas. *Thrown among Strangers: The Making of Mexican Culture in Frontier California.* Berkeley: University of California Press, 1990.

Mott, Frank Luther. *Golden Multitudes: The Story of Best Sellers in the United States.* New York: Macmillan, 1947.

———. *A History of American Magazines.* Vol. 3, *1865–1885.* Cambridge, Mass.: Harvard University Press, 1957.

Moylan, Michele. "Materiality as Performance: The Forming of Helen Hunt Jackson's *Ramona.*" In *Reading Books: Essays on the Material Text and Literature in America,* edited by Moylan and Lane Stiles. Boston: University of Massachusetts Press, 1997.

Nevins, Allan. *The "Evening Post": A Century of Journalism.* 1922. Reprint, New York: Russell & Russell, 1968.

Oandasan, William. "Ramona: Reflected through Indigenous Eyes." *California Historical Courier* 28 (February/March 1986): 7.

Obituary for Ray Palmer. *New York Independent,* April 14, 1887.

Odell, Ruth. *Helen Hunt Jackson (H.H.).* New York: D. Appleton-Century, 1939.

"Our 'Forty Immortals.'" *Critic,* April 12, 1884.

Padillo, Genaro M. *My History, Not Yours: The Formation of Mexican American Autobiography.* Madison: University of Wisconsin Press, 1993.

Perry, T. S. Review of *Bits of Travel at Home,* by Jackson. *Atlantic Monthly,* December 1878.

Pratt, Mary Louise. *Imperial Eyes: Travel Writing and Transculturation.* London: Routledge, 1992.

Prucha, Francis Paul. *The Great Father: The United States Government and the American Indians.* Abridged ed. Lincoln: University of Nebraska Press, 1984.

Q. "An Indian Commission." *San Diego Union,* June 1, 1883.

Rawls, James J. *Indians of California: The Changing Image.* Norman: University of Oklahoma Press, 1984.

Review of *A Century of Dishonor,* by Jackson. *Nation,* March 3, 1881.

Review of *Everyday Topics,* by Josiah Holland. *Nation,* June 21, 1877.

Review of *Mercy Philbrick's Choice,* by Jackson. *Saturday Review,* November 4, 1876.

Review of *Nelly's Silver Mine,* by Jackson. *Atlantic Monthly,* December 1878.

Review of *Saxe Holm's Stories, First Series,* by Jackson. *Publisher's Weekly,* October 25, 1873.

Review of *Verses,* by Jackson. *Nation,* March 16, 1871.

Review of *Verses,* expanded ed., by Jackson. *Boston Daily Advertiser,* December 22, 1873.

Reviews of *Bits of Talk about Home Matters,* by Jackson. HHJ1, box 6, fd 12.

Reviews of *Bits of Travel,* by Jackson. HHJ1, box 6, fd 11.

Reviews of *Hetty's Strange History,* by Jackson. HHJ1, box 6, fd. 14.

Reviews of Jackson's poetry. HHJ1, box 6, fd. 24.

Reviews of *Mercy Philbrick's Choice,* by Jackson. HHJ1, box 6, fd. 14.

Reviews of *Saxe Holm* stories, by Jackson. HHJ1, box 6, fds. 13 and 24.

Rollins, Alice Wellington. "Authors at Home: Mrs. Jackson ('H.H.') at Colorado Springs." *Critic,* April 25, 1885.

Roosevelt, Theodore. *The Winning of the West.* 4 vols. New York: G. P. Putnam's Sons, 1889–96.

Rosaldo, Renato. *Culture and Truth: The Remaking of Social Analysis.* Boston: Beacon Press, 1989.

Rothman, Sheila M. *Living in the Shadow of Death: Tuberculosis and the Social Experience of Illness in American History.* New York: HarperCollins, 1994.

[Sanborn, Frank]. Editorial on Jackson's review of Eugene Benson's *Gaspara Stampa.* In "Nature, Arts, and Letters." *Springfield Republican,* November 20, 1881.

Samuels, Shirley, ed. *The Culture of Sentiment: Race, Gender, and Sentimentality in Nineteenth-Century America.* New York: Oxford University Press, 1992.

"Saxe Holm Evolved." *Springfield Republican,* May 25, 1878.

Scheick, William J. *The Half-Blood: A Cultural Symbol in Nineteenth-Century American Fiction.* Lexington: University Press of Kentucky, 1979.

Shinn, Millicent. "The Verse and Prose of 'H.H.'" *Overland Monthly,* September 1885.

Shipek, Florence Connolly. *Pushed into the Rocks: Southern California Indian Land Tenure, 1769–1986.* Lincoln: University of Nebraska Press, 1987.

Showalter, Elaine. *Sister's Choice: Tradition and Change in American Women's Writing.* Oxford: Clarendon Press, 1991.

Smith-Rosenberg, Carroll. *Disorderly Conduct: Visions of Gender in Victorian America.* New York: Alfred A. Knopf, 1985.

Spiller, Robert, et al. *Literary History of the United States.* Rev. ed. New York: Macmillan, 1953.

Starr, Kevin. *Inventing the Dream: California through the Progressive Era.* 1985. Reprint, New York: Oxford University Press, 1986.

Stebbins, Emma, ed. *Charlotte Cushman: Her Letters and Memories of Her Life.* 1879. Reprint, New York: Benjamin Bloom, 1972.

Sundquist, Eric J. "Realism and Regionalism." In *Columbia Literary History of the United States,* edited by Emory Elliott. New York: Columbia University Press, 1988.

"The Ten Questions." *Youth's Companion,* March 1, 1839.

Tibbles, Thomas Henry. *Standing Bear and the Ponca Chiefs.* With an introduction by Susette La Flesche. Edited with a new introduction by Kay Graber. Lincoln: University of Nebraska Press, 1995. Originally published under the pseudonym "Zylyff" as *The Ponca Chiefs: An Indian's Attempt to Appeal from the Tomahawk to the Courts* (Boston: Lockwood, Brooks, 1879).

"To the Editor of the Youth's Companion." *Youth's Companion,* February 22, 1839.

Tompkins, Jane. *Sensational Designs: The Cultural Work of American Fiction, 1790–1860.* New York: Oxford University Press, 1985.

Tourgée, Albion. "A Study in Civilization." *North American Review,* September 1886.

"Trouble in the Indian Service." *San Bernardino Times,* date unknown. Enclosed in Jackson to Hiram Price, July 27, 1883, NatArch, #14177-1883.

Tsosie, Rebecca. "Changing Women: The Crosscurrents of American Indian Feminine Identity." In *Unequal Sisters: A Multi-Cultural Reader in U.S. Women's History,* edited by Vicki L. Ruiz and Ellen Carol DuBois. 2d ed. New York: Routledge, 1994.

Tyler, William S. *A History of Amherst College during the Administrations of Its First Five Presidents from 1821 to 1891.* New York: Frederick H. Hitchcock, 1895.

Walker, Cheryl. *The Nightingale's Burden: Women Poets and American Culture before 1900.* Bloomington: Indiana University Press, 1982.

Warner, Charles Dudley. *In the Wilderness.* Boston: Houghton, Mifflin, 1878.

———, ed. *A Library of the World's Best Literature, Ancient and Modern.* Hamilton Wright Mabie, Lucia Gilbert Runkle, and George Henry Warner, associate eds. 45 vols. New York: International Society, 1896.

Weiss, John. "Some Lover's Clear Day." *Galaxy,* May 1867.

Wells, Anna Mary. *Dear Preceptor: The Life and Times of Thomas Wentworth Higginson.* Boston: Houghton Mifflin, 1963.

Welter, Barbara. *Dimity Convictions: The American Woman in the Nineteenth Century.* Athens: Ohio University Press, 1976.

Wills, Mary H. *A Winter in California.* Norristown, Pa.: the author, 1889.

Winter, William. *Wanderers: The Poems of William Winter.* New ed. New York: Macmillan, 1893.

Wolff, Cynthia Griffin. *Emily Dickinson.* 1986. Reprint, Reading, Mass.: Addison-Wesley, 1988.

Woolsey, Sarah. *See* Coolidge, Susan.

Index

"The Abbot Paphnutius" (HHJ), 163
Abbott, Gorham, 70
Abbott, Jacob, 70; *The Bible Class Book,*
    49–50, 67
Abbott, Jane, 67
Abbott, Jennie, 67, 112
Abbott, John Stevens Cabot, 294n.8; and
    literary education of HHJ, 67–68, 69,
    70; reputation of, 116; *The School-
    girl,* 67–68, 138; success of, 70; on
    women writers, 98
Abbott Institute (NYC), 66–68, 69–70
abolitionism, 84–85
"Acquainted with Grief" (HHJ), 132
Act for the Relief of the Mission Indians in
    the State of California (1891), 250,
    276
Adam Bede (Eliot), 192
"An Afternoon in the Ghetto of Rome"
    (HHJ), 249
"An Afternoon's Chances in Bethlehem"
    (HHJ), 154, 163, 325n.137
"A-Hunting of the Deer" (C. D. Warner),
    261
"Alamosa" (HHJ), 175, 179, 180, 322n.91
Alcott, Amos Bronson, 108
Alcott, Louisa May, 108, 110, 200,
    212–13
Alcott, May, 168

Alcott, William Andrus: *Stories of Eliot
    and the Indians,* 226
Aldrich, Thomas Bailey, 35, 109, 110, 124,
    250, 287n.94, 301n.77
Alec Forbes of Howglen (MacDonald), 189
Alegre, Francisco Javier: *Historia de la
    Compañia de Jesus en Nueva-España,*
    236
Alise (a friend), 265
America, HHJ's travel writings on. *See
    under* travel writings of HHJ; *and also
    names of specific places*
American Ethnological Society, 236
American expansion, 24–25, 28–29. *See
    also* travel writings of HHJ
"Americanism in Literature" (Higginson),
    101
American Novel (Van Doren), 31
American Sonnets (Higginson), 274
American Woman's Home (Beecher), 138
"American Women" (HHJ), 142,
    307n.103
Amherst (Mass.), 11, 45, 290n.4
Amherst College (Mass.), 45–47, 84, 156
Among the Isles of Shoals (Thaxter),
    305n.44
"Among the Skylines" (HHJ), 112,
    301n.77
Anderson, Benedict, 38

351

Andover Theological Seminary, 44, 67
Anthony, Susan B., 141–42
Apis, Pablo, Temecula chief, 250
Apponyi, Flora Haynes, 268–69, 269–70
Archer, Anne, 1
"Ariadne's Farewell" (HHJ), 125, 130
Aspendale (Preston), 189
assimilationism, 27–28
Astoria (Irving), 311n.20
Atchison, Topeka, and Santa Fe Railroad, 240, 275–76
Atherton, Gertrude, 275
Atlantic Monthly, 35, 108, 109; on A Century of Dishonor, 235; HHJ's writings for, 23–24, 37, 110, 111, 112, 115, 288n.108, 301n.77; pay rates of, 112; on Ramona, 260; reputation/readership of, 111, 115; travel writings of HHJ in, 159, 161, 163, 173, 231, 236, 240, 249–50
"Aunt Betsy" (D. Fiske), 62
"Aunty Lane" (HHJ), 181–82, 188, 236
Aurora Leigh (E. B. Browning), 208
Austin, Mary, 275
authorial enthusiasm, 188, 190

"A Ballad of the Gold Country" (HHJ), 129
Bancroft, Hubert Howe, 164, 240, 242, 274
Banfield, Ann (HHJ's niece), 326n.21
Banfield, Ann (née Fiske; HHJ's sister), 5; birth of, 45; childhood of, 12; and Lavinia Dickinson, 144; finances/inheritance of, 44, 112, 289n.1; housekeeping by, 77; personality of, 17; racial attitudes of, 83; relationship with HHJ, 12, 93, 112, 138; travelogues sent by HHJ to, 159, 231
Banfield, Edith (HHJ's niece), 326n.21
Banfield, Everett (HHJ's brother-in-law), 112
Banfield, Helen (HHJ's niece), 12, 139, 271, 273–74, 326n.21
Banfield, Mary (HHJ's niece), 326n.21
Barr, Amelia Edith, 270
Bartlett, Helen, 6, 282n.13
Bartlett, J. Russell: Personal Narrative of Explorations and Incidents in Texas, New Mexico, California, Sonora, and Chihuahua, 236
"The Basin of Minas, and Evangeline's home" (HHJ), 251–52
Bathmendi: A Persian Tale (HHJ), 120
Baym, Nina, 286n.91
Beecher, Catharine: American Woman's Home, 138
Beecher, Edward, 189

Beecher, Lyman, 189
Bercovitch, Sacvan, 259
Berkeley Hotel (NYC), 21, 253
Bethlehem (N.H.), 151, 153–55
"A Bethlehem of Today" (HHJ), 154, 157–58
Between Whiles (HHJ), 217, 268
The Bible Class Book (N. Fiske and Jacob Abbott), 49–50, 67
Bishop, Isabella Bird: Lady's Life in the Rocky Mountains, 176
Bits of Talk about Home Matters (HHJ), 133–34, 136–38, 141, 200
Bits of Talk in Verse and Prose for Young Folks (HHJ), 135, 212
Bits of Travel (HHJ), 163, 231. See also titles of individual essays
Bits of Travel at Home (HHJ), 111, 173, 313n.74. See also titles of individual essays
The Black Image in White Mind (Fredrickson), 179
Black Legend, 179–80
blacks, racism toward, 82
Blake, Lillie Devereux, 307n.107
Bleak House (Dickens), 306n.68
Boericke, A. T., 270, 272, 273
"Bon Voyage" (HHJ), 122
book reviews of HHJ, 93, 189–90, 191, 200, 252, 324n.128
"Border Lands" (HHJ), 129
borderlands historians, 320n.68
Boston, 67, 68, 83, 108–10
Boston Daily Advertiser, 208
Boston Indian Citizenship Committee, 227, 263
Boston Post, 134
Botta, Anne Lynch, 94, 110; Leaves from the Diary of a Recluse, 79–80; literary salon of, 80, 296n.81
Botta, Vincenzo, 80
Bowdoin College (Maine), 67
Bowen, Henry, 116
Bowles, Samuel, 169, 171, 195, 316n.45; Our New West, 176
"Breakfast in San Juan Capistrano" (HHJ), 249
Breaking Boundaries: New Perspectives on Women's Regional Writing, 37–38
"Breaking the Will" (HHJ), 136
Brevoort Hotel (NYC), 21
Bridget (an employee), 83
Brodhead, Richard, 34, 38
Brooks, Noah, 227
Bross, Jessy, 168, 267
Brown, Emma: "A Day With Helen Hunt Jackson," 313n.72
Browning, Elizabeth Barrett, 101, 129, 305n.48; Aurora Leigh, 208

Browning, Robert: *Men and Women,* 78
Bruce, Georgia, 312n.47
Brunson and Wells, 248, 323n.113
Bryant, William Cullen, 80; *Popular History of the United States,* 237
Bulwer-Lytton, Edward: *My Novel,* 251
Bunyan, John: *Pilgrim's Progress,* 58
"A Burial Service" (HHJ), 131
Burleigh, Celia, 195–96
Burnett, Frances Hodgson, 112
Burnett, Peter, 28
Burns, Robert, 7, 128
"A Burns Pilgrimage" (HHJ), 7
Butler, Dr., 89, 298n.123
Byers, William, 176, 228
"By Horse Cars into Mexico" (HHJ), 180, 240

Cahuilla Indians, 247, 250
Calder, Alma, 196
California: dystopian portraits of, 3, 277 (see also *Ramona*); gold rush in, 164; Indian population of, 245 (*see also* Mission Indians); HHJ's travel writings on (*see under* travel writings of HHJ); racism toward Native Americans in, 28–29, 157; tourism of, 164
California: A History of Upper and Lower California (Forbes), 244–45
California, In-doors and Out (Farnham), 164, 312n.47
Californios (nineteenth-century Hispanic Californians), 242, 286n.80, 325n.134. See also *Ramona*
Calvinism, 11, 87, 119, 128, 152, 284n.66
The Cambridge History of American Literature, 31
capitalism, 37–38, 325n.134
"The Captain of the 'Heather Bell'" (HHJ), 268
"Captain Pablo's Story" (HHJ), 250
Carlyle, Thomas: *Sartor Resartus,* 73
Carr, Jeanne, 142, 239
Carroll, Lewis, 212–13
Cary, Alice, 80
Cary, Phoebe, 80
Castillo, José Jesus, 247
Cate, Dr., 168–69
Catholics, 82–83, 162–63, 243
Central Pacific Railroad, 164
Century Magazine, 110; HHJ's writings for, 27, 29, 110–11, 112; reputation/readership of, 111; travel writings of HHJ for, 231, 236, 239, 240–47
A Century of Dishonor (HHJ), 252, 324n.133; critical reception of,

286n.88; HHJ on, 270, 272; proofreading of, 107, 297n.86; reformist goals of, 226–30, 234–35; sales of, 111; success of, 259, 276
"Chance Days in Oregon" (HHJ), 249
Channing, Mary, 22, 97, 101, 102–3, 220
Channing, William Ellery, 101
Les Chansons des rues et des bois (Hugo), 119–20
Charles III, king of Spain, 243
Chase, Richard, 286n.90
Cherokee Indians, 156, 226. See also *A Century of Dishonor*
"Chester Streets" (HHJ), 232
Cheyenne Indians. See *A Century of Dishonor*
"Cheyenne Mountain" (HHJ), 127
Child, Lydia Maria, 80
"Children in Nova Scotia" (HHJ), 134
children's writers, 213
Chinatown (San Francisco), 166–67
"The Chinese Empire" (HHJ), 166
Chivington, John, 228
"Choir Invisible" (Eliot), 305n.48
Christian communism, 177
Christian submission. *See under* Fiske, Deborah; Fiske, Nathan Welby; Jackson, Helen Hunt
Christian Union: HHJ's writings for, 110, 136, 236; *Ramona* serialized in, 259–60; reputation/readership of, 110
"A Christmas Tree for Cats" (HHJ), 183
Civil War, 15, 37, 225; HHJ's volunteer work during, 81; HHJ's writings on, 37, 186–87
Clark, Charles, 71
Clarke, James Freeman, 125
Clarke, Lilian, 152–53, 158–59
Clarke, Sarah, 125, 152–53, 158–59
class, HHJ's sensitivity to, 267
Closet Hours (R. Palmer), 70
Colonial History of the City of San Francisco (Dwinelle), 244
Colorado, 24–25; development of, 24, 168–69, 174–76, 178–81; HHJ's travel writings on (*see under* travel writings of HHJ); racism toward Native Americans in, 28
Colorado: A Summer Trip (Taylor), 176
"A Colorado Road" (HHJ), 180
Colorado Springs (Col.), 24–25, 169–70, 220–21
"Colorado Springs" (HHJ), 169, 178, 179
Colorado Territory, 168–69
"Coming Across" (HHJ), 125
Common Sense about Women (Higginson), 98

"Concord, May 31, 1882" (Woolsey), 297n.85

"Confession of Faith" (HHJ), 121

Congregationalism, 87, 152. See also Fiske, Nathan Welby

"Consecration" (HHJ), 74, 79

Contemporaries (Higginson), 274

Conway, Ellen, 89–90

Conway, Moncure: abolitionism of, 225; on aging, 209; on "Draxy Miller's Dowry," 192; The Earthward Pilgrimage, 86; The Gospel of Art, 86; on HHJ's poetry, 124; and literary education of HHJ, 85–86, 88–90, 298n.124; reputation of, 116; on the Saxe Holm mystery, 196, 198

"The Cook of the Buckeye Mine" (HHJ), 232, 233, 271

Coolbrith, Ina, 274

Coolidge, Susan. See Woolsey, Sarah

Cooper, James Fenimore, 324n.128

Cornelius, Elias, 44–45

"Coronation" (HHJ), 125

Coronel, Antonio F., 238, 241–42, 244, 246, 261, 262, 323n.113; "Cosas de California," 242

Coronel, Mariana (Mary Burton Williamson), 238, 242, 262, 323n.113

Corot, Jean-Baptiste-Camille, 35

"Corporal Punishment" (HHJ), 134

"Cosas de California" (A. Coronel), 242

Coultrap-McQuin, Susan, 183–84

Cowles, Eunice, 65

Cowles, John, 65

Cowper, William, 58

"The Cradle of Peace" (HHJ), 174

Crespí, Juan, 244

Critic, 116

"A Critical Opinion of the Last Literary Venture" (HHJ), 311n.28

Cronyn, David, 239

"Crossed Threads" (HHJ), 122

Cushman, Charlotte: and HHJ, 103–7, 131–32, 142–43, 170–71, 299n.33; and Higginson, 105–7; and literary career of HHJ, 105; on the Saxe Holm stories, 194–95; on "Spinning," 122

Custer, Elizabeth, 30

Dakota Territory, 26, 223

Dall, Caroline, 143; "The Story of Indian Wrongs," 235

Dame, Hannah, 21, 95

Davenport, Ruth, 297n.86

Davidson, Cathy N., 287n.98

Davis, Carlyle Channing, 28

Davis, Rebecca Harding, 235

Dawes, Henry, 28

Dawes General Allotment Act (1887), 27, 28

"A Day in Trinidad" (HHJ), 179–80

Day of the Locust (West), 277

"A Day with Helen Hunt Jackson" (Brown), 313n.72

"A Day with the Cahuillas" (HHJ), 250

de Coursey, Mrs. Gerald, 220

De Forest, John: Kate Beaumont, 35–36; Overland, 35–36, 189

Deirdre (Joyce), 128

de Kay, Helena, 197

Delaware Indians. See A Century of Dishonor

del Rio, Dolores, 2

del Valle, Señor, 276

de Mofras, Duflot: Exploration du Territoire de L'Orégon, 244

Denver and Rio Grande Railroad, 169, 170, 175–76, 178–79, 203, 265, 270

Department of the Interior, 227–28

dialect literature, 289n.114

Diaz, Abby Morton, 143

Dickens, Charles, 315n.24; Bleak House, 306n.68; Dombey and Son, 66

Dickinson, Austin (Emily's brother), 144, 145

Dickinson, Edward (Emily's father), 144, 145

Dickinson, Emily, 22–23, 32, 124; and HHJ, 144–47, 308nn.115,118, 309nn.119,124, 310n.134; on HHJ's death, 145, 274; and Higginson, 145, 146, 309n.124; and Niles, 200; and the Saxe Holm mystery, 197; as source for Mercy Philbrick's Choice, 317n.70; "Success," 147, 309n.129

Dickinson, Lavinia (Emily's sister), 144, 308n.116

Dickinson, Samuel Fowler (Emily's grandfather), 145

Didion, Joan, 3

Diego, Juan, 247, 249, 250, 276

diversity, 37

divorce, 269

Dodge, Mary Abigail ("Gail Hamilton"), 212

Dodge, Mary Mapes ("Lizzie"), 135, 141, 212–13; on HHJ's death, 274

Dombey and Son (Dickens), 66

domestic essays of HHJ, 26–27, 93, 117, 133–38; on cheerfulness, 134–35; for children, 135–36; on children's rights, 133–34; for the Christian Union, 136; H.H. signature used for, 133; on homemaking, 137–38; moral agenda of, 118–19, 133, 135, 136; on motherhood/child rearing, 133, 136,

137–38; for the *New York Evening Post,* 133–34; for the *New York Independent,* 133, 134–35; popularity of, 118; traditionalism of, 137–38, 139. *See also* Jackson, Helen Hunt, works by; *and titles of specific essays*
domestic literature, 32
Donovan, Josephine, 37–38
Douglas, Ann, 286n.91
"Down the Arkansas River to New York" (HHJ), 173
"Draxy Miller's Dowry" (HHJ), 79, 184, 187–88, 192, 199, 220, 317n.70
Dream Life (Mitchell), 71
"Dreams" (HHJ), 120–21
Dr. Grimshawe's Secret (Hawthorne), 5
Dundy, Elmer S., 223, 227
Dwinelle, John Whipple: *Colonial History of the City of San Francisco,* 244
dystopian literature, 3, 277

The Earthward Pilgrimage (Conway), 86
Eastman, Charles, 275
"Echoes in the City of Angels" (HHJ), 237, 240, 241–43, 254
"Eden, Formerly on the Euphrates" (HHJ), 178, 314n.90
Egan, Richard, 323n.113
"The Elder's Wife" (HHJ), 16, 183, 184, 187
Elements of Criticism (Kames), 66, 251
Eliot, George, 129, 190, 209; *Adam Bede,* 192; "Choir Invisible," 305n.48; *Felix Holt,* 191; and Lewes, 192, 315n.24; *The Spanish Gypsy,* 305n.48
Ellis, Ruth, 195–96
"Elspeth Dynor" (HHJ), 26, 81, 177, 215, 216–20, 254, 272, 305n.48
Emerson, Ralph Waldo, 23, 287n.94; at Anne Botta's salon, 80; and HHJ, 108, 124–26, 304nn.24,30, 305n.48; "Introductory Lecture on the Times," 73; "Man the Reformer" lecture, 102; *Nature,* 89; *Parnassus,* 125; Transcendentalism of, 88–89, 126, 311n.28; in Yosemite, 168
"Emigravit" (HHJ), 122, 272
The English Governess at the Siamese Court (Leonowens), 130, 305n.54
Epictetus, 97, 213
Eschenburg, Johann Joachim: *Handbuch der klassischen Literatur,* 48, 291n.26
"Esther Wynn's Love-Letters" (HHJ), 131, 184, 193, 311n.21, 317n.70
"Ethics of Home" (HHJ), 136
Ethnographic Museum (Copenhagen), 233–34

Europe, HHJ's travels in, 23, 158–59; HHJ's travel writings on (*see under* travel writings of HHJ); tradition of travel writing on, 159
Evangeline (Longfellow), 251–52, 261
Evans, Augusta Jane: *St. Elmo,* 208
evolution, 135
Exploration du Territoire de L'Orégon (de Mofras), 244
"The Expression of Rooms" (HHJ), 135

Faderman, Lillian, 103
fantasy heritage, 275
"Farmer Bassett's Romance" (HHJ), 184, 186
"Farmer Worrall's Case" (HHJ), 268
Farnham, Eliza: *California, In-doors and Out,* 164, 312n.47
"The Fate of Saboba" (HHJ), 250
"Father Junipero and His Work" (HHJ), 240, 241, 243–44, 246
Felix Holt (Eliot), 191
Fénelon, François: *Treatise on the Education of Daughters,* 138
Fetterley, Judith, 37–38, 288n.110
"A Few Words to 'Poor Susan'" (D. Fiske), 62
Field, Kate (*pseud.* Straws, Jr.), 95–96, 102–3, 139, 307n.107; on HHJ's death, 274
Fields, Annie, 108–9, 112, 125, 243, 287n.94
Fields, James T., 109, 115, 140, 287n.94; on American regionalism, 173; and HHJ's *Verses,* 105, 108, 120, 303n.6; travelogues sent by HHJ to, 159. See also *Atlantic Monthly*
Fields, Osgood and Company, 120
"The First Time" (HHJ), 52, 136, 196–97, 206–7, 292n.57
Fiske, Charles, 289n.1
Fiske, David Vinal (HHJ's brother), 46
Fiske, Deborah Vinal (HHJ's mother): "Aunt Betsy," 62; background of, 157; and the Beechers, 189; Calvinism of, 11, 56–57, 58, 62–63; on Catholics, 82–83; cat letters of, 63–64, 183, 268; on Christian submission, 11, 19, 56–58; death of, 14, 16, 53, 57, 292n.57; education of HHJ by, 58–59; "A Few Words to 'Poor Susan,'" 62; health of, 12–14, 20, 57, 63; housekeeping of, 63; influence on HHJ, 44, 46, 57; influence on HHJ's literary career, 56, 58–59, 64; on Irish servants, 82; "A Letter from a Little Girl Who Did Nothing but Play," 61; letters of, 57–58, 59–60; literary

Hunt, Edward *(continued)*
    HHJ, 15, 74–75; literary interests of,
    77–78; marriage to HHJ, 15, 75–77,
    85; racial attitudes of, 81–82, 176,
    225; separations from HHJ, 15–16; on
    Stowe's *Uncle Tom's Cabin*, 84–85;
    *Union Foundations: A Study of
    American Nationality as a Fact of
    Science*, 82, 225; Unitarianism of, 85,
    87–88
Hunt, Molly (HHJ's sister-in-law), 74,
    159, 225, 274
Hunt, Murray (HHJ's son), 15, 77
Hunt, Warren Horsford ("Rennie"; HHJ's
    son), 15–16, 18, 77, 89, 93, 271,
    312n.35
Hunt, Washington (HHJ's brother-in-law),
    74
Hunt, William Morris, 36, 95, 189,
    315n.24
The Hunter Cats of Connorloa (HHJ),
    268
Hutchinson, Elizabeth, 143
"Hysteria in Literature" (HHJ), 32–33,
    133

idealism, 189–90
Independent. See *New York Independent*
Indian reform work of HHJ, 135, 220–30;
    and assimilation, 27–28, 285n.71; and
    the Boston Indian Citizenship
    Committee, 227; for Cherokee
    Indians, 226; and childhood of HHJ,
    225–26; criticism of, 29, 286n.78; and
    the Dawes General Allotment Act, 27,
    28; earlier views on improving society,
    26–27, 225; and the Ethnographic
    Museum, 233–34; via fiction, 251–52,
    261, 268, 322n.97 (see also *Ramona*);
    friends' sympathies with, 225, 227,
    234, 235; goals of, 27, 224;
    Humphrey's influence on, 226;
    William Jackson's support of, 228–29,
    234; Kames's influence on, 66, 251;
    and La Flesche, 26, 221, 224, 251;
    and land/reservations, 28–29, 230,
    246, 247, 248, 285n.73; for the
    Mission Indians, 27, 28–29, 237–38,
    240, 247–49, 250–51; and the moral
    value of art, 220–21; and Native
    Americans vs. U.S. government, 223,
    266–67 (see also *A Century of
    Dishonor*); for the Piegans, 266–67;
    for the Poncas, 26–27, 221, 223–24,
    226–27, 234, 318n.2; and racial
    attitudes of HHJ, 225–26; Reid's
    support of, 110, 227; results of, 276;
    and Schurz, 227–28, 234, 235; and

Standing Bear, 26, 221, 224, 318n.2;
    for the Utes, 227–28; and the
    Women's National Indian Association,
    227, 285n.71; for *Youth's Compan-
    ion*, 267
Indian rights, 26–28, 155, 223,
    285nn.71,73. See also Indian reform
    work of HHJ
"Indian Rights and Our Duties"
    (Humphrey), 226
Indian Rights Association, 285n.71
Indian Territory (Oklahoma), 26, 27, 223
industrialization, 23–24, 37–38, 154–55,
    178, 180
Ingelow, Jean, 200
"The Inhumanities of Parents" (HHJ), 134
Innocents Abroad (Twain), 160, 161,
    312n.35
"The Inn of the Golden Pear" (HHJ), 217
intermarriage, 262, 325n.136
"In the Dark" (HHJ), 121
In the Tennessee Mountains (Murfree), 270
"In the White Mountains" (HHJ), 153,
    154, 190–91, 311n.28
"Introductory Lecture on the Times"
    (Emerson), 73
Ipswich (Mass.), 65–67
Ipswich Female Seminary (Mass.), 54–55,
    65–66
Irish people, racism toward, 82, 83, 162
Irving, Washington, 99, 200; *Astoria*,
    311n.20; influence of, 158, 161, 190,
    311n.20; "The Legend of Sleepy
    Hollow," 158, 310n.19; "Rip Van
    Winkle," 23, 153, 158, 311n.20; *The
    Sketch Book of Geoffrey Crayon,
    Gent.*, 153, 158, 161

Jackson, Andrew, 226
Jackson, Helen Hunt (née Fiske): abolition-
    ism of, 84–85; accident/physical
    decline of, 265–66, 273; on
    aging/death, 209–10; in Amherst, 39;
    as an "artist," 35; art studies of, 77;
    birth of, 11, 45, 282n.1; on blacks,
    178; in Boston, 39; on Catholics,
    162–63, 243; cheerfulness/humor of,
    18–19, 44, 57, 59, 97; childhood/up-
    bringing of, 11–12, 50, 118–19; and
    Christian submission, 16–18, 19,
    38–39, 56, 93, 97, 121–23, 128, 270;
    on cities, 39; in Colorado Springs,
    24–25, 39, 169–70, 220–21; in
    Colorado Territory, 168–69;
    criticism/dismissal of, 29, 31–32,
    286n.78,88; and Cushman, 103–7,
    131–32, 142–43, 170–71, 299n.33;
    date books of, 5, 281n.2; death of,

Jackson, Helen Hunt, works by
(continued)
to New York," 173; "Draxy Mille
Dowry," 79, 184, 187–88, 192, 199,
220, 317n.70; "Dreams," 120–21;
"Echoes in the City of Angels," 237,
240, 241–42, 254; "Eden, Formerly
on the Euphrates," 178, 314n.90;
"The Elder's Wife," 16, 183, 184,
187; "Elspeth Dynor," 26, 81, 177,
215, 216–20, 254, 272, 305n.48;
"Emigravit," 122; "Esther Wynn's
Love-Letters," 131, 184, 193,
311n.21, 317n.70; "Ethics of Home,"
136; "The Expression of Rooms,"
135; "Farmer Bassett's Romance,"
184, 186; "Farmer Worrall's Case,"
268; "The Fate of Saboba," 250;
"Father Junipero and His Work,"
240, 241, 243–44, 246; "The First
Time," 52, 136, 196–97, 206–7,
292n.57; "Four Days with Sanna,"
230; "A Four Leaved Clover," 37,
184, 186, 191, 201–2; "Freedom,"
178; "Fretting," 134–35; "Friends of
the Prisoners," 18; "From Chicago to
Ogden," 165; "From Ogden to San
Francisco," 165; "Funeral March,"
105; "A German Landlady," 161,
162–63, 312n.36; "Glass Houses," 6,
133; "A Glimpse of the Queen of
England," 312n.36; *Glimpses of Three
Coasts,* 231, 240, 311n.20; "Good-by,
Leather Stockings!" 141–42; "Habeas
Corpus," 273; heroines in, 25–26,
284n.66; *Hetty's Strange History,* 26,
183, 191, 200, 210–12, 219, 259,
271; "Hide and Seek Town,"
310n.14; "Holy Cross Village and
Mrs. Pope's," 164; "How One
Woman Kept her Husband," 184,
193; *The Hunter Cats of Connorloa,*
268; "Hysteria in Literature," 32–33,
133; "The Inhumanities of Parents,"
134; "The Inn of the Golden Pear,"
217; "In the Dark," 121; "In the
White Mountains," 153, 154, 190–91,
311n.28; "Joe Hale's Red Stockings,"
37, 81, 184, 186–87; "Joy," 125;
"Justifiable Homicide in Southern
California," 250; "Just out of Sight,"
121; "The Kansas & Colorado
Building at the Centennial Exposition," 178–79; "The Katrina Saga,"
37, 230, 288n.108; "The Key of the
Casket," 18, 94; "The King's Friend,"
133; "A Last Prayer," 272–73; "Last
Words," 272, 273; *Letters from a Cat,*
63–64, 268; "Little Bel's Supplement,"
268; "Locusts and Wild Honey," 127;
Mammy Tittleback and Her Family,
268; "Massy Sprague's Daughter,"
215, 216, 311n.21; "A May-Day in
Albano," 160–61; "A Medley," 74;
"A Midsummer Fete in the Pueblo of
San Juan," 112, 301n.77; "The Mill
Has Shut Down," 267; "A Morning in
a Vermont Graveyard," 157, 313n.74;
"Mountain Life: The New Hampshire
Town of Bethlehem," 94, 151, 153,
154; "Mrs. Millington and Her
Librarian," 216; "Mt. Washington in
September," 155; "My Legacy," 121,
125; "My Ship," 122; "The Mystery
of Wilhelm Rutter," 268; "My
Tenants," 128–29; "My Tourmaline,"
184, 191, 201–2; "The Naughtiest
Day of My Life, and What Came of
It," 17, 52, 135–36; "Negative
Selfishness," 134; *Nelly's Silver Mine,*
26, 97, 212–15, 304n.41; "A New
Anvil Chorus," 181; "A New Sleepy
Hollow," 157; "Notes of Travel,"
157, 185–86; "O-Be-Joyful Creek and
Poverty Gulch," 180–81; "Occupation
for Children," 136; "October's Bright
Blue Weather," 127; "The Old Bell,"
106; "The Old-Clothes Monger in
Journalism," 6; "The One-Legged
Dancers," 184; "Outdoor Industries in
Southern California," 240, 241; "An
Out of the Way Place," 154, 311n.21;
"Pansy Billings," 267–68; persever-
ance theme in, 11, 25–26, 38;
"Pheonixiana," 177; "Pi-wy-ack and
Yo-wi-he," 167–68; *Poems,* 120;
"Popsy," 267–68; "A Pot of Gold,"
237; "The Present Condition of the
Mission Indians in Southern Califor-
nia," 240, 246–47; "The Prince's
Little Sweetheart," 268–69; "A Protest
against the Spread of Civilization,"
24, 151, 153–55, 156, 158, 307n.99;
"Queen Eumesia," 249; regionalism
in, 22, 34–37, 38–39, 288n.110,
289n.113 (*see also* travel writings of
HHJ); "The Reign of Archelaus," 134;
religious tolerance in, 163; *Report on
the Conditions and Needs of the
Mission Indians of California,* 27,
248–49, 250–51, 276; "The Republic
of the Family," 134; "Resurgam,"
121; "Rudeness," 134; "Salt Lake
City," 165; *Saxe Holm's Stories, First
Series,* 184; *Saxe Holm's Stories,
Second Series,* 184–86; sentimentalism
of, 32, 33–34, 36; "A Short Cut from
Icicles to Oranges," 237; "Sister

Mary's Story," 215, 216; "The Song He Never Wrote," 272–73; *Sonnets and Lyrics,* 120; "Standing Bear and Bright Eyes," 224, 251; stories, 296n.75 (*see also* Saxe Holm stories); "The Story of Clotilde Danarosch," 215; "Susan Lawton's Escape," 184, 201–2; "The Temecula Exiles," 250; "Three Pennsylvania Women," 249; "Too Much Wheat," 266–67; *Travel at Home,* 145; "Wanted, in New England, An Apostle for Sunshine," 184–85, 220; "The Wards of the United States Government," 225; "Whose Wife Was She?" 183, 184, 185–86, 191, 193; writing style, 99–100, 299n.20; *Zeph,* 269, 272. See also *A Century of Dishonor;* domestic essays of HHJ; literary career of HHJ; literary education of HHJ; *Mercy Philbrick's Choice;* novels of HHJ; poetry of HHJ; *Ramona; Verses*
Jackson, Jean (HHJ's great grand-niece), 4
Jackson, Margaret (HHJ's sister-in-law), 274, 326n.21
Jackson, Mary Ann (HHJ's mother-in-law), 319n.30
Jackson, William S., III ("Bill"; HHJ's great grand-nephew), 4
Jackson, William Sharpless (HHJ's second husband), 4, 5; background of, 169, 176–77; career/finances of, 25, 113–14, 169, 178, 203, 265, 270; on cheerful diligence, 202; HHJ as sometimes unsupportive of career of, 202–3; and HHJ's death, 272, 273, 274; HHJ's farewell letter to, 270–71; introduction to/courtship of HHJ, 169–70; letter writing by, 232–33, 319n.30; marriage to Helen Banfield, 273–74; marriage to HHJ, 107, 113; on Native Americans, 228–29; political aspirations of, 202–3; racial attitudes of, 176–78, 225; religious attitudes of, 177; and the Saxe Holm mystery, 198; on social reform via fiction, 252; as supportive of HHJ, 200, 201–2, 221, 228–29, 234; on verbal affection, 232–33
James, George Wharton, 286n.82
James, Henry, 110, 190, 208
Jane (a cook), 177
Jenkins, Herbert, 31
Jeremiah, 259
Jesuits, 243
Jewett, Sarah Orne, 34–35, 112, 189, 243
"Joe Hale's Red Stockings" (HHJ), 37, 81, 184, 186–87

Johnson, Jenny Abbott, 274, 326n.21
Johnson, Oliver, 110
Johnson, Thomas, 308n.115
Johnston, Mr., 196
Jones, Gavin, 289n.114
Jones, Howard Mumford, 31–32, 286n.90
Jordan, Emaline, 249
journalism, 102
"Joy" (HHJ), 125
Joyce, Robert Dwyer: *Deirdre,* 128
"Justifiable Homicide in Southern California" (HHJ), 250
"Just out of Sight" (HHJ), 121

Kaloolah (Mayo), 71
Kames, Lord: *Elements of Criticism,* 66, 251
"The Kansas & Colorado Building at the Centennial Exposition" (HHJ), 178–79
Kaplan, Amy, 38, 289n.113
Kate Beaumont (De Forest), 35–36
"The Katrina Saga" (HHJ), 37, 230, 288n.108
Katy (a servant), 272
Keats, John, 309n.121
Kempis, Thomas à, 58
"The Key of the Casket" (HHJ), 18, 94
The King and I (Rodgers and Hammerstein), 305n.54
"The King's Friend" (HHJ), 133
Kingsley, Charles: *Yeast,* 71
Kinney, Abbot, 239, 240, 241, 247, 248, 270
Kirkland, Caroline, 69; *A New Home: Who'll Follow?* 189

Lady's Life in the Rocky Mountains (Bishop), 176
La Flesche, Francis, 223
La Flesche, Joseph, Omaha chief, 224
La Flesche, Susette (Inshta Theumba; "Bright Eyes"), 26, 221, 224, 251; "Nedawi," 262, 318n.4
Lamb, Charles, 161, 200
Lamborn, Robert H., 170, 283n.14
"Lars" (Taylor), 124
"A Last Prayer" (HHJ), 272–73
Last Tycoon (Fitzgerald), 277
"Last Words" (HHJ), 272, 273
"Laurel" (R. W. Gilder), 124
Lawson, S. S., 247, 248
Leadville (Col.), 174–75
Leaves from the Diary of a Recluse (Botta), 79–80
Lectures on Christian Doctrine (Peabody), 88

"The Legend of Sleepy Hollow" (Irving), 158, 310n.19
Leonowens, Anna, 143; *The English Governess at the Siamese Court,* 130, 305n.54
"A Letter from a Little Girl Who Did Nothing but Play" (D. Fiske), 61
Letters from a Cat (HHJ), 63–64, 268
"A Letter to a Young Contributor" (Higginson), 99
Lewes, George Henry, 192, 209, 315n.24
Lewis, Edmonia, 178
Lewis, Mr., 196
Lewisohn, Ludwig, 286n.90
Library of the World's Best Literature (C. D. Warner), 274
Life amongst the Modocs (Miller), 324n.128
Life among the Piutes (Winnemucca), 324n.133
The Life and Adventures of Joaquin Murietta (Ridge), 324n.133
Lind, Jenny, 67
Linton, Eliza Lynn: *The True History of Joshua Davidson,* 177
Lippincott, Sara. *See* Greenwood, Grace
literary career of HHJ, 93–117; ambitions/professionalism of HHJ, 98, 107–8, 111, 114, 137, 276; *Atlantic Monthly* writings, 23–24, 37, 80, 110, 111, 112, 115, 288n.108, 301n.77; beginnings of, 18, 22, 93–94, 99–100, 296n.75; book reviews, 93, 189–90, 191, 200, 252, 324n.128; in Boston, 108–9; *Century Magazine* writings, 27, 29, 110–11, 112; character portrayal, 24; *Christian Union* writings, 110; Cushman's role in, 105; earnings from, 111–16, 302nn.90,96; father's influence on, 44, 47, 56, 64, 118–19; fiction, 183 (*see also* novels of HHJ; Saxe Holm stories); *Galaxy* writings, 110–11; goals of writing, 94; *Harper's Monthly* writings, 110–11, 112; *Hearth and Home* writings, 135; H.H. signature, 23–24, 93, 120, 133, 140, 260; Higginson's influence on, 22–23, 94, 95, 96–102, 105, 107–8, 114; Jane Silsbee stories, 215–16, 318n.92; literary circle of HHJ, 80, 86, 95, 108–9, 296n.81; mother's influence on, 44, 56, 58–59, 64; and the *Nation,* 111, 301n.68; in Newport, 94–95, 97, 108; in New York, 109; *New York Evening Post* writings, 22, 23, 94, 110, 115, 296n.75; *New York Independent,* negotiations with, 111, 112, 115–16,
302n.103; *New York Independent* writings, 23, 29, 70, 93, 110, 119, 301n.70; *New York Tribune* writings, 110; perfectionism of HHJ, 100; publishing pace of HHJ, 110; *Scribner's Monthly* writings, 25, 109, 110–11, 112, 199; *St. Nicholas* writings, 112, 135; success/reputation of HHJ, 11, 31, 39, 111, 116–17, 123–24, 289n.118; work habits, 172; *Youth's Companion* writings, 112. *See also* domestic essays of HHJ; poetry of HHJ; travel writings of HHJ
literary education of HHJ, 65–90, 295n.52; John Abbott's role in, 67–68, 69, 70; at the Abbott Institute, 66–68, 69–70; and activism of HHJ, 81; in Albany, 70–73; and ambitions of HHJ, 69, 73, 78; and anxieties of HHJ, 71–73, 295n.36; Carlyle's *Sartor Resartus,* 73; characterization, 73–74; in Charlestown, 68–69, 294n.16; composition studies, 66; Conway's role in, 85–86, 88–90, 298n.124; Emerson's "Introductory Lecture on the Times," 73; Emerson's *Nature,* 89; *Essays on the Difficulties of the Pentateuch,* translation of, 74; father's role in, 43–44, 52–53; Hawthorne's fiction, 77; Higginson's role in, 97–102; and hospital volunteer work of HHJ, 81; Kames's *Elements of Criticism,* 66; letters, 73, 74; literary circle of HHJ, 80, 86, 296n.81; at Miss Austin's school, 66; mother's role in, 43–44, 59; in New York City, 66–67, 69, 80; Ray Palmer's role in, 74, 119–20; *Portfolio,* work on, 69–70; reading, extent of, 77; Stowe's fiction, 77
literary magazines, 102. *See also titles of specific magazines*
literary salons (NYC), 80, 296n.81
Literary World, 208
literature: average sentence length, 100, 299n.20; spiritual enlightenment from, 119
"Literature as Art" (Higginson), 99, 102
"Little Bel's Supplement" (HHJ), 268
Little Brown and Company, 31, 109
Lloyd, Henry Demarest: "The Political Economy of Seventy-Three Million Dollars," 267
local color, 35, 288n.110. *See also* regionalist literature; travel writings of HHJ
"Locusts and Wild Honey" (HHJ), 127
Longfellow, Henry Wadsworth, 67, 86,

108, 227; *Evangeline,* 251–52, 261;
Hiawatha, 251
López, Jesús, 247
Los Angeles, 237, 240, 242, 276
Los Angeles Times, 286n.78
Loved One (Waugh), 277
Lowell, James Russell, 108, 227
Lubo, Ramona, 276, 327n.46
Lucy (a slave), 84
Lummis, Charles Fletcher, 275

Mabie, Hamilton Wright, 270
MacDonald, George: *Alec Forbes of
Howglen,* 189
Malbone (Higginson), 199
Mammy Tittleback and Her Family (HHJ),
268
Manitou Springs (Col.), 170, 284n.51
Manual of Classical Literature (N. Fiske),
11, 48–49, 291n.26
Martí, José, 274–75
Martineau, Harriet, 143
A Masque of Poets, 146–47, 309n.129
"Massy Sprague's Daughter" (HHJ), 215,
216, 311n.21
"A May-Day in Albano" (HHJ), 160–61
The Mayflower (Stowe), 189
Mayo, William Starbuck: *Kaloolah,* 71
McCarthy, Justin: "American Women and
English Women," 307n.103
McCosh, James: *The Method of Divine
Government,* 71
McLeod, Effie, 265–66, 272, 273, 326n.21
McWilliams, Carey, 275
Mechanism in Thought and Morals
(Holmes), 220
"A Medley" (HHJ), 74
Meeker, Nathan C., 227–28
Memoir of Rev. Nathan W. Fiske
(Humphrey), 45, 47, 48, 290n.5
Men and Women (R. Browning), 78
Mercy Philbrick's Choice (HHJ), 203–9,
276; as autobiographical, 25,
79, 118, 139, 203–5, 317n.70;
cheerfulness/diligence in, 204; critical
reception of, 208–9, 212; Emily
Dickinson not a source for, 317n.70;
heroine's flight in, 259; hidden love in,
204–5; Mercy's career choice in,
208–9; moralism of, 206–7; New
England regionalism of, 25–26; Niles
on, 207–8; poetry in, 121, 122, 205;
popularity of, 111, 208; publication
of, 200, 203, 207–8; sales of, 207–8;
setting/plot of, 204–6; style of, 204
The Method of Divine Government
(McCosh), 71
Mexican-American War (1846–1848), 164

"A Midsummer Fete in the Pueblo of San
Juan" (HHJ), 112, 301n.77
Miller, Joaquin, 128, 274, 305n.43; *Life
amongst the Modocs,* 324n.128
"The Mill Has Shut Down" (HHJ),
267
Miss Austin's school (Charlestown, Mass.),
66
Mission Indians (Southern Calif.), 27,
28–29, 237–38, 240, 244–46, 247–49,
250–51, 285n.70
Mission Revival movement, 3
Mitchell, Donald Grant ("Ik Marvel"):
Dream Life, 71; *Reveries of a
Bachelor,* 71
Mora, Francis, 238
moral philosophy, 46–47
More, Hannah, 53
Mormons, 165–66
"A Morning in a Vermont Graveyard"
(HHJ), 157, 313n.74
Morris, William, 124
Morse, Ephraim W., 323n.113
Moses (a Persian minister), 83
Mott, Frank Luther, 301n.71
"Mountain Life: The New Hampshire
Town of Bethlehem" (HHJ), 94, 151,
153, 154
Mount Washington (N.H.), 155
Moylan, Michele, 301n.71
"Mrs. Millington and Her Librarian"
(HHJ), 216
"Mt. Washington in September" (HHJ),
155
Murfree, Mary Noailles, 190; *In the
Tennessee Mountains,* 270
Murillo, Bartolomé Esteban, 35
"My Faith Looks Up to Thee" (R. Palmer),
70
"My Legacy" (HHJ), 121, 125
My Novel (Bulwer-Lytton), 251
"My Ship" (HHJ), 122
"The Mystery of Wilhelm Rutter" (HHJ),
268
My Summer in a Garden (C. D. Warner),
200
"My Tenants" (HHJ), 128–29
"My Tourmaline" (HHJ), 184, 191, 2
01–2
My Wife and I (Stowe), 189–90

Nana (Zola), 190, 315n.17
Nation, 31, 33; on *A Century of Dishonor,*
235; and HHJ, 111, 198, 301n.68; on
Josiah Holland, 199; on *Ramona,*
260; reputation/readership of,
111

Native Americans: Christian conversion of, 226; "noble" imagery of, 324n.128; novels by, 261, 324n.133; racism toward/fear of, 28–29, 30, 155–57, 176, 246, 286n.82; rights of, 26–28, 155, 223, 285nn.71,73 (see also Indian reform work of HHJ); travel writings on, 157, 167–68, 310n.14

Nature (Emerson), 89

"The Naughtiest Day of My Life, and What Came of It" (HHJ), 17, 52, 135–36

"Nedawi" (La Flesche), 262, 318n.4

"Negative Selfishness" (HHJ), 134

Nelly's Silver Mine (HHJ), 26, 97, 212–15, 304n.41

Nevins, Allan, 296n.75

"A New Anvil Chorus" (HHJ), 181

New England Woman's Club, 140–41

A New Home: Who'll Follow? (Kirkland), 189

New Life in New Lands (Greenwood), 176

Newport (R.I.), 22, 94–95, 97, 108, 310n.19

"A New Sleepy Hollow" (HHJ), 157

The New Year's Bargain (Woolsey), 80–81

New York City, 66–67, 80, 83, 108, 109–10, 296n.81

New York Evening Post: domestic essays of HHJ in, 133–34; HHJ's writings for, 22, 23, 94, 110, 115; travel writings of HHJ in, 151, 152, 153

New York Independent: domestic essays of HHJ in, 133, 134–35; HHJ's negotiations with, 111, 112, 115–16, 302n.103; HHJ's writings for, 23, 29, 93, 110, 119, 301n.70; pay rates of, 112; reputation/readership of, 110, 115; travel writings of HHJ in, 153, 154, 159, 162, 163, 164, 172–73, 250

New York Times, 194, 227

New York Tribune, 110, 197

Nez Percé Indians. See *A Century of Dishonor*

Niles, Thomas, 109, 113, 198, 200, 310n.134; and "Elspeth Dynor," 217, 272; and *Hetty's Strange History*, 212; on HHJ's death, 274; on *Mercy Philbrick's Choice*, 207–8; and *Nelly's Silver Mine*, 215; *Zeph* published by, 269, 272

"Notes of Travel" (HHJ), 157, 185–86

Noticia de la California (Venegas), 236

novels of HHJ, 198–221; as autobiographical, 198–99; for children, 213 (see also *Nelly's Silver Mine*); heroines in, 199; personal vs. professional fulfillment in, 208–9; popularity of, 198–99; rural

settings of, 184. *See also* Jackson, Helen Hunt, works by; *and titles of specific novels*

"O-Be-Joyful Creek and Poverty Gulch" (HHJ), 180–81

"Occupation for Children" (HHJ), 136

"October's Bright Blue Weather" (HHJ), 127

Odell, Ruth, 291n.25, 297n.86; *Helen Hunt Jackson (H.H.)*, 4, 31–32

O'Keefe, Father, 238

Old and New, 108

"The Old Bell" (HHJ), 106

"The Old-Clothes Monger in Journalism" (HHJ), 6

Oliphant, Margaret, 212–13

"The One-Legged Dancers" (HHJ), 184

Ordonez de Montalvo, Garcia: *Las Sergas de Esplandiàn,* 236–37

Oregon Trail (Parkman), 236

Osgood, J. R., 23–24, 108

Our New West (Bowles), 176

"Outdoor Industries in Southern California" (HHJ), 240, 241

Out-Door Papers (Higginson), 98–99, 106, 270

"An Out of the Way Place" (HHJ), 154, 311n.21

Overland (De Forest), 35–36, 189

Overland Monthly, 31

Padillo, Genaro M., 242

Palmer, Ann, 70, 71, 75

Palmer, Julius A. (HHJ's guardian), 5, 14–15; and HHJ's finances/inheritance, 44, 114, 289n.1; relationship with HHJ, 43, 68, 69, 152, 164

Palmer, Julius A., Jr., 289n.1

Palmer, Lucy, 14, 15, 75, 77, 152, 164

Palmer, Ray: *Closet Hours,* 70; and HHJ, 15, 75; and literary education of HHJ, 74, 119–20; "My Faith Looks Up to Thee," 70; reputation of, 116; *Spiritual Improvements,* 70

Palmer, William Jackson, 169

Paloú, Father: *La Vida de Junípero Serra,* 244

"Pansy Billings" (HHJ), 267–68

Parish, Fanny, 220

Parker House (Boston), 21

Parkman, Francis, 235; *Oregon Trail,* 236

Park Street Church (Boston), 152

Parnassus (Emerson), 125

Parton, Sara Willis ("Fanny Fern"): *Ruth Hall,* 208

Pascal, Blaise, 58

Peabody, Andrew Preston: *Lectures on Christian Doctrine,* 88
Pearson, Virginia King, 220
Personal Narrative of Explorations and Incidents in Texas, New Mexico, California, Sonora, and Chihuahua (J. R. Bartlett), 236
Petrarca, Francesco, 101
Phelps, Elizabeth Stuart, 189, 274
"Pheonixiana" (HHJ), 177
Pickford, Mary, 2
Pico, Pío, 237
Pico House (Los Angeles), 237
Piegan Indians, 266–67
Pilgrim's Progress (Bunyan), 58
pioneers, 176
Pittsfield Academy (Mass.), 51
"Pi-wy-ack and Yo-wi-he" (HHJ), 167–68
Ploughed Under (Harsha), 252
Poe, Edgar Allan, 80
Poems (HHJ), 120
Poems of Passion (Wilcox), 131
poetry of HHJ, 23, 25, 51, 78, 93, 117–33; for children, 135; Conway on, 124; critical reception of, 129; earnings from, 120, 303n.6; Emerson's admiration for/influence on, 125–26; expressiveness/style of, 120; Higginson on, 39, 79, 96, 101, 132–33, 274, 296n.75; intellectually ambiguous, 120; light verse, 120; of love/passion, 129–32; moral agenda of, 118–19, 132–33, 147; nature poems, 126–27, 128–29; popularity/success of, 118, 119, 120, 276; regionalist, 128; sonnets, 120–21; spiritual/Christian, 121–23, 124, 128–29; Transcendentalist, 126, 127, 128; translations from French, 119–20; on women's themes, 129, 132. *See also* Jackson, Helen Hunt, works by; *and titles of specific poems*
"The Political Economy of Seventy-Three Million Dollars" (Lloyd), 267
polygamy, 165–66
The Ponca Chiefs (Tibbles), 224, 324n.128
Poncas Indians, 26–27, 221, 223–24, 226–27, 234, 318n.2. See also *A Century of Dishonor*
"Poor Susan" (D. Fiske), 61–62
"Popsy" (HHJ), 267–68
Popular History of the United States (Bryant), 237
Portfolio (HHJ, ed.), 69–70
"A Pot of Gold" (HHJ), 237
Pre-Raphaelites, 124
"The Present Condition of the Mission Indians in Southern California" (HHJ), 240, 246–47

Preston, Harriet Waters: *Aspendale,* 189
Price, Hannah Jackson (HHJ's sister-in-law), 171–72, 274, 326n.21
Price, Hiram, 247, 248
"Prince Deukalion" (Taylor), 124
"The Prince's Little Sweetheart" (HHJ), 268–69
Prometheus Unbound (Shelley), 73
"A Protest against the Spread of Civilization" (HHJ), 24, 151, 153–55, 156, 158, 307n.99
Pryse, Marjorie, 37–38, 288n.110
Publishers Weekly, 134
Pynchon, Thomas, 3

"Queen Eumesia" (HHJ), 249
"The Queen of California" (Hale), 236–37
Quinton, Amelia Stone, 234, 235

racism, 82, 179–80. *See also under* Native Americans
railroads, 37, 155, 164, 175–76, 180, 237, 267. *See also names of specific railroads*
Ramona (HHJ), 252–64; Alessandro in, 256–57, 258; Alessandro's nickname for Ramona, 323n.113; as American jeremiad, 259; Angus Phail in, 256, 323n.118; Aunt Ri in, 263–64; as autobiographical, 256; the baby's death in, 258; as a best-seller, 111, 301n.71; California in, 259, 277; character portrayal in, 29–31, 261, 286n.82; completion of, 253; critical reception of, 31–32, 35, 260, 274, 286n.90; dialect in, 39, 262; Emily Dickinson on, 145; domesticity in, 262–63; Father Gaspara in, 257; Father Salvierderra in, 254; Felipe in, 256, 258–59; film/dramatic adaptations of, 2, 275; goals of, 259–61, 262, 264; HHJ on, 270, 275; illustrations for, 320n.56; intermarriages in, 262–63; land loss in, 254–55; literary influences on, 260–61, 324n.128; misinterpretation of, 275; nostalgia of, 261–62; plot of, 252–53; popularity/influence of, 2–3, 30, 31, 39, 275–77; power of, 254, 276–77; publication by Roberts Brothers, 260; racial tolerance in, 262–64; Ramona in, 256–57, 263; Ramona and Alessandro's marriage in, 257–58, 262–63; Ramona and Felipe's marriage in, 259, 262; reformist goals of, 27, 30; regionalism of, 29, 34, 35; Saboba in, 257–58; Señora

Ramona (HHJ) *(continued)*
    Moreno in, 255–57, 258, 261–62;
    sentimentalism of, 34, 276–77;
    serialization in *Christian Union*,
    259–60; setting of, 254, 261,
    323n.116; solidarity with oppressed
    groups in, 39; sources/research for, 3,
    30, 238, 247, 249, 252, 322n.91,
    323n.113; Temecula ejection in, 257,
    323n.120; title of, 260; tourism
    encouraged by, 276; translation of,
    274–75; on U.S. imperialism, 29–30,
    261–62, 277; work methods for,
    252–53, 323n.113
"Ramona" (song; Wayne and Gilbert), 2
Ramona Myth, 275, 276
Ramona Pageant (Hemet, Calif.), 1–2, 3
Rancho Camulos (Ventura County, Calif.),
    3, 238, 276
Reade, Charles: *A Terrible Temptation*,
    315n.17
realism, 188, 189–90, 275, 289n.113. *See
    also* regionalist literature; travel
    writings of HHJ
Rebecca of Sunnybrook Farm (Wiggin),
    139
regionalist literature, 34–35, 188–89,
    287n.98; and the Civil War, 37;
    dialogue in, 37; HHJ on, 35–36, 37;
    and nationhood/colonialism, 38;
    subversiveness of, 37–38; sympathy
    with local subjects in, 38–39,
    288n.110. *See also* travel writings of
    HHJ
Reid, Hugo, 323n.118
Reid, Whitelaw, 6, 110, 154, 301n.68
"The Reign of Archelaus" (HHJ), 134
Renan, Ernest, 163
*Report of the Exploring Expedition to the
    Rocky Mountains in the Year 1842*
    (Frémont), 236
*Report on the Conditions and Needs of the
    Mission Indians of California* (HHJ),
    27, 248–49, 250–51, 276
"The Republic of the Family" (HHJ), 134
"Resurgam" (HHJ), 121
Reveries of a Bachelor (Mitchell), 71
Richards, C. A. L., 300n.55
Richardson, Abbie Sage, 220
Rideing, William H., 267
Ridge, John Rollin: *The Life and Adven-
    tures of Joaquin Murietta*, 324n.133
Ripley, George, 109
"Rip Van Winkle" (Irving), 23, 153, 158,
    311n.20
Roberts Brothers (Boston), 26, 31, 109,
    113, 120, 135, 200. See also *Mercy
    Philbrick's Choice; Ramona*
Rocky Mountain News, 176

Rocky Mountains, 170
Rodgers, Richard: *The King and I*,
    305n.54
Rollins, Alice Wellington, 6, 138–39, 274,
    282n.14, 307n.96
Romanticism, 36, 188, 189, 190
Roosevelt, Theodore, 286n.88
Root, Henry, 15, 71–74, 75, 79, 86, 144,
    295n.36
Rossetti, Christina, 101, 129, 200,
    305n.48
Rossetti, Dante Gabriel, 124, 256
Rothman, Sheila M., 282n.2
"Rudeness" (HHJ), 113
Ruiz de Burton, María Amparo, 261; *The
    Squatter and the Don*, 325n.134
Runkle, Lucia Gilbert Calhoun ("Bertie"),
    95–96, 110, 112, 152–53, 168, 274
Ruskin, John: *Stones of Venice*, 311n.33
Ruth Hall (Parton), 208

"Salt Lake City" (HHJ), 165
Samuels, Shirley, 32
San Bernardino, 240
San Bernardino Times, 286n.78
Sanchez, Francisco de Jesús, 238, 254
Sand, George, 143, 200
Sand Creek Massacre (1864), 228, 236
Sandham, Henry, 239, 320n.56
San Diego, 238–39, 240
San Diego Union, 286n.78
San Francisco, 164–65, 166–67
San Gabriel mission (Calif.), 323n.118
San Luis Rey Star, 29
San Pasqual (Calif.), 246, 321n.82,
    323n.116
Santa Barbara, 238, 240
San Ysidro Canyon (Calif.), 248
Sarah Ann (a servant), 83
Sartor Resartus (Carlyle), 73
Saturday Review, 208
Saunders, Alvin, 28
Savage, Thomas, 242
Saxe Holm's Stories, First Series (HHJ),
    184
Saxe Holm's Stories, Second Series (HHJ),
    184–86
Saxe Holm stories, 183–98; as autobio-
    graphical, 192–93, 194, 195;
    character portrayal in, 192–93;
    cheerfulness/industry in, 26, 188, 192;
    critical reception of, 184, 193–94,
    198; dialect/vernacular in, 187;
    earnings from, 112; idealism of,
    193–94; identity of Saxe Holm, 25,
    183–84, 194–98, 201, 297n.86; later
    works, 268; love/passion in, 131, 132,
    191, 193, 194; popularity of, 25, 184,

193–94; proofreading of, 300n.55; rural settings of, 184; Saxe Holm pseudonym, meaning of, 194; sentimentalism vs. realism in, 188, 194; style of, 99. *See also* Jackson, Helen Hunt, works by; *and titles of specific stories*
"The Sceptre" (Winter), 127–28
Scholfield, Ann (HHJ's cousin), 59–60, 65–66, 271
Scholfield, Ellen, 62
The School-girl (John Abbott), 67–68, 138
Schurz, Carl, 227–28, 234, 235
Scribner's Monthly, 108; HHJ's writings for, 25, 109, 110–11, 112, 199 (*see also* Saxe Holm stories); pay rates of, 112; reputation/readership of, 111, 184
Scudder, Horace, 35
Sea Miner (a weapon), 16, 283n.27
"A Second Celestial Railroad," 155, 190–91
Sedgwick, Catharine, 80
sentimentalism, 32–34, 188, 286n.91, 287n.98
Las Sergas de Esplandiàn (Ordonez de Montalvo), 236–37
Serra, Junipero, 238, 243
Severn, Joseph, 145, 309n.121
sexism, literary, 208
Shakespeare, William, 53, 292n.51
Shaw, Flora, 212–13
Shelley, Percy Bysshe: *Prometheus Unbound,* 73
Sheriff, Mary, 248, 249, 323n.113
"A Short Cut from Icicles to Oranges" (HHJ), 237
short stories. *See* Saxe Holm stories
Short Studies of American Authors (Higginson), 101, 125, 199, 274
"The Shoshone Oath" (HHJ), 129
Sigourney, Lydia, 129
"The Singer's Hills" (HHJ), 126
Sioux Indians. See *A Century of Dishonor*
"Sister Mary's Story" (HHJ), 215, 216
The Sketch Book of Geoffrey Crayon, Gent. (Irving), 153, 158, 161
slavery, 84
Snell, Mary, 17
Snell, Rebecca, 12
"The Snow-Image" (Hawthorne), 191
Soboba (Calif.), 247, 248
Soboba Indians, 285n.73
"Some Lover's Clear Day" (Weiss), 129, 305n.50
"The Song He Never Wrote" (HHJ), 272–73
"Sonnet, To One Who Complained of a

Poet for Not Writing about Nature" (HHJ), 127
Sonnets and Lyrics (HHJ), 120
Southern Pacific Railroad, 237, 275–76
Southworth, E. D. E. N., 33, 112
Spanish Colonial Revival movement, 3
The Spanish Gypsy (Eliot), 305n.48
spas, 284n.51
"Spinning" (HHJ), 122–23, 188
Spiritual Improvements (R. Palmer), 70
Sprague, Mary, 18–19, 71
Springfield Republican, 130, 195, 197
The Squatter and the Don (Ruiz de Burton), 325n.134
Staël, Germaine de, 68, 143
Stampa, Gaspara, 129–30
Standing Bear, Ponca chief, 26, 221, 224, 318n.2
"Standing Bear and Bright Eyes" (HHJ), 224, 251
Stanton, Elizabeth Cady, 141–42
Starr, Kevin, 275
"A State without a Debt" (HHJ), 178–79
Stearns, Nelly, 158–59
Stearns, Priscilla, 152–53, 158–59
Stebbins, Emma, 104, 299n.33
Stedman, Edmund Clarence, 80, 109, 124
Steen, Susanna ("Sanna"), 230
Stegner, Wallace, 286n.90
Steinbeck, John: *Grapes of Wrath,* 277
St. Elmo (Evans), 208
Stevenson, Robert Louis: *Travels with a Donkey in the Cévennes,* 311n.34
St. Nicholas, 112, 135, 141, 197, 249
Stoddard, Charles Warren, 305n.43
Stoddard, Elizabeth, 80, 142, 189
Stoddard, Richard, 80, 109, 124, 189
stoicism, 97
Stone, Lucy, 143
"The Stone-Mason's Garden of Eden" (HHJ), 313n.72
Stones of Venice (Ruskin), 311n.33
Stories of Eliot and the Indians (W. A. Alcott), 226
stories of HHJ, 296n.75. *See also* Saxe Holm stories
The Story of Aleck (N. Fiske), 49, 52–53
"The Story of Boon" (HHJ), 130–31
"The Story of Clotilde Danarosch" (HHJ), 215
"The Story of Indian Wrongs" (Dall), 235
Stowe, Harriet Beecher, 34, 77, 116, 253–54; *The Mayflower,* 189; *My Wife and I,* 189–90; *Uncle Tom's Cabin,* 32, 84–85, 251, 252, 260
Straws, Jr. *See* Field, Kate
suffrage, 141–42, 307n.99
Sundquist, Eric, 38, 287n.98
"Sunshine and Petrarch" (Higginson), 101

"Susan Lawton's Escape" (HHJ), 184, 201–2
"A Symphony in Yellow and Red" (HHJ), 174

Taylor, Bayard, 80, 109; *Colorado: A Summer Trip,* 176; "Lars," 124; "Prince Deukalion," 124
Teller, Henry, 29, 234, 240, 248
Temecula (Calif.), 239, 246–47, 323nn.113, 116
"The Temecula Exiles" (HHJ), 250
Temple, Sam, 249, 250, 323n.113
"Ten Questions That I Wish Nobody Would Ever Ask Me Again" (D. Fiske), 61, 293n.98
Ten Times One Is Ten (Hale), 119, 302n.2
A Terrible Temptation (Reade), 315n.17
Thacher, Mary, 220
Thaxter, Celia, 128; *Among the Isles of Shoals,* 305n.44
Thibault, Sara, 270, 273
Thomas, Edith M., 144, 274
Thoreau, Henry David: *A Week on the Concord and Merrimack Rivers,* 311n.28
"Thought" (HHJ), 125
"Three Kisses of Farewell" (HHJ), 131, 132
"Three Pennsylvania Women" (HHJ), 249
Tibbles, Thomas Henry, 223, 318n.4; *The Ponca Chiefs,* 224, 324n.128
Ticknor, Mary J., 247, 249
"To Leadville" (HHJ), 174–75, 181
Tompkins, Jane, 32
"Too Much Wheat" (HHJ), 266–67
Tourgée, Albion, 274; *A Fool's Errand,* 252
The Training of Children (HHJ), 136
Transcendentalism, 88–89, 124, 126, 160, 311n.28
transportation, 37
Travel at Home (HHJ), 145. See also *Bits of Travel at Home*
travel by women, 152–53
travel literature, 161, 311nn.33,34. See also travel writings of HHJ
Travels with a Donkey in the Cévennes (Stevenson), 311n.34
travel writings of HHJ, 23–24, 29, 36–37, 39, 93, 96, 99–100, 151–82, 296n.75; on America, 23–25, 29, 151–58, 163–68, 172–76, 178–82; for the *Atlantic Monthly,* 159, 161, 163, 173, 231, 236, 240, 249–50; on California, 29, 164–68, 236–38, 240–44, 249–50; for *Century Magazine,* 231, 236, 239, 240–41, 243, 249; character portrayal in, 158–59, 161–62, 163; on the Chinese, 166–67, 180, 249; for the *Christian Union,* 236; on Colorado, 25, 172–76, 178–82; critical reception of, 173; dialect in, 158, 161–62; diversity/ethnicity in, 157–58, 165, 176, 249; on Europe, 23–24, 158–63, 311nn.28,33; female subjects in, HHJ's identification with, 161–62, 163, 192, 312n.36; on Franciscan missions, 243–45; goals of, 152; on Hispanic residents of Colorado, 175–76, 180; Irving's influence on, 158, 161, 190, 311n.20; William Jackson's influence on, 178; late, 230–33, 236; on Native Americans, 157, 167–68, 240, 244–45, 249–50, 310n.14; for the *New York Evening Post,* 151, 152, 153; for the *New York Independent,* 153, 154, 159, 162, 163, 164, 172–73, 250; popularity of, 163–64; racial attitudes/tolerance in, 179–80, 242–43, 249–50; as source material for fiction, 311n.21; for the *St. Nicholas,* 249; style of, 159, 160, 161; tourism popularized by, 154; on Transcendentalism, 160, 311n.28; on women, 181–82; work methods for, 231–32; on Yosemite, 167–68. See also Jackson, Helen Hunt, works by; and titles of specific essays
Treatise on the Education of Daughters (Fénelon), 138
"Tribute: R. W. E." (HHJ), 125
Trimble, Mary, 104, 239–40
Trowbridge, William, 283n.27
The True History of Joshua Davidson (Linton), 177
"Tryst" (HHJ), 131
tuberculosis, 13–14
Tufts, Charles, 289n.1
"A Turkish Bath and a Parcel of Old Love Letters" (HHJ), 311n.21
Twain, Mark: *The Gilded Age,* 201; *Innocents Abroad,* 160, 161, 312n.35; and the Saxe Holm mystery, 197
Twining, Alexander, 283n.27
Tyler, E., 51
Tyler, William S., 51

Ubach, Anthony, 239, 257
Uncle Tom's Cabin (Stowe), 32, 84–85, 251, 252, 260
Union Foundations: A Study of American Nationality as a Fact of Science (E. Hunt), 82, 225

Union Pacific Railroad, 164
Unitarianism, 87
United States–Mexican Boundary Survey
(1850–1853), 236
Ute Indians, 28; White River (Col.),
227–28

Van Doren, Carl: *American Novel*, 31
Van Winkle, Rip (*pseud.*). *See* Jackson,
Helen Hunt
Venegas, Miguèl: *Noticia de la California*,
236
Venetian Life (Howells), 311n.33
Ventura (Calif.), 240
Verses (HHJ): advertising for, 307n.96;
critical reception of, 111; Emily
Dickinson on, 145; Emerson on, 125;
and James T. Fields, 105, 108, 120,
303n.6
Victoria, queen of Great Britain and
Ireland, 312n.36
"A Victory of Love" (HHJ), 136
La Vida de Junípero Serra (Paloú), 244
Vinal, David (HHJ's grandfather), 12, 14,
44, 68–69, 94, 289n.1
Vinal, Martha (HHJ's great aunt), 13, 15,
49, 57
Vinal, Otis (HHJ's great uncle), 13
"Vintage" (HHJ), 131–32
"A Visit to Borioboola Gha: The School
System There" (HHJ), 133–34,
306n.68

Wabash railroad, 267
Wagner-Martin, Linda, 287n.98
"Wa-ha-toy-a; or, Before the Graders"
(HHJ), 175
Walsenburg (Col.), 175–76
"Wanted: A Home" (HHJ), 137, 139, 141
"Wanted, in New England, An Apostle for
Sunshine" (HHJ), 184–85, 220
Ward, William Hayes, 110, 115, 116, 134,
171, 195, 202
"The Wards of the United States Govern-
ment" (HHJ), 225
Warner, Charles Dudley, 6, 283n.14,
307n.96; "A-Hunting of the Deer,"
261; *The Gilded Age*, 201; " 'H.H.' in
Southern California," 274; and HHJ,
200–201; on HHJ's death, 274; and
Indian rights, 227; *Library of the
World's Best Literature*, 274; *My
Summer in a Garden*, 200; and the
Saxe Holm mystery, 201
Warner, Susan, 200; *The Wide, Wide
World*, 71

Washburn, Royal, 46
water cures, 284n.51
Waugh, Evelyn, 3; *Loved One*, 277
Wayne, Mabel: "Ramona," 2
"The Way to Sing" (HHJ), 304n.36
Webster, Will, 323n.113
*A Week on the Concord and Merrimack
Rivers* (Thoreau), 311n.28
Weiss, John: "Some Lover's Clear Day,"
129, 305n.50
Welch, Raquel, 1
Wells, Anna Mary, 103
Welter, Barbara, 33
West, Nathanael, 3; *Day of the Locust*,
277
"What a Useful Young Lady!" (D. Fiske),
61
Whipple, Mrs. D. J., 266
White Mountains (N.H.), 153
Whitman, Walt, 124
Whittier, John Greenleaf, 5, 108, 281n.5;
and Indian rights, 227
"Whose Wife Was She?" (HHJ), 183, 184,
185–86, 191, 193
The Wide, Wide World (S. W. Warner), 71
Wiggin, Kate Douglas: *Rebecca of
Sunnybrook Farm*, 139
Wilcox, Ella Wheeler: *Poems of Passion*,
131
Wilkes, Mrs., 143
Willis, Katy, 83–84
Wilson, B. D., 244
Winnebago Indians. *See A Century of
Dishonor*
Winnemucca, Sarah, 230; *Life among the
Piutes*, 324n.133
Winter, William: "The Golden Silence,"
127–28, 304n.36; "The Sceptre,"
127–28
Wolf, Louis, 239, 262
Wolf, Ramona, 239, 262, 327n.46
Wolff, Cynthia Griffin, 290n.4, 308n.115
"A Woman's Battle" (HHJ), 128
Woman's Journal, 98, 143, 195
women: as authors, 98, 138, 143–44, 153;
rights of, 268–69; travel by, 152–53
Women's National Indian Association
(WNIA), 227, 285n.71
women's rights movement, 141–42,
307n.99
Woolsey, Sarah ("Sally"; *pseud.* Susan
Coolidge), 17, 21, 22, 44, 95,
297n.86, 307n.107, 312n.35;
"Concord, May 31, 1882," 297n.85;
on HHJ's death, 274; on HHJ's
marriage to Jackson, 171; HHJ's
support of, 112, 144; *The New Year's
Bargain*, 80–81; and Niles, 200; on

Woolsey, Sarah *(continued)*
    Ramona, 256; research materials sent
    to, 271; and the Saxe Holm mystery,
    197; travelogues sent by HHJ to, 159;
    travels with HHJ, 152–53, 164;
    tribute to HHJ by, 274
Wordsworth, William, 126–27
The Works of Epictetus (Higginson), 97
Wormeley, Katherine, 78, 296n.70

Yeast (Kingsley), 71
Yosemite (Calif.), 167–68
Youth's Companion, 60–62, 63, 112,
    267

Zeph (HHJ), 269, 272
Zola, Émile: *Nana,* 190,
    315n.17

Compositor:	Rainsford Type
Text:	9.5/12.75 Sabon
Display:	Chaparral
Printer and Binder:	Malloy Lithographing, Inc.
Indexer:	Carol Roberts